FIFTEENTH EDITION

GLOBAL STUDIES

Latin America and the Caribbean

Paul B. Goodwin

University of Connecticut, Storrs

Series Consultant
Christopher J. Sutton
Western Illinois University

OTHER BOOKS IN THE GLOBAL STUDIES SERIES

- Africa
- China
- Europe
- India and South Asia
- Japan and the Pacific Rim
- The Middle East
- Russia and the Near Abroad

Mc Graw Hill

Connect
Learn
Succeed™

GLOBAL STUDIES: LATIN AMERICA AND THE CARIBBEAN, FIFTEENTH EDITION

Published by McGraw-Hill, a business unit of The McGraw-Hill Companies, Inc., 1221 Avenue of the Americas, New York, NY 10020. Copyright © 2013 by The McGraw-Hill Companies, Inc. All rights reserved. Printed in the United States of America. Previous editions © 2011, 2009, and 2007. No part of this publication may be reproduced or distributed in any form or by any means, or stored in a database or retrieval system, without the prior written consent of The McGraw-Hill Companies, Inc., including, but not limited to, in any network or other electronic storage or transmission, or broadcast for distance learning.

Some ancillaries, including electronic and print components, may not be available to customers outside the United States.

This book is printed on acid-free paper.

Global Studies® is a registered trademark of the McGraw-Hill Companies, Inc.

Global Studies is published by the **Contemporary Learning Series** group within the McGraw-Hill Higher Education division.

1 2 3 4 5 6 7 8 9 0 QDB/QDB 1 0 9 8 7 6 5 4 3 2

MHID: 0-07-802626-1
ISBN: 978-0-07-802626-3
ISSN: 1061-2831

Managing Editor: *Larry Loeppke*
Senior Developmental Editor: *Debra A. Henricks*
Content Licensing Specialist: *Rita Hingtgen*
Project Manager: *Erin Melloy*
Design Coordinator: *Brenda Rolwes*
Cover Graphics: *Rick D. Noel*
Buyer: *Jennifer Pickel*
Media Project Manager: *Sridevi Palani*

Compositor: Laserwords Private Limited
Cover Image: Photo © www.danheller.com

Author/Editors

Dr. Paul B. Goodwin

Dr. Paul B. Goodwin is a professor emeritus of Latin American history at the University of Connecticut, Storrs. Dr. Goodwin has written, reviewed, and lectured extensively at universities in the United States and many other countries. His particular areas of interest are modern Argentina and Anglo–Latin American relations. Dr. Goodwin has authored or edited three books and numerous articles.

Series Consultant
Dr. Christopher J. Sutton

Dr. Christopher J. Sutton is professor of geography at Western Illinois University. Born in Virginia and raised in Illinois, he received his bachelor's degree (1988) and master's degree (1991) in Geography from Western Illinois University. In 1995 he earned his PhD in Geography from the University of Denver. Along with serving as a consultant for the Global Studies series, Dr. Sutton is co-author of McGraw-Hill's *Student Atlas of World Geography* and *Student Atlas of World Politics*. A broadly trained geographer who has authored numerous research articles and educational materials, his areas of interest include cartographic design, cultural geography, and urban transportation. Dr. Sutton has served as chairperson of the WIU Department of Geography and as president of the Illinois Geographical Society.

Academic Advisory Board

Members of the Academic Advisory Board are instrumental in the final selection of articles for each edition of *Global Studies*. Their review of articles for content, level, and appropriateness provides critical direction to the editors and staff. We think that you will find their careful consideration well reflected in this volume.

Global Studies: Latin America and the Caribbean
Fifteenth Edition

Contents

Global Studies: Latin America and the Caribbean

UNIT 1 — Latin America: Myth and Reality — 2

UNIT 2 — Central America: Lands in Turmoil — 20

UNIT 3 — South America: An Imperfect Prism — 70

UNIT 4 — The Caribbean: Sea of Diversity — 156

Articles from the World Press

Regional Articles

Mexico

Central America

Caribbean

Preface

USING GLOBAL STUDIES: LATIN AMERICA AND THE CARIBBEAN

The Global Studies Series

The Global Studies series was designed to provide readers with a basic knowledge and understanding of the regions and countries of the world. Each volume provides a foundation of information—geographic, cultural, economic, political, historical, and religious—that will allow readers to better assess the current and future problems within these countries and regions and to comprehend how events there might affect their own wellbeing. In short, these volumes present the background information necessary to respond to the realities of our global age.

Each of the volumes in the Global Studies series is crafted under the careful direction of an author/editor who is an expert in the area under study. The author/ editors teach and conduct research and have traveled extensively through the regions about which they are writing.

Major Features of the Global Studies Series

The Global Studies volumes are organized to provide concise information on the regions and countries within those areas under study. The major sections and features of the books are described here.

Regional Essays

For *Global Studies: Latin America and the Caribbean,* the author/editor has written five essays "Latin America: Myth and Reality," "Mexico: A Country Challenged," "Central America: Lands in Turmoil," "South America: An Imperfect Prism," and "The Caribbean: Sea of Diversity." Regional maps accompany the essays.

Country Reports

Concise reports are written for each of the countries within the region under study. These reports are the heart of each Global Studies volume. *Global Studies: Latin America and the Caribbean* Fifteenth Edition, contains 33 country reports, including the essay on Mexico.

Each country report is comprised of: a detailed map visually positioning the country among its neighboring states; a current essay providing important historical, geographical, political, cultural, and economic information; a timeline of key historical events; and a summary of statistical information. "Did you Know?" boxes offer interesting facts to further engage student interest, and "Further Investigation" boxes provide references to encourage students to explore a topic more deeply. Finally, Snapshot boxes summarize the country in terms of its development, freedom, health/welfare, and achievements.

A Note on the Statistical Reports

The statistical information provided for each country has been drawn from a wide range of sources. (The most frequently referenced are listed in the bibliography.) Every effort has been made to provide the most current and accurate information available. However, sometimes the information cited by these sources differs to some extent; and, all too often, the most current information available for some countries is somewhat dated. Aside from these occasional difficulties, the statistical summary of each country is generally quite complete and up to date. Care should be taken, however, in using these statistics (or, for that matter, any published statistics) in making hard comparisons among countries. Comparable statistics for the United States and Canada, can be found in Appendixes A and B.

Articles From the World Press

A collection of carefully selected articles from a broad range of international periodicals and newspapers are reprinted in this volume. The articles have been chosen for currency, interest, and their differing perspectives on the subject countries. Learning Objectives and Challenge Questions accompany each article to enhance student learning and comprehension.

Internet References

An extensive annotated list of websites can be found in this edition of *Global Studies: Latin America and the Caribbean.* In addition, country specific websites are provided at the end of most country reports. All of the website addresses were correct and operational at press time. Instructors and students alike are urged to refer to those sites often to enhance their understanding of the region and to keep up with current events.

Glossary, Bibliography, Index

At the back of each Global Studies volume, readers will find a glossary of terms and abbreviations, which provides a quick reference to the specialized vocabulary of the area under study and to the standard abbreviations used throughout the volume.

Following the glossary is a bibliography, which lists general works, national histories, and current-events publications and periodicals that provide regular coverage on Latin America and the Caribbean.

The index at the end of the volume is an accurate reference to the contents of the volume. Readers seeking specific information and citations should consult this standard index.

Currency and Usefulness

Global Studies: Latin America and the Caribbean, like the other Global Studies volumes, is intended to provide the most current and useful information available necessary to understand the events that are shaping the cultures of the region today.

This volume is revised on a regular basis. If you have an idea that you think will make the next edition more useful, an article or bit of information that will make it more current, or a general comment on its organization, content, or features, please send it in for serious consideration.

Guided Tour

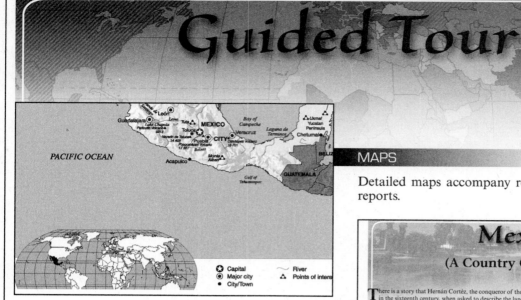

MAPS

Detailed maps accompany regional essays and country reports.

Mexico
(A Country Challenged)

There is a story that Hernán Cortéz, the conqueror of the Aztec Empire in the sixteenth century, when asked to describe the landscape of New Spain (Mexico), took a piece of paper in his hands and crumpled it. The analogy is apt. Mexico is a tortured land of mountains and valleys, of deserts in the north and rain forests in the south. Geography has helped to create an intense regionalism in Mexico, and the existence of hundreds of *patrias chicas* ("little countries") has hindered national integration.

Much of Mexico's territory is vulnerable to earthquakes and volcanic activity. In 1943, for example, a cornfield in one of Mexico's richest agricultural zones sprouted a volcano instead of maize. In 1982, a severe volcanic eruption in the south took several hundred lives, destroyed thousands of head of livestock, and buried crops under tons of ash. Thousands of people died when a series of earthquakes struck Mexico City in 1985.

Mexico is a nation of climatic extremes. Much-needed rains often fall so hard that most of the water runs off before it can be absorbed by the soil. When rains fail to materialize, crops die in the fields. The harsh face of the land, the unavailability of water, and erosion limit the agricultural potential of Mexico. Only 10 to 15 percent of Mexico's land can be planted with crops, but because of unpredictable weather or natural disasters, good harvests can be expected from only 6 to 8 percent of the land in

TIMELINE
1519
Hernán Cortés lands at Vera Cruz
1521
Destruction of the Aztec Empire
1810
Mexico proclaims its independence from Spain
1846–1848

REGIONAL ESSAYS AND COUNTRY REPORTS

Concise regional essays and country reports include historical, cultural, religious, political, and economic information, along with detailed maps and statistics.

TIMELINE
1519
Hernán Cortés lands at Vera Cruz
1521
Destruction of the Aztec Empire
1810
Mexico proclaims its independence from Spain
1846–1848
War with the United States; Mexico loses four-fifths of its territory
1862–1867
The French take over the Mexican throne and

TIMELINE

A timeline of key historical events is included with each country report.

DID YOU KNOW?

Did You Know? boxes offer interesting facts to engage student interest

? DID YOU KNOW?
The dance known as the tango had its origins in the bars and brothels of Buenos Aires in the 19th century. It gained respectability around the turn of the century when it became popular in Paris. The dance has since become one of Argentina's national symbols and is embraced by all levels of society.

FURTHER INVESTIGATION
For more information on the tango, visit www.history-of-tango.com/

FURTHER INVESTIGATION

Further Investigation boxes encourage students to explore a topic more deeply.

Statistical information from a wide range of sources is provided for each country.

Statistics

Geography

Area in Square Miles (Kilometers): 764,000 (1,978,000) (about 3 times the size of Texas)

Capital (Population): Mexico City (19,310,000 including suburbs)

Environmental Concerns: Scarce freshwater resources; water pollution; deforestation; soil erosion; serious air pollution

Geographical Features: high, rugged mountains; low coastal plains; high plateaus; desert

Climate: varies from tropical to desert

People

Population

Total: 113,724,226 (2010 est.)

Annual Growth Rate: 1.1%

Rural/Urban Population Ratio: 22/78

Major Languages: Spanish; various Maya, Nahuatl, and other regional indigenous languages

Ethnic Makeup: 60% Mestizo; 30% Amerindian; 9% white; 1% others

Religions: 76.5% Roman Catholic; 6.3% Protestant; 13.8% unspecified or none

Health

Life Expectancy at Birth: 73 years (male); 79 years (female)

Infant Mortality Rate (Ratio): 17.29/1,000

Government

Type: federal republic

Independence Date: September 16, 1810 (from Spain)

Head of State/Government: President Felipe Calderón is both head of state and head of government

Political Parties: Institutional Revolutionary Party; National Action Party; Party of the Democratic Revolution; Workers Party; Convergence for Democracy; Labor Party; Mexican Green Ecological Party; others.

Suffrage: universal and compulsory at 18

Military

Military Expenditures (% of GDP): 0.5%

Current Disputes: none

Economy

Currency ($U.S. Equivalent): 13.64 pesos = $1

Per Capita Income/GDP: $13,900/$1.567 trillion

GDP Real Growth Rate: −5.5%

Inflation Rate: 4.2%

Unemployment Rate: 5.4%; underemployment: +/− 25%

Labor Force: 47 million

Natural Resources: petroleum; silver; copper; gold; lead; zinc; natural gas; timber

Agriculture: corn; wheat; soybeans; rice; beans; cot-

Snapshot: MEXICO

Summarized below is a quick look at the country with regard to its development, freedom, health/welfare, and achievements.

Development

Mexico's state-owned oil company, PEMEX, is badly in need of money both to invest in upgrades to an aging infrastructure and to explore for new oil fields to replace those that are nearly played out. Mexicans, however, are loath to invite the participation of foreign oil companies in an industry that many view as a "sacred" symbol of their sovereignty.

Freedom

from Free to Partly Free due to the targeting of local officials by organized crime groups and the government's inability to protect citizens' rights in the face of criminal violence.

Health/Welfare

In 2005 the Mexican congress passed legislation that promised universal health coverage for all its citizens. By September 2011 about 51 million people had enrolled in the program.

Achievements

Mexican writers and artists have won world acclaim. The works of novelists such as Carlos Fuentes, Mariano Azuela, and Juan Rulfo have been translated into many languages. The graphic-art styles of Posada and the mural art of Diego

Snapshot boxes summarize each country with regard to its development, freedom, health/welfare, and achievements.

A collection of carefully selected articles from the world press introduces students to relevant topics affecting the modern culture of the region.

---

1   The Paradoxes of Latin America

Mario Vargas Llosa

Learning Objectives

After reading this article, you will more clearly understand the following:

- Latin American identities
- Cultural diversity
- Myths and stereotypes
- *Mestizaje* (racial mixing)

What does it mean to feel you are Latin American? It means being aware that the territorial boundaries dividing our nations are artificial, imposed arbitrarily during the colonial period. And neither our leaders during the emancipation period nor the republican governments that followed bothered to correct that situation. In fact, they often worsened things by further separating and isolating societies whose commonalities were deeper than their petty differences. This balkanization of Latin America, unlike what took place in North America, where the Thir-

traditions—Quechua and Aymara—are the patrimony of vast social conglomerations, others, like the Amazonian cultures, survive in small communities, sometimes just a handful of families.

Fortunately, *mestizaje*—racial mixing—extends in all directions, bringing these two worlds together. In some countries, Mexico for example, *mestizaje* has integrated the bulk of society both culturally and racially. It represents the greatest achievement of the Mexican Revolution—transforming the two ethnic extremes, Native Americans and Europeans, into minorities. This integration is less dynamic in the other countries, but it is still going on and it will ultimately give Latin America the distinctive identity of a *mestizo* continent. But let's hope it does so without making it totally uniform and erasing its subtle differences, though that is certainly possible in this century of globalization and interdependence among nations.

What is imperative is that, sooner rather than later, liberty and legality will be conjoined, thanks to democracy. Then all Latin Americans, regardless of race, language, religion and culture, will be equal before the law, will enjoy the same rights and opportunities, and will coexist in

Learning Objectives and ***Challenge Questions*** accompany each article to further enhance learning and comprehension.

Challenge Questions

After reading this article, you will be able to answer the following questions:

1. Is Latin America a "western" culture or something else?
2. Is there a Latin American identity?
3. How can we explain the paradox between Latin American political and social "underdevelopment" and the region's extraordinary literary and artistic originality?
4. How can we understand the tension between nationalism and cultural integration?

Internet References

(Some websites continually change their structure and content, so the information listed here may not always be available.)

GENERAL SITES

CNN Online Page

www.cnn.com

U.S. 24-hour video news channel. News is updated every few hours.

C-SPAN Online

www.c-span.org

See especially C-SPAN International on the Web for International Programming Highlights and archived C-SPAN programs.

GlobalEdge

http://globaledge.msu.edu/ibrd/ibrd.asp

Connect to several international business links from this site. Included are links to a glossary of international trade terms, exporting data, international trade, current laws, and data on GATT, NAFTA, and MERCOSUR.

UN Environmental Programme (UNEP)

www.unep.org

Official site of UNEP with information on UN environmental programs, products, services, events, and a search engine.

U.S. Agency for International Development (USAID)

www.usaid.gov

Graphically presented U.S. trade statistics with Latin America and the Caribbean.

U.S. Central Intelligence Agency Home Page

www.cia.gov/library/publications/the-world-factbook/

This site includes publications of the CIA, such as the World Factbook, Factbook on Intelligence, Handbook of International Economic Statistics, CIA Maps and Publications, and much more.

U.S. Department of State Home Page

www.state.gov/www/ind.html

Organized alphabetically (i.e., Country Reports, Human

Internet References direct students to additional information.

This map provides a graphic picture of where the countries of the world are located, the relationship they have with their region and neighbors, and their positions relative to major powers and power blocs. Certain areas have been focused on to illustrate these crowded regions more clearly. Latin America and the Caribbean is shaded for emphasis.

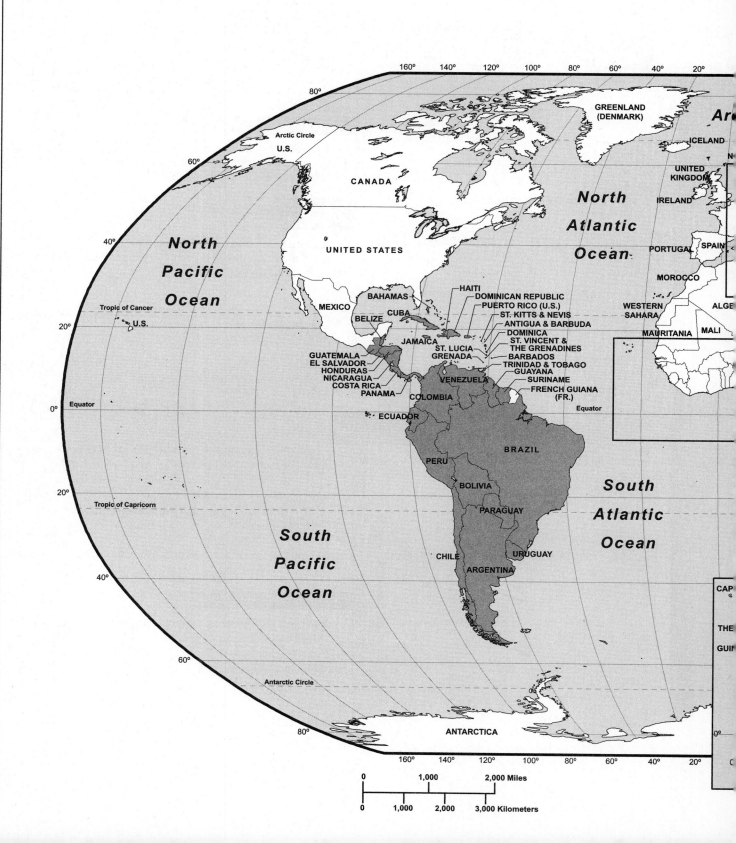

Inset map (Europe/Middle East):
NORWAY, SWEDEN, ESTONIA, DENMARK, LATVIA, RUSSIA, LITHUANIA, NETHERLANDS, BELARUS, BELGIUM, POLAND, GERMANY, UKRAINE, LUX., LIECHT., CZECHIA, SLOVAKIA, MOLDOVA, FRANCE, SWITZ., AUSTRIA, HUNGARY, SLOVENIA, ROMANIA, SAN MARINO, CROATIA, SERBIA, MONACO, ITALY, MONT., BULGARIA, AZERBAIJAN, ANDORRA, KOSOVO, MAC., GEORGIA, ARMENIA, VATICAN CITY, ALBANIA, GREECE, TURKEY, IRAN, TUNISIA, MALTA, CYPRUS, SYRIA, IRAQ, LEBANON, ISRAEL, JORDAN, KUWAIT, ALGERIA, LIBYA, EGYPT, SAUDI ARABIA

0, 300, 600 Miles
0, 300, 600 Kilometers

Main map:
Arctic Circle

RUSSIA

FINLAND, SWEDEN

KAZAKHSTAN, MONGOLIA, JAPAN, North Pacific Ocean

UZBEKISTAN, TAJIKISTAN, KYRGYZSTAN, TURKMENISTAN

AFGHANISTAN, NEPAL, CHINA, BHUTAN, TAIWAN

IRAN, PAKISTAN, BAHRAIN, LAOS, Tropic of Cancer

EGYPT, SAUDI ARABIA, QATAR, U.A.E., OMAN, INDIA, BANGLADESH, MYANMAR, THAILAND, VIETNAM, PHILIPPINES, LIBYA, CHAD, ERITREA, YEMEN, DJIBOUTI

SUDAN, SOUTH SUDAN, ETHIOPIA, SOMALIA, C.A.R., SRI LANKA, CAMBODIA, BRUNEI, MALAYSIA, PALAU, MICRONESIA, MALDIVES, KIRIBATI, NAURU

UGANDA, SINGAPORE, Equator

DEM. REP. OF THE CONGO, KENYA, RWANDA, BURUNDI, SEYCHELLES, INDONESIA, PAPUA NEW GUINEA, SOLOMON ISLANDS

TANZANIA, MALAWI, COMOROS, TIMOR-LESTE, VANUATU, FIJI

ANGOLA, ZAMBIA, MADAGASCAR, Indian Ocean, Tropic of Capricorn, TONGA

ZIMBABWE, NAMIBIA, BOTSWANA, MOZAMBIQUE, MAURITIUS, AUSTRALIA

SOUTH AFRICA, SWAZILAND, LESOTHO

NEW ZEALAND

Antarctic Circle

Inset map (Africa):
MAURITANIA, MALI, NIGER, SENEGAL, CHAD, BURKINA FASO, GUINEA, BENIN, NIGERIA, COTE D'IVOIRE, TOGO, GHANA, CAMEROON, LIBERIA, A LEONE, EQUATORIAL GUINEA, SÃO TOMÉ & PRÍNCIPE, GABON, CONGO REP.

800 Miles
1,000 Kilometers

1

Latin America

Bahamas

Gulf of
Mexico

ATLANTIC
OCEAN

Mexico

Cuba

Dominican
Republic

Puerto Rico (U.S.)

Jamaica

Haiti

Antigua and Barbuda

Belize

St. Kitts and Nevis

Dominica

Honduras

Caribbean
Sea

St. Lucia

Guatemala

St. Vincent and
the Grenadines

Barbados

El Salvador

Nicaragua

Grenada

Costa Rica

Panama

Trinidad and Tobago

Venezuela

Guyana

Suriname

French Guiana (Fr.)

Colombia

Ecuador

PACIFIC
OCEAN

Peru

Brazil

Bolivia

Paraguay

Chile

Uruguay

Argentina

ATLANTIC
OCEAN

0   500   1,000   1,500 Miles

0   500   1,000   1,500   2,000 Kilometers

Latin America
Myth and Reality

Much of the world still tends to view Latin Americans in terms of stereotypes. Latin American leaders are in many cases still perceived as dictators or demagogues, either from the left or the right sides of the political spectrum with scant attention paid to their actual goals and policies. The popular image of the mustachioed bandit sporting a large sombrero and draped with cartridge belts has been replaced by the figure of the modern-day guerrilla or drug lord, but the same essential image, of lawlessness and violence, persists. Another common stereotype is that of the lazy Latin American who constantly puts things off until *mañana* ("tomorrow"). The implied message here is that Latin Americans lack industry and do not know how to make the best use of their time. A third widespread image is that of the Latin lover and the cult of *machismo* (manliness).

Many of those outside the culture find it difficult to conceive of Latin America as a mixture of peoples and cultures, each one distinct from the others. Indeed, it was not so long ago that then–U.S. president Ronald Reagan, after a tour of the region, remarked with some surprise that all of the countries were "different." Stereotypes spring from ignorance and bias; images are not necessarily a reflection of reality. In the words of Spanish philosopher José Ortega y Gasset: "In politics and history, if one takes accepted statements at face value, one will be sadly misled."

■ THE LATIN AMERICAN REALITY

The reality of Latin America's multiplicity of cultures is, in a word, complexity. Europeans, Africans, Asians, and the indigenous peoples of Latin America have all contributed substantially to these cultures. If one sets aside non-Hispanic influences for a moment, it may be possible to argue, as does historian Claudio Veliz, that "the Iberian [Spanish and Portuguese] inheritance is an essential part of our lives and customs; Brazil and Spanish America [i.e., Spanish-speaking] have derived their personality from Iberia."

Many scholars would disagree. For example, political scientist Lawrence S. Graham argues that "what is clear is that generalizations about Latin American cultural unity are no longer tenable." And that "one of the effects of nationalism has been to . . . lead growing numbers of individuals within the region to identify with their own nation-state before they think in terms of a more amorphous land mass called Latin America."

Granted, Argentines speak of their Argentinity and Mexicans of their *Mejicanidad*. It is true that there are profound differences that separate the nations of the region. But there exists a cultural bedrock that ties Latin America to Spain and Portugal, and beyond—to the Roman Empire and the great cultures of the Mediterranean world. African influence, too, is substantial in many parts of the region. Latin America's Indians, of course, trace their roots to indigenous sources. In countries such as Bolivia, however, where indigenous peoples are in the majority, in recent years there has emerged a strong movement that exalts indigenous cultures over those derived from the West.

In Latin America, the family is an important element in the cultural context.

To understand the nature of Latin American culture, one must remember that there exist many exceptions to the generalizations; the cultural mold is not rigid. Much of what has happened in Latin America, including the evolution of its cultures, is the result of a fortunate—and sometimes an unfortunate—combination of various factors.

■ THE FAMILY

Let us first consider the Latin American family. The family unit has, for the most part, survived Latin America's uneven economic development and the pressures of modernization. Family ties are strong and dominant. These bonds are confined not only to the nuclear family

3

(Royalty-Free/Corbis/DALIND085)

The role of the indigenous woman in Latin America has been defined by centuries of tradition. This woman is carrying a bundle of firewood, just as her ancestors did.

of father, mother, children, and grandparents but also present in the extended family (a network of second cousins, godparents, and close friends of blood relatives). In times of difficulty the family can usually be counted on to help. Ideally it is a fortress against the misery and uncertainty of the outside world; it is the repository of dignity, honor, and respect.

Sadly, violence, drugs, gangs, extreme poverty, emigration, and the need to flee have compromised the ideal world in many parts of the region. Guerrilla warfare in Central America and Colombia, for example, has shattered families and forced thousands to become refugees. Drug gangs in the impoverished *favelas* of Brazil's major cities have torn apart neighborhoods and families. Extreme poverty and lack of opportunity have caused additional thousands of people to flee their countries in makeshift boats or to emigrate north to the United States and Canada. This, too, often divides families.

■ AN URBAN CIVILIZATION

In a region where the interaction of networks of families is the rule and where frequent human contact is sought out, it is not surprising to find that Latin Americans are, above all, an urban people. There are more cities of over half a million people in Latin America than in the United States.

Latin America's high percentage of urban dwellers is unusual, for urbanization is usually associated with industrialization. In Latin America, urban culture was not created by industrial growth; it actually predated it. As soon as the opportunity presented itself, the Spanish conquerors of the New World, in Veliz's words, "founded cities in which to take refuge from the barbaric, harsh, uncivilized, and rural world outside. . . . For those men civilization was strictly and uniquely a function of well-ordered city life."

The city, from the Spanish conquest until the present, has dominated the social and cultural horizon of Latin America. Opportunity is found in the city, not in the countryside. This cultural fact of life, in addition to economic motives, accounts for the continuing flow of population from rural to urban areas in Latin America.

■ A WORLD OF APPEARANCES

Because in their urban environment Latin Americans are in close contact with many people, appearances are important to them. There is a constant quest for prestige, dignity, status, and honor. People are forever trying to impress one another with their public worth. Hence, it is not unusual to see a blue-collar worker traveling to work dressed in a suit, briefcase in hand. It is not uncommon to see jungles of television antennas over shantytowns, although many are not connected to anything.

It is a society that, in the opinion of writer Octavio Paz, hides behind masks. Latin Americans convey an impression of importance, no matter how menial their position. Glen Dealy, a political scientist, writes: "And those of the lower class who must wait on tables, wash cars, and do gardening for a living can help to gain back a measure of self-respect by having their shoes shined by someone else, buying a drink for a friend . . . , or concealing their occupation by wearing a tie to and from work."

■ MACHISMO

Closely related to appearances is *machismo*. The term is usually understood solely, and mistakenly, in terms of virility—the image of the Latin lover, for example. But machismo also connotes generosity, dignity, and honor. In many respects, macho behavior is indulged in because of social convention; it is expected of men. Machismo is also a cultural trait that cuts through class lines, for the macho is admired regardless of his social position.

■ THE ROLE OF WOMEN

If the complex nature of machismo is misunderstood by those outside the culture, so too is the role of women. The commonly held stereotype is that Latin American women are submissive and that the culture is dominated by males. Again, appearances mask a far more complex reality, for Latin American cultures actually allow for strong female roles. Political scientist Evelyn Stevens, for example, has found that *marianismo*—the female counterpart of machismo—permeates all strata of Latin American society. Marianismo is the cult of feminine spiritual superiority that "teaches that women are semi-divine, morally superior to and spiritually stronger than men."

When Mexico's war for independence broke out in 1810, a religious symbol—the Virgin of Guadalupe—was identified with the rebels and became a rallying point for the first stirrings of Mexican nationalism. It was not uncommon in Argentine textbooks to portray Eva Perón (1919–1952), President Juan Perón's wife, in the image of the Virgin Mary, complete with a blue veil and halo. In less religious terms, one of Latin America's most popular novels, *Doña Barbara,* by Rómulo Gallegos, is the

(United Nations Photo/Jerry Frank (UN160755))

Agriculture is the backbone of much of Latin America's cultures and economies. These workers are harvesting sugarcane on a plantation in the state of Pernambuco, Brazil.

story of a female *caudillo* ("man on horseback") on the plains of Venezuela. One need not look to fiction, for in 2006 Chile elected a woman as president. Importantly, she won on her own merits: equally important, she was careful to cultivate an image of a caring mother. More recently Argentina elected its first woman president. Substantial numbers of women may now be counted as members of congress in several countries.

The Latin American woman dominates the family because of a deep-seated respect for motherhood. Personal identity is less of a problem for her because she retains her family name upon marriage and passes it on to her children. Women who work outside the home are also supposed to retain respect for their motherhood, which is sacred. In any conflict between a woman's job and the needs of her family, the employer, by custom, must grant her a leave to tend to the family's needs. Recent historical scholarship has also revealed that Latin American women have long enjoyed rights denied to women in other, more "advanced" parts of the world. For example, Latin American women were allowed to own property and to sign for mortgages in their own names even in colonial days. In the 1920s, they won the right to vote in local elections in Yucatán, Mexico, and in San Juan, Argentina.

Here again, though, appearances can be deceiving. Many Latin American constitutions guarantee equality of treatment, but reality is burdensome for women in many parts of the region. They do not have the same kinds of access to jobs that men enjoy; they seldom receive equal pay for equal work; and family life, at times, can be brutalizing.

◼ WORK AND LEISURE

Work, leisure, and concepts of time in Latin America correspond to an entirely different cultural mind-set than exists in Northern Europe and North America. The essential difference was demonstrated in a North American television commercial for a wine, in which two starry-eyed people were portrayed giving the Spanish toast *Salud, amor, y pesetas* ("Health, love, and money"). For a North American audience, the message was appropriate. But the full Spanish toast includes the tag line *y el tiempo para gozarlos* ("and the time to enjoy them").

In Latin America, leisure is viewed as a perfectly rational goal. It has nothing to do with being lazy or indolent. Indeed, in *Ariel,* by writer José Enrique Rodó, leisure is described within the context of the culture: "To think, to dream, to admire—these are the ministrants that haunt my cell. The ancients ranked them under the word *otium,* well-employed leisure, which they deemed the highest use of being truly rational, liberty of thought emancipated of all ignoble chains. Such leisure meant that use of time which they opposed to mere economic activity as the expression of a higher life. Their concept of dignity was linked closely to this lofty conception of leisure." Work, by contrast, is often perceived as a necessary evil.

CONCEPTS OF TIME

Latin American attitudes toward time also reveal the inner workings of the culture. Exasperated North American businesspeople have for years complained about the *mañana, mañana* attitude of Latin Americans. People often are late for appointments; sometimes little *appears* to get done.

For the North American who believes that time is money, such behavior appears senseless. However, Glen Dealy, in his perceptive book *The Public Man,* argues that such behavior is perfectly rational. A Latin American man who spends hours over lunch or over coffee in a café is not wasting time. For here, with his friends and relatives, he is with the source of his power. Indeed, networks of friends and families are the glue of Latin American society. "Without spending time in this fashion he would, in fact, soon have fewer friends. Additionally, he knows that to leave a café precipitously for an 'appointment' would signify to all that he must not keep someone else waiting—which further indicates his lack of importance. If he had power and position the other person would wait upon his arrival. It is the powerless who wait." Therefore, friends and power relationships are more important than rushing to keep an appointment. The North American who wants the business deal will wait. In a sense, then, the North American is the client and the Latin American is the *patrón* (the "patron," or wielder of power).

Perceptions of time in Latin America also have a broader meaning. North American students who have been exposed to Latin American literature are almost always confused by the absence of a "logical," chronological development of the story. Time, for Latin Americans, tends to be circular rather than linear. That is, the past and the present are perceived as equally relevant—both are points on a circle. The past is as important as the present.

MYTH AND REALITY MERGE

The past that is exposed in works of Latin American literature as well as scholarly writings reflects wholly different attitudes toward what people from other cultures identify as reality. For example, in Nobel Prize–winning writer Gabriél García Márquez's classic novel *One Hundred Years of Solitude*—a fictional history of the town of Macondo and its leading family—fantasy and tall tales abound. But García Márquez drew his inspiration from stories he heard at his grandmother's knee about Aracataca, Colombia, the real town in which he grew up. The point here is that the fanciful story of the town's origins constitutes that town's memory of its past. The stories give the town a common heritage and memory.

From a North American or Northern European perspective, the historical memory is faulty. From the Latin American perspective, however, it is the perception of the past that is important, regardless of its factual accuracy. Myth and reality, appearances and substance, merge.

POLITICAL CULTURE

The generalizations drawn here about Latin American society apply also to its political culture, which is essentially authoritarian and oriented toward power and power relationships. Ideology—be it liberalism, conservatism, or communism—is little more than window dressing. It is the means by which contenders for power can be separated. As Claudio Veliz has noted, regardless of the aims of revolutionary leaders, the great upheavals in Latin America in the twentieth century, without exception, ended up by strengthening the political center, which is essentially authoritarian. This was true of the Mexican Revolution (1910), the Bolivian Revolution (1952), the Cuban Revolution (1958), and the Nicaraguan Revolution (1979). At this moment populist movements in Venezuela, Bolivia, and Ecuador have all strengthened executive power. Indeed, the apparent "moral superiority" of political leaders is used to justify constitutional changes to allow presidents to serve extended terms. Ecuador's current president campaigned with a slogan proclaiming that he was "God's envoy."

Ideology has never been a decisive factor in the historical and social reality of Latin America. But charisma and the ability to lead are crucial ingredients. José Velasco Ibarra, five times the president of Ecuador in the twentieth century, once boasted: "Give me a balcony and I will be president!" He saw his personality, not his ideology, as the key to power.

In the realm of national and international relations, Latin America often appears to those outside the culture to be in a constant state of turmoil and chaos. It seems that every day there are reports that a prominent politician has fallen from power, border clashes have intensified, or guerrillas have taken over another section of a country. But the conclusion that chaos reigns in Latin America is most often based on the visible political and social violence, not on the general nature of a country. Political violence is often local in nature, and the social fabric of the country is bound together by the enduring social stability of the family. Again, there is the dualism of what *appears to be* and what *is*.

Much of this upheaval can be attributed to the division in Latin America between the people of Mediterranean background and the indigenous Indian populations. There may be several hundred minority groups within a single country. The problems that may arise from such intense internal differences, however, are not always necessarily detrimental, because they contribute to the texture and color of Latin American culture.

SEEING BEHIND THE MASK

In order to grasp the essence of Latin America, one must ignore the stereotypes, appreciate appearances for what they are, and attempt to see behind the mask. Although Latin America must be appreciated as an amalgam of cultures, it is largely dominated by behavior that is essentially a derivative of Mediterranean Western models.

A Latin American worldview tends to be dualistic. The family constitutes the basic unit; here one finds generosity, warmth, honor, and love. Beyond the walls of the home, in the world of business and politics, Latin Americans don their masks and enter "combat." It is a world of power relationships, of macho bravado, and of appearances. This dualism is deep-seated; scholars such as Richard Morse and Glen Dealy have traced its roots to the Middle Ages. For Latin Americans, one's activities are compartmentalized into those fit for the City of God, which corresponds to religion, the home, and one's intimate circle of friends; and those appropriate for the City of Man, which is secular and often ruthless and corrupt.

North Americans, who tend to measure both their public and private lives by the same yardstick, often interpret Latin American dualism as hypocrisy. Nothing could be further from the truth.

For the Latin American, life exists on several planes, has purpose, and is perfectly rational. Indeed, one is tempted to suggest that many Latin American institutions—particularly the supportive network of families and friends—are more in tune with a world that can alienate and isolate than are our own. As you will see in the following reports, the social structure and cultural diversity of Latin America add greatly to its character and, paradoxically, to its stability.

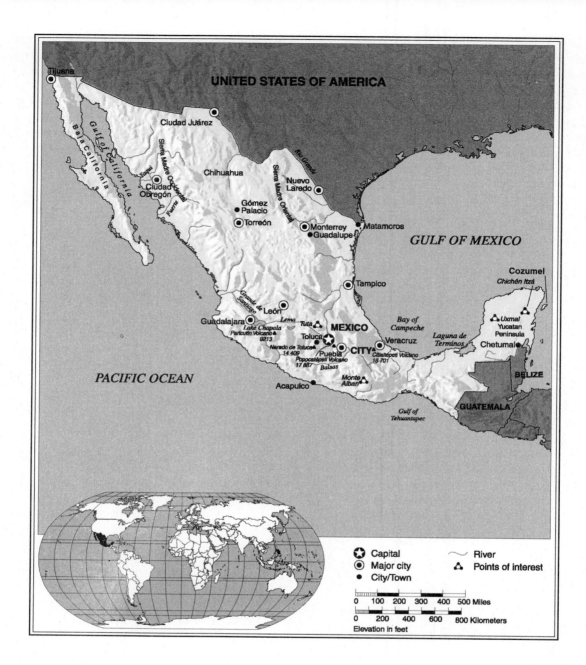

UNITED STATES OF AMERICA

Tijuana

Ciudad Juárez

Gulf of California

Baja California

Yaqui

Ciudad Obregón

Fuerte

Chihuahua

Sierra Madre Occidental

Sierra Madre Oriental

Rio Grande

Nuevo Laredo

Gómez Palacio

Torreón

Monterrey

Guadalupe

Matamoros

GULF OF MEXICO

Tampico

Cozumel

Chichén Itzá

Grande de Santiago

León

Lema

Tuta

MEXICO

Bay of Campeche

Uxmal

Yucatan Peninsula

Guadalajara

Lake Chapala

Paricutín Volcano 9213

Toluca

Nevado de Toluca 14,409

Popocatépetl Volcano 17,887

Puebla

CITY

Balsas

Citlaltépetl Volcano 18,701

Veracruz

Laguna de Terminos

Chetumal

BELIZE

PACIFIC OCEAN

Acapulco

Monte Albán

Gulf of Tehuantepec

GUATEMALA

☆ Capital

◉ Major city

● City/Town

∼ River

△ Points of interest

0 100 200 300 400 500 Miles

0 200 400 600 800 Kilometers

Elevation in feet

Mexico
(A Country Challenged)

There is a story that Hernán Cortéz, the conqueror of the Aztec Empire in the sixteenth century, when asked to describe the landscape of New Spain (Mexico), took a piece of paper in his hands and crumpled it. The analogy is apt. Mexico is a tortured land of mountains and valleys, of deserts in the north and rain forests in the south. Geography has helped to create an intense regionalism in Mexico, and the existence of hundreds of *patrias chicas* ("little countries") has hindered national integration.

Much of Mexico's territory is vulnerable to earthquakes and volcanic activity. In 1943, for example, a cornfield in one of Mexico's richest agricultural zones sprouted a volcano instead of maize. In 1982, a severe volcanic eruption in the south took several hundred lives, destroyed thousands of head of livestock, and buried crops under tons of ash. Thousands of people died when a series of earthquakes struck Mexico City in 1985.

Mexico is a nation of climatic extremes. Much-needed rains often fall so hard that most of the water runs off before it can be absorbed by the soil. When rains fail to materialize, crops die in the fields. The harsh face of the land, the unavailability of water, and erosion limit the agricultural potential of Mexico. Only 10 to 15 percent of Mexico's land can be planted with crops, but because of unpredictable weather or natural disasters, good harvests can be expected from only 6 to 8 percent of the land in any given year. Hurricanes have also taken a toll on Mexico's Atlantic and Pacific coasts. In 2005 severe storms struck Cancun where they not only wreaked havoc with the lucrative tourism industry but also caused significant losses in farming areas in the south.

■ MEXICO CITY

Mexico's central region has the best cropland. It was here that the Aztecs built their capital city, the foundations of which lie beneath the current Mexican capital, Mexico City. Given their agricultural potential as well as its focus as the commercial and administrative center of the nation, Mexico City and the surrounding region have always supported a large population. For decades, Mexico City has acted as a magnet for rural poor who have given up attempts to eke out a living from the soil. In the 1940s and 1950s, the city experienced a great population surge. In that era, however, it had the capacity to absorb the tens of thousands of migrants, and so a myth of plentiful money and employment was created. Even today, that myth exercises a strong influence in the countryside; it partially accounts for the tremendous growth of the city and its greater metropolitan area, now home to approximately 20 million people.

The size and location of Mexico City have spawned awesome problems. Because it lies in a valley surrounded by mountains, air pollution is trapped. Mexico City has the worst smog in the Western Hemisphere. It has been suggested that breathing the air in Mexico City is the equivalent of smoking five packs of cigarettes a day. Traffic congestion is among the worst in the world. And essential services—including the provision of drinkable water, electricity, and sewers—have failed to keep pace with the city's growth in population.

TIMELINE

1519
Hernán Cortés lands at Vera Cruz

1521
Destruction of the Aztec Empire

1810
Mexico proclaims its independence from Spain

1846–1848
War with the United States; Mexico loses four-fifths of its territory

1862–1867
The French take over the Mexican throne and install Emperor Maximillian

1876–1910
Era of dictator Porfirio Díaz: modernization

1910–1917
The Mexican Revolution

1934–1940
Land distribution under President Cárdenas

1938
Nationalization of foreign petroleum companies

1955
Women win the right to vote

1968
The Olympic Games are held in Mexico City; riots and violence

1980s
Severe economic crisis; the peso is devalued; inflation soars; the foreign-debt crisis escalates; Maya insurgency in the state of Chiapas

1990s
NAFTA is passed: the PRI loses ground in legislative, gubernatorial, and municipal elections

2000s
Presidential elections held in July 2012
Death toll from drug violence surpasses 40,000

(Pixtal/age fotostock)

Between 1960 and 1980 the population of Mexico City more than doubled.

Social and Cultural Changes

Dramatic social and cultural changes have accompanied Mexico's population growth. These are particularly evident in Mexico City, which daily becomes less Mexican and more cosmopolitan and international.

As Mexico City has become more worldly, English words have become more common in everyday vocabulary. "Okay," "coffee break," and "happy hour" are some examples of English idioms that have slipped into popular usage. In urban centers, quick lunches and coffee breaks have replaced the traditional large meal that was once served at noon. For most people, the afternoon siesta ("nap") is a fondly remembered custom of bygone days.

Mass communication has had an incalculable impact on culture. Television commercials primarily use models who are ethnically European in appearance—preferably white, blue-eyed, and blonde. As if in defiance of the overwhelmingly Mestizo (mixed Indian and white) character of the population, Mexican newspapers and magazines carry advertisements for products guaranteed to lighten one's skin. Success has become associated with light skin.

Once a symbol of success was ownership of a television. Anntennas covered rooftops even in the poorest urban slums. Acute observers have noted, however, that many of the antennas were not connected to anything; the residents of many hovels merely wanted to convey the impression that they can afford one. Today, possession of cell phones or other electronic devices is an essential part of one's image.

Television, however, has helped to educate the illiterate. Some Mexican soap operas, for instance, incorporate educational materials. On a given day, a show's characters may attend an adult-education class that stresses basic reading and writing skills. Both the television characters and the home-viewing audience sit in on the class. Literacy is portrayed as being essential to one's success and well-being. Mexican *telenovelas,* or "soaps," have a special focus on teenagers and problems common to adolescents. Solutions are advanced within a traditional cultural context and reaffirm the central role of the family.

Cultural Survival: Compadrazgo

Despite these obvious signs of change, distinct Mexican traditions and customs have not only survived Mexico's transformation but have also flourished because of it. The chaos of city life, the hundreds of thousands of migrants uprooted from rural settings, and the sense of isolation and alienation common to city dwellers the world over are in part eased by the Hispanic institution of *compadrazgo* ("cogodparenthood" or "sponsorship").

Compadrazgo is found at all levels of Mexican society and in both rural and urban areas. It is a device for building economic and social alliances that are more enduring than simple friendship. Furthermore, it has a religious dimension as well as a secular, or everyday, application. In addition to basic religious occasions (such as baptism, confirmation, first communion, and marriage), Mexicans seek sponsors for minor religious occasions, such as the blessing of a business, and for events as common as a graduation or a boy's first haircut.

Anthropologist Robert V. Kemper observes that the institution of compadrazgo reaches across class lines and knits the various strands of Mexican society into a whole cloth. Compadrazgo performs many functions, including providing assistance from the more powerful to the less powerful and, reciprocally, providing homage from the less powerful to the more powerful. The most common choices for *compadres* are neighbors, relatives, fellow migrants, coworkers, and employers. A remarkably flexible institution, compadrazgo is perfectly compatible with the tensions and anxieties of urban life.

Yet even compadrazgo—a form of patron/client relationship—has its limitations. As Mexico City has sprawled ever wider across the landscape, multitudes of new neighborhoods have been created. Many are the result of well-planned land seizures, orchestrated by groups of people attracted by the promise of the city. Technically, such land seizures are illegal, and a primary goal of the *colonos* (inhabitants of these low-income communities) is legitimization and consequent community participation.

Beginning in the 1970s, colonos forcefully pursued their demands for legitimization through protest movements and demonstrations, some of which revealed a surprising degree of radicalism. In response, the Mexican government adopted a two-track policy: It selectively repressed the best-organized and most radical groups of colonos, and it tried to co-opt the remainder through negotiation. In the early 1980s, the government created "Citizen Representation" bodies, official channels within Mexico City through which colonos could participate, within the system, in the articulation of their demands.

From the perspective of the colonos, the establishment of the citizen organizations afforded them an additional means to advance their demands for garbage collection, street paving, provision of potable water, sewage removal, and, most critically, the regularization of land tenure—that is, legitimization. In the government's view, representation for the colonos served to win supporters for the Mexican political structure, particularly the authority of the official ruling party, at a time of outspoken challenge from other political sectors.

Citizens are encouraged to work within the system; potential dissidents are transformed through the process of co-optation into collaborators. In today's Mexico City, then, patronage and clientage have two faces: the traditional one of compadrazgo, the other a form of state paternalism that promotes community participation.

◼ THE BORDER

In the past few decades, driven by poverty, unemployment, and underemployment, many Mexicans have chosen not Mexico City but the United States as the place to improve their lives. Mexican workers in the United States are not a new phenomenon. During World War II, the presidents of both nations agreed to allow Mexican workers, called *braceros,* to enter the United States as agricultural workers. They were strictly regulated. In contrast, the new wave of migrants is largely unregulated. Each year, hundreds of thousands of undocumented Mexicans illegally cross the border in search of work. It has been estimated that at any given time, between 4 million and 6 million Mexicans pursue an existence as illegal aliens in the United States.

Thousands of Mexicans are able to support families with the fruits of their labors, but, as undocumented workers, they are not protected by the law. Many are callously exploited by those who smuggle them across the border as well as by employers in the United States. For the Mexican government, however, such mass emigration has been a blessing in disguise. It has served as a kind of sociopolitical safety valve, and it has resulted in an inflow of dollars sent home by the workers.

In recent years, U.S. companies and the governments of Mexican states along the border have profited from the creation of assembly plants known as *maquiladoras.* Low wages and a docile labor force are attractive to employers, while the Mexican government reaps the benefits of employment and tax dollars. Despite the appearance of prosperity along the border, it must be emphasized that chronic unemployment in other parts

(Courtesy of Heather Haddon)

Mexican women won the right to vote in 1955. This woman demonstrates her political consciousness in response to an especially disputed gubernatorial election in the state of Oaxaca in August 2004.

of Mexico ensures the misery of millions of people. The North American Free Trade Agreement (NAFTA) hoped to alter these harsh realities, but after more than a decade real wages are lower, the distribution of income has become more unequal, and Mexicans still cross the U.S. border in large numbers. U.S. immigration policy has only served, from the Mexican perspective, to exacerbate the problem. Increased patrols, the construction of a high wall along the border, and the increased deportation of undocumented workers from the United States has worsened Mexico's problem with an excess labor supply. Drug smuggling along the border has added additional elements of violence and corruption and strained relations between the two nations. Mexico's struggle against gangs of drug dealers and its concomitant bloodshed has shown ominous signs of crossing the border.

THE INDIAN "PROBLEM"

During the 1900s, urbanization and racial mixing changed the demographic face of Mexico. A government official once commented: "A country predominately Mestizo, where Indian and white are now minorities, Mexico preserves the festivity and ceremonialism of the Indian civilizations and the religiosity and legalism of the Spanish Empire." The quotation is revealing, for it clearly identifies the Indian as a marginal member of society, as an object of curiosity.

In Mexico, as is the case with indigenous peoples in most of Latin America, Indians in many quarters are viewed as obstacles to national integration and economic progress. There exist in Mexico more than 200 distinct Indian tribes or ethnic groups, who speak more than 50 languages or dialects. In the view of "progressive"

Mexicans, the "sociocultural fragmentation" caused by the diversity of languages fosters political misunderstanding, insecurity, and regional incomprehension. Indians suffer from widespread discrimination. Language is not the only barrier to their economic progress. They have long endured the unequal practices of a ruling white and Mestizo elite. Indians may discover, for example, that they cannot expand a small industry, such as a furniture-making enterprise, because few financial institutions will lend a large amount of money to an Indian.

NATIONAL IDENTITY

Mexico's Mestizo face has had a profound impact on the attempts of intellectuals to understand the meaning of the term "Mexican." The question of national identity has always been an important theme in Mexican history; it became a particularly burning issue in the aftermath of the Revolution of 1910. Octavio Paz believes that most Mexicans have denied their origins: They do not want to be either Indian or Spaniard, but they also refuse to see themselves as a mixture of both. One result of this essential denial of one's ethnic roots is a collective inferiority complex. The Mexican, Paz writes, is insecure. To hide that insecurity, which stems from his sense of "inferiority," the Mexican wears a "mask." Machismo (the cult of manliness) is one example of such a mask. In Paz's estimation, aggressive behavior at a sporting event, while driving a car, or in relationships with women reflects a deep-seated identity crisis.

Perhaps an analogy can be drawn from Mexican domestic architecture. Traditional Mexican homes are surrounded by high, solid walls, often topped with shards of glass and devoid of windows looking out onto the street. From the outside, these abodes appear cold and inhospitable. Once inside (once behind the mask), however, the Mexican home is warm and comfortable. Here, appearances are set aside and individuals can relax and be themselves. By contrast, many homes in the United States have vast expanses of glass that allow every passerby to see within. That whole style of open architecture, at least for homes, is jolting for many Mexicans (as well as other Latin Americans).

THE FAILURE OF THE 1910 REVOLUTION

In addition to the elusive search for Mexican identity, one of Mexican intellectuals' favorite themes is the Revolution of 1910 and what they perceive as its shortcomings. That momentous struggle (1910–1917) cost more than 1 million lives, but it offered Mexico the promise of a new society, free from the abuses of past centuries. It began with a search for truth and honesty in government; it ended with an assertion of the dignity and equality of all men and women.

The goals of the 1910 Revolution were set forth in the Constitution of 1917, a remarkable document—not only in its own era, but also today. *Article 123,* for example, which concerns labor, includes the following provisions: an eight-hour workday, a general minimum wage, and a six-week leave with pay for pregnant women before the approximate birth date plus a six-week leave with pay following the birth. During the nursing period, the mother must be given extra rest periods each day for nursing the baby. Equal wages must be paid for equal work, regardless of sex or nationality. Workers are entitled to a participation in the profits of an enterprise (i.e., profit sharing). Overtime work must carry double pay. Employers are responsible for and must pay appropriate compensation for injuries received by workers in the performance of their duties or for occupational diseases. In 1917, such provisions were viewed as astounding and revolutionary.

Unfulfilled Promises

Unfortunately, many of the goals of 1917 have yet to be achieved. A number of writers, frustrated by the slow pace of change, concluded long ago that the Mexican Revolution was dead. Leading thinkers and writers, such as Carlos Fuentes, have bitterly criticized the failure of the Revolution to shape a more equitable society. Corruption, abuse of power, and self-serving opportunism characterize Mexico today.

One of the failed goals of the Revolution, in the eyes of critics, was an agrarian-reform program that fell short of achieving a wholesale change of land ownership or even of raising the standard of living in rural areas. Over the years, however, small-scale agriculture has sown the seeds of its own destruction. Plots of land that are barely adequate for subsistence farming have been further divided by peasant farmers anxious to satisfy the inheritance rights of their sons. More recently, government price controls on grain and corn have driven many marginal producers out of the market and off their lands.

Land Reform: One Story

Juan Rulfo, a major figure in the history of postrevolutionary literature, captured the frustration of peasants who have "benefited" from agrarian reform. "But sir," the peasant complained to the government official overseeing the land reform, "the earth is all washed away and hard. We don't think the plow will cut into the earth . . . that's like a rock quarry. You'd have to make with a pick-axe to plant the seed, and even then you can't be sure that anything will come up. . . ." The official, cold and indifferent, responded: "You can state that in writing. And now you can go. You should be attacking the large-estate owners and not the government that is giving you the land."

More frequently, landowners have attacked peasants. During the past several years in Mexico, insistent peasant demands for a new allocation of lands have been the occasion of a number of human-rights abuses—some of a very serious character. Some impatient peasants who have occupied lands in defiance of the law have been killed or have "disappeared." In one notorious case in 1982, 26 peasants were murdered in a dispute over land in the state of Puebla. The peasants, who claimed legal title to the land, were killed by mounted gunmen, reportedly hired by local ranchers. Political parties reacted to the massacre in characteristic fashion—all attempted to manipulate the event to their own advantage rather than to address the problem of land reform. Yet years later, paramilitary bands and local police controlled by political bosses or landowners still routinely threatened and/or killed peasant activists. Indeed, access to the land was a major factor in the Maya uprising in the southern state of Chiapas that began in 1994 and, in 2012, though dormant, remains unresolved.

The Promise of the Revolution

While critics of the 1910 Revolution are correct in identifying its failures, the Constitution of 1917 represents more than dashed hopes. The radical nature of the document allows governments (should they desire) to pursue aggressive egalitarian policies and still be within the law. For example, when addressing citizens, Mexican public officials often invoke the Constitution—issues tend to become less controversial if they are placed within the broad context of 1917. When President Adolfo López Mateos declared in 1960 that his government would be "extremely leftist," he quickly added that his position would be "within the Constitution." But some authorities argue that constitutional strictures can inhibit needed change. For example, the notoriously inefficient state petroleum monopoly (PEMEX) has been critically short of investment capital for years. To allow private companies to invest in the oil industry would require a constitutional change that many Mexicans equate to a form of *vendepatria* (selling out the country). Indeed, Congress routinely rejected discussions of even limited private participation in a national industry.

Women's Rights

Although the Constitution made reference to the equality of women in Mexican society, it was not until World War II that the women's-rights movement gathered strength. Women won the right to vote in Mexico in 1955; by the 1970s, they had challenged laws and social customs that were prejudicial to women. Some women have served on presidential cabinets, and one became governor of the state of Colima. The most important victory for women occurred in 1974, however, when the Mexican Congress passed legislation that, in effect, asked men to grant women full equality in society—including jobs, salaries, and legal standing. Some improvement has occurred in terms of the percentage of women who have been elected to congress. Indeed, in terms of percentage, more women hold congressional seats in Mexico than in the United States.

But attitudes are difficult to change with legislation, and much social behavior in Mexico still is sexist. The editor of the Mexican newspaper *Noroeste* asserted that the most important challenge that confronted former president Vicente Fox was to "break the paternalistic culture." For the most part, that has not happened and, according to the *World Economic Forum,* women fall behind men "in key measures of social well-being," such as education, health, and economic participation.

Many Mexican men feel that there are male and female roles in society, regardless of law. Government, public corporations, private businesses, the Roman Catholic Church, and the armed forces represent important areas of male activity. The home, private religious rituals, and secondary service roles represent areas of female activity. One is clearly dominant, the other subordinate.

The Role of the Church

Under the Constitution of 1917, no religious organization is allowed to administer or teach in Mexico's primary, secondary, or normal (higher education) schools; nor may clergy participate in the education of workers or peasants. Yet between 1940 and 1979, private schools expanded to the point where they enrolled 1.5 million of the country's 17 million pupils. Significantly, more than half of the private-school population attended Roman Catholic schools. Because they exist despite the fact that they are prohibited by law, the Catholic schools demonstrate the kinds of accommodation and flexibility that are possible in Mexico. It is in the best interests of the ruling party to satisfy as many interest groups as is possible.

From the perspective of politicians, the Roman Catholic Church has increasingly tilted the balance in the direction of social justice in recent years. Some Mexican bishops have been particularly outspoken on the issue, but when liberal or radical elements in the Church embrace social change, they may cross into the jurisdiction of the state. Under the Constitution, the state is responsible for improving the welfare of its people. Some committed clergy, however, believe that religion must play an active role in the transformation of society; it must not only have compassion for the poor but must also act to relieve poverty and eliminate injustice.

In 1991, Mexican bishops openly expressed their concern about the torture and mistreatment of prisoners, political persecution, corruption, discrimination against indigenous peoples, mistreatment of Central American refugees, and electoral fraud. In previous years, the government would have reacted sharply against such charges emanating from the Church. But, in this case, there had been a significant rapprochement between the Catholic Church and the state in Mexico. The new relationship culminated with the exchange of diplomatic representatives and Pope John Paul II's successful and popular visit to Mexico in 1990. Despite better relations at the highest level, in 1999 the bishop of Chiapas vigorously criticized the government for backing away from a 1996 accord between the state and leaders of a guerrilla insurgency and returning to a policy of violent repression.

■ MEXICO'S STABILITY

The stability of the Mexican state, as has been suggested, depends on the ability of the ruling elite to maintain a state of relative equilibrium among the multiplicity of interests and demands in the nation. The whole political process is characterized by bargaining among elites with various views on politics, social injustice, economic policy, and the conduct of foreign relations.

It was the Institutional Revolutionary Party (PRI), which held the presidency from 1929 until 2000, that set policy and decided what was possible or desirable. All change was generated from above, from the president and his advisers. Although the Constitution provides for a federal system, power was effectively centralized. In the words of one authority, Mexico, with its one-party rule, was not a democracy but, rather, "qualified authoritarianism." In the PRI era, Peruvian author Mario Vargas Llosa referred to Mexico as a "perfect dictatorship." Indeed, the main role of the PRI in the political system was political domination, not power sharing. Paternalistic and all-powerful, the state controlled the bureaucracies that directed the labor unions, peasant organizations, student groups, and virtually every other dimension of organized society. Even though the PRI lost the presidency in 2000, its adherents remain influential in Mexico's power centers.

Historically, politicians have tended to be more interested in building their careers than in responding to the demands of their constituents. According to political scientist Peter Smith, Mexican politicians are forever bargaining with one another, seeking favors from their superiors, and communicating in a language of "exaggerated deference." They have learned how to maximize power and success within the existing political structure. By following the "rules of the game," they move ahead. The net result is a consensus at the upper echelons of power.

In the past few decades, that consensus has been undermined. One of the great successes of the Revolution of 1910 was the rise to middle-class status of millions of people. But recent economic crises alienated that upwardly mobile sector from the PRI. People registered their dissatisfaction at the polls; in 1988, in fact, the official party finished second in Mexico City and other urban centers. In 1989, the PRI's unbroken winning streak of 60 years, facilitated by widespread electoral corruption, was broken in the state of Baja California del Norte, where the right-wing National Action Party (PAN) won the governorship. A decade of worrisome political losses prompted the PRI to consider long overdue reforms. That concern did not prevent the PRI from flagrant electoral fraud in 1988 that handed the presidency to Carlos Salinas Gortari. When it seemed apparent that the PRI would lose, the vote count was interrupted because of "computer failures." In the words of the recent autobiography of former president Miguel de la Madrid, who presided over the fraud, he was told by the PRI president: "You must proclaim the triumph of the PRI. It is a tradition that we cannot break without alarming the citizens." That "tradition" was about to end. Clearly, the PRI had lost touch with critical constituencies who were interested in fundamental change rather than party slogans and were fed up with the rampant corruption of PRI functionaries. Opposition parties continued to win elections.

In the summer of 1997, the left-of-center Party of the Democratic Revolution (PRD) scored stunning victories in legislative, gubernatorial, and municipal elections. For the first time, the PRI lost its stranglehold on the Chamber of Deputies, the lower house of Congress. Significantly, Cuauhtemoc Cardenas of the PRD was swept into power as mayor of Mexico City in the first direct vote for that position since 1928. In gubernatorial contests, the PAN won two elections and controlled an impressive seven of Mexico's 31 governorships.

Within the PRI, a new generation of leaders now perceived the need for political and economic change. President Ernesto Zedillo, worried about his party's prospects in the general elections of 2000, over the objections of old-line conservatives pushed a series of reforms in the PRI. For the first time, the party used state primaries and a national convention to choose the PRI's presidential candidate. This democratization of the party had its reflection in Zedillo's stated commitment to transform Mexican politics by giving the opposition a fair playing field. Voting was now more resistant to tampering and, as a consequence, the three major parties had to campaign for the support of the voters.

In July 2000, Vicente Fox headed a coalition of parties that adopted the name Alliance for Change and promised Mexico's electorate a "Revolution of Hope." It was a formula for success, as the PRI was swept from power. Although Fox was labeled a conservative, his platform indicated that he was above all a pragmatic politician who realized that his appeal and policies had to resonate with a wide range of sectors. Mexican voters saw in Fox someone who identified with human rights, social activism, indigenous rights, women, and the poor. He promised to be a "citizen president." Pundits described his election as a shift from an "imperial presidency" to an "entrepreneurial presidency." Indeed, Fox's economic policies, if implemented, would have promoted an annual growth rate of 7 percent, lowered inflation, balanced the budget, raised tax revenues, and improved the standard of living for Mexico's poor (who number 40 million). The private sector, in his vision, would drive the economy; strategic sectors of the economy, notably electricity generation and petrochemicals, would be opened to private capital. Labor reforms would be initiated that would link salaries to productivity.

President Fox also promised a renewed dialogue with rebels in the southern state of Chiapas. There, beginning in 1994, Maya insurgents had rebelled against a government that habitually supported landowners against indigenous peoples, essentially marginalizing the latter. Led by Subcomandante Marcos, a shrewd and articulate activist who quickly became a hero not only in Chiapas but also in much of the rest of Mexico, the rebels symbolized widespread dissatisfaction with the promises of the PRI. A series of negotiations with the government from time to time interrupted the climate of violence and culminated in 1996 with the Agreements of San Andres. The government assured the Maya of their independence over issues of local governance. But lack of implementation of the agreements, in combination with attacks by the military on the Maya, doomed the accord from the outset.

The inability of President Fox to implement fully his programs, Mexico's far-from-satisfactory economic performance (actual GDP growth in 2007 was only 3%), and a general trend in Latin America that has put populist regimes in power, set the stage for an interesting and contentious general election in July 2006. The election, which was likely the cleanest in Mexican history, was also the closest, with PAN candidate Felipe Calderón apparently winning by half a percent of the votes. Calderón, who did well in the north and among middle and upper-class voters, favored a free-market approach to the economy and wanted to allow the participation of private investment in the state-controlled energy markets. His economic priorities included job creation and the reduction of poverty, and in 2007 he won congressional support for fiscal and pension reforms. Runner-up Andrés Manuel López Obrador, a populist, favored the involvement of the state in public works projects to stimulate construction and ease unemployment. He also advocated broad-ranging social programs to address the plight of millions of impoverished Mexicans. The PRI finished a distant third. It is clear that the election revealed a polarized nation, divided geographically between the north and the south, and between the rich and the poor. President Calderon, in part because of difficult economic times, failed to generate either job creation or a reduction in poverty levels. His party might not survive elections scheduled for July 2012.

■ ORGANIZED LABOR

Organized labor provides an excellent example of the ways in which power is wielded in Mexico and how social change occurs. Mexican trade unions have the right to organize, negotiate, and strike. Most unions historically have not been independent of the government. The major portion of the labor movement is still affiliated with the PRI through an umbrella organization known as the Confederation of Mexican Workers (CTM). The Confederation, with a membership of 3.5 million, is one of the PRI's most ardent supporters. Union bosses truck in large crowds for campaign rallies, help PRI candidates at election time, and secure from union members approval of government policies. Union bosses have been well rewarded by the system they have helped to support. Most have become moderately wealthy and acquired status and prestige. Fully one-third of Mexico's senators and congressional representatives, as well as an occasional governor, come from the ranks of union leadership.

Such a relationship must be reciprocal if it is to function properly. The CTM has used an impressive array of left-wing slogans for years to win gains for its members. It has projected an aura of radicalism when, in fact, it is not. The image is important to union members, however, for it gives them the feeling of independence from the government, and it gives a role to the true radicals in the movement. In the 1980s, cracks began to appear in the foundation of union support for the government. The economic crisis of that decade resulted in sharp cutbacks in government spending. Benefits and wage increases fell far behind the pace of inflation; layoffs and unemployment led many union members to question the value of their special relationship with the PRI. Indeed, during the 1988 elections, the Mexican newspaper *El Norte* reported that Joaquín Hernández Galicia, the powerful leader of the Oil Workers' Union, was so upset with trends within the PRI that he directed his membership to vote for opposition candidates. Not surprisingly, then, President Salinas responded by naming a new leader to the Oil Workers' Union.

Independent unions outside the Confederation of Mexican Workers capitalized on the crisis and increased their memberships. For the first time, these independent unions possessed sufficient power to challenge PRI policies. To negate the challenge from the independents, the CTM invited them to join the larger organization. Incorporation of the dissidents into the system is seen as the only way in which the system's credibility can be maintained. It illustrates the state's power to neutralize opposing forces by absorbing them into its system. The demands of labor today are strong, which will present a significant challenge to the Calderón government. If labor is to win benefits, it will have to collaborate, but the government must also be prepared for a reciprocal relationship.

■ ECONOMIC CRISIS

As has been suggested, a primary threat to the consensus politics of the PRI came from the economic crisis that began to build in Mexico and other Latin American countries (notably Brazil, Venezuela, and Argentina) in the early 1980s. In the 1970s, Mexico undertook economic policies designed to foster rapid and sustained industrial growth. Credit was readily available from international lending agencies and banks at low rates of interest. Initially, the development plan seemed to work, and Mexico achieved impressive economic growth rates, in the range of 8 percent per year. The government, confident in its ability to pay back its debts from revenues generated by the vast deposits of petroleum beneath Mexico, recklessly expanded its economic infrastructure.

A glut on the petroleum market in late 1981 and 1982 led to falling prices for Mexican oil. Suddenly, there was not enough money available to pay the interest on loans that were coming due, and the government had to borrow more money—at very high interest rates—to cover the unexpected shortfall. By the end of 1982, between 35 and 45 percent of Mexico's export earnings were devoured in -interest payments on a debt of

$80 billion. Before additional loans could be secured, foreign banks and lending organizations, such as the International Monetary Fund, demanded that the Mexican government drastically reduce state spending. This demand translated into layoffs, inadequate funding for social-welfare programs, and a general austerity that devastated the poor and undermined the high standard of living of the middle class.

Although political reform was important to then-president Salinas, he clearly recognized that economic reform was of more compelling concern. Under Salinas, the foreign debt was renegotiated and substantially reduced.

It was hoped that the North American Free Trade Agreement (NAFTA) among Mexico, the United States, and Canada would shore up the Mexican economy and generate jobs. After a decade there is a wide range of disagreement over NAFTA's success. The Carnegie Endowment of International Peace concluded in November 2003 that the agreement failed to generate significant job growth and actually hurt hundreds of thousands of subsistence farmers who could not compete with "highly efficient and heavily subsidized American farmers." A World Bank report argued that NAFTA had "brought significant economic and social benefits to the Mexican economy," and that Mexico would have been worse off without the pact. Part of the problem lies with the globalization of the economy. Mexico has lost thousands of jobs to China as well as El Salvador, where labor is 20 percent cheaper and less strictly regulated. Five hundred of Mexico's 3,700 maquiladoras have closed their doors since 2001. Opposition politicians, nationalists, and those concerned with the more negative aspects of capitalism have generally fought all free-trade agreements, which they see as detrimental to Mexico's sovereignty and independence of action. Perhaps the most interesting development is not economic, but political. Analysts have noted that NAFTA has contributed to a trend toward more representative government in Mexico and that globalization of the economy undercut the state-centered regime of the PRI. Despite advances in some areas, there are still far too many Mexicans whose standard of living is below the poverty level. Of the 40 million poor, 18 million are characterized as living in "extreme poverty." Income distribution is skewed, with the richest 20 percent of the population in control of 58 percent of the nation's wealth, while the poorest 20 percent control only 4 percent.

Many of those unemployed workers, now estimated at 150,000 per year, will continue to make their way to the U.S. border, which remains accessible despite the passage of immigration-reform legislation and more rigorous patrolling of the border. Others will be absorbed by the so-called informal sector, or underground economy. When walking in the streets of Mexico City, one quickly becomes aware that there exists an economy that is not recognized, licensed, regulated, or "protected" by the government. This informal sector of the economy produces 25 to 35 percent of Mexico's gross domestic product and served as a shield for millions of Mexicans who might otherwise have been reduced to destitution. According to George Grayson, "Extended families, which often have several members working and others hawking lottery tickets or shining shoes, establish a safety net for upward of one-third of the workforce in a country where social security coverage is limited and unemployment compensation is nonexistent."

FOREIGN POLICY

The problems created by Mexico's economic policy have been balanced by a visibly successful foreign policy. Historically, Mexican foreign policy, which is noted for following an independent course of action, has been used by the government for domestic purposes. In the 1980s, President Miguel de la Madrid identified revolutionary nationalism as the historical synthesis, or melding, of the Mexican people. History, he argued, taught Mexicans to be nationalist in order to resist external aggression, and history made Mexico revolutionary in order to enable it to transform unequal social and economic structures. These beliefs, when tied to the formulation of foreign policy, have fashioned policies with a definite leftist bias. The country has often been sympathetic to social change and has identified, at least in principle, with revolutionary causes all over the globe. The Mexican government opposed the economic and political isolation of Cuba that was so heartily endorsed by the United States. It supported the Marxist regime of Salvador Allende in Chile at a time when the United States was attempting to destabilize his government. Mexico was one of the first nations to break relations with President Anastasio Somoza of Nicaragua and to recognize the legitimacy of the struggle of the Sandinista guerrillas. In 1981, Mexico joined with France in recognizing the opposition front and guerrilla coalition in El Salvador. In the 1990s Mexico, together with several other Latin American countries, urged a negotiated solution to the armed conflict in Central America. Even though the populist candidate did not win the presidential election in 2006, the Calderón government did not distance itself from other populist regimes in Latin America.

Mexico's traditional leftist foreign policy balances conservative domestic policies. A foreign policy identified with change and social justice has the effect of softening the impact of leftist demands in Mexico for land reform or political change. Mexicans, if displeased with government domestic policies, were soothed by a vigorous foreign policy that placed Mexico in a leadership role, often in opposition to the United States. In economic matters, Mexico's foreign policy will tend more toward centrism, especially with regard to the negotiation of free-trade agreements. Indeed, in 2008, Mexico had in place 12 free-trade agreements with 40 countries.

HARD TIMES

Mexico's future is fraught with uncertainty. In December 1994, the economy collapsed after the government could no longer sustain an overvalued peso. In just a few months, the peso fell in value by half, while the stock market, in terms of the peso, suffered a 38 percent drop. The crash was particularly acute because the Salinas government had not invested foreign aid in factories and job creation, but had instead put most of the money into Mexico's volatile stock market. It then proceeded to spend Mexico's reserves to prop up the peso when the decline gathered momentum. Salinas's successor, President Ernesto Zedillo, had to cut public spending, sell some state-owned industries, and place strict limits on wage and price increases.

To further confound the economic crisis, the Maya insurgency in Chiapas succeeded in generating much antigovernment support in the rest of Mexico. President Zedillo claimed that the rebels, who call themselves the Zapatista Army of National Liberation (EZLN, named for Emiliano Zapata, one of the peasant leaders of the Mexican Revolution), were "neither popular, nor indigenous, nor from Chiapas." Nobel Laureate Octavio Paz condemned the uprising as an "interruption of Mexico's ongoing political and economic liberalization." The interests of the EZLN leadership, he said, were those of intellectuals rather than those of the peasantry. In other words, what happened in Chiapas was an old story of peasant Indians being used by urban intellectuals—in this instance, to challenge the PRI. Indeed, the real identity of "Subcomandante Marcos" was revealed as Rafael Sebastian Guillen Vicente, a former professor from a rich provincial family who had worked with Tzotzil and Tzeltal Maya Indians since 1984.

George Collier, however, argues that the rebellion is a response to changing governmental policies, agricultural modernization, and cultural and economic isolation. While the peasants of central Chiapas profited from PRI policies, those in the eastern part of the state were ignored. Thus, the rebellion, in essence, was a demand to be included in the largesse of the state. The demands of the EZLN were instructive: democratic reform by the state, limited autonomy for indigenous communities, an antidiscrimination law, teachers, clinics, doctors,

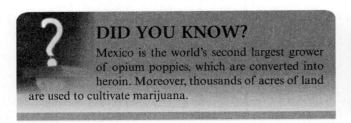

DID YOU KNOW?

Mexico is the world's second largest grower of opium poppies, which are converted into heroin. Moreover, thousands of acres of land are used to cultivate marijuana.

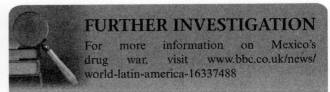

FURTHER INVESTIGATION

For more information on Mexico's drug war, visit www.bbc.co.uk/news/world-latin-america-16337488

Snapshot: MEXICO

Summarized below is a quick look at the country with regard to its development, freedom, health/welfare, and achievements.

Development

Mexico's state-owned oil company, PEMEX, is badly in need of money both to invest in upgrades to an aging infrastructure and to explore for new oil fields to replace those that are nearly played out. Mexicans, however, are loath to invite the participation of foreign oil companies in an industry that many view as a "sacred" symbol of their sovereignty.

Freedom

Freedom House reported in 2011 that "Mexico's political rights rating declined from 2 to 3 and its status changed from Free to Partly Free due to the targeting of local officials by organized crime groups and the government's inability to protect citizens' rights in the face of criminal violence.

Health/Welfare

In 2005 the Mexican congress passed legislation that promised universal health coverage for all its citizens. By September 2011 about 51 million people had enrolled in the program.

Achievements

Mexican writers and artists have won world acclaim. The works of novelists such as Carlos Fuentes, Mariano Azuela, and Juan Rulfo have been translated into many languages. The graphic-art styles of Posada and the mural art of Diego Rivera, José Clemente Orozco, and David Siqueiros are distinctively Mexican.

---

electricity, better housing, child-care centers, and a radio station for indigenous peoples. Only vague statements were made about subdivision of large ranches.

During the presidential campaign of 2000, Fox promised to address the complaints raised by the EZLN. Legislation introduced in Congress in the spring of 2001 was designed to safeguard and promote the rights of indigenous peoples. To call attention to the debate, the Zapatistas, with government protection, embarked on a two-week-long march to Mexico City. Significantly, the marchers carried not only the flag of the EZLN but also that of -Mexico. But Congress felt that the legislation could damage the nation's unity and harm the interests of local landlords in the south. When a watered-down version of the legislation was passed, Subcomandante Marcos vowed to continue the rebellion. President Fox urged that the talks continue and publicly complained about the congressional action. This was an astute move, because the EZLN could lose an important ally if it adopted an intransigent position.

On the other hand, the Zapatistas were in danger of fading into the background if they lost the ability to attract the attention of the media. Indeed, the government has essentially ignored them in recent years and much Zapatista support in Mexico has shifted to the populism of the PRD. It is no surprise that Subcomandante Marcos emerged from the jungle and embarked on a nationwide tour in 2006, not only to prevent his movement from becoming irrelevant in the minds of Mexicans, but also to attack the PRD presidential candidate as a "traitor" who would betray Mexico's indigenous peoples.

In summary, the insurgency can be seen to have several roots and to serve many purposes. It is far more complex than a "simple" uprising of an oppressed people.

■ THE FUTURE

Journalist Igor Fuser, writing in the Brazilian newsweekly *Veja,* observed: "For pessimists, the implosion of the PRI is the final ingredient needed to set off an apocalyptic bomb composed of economic recession, guerrilla war, and the desperation of millions of Mexicans facing poverty. For optimists, the unrest is a necessary evil needed to unmask the most carefully camouflaged dictatorship on the planet."

The elections of 2000 and 2006 tore away that mask, but persistent problems remain. Corruption, endemic drug-related violence, poverty, unemployment and underemployment, high debt, and inflation are daunting. President Calderón inherited a difficult set of problems and a polarized electorate. His most serious challenge was the corruption and horrific violence spawned by the drug trade. Rival gangs are at war as they seek to control the lucrative traffic, and the death toll over the past few years now stands at approximately 40,000. So pervasive is the violence that it has had a profound impact on folk culture in the effected areas. La Santa Muerte (the Death Saint) has a large corpus of believers among the "foot-soldiers" of the gangs who feel that if you pay her homage she will protect you. Well-financed and heavily armed, the drug lords will be difficult to eliminate so long as there is a demand for their wares.

Statistics

Geography

Area in Square Miles (Kilometers): 764,000 (1,978,000) (about 3 times the size of Texas)

Capital (Population): Mexico City (19,310,000 including suburbs)

Environmental Concerns: Scarce freshwater resources; water pollution; deforestation; soil erosion; serious air pollution

Geographical Features: high, rugged mountains; low coastal plains; high plateaus; desert

Climate: varies from tropical to desert

People

Population

Total: 113,724,226 (2010 est.)

Annual Growth Rate: 1.1%

Rural/Urban Population Ratio: 22/78

Major Languages: Spanish; various Maya, Nahuatl, and other regional indigenous languages

Ethnic Makeup: 60% Mestizo; 30% Amerindian; 9% white; 1% others

Religions: 76.5% Roman Catholic; 6.3% Protestant; 13.8% unspecified or none

Health

Life Expectancy at Birth: 73 years (male); 79 years (female)

Infant Mortality Rate (Ratio): 17.29/1,000

Physicians Available (Ratio): 2.9/1,000

Education

Adult Literacy Rate: 86.1%

Compulsory (Ages): 6–12; free

Communication

Telephones: 19,892,000 main lines

Daily Newspaper Circulation: 115 per 1,000 people

Cell Phones: 91,363,000

Internet Users: 31,020,000

Transportation

Roadways in Kilometers (Miles): 235,760 (146,439)

Railroads in Kilometers (Miles): 17,665 (10,977)

Usable Airfields: 1,819

Government

Type: federal republic

Independence Date: September 16, 1810 (from Spain)

Head of State/Government: President Felipe Calderón is both head of state and head of government

Political Parties: Institutional Revolutionary Party; National Action Party; Party of the Democratic Revolution; Workers Party; Convergence for Democracy; Labor Party; Mexican Green Ecological Party; others.

Suffrage: universal and compulsory at 18

Military

Military Expenditures (% of GDP): 0.5%

Current Disputes: none

Economy

Currency ($U.S. Equivalent): 13.64 pesos = $1

Per Capita Income/GDP: $13,900/$1.567 trillion

GDP Real Growth Rate: −5.5%

Inflation Rate: 4.2%

Unemployment Rate: 5.4%; underemployment: +/− 25%

Labor Force: 47 million

Natural Resources: petroleum; silver; copper; gold; lead; zinc; natural gas; timber

Agriculture: corn; wheat; soybeans; rice; beans; cotton; coffee; fruit; tomatoes; livestock products; wood products

Industry: food and beverages; tobacco; chemicals; iron and steel; petroleum; mining; textiles; clothing; motor vehicles; consumer durables; tourism

Exports: $298.5 billion (primary partners United States, Canada)

Imports: $301.5 billion (primary partners United States, Japan, China)

Suggested Website

www.cia.gov/cia/publications/factbook/geos/mx.html#geo

Central America

0   100   200   300 Miles
0 100 200 300 400 Kilometers

Much of Central America shares important historical milestones. In 1821, the states of Guatemala, Honduras, El Salvador, Costa Rica, and Nicaragua declared themselves independent of Spain. In 1822, they joined the Empire of Mexico; in 1823, they formed the United Provinces of Central America. This union lasted until 1838, when each member state severed its relations with the federation and went its own way. Since 1838, there have been more than 25 attempts to restore the union—but to no avail.

Central America

Lands in Turmoil

■ LIFE IN THE MOUTH OF THE VOLCANO

Sons of the Shaking Earth, a well-known study of Middle America by anthropologist Eric Wolf, captures in its title the critical interplay between people and the land in Central America. It asserts that the land is violent and that the inhabitants of the region live in an environment that is often shaken by natural disaster.

The dominant geographical feature of Central America is the impressive and forbidding range of volcanic mountains that runs from Mexico to Panama. These mountains have always been obstacles to communication, to the cultivation of the land, and to the national integration of the countries in which they lie. The volcanoes rest atop major fault lines; some are dormant, others are active, and new ones have appeared periodically. Over the centuries, eruptions and earthquakes have destroyed thousands of villages. Some have recovered, but others remain buried beneath lava and ash. Nearly every Central American city has been destroyed at one time or another; and some, such as Managua, Nicaragua, have suffered repeated devastation.

An ancient Indian philosophy speaks of five great periods of time, each doomed to end in disaster. The fifth period, which is the time in which we now live, is said to terminate with a world-destroying earthquake. "Thus," writes Wolf, "the people of Middle [Central] America live in the mouth of the volcano. Middle America . . . is one of the proving grounds of humanity."

Earthquakes and eruptions are not the only natural disasters that plague the region. Rains fall heavily between May and October each year, and devastating floods are common. On the Caribbean coast, hurricanes often strike in the late summer and early autumn, threatening coastal cities and leveling crops.

The constant threat of natural disaster has had a deep impact on Central Americans' views of life and development. Death and tragedy have conditioned their attitudes toward the present and the future.

■ GEOGRAPHY

The region is not only violent but also diverse. In political terms, Central America consists of seven independent nations: Belize, Costa Rica, El Salvador, Guatemala, Honduras, Nicaragua, and Panama. With the exception of Costa Rica and Panama, where national borders coincide with geographical and human frontiers, political boundaries are artificial and were marked out in defiance of both the lay of the land and the cultural groupings of the region's peoples.

Geographically, Central America can be divided into four broad zones: Petén–Belize; the Caribbean coasts of Guatemala, Honduras, and Nicaragua; the Pacific volcanic region; and Costa Rica–Panama.

The northern Guatemalan territory of Petén and all of Belize are an extension of Mexico's Yucatán Peninsula. The region is heavily forested with stands of mahogany, cedar, and pine, whose products are a major source of revenue for Belize.

The Caribbean lowlands, steamy and disease-ridden, are sparsely settled. The inhabitants of the Caribbean coast in Nicaragua include Miskito Indians and the descendants of English-speaking blacks who first settled the area in the seventeenth century. The Hispanic population there was small until recently. Coastal Honduras is more heavily populated and marginally more prosperous than the rest of the country because of the banana industry. Coffee also is a significant source of revenue. But the coast is vulnerable to hurricanes and "blow-downs" of the banana trees is a frequent occurrence. Honduras, overall, is a very poor country.

The Pacific volcanic highlands are the cultural heartland of Central America. Here, in highland valleys noted for their spring like climate, live more than 80 percent of the population of Central America; here are the largest cities. In cultural terms, the highlands are home to the whites, mixed bloods, Hispanicized Indians known as Ladinos, and pure-blooded Indians who are descended from the Maya. These highland groups form a striking ethnic contrast to the Indians (such as the Miskito), mulattos, and blacks of the coastlands. The entire country of El Salvador falls within this geographical zone. Unlike its neighbors, there is a uniformity to the land and people of El Salvador.

The fourth region, divided between the nations of Costa Rica and Panama, constitutes a single geographical unit. Mountains form the spine of the isthmus. In Costa Rica, the Central Mesa has attracted 70 percent of the nation's population, because of its agreeable climate.

■ CLIMATE AND CULTURE

The geographic and biological diversity of Central America—with its cool highlands and steaming lowlands, its incredible variety of microclimates and environments, its seemingly infinite types of flora and fauna, and

Central American Indians are firmly tied to their traditional beliefs and have strongly resisted the influence of European culture, as evidenced by this Cuna woman.

its mineral wealth—has been a major factor in setting the course of the cultural history of Central America. Before the Spanish conquest, the environmental diversity favored the cultural cohesion of peoples. The products of one environmental niche could easily be exchanged for the products of another. In a sense, valley people and those living higher up in the mountains depended on one another. Here was one of the bases for the establishment of the advanced culture of the Maya.

The cultural history of Central America has focused on the densely populated highlands and Pacific plains—those areas most favorable for human occupation. Spaniards settled in the same regions, and centers of national life are located there today. But if geography has been a factor in bringing peoples together on a local level, it has also contributed to the formation of regional differences, loyalties, interests, and jealousies. Neither Maya rulers nor Spanish bureaucrats could triumph over the natural obstacles presented by the region's harsh geography. The mountains and rain forests have mocked numerous attempts to create a single Central American state.

■ CULTURES IN CONFLICT

Although physical geography has interacted with culture, the contact between Indians and Spaniards since the sixteenth century has profoundly shaped the cultural face of today's Central America. According to historian Ralph Woodward, the religious traditions of the indigenous peoples, with Christianity imperfectly superimposed over them, "together with the violence of the Conquest and the centuries of slavery or serfdom which followed, left clear impressions on the personality and mentality of the Central American Indian."

To outsiders, the Indians often appear docile and obedient to authority, but beneath this mask may lie intense emotions, including distrust and bitterness. The Indians' vision is usually local and oriented toward the village and family; they do not identify themselves as Guatemalan or Nicaraguan. When challenged, Indians have fought to defend their rights, and a long succession of rebellions from colonial days until the present attests to their sense of what is just and what is not. The Indians, firmly tied to their traditional beliefs and values, have tried to resist modernization, despite government programs and policies designed to counter what urbanized whites perceive as backwardness and superstition.

Population growth, rather than government programs and policies, has had a great impact on the region's Indian peoples and has already resulted in the recasting of cultural traditions. Peasant villages in much of Central America have traditionally organized their ritual life around the principle of *mayordomía,* or sponsorship. Waldemar Smith, an anthropologist who has explored the relationship between the *fiesta* (ceremony) system and economic change, has shown the impact of changing circumstances on traditional systems. In any Central American community in any given year, certain families are appointed *mayordomos,* or stewards, of the village saints; they are responsible for organizing and paying for the celebrations in their names. This responsibility ordinarily lasts for a year. One of the outstanding features of the fiesta system is the phenomenal costs that the designated family must bear. An individual might have to expend the equivalent of a year's earnings or more to act as a sponsor in a community fiesta. Psychological and social burdens must also be borne by the mayordomos, for they represent their community before its saints. Mayordomos, who in essence are priests for a year, are commonly expected to refrain from sexual activity for long periods as well as to devote much time to ritual forms.

The office, while highly prestigious, can also be dangerous. Maya Indians, for example, believe that the saints use the weather as a weapon to punish transgressions, and extreme weather is often traced to ritual error or sins on the part of the mayordomo, who might on such occasions actually be jailed.

Since the late 1960s, the socioeconomic structure of much of the area heavily populated by Indians has changed, forcing changes in traditional cultural forms, including the fiesta system. Expansion of markets and

(Courtesy of Omar Sahyoun)

An estimated 40 million children throughout Latin America between three and 18 are living and working on the streets. Children, as pictured above, sell trinkets to supplement the family income where parents earn well below a living wage.

educational opportunity, the absorption of much of the workforce in seasonal plantation labor, more efficient transportation systems, and population growth have precipitated change. Traditional festivals in honor of a community's saints have significantly diminished in importance in a number of towns. Costs have been reduced or several families have been made responsible for fiesta sponsorship. This reflects not only modernization but also crisis. Some communities have become too poor to support themselves—and the expensive fiestas have, naturally, suffered.

This increasing poverty is driven in part by population growth, which has exerted tremendous pressure on people's access to land. Families that cannot be sustained on traditional lands must now seek seasonal wage labor on sugarcane, coffee, or cotton plantations. Others emigrate. Ominously, some turn to drug trafficking. The net result is a culture under siege. Thus, while the fiestas may not vanish, they are surely in the process of change.

The Ladino World

The word *Ladino* can be traced back to the Roman occupation of Spain. It referred to someone who had been "Latinized" and was therefore wise in the ways of the world. The word has several meanings in Central America. In Guatemala, it refers to a person of mixed blood, or *Mestizo*. In most of the rest of Central America, however, it refers to an Indian who has adopted white culture.

The Ladinos are caught between two cultures, both of which initially rejected them. The Ladinos attempted to compensate for their lack of cultural roots and cultural identity by aggressively carving out a place in Central American society. Often acutely status-conscious, Ladinos typically contrast sharply with the Indians they physically resemble. Ladinos congregate in the larger towns and cities, speak Spanish, and seek a livelihood as shopkeepers or landowners. They compose the local elite in Guatemala, Nicaragua, Honduras, and El Salvador (the latter country was almost entirely Ladinoized by the end of the nineteenth century), and they usually control regional politics. They are often the most aggressive members of the community, driven by the desire for self-advancement. Their vision is frequently much broader than that of the Indian; they have a perspective that includes the capital city and the nation. The vast majority of the population speak Spanish; few villages retain the use of their original, native tongues.

The Elite

For the elite, who are culturally "white," the city dominates their social and cultural horizons. For them, the world of the Indian is unimportant—save for the difficult questions of social integration and modernization. Businesspeople and bureaucrats, absentee landlords, and the professional class of doctors, lawyers, and engineers constitute an urban elite who are cosmopolitan and sophisticated. Wealth, status, and "good blood" are the keys to elite membership.

The Disadvantaged

The cities have also attracted disadvantaged people who have migrated from poverty-stricken rural regions in search of economic opportunity. Many are self-employed as peddlers, small-scale traders, or independent craftspeople. Others seek low-paying, unskilled positions in industry, construction work, and transportation. Most live on the edge of poverty and are the first to suffer in times of economic recession. But there exist Hispanic institutions in this harsh world that help people of all classes to adjust. In each of the capital cities of Central America, lower-sector people seek help and sustenance from the more advantaged elements in society. They form economic and social alliances that are mutually beneficial. For example, a tradesman might approach a well-to-do merchant and seek advice or a small loan. In return, he can offer guaranteed service, a steady supply of crafts for the wholesaler, and a price that is right. It is a world built on mutual exchanges.

These networks, when they function, bind societies together and ease the alienation and isolation of the less advantaged inhabitants. Of course, networks that cut through class lines can effectively limit class action in pursuit of reforms; and, in many instances, the networks do not exist or are exploitive.

(World Bank/Curt Carnemark/MX001S01)

The migration of poor rural people to Central American urban centers has caused large numbers of squatters to take up residence in slums.

■ POPULATION MOVEMENT

For many years, Central Americans have been peoples in motion. Migrants who have moved from rural areas into the cities have often been driven from lands they once owned, either because of the expansion of landed estates at the expense of the smaller landholdings, population pressure, or division of the land into plots so small that subsistence farming is no longer possible. Others have moved to the cities in search of a better life.

Population pressure on the land is most intense in El Salvador. No other Latin American state utilizes the whole of its territory to the extent that El Salvador does. Most of the land is still privately owned and is devoted to cattle farming or to raising cotton and coffee for the export market. There is not enough land to provide crops for a population that has grown at one of the most rapid rates in the Western Hemisphere. There are no unpopulated lands left to occupy. Agrarian reform, even if successful, will still leave hundreds of thousands of peasants without land.

Many Salvadorans have moved to the capital city of San Salvador in search of employment. Others have crossed into neighboring countries. In the 1960s, thousands moved to Honduras, where they settled on the land or were attracted to commerce and industry. By the end of that decade, more than 75 percent of all foreigners living in Honduras had crossed the border from El Salvador. Hondurans, increasingly concerned by the growing presence of Salvadorans, acted to stem the flow and passed restrictive and discriminatory legislation against the immigrants. The tension, an ill-defined border, and festering -animosity ultimately brought about a brief war between Honduras and El Salvador in 1969.

Honduras, with a low population density (about 139 persons per square mile, as compared to El Salvador's 721), has attracted population not only from neighboring countries but also from the Caribbean. Black migrants from the "West Indian" Caribbean islands known as the Antilles have been particularly attracted to Honduras's north coast, where they have been able to find employment on banana plantations or in the light industry that has increasingly been established in the area. The presence of these Caribbean peoples in moderate numbers has more sharply focused regional differences in Honduras. The coast, in many respects, is Caribbean in its peoples' identity and outlook; while peoples of the highlands of the interior identify with the capital city of Tegucigalpa, which is Hispanic in culture.

■ THE REFUGEE PROBLEM

Recent turmoil in Central America created yet another group of people on the move—refugees from the fighting in their own countries or from the persecution by extremists of the political left and right. For example, thousands of Salvadorans crowded into Honduras's western province. In the south, Miskito Indians, fleeing from Nicaragua's Sandinista government, crossed the Río Coco in large numbers. Additional thousands of armed Nicaraguan counterrevolutionaries camped along the border. Only in 1990–1991 did significant numbers of Salvadorans move back to their homeland. With the declared truce between Sandinistas and Contras and the election victory of Violeta Chamorro, Nicaraguan refugees were gradually repatriated. Guatemalan Indians sought refuge in southern Mexico, and Central Americans of all nationalities resettled in Costa Rica and Belize.

El Salvadorans, who began to emigrate to the United States in the 1960s, did so in much greater numbers with the onset of the El Salvadoran Civil War, which killed approximately 70,000 people and displaced about 25 percent of the nation's population. The Urban Institute, a Washington, D.C.–based research group, estimated in 1986 that there were then about ¾ million El Salvadorans—of a total population of just over 5 million—living in the United States. Those emigrants became a major source of dollars for El Salvador; it is estimated that they now send home about $500 million a year.

While that money has undoubtedly helped to keep the nation's economy above water, it has also generated, paradoxically, a good deal of anti–U.S. sentiment in El Salvador. Lindsey Gruson, a reporter for *The New York Times,* studied the impact of expatriate dollars in Intipuca, a town 100 miles southwest of the capital, and concluded that they had a profound impact on Intipuqueño culture. The influx of money was an incentive not to work, and townspeople said that the "free" dollars "perverted cherished values" and were "breaking up many families."

■ THE ROOTS OF VIOLENCE

Central America still feels the effects of civil war and violence. Armies, guerrillas, and terrorists of the political left and right have exacted a high toll on human lives and property. The civil wars and guerrilla movements that spread violence to the region sprang from each of the societies in question.

A critical societal factor was (and remains) the emergence of a middle class in Central America. In some respects, people of the middle class resemble the Mestizos or Ladinos, in that their wealth and position have placed them above the masses. But, like the Mestizos and Ladinos, they have been denied access to the upper reaches of power, which is the special preserve of the elite. Since World War II, it has been members of the middle class who have called for reform and a more equitable distribution of the national wealth. They have also attempted to forge alliances of opportunity with workers and peasants.

Nationalistic, assertive, restless, ambitious, and, to an extent, ruthless, people of the middle class (professionals, intellectuals, junior officers in the armed forces, office workers, businesspeople, teachers, students, and skilled workers) demand a greater voice in the political world. They want governments that are responsive to their interests and needs; and, when governments have proven unresponsive or hostile, elements of the middle class have chosen confrontation.

In the civil war that removed the Somoza family from power in Nicaragua in 1979, for example, the middle class played a critical leadership role. Guerrilla leaders in El Salvador were middle class in terms of their social origins, and there was significant middle-class participation in the unrest in Guatemala.

Indeed, Central America's middle class is among the most revolutionary groups in the region. Although middle-class people are well represented in antigovernment forces, they also resist changes that would tend to elevate those below them on the social scale. They are also significantly represented among right-wing groups, whose reputation for conservative views is accompanied by systematic terror.

Other societal factors also figure prominently in the violence in Central America. The rapid growth of population since the 1960s has severely strained each nation's resources. Many rural areas have become overpopulated, poor agricultural practices have caused extensive soil erosion, the amount of land available to subsistence farmers is inadequate, and poverty and misery are pervasive. These problems have combined to compel rural peoples to migrate to the cities or to whatever frontier lands are still available. In Guatemala, government policy drove Indians from ancestral villages in the highlands to "resettlement" villages in the low-lying, forested Petén to the north. Indians displaced in this manner often—not surprisingly—joined guerrilla movements. They were not attracted to insurgency by the allure of socialist or communist ideology; they simply responded to violence and the loss of their lands with violence against the governments that pursued such policies.

The conflict in this region does not always pit landless, impoverished peasants against an unyielding elite. Some members of the elite see the need for change. Most peasants have not taken up arms, and the vast majority wish to be left in peace. Others who desire change may be found in the ranks of the military or within the hierarchy of the Roman Catholic Church. Reformers are drawn from all sectors of society. It is thus more appropriate to view the conflict in Central America as a civil war rather than a class struggle, as civil wars cut through the entire fabric of a nation.

Today's criminal violence in urban areas of Central America, and particularly in El Salvador and Honduras, is not only a direct consequence of the years of civil war, but also a result of the tremendous growth of drug trafficking in the region. Young children of refugees, who relocated to large United States cities as adolescents, often imitated the gang culture to which they were exposed. When they returned to Central America and encountered a society that they did not recognize, they could not find jobs and the gang culture was replicated. Some of those gangs evolved into drug trafficking and dealing cartels. Indeed, violent crime, most of which was attributed to youth gangs, was a central issue in presidential elections in Honduras in 2005.

■ ECONOMIC PROBLEMS

Central American economies, always fragile, have in recent years been plagued by a combination of vexing problems. Foreign debt, inflation, currency devaluations, recession, and, in some instances, outside interference have had deleterious effects on the standard of living in all the countries. Civil war, insurgency, corruption and mismanagement, and population growth have added fuel to the crisis—not only in the region's economies but also in their societies. Nature, too, has played an important contributory role in the region's economic and social malaise. Hurricane Mitch, which struck Central American in 1998, killed thousands, destroyed crops and property, and disrupted the infrastructure of roads and bridges in Honduras, Nicaragua, Guatemala, and El Salvador. Ten years later, in 2008, Hurricane Ida wreaked havoc in the same region.

Civil war in El Salvador brought unprecedented death and destruction and was largely responsible for economic deterioration and a decline of well over one-third of per capita income from 1980 to 1992. Today (2010) the official unemployment rate is nearly 8 percent but underemployment is a much more significant factor in the economy. The struggle of the Sandinista government of Nicaragua against U.S.–sponsored rebels routinely consumed 60 percent of government spending; even with peace, much of the budget was earmarked for economic recovery. Nicaragua remains the poorest nation in Central America. In Guatemala, a savage civil war lasted more than a generation; took more than 140,000 lives; strained the economy; depressed wages; and left unaddressed pressing social problems in education, housing, and welfare. Although the violence has subsided, the lingering fears conditioned by that violence have not. U.S. efforts to force the ouster of Panamanian strongman Manuel Antonio Noriega through the application of economic sanctions probably harmed middle-class businesspeople in Panama more than Noriega.

Against this backdrop of economic malaise there have been some creative attempts to solve, or at least to confront, pressing problems. In 1987, the Costa Rican government proposed a series of debt-for-nature swaps to international conservation groups, such as the Nature Conservancy. The first of the transactions took place in 1988, when several organizations purchased more than $3 million of Costa Rica's foreign debt at 17 percent of face value. The plan called for the government to exchange with the organizations part of Costa Rica's external debt for government bonds; the conservation groups would then invest the earnings of the bonds in the management and protection of Costa Rican national parks. According to the National Wildlife Federation, while debt-for-nature swaps are not a cure-all for the Latin American debt crisis, at least the swaps can go some distance toward protecting natural resources and encouraging ecologically sound, long-term economic development.

■ INTERNAL AND EXTERNAL DIMENSIONS OF CONFLICT

The continuing violence in much of Central America suggests that internal dynamics are perhaps more important than the overweening roles formerly ascribed to Havana, Moscow, and Washington. The removal of foreign "actors" from the stage lays bare the real reasons for violence in the region: injustice, power, greed, revenge, and racial and ethnic discrimination. Havana, Moscow, and Washington, among others, merely used Central American violence in pursuit of larger policy goals. And Central American governments and guerrilla groups were equally adept at using foreign powers to advance their own interests, be they revolutionary or reactionary.

Panama offers an interesting scenario in this regard. It, like the rest of Central America, is a poor nation comprised of subsistence farmers, rural laborers, urban workers, and unemployed and underemployed people dwelling in the shantytowns ringing the larger cities. For years, the pressures for reform in Panama were skillfully rechanneled by the ruling elite toward the issue of the Panama Canal. Frustration and anger were deflected from the government, and an outdated social structure was attributed to the presence of a foreign power—the United States—in what Panamanians regarded as their territory.

Central America, in summary, is a region of diverse geography and is home to peoples of many cultures. It is a region of strong local loyalties; its problems are profound and perplexing. The violence of the land is matched by the violence of its peoples as they fight for something as noble as justice or human rights, or as ignoble as political power or self-promotion.

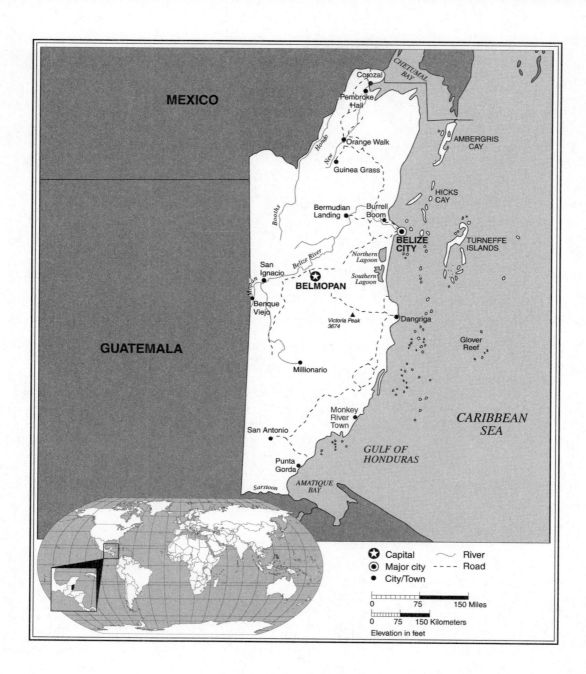

MEXICO

Corozal

Pembroke
Hall

Hondo

New

Orange Walk

AMBERGRIS
CAY

Guinea Grass

CHETUMAL
BAY

Booths

HICKS
CAY

Bermudian
Landing

Burrell
Boom

BELIZE
CITY

TURNEFFE
ISLANDS

Belize River

Northern
Lagoon

San
Ignacio

Mopán

Southern
Lagoon

BELMOPAN

Benque
Viejo

Victoria Peak
3674

Dangriga

Glover
Reef

GUATEMALA

Millionario

CARIBBEAN
SEA

Monkey
River
Town

San Antonio

GULF OF
HONDURAS

Punta
Gorda

Sarstoon

AMATIQUE
BAY

⊛ Capital — River
◉ Major city ---- Road
● City/Town

0   75   150 Miles
0   75   150 Kilometers
Elevation in feet

Belize

THE "HISPANICIZATION" OF A COUNTRY

Belize was settled in the late 1630s by English woodcutters who also indulged in occasional piracy at the expense of the Spanish crown. The loggers were interested primarily in dyewoods, which, in the days before chemical dyes, were essential to British textile industries. The country's name is derived from Peter Wallace, a notorious buccaneer who, from his base there, haunted the coast in search of Spanish shipping. The natives shortened and mispronounced Wallace's name until he became known as "Belize."

As a British colony (called British Honduras), Belize enjoyed relative prosperity as an important entrepôt, or storage depot for merchandise, until the completion of the Panama Railway in 1855. With the opening of a rail route to the Pacific, commerce shifted south, away from Caribbean ports. Belize entered an economic tailspin (from which it has never entirely recovered). Colonial governments attempted to diversify the colony's agricultural base and to attract foreign immigration to develop the land. But, except for some Mexican settlers and a few former Confederate soldiers who came to the colony after the U.S. Civil War, the immigration policy failed. Economically depressed, its population exposed to the ravages of yellow fever, malaria, and dengue (a tropical fever), Belize was once described by British novelist Aldous Huxley in the following terms: "If the world had ends, Belize would be one of them."

Living conditions improved markedly by the 1950s, and the colony began to move toward independence from Great Britain. Although self-governing by 1964, Belize did not become fully independent until 1981, because of Guatemalan threats to invade what it considered a lost province, stolen by the British.

For most of its history Belize has been culturally British with Caribbean overtones. English common law is practiced in the courts, and politics are patterned on the English parliamentary system. A large percent of the people are Protestants. The Belizeans are primarily working-class poor and middle-class shopkeepers and merchants. There is no great difference between the well-to-do and the poor in Belize, and few people fall below the absolute poverty line.

Nearly 50 percent of the population are classified as Mestizo and 25 percent are Creole (black and English mixture). The Garifuna (black and Indian mixture) who comprise about 6 percent of the population, originally inhabited the Caribbean island of St. Vincent. In the eighteenth century, they joined with native Indians in an uprising against the English authorities. As punishment, virtually all the Garifuna were deported to Belize.

Despite a pervasive myth of racial democracy in Belize, discrimination exists. Belize is not a harmonious, multiethnic island in a sea of violence. For example, sociologist Bruce Ergood notes that in Belize it "is not uncommon to hear a light Creole bad-mouth 'blacks,' even though both are considered Creole. This reflects a vestige of English colonial attitude summed up in the saying, 'Best to be white, less good to be mulatto, worst to be black. . . .'"

TIMELINE

1638
Belize is settled by English logwood cutters
1884
Belize is declared an independent Crown colony
1972
Guatemala threatens to invade
1981
Independence from Great Britain
1990s
Belize becomes an ecotourism destination
2000s
Guatemala continues territorial claims to Belize
Negotiations with Guatemala over border issues continue

Snapshot: BELIZE

Summarized below is a quick look at the country with regard to its development, freedom, health/welfare, and achievements.

Development

Belize has combined its tourism and environmental-protection offices into one ministry, which holds great promise for ecotourism. Large tracts of land have been set aside to protect jaguars and other endangered species. But there is also pressure on the land from rapid population growth.

Freedom

Freedom House reported that in 2010 the Supreme Court 'ruled in favor of indigenous Mayan communities' constitutionally protected property and cultural rights, including the right to block development and mining activities on communal land."

Health/Welfare

In a speech to the Christian Workers Union, former Prime Minister Said Musa noted: "Higher wages will not mean much if families cannot obtain quality and affordable health care services. What good are higher wages if there are not enough classrooms in which to place the children? What good are higher wages if we are forced to live in fear of the criminal elements in society? A workers' movement must . . . concern itself not only with wages but also with the overall quality of life of its members."

Achievements

Recent digging by archaeologists has uncovered several Maya sites that have convinced scholars that the indigenous civilization in the region was more extensive and refined than experts had previously believed.

A shift in population occurred in the 1980s because of the turmoil in neighboring Central American states. For years, well-educated, English-speaking Creoles had been leaving Belize in search of better economic opportunities in other countries; but this was more than made up for by the inflow of perhaps as many as 40,000 Latin American refugees fleeing the fighting in the region. Spanish is now the primary language of a significant percentage of the population, and some Belizeans are concerned about the "Hispanicization" of the country.

Women in Belize suffer discrimination that is deeply rooted in the cultural, social, and economic structures of the society, even though the government promotes their participation in the nation's politics and development process. Great emphasis is placed on education and health care. Tropical diseases, once the primary cause of death in Belize, were brought under control by a government program of insect spraying. Better health and nutritional awareness are emphasized in campaigns to encourage breastfeeding and the selection and preparation of meals using local produce.

With the new millennium, Belize has increasingly turned its attention to the impact of globalization. Concern was expressed by the government about job security and the need for education and training in the skills necessary to compete in a global marketplace. National Trade Union Congress president Dorene Quiros noted that "global institutions are not meeting the basic needs of people," and promises by international organizations to do better have produced only modest results. Worrying, too, is the rising incidence of violent urban crime and growing involvement in the South American drug trade.

In 2006 petroleum was discovered in the western part of the country close to the border with Guatemala. With expectations that the oil field could yield about 50,000 barrels of oil per day, exports could provide a modest boost to the economy. But the discovery could lead to friction with Guatemala. Although Guatemala recognized the independence of Belize in 1992, the oil was found in a disputed border area.

Potential oil revenues are still in the future. In the meantime, tourism forms the backbone of the economy. Ongoing problems include a large foreign debt, high levels of poverty and a growing incidence of urban crime. Even though Belize has the second highest per capita income in the region, there is a huge imbalance between the rich and the poor. Belize has also become an increasingly significant transit point for South America's drug trade (primarily cocaine) and trafficking in men, women, and children for commercial sexual exploitation.

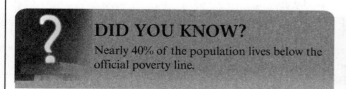

DID YOU KNOW?

Nearly 40% of the population lives below the official poverty line.

FURTHER INVESTIGATION

For more information on health issues, visit www.who.int/country/blz/en

Statistics

Geography

Area in Square Miles (Kilometers): 8,866 (22,963) (about the size of Massachusetts)

Capital (Population): Belmopan (7,100)

Environmental Concerns: deforestation; water pollution

Geographical Features: flat, swampy coastal plain; low mountains in south

Climate: tropical; very hot and humid

People

Population

Total: 321,115 (2011 est.)

Annual Growth Rate: 2.0%

Rural/Urban Population Ratio: 48/52

Ethnic Makeup: 48.7% Mestizo; 24.9% Creole; 10.6% Maya; 6.1% Garifuna; 9.7% others

Major Languages: Spanish 46%; Creole 32.9%; Maya dialects 8.9%; English 3.9% (official)

Religions: 49.6% Roman Catholic; 27% Protestant; 14% others; 9.4% unaffiliated

Health

Life Expectancy at Birth: 66 years (male); 70 years (female)

Infant Mortality Rate (Ratio): 21.95/1,000

Physicians Available (Ratio): 0.83/1000

Education

Adult Literacy Rate: 77%

Compulsory (Ages): 5–14

Communication

Telephones: 30,300 main lines

Cell Phones: 194,200

Internet Users: 36,000

Transportation

Highways in Miles (Kilometers): 1,723 (2,872)

Railroads in Miles (Kilometers): none

Usable Airfields: 44

Government

Type: parliamentary democracy

Independence Date: September 21, 1981 (from the United Kingdom)

Head of State/Government: Governor General Sir Colville Young (represents Queen Elizabeth II); Prime Minister Dean Barrow

Political Parties: People's United Party; United Democratic Party; National Alliance for Belizean Rights

Suffrage: universal at 18

Military

Military Expenditures (% of GDP): 1.4%

Current Disputes: border dispute with Guatemala

Economy

Currency ($U.S. Equivalent): 2.00 Belize dollars = $1

Per Capita Income/GDP: $8,400/$2.651 billion

GDP Growth Rate: +1.5%

Inflation Rate: 0.9%

Unemployment Rate: 13.1%

Labor Force: 120,500

Natural Resources: arable land; timber; fish; hydropower

Agriculture: bananas; cocoa; citrus fruits; sugarcane; lumber; fish; cultured shrimp

Industry: garment production; food processing; tourism; construction

Exports: $475 million (f.o.b.) (primary partners, United States, United Kingdom, Costa Rica)

Imports: $647 million (f.o.b.) (primary partners United States, Mexico, United Kingdom)

Suggested Website

www.cia.gov/cia/publications/factbook/geos/bh.html#Geo

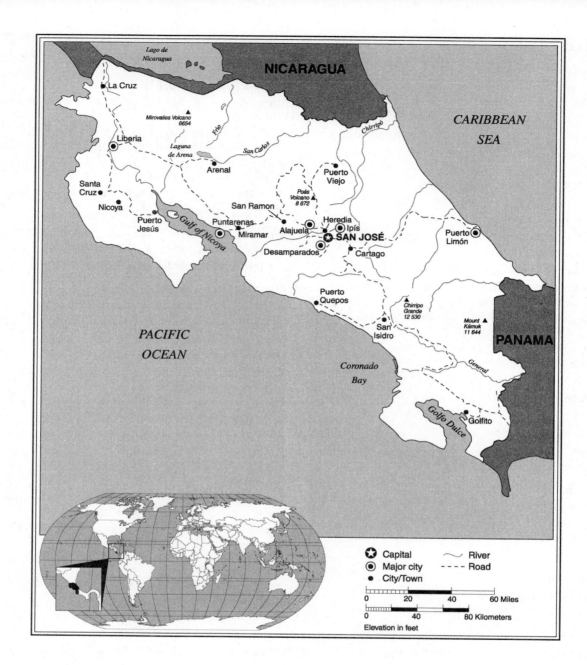

NICARAGUA

CARIBBEAN
SEA

*Lago de
Nicaragua*

La Cruz

*Mirovalles Volcano
6654*

Liberia

Frio

San Carlos

Chirripó

*Laguna
de Arena*

Arenal

Santa
Cruz

San Ramon

*Poás
Volcano* ▲
8 872

Puerto
Viejo

Nicoya

Puerto
Jesús

Gulf of Nicoya

Puntarenas

Miramar

Alajuela

Heredia

Ipís

SAN JOSÉ

Puerto
Limón

Desamparados

Cartago

PACIFIC

OCEAN

Puerto
Quepos

San
Isidro

*Chirripó
Grande
12 530* ▲

Mount ▲
*Kámuk
11 644*

PANAMA

*Coronado
Bay*

General

Golfo Dulce

Golfito

★ Capital

~ River

◎ Major city

- - - Road

● City/Town

| 0 | | 20 | | 40 | | 60 Miles |

| 0 | | 40 | | | 80 Kilometers |

Elevation in feet

Costa Rica

(Republic of Costa Rica)

COSTA RICA: A DIFFERENT TRADITION?

Costa Rica has often been singled out as politically and socially unique in Latin America. It is true that the nation's historical development has not been as directly influenced by Spain as its neighbors' have, but this must not obscure the essential Hispanic character of the Costa Rican people and their institutions. Historian Ralph Woodward observes that historically, Costa Rica's "uniqueness was the product of her relative remoteness from the remainder of Central America, her slight economic importance to Spain, and her lack of a non-white subservient class and corresponding lack of a class of large landholders to exploit its labors." Indeed, in 1900, Costa Rica had a higher percentage of farmers with small- and medium-range operations than any other Latin American country.

The nature of Costa Rica's economy allowed a wider participation in politics and fostered the development of political institutions dedicated to the equality of all people, which existed only in theory in other Latin American countries. Costa Rican politicians, since the late nineteenth century, have endorsed programs that have been largely middle class in content. The government has consistently demonstrated a commitment to the social welfare of its citizens.

AN INTEGRATED SOCIETY

Despite the recent atmosphere of crisis and disintegration in Central America, Costa Rica's durable democracy has avoided the twin evils of oppressive authoritarianism and class warfare. But what might be construed as good luck is actually a reflection of Costa Rica's history. In social, racial, linguistic, and educational terms, Costa Rica is an integrated country without the fractures and cleavages that typify the rest of the region.

Despite its apparent uniqueness, Costa Rica is culturally an integral part of Latin America and embodies what is most positive about Hispanic political culture. The government has long played the role of benevolent patron to the majority of its citizens. Opposition and antagonism have historically been defused by a process of accommodation, mutual cooperation, and participation. In the early 1940s, for example, modernizers who wanted to create a dynamic capitalist economy took care to pacify the emerging labor movement with appropriate social legislation and benefits. Moreover, to assure that development did not sacrifice social welfare, the state assumed a traditional role with respect to the economy—that is, it took an active role in the production and distribution of income. After much discussion, in 1993, the Costa Rican Congress authorized the privatization of the state-owned cement and fertilizer companies. In both cases, according to *Regional Latin American Report: Costa Rica* "a 30% stake [would] be reserved for employees, 20% [would] be offered to private investors, and the remainder [would] be shared out between trade unions . . . and cooperatives." Tight controls were retained on banking, insurance, oil refining, and public utilities.

Women, who were granted the right to vote in the 1940s, have participated freely in Costa Rica's elections. In 2010, the nation elected its first woman president, Laura Chinchilla. Women have also served as a vice

TIMELINE

1522
Spain establishes its first settlements in Costa Rica

1821
Independence from Spain

1823
Costa Rica is part of the United Provinces of Central America

1838
Costa Rica becomes independent as a separate state

1948
Civil war; reforms; abolition of the army

1980s
Costa Rica takes steps to protect its tropical rain forests and dry forests

1990s
Ecotourism to Costa Rica increases

2000s
Two former presidents jailed on corruption charges
Laura Chinchilla elected first woman president in 2010

(Phillippe Colombi/Getty Images)

Modern growing and distribution techniques are making more and better produce available, both for export and for the domestic market. Here a man is seen packing pineapples into boxes in a processing plant in Costa Rica.

president, minister of foreign commerce, and president of the Legislative Assembly. In 2007 more than 38 percent of the seats in the Legislative Assembly were held by women. Although in broader terms the role of women is primarily domestic, they are legally unrestricted. Equal work, in general, is rewarded by equal pay for men and women. But women also hold, as a rule, lower-paying jobs.

■ POLITICS OF CONSENSUS

Costa Rica's political stability is assured by the politics of consensus. Deals and compacts are the order of the day among various competing elites. Political competition is open, and participation by labor and peasants is expanding. Election campaigns provide a forum to air differing viewpoints, to educate the voting public, and to keep politicians in touch with the population at large.

Costa Rica frequently has had strong, charismatic leaders who have been committed to social democracy and have rejected a brand of politics grounded in class differences. The country's democracy has always reflected the paternalism and personalities of its presidents.

This tradition was again endorsed when José María Figueres Olsen won the presidential election on February 6, 1994. Figueres was the son of the founder of the modern Costa Rican democracy, and he promised to return to a reduced version of the welfare state. But, by 1996, in the face of a sluggish economy, the populist champion adopted policies that were markedly pro-business. As a result, opinion polls rapidly turned against him. In the

1998 presidential election, an unprecedented 13 political parties ran candidates, which indicated to the three leading parties that citizens no longer believed in them and that political reforms were in order.

A low voter turnout of 65 percent in presidential elections in 2006 signaled further dissatisfaction with the nation's traditional parties. In 2004 evidence of high-level corruption resulted in the jailing of two former presidents on charges of graft. Although former president (1986–1990) and Nobel Prize–winner Oscar Arias was expected to win easily, the vote was evenly split. Only after a manual recount and a series of legal challenges did Otton Solis concede defeat.

Other oft-given reasons for Costa Rica's stability are the high levels of tolerance exhibited by its people and the absence of a military establishment. Costa Rica has had no military establishment since a brief civil war in 1948. Government officials have long boasted that they rule over a country that has more teachers than soldiers. There is also a strong public tradition that favors demilitarization. Costa Rica's auxiliary forces, however, could form the nucleus of an army in a time of emergency.

The Costa Rican press is among the most unrestricted in Latin America, and differing opinions are openly expressed. Human-rights abuses are virtually nonexistent in the country, but there is a general suspicion of Communists in this overwhelmingly middle-class, white society. And some citizens are concerned about the antidemocratic ideas expressed by ultra-conservatives.

The aftermath of Central America's civil wars is still being felt. Although thousands of refugees returned to Nicaragua with the advent of peace, many thousands more remained in Costa Rica. Economic malaise in Nicaragua combined with the devastation of Hurricane Mitch in 1998 sent thousands of economic migrants across the border into Costa Rica. "Ticos" are worried by the additional strain placed on government resources in a country where more than 80 percent of the population are covered by social-security programs, and approximately 60 percent are provided with pensions and medical benefits.

The economy has been under stress since 1994, and President Figueres was forced to reconsider many of his statist policies. While the export sector remained healthy, domestic industry languished and the internal debt ballooned. The Costa Rican–American Chamber of Commerce observed that "Costa Rica, with its tiny $8.6 billion GDP and 3.5 million people, cannot afford a government that consistently overspends its budget by 5 percent or more and then sells short-term bonds, mostly to state institutions, to finance the deficit." In 1997, there was a vigorous debate over the possible privatization of many state entities in an effort to reduce the debt quickly. But opponents of privatization noted that state institutions were important contributors to the high standard of living in the country.

Acknowledging that the world had entered a new phase of development, President Miguel Angel Rodríguez introduced a new economic program in January 2001. Called *Impulso* ("Impulse"), the plan, as reported in *The Tico Times,* noted that for Costa Rica to compete in the new global economy, "knowledge, technology, quality of human resources and the development of telecommunication and transportation infrastructures are fundamental determinants of national prosperity." The old model of economic development, which, according to the president, was characterized by "a diversification of exports, liberalized markets and high levels of foreign investment," must be replaced with a fresh approach "rooted in advanced technological development, a highly qualified labor force, and exports of greater value." President Abel Pacheco, elected in April 2002, embraced a similar approach to economic development. But he was unable to fulfill his promises in part because of falling commodity prices and continued trade and fiscal deficits and in part because of political opposition to tax reforms, privatization of some sectors of the economy, and his free trade philosophy. President Arias was also committed to free trade. Costa Rica, in October 2007, narrowly voted to join the Central American Free Trade Agreement with the United States. This close vote, together with President Arias' razor thin victory in the presidential elections of 2006, signal the need for compromise and flexibility in the country's economic policy.

■ THE ENVIRONMENT

At a time when tropical rain forests globally are under assault by developers, cattle barons, and land-hungry peasants, Costa Rica has taken concrete action to protect

its environment. Minister of Natural Resources Álvaro Umana was one of those responsible for engineering an imaginative debt-for-nature swap. In his words: "We would like to see debt relief support conservation . . . a policy that everybody agrees is good." Since 1986, the Costa Rican government has authorized the conversion of $75 million in commercial debt into bonds. Interest generated by those bonds has supported a variety of projects, such as the enlargement and protection of La Amistad, a 1.7 million-acre reserve of tropical rain forest.

About 13 percent of Costa Rica's land is protected currently in a number of national parks. It is hoped that very soon about 25 percent of the country will be designated as national parkland in order to protect tropical rain forests as well as the even more endangered tropical dry forests.

Much of the assault on the forests typically has been dictated by economic necessity and/or greed. In one all-too-common scenario, a small- or middle-sized cacao grower discovers that his crop has been decimated by a blight. Confronted by disaster, he will usually farm the forest surrounding his property for timber and then torch the remainder. Ultimately, he will likely sell his land to a cattle rancher, who will transform what had once been rain forest or dry forest into pasture.

In an effort to break this devastating pattern, at least one Costa Rican environmental organization has devised a workable plan to save the forests. Farmers are introduced to a variety of cash crops so that they will not be totally dependent on a single crop. Also, in the case of cacao, for example, the farmer will be provided with a disease- or blight-resistant strain to lessen further the chances of crop losses and subsequent conversion of land to cattle pasture.

Scientists in Costa Rica are concerned that tropical forests are being destroyed before their usefulness to humankind can be fully appreciated. Such forests contain a treasure trove of medicinal herbs. In Costa Rica, for example, there is at least one plant common to the rain forests that might be beneficial in the struggle against AIDS.

Snapshot: COSTA RICA

Summarized below is a quick look at the country with regard to its development, freedom, health/welfare, and achievements.

Development

In recent years the country has moved away from its traditional dependence on exports of coffee, bananas, and beef. Tourism is now Costa Rica's main source of revenue. Over 200 multinational companies have established themselves in a wide range of industries, including advanced manufacturing and medical devices and services.

Freedom

In 2010 Freedom House noted that Costa Rica's media are "generally free from state interference. There are six privately owned dailies, and both public and commercial broadcast outlets are available, including at least four private television stations and more than 100 private radio stations. Abuse of government advertising and direct pressure from senior officials to influence media content has been reported." A February 2010 Supreme Court ruling removed prison terms for defamation; internet access is unrestricted.

Health/Welfare

Costa Ricans enjoy the highest standard of living in Central America. But Costa Rica's indigenous peoples, in part because of their remote location, have inadequate schools, health care, and access to potable water. Sixteen percent of the population live in poverty.

Achievements

In a region torn by civil war and political chaos, Costa Rica's years of free and democratic elections stand as a remarkable achievement in political stability and civil rights. President Óscar Arias was awarded the Nobel Peace Prize in 1987; he remains a respected world leader.

Statistics

Geography

Area in Square Miles (Kilometers): 19,700 (51,022) (about the size of West Virginia)

Capital (Population): San José (1,400,000) (metropolitan area)

Environmental Concerns: deforestation; soil erosion

Geographical Features: coastal plains separated by rugged mountains

People

Population

Total: 4,576,582 (2011 est.)

Annual Growth Rate: 1.3%

Rural/Urban Population Ratio: 26/64

Major Language: Spanish

Ethnic Makeup: 94% white (including a few Mestizos); 3% black; 1% Indian; 1% Chinese

Religions: 76.3% Roman Catholic; 13.7% Evangelical; 5% others

Health

Life Expectancy at Birth: 75 years (male); 80 years (female)

Infant Mortality Rate (Ratio): 8.77/1,000

Physicians Available (Ratio): 9.45/1000

Education

Adult Literacy Rate: 95%

Compulsory (Ages): 6–15; free

Communication

Telephones: 1,482,000 main lines

Daily Newspaper Circulation: 102 per 1,000 people

Cell Phones: 3,035,000

Internet Users: 1,485,000

Transportation

Roadways in Kilometers (Miles): 10,886 (6,764)

Railroads in Kilometers (Miles): 278 (173) None in use

Usable Airfields: 151

Government

Type: democratic republic

Independence Date: September 15, 1821 (from Spain)

Head of State/Government: President Laura Chinchilla is both head of state and head of government

Political Parties: Citizen Action Party; Libertarian Movement; National Liberation Party; others

Suffrage: universal and compulsory at 18

Military

Military Expenditures (% of Central Government Expenditures): 0.4%

Current Hostilities: none

Economy

Currency ($U.S. Equivalent): 513 colons = $1

Per Capita Income/GDP: $11,300/$51.17 billion

GDP Growth Rate: 4.2%

Inflation Rate: 5.7%

Unemployment Rate: 7.3%

Labor Force: 2,052,000

Natural Resources: hydropower

Agriculture: coffee; bananas; sugar; corn; rice; beans; potatoes; beef; timber

Industry: microprocessors; food processing; textiles and clothing; construction materials; fertilizer; plastic products; tourism

Exports: $12.9 billion (primary partners United States, China, Netherlands, United Kingdom)

Imports: $10.9 billion (primary partners United States, Japan, China, Mexico)

Suggested Website

www.cia.gov/cia/publications/factbook/geos/cs.html

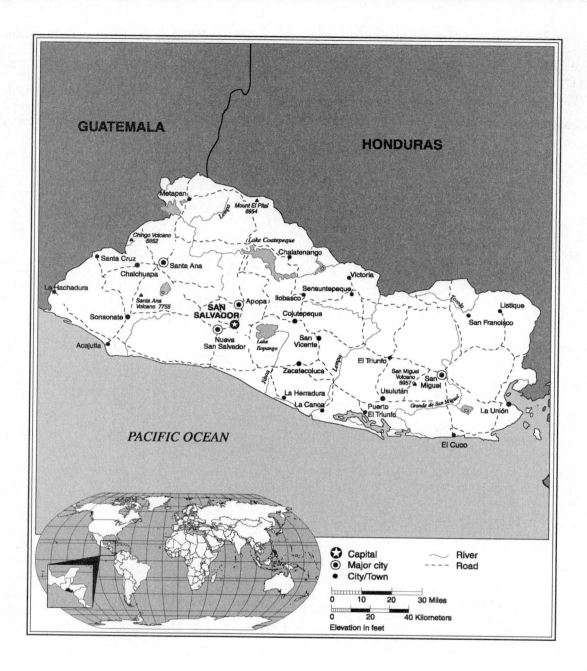

GUATEMALA

HONDURAS

Metapan

Mount El Pital
8954

Chingo Volcano
5852

Lake Coatepeque

Santa Cruz

Chalatenango

Santa Ana

Chalchuapa

Victoria

La Hachadura

Sensuntepeque

Santa Ana
Volcano 7755

Ilobasco

Apopa

Listique

SAN
SALVADOR

Cojutepeque

San Francisco

Sonsonate

Acajutla

Nueva
San Salvador

Lake
Ilopango

San
Vicente

El Triunfo

Zacatecoluca

San Miguel
Volcano
6957

San
Miguel

La Herradura

Usulután

La Union

La Canoa

Puerto
El Triunfo

Grande de San Miguel

PACIFIC OCEAN

El Cuco

★ Capital

◎ Major city

● City/Town

〜 River

- - - Road

0   10   20   30 Miles

0   20   40 Kilometers

Elevation in feet

El Salvador
(Republic of El Salvador)

EL SALVADOR: A TROUBLED LAND

El Salvador, the smallest country in Central America, was engaged until 1992 in a civil war that cut through class lines, divided the military and the Roman Catholic Church, and severely damaged the social and economic fabric of the nation. It was the latest in a long series of violent sociopolitical eruptions that have plagued the country since its independence in 1821.

In the last quarter of the nineteenth century, large plantation owners—spurred by the sharp increase in the world demand for coffee and other products of tropical agriculture—expanded their lands and estates. Most of the new land was purchased or taken from Indians and Mestizos (those of mixed white and Indian blood), who, on five occasions between 1872 and 1898, took up arms in futile attempts to preserve their land. The once-independent Indians and Mestizos were reduced to becoming tenant farmers, sharecroppers, day laborers, or peons on the large estates. Indians, when deprived of their lands, also lost much of their cultural and ethnic distinctiveness. Today, El Salvador is an overwhelmingly Mestizo society.

The uprooted peasantry was controlled in a variety of ways. Some landowners played the role of *patrón* and assured workers the basic necessities of life in return for their labor. Laws against "vagabonds" (those who, when stopped by rural police, did not have a certain amount of money in their pockets) assured plantation owners a workforce and discouraged peasant mobility.

To enforce order further, a series of security organizations—the National Guard, the National Police, and the Treasury Police—were created by the central government. Many of these security personnel actually lived on the plantations and estates and followed the orders of the owner. Although protection of the economic system was their primary function, over time elements of these organizations became private armies.

This phenomenon lay at the heart of much of the "unofficial" violence in El Salvador in recent years. In Salvadoran society, personal loyalties to relatives or local strongmen competed with and often superseded loyalty to government officials. Because of this, the government was unable to control some elements within its security forces.

In an analysis of the Salvadoran Civil War, it is tempting to place the rich, right wing landowners and their military allies on one side; and the poor, the peasantry, and the guerrillas on the other. Such a division is artificial, however, and fails to reflect the complexities of the conflict. Granted, the military and landowners had enjoyed a mutually beneficial partnership since 1945. But there were liberal and conservative factions within the armed forces, and, since the 1940s, there had been some movement toward needed social and economic reforms. It was a military regime in 1949 that put into effect the country's first social-security legislation. In 1950, a Constitution was established that provided for public-health programs, women's suffrage, and extended social-security coverage. The reformist impulse continued in the 1960s, when it became legal to organize opposition political parties.

TIMELINE

1524
Present-day El Salvador is occupied by Spanish settlers from Mexico

1821
Independence from Spain is declared

1822
El Salvador is part of the United Provinces of Central America

1838
El Salvador becomes independent as a separate state

1969
A brief war between El Salvador and Honduras

1970
Guerrilla warfare in El Salvador

1979
Army officers seize power in a coup; civil war

1990s
A cease-fire takes effect on February 1, 1992, officially ending the civil war

2000s
Earthquakes devastate towns and cities, with a heavy loss of life and extensive infrastructure damage
In 2008, Hurricane Ida caused widespread destruction
Mauricio Funes wins the 2009 presidential election. Gang violence escalates in 2011–12

(© Photodisc/PunchStock)

Civil strife disrupted much of El Salvador's agrarian production, and a lack of fishery planning necessitated importing from other parts of the world. With a new and efficient program to take advantage of fish in domestic waters, El Salvador has been able to develop an effective food industry from the sea.

■ A TIME FOR CHANGE

Food production increased in the 1970s by 44 percent, a growth that was second in Latin America only to Brazil's. Although much of the food grown was exported to world markets, some of the revenue generated was used for social programs in El Salvador. Life expectancy increased, the death rate fell, illiteracy declined, and the percentage of government expenditures on public health, housing, and education was among the highest in Latin America.

The programs and reforms, in classic Hispanic form, were generated by the upper classes. The elite believed that state-sponsored changes could be controlled in such a way that traditional balances in society would remain intact and elite domination of the government would be assured.

The origin of El Salvador's civil war may be traced to 1972, when the Christian Democratic candidate for president, José Napoleón Duarte, is believed to have won the popular vote but was deprived of his victory when the army declared the results false and handed the victory to its own candidate. Impatient and frustrated, middle-class politicians and student leaders from the opposition began to consider more forceful ways to oust the ruling class.

By 1979, guerrilla groups had become well established in rural El Salvador, and some younger army officers grew concerned that a successful left-wing popular revolt was a distinct possibility. Rather than wait for revolution from below, which might result in the destruction of the military as an institution, the officers chose to seize power in a coup and manipulate change from above. Once in power, this *junta,* or ruling body, moved quickly to transform the structure of Salvadoran society. A land-reform program, originally developed by civilian reformers and Roman Catholic clergy, was adopted by the military. It would give the campesinos ("peasants") not only land but also status, dignity, and respect.

In its first year, 1980, the land-reform program had a tremendous impact on the landowning elite—37 percent of the lands producing cotton and 34 percent of the coffee--growing lands were confiscated by the government and redistributed. The junta also nationalized the banks and assumed control of the sale of coffee and sugar. Within months, however, several peasant members of the new cooperatives and the government agricultural advisers sent to help them were gunned down. The violence spread. Some of the killings were attributed to government security men in the pay of dispossessed landowners, but most of the killings may have been committed by the army.

In the opinion of a land-reform program official, the army was corrupt and had returned to the cooperatives that it had helped to establish in order to demand money for protection and bribes. When the peasants refused, elements within the army initiated a reign of terror against them.

In 1989, further deterioration of the land-reform program was brought about by Supreme Court decisions and by policies adopted by the newly elected right-wing government of President Alfredo Cristiani. Former landowners who had property taken for redistribution to peasants successfully argued that seizures under the land reform were illegal. Subsequently, five successive land-reform cases were decided by the Supreme Court in favor of former property owners.

Cristiani, whose right-wing National Republican Alliance Party (ARENA) fought hard against land reform, would not directly attack the land-reform program—only be cause such a move would further alienate rural peasants and drive them into the arms of left-wing guerrillas. Instead, Cristiani favored the reconstitution of collective farms as private plots. Such a move, according to the government, would improve productivity and put an end to what authorities perceived as a form of U.S.–imposed "socialism." Critics of the government's policy charged that the privatization plan would ultimately result in the demise of land reform altogether.

Yet another problem was that many of the collectives established under the reform were (and remain) badly in debt. A 1986 study by the U.S. Agency for International Development reported that 95 percent of the cooperatives could not pay interest on the debt they were forced to acquire to compensate the landlords. *New York Times* reporter Lindsey Gruson noted that the world surplus of agricultural products as well as mismanagement by peasants who suddenly found themselves in the unfamiliar role of owners were a large part of the reason for the failures. But the government did not help. Technical assistance was not provided, and the tremendous debt gave the cooperatives a poor credit rating, which made it difficult for them to secure needed fertilizer and pesticides.

Declining yields and, for many families, lives of increasing desperation have been the result. Some peasants must leave the land and sell their plots to the highest bidder. This will ultimately bring about a reconcentration of land in the hands of former landlords.

Other prime farmland lay untended because of the civil war. Violence drove many peasants from the land to the slums of the larger cities. And free-fire zones established by the military (in an effort to destroy the guerrillas' popular base) and guerrilla attacks against cooperatives (in an effort to sabotage the economy and further destabilize the country) had a common victim: the peasantry.

Some cooperatives and individual families failed to bring the land to flower because of the poor quality of the soil they inherited. Reporter Gruson told the story of one family, which was, unfortunately, all too common:

> José . . . received 1.7 acres on a rockpocked slope an hour's walk from his small shack. José . . . used to sell some of his beans and rice to raise a little cash. But year after year his yields have declined. Since he cannot afford fertilizers or insecticides, the corn that survives the torrential rainy season produces pest-infested ears the size of a baby's foot. Now he has trouble feeding his wife and seven children.
>
> "The land is no good," he said. "I've been working it for 12 years and my life has gotten worse every year. I don't have anywhere to go, but I'll have to leave soon."

After the coup, several governments came and went. The original reformers retired, went into exile, or went over to the guerrillas. The civil war continued into 1992, when a United Nations–mediated cease-fire took effect.

■ HUMAN-RIGHTS ISSUES

Twelve years of war had cost 70,000 lives and given El Salvador the reputation of a bloody and abusive country. Tens of thousands of El Salvadorans were uprooted by the violence and many made their way to the United States. Despite the declared truce, the extreme right and left continued to utilize assassination to eliminate or terrorize both each other and the voices of moderation who dared to speak out.

Through 1992, human-rights abuses still occurred on a wide scale in El Salvador. Public order was constantly disrupted by military operations, guerrilla raids, factional hatreds, acts of revenge, personal grudges, pervasive fear, and a sense of uncertainty about the future. State-of-siege decrees suspended all constitutional rights to freedom of speech and press. However, self-censorship, both in the media and by individuals, out of fear of violent reprisals, was the leading constraint on free expression in El Salvador.

Eventually, as *Boston Globe* correspondent Pamela Constable reported, "a combination of war-weariness and growing pragmatism among leaders of all persuasions suggests that once-bitter adversaries have begun to develop a modus vivendi."

Release of the report in 1993 by the UN's "Truth Commission," a special body entrusted with the investigation of human-rights violations in El Salvador, prompted the right wing–dominated Congress to approve an amnesty for those named. But progress has been made in other areas. The National Police have been separated from the Defense Ministry; and the National Guard, Civil Defense forces, and the notorious Treasury Police have been abolished. A new National Civilian Police, comprised of 20 percent of National Police, 20 percent former Farabundo Martí National Liberation Front (FMLN) guerrillas, and 60 percent with no involvement on either side in the civil war, was instituted in 1994.

President Cristiani reduced the strength of the army from 63,000 to 31,500 by February 1993, earlier than provided for by the agreement; and the class of officers known as the *tondona,* who had long dominated the military and were likely responsible for human-rights abuses, were forcibly retired by the president on June 30, 1993. Land, judicial, and electoral reforms followed. Despite perhaps inevitable setbacks because of the legacy of violence and bitterness, editor Juan Comas wrote that "most analysts are inclined to believe that El Salvador's hour of madness has passed and the country is now on the road to hope."

In El Salvador, as elsewhere in Latin America, the Roman Catholic Church was divided. The majority of Church officials backed government policy and supported the United States' contention that the violence in El Salvador was due to Cuban-backed subversion. Other clergy strongly disagreed and argued convincingly that the violence was deeply rooted in historical social injustice.

Another endemic problem that confronts postwar El Salvador is widespread corruption. It is a human-rights issue because corruption and its attendant misuse of scarce resources contribute to persistent or increased poverty and undermine the credibility and stability of government at all levels. According to the nonprofit watchdog group *Probidad,* "El Salvador has a long history of corruption. . . . Before the first of many devastating earthquakes on January 13, 2001, El Salvador was the third poorest country in Latin America. . . . Influence peddling between construction companies and their friends and families in government and other corrupt practices resulted in many unnecessary deaths, infrastructure damage, and irregularities in humanitarian assistance distribution."

ECONOMIC ISSUES

In 1998, President Armando Calderón Sol surprised both supporters and opponents when he launched a bold program of reforms. The first three years of his administration had been characterized by indecision. Political scientist Tommie Sue Montgomery noted that his "reputation for espousing as policy the last viewpoint he has heard has produced in civil society both heartburn and black humor." But a combination of factors created new opportunities for Calderón. The former guerrillas of the FMLN were divided and failed to take advantage of ARENA's apparent weak leadership; a UN–sponsored program of reconstruction and reconciliation was short of funds and, by 1995, had lost momentum; and presidential elections were looming in 1999. A dozen years of war had left the economic infrastructure in disarray. The economy had, at best, remained static, and while the war raged, there had been no attempt to modernize. During his final year in office, Calderón developed reform policies of modernization, privatization, and free-market competition. Interestingly, his reforms generated opposition from former guerrillas, who are now represented in the Legislature by the FMLN, as well as from some members of the traditional conservative economic elite.

Perhaps one result of Calderón's reforms was the decisive victory of ARENA at the polls in 1999, and again in 2004. The FMLN, on the other hand, won municipal and legislative elections in 2003, which gave them the largest voting bloc in Congress, and in 2009 won the presidency in a very close election. An evenly divided electorate revealed a significant polarization between left and right wing parties.

OUT-MIGRATION

El Salvador's civil war set into motion some profound changes in the nation. As noted, thousands of people fled to other countries, and especially to the United States. Once established, other family members tended to follow. Indeed, one of every nine people born in El Salvador will migrate to the United States. Salvadoran sociologist Raymundo Calderón, as reported in the *Los Angeles Times,* stated: "Most of the Salvadorans who have migrated . . . are not well educated. But when they get to the United States, they have access to better housing and better pay. Their view of the world changes, and they communicate this to their families in El Salvador." So many have departed that there is a labor shortage in the agricultural sector that has had to be filled by workers from Honduras and Nicaragua. In November 2005 the nation's minister of agriculture announced that 15,000 foreign workers would be needed to cut sugarcane and harvest the cotton and coffee crops.

The labor shortage is directly related to a more serious issue. *Los Angeles Times* correspondent Hector Tobar notes concerns that Salvadorans are losing their "industrious self-image, a vision celebrated by poets such as Roque Dalton, whose 'Love Poem' recounted the exploits of Salvadoran laborers up and down the Americas." Remittances from the United States to El Salvador, which reached $3.8 billion in 2008, prompted one harvest supervisor for a large sugar refinery to say that money from families in the United States has made Salvadorans "comfortable, and they don't want to work cutting cane." It is estimated that 22.3% of El Salvadoran families receive remittances from abroad. This lament was echoed by the minister of the interior in his comments to a local newspaper: "Today people are telling us that their family remittances are sufficient [to live on]. It's not possible that we are abandoning our own fields and we have to bring in labor from abroad." What the minister finds impossible is that El Salvadoran rural workers, because of a labor surplus, had traditionally sought work in neighboring Honduras. Now the flow of labor is in the other direction. War, natural disasters, and out-migration have changed the very culture of the nation.

Finally, an unwelcome consequence of out-migration is that many youths, exposed to and emulating the gang cultures in several United States cities, have become a serious criminal problem for not only United States authorities, but also for those in El Salvador as gangs have made their appearance in urban areas. Gang violence is largely responsible both for the disappearance of many young people and a homicide rate that is among the highest in the world at 64 per 100,000. A BBC report notes: "Poverty, civil war, natural disaster, and consequent dislocations have left their mark on . . . society, which is among the most violent and crime ridden in the Americas."

On a positive note, financial incentives in the form of free trade zones have stimulated an expansion of the textile and apparel industries, which now provide over 70,000 jobs. A further indication of a shift away from agriculture is the fact that 49 percent of the total labor force is now employed in retail and financial services.

? DID YOU KNOW?

Since 2003 El Salvador has worked hard to liberalize and modernize its trade policies and regulations. Its customs regimen has been overhauled and licensing requirements eased. Progress has been made with respect to the integration of Central American economies.

FURTHER INVESTIGATION

For more information on trade policies, visit www.wto.org/english/tratop_e/tpr_e/tp326_e.htm

Snapshot: EL SALVADOR

Summarized below is a quick look at the country with regard to its development, freedom, health/welfare, and achievements.

Development

Since 2004, the government has pursued a policy of economic diversification, especially in the areas of textile production, international port services, and tourism. Formerly state-controlled enterprises, such as telecommunications, the distribution of electric power, banking, and pension funds, are in the process of privatization. El Salvador was the first regional nation to ratify the Central American Free Trade Agreement.

Freedom

In 2010 Freedom House reported that while "women are granted equal rights under family and property law, they are occasionally discriminated against in practice; women also suffer discrimination in employment. El Salvador remains a source, transit, and destination country for the trafficking of women and children for the purposes of prostitution and forced labor. A 2010 study conducted by the Ministry of Economics found that 10 percent of children between the ages of 5 and 17 were working. Violence against women and children . . . remained widespread."

Health/Welfare

Many Salvadorans suffer from parasites and malnutrition. El Salvador has one of the highest infant mortality rates in the Western Hemisphere, largely because of polluted water. Potable water is readily available to only 10 percent of the population.

Achievements

Despite the violence of war, political power has been transferred via elections at both the municipal and national levels. Elections have helped to establish the legitimacy of civilian leaders in a region usually dominated by military regimes.

Statistics

Geography

Area in Square Miles (Kilometers): 8,292 (21,476) (about the size of Massachusetts)

Capital (Population): San Salvador 1,534,000 (2011 est.)

Environmental Concerns: deforestation; soil erosion; water pollution; soil contamination

Geographical Features: a hot coastal plain in south rises to a cooler plateau and valley region; mountainous in north, including many volcanoes

Climate: tropical; distinct wet and dry seasons

People

Population

Total: 6,070,000 (2011 est.)

Annual Growth Rate: 0.32%

Rural/Urban Population Ratio: 36/64

Ethnic Makeup: 90% Mestizo; Amerindian 1%; white 9%

Major Language: Spanish

Religions: 57.1% Roman Catholic; 25% Protestant groups, none 17%

Health

Life Expectancy at Birth: 70 years (male); 77 years (female)

Infant Mortality Rate (Ratio): 20.3/1,000

Physicians Available (Ratio): 1.6/1000

Education

Adult Literacy Rate: 81.1%

Compulsory (Ages): 7–16; free

Communication

Telephones: 1,000,000 main lines

Daily Newspaper Circulation: 53 per 1,000 people

Cell Phones: 7,700,000

Internet Users: 746,000

Transportation

Roadways in Kilometers (Miles): 10,886 (6,764)

Railroads in Kilometers (Miles): 562 (349) None in use since 2005

Usable Airfields: 65

Government

Type: republic

Independence Date: September 15, 1821 (from Spain)

Head of State/Government: President Mauricio Funes is both head of state and head of government

Political Parties: Farabundo Martí National Liberation Front; National Republican Alliance; National Conciliation Party; Christian Democratic Party; Democratic Convergence; others

Suffrage: universal at 18

Military

Military Expenditures (% of GDP): 0.6%

Current Disputes: border disputes

Economy

Currency ($U.S. Equivalent): 1 colon = $1

Per Capita Income/GDP: $7,200/$43.57 billion

GDP Growth Rate: 0.7%

Inflation Rate: 1.2%

Unemployment Rate: 7.2% Underemployment: Significant underemployment

Labor Force: 2,564,000

Natural Resources: hydropower; geothermal power; petroleum; arable land

Agriculture: coffee; sugarcane; corn; rice; beans; oilseed; cotton; sorghum; beef; dairy products; shrimp

Industry: food processing; beverages; petroleum; chemicals; fertilizer; textiles; furniture; light metals

Exports: $4.577 billion (primary partners United States, Guatemala, Honduras)

Imports: $8,189 billion (primary partners United States, Guatemala, Mexico, Honduras, China)

Suggested Website

http://cia.gov/cia/publications/factbook/index.html

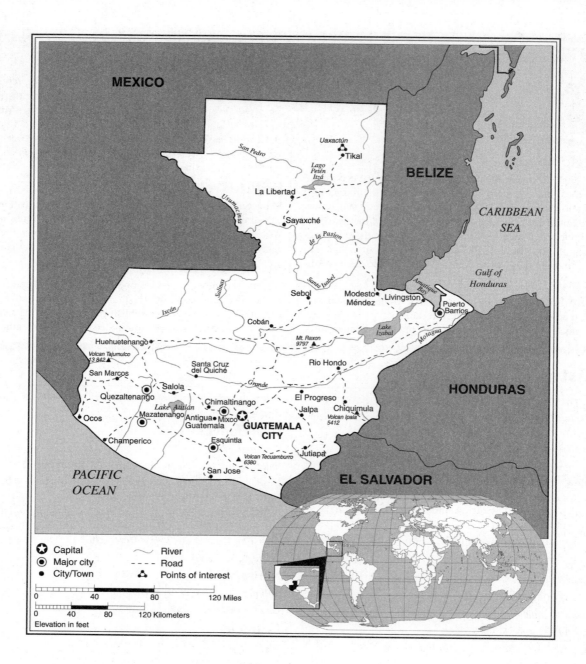

MEXICO

San Pedro

Uaxactún
Tikal

*Lago
Petén
Itzá*

BELIZE

La Libertad

*CARIBBEAN
SEA*

Sayaxché

Usumacinta

de la Pasión

*Gulf of
Honduras*

Salinas

Santa Isabel

Sebol

Modesto
Méndez

Livingston

*Amatique
Bay*

Puerto
Barrios

Iscán

Cobán

*Lake
Izabal*

Motagua

Huehuetenango

Mt. Raxon
9797 ▲

*Volcan Tajumulco
13,842* ▲

Santa Cruz
del Quiché

Rio Hondo

San Marcos

Grande

HONDURAS

Salola

Quezaltenango

Chimaltinango

El Progreso

Lake Atitlán

Mazatenango

Jalpa

Chiquimula

Antigua
Guatemala

Mixco

*Volcan Ipala
5412* ▲

Ocos

GUATEMALA
CITY

Champerico

Esquintla

Jutiapa

*Volcan Tecuamburro
6380* ▲

*PACIFIC
OCEAN*

San Jose

EL SALVADOR

✪ Capital
◉ Major city
● City/Town

∿ River
--- Road
△ Points of interest

| 0 | 40 | 80 | 120 Miles |

| 0 | 40 | 80 | 120 Kilometers |

Elevation in feet

Guatemala
(Republic of Guatemala)

GUATEMALA: PEOPLES IN CONFLICT

Ethnic relations between the descendants of Maya Indians, who comprise 44 percent of Guatemala's population, and whites and Ladinos (Hispanicized Indians) have always been unfriendly and have contributed significantly to the nation's turbulent history. During the colonial period and since independence, Spaniards, Creoles (in Guatemala, whites born in the New World—as opposed to in Nicaragua, where Creoles are defined as native-born blacks), and Ladinos have repeatedly sought to dominate the Guatemalan Indian population, largely contained in the highlands, by controlling the Indians' land and their labor.

The process of domination was accelerated between 1870 and 1920, as Guatemala's entry into world markets hungry for tropical produce such as coffee resulted in the purchase or extensive seizures of land from Indians. Denied sufficient lands of their own, Indians were forced onto the expanding plantations as debt peons. Others were forced to labor as seasonal workers on coastal plantations; many died there because of the sharp climatic differences.

THE INDIAN AND INTEGRATION

Assaulted by the Ladino world, highland Indians withdrew into their own culture and built social barriers between themselves and the changing world outside their villages. Those barriers have persisted until the present.

For the Guatemalan governments that have thought in terms of economic progress and national unity, the Indians have always presented a problem. A 2003 presidential candidate stated: "Indigenous groups do not speak of a 'political system'; they speak of community consensus, and their conception of community is very local. . . . How do you have a functioning nation state, one where indigenous groups participate actively in protecting their political interests, and yet still respect the cultural practices of other indigenous groups for whom participation in Western political institutions is deemed undesirable?"

According to anthropologist Leslie Dow, Jr., Guatemalan governments too easily explain the Indian's lack of material prosperity in terms of the "deficiencies" of Indian culture. Indian "backwardness" is better explained by elite policies calculated to keep Indians subordinate. Social, political, and economic deprivations have consistently and consciously been utilized by governments anxious to maintain the Indian in an inferior status.

Between 1945 and 1954, however, there was a period of remarkable social reform in Guatemala. Before the reforms were cut short by the resistance of landowners, factions within the military, and a U.S. Central Intelligence Agency–sponsored invasion, Guatemalan governments made a concerted effort to integrate the Indian into national life. Some Indians who lived in close proximity to large urban centers such as the capital, Guatemala City, learned that their vote had the power to effect changes to their benefit. They also realized that they were unequal not because of their illiteracy, "backwardness," poverty, or inability to converse in Spanish, but because of governments that refused to reform their political, social, and economic structures.

TIMELINE

1523
Guatemala is conquered by Spanish forces from Mexico

1821
Independence

1822–1838
Guatemala is part of the United Provinces of Central America

1838
Guatemala becomes independent as a separate state

1944
Revolution; many reforms

1954
A CIA–sponsored coup deposes the reformist government

1976
An earthquake leaves 22,000 dead

1977
Human-rights abuses lead to the termination of U.S. aid

1990s
Talks between the government and guerrillas end 36 years of violence

2000s
Economic problems multiply
In 2010 tropical storm Agatha and the eruption of the Pacaya volcano threatened Guatemala's food supply

(USAID/Maureen Taft-Morales)

In recent years, Indians in Guatemela have pursued their rights by excersing their voting power. Here two women display the ink on their index finger indicating they've voted.

In theory, indigenous peoples in Guatemala enjoy equal legal rights under the Constitution. In fact, however, they remain largely outside the national culture, do not speak Spanish, and are not integrated into the national economy. Indian males are far more likely to be impressed into the army or guerrilla units. Indigenous peoples in Guatemala suffered most of the combat-related casualties and repeated abuses of their basic human rights. There remains a pervasive discrimination against Indians in white society. Indians have on occasion challenged state policies that they have considered inequitable and repressive. But if they become too insistent on change, threaten violence or societal upheaval, or support and/or join guerrilla groups, government repression is usually swift and merciless.

■ GUERRILLA WARFARE

A civil war, which was to last for 36 years, developed in 1960. Guatemala was plagued by violence, attributed both to left-wing insurgencies in rural areas and to armed forces' counterinsurgency operations. Led by youthful middle-class rebels, guerrillas gained strength because of several factors: the radical beliefs of some Roman Catholic priests in rural areas; the ability of the guerrillas to mobilize Indians for the first time; and the "demonstration effect" of events elsewhere in Central America. Some of the success is explained by the guerrilla leaders' ability to

converse in Indian languages. Radical clergy increased the recruitment of Indians into the guerrilla forces by suggesting that revolution was an acceptable path to social justice. The excesses of the armed forces in their search for subversives drove other Indians into the arms of the guerrillas. In some parts of the highlands, the loss of ancestral lands to speculators or army officers was sufficient to inspire the Indians to join the radical cause.

According to the *Latin American Regional Report* for Mexico and Central America, government massacres of guerrillas and their actual or suspected supporters were frequent and "characterized by clinical savagery." At times, the killing was selective, with community leaders and their families singled out. In other instances, entire villages were destroyed and all the inhabitants slaughtered. "Everything depends on the army's perception of the local level of support for the guerrillas," according to the report.

To counterbalance the violence, once guerrillas were cleared from an area, the government implemented an "Aid Program to Areas in Conflict." Credit was offered to small farmers to boost food production in order to meet local demand, and displaced and jobless people were enrolled in food-for-work units to build roads or other public projects.

By the mid-1980s, most of the guerrillas' military organizations had been destroyed. This was the result not only of successful counterinsurgency tactics by the Guatemalan military but also of serious errors of judgment by guerrilla leaders. Impatient and anxious for change, the guerrillas had overestimated the willingness of the Guatemalan people to rebel. They also had underestimated the power of the military establishment. Surviving guerrilla units maintained an essentially defensive posture for the remainder of the decade. In 1989, however, the guerrillas regrouped. The subsequent intensification of human-rights abuses and the climate of violence were indicative of the military's response.

There was some hope for improvement in 1993, in the wake of the ouster of President Jorge Serrano, whose attempt to emulate the "self-coup" of Peru's Alberto Fujimori failed. Guatemala's next president, Ramiro de León Carpio, was a human-rights activist who was sharply critical of security forces in their war against the guerrillas of the Guatemalan National Revolutionary Unity (URNG). Peace talks between the government and guerrillas had been pursued with the Roman Catholic Church as intermediary for several years, with sparks of promise but no real change. In July 1993, de León announced a new set of proposals to bring to an end the decades of bloodshed that had resulted in 140,000 deaths. Those proposals were the basis for the realization of a peace agreement worked out under the auspices of the United Nations in December 1996.

But the underlying causes of the violence still must be addressed. Colin Woodard, writing in *The Chronicle of Higher Education,* reported that the peace accords promised to "reshape Guatemala as a democratic, multicultural society." But an estimated 70 percent of the Maya Indians still live in poverty, and more than 80 percent are illiterate. Estuardo Zapeta, Guatemala's first Maya newspaper columnist, writes: "This is a multicultural, multilingual society. . . . As long as we leave the Maya illiterate, we're condemning them to being peasants. And if that happens, their need to acquire farmland will lead us to another civil war." This, however, is only one facet of a multifaceted set of issues. The very complexity of Guatemalan society, according to political scientist Rachel McCleary, "make[s] it extremely difficult to attain a consensus at the national level on the nature of the problems confronting society." But the new ability of leaders from many sectors of society to work together to shape a meaningful peace is a hopeful sign.

Although the fighting has ended, fear persists. Journalist Woodard wrote in July 1997: "In many neighborhoods [in Guatemala City] private property is protected by razor wire and patrolled by guards with pump-action shotguns." One professor at the University of San Carlos observed, "It is good that the war is over, but I am pessimistic about the peace. . . . There is intellectual freedom now, but we are very unsure of the permanence of that freedom. It makes us very cautious."

■ URBAN VIOLENCE

Although most of the violence occurred in rural areas, urban Guatemala did not escape the horrors of the civil war. The following characterization of Guatemalan politics, written by an English traveler in 1839, is still relevant today: "There is but one side to the politics in Guatemala. Both parties have a beautiful way of producing unanimity of opinion, by driving out of the country all who do not agree with them."

During the civil war, right-wing killers murdered dozens of leaders of the moderate political left to prevent them from organizing viable political parties that might challenge the ruling elite. These killers also assassinated labor leaders if their unions were considered leftist or antigovernment. Leaders among university students and professors "disappeared" because the national university had a reputation as a center of leftist subversion. Media people were gunned down if they were critical of the government or the right wing. Left-wing extremists also assassinated political leaders associated with "repressive" policies, civil servants (whose only "crime" was government employment), military personnel and police, foreign diplomats, peasant informers, and businesspeople and industrialists associated with the government.

Common crime rose to epidemic proportions in Guatemala City (as well as in the capitals of other Central American republics). Many of the weapons that once armed the Nicaraguan militias and El Salvador's civil-defense patrols found their way onto the black market, where, according to the Managua newspaper *Pensamiento Propio,* they were purchased by the Guatemalan Army, the guerrillas of the URNG, and criminals.

The fear of official or unofficial violence has always inhibited freedom of the press in Guatemala. Early in the 1980s, the Conference on Hemispheric Affairs noted that restrictions on the print media and the indiscriminate brutality of the death squads "turned Guatemala into a virtual no-man's land for journalists." Lingering fears and memories of past violence tend to limit the exercise of press freedoms guaranteed by the Constitution. The U.S. State Department's Country Reports notes that "the media continues to exercise a degree of self-censorship on certain topics. . . . The lack of aggressive investigative reporting dealing with the military and human rights violations apparently is due to self-censorship."

■ HEALTH CARE AND NUTRITION

In rural Guatemala, half the people have a diet that is well below the minimum daily caloric intake established by the Food and Agricultural Organization. Indeed, in 2009, 43 percent of children under age five were chronically malnourished, one of the highest rates in the world. Growth in the staple food crops (corn, rice, beans, wheat) has failed to keep pace with population growth. Marginal malnutrition is endemic.

Health services vary, depending on location, but are uniformly poor in rural Guatemala. The government has begun pilot programs in three departments to provide basic primary health care on a wide scale. But some of these well-intentioned policies have failed because of a lack of sensitivity to cultural differences. Anthropologist Linda

Snapshot: GUATEMALA

Summarized below is a quick look at the country with regard to its development, freedom, health/welfare, and achievements.

Development

Increased investment and export diversification was one result of the implementation of the Central American Free Trade Agreement in 2006. Ethanol and non-traditional agricultural exports experienced the largest increase. Development was slowed in 2009 with the contraction of the economy because of the global recession but showed signs of recovery in 2011.

Freedom

Freedom House noted that although the constitution guarantees religious freedom, members of indigenous communities have faced discrimination for openly practicing their beliefs. Also, while the government does not interfere with academic freedom, "scholars have received death threats for raising questions about past human rights abuses or continuing injustices."

Health/Welfare

In 2010 the UN reported that Guatemala "continued to battle the threat of famine, particularly in rural areas." Severe malnutrition claimed the lives of at least 6,575 people as a result of rising food prices, prolonged drought, and a decline in migrant remittances linked to the global economic downturn.

Achievements

Guatemalan novelist Miguel Ángel Asturias gained an international reputation for his works about political oppression. In 1967, he was awarded the Nobel Prize for Literature. Rigoberta Menchú Tum won the Nobel Peace Prize in 1992 for her passionate support of the Maya peoples of Guatemala.

Greenberg has observed that the Ministry of Health, as part of its campaign to bring basic health-care services to the hinterlands, introduced midwives who were ignorant of Indian traditions. For Guatemalan Indians, pregnancy is considered an illness that demands specific care, calling for certain foods, herbs, body positions, and interpersonal relations between expectant mother and Indian midwife. In Maya culture, traditional medicine has spiritual, psychological, physical, social, and symbolic dimensions. Ministry of Health workers too often dismissed traditional practices as superstitious and unscientific. Their insensitivity and ignorance created ineffectual health-care programs. In April 2008, President Colom, borrowing programs from Brazil and Mexico, promised to improve healthcare, education and rural development. These programs will provide financial incentives to poor families to keep their children in school and educate parents as to the need for regular health check-ups. But if cultural sensitivities are not addressed the success of such programs is problematical.

■ THE FUTURE

In February 1999, a UN–sponsored Commission for Historical Clarification, in a harsh nine-volume report, blamed the Guatemalan government for acts of genocide against the Maya during the long civil war. The purpose of the report was not to set the stage for criminal prosecutions but to examine the root causes of the civil war and explain how the conflict developed over time. It was hoped that the report signaled the first steps toward national reconciliation and the addressing of human-rights issues, long ignored by those in power.

But the high command of the military and its civilian allies, accused of planning and executing a broad range of atrocities against the Maya, may perceive the report as a threat to their position and their future. In fact, the government has done little to implement the recommendations called for in the 1996 peace accords that ended the civil war. Former President Efraín Rios Montt, who engineered the assault against the Maya during the civil war, lost his congressional seat—and his immunity to prosecution—in 2004.

Not surprisingly, the poor and disadvantaged are increasingly frustrated. Illiteracy, infant mortality and malnutrition are among the highest in Central America while life expectancy is among the lowest. Two-thirds of Guatemala's children live in poverty. Violence remains endemic. Presidential elections in 2007 produced a number of unexpected

? DID YOU KNOW?

Organized gangs in Guatemala have challenged and corrupted the justice system. The nation, according to PBS, has become an epicenter of violence in Central America. Violence against women in particular has hit record levels. Amnesty International reported 717 women were killed in 2009. Of those, many had been raped and mutilated. According to the United Nations, nearly 45 percent of Guatemalan women have suffered some kind of violence in their lifetimes. Abuses that don't end in death are under-reported.

FURTHER INVESTIGATION

For more information on violence against women, visit http://www.pbs.org/newshour/bb/world/jan-june11/guatemala_03-07.html

results that captured in microcosm many of Guatemala's problems and idiosyncrasies. One of the candidates was former Nobel Prize winner Rigoberta Menchú who promised to be an advocate for Guatemala's Maya. Yet she finished sixth in a field of fourteen candidates with only 3 percent of the vote. Many Maya voted for other candidates simply because Menchú is a Quiche Maya from the highlands, distinct in terms of language and dress from the 23 other Maya groups. As one Tz'utujil Maya noted: "She's one of us, but she's not." The candidates who participated in a run-off election pitted two men, a former army general and a businessman, with radically different platforms. The general, Otto

Pérez Molina, promised to rule with a "mano duro" (iron fist) to eliminate the nation's drug traffickers, gang members, and organized crime. The other candidate and eventual winner was Alvaro Colom, described by a *New York Times* reporter as "a gawky policy wonk and businessman who made fighting poverty his campaign's centerpiece." Guatemalans rejected the general in large part because of the past misdeeds and corruption of the military during the years of civil war. President Colom noted that "we had a firm hand for 50 years and it caused more than 250,000 victims in a dirty war." Colom, as noted, is pledged to confront the widespread poverty among Guatemala's indigenous peoples.

Statistics

Geography

Area in Square Miles (Kilometers): 42,000 (108,780) (about the size of Tennessee)

Capital (Population): Guatemala City (2,205,000)

Environmental Concerns: deforestation; soil erosion; water pollution

Geographical Features: mostly mountains, with narrow coastal plains and a rolling limestone plateau (Peten)

Climate: temperate in highlands; tropical on coasts

People

Population

Total: 13,824,463 (2011 est.)

Annual Growth Rate: 2%

Rural/Urban Population Ratio: 51/49

Ethnic Makeup: 59.4% Ladino and white; 44% Amerindian

Major Languages: Spanish; Maya languages

Religions: predominantly Roman Catholic; Protestant and Maya indigenous beliefs

Health

Life Expectancy at Birth: 69 years (male); 72 years (female)

Infant Mortality Rate (Ratio): 26.02/1,000

Physicians Available (Ratio): 0.9/1,000

Education

Adult Literacy Rate: 69%

Compulsory (Ages): 7–14; free

Communication

Telephones: 1,499,000 main lines

Daily Newspaper Circulation: 29 per 1,000 people

Cell Phones: 18,060,000 (2010 est.)

Internet Users: 2,279,000 (2009)

Transportation

Roadways in Kilometers (Miles): 14,095 (8,758)

Railroads in Kilometers (Miles): 552 (343)

Usable Airfields: 402

Government

Type: Constitutional democratic republic

Independence Date: September 15, 1821 (from Spain)

Head of State/Government: President Otto Perez Molina is both head of state and head of government

Political Parties: National Unity for Hope; Grand National Alliance; Patriot Party; Guatemalan Republican Front

Suffrage: universal at 18

Military

Military Expenditures (% of GDP): 0.4%

Current Disputes: border dispute with Belize

Economy

Currency ($U.S. Equivalent): 8.08 quetzals = $1

Per Capita Income/GDP: $5,200/$70.15 billion

GDP Growth Rate: 2.6%

Inflation Rate: 6.6%

Unemployment Rate: 2.2%

Labor Force: 4,146,000

Natural Resources: petroleum; nickel; rare woods; fish; chicle; hydropower

Agriculture: sugarcane; corn; bananas; coffee; beans; cardamom; livestock

Industry: sugar; textiles and clothing; furniture; chemicals; petroleum; metals; rubber; tourism

Exports: $8.566 billion (primary partners, United States El Salvador, Honduras, Mexico)

Imports: $12.86 billion (primary partners, United States Mexico, China, El Salvador)

Suggested Website

www.cia.gov/cia/publications/factbook/index.html

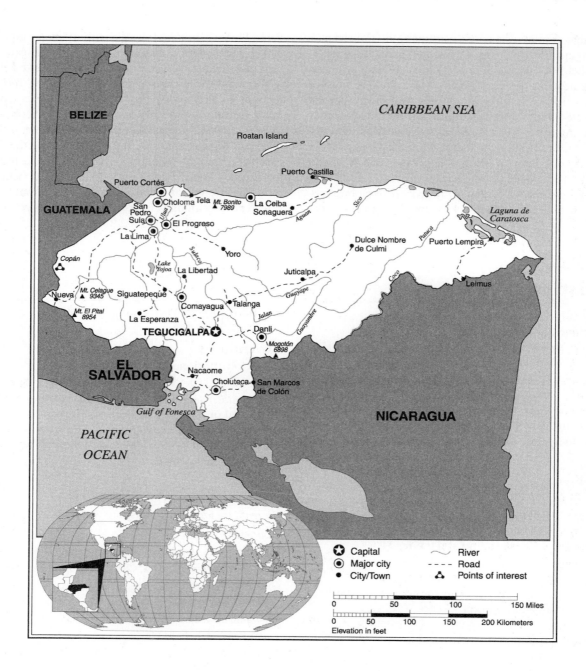

BELIZE

CARIBBEAN SEA

Roatan Island

Puerto Castilla

Puerto Cortés

Choloma Tela   *Mt. Bonito*   La Ceiba
                  7989   Sonaguera
GUATEMALA   San
            Pedro
            Sula   El Progreso
                                              Sico
            La Lima   *Laguna de*
                                                         Caratosca
                       Sulaco   Yoro   Dulce Nombre
Copán   de Culmi   Puerto Lempira
                   Lake   La Libertad   *Patuca*
                   Yojoa
Mt. Celague   Juticalpa   Leimus
Nueva   *9345* Siguatepeque   *Coco*
               Mt. El Pital   Comayagua Talanga   *Guayape*
               8954
          La Esperanza   *Jalan*
                                                      Guayambre
            TEGUCIGALPA ☆   Danli
                                    Mogotón
EL   *6898*
SALVADOR   Nacaome
                    Choluteca San Marcos
                               de Colón   NICARAGUA
        Gulf of Fonesca

PACIFIC

OCEAN

☆ Capital   ～ River
◉ Major city   - - - Road
● City/Town   ⬠ Points of interest

0   50   100   150 Miles
0   50   100   150   200 Kilometers
Elevation in feet

50

Honduras

(Republic of Honduras)

HONDURAS: THE CONTAGION OF VIOLENCE

In political terms, Honduras resembles much of the rest of Central America. Frequent changes of government, numerous constitutions, authoritarian leaders, widespread corruption, and an inability to solve basic problems are common to Honduras and to the region. A historian of Honduras once wrote that his country's history could be "written in a tear."

In terms of social policy, however, Honduras once stood somewhat apart from its neighbors. It was slower to modernize, there were no great extremes of wealth between landowners and the rest of the population, and society appeared more paternalistic and less exploitive than was the case in other Central American states. "Ironically," notes journalist Loren Jenkins, "the land's precarious existence as a poor and unstable backwater has proven almost as much a blessing as a curse." Until recently Honduras lacked the sharp social divisions that helped to plunge Nicaragua, El Salvador, and Guatemala into rebellion and civil war. And Honduran governments have seemed somewhat more responsive to demands for change. Still, Honduras is a poor country. Its people have serious problems—widespread illiteracy, malnutrition, and inadequate health care and housing. The government itself reported an underemployment rate of 30 percent in 2005 and that 70 percent of the nation's population lived in poverty. Those figures had not substantially changed in 2011, when the combined unemployment and underemployment rate stood at 35 percent.

A WILLINGNESS TO CHANGE

In 1962 and 1975, agrarian-reform laws were passed and put into effect with relative success. The Honduran government, with the aid of peasant organizations and organized labor, was able to resettle 30,000 families on their own land. Today, two-thirds of the people who use the land either own it or have the legal right to its use. Labor legislation and social-security laws were enacted in the early 1960s. Even the Honduran military, usually corrupt, has at times brought about reform. An alliance of the military and organized labor in the early 1970s produced a series of reforms in response to pressure from the less advantaged sectors of the population; in 1974, the military government developed a five-year plan to integrate the rural poor into the national economy and to increase social services in the area. The state has often shown a paternalistic face rather than a brutal, repressive one. The capacity for reform led one candidate in the 1981 presidential campaign to comment: "We Hondurans are different. There is no room for violence here."

There are now many signs of change. Agrarian reform slowed after 1976, prompting a peasant-association leader to remark: "In order to maintain social peace in the countryside, the peasants' needs will have to be satisfied to avoid revolt." In 1984, the Honduran government initiated a land-titling program and issued about 1,000 titles per month to landless peasants. The government's agrarian-reform program, which is under the control of the National Agrarian Institute, has always been characterized by the carrot and the stick. While some *campesinos* ("peasants") have been

TIMELINE

1524
Honduras is settled by Spaniards from Guatemala
1821
Independence from Spain
1822–1838
Honduras is part of the United Provinces of Central America
1838
Honduras becomes Independent as a separate country
1969
Brief border war with El Salvador
1980s
Tensions with Nicaragua grow
1990s
Hurricane Mitch causes enormous death and destruction
2000s
AIDS is an increasing problem
Military coup ousts President Manuel Zelaya; Porfirio Lobo elected as the new president; Drug trafficking becomes a serious problem

granted titles to land, others have been jailed or killed. Former military and security personnel apparently murdered several indigenous minority rights leaders in 2004.

Honduran campesinos, according to the *Caribean & Central America Report,* "have had a long and combative history of struggling for land rights." In 1987, hundreds of peasants were jailed as "terrorists" as a result of land invasions. Occupation of privately owned lands has become increasingly common in Honduras and reflects both population pressure on and land hunger of the peasantry. Land seizures by squatters are sometimes recognized by the National Agrarian Institute. In other cases, the government has promoted the relocation of people to sparsely populated regions of the country. Unfortunately, the chosen relocation sites are in tropical rain forests, which are already endangered throughout the region. The government wishes to transform the forests into rubber and citrus plantations or into farms to raise rice, corn, and other crops.

Peasants who fail to gain access to land usually migrate to urban centers in search of a better life. What they find in cities such as the capital, Tegucigalpa, are inadequate social services, a miserable standard of living, and a municipal government without the resources to help. In 1989, Tegucigalpa was deeply in debt, mortgaged to the limit, months behind in wage payments to city workers, and plagued by garbage piling up in the streets. In 2004 the capital city was plagued by a crime wave conducted by youth gangs, drug trafficking, police implication in high-profile crimes, and the murder of street children by death squads.

The nation's economy as a whole fared badly in the late 1980s. But by 1992, following painful adjustments occasioned by the reforms of the government of President Rafael Callejas, the economy again showed signs of growth. Real gross domestic product reached 3.5 percent, and inflation was held in check. Still, unemployment remained a persistent problem; some agencies calculated that two-thirds of the workforce lacked steady employment. A union leader warned: "Unemployment leads to desperation and becomes a time bomb that could explode at any moment."

In addition to internal problems, pressure was put on Honduras by the International Monetary Fund. According to the *Caribbean & Central America Report,* the first phase of a reform program agreed to with the IMF succeeded in stabilizing the economy through devaluation of the lempira (the Honduran currency), public spending cuts, and increased taxes. But economic growth declined, and international agencies urged a reduction in the number of state employees as well as an accelerated campaign to privatize state-owned enterprises. The government admitted that there was much room for reform, but one official complained: "As far as they [the IMF] are concerned, the Honduran state should make gigantic strides, but our position is that this country cannot turn into General Motors overnight."

Opposition to the demands of international agencies was quick to materialize. One newspaper warned that cuts in social programs would result in violence.

Trade-union and Catholic Church leaders condemned the social costs of the stabilization program despite the gains recorded in the credit-worthiness of Honduras.

■ HUMAN AND CIVIL RIGHTS

In theory, despite the continuing violence in the region, basic freedoms in Honduras are still intact. The press is privately owned and free of government censorship. However, journalists have been threatened and killed, and there is a quietly expressed concern about offending the government, and self-censorship is considered prudent. Moreover, it is an accepted practice in Honduras for government ministries and other agencies to have journalists on their payrolls.

Honduran labor unions are free to organize and have a tradition of providing their rank-and-file certain benefits. Unions are allowed to bargain, but labor laws guard against "excessive" activity. A complex procedure of negotiation and arbitration must be followed before a legal strike can be called. If a government proves unyielding, labor will likely pass into the ranks of the opposition.

In 1992, Honduras's three major workers' confederations convinced the private sector to raise the minimum wage by 13.7 percent, the third consecutive year of increases. Nevertheless, the minimum wage, which varies by occupation and location, is not adequate to provide a decent standard of living, especially in view of inflation. One labor leader pointed out that the minimum wage will "not even buy tortillas." To compound workers' problems, the labor minister admitted that about 30 percent of the enterprises under the supervision of his office paid wages *below* the minimum. To survive, families must pool the resources of all their working members. Predictably, health and safety laws are usually ignored. As is the case in the rural sector, the government has listened to the complaints of workers—but union leaders have also on occasion been jailed.

The government is also confronted with the problem of an increasing flow of rural poor into the cities. Employment opportunities in rural areas have declined as landowners have converted cropland into pasture for beef cattle. Because livestock raising requires less labor than growing crops, the surplus rural workers seek to better their opportunities in the cities. But the new migrants have discovered that Honduras's commercial and industrial sectors are deep in recession and cannot provide adequate jobs.

Fortunately, many of the 300,000 refugees from Nicaragua and El Salvador have returned home. With the election of President Violeta Chamorro in Nicaragua, most of the 20,000 rebel Contras laid down their arms and went home, thus eliminating—from the perspective of the Honduran government—a source of much violence in its border regions.

To the credit of the Honduran government, which is under strong pressure from conservative politicians and businesspeople as well as elements within the armed forces for tough policies against dissent, allegations vis-à-vis human-rights abuses are taken seriously. (In one celebrated case, the Inter-American Court of Human Rights, established in 1979, found the government culpable in at least one person's "disappearance" and ordered the payment of an indemnification to the man's family. While not accepting any premise of guilt, the government agreed to pay. More important, according to the COHA *Washington Report,* the decision sharply criticized "prolonged isolation" and "incommunicado detention" of prisoners and equated such abuses with "cruel and inhuman punishment.") Former president Carlos Roberto Reina was a strong advocate of human rights as part of his "moral revolution." In 1995, he took three steps in this direction: A special prosecutor was created to investigate human-rights violations, human-rights inquiries were taken out of the hands of the military and given to a new civilian Department of Criminal Investigation, and promises were made to follow up on cases of disappearances during previous administrations. While Honduras may no longer be characterized as "the peaceable kingdom," the government has not lost touch with its people and still acts out a traditional role of patron.

From the mid-1980s to the mid-1990s, the most serious threat to civilian government came from the military. The United States' Central American policy boosted the prestige, status, and power of the Honduran military, which grew confident in its ability to forge the nation's destiny. With the end of the Contra–Sandinista armed struggle in Nicaragua, there was a dramatic decline in military assistance from the United States. This allowed President Reina to assert civilian control over the military establishment.

Economic assistance from the United States in the 1980s and 1990s had some success in addressing the needs of poverty-stricken Hondurans. But that aid was sharply cut back in the late 1990s. Recently allocated U.S. economic aid, much of which has been motivated by Washington's concerns about drug trafficking, terrorism, and the appearance of "unfriendly" governments in the region, has been skewed by a political agenda and not the needs of Honduras. Such targeted aid does little to alleviate basic social problems, such as poverty or underemployment. Successful Honduran programs, ironically, have languished because of inadequate funding. One program provided access to potable water and was credited with cutting the infant mortality rate by half. Other programs funded vaccinations and primary-education projects. In the words of newspaperman and development expert Juan Ramón Martínez: "Just when you [the United States] started getting it right, you walked away."

President Reina's "moral revolution" also moved to confront the problem of endemic official corruption. In June 1995, Reina alluded to the enormity of the task when he said that if the government went after all of the guilty, "there would not be enough room for them in the prisons." In 1998, just as the Honduran economy was beginning to recover from economic setbacks occasioned by turmoil in the influential Asian financial markets, Hurricane Mitch wreaked havoc on the nation's infrastructure. Roads, bridges, schools, clinics, and homes were destroyed, and thousands of lives were lost.

DID YOU KNOW?

Honduras has become a major transit point for drugs being moved from South America to the United States and Europe. Because drug cartels often pay smugglers with raw cocaine, drug abuse in Honduras has grown.

Freshwater wells had to be reconstructed. Banana plantations were severely damaged. Recovery from this natural disaster was set back in 2008 by Hurricane Ida.

President Ricardo Maduro made a determined effort to crack down on a rampant crime wave. Undoubtedly his focus was sharpened by the loss of his son to criminal violence in 1998. Presidential elections in 2005 were dominated by the growing incidence of violent crime, much of it attributed to youth gangs. Both candidates stressed law and order issues. The candidate of the ruling National Party urged a hard line policy against gangs. He endorsed the government's "Mano Duro" (Tough Hand) Law, by which membership in a gang was made a felony, and sought reinstatement of the death penalty, which had been abolished in 1937. The victor in the elections, the Liberal Party's Manuel Zelaya, is opposed to the death penalty as well as the tough anti-gang legislation. Crime, he argued, in part springs from basic social problems. Poverty and unemployment drive youth into gangs, he asserted. The close results of the election indicate that Hondurans are badly divided over issues of crime and poverty.

Despite a polarized electorate, President Zelaya, a self-proclaimed populist, attempted to utilize a popular referendum to modify the nation's constitution despite a court order not to do so. Zelaya's explanation for rewriting the constitution was, as he said, "to challenge a political system dominated by a few wealthy families who ignored the needs of the disadvantaged." Opposition politicians claimed that Zelaya wanted to eliminate presidential term limits and remain in power indefinitely. Ostensibly, as defenders of the constitution, the military ousted Zelaya in a coup in June 2009 and precipitated a political crisis punctuated by violence. International mediation resulted in a new election and national reconciliation. President Porfirio Lobo took office and pledge to support the work of a Truth Commission, which undertook the task of investigating the coup and its aftermath. As of 2011, ex-President Zelaya remains in exile in the Dominican Republic.

FURTHER INVESTIGATION

For more information on the Honduras drug trade, visit/www.indexmundi.com/honduras/illicit_drugs.html

Snapshot: HONDURAS

Summarized below is a quick look at the country with regard to its development, freedom, health/welfare, and achievements.

Development

The Lobo government is committed to improving tax collection, cutting expenditures, and attracting foreign investment. An IMF Precautionary Stand-By agreement in October 2010 helped to renew multilateral and bilateral donor confidence in Honduras.

Freedom

According to Freedom House, the "period since the June 2009 coup has featured few improvements in rule of law.

Human rights activists, journalists, union leaders, and members of the anticoup movement continued to be targeted in attacks, kidnappings, and assassinations in 2010."

Health/Welfare

Honduras remains one of the region's poorest countries. Serious shortcomings are evident in education and health care, and economic growth is essentially erased by population growth. More than half of the population live in poverty.

Achievements

The small size of Honduras, in terms of territory and population, has produced a distinctive literary style that is a combination of folklore and legend.

Statistics

Geography

Area in Square Miles (Kilometers): 43,267 (112,090) (slightly larger than Tennessee)

Capital (Population): Tegucigalpa (1,000,000)

Environmental Concerns: urbanization; deforestation; land degradation and soil erosion; mining pollution

Geographical Features: mostly mountainous in the interior; narrow coastal plains

Climate: subtropical, but varies with elevation (temperate highlands)

People*

Population

Total: 8,143,564

Annual Growth Rate: 1.9%

Rural/Urban Population Ratio: 48/52

Ethnic Makeup: 90% Mestizo (European and Indian mix); 7% Indian; 2% African; 1% European, Arab, and Asian

Major Language: Spanish

Religions: 97% Roman Catholic; a small Protestant minority

Health

Life Expectancy at Birth: 69 years (male); 72 years (female)

Infant Mortality Rate (Ratio): 20.44/1,000

Physicians Available (Ratio): 0.57/1000

Education

Adult Literacy Rate: 80%

Compulsory (Ages): 7–13; free

Communication

Telephones: 609,500 main lines

Daily Newspaper Circulation: 45 per 1,000 people

Cell Phones: 9,505,000

Internet Users: 731,700

Transportation

Roadways in Kilometers (Miles): 13,603 (8453)

Railroads in Kilometers (Miles): 699 (434)

Usable Airfields: 104

Motor Vehicles in Use: 185,000

Government

Type: democratic constitutional republic

Independence Date: September 15, 1821 (from Spain)

Head of State/Government: President Porfirio Lobo is both head of state and head of government

Political Parties: Liberal Party; National Party of Honduras; Christian Democratic Party; Democratic Unification Party; others

Suffrage: universal and compulsory at 18

Military

Military Expenditures (% of GDP): 0.6%

Current Disputes: boundary disputes with El Salvador and Nicaragua

Economy

Currency ($U.S. Equivalent): 18.9 lempiras = $1

Per Capita Income/GDP: $4,200/$33.63 billion

GDP Real Growth Rate: 2.8%

Inflation Rate: 4.7%

Unemployment Rate: 5.1%; underemployment 30%

Labor Force: 3,394,000

Natural Resources: timber; gold; silver; copper; lead; zinc; iron ore; antimony; coal; fish; hydropower

Agriculture: bananas; coffee; citrus fruits; beef; timber; shrimp

Industry: sugar; coffee; textiles and clothing; wood products

Exports: $5.742 billion (primary partners United States, El Salvador, Germany)

Imports: $8.55 billion (primary partners United States, Guatemala, Mexico, El Salvador)

Suggested Website

www.cia.gov/cia/publications/factbook/geos/ho.html

*Note: Estimates for Honduras explicitly take into account the effects of excess mortality due to AIDS.

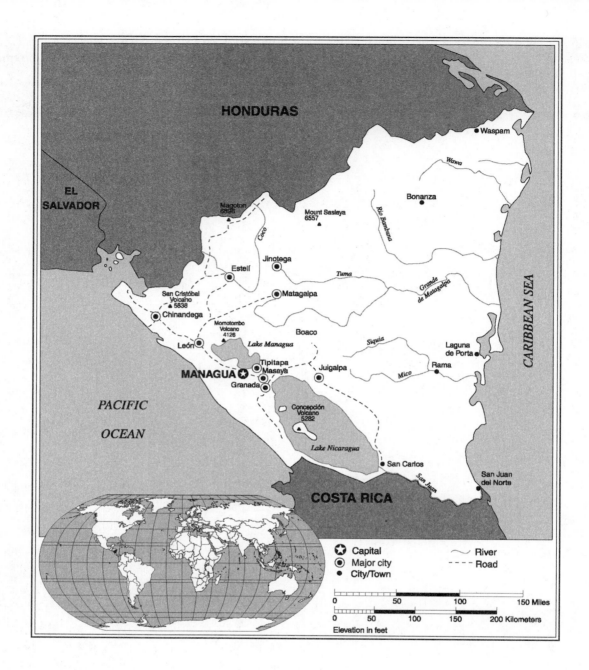

HONDURAS

EL SALVADOR

• Waspam

Wawa

Magoton 6898 ▲

Mount Saslaya 6557 ▲

Bonanza •

Rio Bambana

Jinotega ◉

Estelí ◉

Coco

Tuma

San Cristóbal Volcano ▲ 5838

◉ Matagalpa

Grande de Matagalpa

Chinandega ◉

Momotombo Volcano ▲ 4126

Boaco •

Siquia

Laguna de Porta •

CARIBBEAN SEA

León ◉

Lake Managua

Tipitapa •

Masaya ◉

Juigalpa •

Mico

Rama •

MANAGUA ★

Granada •◉

PACIFIC

OCEAN

Concepción Volcano 5282 ▲

Lake Nicaragua

San Carlos •

San Juan

San Juan del Norte •

COSTA RICA

★ Capital
◉ Major city
• City/Town

〜 River
- - - Road

| 0 | 50 | 100 | 150 Miles |

| 0 | 50 | 100 | 150 | 200 Kilometers |

Elevation in feet

Nicaragua

(Republic of Nicaragua)

NICARAGUA: A NATION IN RECOVERY

Nicaraguan society, culture, and history have been molded to a great extent by the country's geography. A land of volcanoes and earthquakes, the frequency of natural disasters in Nicaragua has profoundly influenced its peoples' perceptions of life, death, and fate. What historian Ralph Woodward has written about Central America is particularly apt for Nicaraguans: Fatalism may be said to be a "part of their national mentality, tempering their attitudes toward the future. Death and tragedy always seem close in Central America. The primitive states of communication, transportation, and production, and the insecurity of human life, have been the major determinants in the region's history. . . ."

Nicaragua is a divided land, with distinct geographic, cultural, racial, ethnic, and religious zones. The west-coast region, which contains about 90 percent of the total population, is overwhelmingly white or Mestizo (mixed blood), Catholic, and Hispanic. The east coast is a sharp contrast, with its scattered population and multiplicity of Indian, Creole (in Nicaragua, native-born blacks), and Hispanic ethnic groups.

The east coast's geography, economy, and isolation from Managua, the nation's capital city, have created a distinct identity among its people. Many east-coast citizens think of themselves as *costeños* ("coast dwellers") rather than Nicaraguans. Religion reinforces this common identity. About 70 percent of the east-coast population, regardless of ethnic group, are members of the Protestant Moravian Church. After a century and a half of missionary work, the Moravian Church has become "native," with locally recruited clergy. Among the Miskito Indians, Moravian pastors commonly replace tribal elders as community leaders. The Creoles speak English and originally arrived either as shipwrecked or escaped slaves or as slave labor introduced by the British to work in the lumber camps and plantations in the seventeenth century. Many Creoles and Miskitos feel a greater sense of allegiance to the British than to Nicaraguans from the west coast, who are regarded as foreigners.

SANDINISTA POLICIES

Before the successful 1979 Revolution that drove the dictator Anastasio Somoza from power, Nicaraguan governments generally ignored the east coast. Revolutionary Sandinistas—who took their name from a guerrilla, Augusto César Sandino, who fought against occupying U.S. forces in the late 1920s and early 1930s—adopted a new policy toward the neglected region. The Sandinistas were concerned with the east coast's history of rebelliousness and separatism, and they were attracted by the economic potential of the region (palm oil and rubber). Accordingly, they hastily devised a bold campaign to unify the region with the rest of the nation. Roads, communications, health clinics, economic development, and a literacy campaign for local inhabitants were planned. The Sandinistas, in defiance of local customs, also tried to organize the local population into mass formations—that is, organizations for youth, peasants, women, wage earners, and the like. It was believed in Managua that such groups would unite the people behind the government and the Revolution and facilitate the economic, political, and social unification of the region.

TIMELINE

1522
Nicaragua is explored by Gil González
1821
Independence from Spain
1823
Nicaragua joins the United Provinces of Central America
1838
Nicaragua becomes independent as a separate state
1855
William Walker and filibusters (U.S. insurgents) invade Nicaragua
1928–1934
Augusto César Sandino leads guerrillas against occupying U.S. forces
1934–1979
Domination of Nicaragua by the Somoza family
1979
Sandinista guerrillas oust the Somoza family
1990s
A cease-fire allows an opening for political dialogue; Hurricane Mitch devastates the country
2000s
Sandinistas win municipal elections in November 2000
2006
Daniel Ortega again elected president
2009
Sandinistas move to change constitutional ban on re-election
Ortega elected for a third term in 2011

(The McGraw-Hill Companies, Inc./Barry Barker, photographer)

A newly constructed concrete highway bridge next to a old road bridge and dirt road, near the border between Costa Rica and Nicaragua. The improvement of highway infrastructure between the two countries will increase trade.

In general, the attempt failed, and regional tensions within Nicaragua persist to this day. Historically, costeños were unimpressed with the exploits of the guerrilla Sandino, who raided U.S. companies along the east coast in the 1930s. When the companies left or cut back on operations, workers who lost their jobs blamed Sandino rather than the worldwide economic crisis of the 1930s. Consequently, there was a reluctance to accept Sandino as the national hero of the new Nicaragua. Race and class differences increased due to an influx of Sandinistas from the west. Many of the new arrivals exhibited old attitudes and looked down on the east-coast peoples as "uncivilized" or "second class."

The Miskito Question

In 1982, the government forced 10,000 Indians from their ancestral homes along the Río Coco because of concern with border security. As a result, many Indians joined the Contras, U.S.–supported guerrillas who fought against the Sandinista regime.

In an attempt to win back the Miskito and associated Indian groups, the government decided on a plan of regional autonomy. The significance of the Sandinista policy was that the government finally appreciated how crucial regional differences are in Nicaragua. Cultural and ethnic differences must be respected if Managua expects to rule its peoples effectively. The lesson learned by the Sandinistas was taken to heart by the subsequent Chamorro government, which was the first in history to appoint a Nicaraguan of Indian background to a ministerial-level position. A limited self-government granted to the east-coast region by the Sandinistas in 1987 has been maintained; local leaders were elected to office in 1990.

A Mixed Record

The record of the Sandinista government was mixed. When the rebels seized power in 1979, they were confronted by an economy in shambles. Nineteen years of civil war had taken an estimated 50,000 lives and destroyed half a billion dollars' worth of factories, businesses, medical facilities, and dwellings. Living standards had tumbled to 1962 levels, and unemployment had reached an estimated 25 percent.

Despite such economic difficulties, the government made great strides in the areas of health and nutrition. A central goal of official policy was to provide equal access to health services. The plan had more success in urban areas than in rural ones. The government emphasized preventive, rather than curative, medicine. Preventive medicine included the provision of clean water, sanitation, immunization, nutrition, and maternal and child care. People were also taught basic preventive medical techniques. National campaigns to wipe out malaria, measles, and polio had reasonable success. But because of restricted budgets, the health system was overloaded, and there was a shortage of medical supplies. In the area of nutrition, basic foodstuffs such as grains, oil, eggs, and milk were paid for in part by the government in an effort to improve the general nutritional level of Nicaraguans.

? DID YOU KNOW?

Nicaragua is divided into two main cultural regions: the west, which was settled by the Spanish and reflects its Spanish heritage, and the east, which more closely identifies with the Anglophone Caribbean.

By 1987, the Sandinista government was experiencing severe economic problems that badly affected all social programs. In 1989, the economy, for all intents and purposes, collapsed. Hyperinflation ran well over 100 percent a month; and in June 1989, following a series of mini-devaluations, the nation's currency was devalued by an incredible 100 percent. Commerce was virtually paralyzed.

The revolutionary Sandinista government, in an attempt to explain the economic debacle, with some justice argued that the Nicaragua that it had inherited in 1979 had been savaged and looted by former dictator Somoza. The long-term costs of economic reconstruction; the restructuring of the economy to redistribute wealth; the trade embargo erected by the United States and North American diplomatic pressure, designed to discourage lending or aid from international institutions such as the International Monetary Fund; and the high cost of fighting a war against the U.S.–supported Contra rebels formed the backdrop to the crisis. Opposition leaders added to this list various Sandinista economic policies that discouraged private business.

The impact of the economic crisis on average Nicaraguans was devastating. Overnight, prices of basic consumer goods such as meat, rice, beans, milk, sugar, and cooking oil were increased 40 to 80 percent. Gasoline prices doubled. Schoolteachers engaged in work stoppages in an effort to increase their monthly wages of about $15, equal to the pay of a domestic servant. (To put the teachers' plight into perspective, note that the cost of a liter of milk absorbed fully 36 percent of a day's pay.)

As a hedge against inflation, other Nicaraguans purchased U.S. dollars on the black market. *Regionews,* published in Managua, noted that conversion of córdobas into dollars was "seen as a better proposition than depositing them in savings accounts."

Economic travail inevitably produces dissatisfaction; opinion polls taken in July 1989 signaled political trouble for the Sandinistas. The surveys reflected an electorate with mixed feelings. While nearly 30 percent favored the Sandinistas, 57 percent indicated that they would not vote for President Daniel Ortega.

The results of the election of 1990 were not surprising, for the Sandinistas had lost control of the economy. They failed to survive a strong challenge from the opposition, led by the popular Violeta Chamorro.

Sandinista land reform, for the most part, consisted of the government's confiscation of the huge estates of the ousted Somoza family. These lands amounted to more than 2 million acres, including about 40 percent of the nation's best farmland. Some peasants were given land, but the government preferred to create cooperatives. This policy prompted the criticism that the state had simply become an old-style landowner. The Sandinistas replied that "the state is not the same state as before; it is a state of producers; we organized production and placed it at the disposal of the people." In 1990, there were several reports of violence between Sandinista security forces and peasants and former Contras who petitioned for private ownership of state land.

The Role of the Church

The Revolution created a sharp division within the Roman Catholic Church in Nicaragua. Radical priests, who believed that Christianity and Marxism share similar goals and that the Church should play a leading role in social change and revolution, were at odds with traditional priests fearful of "godless communism." Since 1979, many radical Catholics had become involved in social and political projects; several held high posts in the Sandinista government.

One priest of the theology of liberation was interviewed by *Regionews.* The interviewer stated that an "atheist could say, "These Catholics found a just revolution opposed by the Church hierarchy. They can't renounce their religion and are searching for a more convenient theology. But it's their sense of natural justice that motivates them." The priest replied: "I think that's evident and that Jesus was also an 'atheist,' an atheist of the religion as practiced in his time. He didn't believe in the God of the priests in the temples who were allied with Caesar. Jesus told of a new life. And the 'atheist' that exists in our people doesn't believe in the God that the hierarchy often offers us. He believes in life, in man, in development. God manifests Himself there. A person who believes in life and justice in favor of the poor is not an atheist." The movement, he noted, would continue "with or without approval from the hierarchy."

The Drift to the Left

As has historically been the case in revolutions, after a brief period of unity and excitement, the victors begin to disagree over policies and power. For a while in Nicaragua, there was a perceptible drift to the left, and the Revolution lost its image of moderation. While radicalization was a dynamic inherent in the Revolution, it was also pushed in a leftward direction by a hostile U.S. foreign policy that attempted to bring down the Sandinista regime through its support of the Contras. In 1987, however, following the peace initiatives of Latin American governments, the Sandinista government made significant efforts to project a more moderate image. *La Prensa,* the main opposition newspaper, which the Sandinistas had shut down in 1986, was again allowed to publish. Radio Católica, another source of opposition to the government, was given permission to broadcast after its closure the year before. And antigovernment demonstrations were permitted in the streets of Managua.

Significantly, President Ortega proposed reforms in the country's election laws in April 1989, to take effect before the national elections in 1990. The new Nicaraguan legislation was based on Costa Rican and Venezuelan models, and in some instances was even more forward-looking.

An important result of the laws was the enhancement of political pluralism, which allowed for the National Opposition Union (UNO) victory in 1990. Rules for organizing political parties, once stringent, were loosened; opposition parties were granted access to the media; foreign funding of political parties was allowed; the system of proportional representation permitted minority parties to maintain a presence; and the opposition was allowed to monitor the elections closely.

The Sandinistas realized that to survive, they had to make compromises. In need of breathing space, the government embraced the Central American Peace Plan designed by Costa Rican president Óscar Arias and designed moderate policies to isolate the United States.

On the battlefield, the cease-fire unilaterally declared by the Sandinistas was eventually embraced by the Contras as well, and both sides moved toward a political solution of their differences. Armed conflict formally ended on June 27, 1990, although sporadic violence continued in rural areas.

■ A PEACEFUL TRANSITION

It was the critical state of the Nicaraguan economy that in large measure brought the Sandinistas down in the elections of 1990. Even though the government of Violeta Chamorro made great progress in the demilitarization of the country and national reconciliation, the economy remained a time bomb.

The continuing economic crisis and disagreements over policy directions destroyed the original base of Chamorro's political support. Battles between the legislative and executive branches of government virtually paralyzed the country. At the end of 1992, President Chamorro closed the Assembly building and called for new elections. But by July 1995, an accord had been reached between the two contending branches of government. Congress passed a "framework law" that created the language necessary to implement changes in the Sandinista Constitution of 1987. The Legislative Assembly, together with the executive branch, are pledged to the passage of laws on matters such as property rights, agrarian reform, consumer protection, and taxation. The July agreement also provided for the election of the five-member Consejo Supremo Electoral (Supreme Electoral Council), which oversaw the presidential elections in November 1996.

The election marked something of a watershed in Nicaraguan political history. Outgoing president Chamorro told reporters at the inauguration of Arnoldo Alemán Lâcayo: "For the first time in more than 100 years & one civilian, democratically elected president will hand over power to another." But the election did not mask the fact that Nicaragua was still deeply polarized and that the Sandinistas only grudgingly accepted their defeat.

President Alemán sought a dialogue with the Sandinistas, and both sides agreed to participate in discussions to study poverty, property disputes occasioned by the Sandinista policy of confiscation, and the need to attract foreign investment.

The Alemán administration confronted a host of difficult problems. In the Western Hemisphere, only Haiti is poorer. Perhaps 80 percent of the population were unemployed or underemployed, and an equal percentage lived below the poverty line. Just as the economy began to show some signs of recovery from years of war, Hurricane Mitch devastated the country in 1998 and profoundly set back development efforts, as all available resources had to be husbanded to reconstruct much of Nicaragua's infrastructure.

Economic malaise compounded by allegations of corruption and illegal enrichment undermined the credibility of the Alemán government. Dissatisfaction among voters was registered at the polls, resulting in Sandinista victories in Managua and nine of 17 provincial capitals in municipal elections in November 2000. A contributing factor was the emergence of the Conservative Party, which split the anti-Sandinista vote. Interestingly, the Sandinista victor in Managua, Herty Lewites, has styled himself as a "revolutionary businessman and defender of social justice"—that is, a popular pragmatist.

Organized labor has shown a similar pragmatic dimension in Nicaragua. Labor leaders have quietly supported both globalization and the policies of the World Trade Organization because of the jobs that would be created. Another effect of globalization, not only in Nicaragua but also throughout the region, has been the further erosion of the *siesta* (nap) tradition. In the words of a Nicaraguan-government official, the emerging world economy demands that "we stay open all day."

The administration of President Enrique Bolaño Geyer, elected in 2002, saw some improvement. There was some economic growth in 2003, private investment increased, and exports rose. For the foreseeable future, however, Nicaragua will remain poor.

President Bolaños became politically isolated, however. His campaign against government corruption, which ensnared former President Alemán, led to his abandonment by his own conservative Constitutionalist Liberal Party. Remarkably, the conservatives allied with Daniel Ortega's Sandinista Party with the object, in the words of *The New York Times,* "to regain power without holding an election that neither man could win." The state electoral commission, under Ortega's direction, "lowered the threshold for averting a runoff election to 35 percent of the vote from 45 percent." Ortega won the 2006 contest, a sign that many Nicaraguans wanted more rapid change. To implement change, however, the Nicaraguan government needs an infusion of aid. Some of that aid has been provided by Venezuela in the form of 10 million barrels of petroleum a year, which is sufficient to meet the country's energy needs. Under the deal, Nicaragua is able to purchase the oil at half the market price and has 23 years to pay off the rest at two percent interest. "The deal," according to *The New York Times,* "hands Nicaragua what amounts to a large low-interest loan every month for infrastructure projects and social programs." Critics charge that the loans are not part of the national budget. Roberto Courtney, the Executive Director of the Nicaraguan Ethics and Transparency lobby that supports openness in government, stated: "It's off the books—no institutions, no controls." Such secrecy opens the door to possible corruption and misuse of the moneys, which the

Snapshot: NICARAGUA

Summarized below is a quick look at the country with regard to its development, freedom, health/welfare, and achievements.

Development

The possibility of the construction of a "dry canal" across Nicaragua has raised the hopes of thousands for a better future. A group of Asian investors is investigating the construction of a 234-mile-long rail link between the oceans to carry container cargo. In 2011 both Iran and Venezuela expressed interest in investment in a canal.

Freedom

The creation in 2008 of Citizens Power Councils by the government concerns opposition leaders who see the councils not as an exercise in direct democracy, but as a ploy by President Ortega to control society and to bypass the wishes of the National Assembly. Councils were given power over government programs and, allegedly, could administer those programs preferentially in the interests of the Sandinista Party.

Health/Welfare

Nicaragua's deep debt and the austerity demands of the IMF have had a strongly negative effect on citizens' health. As people have been driven from the health service by sharp cuts in government spending, the incidence of malnutrition in children has risen. Reported deaths from diarrhea and respiratory problems are also on the increase.

Achievements

The Nicaraguan poet Rubén Dario was the most influential representative of the Modernist movement, which swept Latin America in the late nineteenth century. Dario was strongly critical of injustice and oppression.

Nicaraguan people will not tolerate. If Ortega is to enjoy a successful presidency he must govern for all Nicaraguans and not just the party faithful.

Unfortunately, President Ortega once again moved in the direction of a Sandinista-controlled state. Late in 2009, a Sandinista-stacked court unilaterally decided that a constitutional provision that bans more than two terms for a president did not apply to President Ortega, who decisively won a third term in 2011. Carlos Fernando Chamorro, host of an anti-Ortega television news show stated: "Deep inside he [Ortega] doesn't believe in representative democracy. . . . He will never cede power in a democratic or peaceful way." On the other hand, supporters claim that Ortega has changed and that his government will be a boon to poorer Nicaraguans.

FURTHER INVESTIGATION

For more information on Nicaraguan culture, visit www.nicaragua.com/culture/

Statistics

Geography

Area in Square Miles (Kilometers): 49,985 (129,494) (about the size of New York)

Capital (Population): Managua 934,000

Environmental Concerns: deforestation; soil erosion; water pollution

Geographical Features: extensive Atlantic coastal plains rising to central interior mountains; narrow Pacific coastal plain interrupted by volcanoes

Climate: tropical, but varies with elevation (temperate highlands)

People

Population

Total: 5,666,301 (2011 est.)

Annual Growth Rate: 1.1%

Rural/Urban Population Ratio: 23/57

Ethnic Makeup: 69% Mestizo; 17% white; 9% black; 5% Amerindian

Major Language: Spanish

Religions: 58.5% Roman Catholic; 23.2% Evangelical Protestant, none 15.7%

Health

Life Expectancy at Birth: 70 years (male); 74 years (female)

Infant Mortality Rate (Ratio): 22.64/1,000

Physicians Available (Ratio): 0.37/1000

Education

Adult Literacy Rate: 67.5%

Compulsory (Ages): 7–13; free

Communication

Telephones: 258,000 main lines

Daily Newspaper Circulation: 31 per 1,000 people

Cell Phones: 3,771,000

Internet Users: 199,800

Transportation

Roadways in Kilometers (Miles): 19,036 (11,828)

Railroads in Miles (Kilometers): none

Usable Airfields: 143

Government

Type: republic

Independence Date: September 15, 1821 (from Spain)

Head of State/Government: President Daniel Ortega is both head of state and head of government

Political Parties: Liberal Constitutionalist Party; Nicaraguan Liberal Alliance; Sandinista Renovation Movement; Alliance for the Republic; Sandinista National Liberation Front; many others

Suffrage: universal at 16

Military

Military Expenditures (% of GDP): 0.6%

Current Disputes: territorial or boundary disputes with Colombia, Honduras, and El Salvador

Economy

Currency ($U.S. Equivalent): 20.3 córdobas oros = $1

Per Capita Income/GDP: $3,000/17.71 billion

GDP Growth Rate: 4.5%

Inflation Rate: 5.5%

Unemployment Rate: 7.8% underemployment: 46.5% (2008)

Labor Force: 2,811,000

Natural Resources: gold; silver; copper; tungsten; lead; zinc; timber; fish

Agriculture: coffee; bananas; sugarcane; cotton; rice; corn; tobacco; soya; beans; livestock

Industry: food processing; chemicals; machinery; metals products; textiles and clothing; petroleum; beverages; footwear; wood

Exports: $3.157 billion (primary partners United States, Canada, El Salvador, Venezuela)

Imports: $3.968 billion (f.o.b.) (primary partners United States, Costa Rica, Guatemala, Venezuela)

Suggested Website

www.cia.gov/cia/publications/factbook/index.html

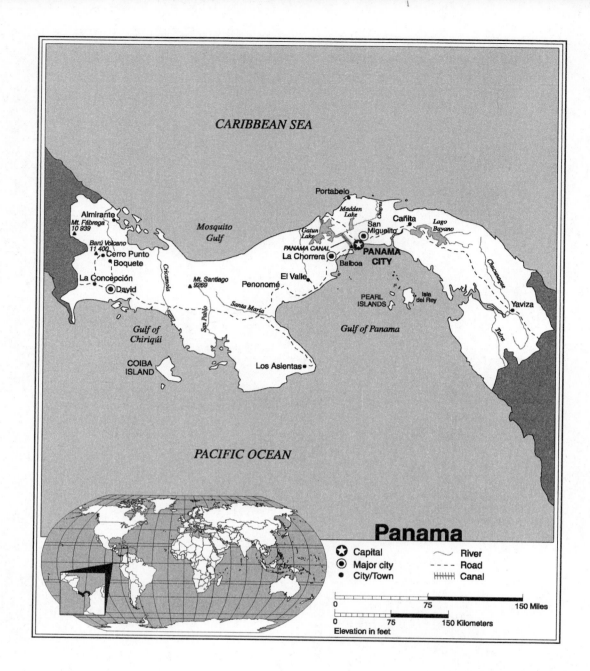

CARIBBEAN SEA

Portabelo

Almirante
Mt. Fábrega
10 939

Barú Volcano
11 400
Cerro Punto
Boquete

La Concepción
David

Mosquito
Gulf

Cricamola

Mt. Santiago
9269

San Pablo

Santa Maria

Gulf of
Chiriqúi

COIBA
ISLAND

Los Asientas

Penonomé

El Valle

Madden
Lake

Gatun
Lake

PANAMA CANAL

La Chorrera

Balboa

Cañita

San
Miguelito

Lago
Bayano

PANAMA
CITY

PEARL
ISLANDS

Isla
del Rey

Gulf of Panama

Chucunaque

Tuira

Yaviza

PACIFIC OCEAN

Panama

⭐ Capital
◉ Major city
● City/Town

〜 River
- - - Road
╫╫╫╫ Canal

0		75		150 Miles

0	75	150 Kilometers

Elevation in feet

Panama

(Republic of Panama)

PANAMA: A NATION AND A CANAL

The Panama Canal, opened to shipping in 1914, has had a sharp impact on Panamanian political life, foreign policy, economy, and society. Panama is a country of minorities and includes blacks, Mestizos (mixed Indian and white), Indians, and Chinese. Many of the blacks and Chinese are the children or grandchildren of the thousands of workers who were brought to Panama to build the canal. Unable to return home, they remained behind, an impoverished people, ignored for decades by a succession of Panamanian governments.

The government has usually been dominated by whites, although all of the country's minorities are politically active. In areas where Indians comprise a majority of the population, they play significant roles in provincial political life. Some, such as the San Blas islanders—famous for the art form known as Mola, which consists of different colored fabrics that are cut away to make designs—live in self-governing districts. Although Indians are not restricted to tribal areas, most remain by choice, reflecting a long tradition of resistance to assimilation and defense of their cultural integrity.

Panama's economy has both profited and suffered from the presence of the canal. Because governments traditionally placed too much reliance on the direct and indirect revenues generated by the canal tolls, they tended to ignore other types of national development. Much of Panama's economic success in the 1980s, however, was the result of a strong service sector associated with the presence of a large number of banks, the Panama Canal, and the Colón Free Zone. Agriculture and industry, on the other hand, usually experienced slow growth rates.

Because of U.S. control of the canal and the Canal Zone, this path between the seas continuously stoked the fires of Panamanian nationalism. The high standard of living and the privileges enjoyed by U.S. citizens residing in the Canal Zone contrasted sharply with the poverty of Panamanians. President Omar Torrijos became a national hero in 1977 when he signed the Panama Canal Treaties with U.S. president Jimmy Carter. The treaties provided for full Panamanian control over the canal and its revenues by 1999.

Panamanian officials spoke optimistically of their plans for the bases they would soon inherit, citing universities, modern container ports, luxury resorts, and retirement communities. But there was much concern over the loss of an estimated $500 million that tens of thousands of American troops, civilians, and their dependents had long pumped into the Panamanian economy. Moreover, while all agreed that the canal itself would be well run, because Panamanians had been phased into its operation, there was pessimism about the lack of planning for ancillary facilities.

In 1995, more than 300 poor, landless people a day were moving into the Zone and were clearing forest for crops. The rain forest in the Canal Basin supplies not only the water essential to the canal but also the drinking water for about 40 percent of Panama's population. Loss of the rain forest could prove catastrophic. One official noted: "If we lose the Canal Basin we do not lose only our water supply, it will also be the end of the Canal itself."

TIMELINE

1518
Panama City is established

1821–1903
Panama is a department of Colombia

1903
Independence from Colombia

1977
The signing of the Panama Canal Treaties

1980s
The death of President Omar Torrijos creates a political vacuum; American troops invade Panama; Manuel Noriega surrenders to face drug charges in the United States

1990s
Mireya Moscoso is elected as Panama's first woman president; the last U.S. troops leave Panama; the Panama Canal passes to wholly local control

2000s
Climatic changes have been accelerated by deforestation

2009
Ricardo Martinelli elected president

2012
Work progresses on expansion of the canal

65

(Courtesy of Dr. Paul Goodwin)

The Panama Canal has been of continuing importance to the country since it opened in 1914. Full control of the canal was turned over to Panama in 1999, marking the end of U.S. involvement and representing a source of Panamanian nationalism.

◼ A RETURN TO CIVILIAN GOVERNMENT

President Torrijos, who died in a suspicious plane crash in 1981, left behind a legacy that included much more than the treaties. He elevated the National Guard to a position of supreme power in the state and ruled through a National Assembly of community representatives.

The 1984 elections appeared to bring to fruition the process of political liberalization initiated in 1978. But even though civilian rule was officially restored, the armed forces remained the real power behind the throne. Indeed, spectacular revelations in 1987 strongly suggested that Defense Forces chief general Manuel Antonio Noriega had rigged the 1984 elections. He was also accused of drug trafficking, gun running, and money laundering.

In February 1988, Noriega was indicted by two U.S. grand juries and charged with using his position to turn Panama into a center for the money-laundering activities of the Medellín, Colombia, drug cartel and providing protection for cartel members living temporarily in Panama.

Attempts by Panamanian president Eric Arturo Delvalle to oust the military strongman failed, and Delvalle himself was forced into hiding. Concerted efforts by the United States to remove Noriega from power—including an economic boycott, plans to kidnap the general and have the CIA engineer a coup, and saber-rattling by the dispatch of thousands of U.S. troops to the Canal Zone—proved fruitless.

The fraud and violence that accompanied an election called by Noriega in 1989 to legitimize his government and the failure of a coup attempt in October ultimately resulted in the invasion of Panama by U.S. troops in

December. Noriega was arrested, brought to the United States for trial, and eventually was convicted on drug-trafficking charges.

The U.S. economic sanctions succeeded in harming the wrong people. Noriega and his cronies were shielded from the economic crisis by their profits from money laundering. But many other Panamanians were devastated by the U.S. policy.

Nearly a decade after the invasion by U.S. troops to restore democracy and halt drug trafficking, the situation in Panama remains problematic. The country is characterized by extremes of wealth and poverty, and corruption is pervasive. The economy is still closely tied to drug-money laundering, which has reached levels higher than during the Noriega years.

Elections in 1994 reflected the depth of popular dissatisfaction. Three-quarters of the voters supported political movements that had risen in opposition to the policies and politics imposed on Panama by the U.S. invasion. The new president, Ernesto Pérez Balladares, a 48-year-old economist and businessman and a former supporter of Noriega, promised "to close the Noriega chapter" in Panama's history. During his term, he pushed ahead with privatization, the development of the Panama Canal Zone, a restructuring of the foreign debt, and initiatives designed to enhance tourism.

Unfortunately, Pérez seemed to have inherited some of the personalist tendencies of his predecessors. In 1998, he pushed for a constitutional change that would have allowed him to run for reelection in 1999. When put to a referendum in August 1998, Panamanians resoundingly defeated the ambitions of the president.

The 1999 elections, without the participation of Pérez, produced a close campaign between Martín

Snapshot: PANAMA

Summarized below is a quick look at the country with regard to its development, freedom, health/welfare, and achievements.

Development

Because many new ships are too large to transit the Canal, the Panamanian government unveiled plans in 2006 to expand it. Work began in 2007 and should be completed by 2014. Such a massive effort requires billions of dollars in new investment, but it is critical to the nation's economy.

Freedom

Freedom House reported that in 2010, "Panama's government approved troubling restrictions on freedoms of assembly, association, and speech, sparking protests from labor unions, journalists, and domestic and international nongovernmental organizations. President Ricardo Martinelli agreed to soften the measures affecting unions in October. Martinelli's popularity declined during the year due to controversial political appointments that were viewed by the opposition as attempts to consolidate power."

Health/Welfare

The Care Group, which is affiliated with Harvard Medical School, Beth Israel Hospital, and Panama's excellent Hospital Nacionál, reached agreement to create the region's first teaching hospital in the area of emergency care. Physicians from all of Latin America have been welcomed to the facility.

Achievements

The Panama Canal, which passed wholly to Panamanian control in 1999, is one of the greatest engineering achievements of the twentieth century. A maze of locks and gates, it cuts through 50 miles of the most difficult terrain on Earth.

Torrijos, the son of Omar, and Mireya Moscoso, the widow of the president who had been ousted by Omar Torrijos. Moscoso emerged as a winner, with 44 percent of the vote, and became Panama's first woman president.

Moscoso opposed many of Pérez's free-market policies and was especially critical of any further plans to privatize state-owned industries. Moscoso identified her administration with the inauguration of a "new era" for Panama's poor. Her social policies stood in direct contrast to the more economically pragmatic approach of her predecessors. Continued domination of the Legislature by the opposition render social reform difficult, but the president felt that she had to intercede on behalf of the poor, who constitute one-third of the population. Diversification of the economy remains a need, as Panama is still overly dependent on canal revenues and traditional agricultural exports. As supplement to the income produced by the canal, the Panama Canal Railway has been refurbished so that it will be able to transport container cargo in less time than it takes for a ship to transit the canal.

■ SOCIAL POLICIES

As is the case in most Latin American nations, Panama's Constitution authorizes the state to direct, regulate, replace, or create economic activities designed to increase the nation's wealth and to distribute the benefits of the economy to the greatest number of people. The harsh reality is that the income of one-third of Panama's population frequently fails to provide for families' basic needs.

Women, who won the right to vote in the 1940s, are accorded equal political rights under the law and hold a number of important government positions, including the presidency. But as in all of Latin America, women do not enjoy the same opportunities for advancement as men. There are also profound domestic constraints to their freedom. Panamanian law, for example, does not recognize community property; divorced or deserted women have no protection and can be left destitute, if that is the will of their former spouses. Many female heads-of-household from poor areas are obliged to work for the government, often as street cleaners, in order to receive support funds from the authorities.

With respect to human rights, Panama's record is mixed. The press and electronic media, while theoretically free, have experienced some harassment. In 1983, the Supreme Court ruled that journalists need not be licensed by the government. Nevertheless, both reporters and editors still exercise a calculated self-censorship, and press conduct in general is regulated by an official Morality and Ethics Commission, whose powers are broad and vague. In 2001, some journalists complained that the Moscoso government used criminal antidefamation laws to intimidate the press in general, and its critics in particular.

In May 2004 Martín Torrijos was elected president with about 47 percent of the vote. Although he was the flag bearer of a political party built by military strongmen, including his father and Noriega, he had promised change. Cloaking himself in the garb of a

? DID YOU KNOW?

When the Panama Canal was built almost 100 years ago, it revolutionized travel and trade. Now expansion of the canal, set to be unveiled in 2014, is a new driving force for ports across the hemisphere that see the need to gear up for the future it promises: an all-water route for oversize ships transiting from Asia to the Atlantic.

populist, Torrijos had presented an image in both the cities and the countryside as the defender of the poor. He had inherited a government widely accused of corruption and a national pension system close to collapse because of overspending. His economic policies embraced a significant reconstruction of the Panama Canal to allow the passage of larger ships. Panama's problems are daunting, and one Panamanian university professor told *The New York Times:* "There is no way [Torrijos] is going to be able to live up to people's expectations. He is going to have a short honeymoon."

Indeed, global recession and charges of corruption in government paved the way for the victory of multimillionaire supermarket owner, Ricardo Martinelli, in the presidential elections in May 2009. Martinelli's victory was especially interesting in that it ran counter to the wave of populist victories in other Latin American nations. His policies include job creation by building ports, highways, and a subway system for Panama City.

FURTHER INVESTIGATION

For more information on the expansion of the Panama Canal, visit www.ticotimes.net/Business-Real-Estate/Panama-Canal-expansion-a-game-changer-_Friday-June-17-2011

Statistics

Geography

Area in Square Miles (Kilometers): 30,185 (78,200) (about the size of South Carolina)

Capital (Population): Panama City (1,340,000)

Environmental Concerns: water pollution; deforestation; land degradation; soil erosion

Geographical Features: interior mostly steep, rugged mountains and dissected upland plains; coastal areas largely plains and rolling hills

Climate: tropical marine

People

Population

Total: 3,460,432 (2011 est.)

Annual Growth Rate: 1.4%

Rural/Urban Population Ratio: 25/75

Major Languages: Spanish; English

Ethnic Makeup: 70% Mestizo; 14% West Indian; 10% white; 6% Indian and others

Religions: 85% Roman Catholic; 15% Protestant and others

Health

Life Expectancy at Birth: 75 years (male); 80 years (female)

Infant Mortality Rate (Ratio): 11.69/1,000

Physicians Available (Ratio): 1.5/1000

Education

Adult Literacy Rate: 92%

Compulsory (Ages): for 6 years between 6–15; free

Communication

Telephones: 553,100 main lines

Daily Newspaper Circulation: 62 per 1,000 people

Cell Phones: 6,496,000

Internet Users: 959,800

Transportation

Roadways in Miles (Kilometers): 6,893 (11,100)

Railroads in Kilometers (Miles): 355 (208)

Usable Airfields: 118

Government

Type: constitutional democracy

Independence Date: November 3, 1903 (from Colombia)

Head of State/Government: President Ricardo Martinelli is both head of state and head of government

Political Parties: Nationalist Republican Liberal Movement; Patriotic Union Party; Democratic Change; others

Suffrage: universal and compulsory at 18

Military

Military Expenditures (% of GDP): 1%

Current Disputes: none

Economy

Currency ($U.S. Equivalent): 1.00 balboa = $1

Per Capita Income/GDP: $13,000/$44.36 billion

GDP Growth Rate: 7.5%

Inflation Rate: 3.5%

Unemployment Rate: 4.2%

Labor Force: 1,485,000

Natural Resources: copper; mahogany forests; shrimp; hydropower

Agriculture: bananas; rice; corn; coffee; sugarcane; vegetables; livestock; fishing

Industry: construction; petroleum; brewing; sugar; canal traffic/ tourism

Exports: $11.33 billion (primary partners Venezuela, South Korea, Ecuador, India, Japan)

Imports: $15.95 billion (primary partners Japan, China, Singapore, United States South Korea)

Suggested Website

www.cia.gov/cia/publications/factbook/index.html

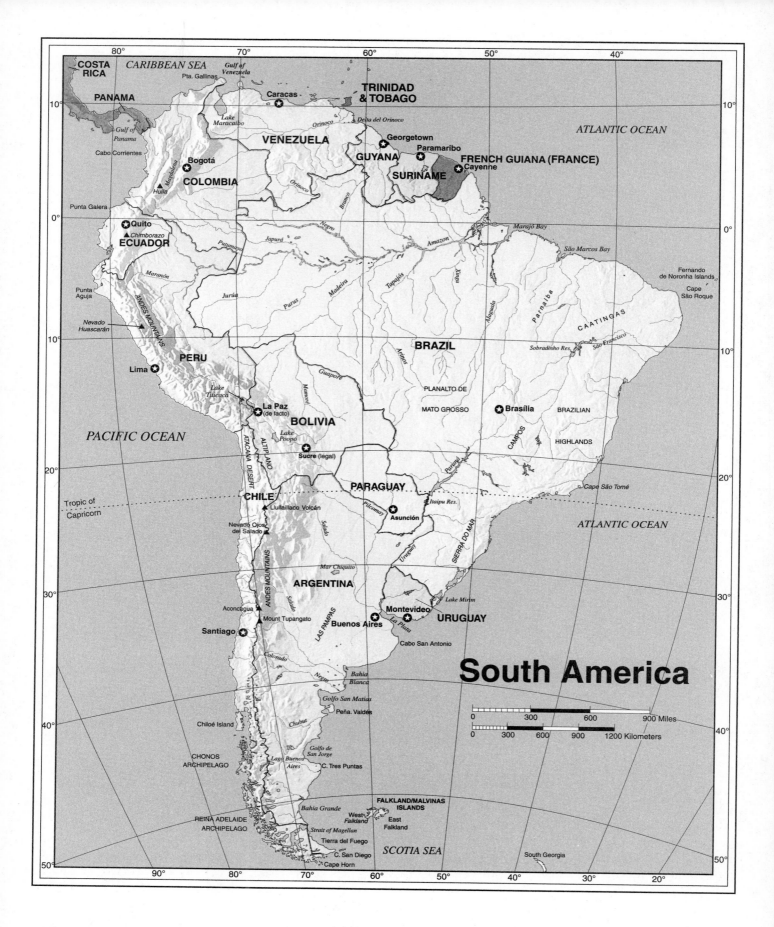

South America

South America

An Imperfect Prism

Any overview of South America must first address the incredible geographic and climatic diversity of the region. Equatorial rain forests are found in Brazil, Ecuador, Colombia, Venezuela, and other countries; and the coastal deserts in Peru and northern Chile are among the driest and most forbidding in the world (naturalist Charles Darwin described the area as "a complete and utter desert"). More hospitable are the undulating pampas and plains of Argentina, Uruguay, central Venezuela, eastern Colombia, and southeastern Brazil. The spine of the continent is formed by the Andes Mountains, majestic and snowcapped. Because of its topography and the many degrees of latitude in which it lies, South America has extremes of temperature, ranging from desert heat to the steaming humidity of the tropics to the cold gales of Tierra del Fuego, which lies close to the Antarctic Circle. To add further to the perils of generalization, wide-ranging differences often occur within a country. Geography has played a critical role in the evolution of each of the nations of South America; it has been one of several major influences in their histories and their cultures.

■ NATURE'S CHALLENGE

Nature has presented the inhabitants of South America with an unrelenting challenge. On the west coast, most of the major cities are located in geologically active zones. All too frequently, earthquakes, tidal waves, volcanic activity, and landslides have taken a staggering toll of human life. And throughout the region, floods and droughts make agriculture a risky business. Periodically, for example, the appearance of a warm current off the coasts of Peru and Ecuador, a phenomenon known as *El Niño,* produces significant atmospheric events worldwide. For Peru and Ecuador, *El Niño* brings devastating floods with heavy loss of life and extensive damage to the area's infrastructure. Further economic damage results from the profound disruption of the fishing industry.

■ REGIONALISM

South America's diverse topography has also helped to foster a deep-seated regionalism that has spawned innumerable civil wars and made national integration an extremely difficult task. In Colombia, for instance, the Andes fan out into three distinct ranges, separated by deep valleys. Each of the nation's three major cities—Bogotá, Medellín, and Cali—dominates a valley and is effectively isolated from the others by the mountains. The broad plains to the east have remained largely

(© Photo Link/Getty Images)

The majestic Andes run along the entire spine of South America. These are in Chile.

undeveloped because of the difficulty of access from the centers of population. Troubling to Colombian governments is the fact that, in terms of topography, the eastern plains are tied to Venezuela and not to the Colombian cities to the west.

Similarly, mountains divide Ecuador, Peru, Bolivia, and Venezuela. In all of these nations, there is a permanent tension between the capital cities and the hinterlands. As is the case in those republics that have large Indian populations, the tension often is as much cultural as it is a matter of geography. But in the entire region, physical geography interacts with culture, society, politics, and economics. Regionalism has been a persistent theme in the history of Ecuador, where there has been an often bitter rivalry between the capital city of Quito, located high in the

(Imagebroker/Alamy)

Football Fountain in front of the central building of the South American football association. Football (soccer) is considered to be the most popular sport in the world. Fans throughout South America often hold a high degree of enthusiasm and national pride in their respective teams.

central mountains, and the port city of Guayaquil. Commonly, port cities, with their window on the world outside, tend to be more cosmopolitan, liberal, and dynamic than cities that are more isolated. Such is the case with free-wheeling Guayaquil, which stands in marked contrast to conservative, traditional, deeply Catholic Quito.

Venezuela boasts six distinct geographical regions, which include mountains and valleys, plains and deserts, rivers and jungles, and a coastline. Historian John Lombardi observes that each of these regions has had an important role in identifying and defining the character of Venezuela's past and present: "Over the centuries the geographical focus has shifted from one region to another in response to internal arrangements and external demands."

THE SOUTHERN CONE

The cultures of the countries of the so-called Southern Cone—Argentina, Uruguay, Paraguay, and Chile—have also been shaped by the geographical environment. Argentina, Uruguay, and Brazil's southern state of Rio Grande do Sul developed subcultures that reflected life on the vast, fertile plains, where cattle grazed by the millions. The *gaucho* ("cowboy") became symbolic of the "civilization of leather." Fierce, independent, a law unto himself, the gaucho was mythologized by the end of the nineteenth century. At a time when millions of European immigrants were flooding into the region, the gaucho emerged as a nationalist symbol of Argentina and Uruguay, standing firm in the face of whatever natives viewed as "foreign."

Landlocked Paraguay, surrounded by powerful neighbors, has for most of its history been an introspective nation, little known to the outside world. Because of its geography, most of Paraguay's population is concentrated near the capital city of Asunción. A third of the nation is tropical and swampy—not suitable for settlement. To the west, the desolate Chaco region, with its lack of adequate sources of drinkable water, is virtually uninhabitable.

Chile, with a coastline 2,600 miles long, is a country of topographic and climatic extremes. If superimposed on a map of North America, Chile would stretch from Mexico's Baja California to the Yukon in Alaska. It is on Chile's border with Argentina that the Andes soar to their greatest heights. Several peaks, including Aconcagua, reach to nearly 23,000 feet in elevation. That mountain barrier has historically isolated Chile from eastern South America and from Europe. The central valley of Chile is the political, industrial, social, and cultural heart of the nation. With the capital city of Santiago and the large port of Valparaíso, the valley holds about 70 percent of Chile's population. The valley's Mediterranean climate and fertile soil have long acted as a magnet for Chileans from other, less hospitable, parts of the country.

BRAZIL

Historian Rollie Poppino has noted that the "major miracle of Brazil is its existence as a single nation." What he implies is that Brazil embraces regions that are so distinct that they could well be separate countries. "There are actually many Brazils within the broad expanse of the national territory, and the implication of uniformity conveyed by their common flag and language is often deceptive." In Brazil, there exists a tremendous range of geographical, racial, cultural, and economic contrasts. But part of the Brazilian "miracle" lies in the ability of its people to accept the diversity as normal. Many Brazilians were unaware of the great differences within their country for years, until the improvement of internal transportation and communications as well as the impact of the mass media informed them not only of their common heritage but also of their profound regional differences.

DIVERSE PEOPLES

In many respects, the peoples of South America are as diverse as its geography. While the populations of Argentina and Uruguay are essentially European, with virtually no Indian intermixture, Chilean society is descended from Spanish conquerors and the Indians they dominated. The Indian presence is strongest in the Andean republics of Bolivia, Peru, and Ecuador—the heart of the ancient Inca civilization. Bolivia is the most Indian, with well over half its population classified as such. Mestizos (mixed white and Indian) constitute about a quarter of the population, and whites make up only about one-tenth.

Three ethnic groups are found among the populations of Colombia and Venezuela: Spanish and Indian predominate, and there are small black minorities. About 60 percent of the populations of both countries are of Mestizo or pardo (mixed blood) origin. One of Brazil's distinctive features is the rich racial mixture of its population. Peoples of Indian, European, African, and Japanese heritage live in an atmosphere largely free of racial enmity, if not degrees of prejudice.

Taken as a whole, the predominant culture is Iberian (that is, Spanish or Portuguese), although many mountain areas are overwhelmingly Indian in terms of ethnic makeup. With the conquest and colonization of South America in the sixteenth century, Spain and Portugal attempted to fasten their cultures, languages, and institutions on the land and its peoples. Spanish cities in South America—laid out in the familiar grid pattern consisting of a large central plaza bordered by a Catholic church, government buildings, and the dwellings of the ruling elite—represented the conscious intention of the conquerors to impose their will, not only on the defeated Indian civilizations but also on nature itself.

By way of contrast, the Brazilian cities that were laid out by early Portuguese settlers tended to be less formally structured, suggesting that their planners and builders were more flexible and adaptable to the new world around them. Roman Catholicism, however, was imposed on all citizens by the central authority. Government, conforming to Hispanic political culture, was authoritarian in the colonial period and continues to be so today. The conquerors created a stratified society of essentially two sectors: a ruling white elite and a ruled majority. But Spain and Portugal also introduced institutions that knit society together. Paternalistic patron–client relationships that bound the weak to the strong were common; they continue to be so today.

■ INDIAN CULTURE

Among the isolated Indian groups of Ecuador, Peru, and Bolivia, Spanish cultural forms were strongly and, for the most part, successfully resisted. Suspicious and occasionally hostile, the Indians refused integration into the white world outside their highland villages. By avoiding integration, in the words of historian Frederick Pike, "they maintain the freedom to live almost exclusively in the domain of their own language, social habits, dress and eating styles, beliefs, prejudices, and myths."

Only the Catholic religion was able to make some inroads, and that was (and still is) imperfect. The Catholicism practiced by Quechua- and Aymara-speaking Indians is a blend of Catholic teachings and ancient folk religion. For example, in an isolated region in Peru where eight journalists were massacred by Indians, a writer who investigated the incident reported in *The New York Times* that while Catholicism was "deeply rooted" among the Indians, "it has not displaced old beliefs like the worship of the *Apus,* or god mountains." When threatened, the Indians are "zealous defenders of their customs and mores." The societies' two cultures have had a profound impact on the literature of Ecuador, Peru, and Bolivia. The plight of the Indian, social injustice, and economic exploitation are favorite themes of these nations' authors.

Other Indian groups more vulnerable to the steady encroachment of "progress" did not survive. In the late nineteenth century, pampas Indians were virtually destroyed by Argentine cavalry armed with repeating rifles. Across the Andes, in Chile, the Araucanian Indians met a similar fate in the 1880s. Unfortunately, relations between the "civilized" world and the "primitive" peoples clinging to existence in the rain forests of Brazil,

Peru, Bolivia, and Venezuela have generally improved little. But beginning in the early 1990s events in Bolivia, Brazil, Ecuador, and Venezuela signaled a marked shift toward greater Indian rights. Bolivians elected an Aymara Indian leader and activist as president in 2006. Indigenous peoples throughout the Amazon Basin, however, are still under almost daily assault from settlers hungry for land, road builders, developers, miners, loggers, and speculators—most of whom care little about the cultures they are annihilating.

■ AFRICAN AMERICAN CULTURE

In those South American countries where slavery was widespread, the presence of a large black population has contributed yet another dimension to Hispanic culture (or, in the case of Guyana and Suriname, English and Dutch culture). Slaves, brutally uprooted from their cultures in Africa, developed new cultural forms that were often a combination of Christian and other beliefs. To insulate themselves against the rigors of forced labor and to forge some kind of common identity, slaves embraced folk religions that were heavily oriented toward magic. Magic helped blacks to face an uncertain destiny, and

(© PhotoLink/Getty Images)

South America's Indian cultures and modern development have never really mixed. The native cultures persist in many areas, as exemplified at a market in Ecuador.

folk religions built bridges between peoples facing a similar, horrible fate. Folk religions not only survived the emancipation of slaves but have remained a common point of focus for millions of Brazilian blacks.

This phenomenon had become so widespread that in the 1970s, the Roman Catholic Church made a concerted effort to win Afro-Brazilians to a religion that was more Christian and less pagan. This effort was partly negated by the development of close relations between Brazil and Africa, which occurred at the same time as the Church's campaign. Brazilian blacks became more acutely aware of their African origins and began a movement of "re-Africanization." So pervasive had the folk religions become that one authority stated that Umbada (one of the folk religions) was now the religion of Brazil. The festival of *Carnaval* ("Carnival") in Rio de Janeiro, Brazil, is perhaps the best-known example of the blending of Christianity with spiritism. Even the samba, a dance form that is central to the Carnaval celebration, had its origins in black folk religions.

■ IMMIGRATION AND CULTURE

Italians, Eastern and Northern Europeans, Chinese, and Japanese have also contributed to the cultural, social, and economic development of several South American nations. The great outpouring of Europe's peoples that brought millions of immigrants to the shores of the United States also brought millions to South America. From the mid-1800s to the outbreak of World War I in 1914, great numbers of Italians and Spaniards, and much smaller numbers of Germans, Russians, Welsh, Scots, Irish, and English boarded ships that would carry them to South America.

Many were successful in the "New World." Indeed, immigrants were largely responsible for the social restructuring of Argentina, Uruguay, and southern Brazil, as they created a large and dynamic middle class where none had existed before.

Italians

Many of the new arrivals came from urban areas, were literate, and possessed a broad range of skills. Argentina received the greatest proportion of immigrants. So great was the influx that an Argentine political scientist labeled the years 1890–1914 the "alluvial era" (flood). His analogy was apt, for by 1914, half the population of the capital city of Buenos Aires were foreign-born. Indeed, 30 percent of the total Argentine population were of foreign extraction. Hundreds of thousands of immigrants also flocked into Uruguay.

In both countries, they were able to move quickly into middle-class occupations in business and commerce. Others found work on the docks or on the railroads that carried the produce of the countryside to the ports for export to foreign markets. Some settled in the interior of Argentina, where they usually became sharecroppers or tenant farmers, although a sizable number were able to purchase land in the northern province of Santa Fe or became truck farmers in the immediate vicinity of Buenos Aires. Argentina's wine industry underwent a rapid transformation and expansion with the arrival of Italians in the western provinces of Mendoza and San Juan. In the major cities of Argentina, Uruguay, Chile, Peru, and Brazil, Italians built hospitals and established newspapers; they formed mutual aid societies and helped to found the first labor unions. Their presence is still strong today, and Italian words have entered into everyday discourse in Argentina and Uruguay.

Other Groups

Other immigrant groups also made their contributions to the formation of South America's societies and cultures. Germans colonized much of southern Chile and were instrumental in creating the nation's dairy industry. In the wilds of Patagonia, Welsh settlers established sheep ranches and planted apple, pear, and cherry trees in the Río Negro Valley.

In Buenos Aires, despite the 1982 conflict over the Falkland Islands, there remains a distinct British imprint. Harrod's is the largest department store in the city, and one can board a train on a railroad built with English capital and journey to suburbs with names such as Hurlingham, Temperley, and Thames. In both Brazil and Argentina, soccer was introduced by the English, and two Argentine teams still bear the names "Newell's Old Boys" and "River Plate." Collectively, the immigrants who flooded into South America in the late nineteenth and early twentieth centuries introduced a host of new ideas, methods, and skills. They were especially important in stimulating and shaping the modernization of Argentina, Uruguay, Chile, and southern Brazil.

In other countries that were bypassed earlier in the century, immigration has become a new phenomenon. Venezuela—torn by political warfare, its best lands long appropriated by the elite, and its economy developing only slowly—was far less attractive than the lands of opportunity to its north (the United States) and south (Argentina, Uruguay, and Brazil). In the early 1950s, however, Venezuela embarked on a broadscale development program that included an attempt to attract European immigrants. Thousands of Spaniards, Portuguese, and Italians responded to the economic opportunity. Most of the immigrants settled in the capital city of Caracas, where some eventually became important in the construction business, retail trade, and the transportation industry.

■ INTERNAL MIGRATION

Paralleling the movement of peoples from across the oceans to parts of South America has been the movement of populations from rural areas to urban centers. In every nation, cities have been gaining in population for years. What prompts people to leave their homes and strike out for the unknown? In the cases of Bolivia and Peru, the very real prospect of famine has driven people out of the highlands and into the larger cities. Frequently, families will plan the move carefully. Vacant lands around

(World Bank/Francis Dobbs/BR005S09)

Slums in Brazil, as is the case with many other Latin American nations, has experienced rapid urbanization. Large numbers of migrants from rural areas have spread into slums on the outskirts of cities, as exemplified by this picture of a section of Colombia's capital, Bogotá. Most of the migrants are poorly paid, and the struggle to meet basic needs precludes political activism.

the larger cities will be scouted in advance, and suddenly, in the middle of the night, the new "settlers" will move in and erect a shantytown. With time, the seizure of the land is usually recognized by city officials and the new neighborhood is provided with urban services. Where the land seizure is resisted, however, violence and loss of life are common.

Factors other than famine also force people to leave their ancestral homes. Population pressure and division of the land into parcels too small to sustain families compel people to migrate. Others move to the cities in search of economic opportunities or chances for social advancement that do not exist in rural regions. Tens of thousands of Colombians illegally crossed into Venezuela in the 1970s and 1980s in search of employment. As is the case with Mexicans who enter the United States, Colombians experienced discrimination and remained on the margins of urban society, mired in low-paying, unskilled jobs. Those who succeeded in finding work in industry were a source of anger and frustration to Venezuelan labor-union members, who resented Colombians who accepted low rates of pay. Other migrants sought employment in the agricultural sector on coffee plantations or the hundreds of cattle ranches that dot the *llanos,* or plains. In summary, a combination of push-and-pull factors are involved in a person's decision to begin a new life.

Since World War II, indigenous migration in South America has rapidly increased urban populations and has forced cities to reorganize. Rural people have been exposed to a broad range of push–pull pressures to move to the cities. Land hunger, extreme poverty, and rural violence might be included among the push factors; while hope for a better job, upward social mobility, and a more satisfying life help to explain the attraction of a city. The phenomenon can be infinitely complex.

In Lima, Peru, there has been a twofold movement of people. While the unskilled and illiterate, the desperately poor and unemployed, the newly arrived migrant, and the delinquent have moved to or remained in inner-city slums, former slum dwellers have in turn moved to the city's perimeter. Although less centrally located, they have settled in more spacious and socially desirable shantytowns. In this way, some 16,000 families created a squatter settlement practically overnight in the south of Lima. Author Hernando DeSoto, in his groundbreaking and controversial book *The Other Path,* captures the essence of the shantytowns: "Modest homes cramped together on city perimeters, a myriad of workshops in their midst, armies of vendors hawking their wares on the street, and countless minibus lines crisscrossing them—all seem to have sprung from nowhere, pushing the city's boundaries ever outward."

Significantly, DeSoto notes, collective effort has increasingly been replaced by individual effort, upward mobility exists even for the inner-city slum dwellers, and urban culture and patterns of consumption have been transformed. Opera, theater, and *zarzuela* (comic opera) have gradually been replaced by movies, soccer, folk festivals, and television. Beer, rice, and table salt are now within the reach of much of the population; consumption of more expensive items, however, such as wine and meat, has declined.

On the outskirts of Buenos Aires there exists a *villa miseria* (slum) built on the bottom and sides of an old clay pit. Appropriately, the *barrio,* or neighborhood, is called La Cava (literally "The Digging"). The people of La Cava are very poor; most have moved there from rural Argentina or from Paraguay. Shacks seem to be thrown together from whatever is available—scraps of wood, packing crates, sheets of tin, and cardboard. There is no source of potable water, garbage litters the narrow alleyways, and there are no sewers. Because of the concave character of the barrio, the heat is unbearable in the summer. Rats and flies are legion. At times, the smells are repulsive. The visitor to La Cava experiences an assault on the senses; this is Latin America at its worst.

But there is another side to the slums of Buenos Aires, Lima, Santiago, and Rio de Janeiro. A closer look at La Cava, for example, reveals a community in transition. Some of the housing is more substantial, with adobe replacing the scraps of wood and tin; other homes double as places of business and sell general merchandise, food, and bottled drinks. One advertises itself as a food store, bar, and butcher shop. Another sells watches and repairs radios. Several promote their merchandise or services in a weekly newspaper that circulates in La Cava and two other *barrios de emergencia* ("emergency"—that is, temporary—neighborhoods). The newspaper addresses items of concern to the inhabitants. There are articles on hygiene and infant diarrhea; letters and editorials plead with people not to throw their garbage in the streets; births and deaths are recorded. The newspaper is a chronicle of progress as well as frustration: people are working together to create a viable neighborhood; drainage ditches are constructed with donated time and equipment; collections and raffles are held to provide materials to build sewers and, in some cases, to provide minimal street lighting; and men and women who have contributed their labor are singled out for special praise.

The newspaper also reproduces municipal decrees that affect the lives of the residents. The land on which the barrio sits was illegally occupied, the stores that service the neighborhood were opened without the necessary authorization, and the housing was built without regard to municipal codes, so city ordinances such as the following aimed at the barrios de emergencia are usually restrictive: "The sale, renting or transfer of *casillas* [homes] within the boundaries of the barrio de emergencia is prohibited; casillas can not be inhabited by single men, women or children; the opening of businesses within the barrio is strictly prohibited, unless authorized by the Municipality; dances and festivals may not be held without the express authorization of the Municipality." But there are also signs of accommodation: "The

Municipality is studying the problem of refuse removal." For migrants, authority and the legal system typically are not helpful; instead, they are hindrances.

Hernando DeSoto found this situation to be true also of Peru, where "the greatest hostility the migrants encountered was from the legal system." Until the end of World War II, the system had either absorbed or ignored the migrants "because the small groups who came were hardly likely to upset the status quo." But when the rural-to-urban flow became a flood, the system could no longer remain disinterested. Housing and education were barred to them, businesses would not hire them. The migrants discovered over time that they would have to fight for every right and every service from an unwilling establishment. Thus, to survive, they became part of the informal sector, otherwise known as the underground or parallel economy.

On occasion, however, municipal laws can work to the advantage of newly arrived migrants. In the sprawling new communities that sprang up between Lima and its port city of Callao, there are thousands of what appear to be unfinished homes. In almost every instance, a second floor was begun but, curiously, construction ceased. The reason for the incomplete projects relates to taxes—they are not assessed until a building is finished.

These circumstances are true not only of the squatter settlements on the fringes of South America's great cities but also of the inner-city slums. Slum dwellers have been able to improve their market opportunities and have been able to acquire better housing and some urban services, because they have organized on their own, outside formal political channels. In the words of sociologist Susan Eckstein, "They refused to allow dominant class and state interests to determine and restrict their fate. Defiance and resistance won them concessions which quiescence would not."

DeSoto found this to be the case with Lima: Migrants, "if they were to live, trade, manufacture, or even consume . . . had to do so illegally. Such illegality was not antisocial in intent, like trafficking in drugs, theft, or abduction, but was designed to achieve such essentially legal objectives as building a house, providing a service, or developing a business."

This is also the story of Buenos Aires's La Cava. To open a shop in the barrio with municipal approval, an aspiring businessperson must be a paragon of patience. Various levels of bureaucracy, with their plethora of paperwork and fees, insensitive municipal officials, inefficiency, and interminable waiting, drive people outside the system where the laws do not seem to conform to social need.

Disturbing, however, is the destruction of the social fabric of some of these "illegal" communities in the environs of Rio de Janeiro. In the *favelas* of this Brazilian city a drug and gang culture has taken root. The accompanying violence has torn families apart and resulted in the deaths of many people who stood in the way drug lords who have appropriated the *favelas* as a base of operations. Government action against the drug gangs became apparent once Rio de Janeiro won the bid for the 2016 Olympics. While some favelas were cleared of drug dealers, it is likely that they moved to other areas.

◼ AN ECCLESIASTICAL REVOLUTION

During the past few decades, there have been important changes in the religious habits of many South Americans. Virtually everywhere, Roman Catholicism, long identified with the traditional order, has been challenged by newer movements such as Evangelical Protestantism and the Charismatics. Within the Catholic Church, the theology of liberation once gained ground. The creation of Christian communities in the barrios, people who bond together to discuss their beliefs and act as agents of change, has become a common phenomenon throughout the region. Base communities from the Catholic perspective instill Christian values in the lives of ordinary people. But it is an active form of religion that pushes for change and social justice. Hundreds of these communities exist in Peru, thousands in Brazil.

◼ NATIONAL MYTHOLOGIES

In the midst of geographical and cultural diversity, the nations of South America have created national mythologies designed to unite people behind their rulers. Part of that mythology is rooted in the wars of independence that tore through much of the region between 1810 and 1830. Liberation from European colonialism imparted to South Americans a sense of their own national histories, replete with military heroes such as José de San Martín, Simón Bolívar, Bernardo O'Higgins, and Antonio José de Sucre, as well as a host of revolutionary myths. This coming to nationhood paralleled what the United States experienced when it won its independence from Britain. South Americans, at least those with a stake in the new society, began to think of themselves as Venezuelans, Chileans, Peruvians, or Brazilians. The architects of Chilean national mythology proclaimed the emergence of a new and superior being who was the result of the symbolic and physical union of Spaniards and the tough, heroic Araucanian Indians. The legacy of Simón Bolívar lives on in particular in Venezuela, his homeland; even today, the nation's foreign policymakers speak in Bolivarian terms about Venezuela's rightful role as a leader in Latin American affairs. In some instances, the mythology generated by the wars for independence became a shield against foreign ideas and customs and was used to force immigrants to become "Argentines" or "Chileans." It was an attempt to bring national unity out of diversity.

Argentines have never solved the question of their identity. Many consider themselves European and hold much of the rest of Latin America in contempt. Following Argentina's loss in the Falklands War with Britain, one scholar suggested that perhaps Argentines should no longer consider themselves as "a forlorn corner of Europe" but should wake up to the reality that they are Latin Americans. Much of Argentine literature reflects this uncertain identity and may help to explain author Jorge Luis Borges's affinity for English gardens and Icelandic sagas. It was also an Argentine military government that invoked Western Catholic civilization in its fight against a "foreign" and "godless" communism in the 1970s.

National mythologies also tend artificially to homogenize a country's history and often ignore large segments of the population and their cultures that differ from the "official" version. Recent events in Bolivia have laid bare long-existing cleavages. The non-Indian elite is clearly concerned by the election of an Aymara as president and his vision of the nation's history and future. The "white" inhabitants of Santa Cruz in eastern Bolivia have loudly proclaimed their cultural, ethnic, and social differences with the indigenous population of the highlands and have talked of secession.

◼ THE ARTIST AND SOCIETY

There is a strongly cultured and humane side of South America. Jeane Franco, an authority on Latin American cultural movements, observes that to "declare oneself an artist in Latin America has frequently involved conflict with society." The art and literature of South America in particular and Latin America in general represent a distinct tradition within the panorama of Western civilization.

The art of South America has as its focus social questions and ideals. It expresses love for one's fellow human beings and "has kept alive the vision of a more just and humane form of society." It rises above purely personal relationships and addresses humanity.

Much change is also evident at the level of popular culture. Andean folk music, for example, is being replaced by the more urban and upbeat chincha music in Peru; and in Argentina, the traditional tango has lost much of its early appeal. Radio and television programs are more and more in the form of soap operas, adventure programs, or popular entertainment, once considered vulgar by cosmopolitan city dwellers. South America is rather like a prism. It can be treated as a single object or region. Yet when exposed to a shaft of sunlight of understanding, it throws off a brilliant spectrum of colors that exposes the diversity of its lands and peoples.

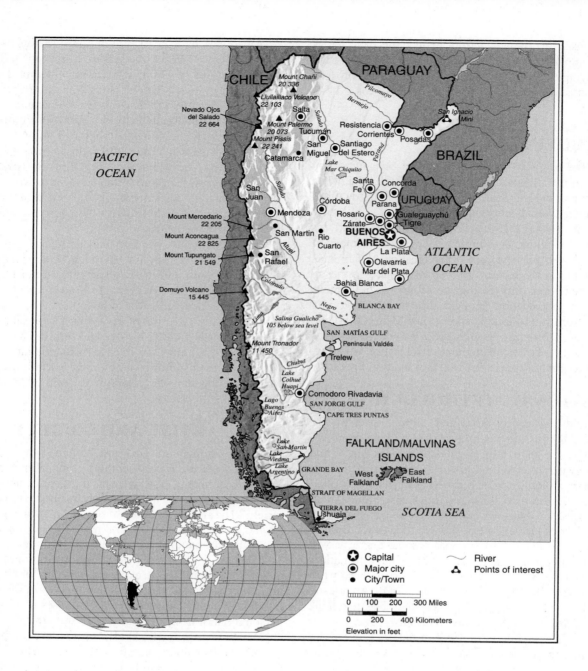

CHILE

PARAGUAY

Pilcomayo

Bermejo

Mount Chañi
20 336

Llullaillaco Volcano
22 103

San Ignacio
Mini

Nevado Ojos
del Salado
22 664

Salta

*PACIFIC
OCEAN*

Resistencia
Corrientes

Posadas

Mount Palermo
20 073

Mount Pissis
22 241

Tucumán

Salado

San
Miguel

Santiago
del Estero

BRAZIL

Catamarca

Lake
Mar Chiquito

Paraná

Santa
Fe

Concordia

San
Juan

Salado

Córdoba

Paraná

URUGUAY

Mount Mercedario
22 205

Mendoza

Rosario

Gualeguaychú

Mount Aconcagua
22 825

San Martin

Aluel

Río
Cuarto

Zárate
Tigre

BUENOS
AIRES

ATLANTIC

Mount Tupungato
21 549

San
Rafael

La Plata

OCEAN

Domuyo Volcano
15 445

Colorado

Olavarria
Mar del Plata

Bahía Blanca

Negro

BLANCA BAY

Lima

Salina Gualicho
105 below sea level

SAN MATÍAS GULF

Mount Tronador
11 450

Peninsula Valdés

Chubut

Trelew

Lake
Colhué
Huapi

Lago
Buenos
Aires

Comodoro Rivadavia

SAN JORGE GULF

CAPE TRES PUNTAS

Lake
San Martin

FALKLAND/MALVINAS
ISLANDS

Lake
Viedma
Lake
Argentino

GRANDE BAY

West
Falkland

East
Falkland

STRAIT OF MAGELLAN

TIERRA DEL FUEGO
Ushuaia

SCOTIA SEA

★ Capital

◉ Major city

● City/Town

∿ River

▲ Points of interest

0   100   200   300 Miles

0   200   400 Kilometers

Elevation in feet

Argentina
(Argentine Republic)

ARGENTINA: THE DIVIDED LAND

Writers as far back as the mid-1800s have perceived two Argentinas. Domingo F. Sarmiento, the president of Argentina in the 1860s, entitled his classic work about the country *Civilization and Barbarism*. More contemporary writers speak of Argentina as a divided land or as a city and a nation. All address the relationship of the capital city, Buenos Aires, to the rest of the country. Buenos Aires is cultured, cosmopolitan, modern, and dynamic. The rural interior is in striking contrast in terms of living standards, the pace of life, and, perhaps, expectations as well. For many years, Buenos Aires and other urban centers have drawn population away from the countryside. Today, Argentina is 88 percent urban.

There are other contrasts. The land is extremely rich and produces a large share of the world's grains and beef. Few Argentines are malnourished, and the annual per capita consumption of beef is comparable to that of the United States. Yet this land of promise, which seemed in the 1890s to have a limitless future, has slowly decayed. Its greatness is now more mythical than real. Since the Great Depression of the 1930s, the Argentine economy has, save for brief spurts, never been able to return to the sustained growth of the late nineteenth and early twentieth centuries.

In the 1990s, the Argentine economy enjoyed a brief period of stability and growth. Inefficient and costly state enterprises were privatized, with the exception of the petroleum industry, traditionally a strategic sector reserved to the state. A peso tied to the dollar brought inflation under control, and the pace of business activity, employment, and foreign investment quickened.

The nation's economy is vulnerable to events in other parts of the world, however. The collapse of the Mexican peso in the early 1990s and the economic crises in Russia and, especially, Asia in the late 1990s had profound negative effects in Argentina. The global slowdown in the new millennium further complicated the economic situation.

By the first quarter of 2002, the economy was in crisis. A foreign debt of $142 billion (which works out to $3,000 for every man, woman, and child in the country), declining export revenues, high unemployment, and the inability of the government to win International Monetary Fund support for additional loans forced a devaluation of the currency.

Argentine economic history has been typified by unrealized potential and unfulfilled promises. Much depends on the confidence of the Argentine people in the leadership and policies of their elected representatives. Five changes of government between December 2001 and March 2002 suggest a wholesale *lack* of confidence.

AUTHORITARIAN GOVERNMENT

In political terms, Argentina has revealed a curious inability to bring about the kind of stable democratic institutions that seemed assured in the 1920s. Since 1930, the military has seized power at least half a dozen times. It must be noted, however, that it has been civilians who have encouraged the generals to play an active role in politics. Historian Robert Potash writes: "The notion that Argentine political parties or other important civilian groups have consistently opposed military takeovers bears little relation to reality."

TIMELINE

1536
Pedro de Mendoza establishes the first settlement at Buenos Aires

1816
Independence of Spain

1865–1870
War with Paraguay

1912
Electoral reform: Compulsory male suffrage

1946–1955 and 1973–1974
Juan Perón is in power

1976–1982
The Dirty War

1980s
War with Great Britain over the Falkland Islands; military mutinies and economic chaos

1990s
Economic crises in Mexico, Russia, and Asia slow the economy

2007
Cristina Fernández de Kirchner elected Argentina's first woman president

2010
Argentina once again begins to agitate over the sovereignty of the Falkland/Malvinas Islands

2011
Fernandez de Kirschner re-elected president

(Flat Earth Images)

Military guard at the Falklands War memorial wall.

Argentina has enjoyed civilian rule since 1983, but the military is still a presence. Indeed, one right-wing faction, the *carapintadas* ("painted faces"), responsible for mutinies against President Raúl Alfonsín in 1987 and 1988, organized a nationwide party and attracted enough votes to rank for a time as an important political force. An authoritarian tradition is very much alive in Argentina, as is the bitter legacy of the so-called Dirty War.

■ THE DIRTY WAR

What made the latest era of military rule different is the climate of political violence that gripped Argentina starting in the late 1960s. The most recent period of violence began with the murder of former president Pedro Aramburu by left-wing guerrillas (Montoneros) who claimed to be fighting on behalf of the popular but exiled leader Juan Perón (president from 1946 to 1955 and from 1973 to 1974). The military responded to what it saw as an armed challenge from the left with tough antisubversion laws and official violence against suspects. Guerrillas increased their activities and intensified their campaign to win popular support.

Worried by the possibility of a major popular uprising and divided over policy, the military called for national elections in 1973, hoping that a civilian government would calm passions. The generals could then concentrate their efforts on destroying the armed left. The violence continued, however, and even the brief restoration of Juan Perón to power failed to bring peace.

In March 1976, with the nation on the verge of economic collapse and guerrilla warfare spreading, the military seized power once again and declared a state of internal war, popularly called the Dirty War. Between 1976 and 1982, between 10,000 and 30,000 Argentine citizens

"disappeared." Torture, the denial of basic human rights, harsh press censorship, officially directed death squads, and widespread fear came to characterize Argentina.

The labor movement—the largest, most effective, and most politically active on the continent—was, in effect, crippled by the military. Identified as a source of leftist subversion, the union movement was destroyed as an independent entity. Collective-bargaining agreements were dismantled, pension plans were cut back, and social-security and public-health programs were eliminated. The military's intent was to destroy a labor movement capable of operating on a national level.

The press was one of the immediate victims of the 1976 coup. A law was decreed warning that anyone spreading information derived from organizations "dedicated to subversive activities or terrorism" would be subject to an indefinite sentence. To speak out against the military was punishable by a 10-year jail term. The state also directed its terrorism tactics against the media, and approximately 100 journalists disappeared. Hundreds more received death threats, were tortured and jailed, or fled into exile. Numerous newspapers and magazines were shut down, and one, *La Opinión,* passed to government control.

The ruling junta justified these excesses by portraying the conflict as the opening battle of "World War III," in which Argentina was valiantly defending Western Christian values and cultures against hordes of Communist, "godless" subversives. It was a "holy war," with all of the unavoidable horrors of such strife.

By 1981, leftist guerrilla groups had been annihilated. Argentines slowly began to recover from the shock of internal war and talked of a return to civilian government. The military had completed its task; the nation needed to rebuild. Organized labor attempted to recreate its structure and threw the first tentative challenges at the regime's handling of the economy. The press carefully criticized both the economic policies of the government and the official silence over the fate of *los desaparecidos* ("the disappeared ones"). Human-rights groups pressured the generals with redoubled efforts.

■ OPPOSITION TO THE MILITARY

Against this backdrop of growing popular dissatisfaction with the regime's record, together with the approaching 150th anniversary of Great Britain's occupation of Las Islas Malvinas (the Falkland Islands), President Leopoldo Galtieri decided in 1982 to regain Argentine sovereignty and attack the Falklands. A successful assault, the military reasoned, would capture the popular imagination with its appeal to Argentine nationalism. The military's tarnished image would regain its luster. Forgiven would be the excesses of the Dirty War. But the attack ultimately failed.

In the wake of the fiasco, which cost thousands of Argentine and British lives, the military lost its grip on labor, the press, and the general population. Military and national humiliation, the continuing economic crisis made even worse by war costs, and the swelling chorus of discontent lessened the military's control over the flow of information and ideas. Previously forbidden subjects—such as the responsibility for the disappearances during the Dirty War—were raised in the newspapers.

The labor movement made a rapid and striking recovery and is now in the forefront of renewed political activity. Even though the movement is bitterly divided into moderate and militant wings, it is a force that cannot be ignored by political parties on the rebound.

The Falklands War may well prove to be a watershed in recent Argentine history. A respected Argentine observer, Torcuato DiTella, argues that the Falklands crisis was a "godsend," for it allowed Argentines to break with "foreign" economic models that had failed in Argentina. Disappointed with the United States and Europe over their support of Great Britain, he concludes: "We belong in Latin America and it is better to be a part of this strife-torn continent than a forlorn province of Europe."

Popularly elected in 1983, President Raúl Alfonsín's economic policies initially struck in bold new directions. He forced the International Monetary Fund to renegotiate Argentina's huge multi-billion-dollar debt in a context more favorable to Argentina, and he was determined to bring order out of chaos.

One of his most difficult problems centered on the trials for human-rights abuses against the nation's former military rulers. According to *Latin American Regional Reports,* Alfonsín chose to "distinguish degrees of responsibility" in taking court action against those who conducted the Dirty War. Impressively, Alfonsín put on trial the highest authorities, to be followed by action against those identified as responsible for major excesses.

Almost immediately, however, extreme right-wing nationalist officers in the armed forces opposed the trials and engineered a series of mutinies that undermined the stability of the administration. In 1987, during the Easter holiday, a rebellion of dissident soldiers made its point, and the Argentine Congress passed legislation that limited the prosecution of officers who killed civilians during the Dirty War to those only at the highest levels. Mini-mutinies in 1988 resulted in further concessions to the mutineers by the Alfonsín government, including reorganization of the army high command and higher wages.

Carlos Menem was supported by the military in the presidential election of May 1989, with perhaps 80 percent of the officer corps casting their votes for the Peronist Party. Menem adopted a policy of rapprochement with the military, which included the 1990 pardon of former junta members convicted of human-rights abuses. Historian Peter Calvert argues that Menem chose the path of amnesty because elements in the armed forces "would not be content until they got it." Rebellious middle-rank officers were well disposed toward Peronists, and Menem's pardon was "a positive gain in terms of the acceptance of the Peronists among the military themselves." In essence, then, Menem's military policy was consistent with other policies in terms of its pragmatic core. And the military seems to have been contained; military spending has

been halved, the army has been reduced from 100,000 to 20,000 soldiers, military enterprises have been divested, and mandatory service has been abandoned in favor of a professional force.

Significant progress has been made with regard to "disappeared" people. In 1992, President Menem agreed to create a commission to deal with the problem of children of the disappeared who were adopted by other families. Many have had their true identities established as a result of the patient work of "The Grandmothers of the Plaza de Mayo" and by the technique of cross-generational genetic analysis. (In 1998, former junta chief Admiral Emilio Massera was arrested on charges of kidnapping—that is, the distribution to families of babies born to victims of the regime.) In 1995, the names of an additional 1,000 people were added to the official list of the missing. Also, a retired military officer revealed his part in pushing drugged prisoners out of planes over the South Atlantic Ocean.

Perhaps the final chapter in the Dirty War is now being written. In 2010 a special tribunal sentenced Renaldo Bignone, the last military president, to 25 years in prison for his part in authorizing more than 300 detention centers, including the notorious Campo de Mayo, where thousands were incarcerated, tortured, and killed. Six other military and police officials implicated in human rights abuses were also jailed. In 2011 more than 20 former military officers, including two presidents, and agents of the government went on trial for excesses committed during the Dirty War. Most received long sentences for crimes against humanity.

■ ECONOMIC TRAVAIL

The Argentine economy under President Alfonsín was virtually out of control. Inflation soared. The sorry state of the economy and spreading dissatisfaction among the electorate forced the president to hand over power to Carlos Menem six months early.

Menem's new government worked a bit of an economic miracle, despite an administration nagged by corruption and early policy indecision, which witnessed the appointment of 21 ministers to nine cabinet positions during his first 18 months in office. In Menem's favor, he was not an ideologue but, rather, an adept politician whose acceptance by the average voter was equaled by his ability to do business with almost anyone. He quickly identified the source of much of Argentina's chronic inflation: the state-owned enterprises. From the time of Perón, these industries were regarded as wellsprings of employment and cronyism rather than as instruments for the production of goods or the delivery of services such as electric power and telephone service. "Ironically," says Luigi Manzetti, writing in *North-South FOCUS,* "it took a Peronist like Menem to dismantle Perón's legacy." While Menem's presidential campaign stressed "traditional Peronist themes like social justice and government investments" to revive the depressed economy, once he was in power, "having inherited a bankrupt state and under pressure from foreign banks and domestic business circles to enact a stiff adjustment program, Menem reversed his stand." He embraced the market-oriented policies of his political adversaries, "only in a much harsher fashion." State-owned enterprises were sold off in rapid-fire order. Argentina thus underwent a rapid transformation, from one of the world's most closed economies to one of the most open.

Economic growth began again in 1991, but the social costs were high. Thousands of public-sector workers lost their jobs; a third of Argentina's population lived below the poverty line, and the gap between the rich and poor tended to increase. But both inflation and the debt were eventually contained, foreign investment increased, and confidence began to return to Argentina.

In November 1993, former president Alfonsín supported a constitutional reform that allowed Menem to serve another term. Menem accepted some checks on executive power, including reshuffling the Supreme Court, placing members of the political opposition in charge of certain state offices, creating a post similar to that of prime minister, awarding a third senator to each province, and shortening the presidential term from six to four years. With these reforms in place, Menem easily won another term in 1995.

Convinced that his mandate should not end with the conclusion of his second term, Menem lobbied hard in 1998 for yet another constitutional reform to allow him to run again. This was not supported by the Supreme Court.

The Radical Party won the elections in 1999. Almost immediately President Fernando de la Rua confronted an economy mired in a deepening recession. Rising unemployment, a foreign debt that stood at 50 percent of gross domestic product, and fears of a debt default prompted the government to announce tax increases and spending cuts to meet IMF debt targets. At the end of 2001, the economic crisis triggered rioting in the streets and brought down the de la Rua administration and three others that followed in rapid succession.

By the end of 2002 the economy was in such shambles that some provinces began to issue their own currencies, farmers resorted to barter—exchanging soy beans for agricultural equipment—and many Argentines seriously considered emigration. Crime rates rose and people lost faith in governments that seemed incapable of positive policies and all-to-susceptible to corruption.

This dismal picture began to change with the election of Néstor Kirchner in May 2003. During his first year in office he called on Congress to begin impeachment proceedings against the widely hated Supreme Court. The justices were accused of producing verdicts that reflected payoffs and political favors. Kirchner also laid siege to Argentina's security forces: he ordered more than 50 admirals and generals into early retirement and dismissed 80 percent of the high command of the notoriously corrupt Federal Police.

Finally, after years of severe malaise, the economy began to turn around in 2003. Kirchner noted that the IMF had abandoned Argentina in 2001 as its economy

spiraled downward. Consequently the Argentine president, in the words of *New York Times* reporter Tony Smith, "felt justified in resolutely refusing to make a series of concessions that negotiators for the monetary fund wanted in exchange for refinancing $21.6 billion in debt that Argentina owes to multilateral institutions. . . ." In March 2005, President Kirchner announced a debt settlement that paid the nation's creditors as little as 30 cents on the dollar. Argentina, in effect, worked out a deal in accord with Argentine economic realities.

■ FOREIGN POLICY

The Argentine government's foreign policy has usually been determined by realistic appraisals of the nation's best interests. From 1946, the country moved between the two poles of pro-West and nonaligned. President Menem firmly supported the foreign-policy initiatives of the United States and the UN. Argentine participation in the Persian Gulf War and the presence of Argentine troops under United Nations command in Croatia, Somalia, and other trouble spots paid dividends: Washington agreed to supply Argentina with military supplies for the first time since the Falklands War in 1982. President Kirchner has assumed an independent posture. The U.S. invasion of Iraq was cast as a violation of international law and Argentina has moved closer to Latin American regimes not in the good graces of Washington, that is, Bolivia, Brazil, Venezuela, and Cuba.

President Kirchner, having stood up to the demands of the IMF, now moved steadily away from Washington's free trade agenda. He has also moved closer to Hugo Chávez of Venezuela and signed a series of economic agreements. By identifying with populist leaders in South America Kirchner established Argentina's independence from the United States.

■ WOMEN AND ARGENTINA'S POLITICAL FUTURE

In 1991, Argentina was the first Latin American country to implement a gender quota law in its lower legislative house, the Chamber of Deputies. The law was extended to the Senate in 2001. Every third name on all party ballots must be a woman. In 2006, 39 percent of the legislature was female and in 2007 Argentina elected its first woman president, Cristina Fernández de Kirchner. This development, which is not confined to Argentina, may be partially explained by the fact that women are seen by

? DID YOU KNOW?

The dance known as the tango had its origins in the bars and brothels of Buenos Aires in the 19th century. It gained respectability around the turn of the century when it became popular in Paris. The dance has since become one of Argentina's national symbols and is embraced by all levels of society.

Snapshot: ARGENTINA

Summarized below is a quick look at the country with regard to its development, freedom, health/welfare, and achievements.

Development

The Economist predicts problems for Argentina's economy in 2012. The factors responsible for rapid growth in 2010—high world prices for commodities, a robust Brazilian economy, and extravagant subsidies—no longer exist. High levels of inflation will also cause difficulties.

Freedom

In December 2011 the government won control of the manufacture, sale, and distribution of newsprint. Media groups called the legislation a death blow for freedom of expression. The Inter-American Press Association saw the move as an attempt by the government "to control the media."

Health/Welfare

In recent years, inflation has had an adverse impact on the amount of state spending on social services. Moreover, the official minimum wage falls significantly lower than the amount considered necessary to support a family.

Achievements

Argentine citizens have won four Nobel Prizes—two for peace and one each for chemistry and medicine. The nation's authors—Jorge Luis Borges, Julio Cortazar, Manuel Puig, and Ricardo Guiraldes, to name only a few—are world-famous.

voters as one way to replace traditional politicians who have promised much but delivered little.

A robust economy in 2010 in part assured Kirchner's re-election in 2011. However, persistently high inflation and a slowing economy spell trouble in 2012. In Kirchner's favor is a political opposition that is hopelessly fractured.

FURTHER INVESTIGATION

For more information on the tango, visit www.history-of-tango.com/

Statistics

Geography

Area in Square Miles (Kilometers): 1,100,000 (2,771,300) (about 4 times the size of Texas)

Capital (Population): Buenos Aires (12,988,000)

Environmental Concerns: soil erosion and degradation; air and water pollution; desertification.

Geographical Features: rich plains of the Pampas in the north; flat to rolling plateau of Patagonia in the south; rugged Andes along western border

Climate: varied; mostly temperate; subantarctic in southwest

People

Population

Total: 41,769,726 (2011 est.)

Annual Growth Rate: 1.0%

Rural/Urban Population Ratio: 8/92

Major Languages: Spanish; Italian; English

Ethnic Makeup: 97% white; 3% Mestizo, Indian, and others

Religions: 90% Roman Catholic (fewer than 20% practicing); 2% Protestant; 2% Jewish; 6% others

Health

Life Expectancy at Birth: 74 years (male); 80 years (female)

Infant Mortality Rate (Ratio): 10.81/1,000

Physicians Available (Ratio): 3.15/1000

Education

Adult Literacy Rate: 97.2%

Compulsory (Ages): 6–14; free

Communication

Telephones: 10,000,000

Daily Newspaper Circulation: 138 per 1,000 people

Cell Phones: 57,300,000

Internet Users: 13,694,000

Transportation

Roadways in Kilometers (Miles): 229,144 (142,384)

Railroads in Kilometers (Miles): 31,902 (19,823)

Usable Airfields: 1,141

Government

Type: republic

Independence Date: July 9, 1816 (from Spain)

Head of State/Government: President Cristina Fernández de Kirchner is both head of state and head of government

Political Parties: Radical Civic Union; Justicialist Party (Peronist); Republican Proposal; various coalitions; others

Suffrage: universal at 18

Military

Military Expenditures (% of GDP): 0.8%

Current Disputes: indefinite boundary with Chile; claims UK-administered South Georgia and South Sandwich Islands, and Falkland Islands (Islas Malvinas); territorial claim in Antarctica

Economy

Currency ($U.S. Equivalent): 3.89 pesos = $1

Per Capita Income/GDP: $14,700/$596 billion

GDP Real Growth Rate: 7.5%

Inflation Rate: 22%

Unemployment Rate: 7.9%

Labor Force: 16,540,000

Natural Resources: fertile plains; lead; zinc; tin; copper; iron ore; manganese; petroleum; uranium

Agriculture: wheat; corn; sorghum; fruits; soybeans; tobacco; tea; livestock

Industry: food processing; motor vehicles; consumer durables; textiles; chemicals and petrochemicals; printing; metallurgy; steel

Exports: $68.13 billion (primary partners Brazil, China, Chile, United States)

Imports: $53.87 billion (primary partners Brazil, United States, China, Germany)

Suggested Website

www.cia.gov/cia/publications/factbook/index.html

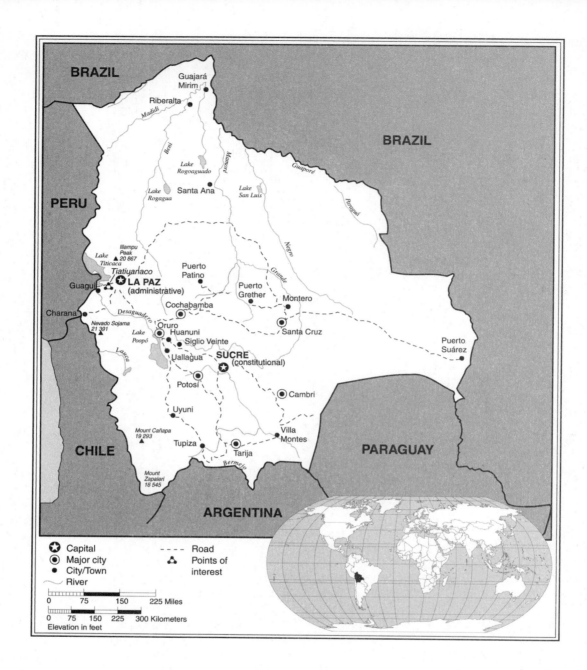

BRAZIL

Guajará
Mirim

Riberalta

Madidi

BRAZIL

Beni

Mamoré

Guaporé

Lake
Rogoaguado

PERU

Lake
Rogagua

Santa Ana

Lake
San Luis

Paraguá

Negro

Grande

Illampu
Peak
▲ 20 867

Lake
Titicaca

Tiatiuanaco

⊕ LA PAZ
(administrative)

Puerto
Patino

Guaqui

Charana

Desaguadero

Nevado Sojama
▲ 21 391

Cochabamba

Puerto
Grether

Montero

Oruro
Huanuni

Lake
Poopó

Santa Cruz

Puerto
Suárez

Lauca

Siglio Veinte

Uallagua

SUCRE
(constitutional)

Potosí

Cambri

Uyuni

Mount Cañapa
▲ 19 293

Tupiza

Villa
Montes

Bermejo

Tarija

PARAGUAY

Mount
Zapaleri
18 545

CHILE

ARGENTINA

⊕ Capital
◉ Major city
● City/Town
〜 River

- - - Road
△ Points of
    interest

| 0 | 75 | 150 | 225 Miles |

| 0 | 75 | 150 | 225 | 300 Kilometers |

Elevation in feet

Bolivia
(Republic of Bolivia)

BOLIVIA: AN INDIAN NATION

Until recently, the images of Bolivia captured by the world's press were uniformly negative. Human-rights abuses were rampant, a corrupt and brutal military government was deeply involved in cocaine trafficking, and the nation was approaching bankruptcy.

Other images might include Bolivia's complex society. So intermixed has this multiethnic culture become that one's race is defined by one's social status. So-called whites, who look very much like the Indians with whom their ancestors intermarried, form the upper classes only because of their economic, social, and cultural positions—that is, the degree to which they have embraced European culture.

Another enduring image fixed in the literature is Bolivia's political instability. The actual number of governments over the past 200 years is about 80, however, and not the 200 commonly noted. Indeed, elected governments have been in power for the past two decades. What outsiders perceive as typical Latin American political behavior clouds what is unusual and positive about Bolivia.

One nineteenth-century leader, Manuel Belzu, played an extremely complex role that combined the forces of populism, nationalism, and revolution. Belzu encouraged the organization of the first trade unions, abolished slavery, promoted land reform, and praised Bolivia's Indian past.

In 1952, a middle-class–led and popularly supported revolution swept the country. The ensuing social, economic, and political reforms, while not erasing an essentially dual society of "whites" and Indians, did significantly ease the level of exploitation. Most of the export industries, including those involved with natural resources, were nationalized. Bolivia's evolution—at times progressive, at times regressive—continues to reflect the impulse for change.

THE SOCIETY: POSITIVE AND NEGATIVE ASPECTS

Bolivia, despite the rapid and startling changes that have occurred in the recent past, remains an extremely poor society. In terms of poverty, life expectancy, death rates, and per capita income, the country ranks among the worst in the Western Hemisphere.

Rights for women have made slow progress, even in urban areas. In 1975, a woman was appointed to the Bolivian Supreme Court; and in 1979, the Bolivian Congress elected Lidia Gueiler Tejada, leader of the lower house, as president. Long a supporter of women's rights, Tejada had drafted and pushed through Congress a bill that created a government ministry to provide social benefits for women and children. That remarkably advanced legislation has not guaranteed that women enjoy a social status equal to that of men, however. Furthermore, many women are likely unaware of their rights under the law.

Bolivia's press is reasonably free, although many journalists are reportedly paid by politicians, drug traffickers, and officials to increase their exposure or suppress negative stories. A few journalists who experienced repression under previous governments still practice self-censorship.

TIMELINE

1538
Spanish settle the altiplano (high plain)

1825
Bolivian declaration of independence of Spain

1879–1880
The War of the Pacific with Chile; Bolivia loses access to the sea

1932–1935
The Chaco War with Paraguay

1952–1964
Reforms: nationalization of mines, land reform, universal suffrage, creation of labor federation

1990s
Privatization of the economy accelerates; labor unrest grips the mining sector Bolivia's indigenous people achieve a new political voice

2000s
President Sánchez de Lozada forced to resign Bolivia's indigenous majority demands economic, political, and social reform
New constitution limits President Morales to a single 5-year term, however he indicated that he wanted to run again in 2014

(Courtesy of Jorge Tutor)

Bolivia has a complex society, tremendously affected by the continued interplay of multiethnic cultures. The influence of indigenous peoples on Bolivia remains strong.

■ URBANIZATION

Santa Cruz has been transformed in the last 50 years from an isolated backwater into a modern city with links to the other parts of the country and to the rest of South America. From a population of 42,000 in 1950, the number of inhabitants quickly rose to half a million in the mid-1980s and is now growing at the rate of about 8 percent a year. Bolivia's second largest city, its population now exceeds that of the de facto capital, La Paz.

Most of the city's population growth has been the result of rural-to-urban migration, a phenomenon closely studied by geographer Gil Green. On paper, Santa Cruz is a planned city, but, since the 1950s, there has been a running battle between city planners and new settlers wanting land. "Due to the very high demand for cheap land and the large amount of flat, empty, nonvaluable land surrounding it, the city has tended to expand by a process of land invasion and squatting. Such invasions are generally overtly or covertly organized by political parties seeking electoral support of the low-income population." In the wake of a successful "invasion," the land is divided into plots that are allocated to the squatters, who then build houses from whatever materials are at hand. Then begins the lengthy process of settlement consolidation and regularization of land tenure. Once again the new land is subdivided and sold cheaply to the low-income population.

Perhaps the pace of urbanization as a result of internal migration is most pronounced in El Alto, which hardly existed on maps 30 years ago. It is now a "city" of 700,000 and overlooks La Paz. The rapid growth actually reflects a profound crisis in Bolivia. Tens of thousands of Aymara and Quechua-speaking miners and peasant farmers have been driven to El Alto by their inability to make a living in rural areas. Over the past five years it has become, in the works of a local newspaper editor, "the capital of social protest in Bolivia." In fact, a rebellion centered in El Alto succeeded in driving President Gonzalo Sánchez from power in 2003 and threatened to do the same to his successor, Carlos Mesa.

The character of what has been termed the "Ideology of Fury" is complex and springs from a broad range of contexts. Perhaps most important, Bolivia's indigenous majority has suffered centuries of neglect and abuse. President Mesa noted as much when he explained the uprising as an "eruption of deeply held positions, over many centuries, that have been accumulating." There appear to have been two more immediate catalysts: U.S. insistence on the eradication of coca and the government's proposal to export natural gas to the United States through the construction of a pipeline to Chile.

With respect to coca cultivation, Bolivian politicians for years have promised to put an end to the trade and substitute other crops such as pineapples, coffee, black pepper, oregano, and passion fruit. Unfortunately most of the government's efforts were put on eradication and not alternative development. The United States, according to economist Jeffrey Sachs, "has constantly made demands on an impoverished country without any sense of reality or an economic framework and strategy to help them in development." The net result was the impoverishment of thousands of peasant farmers, who have since migrated to El Alto and become the taproot of the "Ideology of Fury." What was not appreciated by Washington and Bolivian politicians who were fearful of losing U.S. aid money was that coca is central to indigenous culture. Certainly much is exported in the form of coca paste or cocaine. In the 1990s it was calculated that illegal exports contributed the equivalent of 13 to 15 percent of Bolivia's gross domestic product and that coca by-products accounted for as much as 40 percent of total exports, both legal and illicit. Today, about 400,000 Bolivians are estimated to live off coca and cocaine production. U.S. wishes run afoul of the multifaceted heritage of coca, the sacred plant of the Incas. There is virtually no activity in domestic, social, or religious life in which coca does not play a role; thus, attempts to limit its cultivation have had profound repercussions among the peasantry.

Indigenous resistance to coca eradication now centers on Evo Morales, the head of the coca growers' federation, who emerged victorious in the presidential elections of 2005. Morales's new party, the Movement Toward Socialism, has undertaken the modification of the laws against coca cultivation, regardless of the wishes of the United States. "There has to be a change, to a policy that is truly Bolivian, not one that is imposed by foreigners with the pretext that eradication will put an end to narcotics trafficking," said a member of Congress and an ally of Morales. The president himself coined the phrase: "Yes to coca, no to cocaine."

The second catalyst involved the proposed gas pipeline. While there are good historical reasons for Bolivian antipathy towards Chile (Chile deprived Bolivia its access to the Pacific as a result of territorial adjustments following the War of the Pacific in 1879–1880), resistance to the pipeline also has a social dimension. As reported in *The New York Times,* a Chilean pollster noted: "Part of the democratic process is assuring that people are going to get a piece of the cake, and that has been lacking in Bolivia. Bolivians are suspicious of whoever is making the deal because they think the "elite always puts money in its own pockets, and we are left on the streets with nothing to eat." Regionalism also plays a role in the controversy. Gas-producing regions, those with large deposits of lithium, and even farmers in Santa Cruz who have experienced a boom in soybean exports, now demand a

FURTHER INVESTIGATION

For more information on Bolivia's lack of access to the sea, visit http://ourlatinamerica.blogspot.com/2011/02/bolivia-renews-demands-for-access-to.html

? DID YOU KNOW?

Bolivia, a landlocked country, has a navy and an admiral. The navy operates on Lake Titicaca and symbolically represents Bolivia's desire to recover its access to the sea; lost in a war with Chile.

significant voice in the distribution of the wealth they produce as well as a degree of autonomy from La Paz.

Regional tensions reached a boiling point in May 2008 when Santa Cruz voted on a statute to seek more autonomy from the La Paz government. One provincial legislator who helped draft the statute told a *New York Times* reporter: "We do not want the creation of another republic. But we do want control over our own destiny and our own resources." The statute, if implemented, would accord Santa Cruz the right to elect its own legislature, create its own police force, and raise taxes for public works. It would also allow the province to negotiate royalty rights with energy companies. Part of the drive for autonomy springs from provincial fears that the Morales government plans to break up large rural estates and redistribute land to migrants who have flooded into Santa Cruz from the impoverished highlands.

What is unfolding in Bolivia is the latest manifestation of a problem that has been brewing since the 1950s. Santa Cruz is the economic engine that drives the country and it is in this province that most of the nation's wealth is concentrated. La Paz and the highlands want a greater distribution of that wealth. Some of the strident talk of secession has eased with the surge in energy revenues as a result of the government's new contracts with foreign energy companies.

The success of the indigenous majority in Bolivia in toppling one government and then winning the presidency has both emboldened their leaders, who relish their newfound power, and awakened a sense of racial pride among the Aymara and Quechua. As one unemployed carpenter told reporter Larry Rohter: "They may still say that we are only Indians, but now we can see what is happening and what the Aymara nation can do when it is united."

President Morales will now have to put his rhetoric into action if he is to mollify the demands of an awakened and angry indigenous population. It will be impossible for Bolivia to develop its extensive natural resources in the face of an indigenous and regional resistance that does not take into account their needs. That fact was brought home to the government when Morales' insistence that a highway be built through a lowlands indigenous preserve provoked strong protests and violence. If the government can link development to the creation of jobs, if it finally begins to deliver on years of unfulfilled promises with regard to health care and education, and if it can pursue a coca policy that respects the culture of the majority of the population and stems from Bolivian reality and not Washington's wishes, then perhaps a modus vivendi can be reached. If not, the future will bring further economic malaise and political upheaval.

Snapshot: BOLIVIA

Summarized below is a quick look at the country with regard to its development, freedom, health/welfare, and achievements.

Development

Bolivia recorded the highest growth rate in South America in 2009. During 2010 an increase in world commodity prices resulted in the greatest trade surplus in Bolivia's history. Problems include a lack of foreign investment in the key mining and hydrocarbon sectors and higher food prices.

Freedom

Freedom House reported in 2010 that opposition candidates for political office complained about the "abuse of state resources and a flurry of criminal charges brought against opposition politicians. . . ." Monitors from the European Union characterized elections as "generally free and fair," but they also confirmed misuse of state resources. Judicial paralysis, they noted, left those facing criminal charges with inadequate legal recourse.

Health/Welfare

Provisions against child labor in Bolivia are frequently ignored; many children may be found shining shoes, selling lottery tickets, and as street vendors. Fully 60 percent of the population lives in poverty.

Achievements

The Bolivian author Armando Chirveches, in his political novel *La Candidatura de Rojas* (1909), produced one of the best examples of this genre in all of Latin America. The book captures the politics of the late nineteenth century extraordinarily well.

Statistics

Geography

Area in Square Miles (Kilometers): 424,162 (1,098,160) (about 3 times the size of Montana)

Capital (Population): La Paz (de facto) (1,642,000); Sucre (legal) (281,000)

Environmental Concerns: deforestation; soil erosion; desertification; loss of biodiversity; water pollution

Geographical Features: rugged Andes Mountains with a highland plateau (Altiplano), hills, lowland plains of the Amazon Basin

Climate: varies with altitude; from humid and tropical to semiarid and cold

People

Population

Total: 10,118,683 (2011 est.)

Annual Growth Rate: 1.7%

Rural/Urban Population Ratio: 33/67

Major Languages: Spanish; Quechua; Aymara

Ethnic Makeup: 30% Quechua; 25% Aymara; 30% Mestizo; 15% white

Religions: 95% Roman Catholic; 5% Protestant

Health

Life Expectancy at Birth: 67 years (male); 70 years (female)

Infant Mortality Rate (Ratio): 42.16/1,000

Physicians Available (Ratio): 1.2/1000

Education

Adult Literacy Rate: 86.7%

Compulsory (Ages): 6–14; free

Communication

Telephones: 848,200 main lines

Daily Newspaper Circulation: 69 per 1,000 people

Cell Phones: 7,179,000

Internet Users: 1,103,000

Transportation

Roadways in Kilometers (Miles): 62,479 (38,823)

Railroads in Kilometers (Miles): 3,504 (2,177)

Usable Airfields: 881

Government

Type: republic (Social Unitarian State)

Independence Date: August 6, 1825 (from Spain)

Head of State/Government: President Evo Morales is both head of state and head of government

Political Parties: Movement Toward Socialism; Bolivia-National Convergence; National Unity; Social Alliance

Suffrage: universal and compulsory at 18 if married, at 21 if single

Military

Military Expenditures (% of GDP): 1.3%

Current Disputes: dispute with Chile over water rights; seeks sovereign corridor to the South Pacific Ocean

Economy

Currency ($U.S. Equivalent): 7.0 bolivares = $1

Per Capita Income/GDP: $4,800/47.88 billion

GDP Growth Rate: 4.2%

Inflation Rate: 2.5%

Unemployment Rate: 7.8%; underemployment

Labor Force: 4,614,000

Natural Resources: tin; natural gas; petroleum; zinc; tungsten; antimony; silver; iron; lead; gold; timber; hydropower

Agriculture: soybeans; coffee; coca; cotton; corn; sugarcane; rice; potatoes; timber

Industry: mining; smelting, petroleum; food and beverages; tobacco; handicrafts; clothing

Exports: $6.179 billion (primary partners Brazil, Peru, Colombia, Japan, Argentina)

Imports: $4.992 billion (primary partners Brazil, Argentina, United States, Peru, Chile, China)

Suggested Website

www.cia.gov/cia/publications/factbook/geos/bl.html

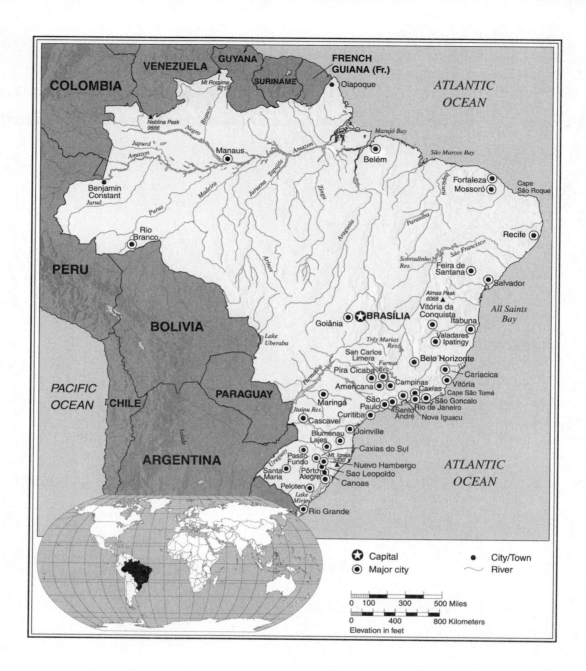

COLOMBIA

VENEZUELA

GUYANA

SURINAME

FRENCH
GUIANA (Fr.)

Mt Roraima
9219

● Oiapoque

ATLANTIC
OCEAN

Neblina Peak
9886

Negro

Branco

Marajó Bay

Amazon

Japurá

● Manaus

● Belém

São Marcos Bay

Amazon

Madeira

Jurena *Tapajós*

Xingu

Fortaleza ◉
Mossoró ◉

Cape
São Roque

Benjamin
Constant

Juruá

Purus

Araguaia

Paraíba

Recife ◉

Rio
Branco ◉

Aripos

São Francisco

Sobradinho
Res.

Feira de
Santana ◉

Salvador ◉

PERU

BOLIVIA

Lake
Uberaba

Paranaíba

Almas Peak
6068 ▲

Goiânia ●

☆BRASÍLIA

Três Marias
Res.

Vitória da
Conquista

Itabuna ◉

All Saints
Bay

Valadares
Ipatingy

PACIFIC
OCEAN

CHILE

PARAGUAY

San Carlos
Limera

Pira Cicaba

Americana ●

Maringa ●

Itaipu Res.

Furnas
Res.

Belo Horizonte ◉

Cariacica

Vitória

Campinas
Caxías

Cape São Tomé

São
Paulo ◉

São Goncalo
Rio de Janeiro

Curitiba ◉

Santo
André

Nova Iguacu

Uruguay

Salado

Cascavel ●

Blumenau
Lajes

Joinville

Caxias do Sul

ARGENTINA

Passo
Fundo

Mt Igreja
5830 ▲

Nuevo Hambergo

Santa
Maria ●

Pôrto
Alegre ◉

Sao Leopoldo

Peloten

Canoas

ATLANTIC
OCEAN

Lake
Mirim

● Rio Grande

| ✪ Capital | ● City/Town |
| ◉ Major city | ⌇ River |

0   100   300   500 Miles

0   400   800 Kilometers

Elevation in feet

Brazil

(Federative Republic of Brazil)

BRAZIL: "ORDER AND PROGRESS"

In 1977, Brazilian president Ernesto Geisel stated that progress was based on "an integrated process of political, social, and economic development." Democracy, he argued, was the first necessity in the political arena. But democracy could only be achieved "if we also further social development . . . , if we raise the standard of living of Brazilians." The standard of living, he continued, "can only be raised through economic development."

It was clear from his remarks that the three broad objectives of democratization, social progress, and economic development were interconnected. He could not conceive of democracy in a poor country or in a country where there were "gaps, defects, and inadequacies in the social realm."

CONCEPTS OF PROGRESS

Geisel's comments offer a framework within which to consider not only the current situation in Brazil but also historical trends that reach back to the late nineteenth century—and, in some instances, to Portugal. Historically, most Brazilians have believed that progress would take place within the context of a strong, authoritarian state. In the nineteenth century, for example, a reform-minded elite adapted European theories of modernization that called for government-sponsored changes. The masses would receive benefits from the state; in this way, the elite reasoned, pressure for change from the poorer sectors of society would be eliminated. There would be progress with order. *Ordem e Progresso* ("Order and Progress") is the motto that graces the Brazilian flag; the motto is as appropriate today as it was in 1889, when the flag first flew over the new republic.

The tension among modernization, social equity, and order and liberty was first obvious in the early 1920s, when politically isolated middle-class groups united with junior military officers (*tenentes*) to challenge an entrenched ruling class of coffee-plantation owners. By the mid-1920s, the tenentes, bent on far-reaching reforms, conceived a new role for themselves. With a faith that bordered at times on the mystical and a philosophy that embraced change in the vaguest of terms, they felt that only the military could shake Brazil from its lethargy and force it to modernize. Their program demanded the ouster of conservative, tradition-minded politicians; an economic transformation of the nation; and, eventually, a return to strong, centralized constitutional rule. The tenentes also proposed labor reforms that included official recognition of trade unions, a minimum wage and maximum workweek, restraints on child labor, land reform, nationalization of natural resources, and a radical expansion of educational facilities. Although the tenentes were frustrated in their attempts to mold policy, many of their reforms were taken up by Getulio Vargas, who seized power in 1930 and imposed a strong, authoritarian state on Brazil.

THE 1964 REVOLUTION

In some respects, the goals of the tenentes were echoed in 1964, when a broad coalition of civilians—frustrated by an economy that seemed to be disintegrating, concerned with the "leftist" slant of the government of João Goulart, and worried about a social revolution that might well challenge the status

FURTHER INVESTIGATION
For more information on Carnival, visit http://www.brazilcarnival.com/aboutus/carnival-history.html

DID YOU KNOW?
Brazil's famous Carnival celebrations are a time to release pent-up frustrations and to immerse oneself in song and dance. Some critics argue that it is really a form of "social control" and is an emotional safety valve for the disadvantaged. However, Carnival is also a popular mass art form embraced by most Brazilians.

and prestige of the wealthy and the middle classes—called on the military to impose order on the country.

The military leaders did not see their intervention as just another coup but, rather, as a revolution. They foresaw change but believed that it would be dictated from above. Government was highly centralized, the traditional parties were virtually frozen out of the political process, and the military and police ruthlessly purged Brazil of elements considered "leftist" or "subversive." (The terms were used interchangeably.) Order and authority triumphed over liberty and freedom. The press was muzzled, and human-rights abuses were rampant.

Brazil's economic recovery eventually began to receive attention. The military gave economic growth and national security priority over social programs and political liberalization. Until the effects of the oil crisis generated by the Organization of Petroleum Exporting Countries (OPEC) in 1973 began to be felt, the recovery of the Brazilian economy was dubbed a "miracle," with growth rates averaging 10 percent a year.

The benefits of that growth went primarily to the upper and middle classes, who enjoyed the development of industries based largely on consumer goods. Moreover, Brazil's industrialization was flawed. It was heavily dependent on foreign investment, foreign technology, and foreign markets. It required large investments in machinery and equipment but needed little labor, and it damaged the environment through pollution of the rivers and air around industrial centers. Agriculture was neglected to the point that even basic foodstuffs had to be imported.

■ THE IMPACT OF RURAL-TO-URBAN MIGRATION

The stress on industrialization tremendously increased rural-to-urban migration and complicated the government's ability to keep up with the expanded need for public health and social services. In 1970, nearly 56 percent of the population were concentrated in urban areas; by 2011, 87 percent of the population were so classified. These figures also illustrate the inadequacies of an agrarian program based essentially on a "moving frontier." Peasants

[IMS Communications Ltd./Capstone Design/FlatEarth Images]

View over Rio de Janeiro with a tram taking people high above the city and water below, possibly to Sugarloaf Mountain.

evicted from their plots have run out of new lands to exploit, unless they move to the inhospitable Amazon region. As a result, many have been attracted by the cities.

The pressure of the poor on the cities, severe shortages of staple foods, and growing tension in rural areas over access to the land forced the government to act. In 1985, the civilian government of José Sarney announced an agrarian-reform plan to distribute millions of acres of unused private land to peasants. Implementation of the reform was not easy, and confrontations between peasants and landowners occurred.

■ MILITARY RULE IS CHALLENGED

Nineteen seventy-four was a crucial year for the military government of Brazil. The virtual elimination of the urban-guerrilla threat challenged the argument that democratic institutions could not be restored because of national security concerns.

Pressure grew from other quarters as well. Many middle- and upper-class Brazilians were frightened by the huge state-controlled sector in the economy that had

[© Photodisc/PunchStock]

By the late 1980s, agrarian reforms that were designed to establish peasants in plots of workable land had caused the depletion of Brazilian jungle and, as space and opportunities diminished, there was a large movement of these people to the cities. The profound urban crowding in Brazil is illustrated by this photo of a section of Rio de Janeiro.

been carved out by the generals. The military's determination to promote the rapid development of the nation's resources, to control all industries deemed vital to the nation's security, and to compete with multinational corporations concerned Brazilian businesspeople, who saw their role in the economy decreasing.

Challenges to the military regime also came from the Roman Catholic Church, which attacked the government for its brutal violations of human rights and constantly called for economic and social justice. One Brazilian bishop publicly called the government "sinful" and in "opposition to the plans of God" and noted that it was the Church's moral and religious obligation to fight it. After 1974, as Brazil's economic difficulties mounted, the chorus of complaints grew insistent.

■ THE RETURN OF DEMOCRACY

The relaxation of political repression was heralded by two laws passed in 1979. The Amnesty Bill allowed for the return of hundreds of political exiles; the Party Reform Bill in essence reconstructed Brazilian politics. Under the provisions of the Party Reform Bill, new political parties could be established—provided they were represented in nine states and in 20 percent of the counties of those states. The new parties were granted the freedom to formulate political platforms, as long as they were not ideological and did not favor any single economic class. The Communist Party was outlawed, and the creation of a workers' party was expressly forbidden. (Communist parties were legalized again in 1985.)

The law against the establishment of a workers' party reflected the regime's concern that labor, increasingly anxious about the state of the economy, might withdraw its traditional support for the state. Organized labor had willingly cooperated with the state since the populist regime of Getulio Vargas (1937–1945). For Brazilian workers in the 1930s, the state was their "patron," the source of benefits. This dependence on the government, deeply rooted in Portuguese political culture, replaced the formation of a more independent labor movement and minimized industrial conflict. The state played the role of mediator between workers and management. President Vargas led the workers to believe that the state was the best protector of their interests. (Polls have indicated that Brazilian workers still cling to that belief.)

If workers expect benefits from the state, however, the state must then honor those expectations and allocate sufficient resources to assure labor's loyalty. A deep economic crisis, such as those that occurred in the early 1960s, in the early 1990s, and again between 2001–2003 and 2008–2009 endangered the state's control of labor. In 1964, organized labor supported the coup, because workers felt that the civilian regime had failed to perform its protective function. This phenomenon also reveals the extremely shallow soil in which Brazilian democracy has taken root.

Organized labor tends not to measure Brazilian governments in political terms, but within the context of the state's ability to address labor's needs. For the rank-and-file worker, it is a question not of democracy or military authoritarianism, but of bread and butter. President Sarney, in an effort to keep labor loyal to the government, sought the support of union leaders for a proposal to create a national pact with businesspeople, workers, and his government. But pervasive corruption, inefficient government, and a continuing economic crisis eventually eroded the legitimacy of the elites and favored nontraditional parties in the 1989 election. The candidacy of Luís Inácio da Silva, popularly known as Lula and leader of the Workers' Party, "was stunning evidence of the Brazilian electorate's dissatisfaction with the conduct of the country's transition to democracy and with the political class in general." He lost the election by a very narrow margin. In 2002, he won the election and promised to "end hunger."

Workers continue to regard the state as the source of benefits, as do other Brazilians. Many social reformers, upset with the generals for their neglect of social welfare, believe that social reform should be dispensed from above by a strong and paternalistic state. Change is possible, even welcome—but it must be the result of compromise and conciliation, not confrontation or nonnegotiable demands.

■ THE NEW CONSTITUTION

The *abertura* (political liberalization) of Brazil climaxed in January 1985 with the election of President Sarney, a civilian, following 21 years of military rule. Importantly, the Brazilian military promised to respect the Constitution and promised a policy of nonintervention in the political process. In 1987, however, with the draft of a new constitution under discussion, the military strongly protested language that removed its responsibility for internal law and order and restricted the military's role to that of defense of the nation against external threats. According to *Latin American Regional Reports: Brazil,* the military characterized the draft constitution as "confused, inappropriate, at best a parody of a constitution, just as Frankenstein was a gross and deformed imitation of a human being."

Military posturing aside, the new Constitution went into effect in October 1988. It reflects the input of a wide range of interests: The Constituent Assembly—which also served as Brazil's Congress—heard testimony and suggestions from Amazonian Indians, peasants, and urban poor as well as from rich landowners and the military. The 1988 Constitution is a document that captures the byzantine character of Brazilian politics and influence peddling and reveals compromises made by conservative and liberal vested interests.

The military's fears about its role in internal security were removed when the Constituent Assembly voted constitutional provisions to grant the right of the military independently to ensure law and order, a responsibility it historically has claimed. But Congress also arrogated to itself the responsibility for appropriating federal monies.

This is important, because it gives Congress a powerful check on both the military and the executive office.

Nationalists won several key victories. The Constituent Assembly created the concept of "a Brazilian company of national capital" that can prevent foreigners from engaging in mining, oil-exploration risk contracts, and biotechnology. Brazilian-controlled companies were also given preference in the supply of goods and services to local, state, and national governments. Legislation reaffirmed and strengthened the principle of government intervention in the economy should national security or the collective interest be at issue.

Conservative congressional representatives were able to prevail in matters of land reform. They defeated a proposal that would have allowed the compulsory appropriation of property for land reform. Although a clause that addressed the "social function" of land was included in the Constitution, it was clear that powerful landowners and agricultural interests had triumphed over Brazil's landless peasantry.

In other areas, however, the Constitution is remarkably progressive on social and economic issues. The workweek was reduced to a maximum of 44 hours, profit sharing was established for all employees, time-and-a-half was promised for overtime work, and paid vacations were to include a bonus of 30 percent of one's monthly salary. Day-care facilities were to be established for all children under age six, maternity leave of four months and paternity leave of five days were envisaged, and workers were protected against "arbitrary dismissal." The Constitution also introduced a series of innovations that would increase significantly the ability of Brazilians to claim their guaranteed rights before the nation's courts and ensure the protection of human rights, particularly the rights of Indians and peasants involved in land disputes.

Despite the ratification of the 1988 Constitution, a functioning Congress, and an independent judiciary, the focus of power in Brazil is still the president. A legislative majority in the hands of the opposition in no way erodes the executive's ability to govern as he or she chooses. Any measure introduced by the president automatically becomes law after 40 days, even without congressional action. Foreign observers perceive "weaknesses" in the new parties, which in actuality are but further examples of well-established political practices. The parties are based on personalities rather than issues, platforms are vague, goals are so broad that they are almost illusions, and party organization conforms to traditional alliances and the "rules" of patronage. Democratic *forms* are in place in Brazil; the *substance* remains to be realized.

The election of President Fernando Collor de Mello, who assumed office in March 1990, proves the point. As political scientist Margaret Keck explains, Collor fit well into a "traditional conception of elite politics, characterized by fluid party identifications, the predominance of personal relations, a distrust of political institutions, and reliance on charismatic and populist appeals to *o povo,* the people." Unfortunately, such a system is open to abuse; revelations of widespread corruption that reached all the way to the presidency brought down Collor's government in 1992 and gave Brazilian democracy its most difficult challenge to date. Populist President Lula da Silva's government was also dogged by charges of corruption. In September 2005 thousands of protesters, including workers, students, and businessmen took to the streets and accused the ruling Workers' Party of bribing lawmakers and complicity in illicit campaign funding. Such scandals bring to light a range of strengths and weaknesses that presents insights into the Brazilian political system.

■ THE PRESS AND THE PRESIDENCY

Brazil's press was severely censored and harassed from the time of the military coup of 1964 until 1982. Not until passage of the Constitution of 1988 was the right of free speech and a free press guaranteed. It was the press, and in particular the news magazine *Veja,* that opened the door to President Collor's impeachment. In the words of *World Press Review,* "Despite government pressure to ease off, the magazine continued to uncover the president's malfeasance, tugging hard at the threads of Collor's unraveling administration. As others in the media followed suit, Congress was forced to begin an investigation and, in the end, indict Collor." The importance of the event to Brazil's press, according to *Veja* editor Mario Sergio Conti, is that "It will emerge with fewer illusions about power and be more rigorous. Reporting has been elevated to a higher plane. . . ."

While the failure of Brazil's first directly elected president in 29 years was tragic, it should not be interpreted as the demise of Brazilian democracy. Importantly, according to Brazilian journalist Carlos Eduardo Lins da Silva, writing in *Current History,* many "Brazilians and outside observers saw the workings of the impeachment process as a sign of the renewed strength of democratic values in Brazilian society. They were also seen as a healthy indicator of growing intolerance to corruption in public officials."

The military has to date allowed the constitutional process to dictate events. For the first time, most civilians do not see the generals as part of the solution to political shortcomings. But many Brazilians still assume that most politicians are "crooked."

■ THE RIGHTS OF WOMEN AND CHILDREN

Major changes in Brazilian households have occurred over the last decade as the number of women in the workforce has dramatically increased. In 1990, just over 35 percent of women were in the workforce, and the number was expected to grow. As a result, many women are limiting the size of their families. More than 20 percent use birth-control pills, and Brazil is second only to China in the percentage of women who have been sterilized. The traditional family of 5.0 or more children has shrunk to an average of 3.4. With two wage earners, the standard of living has risen slightly for some families. Many homes now have electricity and running water. Television sales increased by more than 1,000 percent in the last decade.

In relatively affluent, economically and politically dynamic urban areas, women are more evident in the professions, education, industry, the arts, media, and political life. In rural areas, however, especially in the northeast, traditional cultural attitudes, which call upon women to be submissive, are still well entrenched.

Women are routinely subjected to physical abuse in Brazil. Americas Watch, an international human-rights group, reports that more than 70 percent of assault, rape, and murder cases take place in the home and that many incidents are unreported. Even though Brazil's Supreme Court struck down the outmoded concept of a man's "defense of honor," local courts routinely acquit men who kill unfaithful wives. Brazil, for all intents and purposes, is still a patriarchy.

Children are also in many cases denied basic rights. According to official statistics, almost 18 percent of children between the ages of 10 and 14 are in the labor force, and they often work in unhealthy or dangerous environments. Violence against urban street children reached frightening proportions in the 1990s. Between January and June 1992, 167 minors were killed in Rio de Janeiro; 306 were murdered in São Paulo over the first seven months of the year. In July 1993, the massacre in a single night of seven street children in Rio de Janeiro resulted, for a time, in cries for an investigation of the matter. In February 1997, however, five children were murdered on the streets of Rio.

THE STATUS OF BLACKS

Scholars continue to debate the actual status of blacks in Brazil. Not long ago, an elected black member of Brazil's federal Congress blasted Brazilians for their racism. However, argues historian Bradford Burns, Brazil probably has less racial tension and prejudice than other multiracial societies.

A more formidable barrier, Burns says, may well be class. "Class membership depends on a wide variety of factors and their combination: income, family history and/or connections, education, social behavior, tastes in housing, food and dress, as well as appearance, personality and talent." But, he notes, "The upper class traditionally has been and still remains mainly white, the lower class principally colored." Upward mobility exists and barriers can be breached. But if such advancement depends upon a symbolic "whitening out," does not racism still exist?

This point is underscored by the 1988 celebration of the centennial of the abolition of slavery in Brazil. In sharp contrast to the government and Church emphasis on racial harmony and equality were the public protests by militant black groups claiming that Brazil's much-heralded "racial democracy" was a myth. In 1990, blacks earned 40 percent less than whites in the same professions.

THE INDIAN QUESTION

Brazil's estimated 200,000 Indians have suffered greatly in recent decades from the gradual encroachment of migrants from the heavily populated coastal regions and from government efforts to open the Amazon region to economic development. Highways have penetrated Indian lands, diseases for which the Indians have little or no immunity have killed thousands, and additional thousands have experienced a profound culture shock. Government efforts to protect the Indians have been largely ineffectual.

The two poles in the debate over the Indians are captured in the following excerpts from *Latin American Regional Reports: Brazil.* A Brazilian army officer observed that the "United States solved the problem with its army. They killed a lot of Indians. Today everything is quiet there, and the country is respected throughout the world." And in the words of a Kaingang Indian woman: "Today my people see their lands invaded, their forests destroyed, their animals exterminated and their hearts lacerated by this brutal weapon that is civilization."

Sadly, the assault against Brazil's Indian peoples has accelerated, and disputes over land have become more violent. Yanomamö Indians have been devastated by diseases, particularly malaria, and by mercury poisoning as a result of prospecting activities upriver from Yanomamö settlements. In 1991, cholera began to spread among indigenous Amazon peoples, due to medical waste dumped into rivers in cholera-ridden Peru and Ecuador. In 2008, Tikuna Indians fought to protect their youth from drug and alcohol abuse. Narco-traffickers routinely recruit young Indians to transport drugs from Colombia and Peru into Brazil. Also, the increased proximity of some tribes to non-Indian communities with their western ideas and wares threatens the very existence of their culture.

The Constitution devotes an entire chapter to the rights of Indians. For the first time in the country's history, Indians have the authority to bring suits in court to defend their rights and interests. In all such cases, they will be assisted by a public prosecutor. Even though the government established a large protected zone for Brazil's Yanomamö Indians in 1991, reports of confrontations between Indians and prospectors have persisted to the present day. There are also Brazilian nationalists who insist that a 150-mile-wide strip along the border with Venezuela be excluded from the reserve as a matter of national security. The Yanomamö cultural area extends well into Venezuela; such a security zone would bisect Yanomamö lands.

THE BURNING OF BRAZIL

Closely related to the destruction of Brazil's Indians is the destruction of the tropical rain forests. The burning of the forests by peasants clearing land in the traditional slash-and-burn method, or by developers and landowners constructing dams or converting forest to pasture, has become a source of worldwide concern and controversy.

Ecologists are horrified by the mass extinction of species of plants, animals, and insects, most of which

(World Bank/Julio Pantoja/JPBR-1512-3-B)

A family makes its way down a mud-filled road in Vila da Canpas in the Amazon region of Brazil, near Manaus. For many, the only transportation available is by foot.

have not even been catalogued. The massive annual burning (equivalent in one recent year to the size of Kansas) also fuels the debate on the greenhouse effect and global warming. The problem of the burning of Brazil is indeed global, because we are all linked to the tropics by climate and the migratory patterns of birds and animals.

World condemnation of the destruction of the Amazon basin has on occasion produced a strong xenophobic reaction in Brazil. Foreign Ministry Secretary-General Paulo Tarso Flecha de Lima once informed a 24-nation conference on the protection of the environment that the "international community cannot try to strangle the development of Brazil in the name of false ecological theories." He further noted that foreign criticism of his government in this regard was "arrogant, presumptuous and aggressive." The Brazilian military, according to *Latin American Regional Reports: Brazil,* has adopted a high-profile posture on the issue. The military sees the Amazon as "a kind of strategic reserve vital to national security interests." Any talk of transforming the rain forests into an international nature reserve is rejected out of hand.

Over the next decade, however, Brazilian and foreign investors will create a 2.5 million-acre "green belt" in an already devastated area of the Amazon rain forest. Fifty million seedlings have been planted in a combination of natural and commercial zones. It is hoped that responsible forestry will generate jobs to maintain and study the native forest and to log the commercial zones. Steady employment would help to stem the flow of migrants to cities and to untouched portions of the rain forest. On

the other hand, to compound the problem, landless peasants in 16 of Brazil's states launched violent protests in May 2000 to pressure the government to provide land for 100,000 families, as well as to grant millions of dollars in credits for poor rural workers.

■ FOREIGN POLICY

If Brazil's Indian and environmental policies leave much to be desired, its foreign policy has won it respect throughout much of Latin America and the developing world. Cuba, Central America, Angola, and Mozambique seemed far less threatening during the Cold War to the Brazilian government than they did to Washington. Brazil is more concerned about its energy needs, capital requirements, and trade opportunities.

President Lula da Silva's foreign policy was characterized by the United States as "leftward" leaning, especially since it moved closer to other populist governments in the region, such as Venezuela (Hugo Chavez), or Bolivia (Evo Morales). Closer relations established with Cuba and Iran. Lula attacked the United States' occupation of Iraq and was distrustful of Washington's free-trade agenda. It must be understood that Brazil's current foreign policy, both in terms of its economic and political contexts, has another dimension. Standing up to the United States plays well at home and in the region and may be used to balance domestic policies that fall short of the radical solutions many of his followers expected. Lula himself disdained political labels such as "leftist" and, as he told a *New York*

Snapshot: BRAZIL

Summarized below is a quick look at the country with regard to its development, freedom, health/welfare, and achievements.

Development

Sound economic policies, including a floating exchange rate, attention to inflationary pressures, and conservative fiscal practices produced record trade surpluses between 2003 and 2007. Global recession in 2008–2009 plunged the growth rate into negative figures, but 5 percent growth was expected in 2010.

Freedom

Brazil has one of the highest homicide rates in the world. Most violent crime in the country, according to Freedom House, is related to the illegal drug trade. "Highly organized and well-armed drug gangs frequently fight against the military police as well as private militias comprising off-duty police officers, prison guards, and firefighters. These militias have intimidated human rights activists and residents by instituting their own form of extortion, sometimes charging citizens a mandatory tax for ousting drug traffickers from their areas or actually selling weapons to drug dealers."

Health/Welfare

The quality of education in Brazil varies greatly from state to state, in part because there is no system of national priorities. The uneven character of education has been a major factor in the maintenance of a society that is profoundly unequal. The provision of basic health needs remains poor, and land reform is a perennial issue.

Achievements

Brazil's cultural contributions to the world are many. Authors such as Joaquim Maria Machado de Assis, Jorge Amado, and Graciliano Ramos are evidence of Brazil's high rank in terms of important literary works. Brazilian music has won millions of devotees throughout the world, and Brazil's *Cinema Novo* (New Cinema) has won many awards.

Times reporter, the class struggle was about results for the people and he didn't care if it was called "Socialism or Christianity or simply ethics." Brazil's foreign policy likewise should not be labeled but seen as one of pragmatism. It is expected that President Rousseff will continue Lula's approach to foreign policy.

▪ ECONOMIC POLICY

In mid-1993, Finance Minister Fernando Henrique Cardoso announced a plan to restore life to an economy in shambles. The so-called Real Plan, which pegged the new Brazilian currency (the real) to the dollar, brought an end to hyperinflation and won Cardoso enough popularity to carry him to the presidency. Inflation, which had raged at a rate of 45 percent per month in July 1994, was only 2 percent per month in February 1995. His two-to-one victory in elections in October 1994 was the most one-sided win since 1945.

President Cardoso transformed the economy through carefully conceived and brilliantly executed constitutional reforms. A renovated tax system, an overhauled social-security program, and extensive privatization of state-owned enterprises were supported by a new generation of legislators pledged to support broad-based reform.

But, as was the case in much of Latin America in 1995, Mexico's financial crisis spread quickly to affect Brazil's economy, in large measure because foreign investors were unable to distinguish between Mexico and other Latin American nations. A similar problem occurred in 1998 with the collapse of Asian financial markets. Again, foreign investors shied away from Brazil's economy, and President Cardoso was forced to back away from a promise not to devalue the real. With devaluation in 1999 and signs of recovery in Asian markets, Brazil's economic prospects brightened considerably. Exports rose, and Brazil was able to finance its foreign debt through bond issues. In 2000 and 2001, however, the economy slowed, and concerns were expressed about energy supplies and costs, and the default of Brazil's major trading partner, Argentina, on its foreign debt. Economic uncertainty emboldened Congress to initiate a probe against corruption in government. Life for average Brazilians remained difficult. Cardoso's loss of popularity opened the door to the political opposition who were able to capitalize on presidential elections in 2002, when Luis Inacio da Silva, or "Lula" as he is popularly known, won a resounding triumph at the polls.

Lula, who worried many foreign observers because of his "leftist" ideology attacked Brazil's myriad problems in a pragmatic fashion. Labor unions, who supported his presidency and expected all of the benefits of political patronage, have been somewhat disillusioned. Lula, in attempt to bring the nation's spending under control, significantly culled the public workforce. With regard to the economy, his policies were not "leftist" but more closely adhered to classical economic approaches. This calmed the fears of foreign investors.

The lament of Brazilian journalist Lins da Silva is still accurate: "Brazilian elites have once again shown how capable they are of solving political crises in a creative and peaceful manner but also how unwilling to promote change in inequitable social structures." The wealth of the nation still remains in the hands of a few, and the educational system has failed to absorb and train as many citizens as it should. Police continue routinely to abuse their power. Lula, who's own family roots lie in the favelas, was deeply sensitive to the needs of Brazil's poor and disadvantaged. He made a point of visiting the slums, of listening to the complaints and needs of people, of behaving, in short, like the classic "patron." President Rousseff is cut from the same cloth and has promised to eradicate poverty.

On a positive note, Brazil's progress in the struggle against AIDS, a disease that contributed to the deaths of 9,600 people in Brazil in 1996, is among the best in the world. In simple terms, the government uses language in the Paris Convention of 1883 to produce low-cost generic drugs similar to costlier medications manufactured abroad. Everyone in Brazil infected with the HIV virus is provided with a "cocktail" of drugs, and with training in how to take them effectively. More than 100,000 Brazilians are on the drug regimen, at an annual cost of $163 million. In 2000, AIDS–related deaths declined to 1,200, and the rate of transmission was sharply reduced.

At a broader level, Brazil has prospered from its membership in Mercosur, a regional trade organization that consists of Argentina, Brazil, Paraguay, and Uruguay. The success of Mercosur has expanded relations with other countries, especially Chile, which became an "associate" member in 1997. Lula, like Cardoso before him, was opposed to Washington's efforts to forge a Free Trade Area of the Americas (FTAA), in part because Mercosur and Brazil consider Europe a more important market and do not send a high percentage of their exports to the United States. Brazil has kept the pressure on other South American governments to convince them to join with Mercosur, not only in a "South American Free Trade Agreement," but in closer ties with the European Union. This independent policy has provided Brazil with leverage in the era of globalization.

Brazil has also become a leader in the use of ethanol as a fuel. Derived from cane sugar, it is used by approximately 80 percent of all vehicles. On the negative side, the use of land to produce fuel has resulted in higher food prices, a fact not lost on tens of thousands of Brazilians who live in poverty.

Statistics

Geography

Area in Square Miles (Kilometers): 3,285,670 (8,512,100) (slightly smaller than the United States)
Capital (Population): Brasília (3, 789,000) (2011 est.)
Environmental Concerns: deforestation; water and air pollution; land degradation
Geographical Features: mostly flat to rolling lowlands in the north; some plains, hills, mountains, and a narrow coastal belt
Climate: mostly tropical or semitropical; temperate zone in the south

People*

Population

Total: 203,429,773 (2011 est.)
Annual Growth Rate: 1.1%
Rural/Urban Population Ratio: 13/87
Ethnic Makeup: 53.7% white; 38% mixed; 6.2% black; 1% others
Major Languages: Portuguese; Spanish; English; French
Religions: 70% nominal Roman Catholic; Protestant 15.4%, others

Health

Life Expectancy at Birth: 69 years (male); 76 years (female)
Infant Mortality Rate (Ratio): 21.17/1,000
Physicians Available (Ratio): 1.7/1000

Education

Adult Literacy Rate: 88%
Compulsory (Ages): 7–14; free

Communication

Telephones: 42,141,000 main lines
Daily Newspaper Circulation: 47 per 1,000 people
Cell Phones: 202,944,000
Internet Users: 75,982,000

Transportation

Roadways in Kilometers (Miles): 1,751,868 (1,088,560)
Railroads in Kilometers (Miles): 29,295 (18,203)
Usable Airfields: 4,072

Government

Type: federal republic
Independence Date: September 7, 1822 (from Portugal)
Head of State/Government: President Dilma Rousseff is both head of state and head of government
Political Parties: Brazilian Democratic Movement Party; Democrats; Workers' Party; Brazilian Workers' Party; Democratic Labor Party; others
Suffrage: voluntary at 16; compulsory between 19 and 70; voluntary over 70

Military

Military Expenditures (% of GDP): 1.7%
Current Disputes: boundary disputes with Uruguay

Economy

Currency ($U.S. Equivalent): 1.77 reals = $1
Per Capita Income/GDP: 10,800/2.172 trillion
GDP Growth Rate: 7.5%
Inflation Rate: 5%
Unemployment Rate: 6.7%
Labor Force: 102,200,000
Natural Resources: bauxite; gold; iron ore; manganese; nickel; phosphates; platinum; tin; uranium; petroleum; hydropower; timber
Agriculture: coffee; rice; corn; sugarcane; soybeans; cotton; manioc; oranges
Industry: textiles; shoes; chemicals; cement; lumber; iron ore; tin; steel; aircraft; motor vehicles and parts; other machinery and equipment
Exports: $201.9 billion (primary partners China, United States, Argentina, Netherlands, Germany)
Imports: $181.7 billion (primary partners United States, China, Argentina, Germany, South Korea)

Suggested Website

http://www.cia.gov/cia/publications/factbook/geos/br.html

*Note: Estimates explicitly take into account the effects of excess mortality due to AIDS.

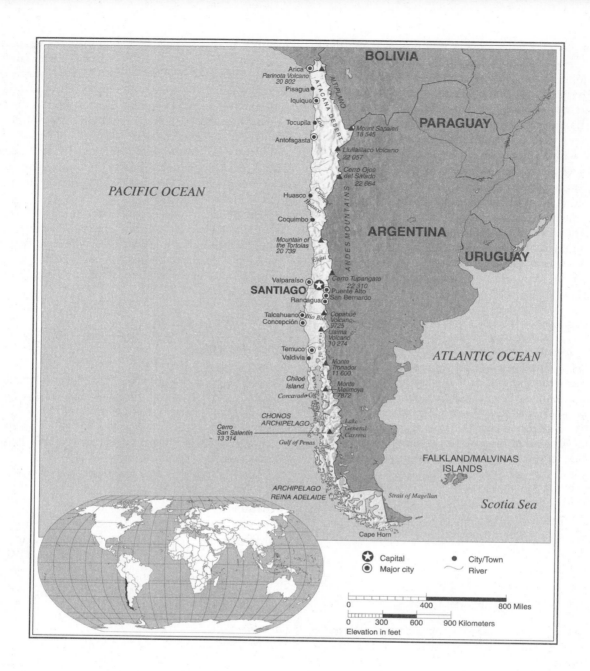

BOLIVIA

PARAGUAY

Arica
Parinota Volcano
20 802
Pisagua
Iquique
Tocupila
Antofagasta

Mount Sapaleri
18 545

Llullaillaco Volcano
22 057

Cerro Ojos
del Salado
22 664

PACIFIC OCEAN

Huasco

Coquimbo

ARGENTINA

Mountain of
the Tortolas
20 739

URUGUAY

Valparaíso
SANTIAGO
Rancagua
Puente Alto
San Bernardo

Cerro Tupangato
22 310

Talcahuano
Concepción

Copahué
Volcano
9725
Llaima
Volcano
10 274

ATLANTIC OCEAN

Temuco
Valdivia

Monte
Tronador
11 600

Chiloé
Island

Monte
Melimoya
7872

Corcavado G.

CHONOS
ARCHIPELAGO

Cerro
San Salentín
13 314

Lake
General
Carrera

Gulf of Penas

FALKLAND/MALVINAS
ISLANDS

ARCHIPELAGO
REINA ADELAIDE

Strait of Magellan

Scotia Sea

Cape Horn

★ Capital
◉ Major city
● City/Town
〰 River

| 0 | 400 | 800 Miles |
| 0 | 300 | 600 | 900 Kilometers |

Elevation in feet

Chile

(Republic of Chile)

CHILE: A NATION ON THE REBOUND

In September 1973, the Chilean military, with the secret support of the U.S. Central Intelligence Agency (CIA), seized power from the constitutionally elected government of President Salvador Allende. Chile, with its long-standing traditions of free and honest elections, respect for human rights, and freedom of the press, was quickly transformed into a brutal dictatorship that arrested, tortured, and killed thousands of its own citizens. In the larger sweep of Chilean history, however, the coup seemed to be the most recent and severe manifestation of a lengthy conflict between social justice, on the one hand, and the requirements of order dictated by the nation's ruling elite, on the other. This was true in the colonial period, when there was conflict between the Roman Catholic Church and landowners over Indian rights. It was also apparent in later confrontations among Marxists, reformers, and conservatives.

FORM, NOT SUBSTANCE

Form, as opposed to substance, had characterized the rule of the Christian Democrats in the 1960s, when they created many separate rural unions, supposedly to address the needs of *campesinos* ("peasants"). A divided union movement in effect became a form of government control that prevented the emergence of a single powerful rural organization.

In the early 1970s, President Allende—despite his talk of socialism and his genuine attempt to destroy the institutions and values of an old social order—used as his weapon of transformation a centralized bureaucracy that would have been recognized by sixteenth-century viceroys and nineteenth-century presidents. Allende's attempts to institute far-reaching social change led to a strong reaction from powerful sectors of Chilean society who felt threatened.

THE 1973 COUP D'ETAT

When the military ousted Allende, it had the support of many Chileans, including the majority of the middle class, who had been hurt by the government's economic policies, troubled by continuous political turmoil, and infuriated by official mismanagement. The military, led by General Augusto Pinochet, began a new experiment with another form of centrist rule: military authoritarianism. The generals made it clear that they had not restored order merely to return it to the "discredited" constitutional practices of the past. They spoke of regeneration, of a new Chile, and of an end to the immorality, corruption, and incompetence of all civilian politics. The military announced in 1974 that, "guided by the inspiration of [Diego] Portales"—one of nineteenth-century Chile's greatest civilian leaders—"the government of Chile will energetically apply the principle of authority and drastically punish any outburst of disorder and anarchy."

The political, economic, and social reforms proposed by the military aimed at restructuring Chile to such an extent that there would no longer be a need for traditional political parties. Economic policy favored free and open competition as the main regulator of economic and social life. The Chilean state rid itself of hundreds of state-owned corporations, struck

TIMELINE

1541
The founding of Santiago de Chile
1818
Independence of Spain is proclaimed
1964–1970
Revolution in Liberty dramatically alters Chilean society
1973
A military coup ousts President Salvador Allende; General Augusto Pinochet becomes president
1988
Pinochet is voted out—and goes
1990s
Asian financial woes cut into Chilean economic growth
2000s
Ricardo Lagos, a moderate Socialist, wins the presidency in December 1999–January 2000 elections
Lagos government accelerates prosecution of human-rights abusers
2006
Chile elects its first woman president, Michelle Bachelet
2010
Conservative Sebastián Piñera assumes presidency; magnitude 8.8 earthquake jolts south-central Chile

(Department of Defense photo by R. D. Ward)

Michelle Bachelet was Chile's first woman president (2006–2010).

down tariffs designed to protect Chilean industry from foreign competition, and opened the economy to widespread foreign investment. The changes struck deeply at the structure of the Chilean economy and produced a temporary but sharp recession, high unemployment, and hundreds of bankruptcies. A steep decline in the standard of living for most Chileans was the result of the government's anti-inflation policy.

Social-welfare programs were reduced to a minimum. The private sector was encouraged to assume many functions and services once provided by the state. Pensions were moved entirely to the private sector as all state programs were phased out. In this instance, the state calculated that workers tied through pensions and other benefits to the success of private enterprise would be less likely to be attracted to "non-Chilean" ideologies such as Marxism, socialism, and even Christian democracy. State-sponsored health programs were also cut to the bone, and many of the poor now paid for services once provided by the government.

■ THE DEFEAT OF A DICTATOR

To attain a measure of legitimacy, Chileans expected the military government to produce economic achievement. By 1987, and continuing into 1989, the regime's economic policies seemed successful; the economic growth rate for 1988 was an impressive 7.4 percent. However, it masked critical weaknesses in the Chilean economy. For example, much of the growth was overdependent on exports of raw materials—notably, copper, pulp, timber, and fishmeal.

Modest economic success and an inflation rate of less than 20 percent convinced General Pinochet that he could take his political scenario for Chile's future to the

voters for their ratification. But in the October 5, 1988, plebiscite, Chile's voters upset the general's plans and decisively denied him an additional eight-year term. (He did, however, continue in office until the next presidential election determined his successor.) The military regime (albeit reluctantly) accepted defeat at the polls, which signified the reemergence of a deep-rooted civic culture and long democratic tradition.

Where had Pinochet miscalculated? Public-opinion surveys on the eve of the election showed a sharply divided electorate. Some political scientists even spoke of the existence of "two Chiles." In the words of government professor Arturo Valenzuela and *Boston Globe* correspondent Pamela Constable, one Chile "embraced those who had benefited from the competitive economic policies and welfare subsidies instituted by the regime and who had been persuaded that power was best entrusted to the armed forces." The second Chile "consisted of those who had been victimized by the regime, who did not identify with Pinochet's anti-Communist cause, and who had quietly nurtured a belief in democracy." Polling data from the respected Center for Public Policy Studies showed that 72 percent of those who voted against the regime were motivated by economic factors. These were people who had lost skilled jobs or who had suffered a decrease in real wages. While Pinochet's economic reforms had helped some, it had also created a disgruntled mass of downwardly mobile wage earners.

Valenzuela and Constable explain how a dictator allowed himself to be voted out of power. "To a large extent Pinochet had been trapped by his own mythology. He was convinced that he would be able to win and was anxious to prove that his regime was not a pariah but a legitimate government. He and other officials came to believe their own propaganda about the dynamic new Chile they had created." The closed character of the regime, with all lines of authority flowing to the hands of one man, made it "impossible for them to accept the possibility that they could lose." And when the impossible occurred and the dictator lost an election played by his own rules, neither civilians on the right nor the military were willing to override the constitutional contract they had forged with the Chilean people.

In March 1990, Chile returned to civilian rule for the first time in almost 17 years, with the assumption of the presidency by Patricio Aylwin. His years in power revealed that tensions still existed between civilian politicians and the military. In 1993, for example, General Pinochet mobilized elements of the army in Santiago—a move that, in the words of the independent newspaper *La Época,* "marked the crystallization of long- standing hostility" between the Aylwin government and the army. The military had reacted both to investigations into human-rights abuses during the Pinochet dictatorship and proposed legislation that would have subordinated the military to civilian control. On the other hand, the commanders of the navy and air force as well as the two right-wing political parties refused to sanction the actions of the army.

(Courtesy of Paul B. Goodwin)

Chilean Vineyard. Wine has become a major export.

President Aylwin regained the initiative when he publicly chastised General Pinochet. Congress, in a separate action, affirmed its supremacy over the judiciary in 1993, when it successfully impeached a Supreme Court justice for "notable dereliction of duty." The court system had been notorious for transferring human-rights cases from civil to military courts, where they were quickly dismissed. The impeachment augured well for further reform of the judicial branch.

Further resistance to the legacy of General Pinochet was expressed by the people when, on December 11, 1993, the center-left coalition candidate Eduardo Frei Ruiz-Tagle won the Chilean presidential election, with 58 percent of the vote. As part of his platform, Frei had promised to bring the military under civilian rule. The parliamentary vote, however, did not give him the two-thirds majority needed to push through such a reform. The trend toward civilian government, though, seemed to be continuing.

Perhaps the final chapter in Pinochet's career began in November 1998, while the former dictator was in London for medical treatment. At that time, the British government received formal extradition requests from the governments of Spain, Switzerland, and France. The charges against Pinochet included attempted murder, conspiracy to murder, torture, conspiracy to torture, hostage taking, conspiracy to take hostages, and genocide, based on Pinochet's alleged actions while in power.

British courts ruled that the general was too ill to stand trial, and Pinochet returned to Chile. In May 2004 a Chilean appeals court revoked Pinochet's immunity from prosecution. Still, in November 2005 Pinochet was arrested on charges of tax fraud and passport forgery in connection with secret bank accounts he maintained under false names in other countries. Almost simultaneously a Chilean judge indicted him on human-rights abuses. Previously, the army had accepted blame for human-rights abuses during the Pinochet era. As the army commander wrote in a Santiago newspaper: "The Chilean Army Chile has taken the difficult but irreversible decision to assume responsibility for all punishable and morally unacceptable acts in the past attributed to it as an institution. . . . Never and for no one can there be any ethical justification for violations of human rights." Importantly, the army's admissions is reassuring to those who wish to pursue human-rights issues but were fearful of the military's possible reaction. Pinochet's death in 2006, before he could be brought to trial, only partially closed this sad chapter in Chile's history.

The election of a conservative president, Sebastián Piñera in 2010, gives a once-discredited right wing in Chilean politics the chance to lay the ghost of Pinochet to rest and become a force for the continued modernizaton of the nation. While his campaign stressed law and order, it also promised job creation. Moreover, in the wake of the devastating earthquake of 2010, Piñera assumed the label the "reconstruction president."

THE ECONOMY

By 1998, the Chilean economy had experienced 13 consecutive years of strong growth. But the Asian financial crisis of that year hit Chile hard, in part because 33 percent of the nation's exports in 1997 went to Asian markets. Copper prices tumbled; and because the largest copper mine is government-owned, state revenues contracted sharply. Following a sharp recession in 1999, the economy once again began to grow. However, domestic recovery has been slow. Unemployment remained high at 9 percent of the workforce, and a growth rate of 5.5 percent did not produce sufficient revenue to finance President Lagos's planned social programs and education initiatives. The sluggish global economy in 2001 was partly to blame, as prices fell for copper, Chile's number-one export.

Snapshot: CHILE

Summarized below is a quick look at the country with regard to its development, freedom, health/welfare, and achievements.

Development

Chile's economy began to rebound in the fourth quarter of 2009, and GDP grew more than 5% in 2010. It achieved this growth despite the magnitude 8.8 earthquake that struck Chile in February 2010. The earthquake and subsequent tsunamis it generated caused considerable damage. The Chilean Ministry of Finance estimated the total immediate losses were close to 17% of GDP.

Freedom

The constitution establishes freedom of speech and of the media, which is usually respected by the authorities. Media independence is reflected in criticism of the government and treatment of sensitive issues. Chile ranked 33rd out of 178 countries in Reporters Without Borders' 2010 world press freedom index. The media "suffer from an extraordinary concentration of ownership," with most outlets owned by two companies, noted the watchdog.

Health/Welfare

Since 1981, all new members of Chile's labor force have been required to contribute 10 percent of their monthly gross earnings to private-pension-fund accounts, which they own. Unfortunately, in 2006 new retirees discovered that their pensions fell far below the guaranteed threshold. One reason was that expenses for managing the funds consumed as much as 33 percent of workers' contributions.

Achievements

Chile's great literary figures, such as Gabriela Mistrál and Pablo Neruda, have a great sympathy for the poor and oppressed. Other major Chilean writers, such as Isabel Allende and Ariel Dorfman, have won worldwide acclaim.

Although there is still a large gap between the rich and poor in Chile, those living in poverty has been reduced from 40 percent to 20 percent over the course of the last decade. The irony is that Chile's economic success story is built on the economic model imposed by the Pinochet regime. "Underlying the current prosperity," writes *New York Times* reporter Larry Rohter, "is a long trail of blood and suffering that makes the thought of reversing course too difficult to contemplate." Many Chileans want to bury the past and move on—but the persistence of memory will not allow closure at this time. Chile has chosen to follow its own course with respect to economic policy. While many of its neighbors in the Southern Cone—notably Argentina, Brazil, Bolivia, Peru, Ecuador, and Venezuela—have moved away from free trade and open markets, Chile remains firmly wed to both.

President Michelle Bachelet, Chile's first woman president, who served in the outgoing Lagos government first as minister of health and then as minister of defense, remained committed to close ties to the United States and to free trade. As a -Socialist she strove to meet the needs of women and the poor—but she also kept in place economic policies that made the -Chilean economy one of the most dynamic in the region. Unemployment fell to 7 -percent at the end of 2007 but in 2010 rose to 10 -percent largely as a consequence of the global recession. Bachelet also amassed a $20 billion Economic and Social Stabilization Fund to provide for social spending. A portion of the high revenues generated by the state-owned copper industry provides money for the fund. That fund is how available for the reconstruction of those parts of Chile hit hard by the earthquake of February 2010, and relief for those civilians who lost homes and employment.

Not all Chileans were pleased with Bachelet's policies. Some were opposed to social change and others felt that change had not occurred as quickly as they expected. Gender was certainly an issue both during her campaign for the presidency and throughout her administration. In an interview with journalist David Rieff she stated that "women say that my election represents a cultural break with the past—a past of sexism, of misogyny." That past exists in the present as Bachelet's male critics complained about her apparent "indecisiveness" in the wake of the earthquake when she hesitated to call in the military to put a halt to widespread looting.

Peruvian novelist and politician Mario Vargas Llosa observes that while Chile "is not paradise," it does have a "stability and economic dynamism unparalleled in Latin America." Indeed, "Chile is moving closer to Spain and Australia and farther from Peru or Haiti." He suggests that there has been a shift in Chile's political culture. "The ideas of economic liberty, a free market open to the world, and private initiative as the motor of progress have become embedded in the people of Chile."

Chilean novelist Ariel Dorfman has a different perspective: "Obviously it is better to be dull and virtuous than bloody and Pinochetista, but Chile has been a very gray country for many years now. Modernization doesn't always have to come with a lack of soul, but I think there is a degree of that happening."

◼ SIGNS OF CHANGE

Although the Chilean Constitution was essentially imposed on the nation by the military in 1980, there are signs of change. The term for president was reduced from eight to six years in 1993; and in 1997, the Chamber of Deputies, the lower house of the Legislature, approved legislation to further reduce the term of a president to four years, with a prohibition on reelection. Military courts, which have broader peacetime jurisdiction than most other countries in the Western Hemisphere, have also come under scrutiny by politicians. According to *Revista Hoy,* as summarized by *CHIP News,* military justice reaches far beyond the ranks. If, for example, several people are involved in the commission of a crime and one of the perpetrators happens to be a member of the military, all are tried in a military court. Another abuse noted by politicians is that the military routinely uses the charge of sedition against civilians who criticize it. A group of Christian Democrats wants to limit the jurisdiction of the military to military crimes committed by military personnel; eliminate the participation of the army prosecutor in the Supreme Court, where he sits on the bench in cases related to the military; grant civilian courts the authority to investigate military premises; and accord civilian courts jurisdiction over military personnel accused of civilian-related crimes. The military itself, in 2004, in an effort to improve its tarnished image has worked in the background to hold accountable those officers involved in human-rights abuses in the past.

Another healthy sign of change is a concerted effort by the Chilean and Argentine governments to discuss issues that have been a historical source of friction between the two nations. Arms escalation, mining exploration and exploitation in border areas, and trade and investment concerns were on the agenda. The Chilean foreign relations minister and the defense minister sat down with their Argentine counterparts in the first meeting of its kind in the history of Argentine–Chilean relations.

■ IMPACT OF THE EARTHQUAKE OF 2010

In February 2010, a massive 8.8 magnitude earthquake, one of the ten strongest ever recorded, struck south central Chile. Hundreds were killed and devastation widespread. An accompanying tsunami annihilated coastal fishing villages. Perhaps one-third of the fishing industry in the impacted area was destroyed, as well as 12 percent of the stock of the wine industry. The pulp and paper industries also suffered substantial losses. Chile's second largest city and an industrial center, Concepción, suffered extensive damage. On a positive note, Chile possesses the resources to meet the human and material challenges. Recovery was well underway in 2011.

Statistics

Geography

Area in Square Miles (Kilometers): 292,280 (756,945) (about twice the size of Montana)

Capital (Population): Santiago 5,883,000 (urban)

Environmental Concerns: air and water pollution; deforestation; loss of biodiversity; soil erosion; desertification

Geographical Features: low coastal mountains; a fertile central valley; rugged Andes Mountains in the east

Climate: temperate; desert in the north; Mediterranean in the center; cool and damp in the south

People

Population

Total: 16,888,760 (2011 est.)

Annual Growth Rate: 0.83%

Rural/Urban Population Ratio: 11/89

Major Language: Spanish

Ethnic Makeup: 95% European and Mestizo; 3% Mapuche; 2% others

Religions: 70% Roman Catholic; 15% Evangelical; 8.3% none

Health

Life Expectancy at Birth: 74 years (male); 81 years (female)

Infant Mortality Rate (Ratio): 7.34/1,000

Physicians Available (Ratio): 1.09/1000

Education

Adult Literacy Rate: 95.7%

Compulsory (Ages): for 8 years; free

Communication

Telephones: 3,458,000 main lines

Daily Newspaper Circulation: 101 per 1,000 people

Cell Phones: 19,852,000

Internet Users: 7,009,000

Transportation

Roadways in Kilometers (Miles): 79,606 (49,464)

Railroads in Kilometers (Miles): 6,585 (4,092)

Usable Airfields: 366

Government

Type: republic

Independence Date: September 18, 1810 (from Spain)

Head of State/Government: President Sebastián Piñera is both head of state and head of government

Political Parties: Coalitions of parties included in the broad-based Alliance for Chile and the Coalition of Parties for Democracy

Suffrage: universal and compulsory at 18

Military

Military Expenditures (% of GDP): 2.7%

Current Disputes: boundary or territorial disputes with Argentina, and Bolivia; territorial claim in Antarctica

Economy

Currency ($U.S. Equivalent): 525.3 pesos = $1

Per Capita Income/GDP: 15,400/$257.9 billion

GDP Growth Rate: 5.3%

Inflation Rate: 1.4%

Unemployment Rate: 7.1%

Labor Force: 7,918,000

Natural Resources: copper; timber; iron ore; nitrates; precious metals; molybdenum; fish; hydropower

Agriculture: wheat; corn; grapes; beans; sugar beets; potatoes; fruit; beef; poultry; wool; timber; fish

Industry: copper and other minerals; foodstuffs; fish processing; iron and steel; wood and wood products; transport equipment; cement; textiles

Exports: $71.03 billion (primary partners China, Japan, United States, Brazil, South Korea)

Imports: $55.17 billion (primary partners United States, China, Argentina, Brazil, South Korea, Japan)

Suggested Website

www.cia.gov/cia/publications/factbook/geos.ci.html

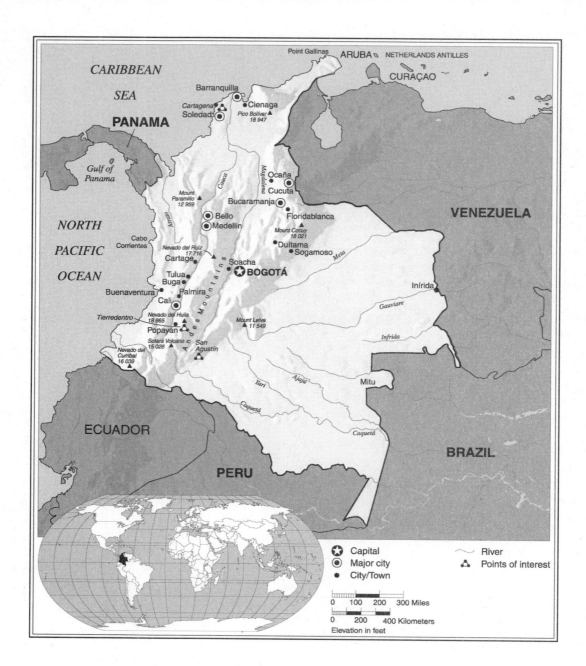

CARIBBEAN

SEA

PANAMA

Point Gallinas
ARUBA
NETHERLANDS ANTILLES
CURAÇAO

Barranquilla
Cartagena
Soledad
Cienaga
Pico Bolívar
18 947

Gulf of
Panama

NORTH

PACIFIC

OCEAN

Mount
Paramillo
12 959

Cauca

Magdalena

Ocaña
Cucuta

Bucaramanja

Floridablanca

Mount Cocuy
18 021

Duítama
Sogamoso

VENEZUELA

Bello
Medellin

Cabo
Corrientes

Nevado del Ruiz
17 716
Cartage

Tulua
Buga
Palmira

Buenaventura
Cali

Tierredentro

Nevado del Huila
18 865

Popayán

Sotará Volcano
15 026

Nevado del
Cumbal
16 039

Soacha
BOGOTÁ

Meta

Inírida

Gauviare

San
Agustín

Mount Leiva
11 549

Infrida

Yari

Ajaja

Mitu

ECUADOR

PERU

Caquetá

Caquetá

BRAZIL

Capital
Major city
City/Town

River
Points of interest

0   100   200   300 Miles

0   200   400 Kilometers

Elevation in feet

Colombia
(Republic of Colombia)

COLOMBIA: THE VIOLENT LAND

Colombia has long been noted for its violent political history. The division of political beliefs in the mid-nineteenth century into conservative and liberal factions produced not only debate but also civil war. To the winner went the presidency and the spoils of office. That competition for office came to a head during the savage War of the Thousand Days (1899–1902). Nearly half a century later, Colombia was again plagued by political violence, which took perhaps 200,000 lives. Although on the surface it is distinct from the nineteenth-century civil wars, *La Violencia* ("The Violence," 1946–1958) offers striking parallels to the violence of the 1800s. Competing factions were again led by conservatives and liberals, and the presidency was the prize. Explanations for this phenomenon have tended to be at once simple and powerful. Colombian writers blame a Spanish heritage and its legacy of lust for political power.

Gabriel García Márquez, in his classic novel *One Hundred Years of Solitude*, spoofed the differences between liberals and conservatives. "The Liberals," said Aureliano Buendia's father-in-law, "were Freemasons, bad people, wanting to hang priests, to institute civil marriage and divorce, to recognize the rights of illegitimate children as equal to those of legitimate ones, and to cut the country up into a federal system that would take power away from the supreme authority." On the other hand, "the Conservatives, who had received their power directly from God, proposed the establishment of public order and family morality. They were the defenders of the faith of Christ, of the principle of authority, and were not prepared to permit the country to be broken down into autonomous entities." Aureliano, when later asked if he was a Liberal or a Conservative, quickly replied: "If I have to be something I'll be a Liberal, because the Conservatives are tricky."

THE ROOTS OF VIOLENCE

The roots of the violence are far more complex than a simple quest for spoils caused by a perceived "flaw" in national character. Historian Charles Bergquist has shown that "divisions within the upper class and the systematic philosophical and programmatic positions that define them are not merely political manifestations of cultural traits; they reflect diverging economic interests within the upper class." These opposing interests developed in both the nineteenth and twentieth centuries. Moreover, to see Colombian politics solely as a violent quest for office ignores long periods of relative peace (1902–1935). But whatever the underlying causes of the violence, it has profoundly influenced contemporary Colombians.

La Violencia was the largest armed conflict in the Western Hemisphere since the Mexican Revolution (1910–1917). It was a civil war of ferocious intensity that cut through class lines and mobilized people from all levels of society behind the banner of either liberalism or conservatism. That elite-led parties were able to win popular support was evidence of their strong organization rather than their opponents' political weakness.

These multiclass parties still dominate Colombian political life, although the fierce interparty rivalry that characterized the civil wars of the

TIMELINE

1525
The first Spanish settlement at Santa Marta
1810
Independence from Spain
1822
The creation of Gran Colombia (including Venezuela, Panama, and Ecuador)
1830
Independence as a separate country
1899–1902
War of the Thousand Days
1946–1958
La Violencia; nearly 200,000 lose their lives
1957
Women's suffrage
1980s
The drug trade becomes big business
1990s
Violence hampers progress; an earthquake kills or injures thousands in central Colombia
2000s
Colombia's violence threatens to involve its neighbors
2008
Growing tensions with neighboring Venezuela and Ecuador
2010
President Juan Manuel Santos elected president
2011
Leader of the FARC killed

111

nineteenth century as well as La Violencia has been stilled. In 1957, Colombia's social elite decided to bury partisan differences and devised a plan to end the widespread strife. Under this National Front agreement, the two parties agreed to divide legislative and bureaucratic positions equally and to alternate the presidency every four years from 1958 to 1974. This form of coalition government proved a highly successful means of elite compromise.

■ THE IMPACT OF LA VIOLENCIA

The violence has left its imprint on the people of Colombia in other ways. Some scholars have suggested that peasants now shun political action because of fear of renewed violence. Refugees from La Violencia generally experienced confusion and a loss of values. Usually, rising literacy rates, improved transportation and communications, and integration into the nation's life produce an upsurge of activism as people clamor for more rapid change. This has not been the case in rural Colombia. Despite guerrilla activity in the countryside—some of which is a spin-off from La Violencia, some of which until recently had a Marxist orientation, and some of which is banditry—the guerrillas have not been able to win significant rural support.

La Violencia also led to the professionalization and enlargement of the Colombian armed forces in the late 1950s and early 1960s. Never a serious participant in the nation's civil wars, the military acquired a new prestige and status unusual for Colombia. It must be considered an important factor in any discussion of Colombian politics today.

A standoff between guerrillas and the military prompted the government of Virgilio Barco to engage reluctantly in a dialogue with the insurgents, with the ultimate goal of peace. In 1988, he announced a three-phase peace plan to end the violence, to talk about needed reforms, and ultimately to reincorporate guerrillas into society. This effort came to fruition in 1991, when the guerrilla movement M-19 laid down its arms after 16 years of fighting and engaged in political dialogue. Other guerrilla groups, notably the long-lived (since 1961) Colombian Revolutionary Armed Forces (FARC) and the National Liberation Army (ELN), led by a Spanish priest, chose to remain in the field.

Numbering perhaps 10,000, at its height, the guerrillas claim that their armed insurgency is about social change; but as *The Economist* has observed, lines between revolution and crime are increasingly blurred. Guerrillas ambush army units, attack oil pipelines, engage in blackmail, and kidnap rich ranchers and foreign oil executives for ransom. Some guerrillas are also in the pay of the drug traffickers and collect a bounty for each helicopter they shoot down in the government's campaign to eradicate coca-leaf and poppy fields.

■ DRUGS AND DEATH

The guerrillas have a different perspective. One FARC leader asserted in an interview with the Colombian news weekly *Semana* that the guerrillas had both political and social objectives. Peace would come only if the government demilitarized large portions of the country and took action against the paramilitary organizations, some of them private and some of them supported by elements within the government. President Andrés Pastrana, who feared losing control of the country as well the credibility of his government, began to press for peace talks in January 1999 and, as a precondition to peace, agreed to demilitarize—that is, to withdraw government soldiers from a number of municipalities in southern Colombia. The United States objected that any policy of demilitarization would result in looser counter-narcotics efforts and urged a broader program to eradicate coca crops through aerial spraying. Critics of the policy claim that crop eradication plays into the hands of the guerrillas, who come to the support of the peasants who grow the coca. There is substance in the criticism, for by late 1999 FARC guerrillas controlled about 40 percent of the countryside.

FARC leaders, contrary to reports of foreign news media, disingenuously claim not to be involved in drug trafficking and have offered their own plan to counter the drug problem. It would begin with a government development plan for the peasants. In the words of a FARC leader: "Thousands of peasants need to produce and grow drugs to live, because they are not protected by the state." Eradication can succeed only if alternative crops can take the place of coca. Rice, corn, cacao, or cotton might be substituted. "Shooting the people, dropping bombs on them, dusting their sown land, killing birds and leaving their land sterile" is not the solution.

The peace talks scheduled between the government and the guerrillas in 1999 stalled and then failed, in large measure because of distrust on the part of FARC. Although a large portion of southern Colombia was demilitarized, the activities of paramilitary organizations were not curbed, and the United States sought to intensify its eradication policy. In the meantime, the Colombian Civil War entered its fourth decade.

In addition to the deaths attributed to guerrilla warfare, literally hundreds of politicians, journalists, judges, and police officers have been murdered in Colombia. It has been estimated that 10 percent of the nation's homicides are politically motivated. Murder is the major cause of death for men between ages 15 and 45. The violence resulted in 250,000 deaths in the 1990s; 300,000 people have left the country; and, since the late 1980s, 1½ million have been internally displaced or become refugees. While paramilitary violence accounts for many deaths, drug trafficking and the unraveling of Colombia's fabric of law are responsible for most. As political scientist John D. Martz writes: "Whatever the responsibility of the military or the rhetoric of government, the penetration of Colombia's social and economic life by the drug industry [is] proving progressively destructive of law, security and the integrity of the political system." Colombian political scientist Juan Gabriel Tokatlian echoed these sentiments in 2001 when he wrote: "The state is losing sovereignty and legitimacy. The left-wing guerrillas and the right-wing paramilitaries control more territory than the government."

Drug traffickers, according to *Latin American Update,* "represent a new economic class in Colombia; since 1981 'narcodollars' have been invested in real estate and large cattle ranches." The newsmagazine *Semana* noted that drug cartels had purchased 2.5 million acres of land since 1984 and now own one-twelfth of the nation's productive farmland in the Magdalena River Basin. More than 100,000 acres of forest have been cut down to grow marijuana, coca, and opium poppies. Of particular concern to environmentalists is the fact that opium poppies are usually planted in the forests of the Andes at elevations above 6,000 feet. "These forests," according to Semana, "do not have great commercial value, but their tree cover is vital to the conservation of the sources of the water supply." The cartels also bought up factories, newspapers, radio stations, shopping centers, soccer teams, and bullfighters. The emergence of Medellín as a modern city of gleaming skyscrapers and expensive cars reflected the enormous profits of the drug business.

Political scientist Francisco Leal Buitrago argues that while trafficking in narcotics in the 1970s was economically motivated, it had evolved into a social phenomenon by the 1980s. "The traffickers represent a new social force that wants to participate like other groups—new urban groups, guerrillas and peasant movements. Like the guerrillas, they have not been able to participate politically. . . ."

Domestic drug consumption has also emerged as a serious problem in Colombia's cities. *Latin American Regional Reports* notes that the increase in consumption of the Colombian form of crack, known as *bazuko,* "has prompted the growth of gangs of youths in slum areas running the bazuko business for small distributors." In Bogotá, police reported that more than 1,500 gangs operated from the city's slums.

■ URBANIZATION

As is the case in other Andean nations, urbanization has been rapid in Colombia. But the constantly spreading slums on the outskirts of the larger cities have not produced significant urban unrest or activism. Most of the migrants to the cities are first generation and are less frustrated and demanding than the general urban population. The new migrants perceive an improvement in their status and opportunities simply because they have moved into a more hopeful urban environment. Also, since most of the migrants are poorly paid, their focus tends to be on daily survival, not political activism.

Migrants make a significant contribution to the parallel Colombian economy. As is the case in Peru and other South American countries, the informal sector amounts to approximately 30 percent of gross domestic product.

The Roman Catholic Church in Colombia has also tended to take advantage of rapid urbanization. Depending on the individual beliefs of local bishops, the Church has to a greater or lesser extent embraced the migrants, brought them into the Church, and created or instilled a sense of community where none existed before. The Church has generally identified with the expansion and change taking place and has played an active social role.

Marginalized city dwellers are often the targets of violence. Hired killers, called *sicarios,* have murdered hundreds of petty thieves, beggars, prostitutes, indigents, and street children. Such "clean-up" campaigns are reminiscent of the activities of the Brazilian death squads since the 1960s. An overloaded judicial system and interminable delays have contributed to Colombia's high homicide rate. According to government reports, lawbreakers have not been brought to justice in 97 to 99 percent of *reported* crimes. (Perhaps three-quarters of all crimes remain unreported to the authorities.) Increasingly, violence and murder have replaced the law as a way to settle disputes; private "justice" is now commonly resorted to for a variety of disputes.

■ SOCIAL CHANGE

Government has responded to calls for social change and reform. President Virgilio Barco sincerely believed that the eradication of poverty would help to eliminate guerrilla warfare and reduce the scale of violence in the countryside. Unfortunately, his policies lacked substance, and he was widely criticized for his indecisiveness.

President César Gaviria felt that political reform must precede social and economic change and was confident that Colombia's new Constitution would set the process of national reconciliation in motion. The constitutional debate generated some optimism about the future of liberal democracy in Colombia. As Christopher Abel writes, it afforded a forum for groups ordinarily denied a voice in policy formulation—"to civic and community movements in the 40 and more intermediate cities angry at the poor quality of basic public services; to indigenous movements. . . .; and to cooperatives, blacks, women, pensioners, small businesses, consumer and sports groups."

Violence and unrest have thwarted all of these efforts. Since the mid-1980s, according to a former Minister of Defence writing in 2000, 200 car bombs had exploded in Colombian cities, an entire democratic left of center party (the Unión Patriotica) had been eliminated by right-wing paramilitaries, and 4 presidential candidates, 200 judges and investigators, half of the supreme court justices, 1,200 police, 151 journalists, and 300,000 ordinary Colombians had been murdered.

While some scholars have described Colombia as a "failed state" others perceptively note that the focus should be on what holds the nation together in the face of unprecedented assaults. In the words of political scientist Malcolm Deas, Colombia is more united than fragmented, ethnically and religiously homogeneous, and its regional differences, while real, are not especially divisive. President Alvaro Uribe, a tough-minded pragmatist, has worked hard to restore the rule of law to Colombia. His first year in office resulted in a significant reduction in murder and kidnapping and attacks by guerrillas, as well as acreage devoted to coca cultivation. Economic recovery was underway, as is indicated by the increased amount of highway traffic. Colombians, for the first time in years, felt more secure and, in 2004, 80 percent of the voting population supported Uribe. A reflection of both his popularity and success was the decision of Colombia's Congress to pass an amendment to the Constitution that would allow Uribe to run for reelection in 2006. As was expected, Uribe won a second term and won praise for his campaign against the guerrillas as well as some success in reducing the incidence of murder and kidnapping. The courts turned down his request to run for a third term in 2010, and his heir-apparent, Manuel Santos, a former defense minister, won the presidency in a tough political campaign. The anti-guerrilla policy of Santos produced dramatic results in 2011 with the death of FARC's number one commander in a military raid. Santos said: "I want to send a message to every member of this organization [FARC]: demobilize. Because if you don't, as we've said so many times and as we've shown, you will end up in jail or a grave." On the other hand, FARC has proven to be remarkably resilient.

ECONOMIC POLICIES

Colombia has a mixed economy. While state enterprises control domestic participation in the coal and oil industries and play a commanding role in the provision of electricity and communications, most of the economy is dominated by private business. At this point, Colombia is a moderate oil producer. A third of the nation's legal exports comes from the coffee industry, while exports of coal, cut flowers, seafood, and other nontraditional exports have experienced significant growth. In that Colombia is not saddled with an onerous foreign debt, its economy is relatively prosperous.

Contributing to economic success is the large informal sector. Also of tremendous importance are the profits from the illegal-drug industry. *The Economist* estimated that Colombia grossed perhaps $1.5 billion in drug sales in 1987, as compared to official export earnings of $5.5 billion. Indeed, over the past 20 years, profits from drug trafficking have grown to encompass between 25 and 35 percent of Colombia's legal exports. Perhaps half the profits are repatriated—that is, converted from dollars into local currency. An unfortunate side effect of the inflow of cash is widespread corruption in virtually all of the nation's institutions.

FOREIGN POLICY

In the foreign-policy arena, President Barco's policies were attacked as low-profile, shallow, and too closely aligned to the policies of the United States. While Presidents Gaviria and Samper tried to adopt more independent foreign policy lines, especially in terms of the drug trade, Presidents Pastrana, Uribe, and Santos have welcomed United States aid against drug trafficking and its attendant evils.

With an uneasy peace reigning in Central America, Colombia's focus has turned increasingly toward its neighbors and a festering territorial dispute with Venezuela over waters adjacent to the Guajira Peninsula. Colombia has proposed a multilateral solution to the problem, perhaps under the auspices of the International Court of Justice. Venezuela continues to reject a multilateral approach and seeks to limit any talks to the two countries concerned. It is likely that a sustained deterioration of internal conditions in either Venezuela or Colombia will keep the territorial dispute in the forefront. A further detriment to better relations with Venezuela is the justified Venezuelan fear that Colombian violence as a result of guerrilla activity, military sweeps, and drugs will cross the border. As it is, thousands of Colombians have fled to Venezuela to escape their violent homeland. Venezuela's president recently infuriated Colombia's government when he independently opened negotiations with guerrillas and implied that they had more power than did President Uribe. Tensions between the two countries intensified briefly in 2008 when Colombia, following a raid into Ecuador to root out a guerrilla camp, discovered evidence that Venezuela's President Chavez apparently funded FARC.

THE CLOUDED FUTURE

Francisco Leal Buitrago, a respected Colombian academic, argues forcefully that his nation's crisis is, above all, "political": "It is the lack of public confidence in the political regime. It is not a crisis of the state itself . . . , but in the way in which the state sets the norms—the rules for participation—for the representation of public opinion. . . ."

Constitutional reforms have taken place in Colombia, but changes in theory must reflect the country's tumultuous realities. Many of those in opposition have looked for a political opening but in the meantime continue to wage an armed insurgency against the government. Other problems, besides drugs, that dog the

FURTHER INVESTIGATION

For more information on Colombian emeralds, visit http://gosouthamerica.about.com/cs/southamerica/a/Colemeralds.htm

Snapshot: COLOMBIA

Summarized below is a quick look at the country with regard to its development, freedom, health/welfare, and achievements.

Development

According to the CIA World Factbook the Santos administration has highlighted five "locomotives" to stimulate economic growth: extractive industries, agriculture, infrastructure, housing, and innovation. Colombia is third largest exporter of oil to the United States. President Santos, inaugurated in August 2010, also introduced unprecedented legislation to better distribute extractive industry royalties and compensate Colombians who lost their land due to decades of violence. He also seeks to build on improvements in domestic security and on President Uribe's promarket economic policies.

Freedom

Many journalists were harassed or endangered during 2010. A journalist, who had been threatened before, believes an attempt on his life was connected to his reports on local operations of drug gangs. Freedom House reports that terrorism continues to be a problem in Colombia, and it affects press freedom. Reporters in community media appear at an increasing risk in rural areas, often forced to rely on self-censorship to protect their lives.

Health/Welfare

The United Nations wants Colombia to improve conditions for women, especially those who are victims of the country's armed conflict, the organization said in its 2010 Women's Day report.

According to official figures, more than one million women in Colombia are displaced by violence. In many cases women are forced to flee their homes to avoid themselves or their children being recruited by illegal armed groups like the FARC.

Achievements

Colombia has a long tradition in the arts and humanities and has produced international figures such as the Nobel Prize–winning author Gabriel Garc'a Márquez; the painters and sculptors Alejandro Obregón, Fernando Botero, and Edgar Negret; the poet León de Greiff; and many others well known in music, art, and literature.

---

government include corruption, violence, slow growth, high unemployment, a weak currency, inflation, and the need for major reforms in banking. To get the economy on track, the International Monetary Fund has recommended that Colombia broaden its tax base, enhance municipal tax collections, get tough on tax evasion, and reduce spending.

Endemic violence and lawlessness, the continued operation of guerrilla groups, the emergence of mini-cartels in the wake of the eclipse of drug kingpins, and the attitude of the military toward conditions in Colombia all threaten any kind of progress. Recent violence (March 2010) includes a deadly car bomb attack in the port city of Buenaventura, attributed to the guerrilla group FARC, and a homicide rate that rose 16 percent in 2009 after several years of decline. Ominously, paramilitary groups have transformed into criminal organizations with connections to the cocaine trade. As was the case in earlier years with the drug cartels, the money generated by the illegal trade is used to buy into legitimate businesses. The hard-line antidrug trafficking policy of the United States adds another complicated, and possibly counterproductive, dimension to the difficult task of governing Colombia.

Statistics

Geography

Area in Square Miles (Kilometers): 440,000 (1,139,600) (about 3 times the size of Montana)

Capital (Population): Bogotá 8,262,000 (urban)

Environmental Concerns: deforestation; soil damage; air pollution

Geographical Features: flat coastal lowlands; central highlands; high Andes Mountains; eastern lowland plains

Climate: tropical on coast and eastern plains; cooler in highlands

People

Population

Total: 44,725,543 (2011 est.)

Annual Growth Rate: 1.15%

Rural/Urban Population Ratio: 25/75

Major Language: Spanish

Ethnic Makeup: 58% Mestizo; 20% white; 14% mulatto; 4% African; 3% African Indian; 1% Indian

Religions: 90% Roman Catholic; 10% other

Health

Life Expectancy at Birth: 71 years (male); 78 years (female)

Infant Mortality Rate (Ratio): 16.39/1,000;

Physicians Available (Ratio): 1.35/1000

Education

Adult Literacy Rate: 90.4%

Compulsory (Ages): for 5 years between 6 and 12; free

Communication

Telephones: 6,809,000 main lines

Daily Newspaper Circulation: 55 per 1,000 people

Cell Phones: 43,405,000

Internet Users: 22,538,000

Transportation

Roadways in Kilometers (Miles): 112,998 (70,207)

Railroads in Kilometers (Miles): 3,304 (2,053)

Usable Airfields: 990

Government

Type: republic

Independence Date: July 10, 1810 (from Spain)

Head of State/Government: President Juan Manuel Santos is both head of state and head of government

Political Parties: Liberal Party; Conservative Party; Alternative Democratic Pole; Radical Change; Social National Unity Party

Suffrage: universal at 18

Military

Military Expenditures (% of GDP): 3.4%

Current Disputes: civil war; maritime boundary dispute with Venezuela; territorial disputes with Nicaragua

Economy

Currency ($U.S. Equivalent): 1870 pesos = $1

Per Capita Income/GDP: 9,800/435.4 billion

GDP Growth Rate: 4.3%

Inflation Rate: 2.3%

Unemployment Rate: 12%

Labor Force: 21,780,000

Natural Resources: petroleum; natural gas; coal; iron ore; nickel; gold; copper; emeralds; hydropower

Agriculture: coffee; cut flowers; bananas; rice; tobacco; corn; sugarcane; cocoa beans; oilseed; vegetables; forest products; shrimp farming

Industry: textiles; food processing; petroleum; clothing and footwear; beverages; chemicals; cement; gold; coal; emeralds

Exports: $40.78 billion (primary partners United States, European Union, China, Ecuador, Portugal)

Imports: $38.64 billion (primary partners United States, China, Mexico, Brazil, Germany)

Suggested Website

www.cia.gov/cia/publications/factbook/index.htm

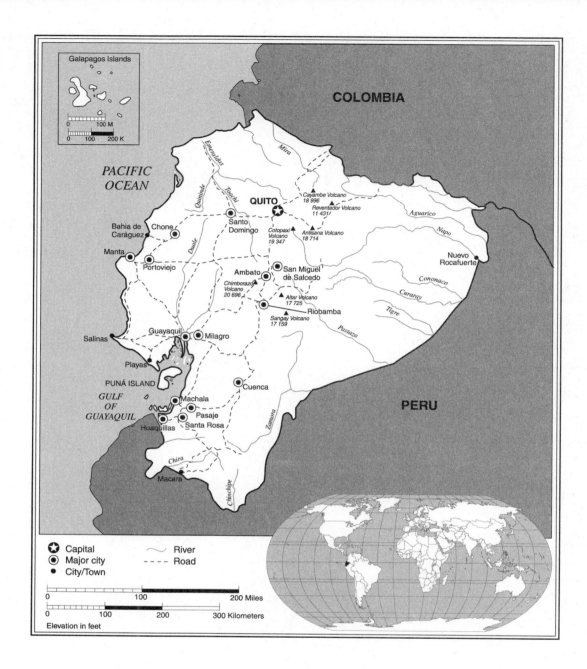

Galapagos Islands

0   100 M

0   100   200 K

PACIFIC
OCEAN

COLOMBIA

Emeraldas

Mira

Quininde

Toachi

QUITO

Cayambe Volcano
18 996

Reventador Volcano
11 431

Aguarico

Bahia de
Caráguez

Chone

Santo
Domingo

Cotopaxi
Volcano
19 347

Antisana Volcano
18 714

Napo

Duale

Manta

Portoviejo

Nuevo
Rocafuerte

Ambato

San Miguel
de Salcedo

Chimborazo
Volcano
20 696

Altar Volcano
17 725

Riobamba

Sangay Volcano
17 159

Cononaco

Curaray

Tigre

Pastaza

Salinas

Guayaquil

Milagro

Playas

PUNÁ ISLAND

GULF
OF
GUAYAQUIL

Machala

Cuenca

PERU

Pasaje

Santa Rosa

Huaquillas

Zamora

Chira

Macara

Chinchipe

★ Capital

◉ Major city

● City/Town

∼ River

--- Road

0   100   200 Miles

0   100   200   300 Kilometers

Elevation in feet

Ecuador

(Republic of Ecuador)

ECUADOR: A LAND OF CONTRASTS

Several of Ecuador's great novelists have had as the focus of their works the exploitation of the Indians. Jorge Icaza's classic *Huasipungo* (1934) describes the actions of a brutal landowner who first forces Indians to work on a road so that the region might be "developed" and then forces them, violently, from their plots of land so that a foreign company's operations will not be impeded by a troublesome Indian population.

That scenario, while possible in some isolated regions, is for the most part unlikely in today's Ecuador. In recent years, despite some political and economic dislocation, Ecuador has made progress in health care, literacy, human rights, freedom of the press, and representative government. Indigenous peoples have been particularly active and over the past decade have demanded cultural rights. An indigenous political party, Pachakutik, has identified with Ecuador's nonindigenous poor and won several seats in Congress. In protest against an economic program of austerity and reflecting ethnic and social conflict, several of these groups in league with mid-level army officers moved to topple President Jamil Mahuad from power in January 2000. It was South America's first successful coup in a quarter of a century. In April 2005 President Lucio Gutierrez, who was behind the coup, was himself ousted from the executive office. He lost the support of indigenous leaders, middle-class homemakers, and students who were angry both over his inability to deliver on promises made and widespread corruption. Austerity policies have hurt the indigenous poor and Ecuador's large public debt has hamstrung social programs.

Although Ecuador is still a conservative, traditional society, it has shown an increasing concern for the plight of its rural inhabitants, including the various endangered Indian groups inhabiting the Amazonian region. The new attention showered on rural Ecuador—traditionally neglected by policymakers in Quito, the capital city—reflects in part the government's concern with patterns of internal migration. Even though rural regions have won more attention from the state, social programs continue to be implemented only sporadically.

Two types of migration are currently taking place: the move from the highlands to the coastal lowlands and the move from the countryside to the cities. In the early 1960s, most of Ecuador's population was concentrated in the mountainous central highlands. Today, the population is about equally divided between that area and the coast, with more than half the nation's people crowded into the cities. So striking and rapid has the population shift been that the director of the National Institute of Statistics commented that it had assumed "alarming proportions" and that the government had to develop appropriate policies if spreading urban slums were not to develop into "potential focal points for insurgency." What has emerged is a rough political parity between regions that has led to parliamentary paralysis and political crisis.

The large-scale movement of people has not rendered the population more homogenous but, because of political parity, has instead fractured the nation. Political rivalry has always characterized relations between Quito, in the highlands (*sierra*), and cosmopolitan Guayaquíl, on the

TIMELINE

1528
First Spanish contact

1822
Ecuador is part of Gran Colombia (with Panama, Venezuela, and Colombia); independence as a separate state

1929
Women's suffrage

1941
A border war with Peru

1990s
Modernization laws aim to speed the privatization of the economy
Popular dissatisfaction with the government's handling of the economy rises

2000s
El Niño devastates the coastal economy; refugees and drug activity spill into Ecuador from Colombia

2006
Rafael Correa elected president

2007
Constituent Assembly begins to rewrite Ecuador's Constitution

2011
Strong economic growth driven by high oil prices

119

(USAID/Satre Comunicaciones)

Men harvesting cacao beans that will be processed into chocolate. Farmers in the Ecuadorian Amazon harvest and process cocoa beans and sell the resulting chocolate worldwide.

DID YOU KNOW?

The Confederation of Indigenous Nationalities of Ecuador (CONAIE) represents most indigenous nationalities. It has successfully developed the capacity to unify indigenous communities to address common problems, such as land, education, poverty, and discrimination.

coast. The presidential election of 1988 illustrated the distinctive styles of the country. Rodrigo Borja's victory was regionally based, in that he won wide support in Ecuador's interior provinces. Usually conservative in its politics, the interior voted for the candidate of the Democratic Left, in part because of the extreme populist campaign waged by a former mayor of Guayaquíl, Abdalá Bucaram. Bucaram claimed to be a man of the people who was persecuted by the oligarchy. He spoke of his lower-class followers as the "humble ones," or, borrowing a phrase from former Argentine president Juan Perón, *los descamisados* ("the shirtless ones"). Bucaram, in the words of political scientist Catherine M. Conaghan, "honed a political style in the classic tradition of coastal populism. He combined promises of concrete benefits to the urban poor with a colorful anti-oligarchic style." Bucaram's style finally triumphed in 1996, when he won election to the presidency.

A similar style and message propelled the country's current president, the charismatic Rafael Correa, to power. He, like Bucaram, addressed the plight of marginalized elements of society and embraced the rhetoric of populism

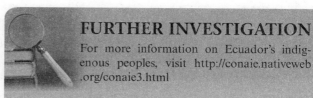

FURTHER INVESTIGATION

For more information on Ecuador's indigenous peoples, visit http://conaie.nativeweb .org/conaie3.html

in his campaign. Correa conceived of himself as "morally superior" and said he was "God's envoy." While he has promised a "citizen's revolution," Correa also seeks to rewrite Ecuador's Constitution with an eye to strengthening the executive office. Venezuela's Hugo Chávez and his professed "Bolivarian Revolution" are admired by Correa, although he is careful to chart an independent course for Ecuador.

■ EDUCATION AND HEALTH

Central to the government's policy of development is education. Twenty-nine percent of the national budget was set aside for education in the early 1980s, with increases proposed for the following years. Adult literacy improved from 74 percent in 1974 to 91 percent by 2009. In the central highlands, however, illiteracy rates of more than 35 percent are still common, largely because Quechua is the preferred language among the Indian peasants.

The government has approached this problem with an unusual sensitivity to indigenous culture. Local Quechua speakers have been enlisted to teach reading and writing in both Quechua and Spanish. This approach has won the support of Indian leaders who are closely involved in planning local literacy programs built around indigenous values.

Health care has also shown steady improvement, but the total statistics hide sharp regional variations. Infant mortality and malnutrition are still severe problems in rural areas. In this sense, Ecuador suffers from a duality found in other Latin American nations with large Indian populations: Social and racial differences persist between the elite-dominated capitals and the Indian hinterlands. Income, services, and resources tend to be concentrated in the capital cities. Ecuador, at least, is attempting to correct the imbalance.

The profound differences between Ecuador's highland Indian and its European cultures is illustrated by the story of an Indian peasant who, when brought to a clinic, claimed that he was dying as the result of a spell. He told the doctor, trained in Western medicine, that, while traveling a path from his highland village down to a valley, he passed by a sacred place, where a witch cast a spell on him. The man began to deteriorate, convinced that this had happened. The doctor, upon examination of the patient, could find no physical reason for the man's condition. Medicine produced no improvements. The doctor finally managed to save his patient, but only after a good deal of compromise with Indian culture. "Yes," he told the peasant, "a witch has apparently cast a spell on you and you are indeed dying." And then the doctor announced: "Here is a potion that will remove the spell." The patient's recovery was rapid and complete. Thus, though modern medicine can work miracles, health-care workers must also be sensitive to cultural differences.

■ THE ECONOMY

Between 1998 and 2000, the Ecuadoran economy was hit hard by two crises. Falling petroleum prices in combination with the ravages of the El Niño phenomenon transformed a $598 million surplus in 1997 into a troubling $830 million deficit in 1998. Petroleum revenues fell to third place, behind exports of bananas and shrimp, which themselves were devastated by bad weather (in the case of shrimp, due to the dramatic warming of waters in the eastern Pacific as a result of El Niño).

President Jamil Mahuad was confronted from the outset of his administration with some daunting policy decisions. A projected growth rate for 1998 of only 1 percent and an inflation rate that soared to 40 percent resulted in budget austerity and an emergency request to Congress to cut spending and prepare legislation for the privatization of Ecuador's telecommunications and electrical industries. The privatization plans raised the ire of nationalists. In the mid-1990s, the government privatized more than 160 state-owned enterprises and, in an effort to modernize and streamline the economy, cut the number of public employees from 400,000 to 260,000.

The sharp economic downturn resulted in severe belt-tightening by the Mahuad government, threw people out of work, produced social and political upheaval, and led to a coup. The military quickly handed over power to the civilian vice president, Gustavo Noboa, to finish out Mahuad's term. Noboa took steps to restore Ecuador's economic viability and adopted some of Mahuad's unpopular policies, including "dollarization" of the economy and continued privatization of state enterprises.

Chronic political instability, which saw the removal of three presidents between 1997 and 2005, has had a negative impact on the government's ability to formulate policies and deliver needed programs on a consistent basis. One result is a continuous drumbeat of opposition from a broad range of Ecuadorans, from the indigenous peoples of the Amazon to the slums around large cities to a large sector of the middle class. The climate for foreign investment has become troublesome and attacks on oil fields and facilities have tended to negate any benefits that might have accrued from rising petroleum prices. President Correa's tighter controls on the private oil industry put a damper on foreign investment and slowed the economy, which had grown at a rate of 5.5 percent between 2002 and 2006.

A combination of global recession and anti-investment policies by the Correa government resulted in a negative 1 percent GDP in 2009. In that year, the government terminated 13 bilateral investment treaties with other nations. The result produced economic uncertainty and discouraged both domestic and foreign investment. However, rebounding oil prices in 2011 and 2012, combined with Chinese loans, have raised expectations that Ecuador's growth rate would approach 6%.

■ BITTER NEIGHBORS

A long legacy of boundary disputes that reached back to the wars for independence created a strained relationship between Ecuador and Peru, which erupted in violence in July 1941. Ecuador initiated an undeclared war against Peru in an attempt to win territory along its southeastern border, in the Marañón River region, and, in the southwest, around the town of Zaramilla. In the 1942 Pact of Peace, Amity, and Limits, which followed a stunning Peruvian victory, Ecuador lost about 120,000 square miles of territory. The peace accord was guaranteed by Argentina, Brazil, Chile, and the United States. In January 1995, the usual tensions that grew each year as the anniversary of the conflict approached were given foundation when fighting again broke out between Peru and Ecuador; Peruvian soldiers patrolling the region had stumbled upon well-prepared and waiting Ecuadoran soldiers. Three weeks later, with the intervention of the guarantors of the original pact, the conflict ended. The Peruvian armed forces were shaken from their smug sense of superiority over the Ecuadorans, and the Ecuadoran defense minister used the fight to support his political pretensions.

The border war sent waves of alarm through the rest of Latin America, in that it reminded more than a dozen nations of boundary problems with their neighbors. Of particular concern were revelations made in 1998 and 1999 that individuals within the Argentine government and the military had sold arms to the Ecuadoran military during the conflict. Argentina was embarrassed because it was one of the original guarantors of the 1942 Pact of Peace.

On October 16, 1998, the legislatures of Ecuador and Peru supported an agreement worked out by other governments in the region to end the border dispute. Under the terms of the agreement, Peru's sovereignty of the vast majority of the contested territory was affirmed. Ecuador won a major concession when it was granted navigation rights on the Amazon River and its tributaries within Peru and the right to establish trading centers on the river. In that both parties benefited from the negotiation, it is hoped that a lasting peace will have been effected.

Relations between Ecuador and Colombia deteriorated in 2008. Colombian troops crossed the border and attacked a guerrilla camp used by FARC (Colombian guerrillas). More broadly, Ecuador has demanded that the United States close its large airbase at Manta, which was used for drug surveillance flights. As a result, the United States moved its aircraft to bases in Colombia.

Snapshot: ECUADOR

Summarized below is a quick look at the country with regard to its development, freedom, health/welfare, and achievements.

Development

MercoPress reported in June 2011 that Ecuador's bonds are rewarding investors with the best performance in Latin America as Chinese loans in the amount of $3 billion and higher oil prices boost confidence in the economy two years after the country defaulted on US $3.2 billion in debt.

Freedom

Freedom House reported that while freedom of expression is generally observed, and the media are outspoken, "the sector is increasingly polarized between the active private media, which is generally sympathetic to the opposition, and the growing set of state-controlled outlets. President Correa often lambastes journalists, and his hostile rhetoric has been blamed for an increase in physical attacks on and harassment of reporters and news outlets." In 2010, press watchdog Fundamedios reported 151 cases of harassment against journalists, a sharp increase over the previous year.

Health/Welfare

Educational and economic opportunities in Ecuador are often not made available to women, blacks, and indigenous peoples. Most of the nation's peasantry, overwhelmingly Indian or Mestizo, are poor. Infant mortality, malnutrition, and epidemic diseases are common among these people.

Achievements

Ecuadoran poets have often made their poetry an expression of social criticism. The so-called Tzántzicos group has combined avant-garde techniques with social commitment and has won a measure of attention from literary circles.

Statistics

Geography

Area in Square Miles (Kilometers): 109,454 (283,560) (about the size of Nevada)

Capital (Population): Quito (1,801,000)

Environmental Concerns: deforestation; soil erosion; desertification; water pollution; pollution from petroleum wastes

Geographical Features: coastal plain; inter-Andean central highlands; flat to rolling eastern jungle

Climate: varied; tropical on the coast and in the inland jungle; cooler inland at higher elevations

People

Population

Total: 15,007,343 (2011 est.)

Annual Growth Rate: 1.44%

Rural/Urban Population Ratio: 33/67

Major Languages: Spanish; Quechua and other Amerindian languages

Ethnic Makeup: 65% Mestizo; 25% Indian; 10% Spanish, black, and others

Religions: 95% Roman Catholic; 5% indigenous and others

Health

Life Expectancy at Birth: 73 years (male); 79 years (female)

Infant Mortality Rate (Ratio): 19.65/1,000

Physicians Available (Ratio): 1.48/1000

Education

Adult Literacy Rate: 91%

Compulsory (Ages): for 6 years between 6 and 14; free

Communication

Telephones: 2,086,000 main lines

Daily Newspaper Circulation: 72 per 1,000 people

Cell Phones: 14,781,000

Internet Users: 3,352,000

Transportation

Roadways in Kilometers (Miles): 43,197 (26,841)

Railroads in Kilometers (Miles): 966 (600)

Usable Airfields: 418

Government

Type: republic

Independence Date: May 24, 1822 (from Spain)

Head of State/Government: President Rafael Correa is both head of state and head of government

Political Parties: Democratic Left; Patriotic Society Party; Pachakutik; Popular Democratic Movement; Alianza PAIS Movement; National Action Institutional; Renewal Party; Rodolsist Party; others

Suffrage: universal and compulsory for literate people ages 18–65; optional for other eligible voters

Military

Military Expenditures (% of GDP): 2.8%

Economy

Currency ($U.S. Equivalent): 1.00 dollar = $1

Per Capita Income/GDP: 7,800/$115 billion

GDP Growth Rate: 3.2%

Inflation Rate: 3.6%

Unemployment Rate: 7.6%;

Labor Force: 4,645,000

Natural Resources: petroleum; fish; timber; hydropower

Agriculture: bananas; coffee; cocoa; rice; potatoes; manioc; plantains; sugarcane; livestock; balsa wood; fish; shrimp

Industry: petroleum; food processing; textiles; metalwork; paper products; wood products; chemicals; plastics; fishing; lumber

Exports: $18.06 billion (primary partners United States, Panama, Peru, Colombia, Russia, Chile)

Imports: $19.64 billion (primary partners United States, Colombia, China, Venezuela, Brazil)

Suggested Website

www.cia.gov/cia/publications/factbook/geos.ec.html

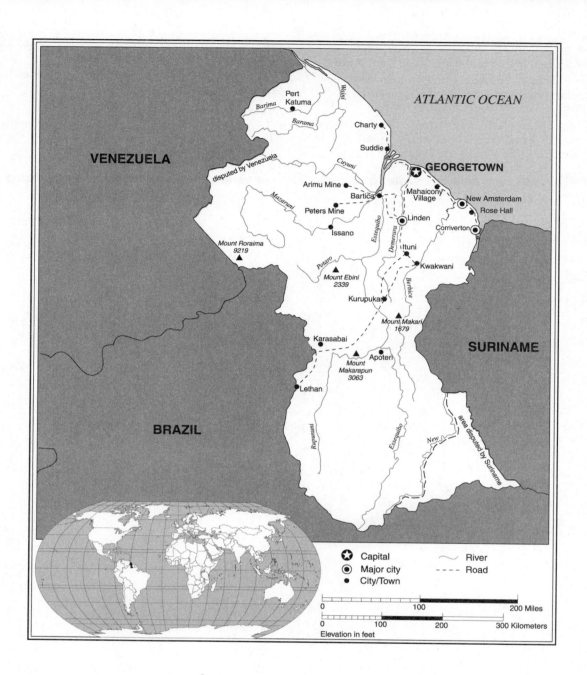

VENEZUELA

ATLANTIC OCEAN

Waini

Pert Katuma

Barima

Barama

Charty

Suddie

GEORGETOWN

Cioyuni

disputed by Venezuela

Arimu Mine

Bartica

Mahaicony Village

New Amsterdam

Rose Hall

Mazaruni

Peters Mine

Linden

Corriverton

Issano

Essequibo

Demerara

Ituni

Potaro

Mount Roraima
9219

Kwakwani

Mount Ebini
2339

Berbice

Kurupukari

Mount Makari
1679

SURINAME

Karasabai

Apoteri

Mount
Makarapun
3063

BRAZIL

Lethan

Rupununi

Essequibo

New

area disputed by Suriname

⊗ Capital

◉ Major city

● City/Town

〜 River

- - - Road

0		100		200 Miles

0	100	200	300 Kilometers

Elevation in feet

Guyana
(Cooperative Republic of Guyana)

GUYANA: RACIAL AND ETHNIC TENSIONS

Christopher Columbus, who cruised along what are now Guyana's shores in 1498, named the region *Guiana*. The first European settlers were the Dutch, who settled in Guyana late in the sixteenth century, after they had been ousted from Brazil by a resurgent Portuguese Crown. Dutch control ended in 1796, when the British gained control of the area. In 1815, as part of the treaty arrangements that brought the Napoleonic Wars to a close, the Dutch colonies of Essequibo, Demerera, and Berbice were officially ceded to the British. In 1831, the former Dutch colonies were consolidated as the Crown Colony of British Guiana.

Guyana is a society deeply divided along racial and ethnic lines. East Indians make up the majority of the population. They predominate in rural areas, constituting the bulk of the labor force on the sugar plantations, and they comprise nearly all of the rice-growing peasantry. They also dominate local businesses and are prominent in the professions. Blacks are concentrated in urban areas, where they are employed in clerical and secretarial positions in the public bureaucracy, in teaching, and in semiprofessional jobs. A black elite dominates the state bureaucratic structure.

Before Guyana's independence in 1966, plantation owners, large merchants, and British colonial administrators consciously favored some ethnic groups over others, providing them with a variety of economic and political advantages. The regime of President Forbes Burnham revived old patterns of discrimination for political gain.

Burnham, after ousting the old elite when he nationalized the sugar plantations and the bauxite mines, built a new regime that simultaneously catered to lower-class blacks and discriminated against East Indians. In an attempt to address the blacks' basic human needs, the Burnham government greatly expanded the number of blacks holding positions in public administration. To demonstrate his largely contrived black-power ideology, Burnham spoke out strongly in support of African liberation movements. The government played to the fear of communal strife in order to justify its increasingly authoritarian rule.

In the mid-1970s, a faltering economy and political mismanagement generated an increasing opposition to Burnham that cut across ethnic lines. The government increased the size of the military, packed Parliament through rigged elections, and amended the Constitution so that the president held virtually imperial power.

There has been some improvement since Burnham's death in 1985. The appearance of newspapers other than the government-controlled *Guyana Chronicle* and the public's dramatically increased access to television have served to curtail official control of the media. In politics, the election of Indo-Guyanese leader Cheddi Jagan to the presidency reflected deep-seated disfavor with the behavior and economic policies of the previous government of Desmond Hoyte. President Jagan identified the nation's foreign debt of $2 billion as a "colossally big problem, because the debt overhang impedes human development."

While president, Hoyte once pledged to continue the socialist policies of the late Forbes Burnham; but in the same breath, he talked about

TIMELINE

1616
The first permanent Dutch settlements on Essequibo River

1815
The Netherlands cedes the territory to Britain

1966
Independence

1985
President Forbes Burnham dies

1990s
The government promises to end racial and ethnic discrimination

2000s
Territorial disputes with Suriname and Venezuela persist
Politics remains bitterly divided along ethnic lines

2006
Disastrous floods caused by high rainfall severely damage coastal agriculture

2011
Donald Ramotar elected president

125

Snapshot: GUYANA

Summarized below is a quick look at the country with regard to its development, freedom, health/welfare, and achievements.

Development

The Economic Commission for Latin America and the Caribbean (ECLAC) in a report released December 21, 2011 said that Guyana's economy continued to post robust growth in 2011 despite the continuing difficulties in the major export markets of the United States and Europe. The report also said that policymakers in Guyana are expected to pursue a low-carbon development strategy. An agreement notes that Guyana will receive some $30 million in financing in 2012 by the Government of Norway and up to $100 million annually through 2020.

Freedom

According to Freedom House "domestic abuse and violence against women in general are widespread. Rape is illegal but often goes unreported and is infrequently prosecuted." The Guyana Human Rights Association "has charged that the legal system's treatment of victims of sexual violence is intentionally humiliating." In May 2010, the Sexual Offenses Act was signed into law, which makes rape gender-neutral and expands its definition to include spousal rape and coercion and child abuse.

Health/Welfare

According to the United Nations Development Program website, Guyana's Human Development Index value for 2011 is 0.633, in the medium human development category, positioning the country at 117 out of 187 countries across the globe. Between 1980 and 2011, the report said the country's HDI value increased from 0.501 to 0.633, an increase of 26.0 percent or an average annual increase of about 0.8 percent.

Achievements

The American Historical Association selected Walter Rodney for the 1982 Beveridge Award for his study of the Guyanese working people. The award is for the best book in English on the history of the United States, Canada, or Latin America. Rodney, the leader of the Working People's Alliance, was assassinated in 1980.

? DID YOU KNOW?

Deep in the jungles of Guyana the Potaro River cascades over the Kaieteur Falls, a drop of 741 feet. The falls are the main attraction in the Kaieteur National Park, established in 1930.

FURTHER INVESTIGATION

For more information on the Kaieteur National Park, visit http://www.kaieteurpark.gov.gy/old/about.html

the need for privatization of the crucial sugar and bauxite industries. Jagan's economic policies, according to *Latin American Regional Reports,* outlined an uncertain course. During his campaign, Jagan stated that government should not be involved in sectors of the economy where private or cooperative ownership would be more efficient. In 1993, however, he backed away from the sale of the Guyana Electric Company and had some doubts about selling off the sugar industry. In Jagan's words: "Privatization and divestment must be approached with due care. I was not elected president to preside over the liquidation of Guyana. I was mandated by the Guyanese people to rebuild the national economy and to restore a decent standard of living." Jagan's policies stimulated rapid socioeconomic progress as Guyana embarked on the road to economic recovery.

Following Jagan's death, new elections were held in December 1997, and Janet Jagan, the ex-president's 77-year-old widow, was named president. In August 1999, she stepped down due to health reasons. She named Finance Minister Bharrat Jagdeo to succeed her.

Jagdeo's presidency pushed infrastructure development and promoted universal primary education. A five-year plan (2003–2007) promised to bring schools to the interior where educational opportunities have been minimal or nonexistent. He also worked toward reducing the racial and ethnic enmity that has plagued the nation. Still, the Afro-Guyanese, who represent less than half of Guyana's population, tend to support the opposition People's National Congress Party, which had held power from 1964 to 1992, and have responded to their lack of power by confronting the government on its policies, sometimes violently.

In the meantime, a divided Guyana may soon be confronted by an aggressive Venezuela, whose president seems intent on reigniting its long-standing border dispute with Guyana. With respect to rival offshore territorial claims between Guyana and Suriname, a UN tribunal has been established to settle the issue. The problem is particularly contentious because of the oil-producing potential of the disputed area.

Statistics

Geography

Area in Square Miles (Kilometers): 82,990 (215,000) (about the size of Idaho)

Capital (Population): Georgetown (132,000)

Environmental Concerns: water pollution; deforestation

Geographical Features: mostly rolling highlands; low coastal plain; savannah in the south

Climate: tropical

People*

Population

Total: 744,768 (2011 est.)

Annual Growth Rate: −0.44

Rural/Urban Population Ratio: 71/29

Major Languages: English; indigenous dialects; Creole; Hindi; Urdu

Ethnic Makeup: 43.5% East Indian, 30% black; 16.7% mixed; 9.1% Amerindian; 2% white and Chinese

Religions: 30.5% Protestant; 28.4% Hindu; 8.1% Roman Catholic; 7.2% Muslim; 25.8% others

Health

Life Expectancy at Birth: 63 years (male); 71 years (female)

Infant Mortality Rate (Ratio): 36.76/1,000

Physicians Available (Ratio): 0.48/1000

Education

Adult Literacy Rate: 91.8%

Compulsory (Ages): 6–14; free

Communication

Telephones: 149,900 main lines

Daily Newspaper Circulation: 97 per 1,000 people

Cell Phones: 555,400

Internet Users: 189,600

Transportation

Roadways in Kilometers (Miles): 7,970 (4,949)

Usable Airfields: 96

Government

Type: republic

Independence Date: May 26, 1966 (from the United Kingdom)

Head of State/Government: President Bharrat Jagdeo; Prime Minister Samuel Hinds

Political Parties: A Partnership for National Unity; People's Progressive Party; Alliance for Change; others

Suffrage: universal at 18

Military

Military Expenditures (% of GDP): 1.8%

Current Disputes: territorial disputes with Venezuela and Suriname

Economy

Currency ($U.S. Equivalent): 204.6 Guyanese dollars = $1

Per Capita Income/GDP: $7,200/5.379 billion

GDP Growth Rate: 4.5%

Inflation Rate: 5.2%

Unemployment Rate: 11% (official: likely higher) Labor Force: 333,900

Natural Resources: bauxite; gold; diamonds; hardwood timber; shrimp; fish

Agriculture: sugar; rice; wheat; vegetable oils; livestock; potential for fishing and forestry

Industry: bauxite; sugar; rice milling; timber; fishing; textiles; gold mining

Exports: $883 million (primary partners United States, Canada, Ukraine, Netherlands, Trinidad and Tobago)

Imports: $1.386 billion (primary partners United States, Trinidad and Tobago, Cuba, China, South Korea)

Suggested Website

www.cia.gov/cia/publications/factbook/geos/gy.html

*Note: Estimates explicitly take into account the effects of excess mortality due to AIDS.

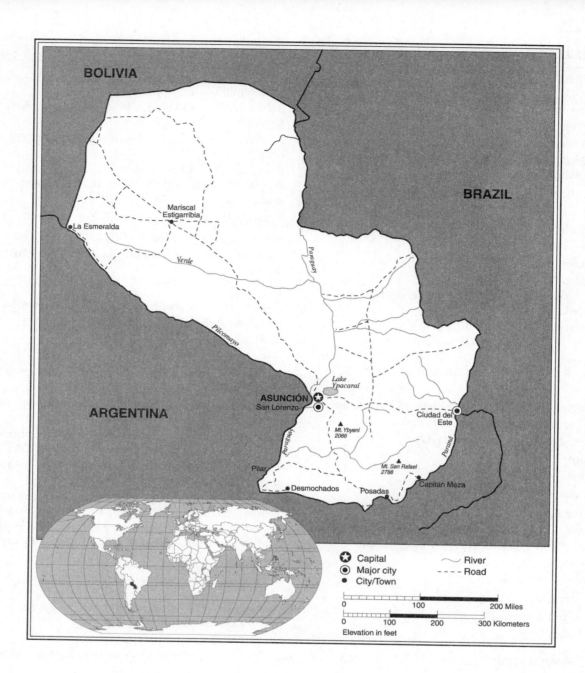

BOLIVIA

BRAZIL

Mariscal
Estigarribia

●La Esmeralda

Verde

Paraguay

Pilcomayo

ARGENTINA

Lake
Ypacaraí

ASUNCIÓN
San Lorenzo

Ciudad del
Este

Paraguay

▲ Mt. Ybyeni
2066

Pilar

▲ Mt. San Rafael
2798

Paraná

Desmochados

Posadas

Capitán Meza

✪	Capital	∿	River
◉	Major city	- - -	Road
●	City/Town		

0   100   200 Miles

0   100   200   300 Kilometers
Elevation in feet

Paraguay
(Republic of Paraguay)

Paraguay is a country of paradox. Although there is little threat of foreign invasion and guerrilla activity is insignificant, a state of siege was in effect for 35 years, ending only in 1989 with the ouster of President (General) Alfredo Stroessner, who had held the reins of power since 1954. Government expenditures on health care in Paraguay are among the lowest in the Western Hemisphere, yet life expectancy is impressive, and infant mortality reportedly has fallen to levels comparable to more advanced developing countries. On the other hand, nearly a third of all reported deaths are of children under five years of age. Educational achievement, especially in rural areas, is low.

Paraguayan politics, economic development, society, and even its statistical base are comprehensible only within the context of its geography and Indo–Hispanic culture. Its geographic isolation in the midst of powerful neighbors has encouraged Paraguay's tradition of militarism and self-reliance—of being led by strongmen who tolerate little opposition. There is no tradition of constitutional government or liberal democratic procedures upon which to draw. Social values influence politics to the extent that politics is an all-or-nothing struggle for power and its accompanying prestige and access to wealth. These political values, in combination with a population that is largely poor and politically ignorant, contribute to the type of paternalistic, personal rule characteristic of a dictator such as Stroessner.

The paradoxical behavior of the Acuerdo Nacional—a block of opposition parties under Stroessner—was understandable within the context of a quest for power, or at least a share of power. Stroessner, always eager to divide and conquer, identified the Acuerdo Nacional as a fruitful field for new alliances. Leaping at the chance for patronage positions but anxious to demonstrate to Stroessner that they were a credible political force worthy of becoming allies, Acuerdo members tried to win the support of unions and the peasantry. At the same time, the party purged its youth wing of leftist influences.

Just when it seemed certain that Stroessner would rule until his death, Paraguayans were surprised in February 1989 when General Andrés Rodríguez—second-in-command of the armed forces, a member of the Traditionalist faction of the Colorado Party, which was in disfavor with the president, and a relative of Stroessner—seized power. Rodríguez's postcoup statements promised the democratization of Paraguay, respect for human rights, repudiation of drug trafficking, and the scheduling of presidential elections. Not surprisingly, General Rodríguez emerged as President Rodríguez. When asked about voting irregularities, Rodríguez indicated that "real" democracy would begin with elections in 1993 and that his rule was a necessary "transition."

"Real" democracy, following the 1993 victory of President Juan Carlos Wasmosy, had a distinct Paraguayan flavor. Wasmosy won the election with 40 percent of the vote; and the Colorado Party, which won most of the seats in Congress, was badly divided. When an opposition victory seemed possible, the military persuaded the outgoing government to push through legislation to reorganize the armed forces. In effect, they were made autonomous.

TIMELINE

1537
Asunci—n founded by the Spanish
1811
Independence is declared
1865–1870
War against the "Triple Alliance": Argentina, Brazil, and Uruguay
1954
General Alfredo Stroessner begins his rule
1961
Women win the vote
1989
Stroessner is ousted in a coup
1990s
A new Constitution is promulgated
2000s
President Fernando Lugo wins the presidency in 2008
2013
Presidential elections scheduled

Snapshot: PARAGUAY

Summarized below is a quick look at the country with regard to its development, freedom, health/welfare, and achievements.

Development

Paraguay's economy experienced accelerated growth between 2009 and 2011. Accurate figures are difficult to obtain because much of the economy is "underground" (informal) and is characterized by thousands of "micro-enterprises" such as smuggling, money-laundering, drugs, arms trafficking, and organized crime. Paraguay is the world's sixth largest producer of soybeans.

Freedom

Paraguay has long been plagued by a corrupt judiciary. Transparency International's 2010 Corruption Perception Index ranked the country 146 out of 176 surveyed. Conflicts between landowners and peasants are a continuing problem. A small guerrilla organization, the Paraguayan People's Army, has allegedly been responsible for a series of kidnappings and murders.

Health/Welfare

The Paraguayan government spends very little on human services and welfare. As a result, its population is plagued by health problems—including poor levels of nutrition, lack of drinkable water, absence of sanitation, and a prevalence of fatal childhood diseases. A 2008 census reported that 88% of the nation's indigenous people lacked access to medical coverage.

Achievements

Paraguay has produced several notable authors, including Gabriel Casaccia and Augusto Roa Bastos. Roa Bastos makes extensive use of religious symbolism in his novels as a means of establishing true humanity and justice.

Political turmoil has continued to characterize Paraguayan politics. Assassination, an attempted coup in 2000, endemic corruption and back room deals are stock in trade. The 2003 victory of President Nicanor Duarte Frutos continued the Colorado's half-century lock on political power.

The problems he faced were serious. Corruption, counterfeiting, contraband, money laundering, and organized crime are entrenched. Despite campaign promises that "there will be no place for people who believe the party and state are there to be abused to the detriment of the country," few Paraguayans expected change. There were other issues that clouded the future. The commercialization of agriculture and high population growth led to a dramatic increase in the number of landless families who have begun to migrate to urban areas where they resettle in shanty towns. Poverty effects nearly 60 percent of the population.

The Colorados failed to resolve Paraguay's basic social problems and, for the first time in 62 years, were voted out of power in 2008. The new president, Fernando Lugo, is a former Roman Catholic bishop and a populist with socialist views. But he eschews comparisons with other populist leaders in the region.

As he stated: "Chávez (president of Venezuela) is a soldier, I am a holy man. Evo (Evo Morales, president of Bolivia) is an Indian, I am not an Indian. Correa (president of Ecuador) is an intellectual, I am not an intellectual. I am simply an individual who feels for the people, feels their pain, their hopes."

◼ THE ECONOMY

It is difficult to acquire accurate statistics about the Paraguayan economy, in part because of the large informal sector and in part because of large-scale smuggling and drug trafficking. It is estimated that 20 percent of the nation's economy has been driven by illicit cross-border trafficking and that almost all of Paraguay's tobacco exports are illicit, counterfeit, or both. President Lugo's attempts to renegotiate Paraguay's contracts for power generated by the Itaipú hydroelectric dam that straddles the border with Brazil have been met with stiff resistance from Brazilian manufacturers who oppose higher prices. Although both countries equally share the electrical output, Paraguay uses only 7 percent and sells the remainder to Brazil at a fixed price that is currently 20 times less than the market rate. A better price would significantly aid Paraguay's economy. There is also concern about the "Brazilianization" of the eastern part of Paraguay, which has developed to the point at which Portuguese is heard as frequently as Spanish or Guaraní, the most common Indian language.

? DID YOU KNOW?

The Itaipú Dam, built between 1975-1991, is the world's largest hydroelectric power plant. In 2000 the facility provided 94% of Paraguay's electricity supply and exported enough kilowatts of electricity to satisfy 20% of Brazil's needs. Negotiations over the price Paraguay charges Brazil for electricity continued in 2012.

FURTHER INVESTIGATION

For further information on the Itaipú Dam go to http://ga.water.usgs.gov/edu/hybiggest.html

Statistics

Geography

Area in Square Miles (Kilometers): 157,048 (406,752) (about the size of California)

Capital (Population): Asunción 1,977,000

Environmental Concerns: deforestation; water pollution; problems with waste disposal

Geographical Features: grassy plains and wooded hills east of Rio Paraguay; Gran Chaco region west of the river; mostly marshy plain near the river; dry forest and thorny scrub elsewhere

Climate: subtropical to temperate

People

Population

Total: 6,459,058 (2011 est.)

Annual Growth Rate: 1.3%

Rural/Urban Population Ratio: 39/61

Major Languages: Spanish; Guaraní; Portuguese

Ethnic Makeup: 95% Mestizo; 5% white and Indian

Religions: 90% Roman Catholic; 8% Protestant

Health

Life Expectancy at Birth: 73 years (male); 79 years (female)

Infant Mortality Rate (Ratio): 23.02/1,000

Physicians Available (Ratio): 1.1/1,000

Education

Adult Literacy Rate: 94%

Compulsory (Ages): 6–12

Communication

Telephones: 405,000 main lines

Daily Newspaper Circulation: 40 per 1,000 people

Cell Phones: 5,915,000

Internet Users: 1,105,000

Transportation

Highways in Kilometers (Miles): 18,320 (29,500)

Railroads in Kilometers (Miles): 36 (22)

Usable Airfields: 800

Government

Type: republic

Independence Date: May 14, 1811 (from Spain)

Head of State/Government: President Fernando Lugo is both head of state and head of government

Political Parties: Colorado Party; Authentic Radical Liberal Party; National Union Movement of Ethical Citizens; Beloved Country

Suffrage: universal and compulsory from 18 to 75

Military

Military Expenditures (% of GDP): 1%

Current Disputes: none

Economy

Currency ($U.S. Equivalent): 4,188 guaranis = $1

Per Capita Income/GDP: $5,500/36.21 billion

GDP Growth Rate: 6.4%

Inflation Rate: 8.9%

Unemployment Rate: 6.6%

Labor Force: 3,085,000

Natural Resources: hydropower; timber; iron ore; manganese; limestone

Agriculture: cotton; sugarcane; soybeans; corn; wheat; tobacco; cassava (tapioca); fruits; vegetables; livestock; timber

Industry: sugar; cement; textiles; beverages; wood products

Exports: $9.756 billion (primary partners Uruguay, Brazil, Chile, Argentina, European Union)

Imports: $12.06 billion (primary partners Brazil, China, United States, Argentina)

Suggested Website

www.cia.gov/cia/publications/factbook/index.html

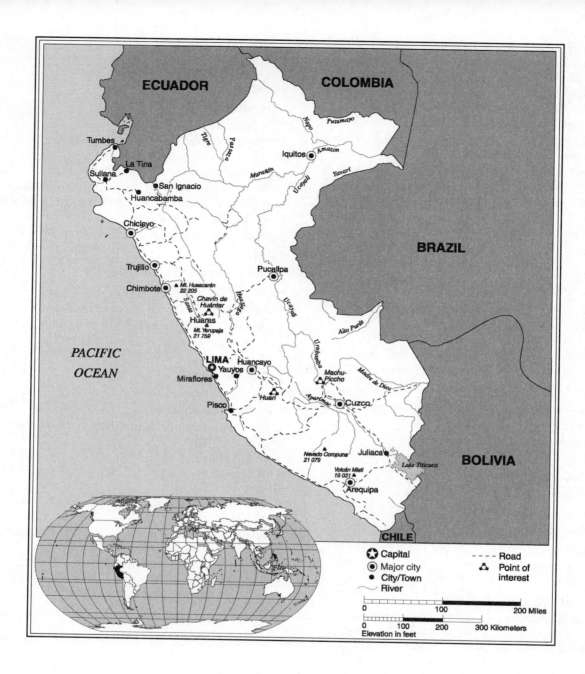

ECUADOR

COLOMBIA

BRAZIL

Tumbes

La Tina

Sullana

San Ignacio

Huancabamba

Chiclayo

Iquitos

Trujillo

Chimbote

Mt. Huascarán
22 205

Chavín de
Huántar

Pucallpa

Huaras

Mt. Yerupajá
21 759

PACIFIC
OCEAN

LIMA

Huancayo

Yauyos

Miraflores

Huari

Machu-
Picchu

Cuzco

Pisco

Nevado Coropuna
21 079

Juliaca

Lake Titicaca

BOLIVIA

Volcán Misti
19 031

Arequipa

CHILE

Napo

Putumayo

Tigre

Pastaza

Marañón

Amazon

Ucayali

Yavarí

Huallaga

Santa

Ucayali

Alto Purús

Urubamba

Madre de Dios

Apurímac

★ Capital

⊙ Major city

● City/Town

∿ River

– – – Road

▲ Point of
   interest

0   100   200 Miles

0   100   200   300 Kilometers

Elevation in feet

Peru
(Republic of Peru)

■ PERU: HEIR TO THE INCAS

The culture of Peru, from pre-Hispanic days to the present, has in many ways reflected the nation's variegated geography and climate. While 55 percent of the nation is covered with jungle, coastal Peru boasts one of the world's driest deserts. Despite its forbidding character, irrigation of the desert is made possible by runoffs from the Andes. This allows for the growing of a variety of crops in fertile oases that comprise about 5.5 percent of the land area.

Similarly, in the highlands, or *sierra,* there is little land available for cultivation. Because of the difficulty of the terrain, only about 7 percent of the land can produce crops. Indeed, Peru contains the lowest per capita amount of arable land in South America. The lack of fertile land has had—and continues to have—profound social and political repercussions, especially in the southern highlands near the city of Ayacucho.

■ THE SUPREMACY OF LIMA

Historically, coastal Peru and its capital city of Lima have attempted to dominate the sierra—politically, economically, and, at times, culturally. Long a bureaucratic and political center, in the twentieth century Lima presided over the economic expansion of the coast. Economic opportunity in combination with severe population pressure in the sierra caused Lima and its port of Callao to grow tremendously in population, if not in services.

Ironically, the capital city has one of the worst climates for dense human settlement. Thermal inversions are common; between May and September, they produce a cloud ceiling and a pervasive cool fog.

Middle- and upper-class city dwellers have always been ignorant of the people of the highlands. Very few know either Quechua or Aymara, the Indian languages spoken daily by millions of Peruvians. Yet this ignorance of the languages—and, by extension, of the cultures—has not prevented government planners or well- meaning intellectuals from trying to impose a variety of developmental models on the inhabitants of the sierra. In the late nineteenth century, for example, modernizers known collectively in Latin America as Positivists sought in vain to transform indigenous cultures by Europeanizing them. Other reformers sought to identify with the indigenous peoples. In the 1920s, a young intellectual named Victor Raúl Haya de la Torre fashioned a political ideology called APRISMO, which embraced the idea of an alliance of Indoamerica to recover the American states for their original inhabitants. While his broader vision proved to be too idealistic, the specific reforms he recommended for Peru were put into effect by reform-minded governments in the 1960s and 1970s. Sadly, reform continued to be developed and imposed from Lima, without an understanding of the rationale behind existing agrarian systems or an appreciation of a peasant logic that was based not on production of a surplus but on attaining a satisfying level of well-being. Much of the turmoil in rural Peru today stems from the agrarian reform of 1968–1979.

TIMELINE

1500
The Inca Empire is at its height
1535
The Spanish found Lima
1821
Independence is proclaimed
1955
Women gain the right to vote
1968
A military coup: far-reaching reforms are pursued
1989
Debureaucratization campaign begins
1990s
El Niño spreads economic havoc and human misery; privatization
2000s
Reappearance of Sendero Luminoso in 2003
2011
Ollanta Humala elected president
2012
Sendero Luminoso admits defeat

AGRARIAN REFORM

From the mid-1950s, rural laborers in the central and southern highlands and on the coastal plantations demonstrated an increasingly insistent desire for agrarian reform. Peasant communities in the sierra staged a series of land invasions and challenged the domination of the large estate, or *hacienda,* from outside. Simultaneously, tenants living on the estates pressured the hacienda system from within. In both cases, peasants wanted land.

The Peruvian government responded with both the carrot and the stick. A military regime, on the one hand, tried to crush peasant insurgency in 1962 and, on the other, passed agrarian reform legislation. The laws had no practical effect, but they did give legal recognition to the problem of land reform. In the face of continued peasant unrest in the south, the military enacted more substantial land laws in 1963, confiscating some property and redistributing it to peasants. The trend toward reform continued with the election of Francisco Belaunde Terry as president of a civilian government.

In the face of continued peasant militancy, Belaunde promised far-ranging reforms, but a hostile Congress refused to provide sufficient funds to implement the proposed reforms. Peasant unrest increased, and the government feared the development of widespread rural guerrilla warfare.

Against this backdrop of rural violence, the Peruvian military again seized power in 1968. To the astonishment of most observers, the military chose not to crush popular unrest but, rather, to embrace reforms. Clearly, the military had become sensitive to the political, social, and economic in-equalities in Peru that had bred unrest. The military was intent on revolutionizing Peru from the top down rather than waiting for revolution from below.

In addition to land reform, the military placed new emphasis on Peru's Indian heritage. Tupac Amaru, an Incan who had rebelled against Spanish rule in 1780–1781, became a national symbol. In 1975, Quechua, the ancient language of the Inca, became Peru's second official language (along with Spanish). School curricula were revised and approached Peru's Indian heritage in a new and positive light.

NATIONALIZATION AND INTEGRATION

Behind the reforms, which were extended to industry and commerce and included the nationalization of foreign enterprises, lay the military's desire to provide for Peru a stable social and political order. The military leaders felt that they could provide better leadership in the quest for national integration and economic development than could "inefficient" civilians. Their ultimate goal was to construct a new society based on citizen participation at all levels.

As is so often the case, however, the reform model was not based on the realities of the society. It was naively assumed by planners that the Indians of the sierra were primitive socialists and wanted collectivized ownership of the land. In reality, each family's interests tended to make it competitive, rather than cooperative, with every other peasant family. Collectivization in the highlands failed because peasant communities outside the old hacienda structure clamored for the return of traditional lands that had been taken from them over the years. The Peruvian government found itself, awkwardly, attempting to defend the integrity of the newly reformed units from peasants who wanted their own land.

THE PATRON

Further difficulties were caused by the disruption of the patron–client relationship in the more traditional parts of the sierra. Hacienda owners, although members of the ruling elite, often enjoyed a tight bond with their tenants. Rather than a boss–worker relationship, the patron–client tie came close to kinship. Hacienda owners, for example, were often godparents to the children of their workers. A certain reciprocity was expected and given. But with the departure of the hacienda owners, a host of government bureaucrats arrived on the scene, most of whom had been trained on the coast and were ignorant of the customs and languages of the sierra. The peasants who benefited from the agrarian reform looked upon the administrators with a good deal of suspicion. The agrarian laws and decrees, which were all written in Spanish, proved impossible for the peasants to understand. Not surprisingly, fewer than half of the sierra peasants chose to join the collectives; and in a few places, peasants actually asked for the return of the hacienda owner, someone to whom they could relate. On the coast, the cooperatives did not benefit all agricultural workers equally, since permanent workers won the largest share of the benefits. In sum, the reforms had little impact on existing trends in agricultural production, failed to reverse income inequalities within the peasant population, and did not ease poverty.

The shortcomings of the reforms—in combination with drought, subsequent crop failures, rising food prices, and population pressure—created very difficult and tense situations in the sierra. The infant mortality rate rose 35 percent between 1978 and 1980, and caloric intake dropped well below the recommended minimum. More than half of the children under age six suffered from some form of malnutrition. Rural unrest continued.

RETURN TO CIVILIAN RULE

Unable to solve Peru's problems and torn by divisions within its ranks, the military stepped aside in 1980, and Belaunde was again elected as Peru's constitutional

(Royalty-Free/CORBIS)

Machu Picchu, a famous Inca ruin, stands atop a 6,750-foot mountain in the Peruvian Andes.

president. Despite the transition to civilian government, unrest continued in the highlands, and the appearance of a left-wing guerrilla organization known as Sendero Luminoso ("Shining Path") led the government to declare repeated states of emergency and to lift civil guarantees.

In an attempt to control the situation, the Ministry of Agriculture won the power to restructure and, in some cases, to liquidate the cooperatives and collectives established by the agrarian reform. Land was divided into small individual plots and given to the peasants. Because the plots can be bought, sold, and mortgaged, some critics argue that the undoing of the reform may hasten the return of most of the land into the hands of a new landed elite.

Civilian rule, however, has not necessarily meant democratic rule for Peru's citizens. This helps to explain the spread of Sendero Luminoso despite its radical strategy and tactics of violence. By 1992, according to Diego García-Sayán, the executive director of the Andean Commission of Jurists, the Sendero Luminoso controlled "many parts of Peruvian territory. Through its sabotage, political assassinations, and terrorist actions, Sendero Luminoso has helped to make political violence, which

used to be rather infrequent, one of the main characteristics of Peruvian society."

Violence was not confined to the guerrillas of Sendero Luminoso or of the Tupac Amaru Revolutionary Movement (MRTA). Economist Javier Iguíñiz, of the Catholic University of Lima, argued that a solution to the violence required an understanding that it flowed from disparate, autonomous, and competing sources, including guerrillas, right-wing paramilitary groups, the Peruvian military and police forces, and cocaine traffickers, "particularly the well-armed Colombians active in the Huallaga Valley." Sendero Luminoso was also active in the Huallaga Valley and profited from taxing drug traffickers. Raúl González, of Lima's Center for Development Studies, observed that as both the drug traffickers and the guerrillas "operate[d] outside the law, there has evolved a relationship of mutual convenience in certain parts of Huallaga to combat their common enemy, the state."

President Alan García vacillated on a policy toward the Sendero Luminoso insurgency. But ultimately, he authorized the launching of a major military offensive against Sendero Luminoso bases thought to be linked to drug trafficking. Later, determined to confront an insurgency that claimed 69,000 victims, President Alberto Fujimori armed rural farmers, known as *rondas campesinas,* to fight off guerrilla incursions. (The arming of peasants is not new to Peru; it is a practice that dates to the colonial period.) Sendero Luminoso reappeared in 2003, but in 2012 finally admitted defeat and sought to negotiate an end to its war with the government. President Humala demanded unconditional surrender, disarmament, and the locations of stockpiles of weaponry. In February 2012 Sendero's leader was wounded and captured.

■ A BUREAUCRATIC REVOLUTION?

Peruvian author Hernando DeSoto's best-selling and controversial book *The Other Path* (as opposed to Sendero Luminoso, or Shining Path), argues convincingly that both left-and right-wing governments in Latin America in general and in Peru in particular are neo-mercantile—that is, both intervene in the economy and promote the expansion of state activities. "Both strengthened the role of the government's bureaucracy until they made it the main obstacle, rather than the main incentive, to progress, and together they produced, without consulting the electorate, almost 99 percent of the laws governing us." There are differences between left- and right-wing approaches: The left governs with an eye to redistributing wealth and well-being to the neediest groups, and the right tends to govern to serve foreign investors or national business interests. "Both, however, will do so with bad laws which explicitly benefit some and harm others. Although their aims may seem to differ, the result is that in Peru one wins or loses by political decisions. Of course, there is a big difference between a fox and a wolf but, for the rabbit, it is the similarity that counts."

DeSoto attacked the bureaucracy head-on when his private research center, the Institute for Liberty and Democracy, drafted legislation to abolish a collection of requirements built on the assumption that citizens are liars until proven otherwise. The law, which took effect in April 1989, reflected a growing rebellion against bureaucracy in Peru. Another law, which took effect in October 1989, radically simplified the process of gaining title to land. (DeSoto discovered that, to purchase a parcel of state-owned land in Peru, one had to invest 56 months of effort and 207 visits to 48 different offices.) The legislation will have an important impact on the slum dwellers of Lima, for it will take much less time to regularize land titles as the result of invasions and seizures. Slum dwellers with land titles, according to DeSoto, invest in home improvements at a rate nine times greater than that of slum dwellers without titles. Slum dwellers who own property will be less inclined to turn to violent solutions to their problems.

The debureaucratization campaign has been paralleled by grassroots social movements that grew in response to a state that no longer could or would respond to the needs of its citizenry. Cataline Romero, director of the Bartolome de Las Cases Institute of Lima, said that "grass-roots social movements have blossomed into political participants that allow historically marginalized people to feel a sense of their own dignity and rights as citizens." Poor people have developed different strategies for survival as the government has failed to meet even their most basic needs. Most have entered the informal sector and have learned to work together through the formation of unions, mothers' clubs, and cooperatives. Concluded Romero: "As crisis tears institutions down, these communities are preparing the ground for building new institutions that are more responsive to the needs of the majority." DeSoto concurs and adds: "No one has ever considered that most poor Peruvians are a step ahead of the revolutionaries and are already changing the country's structures, and what politicians should be doing is guiding the change and giving it an appropriate institutional framework so that it can be properly used and governed."

By 2006 the advances made by the poor in the environs of the large cities was increasingly reflected in the sierras as well. Rolando Arellano, president of a large Peruvian marketing firm, noted: "Being called *serrano* is no longer an insult. That is a very important social change It is a vindication of the sierra tradition." Indeed, what is happening in Peru mirrors what is happening in indigenous communities in Ecuador and Bolivia. Formerly marginalized people have become a political, economic, and consumer force and now have the power to influence decisively elections at the national level.

■ DEMOCRACY AND THE "SELF-COUP"

In April 1992, President Fujimori, increasingly isolated and unable to effect economic and political reforms, suspended the Constitution, arrested a number of opposition leaders, shut down Congress, and openly challenged the power of the judiciary. The military, Fujimori's staunch ally, openly supported the *autogolpe,* or "self-coup," as did business leaders and about 80 percent of the Peruvian people. In the words of political scientist Cynthia McClintock, writing in *Current History,* "Fujimori emerged a new caudillo, destroying the conventional wisdom that institutions, whether civilian or military, had become more important than individual leaders in Peru and elsewhere in Latin America." In 1993, a constitutional amendment allowed Fujimori to run for a second consecutive term.

In April 1995, Fujimori won a comfortable victory, with 64 percent of the vote. This was attributable to his successful economic policies, which saw the

Peruvian economy grow by 12 percent—the highest in the world for 1994—and the campaign against Sendero Luminoso.

This represented the high point of Fujimori's administration. Increasingly dictatorial behavior and a fraudulent election in 2000, coupled with a severe economic slump precipitated by the crisis in Asian financial markets and the chaos wreaked on the infrastructure, coastal agriculture, and fishing industry by the phenomenon known as El Niño, undermined Fujimori's popularity. Rampant corruption was symbolized by one woman who, according to *The Christian Science Monitor,* "became so disgusted with her country's electoral fraud and corruption . . . that she undertook a simple but memorable political protest: handwashing the Peruvian flag in a public square for months on end."

Fujimori's decision to run for a third term, despite a constitutional prohibition, was followed by an election in April 2000 that observers characterized as "rife with fraud." Prodemocracy forces led by Alejandro Toledo, a one-time shoeshine boy, boycotted the run-off election and helped to organize a massive national protest march against Fujimori's swearing-in ceremony. Violence in the streets, press censorship, and revelations of massive corruption by Fujimori's intelligence chief, Vladomiro Montesinos, forced Fujimori to resign from office and flee the country. Interim president Valentin Paniagua began the process of national reconstruction and created several commissions to investigate corruption and human-rights abuses.

Toledo, elected president in 2001, had a rough tenure in office. Despite solid economic growth that averaged 5 percent between 2001 and 2004 and rose to 6.7 percent in 2005, he saw his popularity tumble. Persistent corruption and scandal in government, his failure to deliver on campaign promises of jobs, prosperity, and a return to democracy hamstrung his administration. Troubling also was the reappearance of Sendero Luminoso in 2003. Although small in number they attacked security personnel, took hostages, and initiated a rural campaign to win peasant support. They were well-financed because of their ties to Colombian cocaine traffickers. Indeed, former President Fujimori, whose supporters fondly refer to him as "El Chino"—and whose detractors call him "Chinochet"—still retains a large measure of popularity despite criminal charges. Many people supported Fujimori because he was perceived as strong and decisive. A confident Fujimori, who had fled to Japan to escape criminal charges, appeared in Chile late in 2005 and fully expected to run as a candidate in the 2006 presidential election. But Chilean authorities, at the request of the Peruvian government, detained him while extradition papers were prepared. In 2009, he was sentenced to six years in prison.

The presidential campaign became particularly contentious when Ollanta Humala, a nationalist former army officer, attended a news conference in Caracas, Venezuela, where he was praised by President Hugo Chavez for "joining the battle" against the Free Trade Area of the Americas supported by the United States. Outraged, the Peruvian government withdrew its ambassador from Venezuela for interfering with its election.

Alan Garcia, a former president whose tenure was dogged by corruption and hyperinflation, won the election. In his words: "God, in whom I firmly believe, and the Peruvian people, have given me a second chance." Garcia was above all, a pragmatist, who has the soul of a populist, but is fiscally conservative and politically centrist. When, in May 2008, women protested against rapidly rising food prices, Garcia cut taxes on food imports and ordered the army to deliver parcels of food to Lima's poorest neighborhoods.

In terms of his economic policy he was a supporter of free trade and has invited private capital to invest in a gas-export project worth billions of dollars. He signed trade agreements with the United States, Canada, China, and Singapore and negotiated with half a dozen others. Garcia's foreign policy was centrist. Although something of a populist, he consciously set himself apart from populist regimes in Venezuela and other countries and traded insults with that country's president, Hugo Chávez. In a word, Garcia was a "chameleon" who changed his colors with seamless ease. Peru's newly elected president, Ollanta Humala, like Garcia, is also a political chameleon. During the presidential campaign he abandoned his earlier admiration of Venezuela's Hugo Chávez and noted that the Venezuelan model "isn't applicable in Peru." Instead, he indicated that the more centrist economic and social model of former President Lula of Brazil was better for Peru.

? DID YOU KNOW?

Peru had an exciting and rich pre-Columbian cultural history, as evidenced most dramatically by Machu Picchu and other influences and tangible remains of the Inca empire. In 1985, explorer Gene Savoy discovered another "lost kingdom," Gran Vilaya, in the rain forest in the northern part of Peru. Savoy's expedition found stone complexes and terracing—indications of a well-organized and complex society.

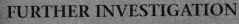
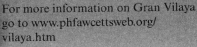

FURTHER INVESTIGATION

For more information on Gran Vilaya go to www.phfawcettsweb.org/vilaya.htm

Snapshot: PERU

Summarized below is a quick look at the country with regard to its development, freedom, health/welfare, and achievements.

Development

Government plans to open large tracts in the Peruvian Amazon to investment, logging, and drilling for petroleum are strongly opposed by indigenous peoples in the effected regions. Similarly, in 2011–2012 indigenous peoples opposed gold mining in the highlands because they feared pollution of their sources for water. Economic growth in these regions would help to stem the flow of sierra dwellers to urban areas.

Freedom

Although President Humala campaigned on a program that promised respect for indigenous rights, those same rights were ignored when the government authorized gold mining in the Sierras. That mining threatened to pollute water supplies.

Health/Welfare

According to the Institute of Development Studies, in the years between 2005–2010 Peru was able to reduce the incidence of malnutrition in children by 5%. In rural areas, "where malnutrition rates are the highest," the drop was almost 10%.

Achievements

Peru has produced a number of literary giants, including José Maria Mariategui, who believed that the "socialism" of the Indians should be a model for the rest of Peru; and Mario Vargas Llosa, always concerned with the complexity of human relationships.

Statistics

Geography

Area in Square Miles (Kilometers): 496,087 (1,285,200) (about the size of Alaska)

Capital (Population): Lima 8,769,000

Environmental Concerns: deforestation; overgrazing; soil erosion; desertification; air and water pollution

Geographical Features: western coastal plain; high and rugged Andes Mountains in the center; eastern lowland jungle of Amazon Basin

Climate: temperate to tropical

People

Population

Total: 29,248,943 (2011 est.)

Annual Growth Rate: 1.09%

Rural/Urban Population Ratio: 23/77

Major Languages: Spanish; Quechua; Aymara

Ethnic Makeup: 45% Indian; 37% Mestizo; 15% white, and others

Religions: 81% Roman Catholic; 12.5% Evangelical

Health

Life Expectancy at Birth: 70 years (male); 74 years (female)

Infant Mortality Rate (Ratio): 22.18/1,000

Physicians Available (Ratio): .92/1,000

Education

Adult Literacy Rate: 92.9%

Compulsory (Ages): 6–11; free

Communication

Telephones: 3,160,000 main lines

Daily Newspaper Circulation: 86 per 1,000 people

Cell Phones: 29,115,000

Internet Users: 9,158,000

Transportation

Roadways in Kilometers (Miles): 78,829 (48,982)

Railroads in Kilometers (Miles): 1,989 (1,236)

Usable Airfields: 211

Government

Type: republic

Independence Date: July 28, 1821 (from Spain)

Head of State/Government: President Ollanta Humala is both head of state and head of government

Political Parties: (coalitions), Gana Peru, Fuerza 2011, Peru Possible, Alliance for Great Change, National Solidarity; others

Suffrage: universal at 18

Military

Military Expenditures (% of GDP): 1.5%

Current Disputes: a boundary dispute with Ecuador was resolved in 1999

Economy

Currency ($U.S. Equivalent): 2.75 New Sols = $1

Per Capita Income/GDP: 10,000/299.7 billion

GDP Real Growth Rate: 6.2%

Inflation Rate: 3%

Unemployment Rate: 6.8% (Lima); extensive underemployment

Labor Force: 10,800,000

Natural Resources: copper; silver; gold; petroleum; timber; fish; iron ore; coal; phosphate; potash

Agriculture: coffee; sugarcane; rice; wheat; potatoes; plantains; coca; livestock; wool; fish

Industry: mining; petroleum; fishing; textiles and clothing; food processing; cement; auto assembly; steel; shipbuilding; metal fabrication

Exports: $43.83 billion (primary partners China, United States, Canada, Japan, Germany, Spain.)

Imports: $36.85 billion (primary partners United States, China, Ecuador, Chile, Colombia)

Suggested Website

www.cia.org/cia/publications/factbook/index.html

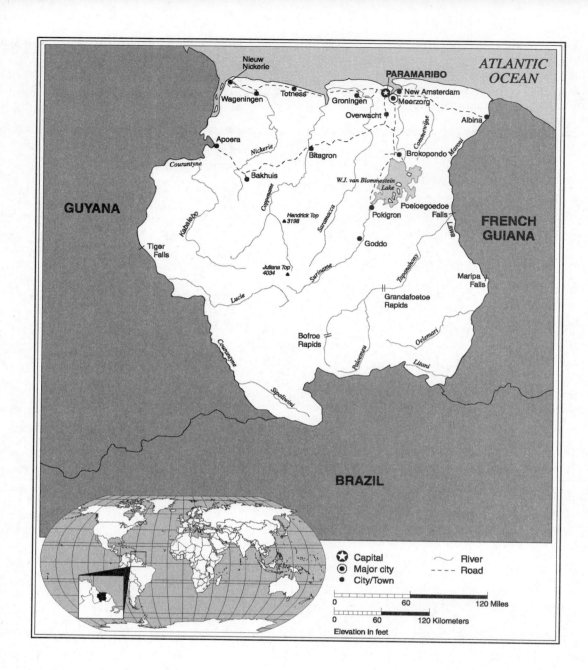

GUYANA

FRENCH
GUIANA

BRAZIL

ATLANTIC
OCEAN

PARAMARIBO

Nieuw
Nickerie

Wageningen

Totness

Groningen

Overwacht

New Amsterdam

Meerzorg

Albina

Apoera

Nickerie

Bitagron

Brokopondo

Bakhuis

W.J. van Blommestein
Lake

Courantyne

Kabalebo

Coppename

Hendrick Top
▲3198

Saramacca

Pokigron

Poeloegoedoe
Falls

Tiger
Falls

Juliana Top
4034 ▲

Suriname

Goddo

Lawa

Maripa
Falls

Lucie

Grandafoetoe
Rapids

Tapanahony

Bofroe
Rapids

Oelemari

Courantyne

Palvemeu

Litani

Sipaliwini

★ Capital
◉ Major city
● City/Town

⁓ River
--- Road

0   60   120 Miles

0   60   120 Kilometers

Elevation in feet

Suriname
(Republic of Suriname)

SURINAME: A SMALL-TOWN STATE

Settled by the British in 1651, Suriname, a small colony on the coast of Guyana, prospered with a plantation economy based on cocoa, sugar, coffee, and cotton. The colony came under Dutch control in 1667; in exchange, the British were given New Amsterdam (Manhattan, New York). The colony was often in turmoil because of Indian and slave uprisings, which took advantage of a weak Dutch power. When slavery was finally abolished, in 1863, plantation owners brought contract workers from China, India, and Java.

On the eve of independence from the Netherlands in 1975, Suriname was a complex, multiracial society. Although existing ethnic tensions were heightened as communal groups jockeyed for power in the new state, other factors cut across racial lines. Even though Creoles (native-born whites) were dominant in the bureaucracy as well as in the mining and industrial sectors, there was sufficient economic opportunity for all ethnic groups, so acute socioeconomic conflict was avoided.

THE POLITICAL FABRIC

Until 1980, Suriname enjoyed a parliamentary democracy that, because of the size of the nation, more closely resembled a small town or extended family in terms of its organization and operation. The various ethnic, political, and economic groups that comprised Surinamese society were united in what sociologist Rob Kroes describes as an "oligarchic web of patron–client relations" that found its expression in government. Through the interplay of the various groups, integration in the political process and accommodation of their needs were achieved. Despite the fact that most interests had access to the center of power, and despite the spirit of accommodation and cooperation, the military seized power early in 1980.

THE ROOTS OF MILITARY RULE

In Kroes's opinion, the coup originated in the army among noncommissioned officers because they were essentially -outside the established social and political system—they were denied their "rightful" place in the patronage network. The officers had a high opinion of themselves and resented what they perceived as discrimination by a wasteful and corrupt government. Their demands for reforms, including recognition of an officers' union, were ignored. In January 1980, one government official talked of disbanding the army altogether.

The coup, masterminded and led by Sergeant Desire Bouterse, who, incidentally, was elected president in 2011, had a vague, undefined ideology. It claimed to be nationalist; and it revealed itself to be puritanical, in that it lashed out at corruption and demanded that citizens embrace civic duty and a work ethic. Ideological purity was maintained by government control or censorship of a once-free media. Wavering between left-wing radicalism and middle-of-the-road moderation, the rapid shifts in Bouterse's ideological declarations suggest that this was a policy designed to keep the opposition off guard and to appease factions within the military.

TIMELINE

1651
British colonization efforts

1667
The Dutch receive Suriname from the British in exchange for New Amsterdam

1975
Independence of the Netherlands

1980s
A military coup

1990s
A huge drug scandal implicates high-level government officials

2000s
The Netherlands extends loan aid

2010
Former dictator Desire Bouterse elected president

Snapshot: SURINAME

Summarized below is a quick look at the country with regard to its development, freedom, health/welfare, and achievements.

Development

The bauxite industry, which had been in decline for 2 decades, now accounts for 15 percent of GDP and 70 percent of export earnings. Gold and oil exports are also significant. Large government deficits remain a problem and in 2011 the currency was devalued by 20% and taxes raised.

Freedom

The Venetiaan government successfully brought to an end the Maroon insurgency of 8 years' duration. Under the auspices of the Organization of American States, the rebels turned in their weapons, and an amnesty for both sides in the conflict was declared.

Health/Welfare

Amerindians and Maroons (the descendants of escaped African slaves) who live in the interior have suffered from the lack of educational and social services, partly from their isolation and partly from insurgency. With peace, however, it is hoped that the health, education, and general welfare of these peoples will improve.

Achievements

Suriname, unlike most other developing countries, has a small foreign debt and a relatively strong repayment capacity. This is substantially due to its export industry.

DID YOU KNOW?

Jewish immigrants from Portuguese Brazil, persecuted because of their religion, settled in Suriname in 1665 and erected the first synagogue in the Western Hemisphere.

The military rule of Bouterse seemed to come to an end early in 1988, when President Ramsewak Shankar was inaugurated. However, in December 1990, Bouterse masterminded another coup. The military and Bouterse remained above the rule of law, and the judiciary was not able to investigate or prosecute serious cases involving military personnel.

With regard to Suriname's economic policy, most politicians see integration into Latin American and Caribbean markets as critical. The Dutch, who suspended -economic aid after the 1990 coup, restored their assistance with the election of President Ronald Venetiaan in 1991. But civilian authorities were well aware of the roots of military rule and pragmatically allowed officers a role in government befitting their self-perceived status.

In 1993, Venetiaan confronted the military when it refused to accept his choice of officers to command the army. Army reform was still high on the agenda in 1995 and was identified by President Venetiaan as one of his government's three great tasks. The others were economic reform necessary to ensure Dutch aid and establish the country's eligibility for international credit; and the need to reestablish ties with the interior to consolidate an Organization of American States–brokered peace, after almost a decade of insurgency.

A loan negotiated with the Dutch in 2001 helped Suriname develop agriculture, bauxite, and the gold-mining industry. Unfortunately the development policy also threatens deforestation, because of timber exports, and the pollution of waterways as a result of careless mining practices. Housing and health care also ranked highly on the government's list of priorities under President Jules Wijdenbosch. The government realized that it could forever depend on the largesse of the Netherlands. The planning and development minister stated that aid had to be sought from other countries. That policy succeeded as significant economic development aid was provided by Belgium and the European Development fund.

Parliamentary elections in 2005 were hotly contested between former President Ronald Venetiaan's New Front coalition and the National Democratic Party of former dictator Desi Bouterse. Ultimately a regional assembly reelected Venetiaan as president. His government faced some difficult problems. Inflation was near 100% when he took office. At the end of his term, it had been reduced to 20%. Other major problems included a health system close to collapse, and a government bureaucracy filled with officeholders who owed their positions to patronage rather than need. Venetiaan introduced austerity measures similar to those he implemented in 1991–96 with some success at that time. During the presidential campaign of 2010 the government dramatically increased social spending in an effort to defeat the candidacy of former army officer Desire Bouterse. That effort failed and Bouterse was elected president. He is unpredictable and has a poor track record with respect to democratic norms.

FURTHER INVESTIGATION

For more information on early Jewish settlement in Suriname go to http://www.suriname-jewish-community.com/our-history.html

Statistics

Geography

Area in Square Miles (Kilometers): 63,037 (163,265) (about the size of Georgia)

Capital (Population): Paramaribo 259,000

Environmental Concerns: deforestation; water pollution; threatened wildlife populations

Geographical Features: rolling hills; a narrow coastal plain with swamps; tropical rain forest

Climate: tropical

People

Population

Total: 491,989 (2011 est.)

Annual Growth Rate: 1.09%

Rural/Urban Population Ratio: 31/69

Major Languages: Dutch; Sranantonga; English; Hindustani

Ethnic Makeup: 37% Hindustani (locally called East Indian); Creole 31%; Javanese 15%; Maroons 10%

Religions: Hindu 27.4%; Protestant 25.2% (mostly Moravian); Roman Catholic 22.8%; Muslim 19.6%; other 5%

Health

Life Expectancy at Birth: 71 years (male); 77 years (female)

Infant Mortality Rate (Ratio): 17.61/1,000

Physicians Available (Ratio): .45/1,000

Education

Adult Literacy Rate: 89.6%

Compulsory (Ages): 6–16; free

Communication

Telephones: 85,000 main lines

Daily Newspaper Circulation: 107 per 1,000 people

Cell Phones: 890,000

Internet Users: 163,000

Transportation

Roadways in Kilometers (Miles): 2,813 (4,530)

Usable Airfields: 51

Government

Type: constitutional democracy

Independence Date: November 25, 1975 (from the Netherlands)

Head of State/Government: President Desire Bouterse is both head of state and head of government

Political Parties: Mega Combination, New front, A-Com, People's Alliance, Party for Democracy and Development in Unity; others

Suffrage: universal at 18

Military

Military Expenditures (% of GDP): 0.6%

Current Disputes: territorial disputes with Guyana and French Guiana

Economy

Currency ($U.S. Equivalent): 3.25 Suriname guilders = $1

Per Capita Income/GDP: $9,500/5.1 billion

GDP Growth Rate: 5%

Inflation Rate: 19.5%

Unemployment Rate: 9.5%

Labor Force: 165,600

Natural Resources: timber; hydropower; fish; kaolin; shrimp; bauxite; gold; nickel; copper; platinum; iron ore

Agriculture: paddy rice; bananas; palm kernels; coconuts; plantains; peanuts; livestock; forest products; shrimp

Industry: bauxite and gold mining; alumina and aluminum production; lumbering; food processing; fishing

Exports: $1.583 billion (primary partners Canada, United States, Belgium, UAE, Netherlands, Norway)

Imports: $1.434 billion (primary partners United States, Netherlands, Trinidad and Tobago, China, Japan, Brazil)

Suggested Website

http://www.cia.gov/cia/publications/factbook/index.html

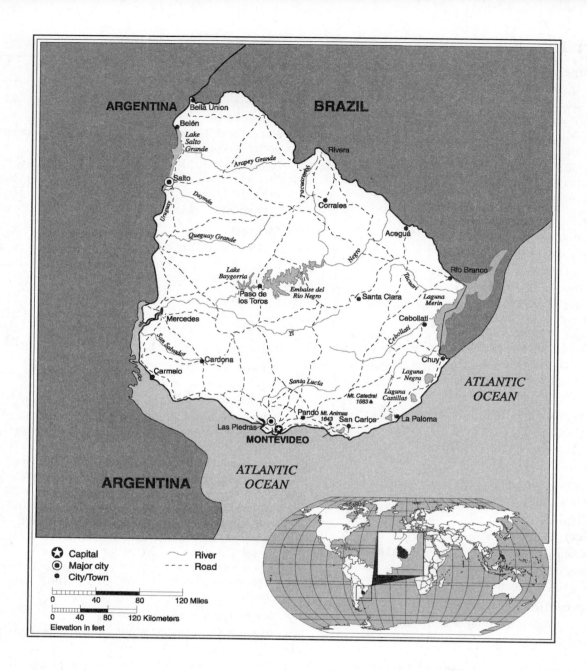

ARGENTINA

BRAZIL

Bella Unión

Belén

*Lake
Salto
Grande*

Rivera

Arapey Grande

Salto

Daymán

Corrales

Aceguá

Queguay Grande

Negro

Río Branco

*Lake
Baygorria*

Paso de
los Toros

*Embalse del
Río Negro*

Santa Clara

Tacuarí

*Laguna
Merin*

Mercedes

Yí

Cebollatí

Cebollatí

San Salvador

Cardona

Chuy

Carmelo

Santa Lucía

*Laguna
Negra*

Mt. Catedral
1683 ▲

*Laguna
Castillas*

**ATLANTIC
OCEAN**

Pando Mt. Animas
1643 San Carlos

La Paloma

Las Piedras

MONTEVIDEO

ARGENTINA

*ATLANTIC
OCEAN*

✪ Capital
◉ Major city
• City/Town

⌇ River
--- Road

0   40   80   120 Miles

0   40   80   120 Kilometers

Elevation in feet

Uruguay
(Oriental Republic of Uruguay)

URUGUAY: MODERATION IN ALL THINGS

The modern history of Uruguay begins with the administration of President José Batlle y Ordoñez. Between 1903 and 1929, Batlle's Uruguay became one of the world's foremost testing grounds for social change, and it eventually became known as the "Switzerland of Latin America." Batlle's Colorado Party supported a progressive role for organized labor and formed coalitions with the workers to challenge the traditional elite and win benefits. Other reforms included the formal separation of church and state, nationalization of key sectors of the economy, and the emergence of mass-based political parties. Batlle's masterful leadership was facilitated by a nation that was compact in size; had a small, educated, and homogeneous population; and had rich soil and a geography that facilitated easy communication and national integration.

Although the spirit of Batllismo eventually faded after his death in 1929, Batlle's legacy is still reflected in many ways. Reports on income distribution reveal an evenness that is uncommon in developing countries. Extreme poverty is unusual in Uruguay, and most of the population enjoy an adequate diet and minimal standards of living. Health care is within the reach of all citizens. And women in Uruguay are granted equality before the law, are present in large numbers at the national university, and have access to professional careers.

But this model state fell on bad times beginning in the 1960s. Runaway inflation, declining agricultural production, a swollen bureaucracy, official corruption, and bleak prospects for the future led to the appearance of youthful middle-class urban guerrillas. Known as Tupamaros, they first attempted to jar the nation to its senses with a Robin Hood–style approach to reform. When that failed, they turned increasingly to terrorism in an effort to destroy a state that resisted reform. The Uruguayan government was unable to quell the rising violence. It eventually called on the military, which crushed the Tupamaros and then drove the civilians from power in 1973.

RETURN TO CIVILIAN RULE

In 1980, the military held a referendum to try to gain approval for a new constitution. Despite extensive propaganda, 60 percent of Uruguay's population rejected the military's proposals and forced the armed forces to move toward a return to civilian government. Elections in 1984 returned the Colorado Party to power, with Julio Maria Sanguinetti as president.

By 1989, Uruguay was again a country of laws, and its citizens were anxious to heal the wounds of the 1970s. A test of the nation's democratic will involved the highly controversial 1986 Law of Expiration, which effectively exempted military and police personnel from prosecution for alleged human-rights abuses committed under orders during the military regime. Many Uruguayans objected and created a pro-referendum commission. They invoked a provision in the Constitution that is

TIMELINE

1624
Jesuits and Franciscans establish missions in the region

1828
Uruguay is established as a buffer state between Argentina and Brazil

1903–1929
The era of President José Batlle y Ordoñez; social reform

1932
Women win the right to vote

1963–1973
Tupamaro guerrillas wage war against the government

1990s
The government endorses sweeping economic and social reforms

2000s
President Batlle struggles with the economy

2004
Tabaré Vázquez becomes president and promises a social transformation

2009
Jose "Pepe" Mujica wins the presidency

2011
Legal decisions open the door for prosecution of those responsible for human rights abuses between 1973–1980

Snapshot: URUGUAY

Summarized below is a quick look at the country with regard to its development, freedom, health/welfare, and achievements.

Development

In November 2007 a pulp mill began operations. Financed by foreign capital in the amount of $1.2 billion, the mill has added 1.6 percent to GDP. Uruguay weathered the global economic recession well and in 2011 had a strong GDP growth rate of 6%.

Freedom

Uruguay's military is constitutionally prohibited from involvement in issues of domestic security unless ordered to do so by civilian authorities. The press is free and unrestricted, as is speech. The political process is open, and academic freedom is the norm in the national university.

Health/Welfare

Between 2002 and the present, the government has pursued social policies that reduced the number of people below the poverty line from 35 percent to 20 percent and halved the unemployment rate.

Achievements

Of all the small countries in Latin America, Uruguay has been the most successful in creating a distinct culture. High levels of literacy and a large middle class have allowed Uruguay an intellectual climate that is superior to many much-larger nations.

---

unique to Latin America: Article 79 states that if 25 percent of eligible voters sign a petition, it would initiate a referendum, which, if passed, would implicitly annul the Law of Expiration. Despite official pressure, the signatures were gathered. The referendum was held on April 16, 1989. It was defeated by a margin of 57 to 43 percent. In 2011, however, there was renewed pressure to annul the Law of Expiration. Uruguay's high court ruled it unconstitutional and congress has acted to pass legislation to make it possible to prosecute those military and police personnel responsible for human rights abuses.

The winds of free-market enterprise and privatization then started to blow through the country. When Sanguinetti regained the presidency in 1994, he was expected, as the leader of the Colorado Party—the party of José Batlle—to maintain the economic status quo. But in 1995, he said that his first priority would be to reform the social-security system, which cannot pay for itself, in large part because people in Uruguay are allowed to retire years earlier than in other countries. Reform was also begun in other sectors of the economy. Government employees were laid off, tariffs were reduced, and a program to privatize state industries was inaugurated. The new policies, according to officials, would produce "a change of mentality and culture" in public administration.

In his first two years in power, Sanguinetti's successor, Jorge Batlle, was unable to bring recession to an end. Low prices for agricultural exports, Argentina's economic malaise, and a public debt that stood at 45 percent of gross domestic product presented the

government with difficult policy decisions. To add to these woes, the appearance of hoof-and-mouth disease in southern Brazil in mid-2001 threatened Uruguay's important beef and wool industries. Once again there was talk of privatization, but a referendum held in December 2003 on the future of ANCAP, the national oil company showed that 62 percent of the electorate wanted no change. Interestingly, these same respondents also opposed monopolies. The failure of the referendum was seen by some political observers as a signal that Batlle would not win reelection in October 2004. That is exactly what happened. What was surprising was neither traditional party won the presidential election. Rather the victor, Tabaré Vázquez, headed up a broad front of political factions that ranged from Communists to Christian Democrats. During the campaign Vázquez's rhetoric promised far-reaching changes that suggested a social transformation of the country. Uruguay's reality, however, is that it does not have the financial resources necessary to support the kinds of domestic programs that featured prominently in campaign speeches. The president indicated that $100 million would be earmarked for the poor. He has also indicated that his government would reopen investigations into the disappearance of people during the years of military rule and reestablish relations with Cuba, raise questions about the wisdom of free-trade agreements, and move closer to populist leaders such as Brazil's Lula and Venezuela's Chavez.

Vazquez, however, once in power pursued pragmatic rather than ideological economic and foreign policies, similar to those followed by Brazil, Chile and Peru. Uruguay, unlike most other Latin American states, successfully weathered the global recession and enjoyed a positive growth rate from 2009 to the present.

Broad Front policies won them the presidency again in 2009. Jose "Pepe" Mujica, a Socialist senator and former guerrilla who fought against the military regime and was incarcerated for 14 years, easily defeated his conservative rival.

The recovery of the Uruguayan economy, a foreign debt that is well under control, and growing investment in the country will provide the government with some of the resources it needs to finance social programs.

? DID YOU KNOW?

Uruguayan literary figures and artists have won worldwide acclaim. Essayist José Enrique Rodó (1872–1917) has been called the greatest modernist prose writer. Short story writer Horacio Quiroga (1878–1937) made the outdoors a popular subject for story material. Artist Joaquin Torres Garcia (1874–1949) studied under Joan Miró and Pablo Picasso. He introduced Picasso's style to South America.

FURTHER INVESTIGATION

For more information on Uruguayan culture go to http://www.discoveruruguay.com/about_uruguay_culture.htm

Statistics

Geography

Area in Square Miles (Kilometers): 68,037 (176,215) (about the size of Washington State)

Capital (Population): Montevideo (1,633,000)

Environmental Concerns: transboundary pollution from Brazilian power plant; water pollution; waste disposal

Geographical Features: mostly rolling plains and low hills; fertile coastal lowland

Climate: warm temperate

People

Population

Total: 3,308,535 (2011 est.)

Annual Growth Rate: 0.23%

Rural/Urban Population Ratio: 8/92

Major Languages: Spanish; Portunol; Brazilero

Ethnic Makeup: 88% white; 8% Mestizo; 4% black

Religions: 47.1% Roman Catholic; 11.1% other Christian, 23% nondenominational, 17.2% atheist or agnostic; 2% Jewish; 30% none indicated or others

Health

Life Expectancy at Birth: 73 years (male); 80 years (female)

Infant Mortality Rate (Ratio): 9.69/1,000

Physicians Available (Ratio): 3.7/1,000

Education

Adult Literacy Rate: 98%

Compulsory (Ages): for 6 years between 6 and 14; free

Communication

Telephones: 962,200 main lines

Daily Newspaper Circulation: 241 per 1,000 people

Cell Phones: 4,437,000

Internet Users: 1,405,000

Transportation

Roadways in Kilometers (Miles): 77,732 (48,300)

Railroads in Kilometers (Miles): 1,243 (2,073)

Usable Airfields: 58

Government

Type: republic

Independence Date: August 25, 1828 (from Brazil)

Head of State/Government: President Jose "Pepe" Mujica is both head of state and head of government

Political Parties: National (Blanco) Party factions; Colorado Party factions; Broad Front Coalition; others

Suffrage: universal and compulsory at 18

Military

Military Expenditures (% of GDP): 1.6%

Current Disputes: boundary disputes with Brazil

Economy

Currency ($U.S. Equivalent): 19.04 Uruguayan pesos = $1

Per Capita Income/GDP: $15,400/$52.02 billion

GDP Growth Rate: 6%

Inflation Rate: 6.7%

Unemployment Rate: 7.9%

Labor Force: 1,636,000

Natural Resources: arable land; hydropower; minor minerals; fisheries

Agriculture: wheat; rice; corn; sorghum; livestock; fish

Industry: food processing; textiles; chemicals; beverages; transportation equipment; petroleum products

Exports: $9.716 billion (primary partners Brazil, Nueva Palmira Free Zone, Argentina, Chile, Russia)

Imports: $10.62 billion (primary partners Brazil, Argentina, China, Venezuela, United States, Russia)

Suggested Website

www.cia.gov/cia/publications/factbook/index.html

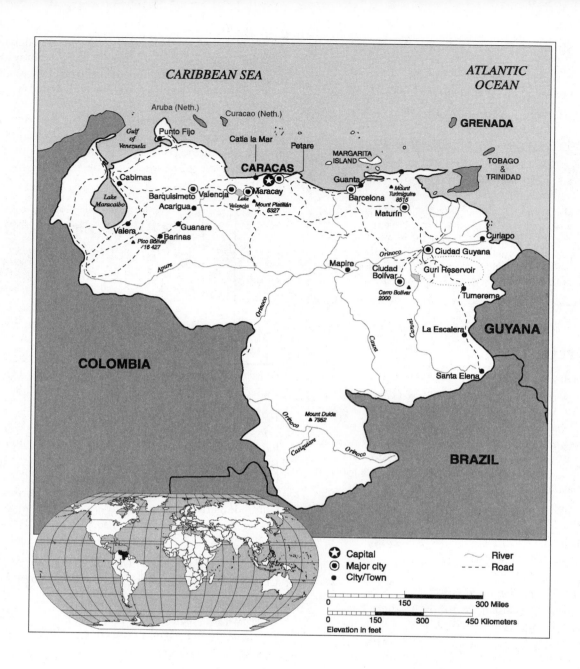

CARIBBEAN SEA

ATLANTIC OCEAN

Aruba (Neth.)

Curacao (Neth.)

GRENADA

Gulf of Venezuela

Punto Fijo

Catia la Mar

Petare

MARGARITA ISLAND

TOBAGO & TRINIDAD

CARACAS

Cabimas

Guanta

Mount Turimiguire 8515

Barquisimeto

Valencia

Maracay

Barcelona

Lake Maracaibo

Acarigua

Lake Valencia

Mount Platillán 6327

Maturín

Valera

Guanare

Curiapo

Barinas

Orinoco

Ciudad Guyana

Pico Bolívar 16 427

Mapire

Ciudad Bolívar

Guri Reservoir

Apure

Orinoco

Cerro Bolívar 2000

Tumeremo

COLOMBIA

Caura

Caroní

La Escalera

GUYANA

Orinoco

Mount Duida 7952

Santa Elena

Casiquiare

Orinoco

BRAZIL

★ Capital

◎ Major city

● City/Town

~ River

--- Road

0   150   300 Miles

0   150   300   450 Kilometers

Elevation in feet

Venezuela
(Bolivarian Republic of Venezuela)

VENEZUELA: CHANGING TIMES

Venezuela is a country in transition. After decades of rule by a succession of *caudillos* (strong, authoritarian rulers), national leaders can now point to four decades of unbroken civilian rule and peaceful transfers of presidential power. Economic growth—stimulated by mining, industry, and petroleum—has, until recently, been steady and, at times, stunning. With the availability of better transportation; access to radio, television, newspapers, and material goods; and the presence of the national government in once-isolated towns, regional diversity is less striking now than a decade ago. Fresh lifestyles and perspectives, dress and music, and literacy and health care are changing the face of rural Venezuela.

THE PROBLEMS OF CHANGE

Such changes have not been without problems—significant ones. Venezuela, despite its petroleum-generated wealth, remains a nation plagued by huge imbalances, inequalities, contradictions, and often bitter debate over the meaning and direction of national development. Some critics note the danger of the massive rural-to-urban population shift and the influx of illegal immigrants the result of Venezuela's rapid economic development or people fleeing the violence in Colombia. Others warn of the excessive dependence on petroleum as the means of development and are concerned about the agricultural output at levels insufficient to satisfy domestic requirements. Venezuela, once a food exporter, periodically has had to import large amounts of basic commodities—such as milk, eggs, and meat—to feed the expanding urban populations. Years of easy, abundant money also promoted undisciplined borrowing abroad to promote industrial expansion and has saddled the nation with a serious foreign-debt problem. Government corruption was rampant and, in fact, led to the impeachment of President Carlos Andrés Pérez in 1993.

THE CHARACTER OF MODERNIZATION

The rapid changes in Venezuelan society have produced a host of generalizations as to the nature of modernization in this Andean republic. Commentators who speak of a revolutionary break with the past—of a "new" Venezuela completely severed from its historic roots reaching back to the sixteenth century—ignore what is enduring about Venezuela's Hispanic culture.

Even before it began producing petroleum, Venezuela was not a sleepy back-water. Its Andean region was always the most prosperous area in the South American continent and was a refuge from the civil wars that swept other parts of the country. There were both opportunity and wealth in the coffee-growing trade. With the oil boom and the collapse of coffee prices in 1929, the Andean region experienced depopulation as migrants left the farms for other regions or for the growing Andean cities. In short, Venezuela's rural economy should not be seen as a static point from which change began but as a part of a dynamic process of continuing change, which now has the production of petroleum as its focus.

TIMELINE

1520
The first Spanish settlement at Cumaná
1822–1829
Venezuela is part of Gran Colombia
1829
Venezuela achieves independence as a separate country
1922
The first productive oil well
1947
Women win the right to vote
1976
Foreign oil companies are nationalized
1980s
Booming public investment fuels inflation; Venezuela seeks renegotiation of foreign debt
1990s
Social and economic crisis grips the nation; Hugo Chavez wins the presidency and sets about to redraft the Constitution; Chavez's government is challenged by massive flooding that leaves more than 30,000 people dead and many more homeless
2000s
A new Constitution is approved
Chavez strengthens executive power; Chavez is reelected
2006
President Chavez reelected
2008
Growing tensions with neighboring Colombia
2010
Venezuela suffers its worst drought in 100 years
2011
President Chávez diagnosed with cancer; Further inroads made on freedom of expression and information

(United States Department of the Interior, Bureau of Mines)

When oil was discovered in Venezuela, rapid economic growth caused many problems in national development. By depending on petroleum as the major source of wealth, Venezuela was at the mercy of the fickle world energy market.

CULTURAL IDENTITY

Historian John Lombardi identifies language, culture, and an urban network centered on the capital city of Caracas as primary forces in the consolidation of the nation. "Across the discontinuities of civil war and political transformation, agricultural and industrial economies, rural life styles and urban agglomerations, Venezuela has functioned through the stable network of towns and cities whose interconnections defined the patterns of control, the directions of resource distribution, and the country's identity."

One example of the country's cultural continuity can be seen by looking into one dimension of Venezuelan politics. Political parties are not organized along class lines but tend to cut across class divisions. This is not to deny the existence of class consciousness—which is certainly ubiquitous in Venezuela—but it is not a major *political* force. Surprisingly, popular support for elections and strong party affiliations are more characteristic of rural areas than of cities. The phenomenon cannot be explained as a by-product of modernization. Party membership and electoral participation are closely linked to party organization, personal ties and loyalties, and charismatic leadership. The party, in a sense, becomes a surrogate *patrón* that has power and is able to deliver benefits to the party faithful.

IMPACTS OF URBANIZATION

Another insight into Hispanic political culture can be found in the rural-to-urban shift in population that has often resulted in large-scale seizures of land in urban areas by peasants. Despite the illegality of the seizures, such actions are frequently encouraged by officials because, they argue, it provides the poor with enough land to maintain political stability and to prevent peasants from encroaching on richer neighborhoods. Pressure by the new urban dwellers at election time usually results in their receiving essential services from government officials. In other words, municipal governments channel resources in return for expected electoral support from the migrants. Here is a classic Hispanic response to challenge from below—to bend, to cooperate.

Cultural values also underlie both the phenomenon of internal migration and the difficulty of providing adequate skilled labor for Venezuela's increasingly technological economy. While the attraction of the city and its many opportunities is one reason for the movement of population out of rural areas, so too is that segment of Venezuelan culture, which belittles the peasant and rural life in general. Similarly, the shortage of skilled labor is the result not only of inadequate training but also of social values that neither reward nor dignify skilled labor.

THE SOCIETY

The rapid pace of change has contributed to a reexamination of the roles and rights of women in Venezuela. In recent years, women have occupied positions in the cabinet and in the Chamber of Deputies; several women deputies have held important posts in political parties.

Yet while educated women are becoming more prominent in the professions, there is a reluctance to employ women in traditional "men's" jobs, and blatant inequality still blemishes the workplace. Women, for example, are paid less than men for similar work. And although modern feminist goals have become somewhat of a social and economic force, at least in urban centers, the traditional roles of wife and mother continue to hold the most prestige, and physical beauty is still often viewed as a woman's most precious asset. In addition, many men seek deference from women rather than embracing social equality. Nevertheless, the younger generations of Venezuelans are experiencing the social and cultural changes that have tended to follow women's liberation in Western industrialized nations: higher levels of education and career skills; broadened intellectualism; increasing freedom and equality for both men and women; relaxed social mores; and the accompanying personal turmoil, such as rising divorce and single-parenthood rates.

Venezuelans generally enjoy a high degree of individual liberty. Civil, personal, and political rights are protected by a strong and independent judiciary. Citizens generally enjoy a free press. There exists the potential for governmental abuse of press freedom, however. Several laws leave journalists vulnerable to criminal charges, especially in the area of libel. Journalists must be certified to work, and certification may be withdrawn by the government if journalists are perceived to stray from the "truth," misquote sources, or refuse to correct "errors." In 2010 new legislation targeted radio, television, and

Caracas, Venezuela, an ultra-modern city of 3.85 million exemplifying the extremes of poverty and wealth that exist in Latin America, sprawls for miles over mountains and valleys.

electronic media and has severely impinged on their freedom of expression and information.

The civil and human rights enjoyed by most Venezuelans have not necessarily extended to the nation's Indian population in the Orinoco Basin. For years, extra-regional forces—in the form of rubber gatherers, missionaries, and developers—have to varying degrees undermined the economic self-sufficiency, demographic viability, and tribal integrity of indigenous peoples. A government policy that stressed the existence of only one Venezuelan culture posed additional problems for Indians.

In 1991, however, President Pérez signed a decree granting a permanent homeland, encompassing some 32,000 square miles in the Venezuelan Amazon forest, to the country's 14,000 Yanomamö Indians. Venezuela will permit no mining or farming in the territory and will impose controls on existing religious missions. President Pérez stated that "the primary use will be to preserve and to learn the traditional ways of the Indians." As James Brooke reported in *The New York Times,* "Venezuela's move has left anthropologists euphoric."

Race relations are outwardly tranquil in Venezuela, but there exists an underlying racism in nearly all arenas. People are commonly categorized by the color of their skin, with white being the most prized. Indeed, race, not economic level, is still a major social-level determinant. This unfortunate reality imparts a sense of frustration and a measure of hopelessness to many of Venezuela's people, in that even those who acquire a good education and career training may be discriminated against in the workplace because they are "of color." Considering that only one-fifth of the population are of white extraction, with 67 percent Mestizos and 10 percent blacks, this is indeed a widespread and debilitating problem.

President Chavez is of mixed racial ancestry and has won broad support among the disadvantaged because he has moved to remove, in the words of Benjamin Keene and Keith Haynes, "the social stigma historically attached to the terms *mulatto, mestizo,* and *black.* This new sense of dignity, not just the hope for improvement in economic status, helped to explain the fierce loyalty of these masses toward their leader." Indicative of an underlying racism among some of those opposed to Chavez are the terms of opprobrium used to describe him, including *el Mono* (the monkey) or *el Negro* (the black).

■ A VIGOROUS FOREIGN POLICY

Venezuela has always pursued a vigorous foreign policy. In the words of former president Luis Herrera Campins: "Effective action by Venezuela in the area of international affairs must take certain key facts into account: economics—we are a producer-exporter of oil; politics—we have a stable, consolidated democracy; and geopolitics—we are at one and the same time a Caribbean, Andean, Atlantic, and Amazonian country." Venezuela has long assumed that it should be the guardian of Simón Bolívar's ideal of creating an independent and united Latin America. The nation's memory of its continental leadership, which developed during the Wars for Independence (1810–1826), has been rekindled in Venezuela's desire to promote the political and economic integration of both the continent and the Caribbean. Venezuela's foreign policy remains true to the Bolivarian ideal of an independent Latin America and it should come as no surprise that President Chavez has adopted the term "Bolivarian Revolution" for his movement. In the Caribbean, Venezuela has invested in industry and provided cut-rate petroleum to Cuba and many microstates. In South America he has established close relations with other populist governments, including those in Brazil, Bolivia, Argentina, and Uruguay. And he has openly challenged the United States with his strong stand against free-trade agreements. Chavez's enmity toward the United States extends to Latin American nations he considers tied to Washington's policies. Colombia's President Uribe, for example, was considered an imperialist lackey and recent evidence suggests that Chavez has monetarily supported Colombian guerrillas.

■ PROMISING PROSPECTS TURN TO DISILLUSIONMENT

The 1980s brought severe turmoil to Venezuela's economy. The boom times of the 1970s turned to hard times as world oil prices dropped. Venezuela became unable to service its massive foreign debt that had ballooned to $45.44 billion at the end of 2007, and to subsidize the "common good" in the form of low gas and transportation prices and other amenities. In 1983, the currency, the bolívar, which had remained stable and strong for many years at 4.3 to the U.S. dollar, was devalued, to an official rate of 14.5 bolívars to the dollar. This was a boon to foreign visitors to the country, which became known as one of the world's greatest travel bargains, but a catastrophe for Venezuelans.

President Jaime Lusinchi of the Democratic Action Party, who took office early in 1984, had the unenviable job of trying to cope with the results of the preceding years of free spending, high expectations, dependence on oil, and spiraling foreign debt. Although the country's gross national product grew during his tenure (agriculture growth contributed significantly, rising from 0.4 percent of gross national product in 1983 to 6.8 percent in 1986), austerity measures were in order. The Lusinchi government was not up to the challenge. Indeed, his major legacy was a corruption scandal at the government agency Recadi, which was responsible for allocating foreign currency to importers at the official rate of 14.5 bolívars to the dollar. It was alleged that billions of dollars were skimmed, with a number of high-level government officials, including three finance ministers, implicated. Meanwhile, distraught Venezuelans watched inflation and the devalued bolívar eat up their savings; the once-blooming middle class started getting squeezed out.

In the December 1988 national elections, another Democratic Action president, Carlos Andrés Pérez, was elected. Pérez, who had served as president from 1974 to 1979, was widely rumored to have stolen liberally from Venezuela's coffers during that tenure. Venezuelans joked at first that "Carlos Andrés is coming back to get what he left behind," but as the campaign wore on, some political observers were dismayed to hear the preponderance of the naive sentiment that "now he has enough and will really work for Venezuela this time."

One of Pérez's first acts upon reentering office was to raise the prices of government-subsidized gasoline and public transportation. Although he had warned that tough austerity measures would be implemented, the much-beleaguered and disgruntled urban populace took to the streets in February 1989 in the most serious rioting to have occurred in Venezuela since it became a democracy. Army tanks rolled down the major thoroughfares of Caracas, the capital; skirmishes between the residents and police and military forces were common; looting was widespread. The government announced that 287 people had been killed. Unofficial hospital sources charge that the death toll was closer to 2,000. A stunned Venezuela quickly settled down in the face of the violence, mortified that such a debacle, widely reported in the international press, should take place in this advanced and peaceable country. But tourism, a newly vigorous and promising industry as a result of favorable currency-exchange rates, subsided immediately; it has yet to recover fully.

On February 4, 1992, another ominous event highlighted Venezuela's continuing political and economic weaknesses. Rebel military paratroopers, led by Hugo Chavez, attacked the presidential palace in Caracas and government sites in several other major cities. The coup attempt, the first in Venezuela since 1962, was rapidly put down by forces loyal to President Pérez, who escaped what he described as an assassination attempt. Reaction within Venezuela was mixed, reflecting widespread discontent with Pérez's tough economic policies, government corruption, and declining living standards. A second unsuccessful coup attempt, on November 27, 1992, followed months of public demonstrations against Pérez's government.

Perhaps the low point was reached in May 1993, when Pérez was suspended from office and impeachment proceedings initiated. Allegedly the president had embezzled more than $17 million and had facilitated other irregularities. Against a backdrop of military unrest, Ramón José Velásquez was named interim president.

In December 1993, Venezuelans elected Rafael Caldera, who had been president in a more prosperous and promising era (1969–1974). Caldera's presidency too was fraught with problems. In his first year, he had to confront widespread corruption in official circles, the devaluation of the bolívar, drug trafficking, a banking structure in disarray, and a high rate of violent crime in Caracas. Indeed, in 1997, a relative of President Caldera was mugged and a Spanish diplomat who had traveled to Caracas to negotiate a trade agreement with Venezuela was robbed in broad daylight.

In an attempt to restore order from chaos, President Caldera inaugurated his "Agenda Venezuela" program to address the difficult problems created by deep recession, financial instability, deregulation, privatization, and market reforms. The plan was showing signs of progress when it was undercut by the collapse of petroleum prices.

The stage was thus set for the emergence of a "hero" who would promise to solve all of Venezuela's ills. In the presidential election of 1998, the old parties were swept from power and a populist—the same Hugo Chavez who had attempted a coup in 1992—won with 55 percent of the popular vote. Those who expected change were not disappointed, although some of Chavez's actions have raised concerns about the future of democracy in Venezuela. A populist and a pragmatist, it is difficult to ascertain where Chavez's often contradictory policies will lead. Since taking power in February 1999, he has placed the army in control of the operation of medical clinics and has put soldiers to work on road and sewer repairs and in school and hospital construction. He has talked about the need to cut costs and uproot what he perceives as a deeply corrupt public sector—but he has refused to downsize the bureaucracy. Chavez supports privatization of the nation's pension fund and electric utilities, but he wants to maintain state control over health care and the petroleum industry.

Perhaps of greater concern is Chavez's successful bid to redraft Venezuela's Constitution, to provide "a better version." He claimed that the document had eroded democracy by allowing a political elite to rule without restraint for decades. Chavez's "democratic" vision demands special powers to revamp the economy without congressional approval. Through clever manipulation of the people by means of his own radio and television shows, and newspaper, Chavez intimidated Congress into granting him almost all the power he wanted to enact financial and economic legislation by decree. A referendum in April 1999 gave him a huge majority supporting the creation of an assembly to redraft the Constitution. A draft was completed in November. The political

opposition was convinced that the new document would allow Chavez to seek a second consecutive term in office, which had been prohibited in Venezuela, and that he was doing nothing less than creating a dictatorship under the cover of democracy and the law. Their fears have been realized, as the new Constitution allows for consecutive six-year terms.

The trend toward more centralized executive authority continued in 2000 and 2001. When the new 1999 Constitution was "reprinted" in March 2000, critics noted substantial changes from the original—changes that enhanced presidential power. In the same month, a group of retired military officers called on President Chavez to halt the politicization of the armed forces. The president's response was to appoint active-duty officers to a range of important positions in the government, including the state-owned petroleum company and foreign ministry. Organized labor complained that Chavez has attempted to transform the labor movement into an appendage of the ruling political party and has ignored union leadership in direct appeals by the government to rank-and-file workers. He has alienated the Catholic hierarchy over abortion and education issues; and the media, while legally free to criticize the government, have felt the need to exercise self-censorship. Perhaps most ominously, Chavez asked for and received from a compliant Legislature permission to rule by decree on a broad spectrum of issues, from the economy to public security. The *Ley Habilitante* allows him to enact legislation without parliamentary debate or even approval.

Equally radical and unpredictable is Chavez's policy toward neighboring Colombia. Chavez opened a dialogue with Colombia's guerrillas and dismissed Colombia's protests with the statement that the guerrillas held effective power.

Chavez clearly sees himself as a major player in the region and seems to enjoy annoying the United States. He is friends with the Castro brothers, made common cause with other populist leaders in Latin America and befriended the radical regime in Iran. Venezuela's longstanding boundary dispute with neighboring Guyana has also been resurrected.

Venezuela's future is wholly unpredictable in large measure because its current government is unpredictable. Growing dissatisfaction with Chavez's strong-arm rule precipitated street violence in early April 2002. For four days he was apparently forced from power by elements in the military, but demonstrations by Chavez's supporters resulted in his return to office. The political opposition mounted a campaign to gather the signatures necessary to

DID YOU KNOW?

Venezuela's Angel Falls are the tallest in the world at 3,212 feet—about 20 times the height of Niagara Falls. They were discovered by an American bush pilot named Jimmie Angel who crash-landed near the falls in the 1930s. He and others in his party, who had been searching for gold, reached civilization after a difficult 11-day journey and reported their find.

FURTHER INVESTIGATION

For more information on the Angel Falls go to http://www.world-of-waterfalls.com/latin-america-angel-falls.html

Snapshot: VENEZUELA

Summarized below is a quick look at the country with regard to its development, freedom, health/welfare, and achievements.

Development

The populist Chavez government, under the ideological umbrella of "21st century Socialism," is in the process of reorganizing the nation's oil industry and takes a larger share from private multinational companies. In January 2010, President Chavez devalued the bol'var in an attempt to increase revenues from petroleum production and stimulate domestic production.

Freedom

Freedom of the press has experienced significant erosion under the current government. Media watchdogs have accused Chavez for, in the words of *BBC News*, "creating a hostile and intimidatory climate for journalists, while some major private media outlets have been have been criticised for playing a direct role in the opposition movement against him. . . ." A controversial media law passed in 2005, ostensibly aimed at improving broadcast standards, also "bans material deemed to harm national security" and is seen by some as an attempt to silence media criticism A 2010 Law on Social Responsibility on Radio, Television, and Electronic Media places severe restrictions on freedom of expression and information.

Health/Welfare

A 1997 survey of children working in the informal sector revealed that 25 percent were between ages 5 and 12; that they worked more than 7 hours a day and earned about $2; and that their "jobs" included garbage collection, lotteries and gambling, and selling drugs. Fewer than half attended school. President Chavez has created 6,840 cooperatives that now employ 210,000 people, many of them who previously were unemployed or underemployed. Pro-active health programs have, as of 2008, virtually eliminated yellow fever and typhus in Venezuela.

Achievements

Venezuela's great novelists, such as Rómulo Gallegos and Artúro Uslar Pietri, have been attracted by the barbarism of the backlands and the lawlessness native to rural regions. Gallegos's classic *Doña Barbara*, the story of a female regional chieftain, has become world-famous.

---

force a recall vote in August 2004. Chavez emerged as the winner and announced that he would run for another six-year term in elections in 2006. Chavez's victory emboldened him to again seek constitutional changes that would essentially allow him to remain in office for as long as he wished. Unexpectedly, an electorate that is increasingly concerned by his policies voted down his proposed reforms. More to the point, many of Chavez's supporters among the poor voted against the president. Promised social programs have not been implemented and inflation eats away already meager incomes. It might be surmised that much of Chavez's fiery rhetoric on the international stage is designed to deflect attention from growing domestic difficulties. Another source of uncertainty was the news that Chavez was diagnosed with cancer, although he shows no signs of wanting to relinquish power.

Statistics

Geography

Area in Square Miles (Kilometers): 352,143 (912,050) (about twice the size of California)

Capital (Population): Caracas (3,051,000)

Environmental Concerns: water, sewage, air, oil, and urban pollution; deforestation; soil degradation

Geographical Features: a flat coastal plain and the Orinoco Delta are bordered by Andes Mountains and hills; plains (llanos) extend between the mountains and the Orinoco; Guyana Highlands and plains are south of the Orinoco

Climate: varies from tropical to temperate

People

Population

Total: 27,635,743 (2011 est.)

Annual Growth Rate: 1.5%

Rural/Urban Population Ratio: 7/93

Major Languages: Spanish; indigenous dialects

Ethnic Makeup: 67% Mestizo; 21% white; 10% black; 2% Indian

Religions: 96% nominally Roman Catholic; 4% Protestant and others

Health

Life Expectancy at Birth: 71 years (male); 77 years (female)

Infant Mortality Rate (Ratio): 20.6/1,000

Physicians Available (Ratio): 1.94/1,000

Education

Adult Literacy Rate: 93%

Compulsory (Ages): 5–15; free

Communication

Telephones: 7,083,000 main lines

Daily Newspaper Circulation: 215 per 1,000 people

Cell Phones: 27,880,000

Internet Users: 8,918,000

Transportation

Roadways in Kilometers (Miles): 96,155 (59,748)

Railroads in Kilometers (Miles): 682 (424)

Usable Airfields: 409

Government

Type: republic

Independence Date: July 5, 1811 (from Spain)

Head of State/Government: President Hugo Chavez Frias is both head of state and head of government

Political Parties: Democratic Action; Movement Toward Socialism; United Socialist Party of Venezuela; Fatherland for All; Christian Democratic Party; Democratic Action, others

Suffrage: universal at 18

Military

Military Expenditures (% of GDP): 1.2%

Current Disputes: territorial disputes with Guyana and Colombia

Economy

Currency ($U.S. Equivalent): 4.428 bolívars = $1

Per Capita Income/GDP: $12,400/$368.8 billion

GDP Growth Rate: 2.8%

Inflation Rate: 28.9%

Unemployment Rate: 8.5%

Labor Force: 13,400,000

Natural Resources: petroleum; natural gas; iron ore; gold; bauxite; other minerals; hydropower; diamonds

Agriculture: corn; sorghum; sugarcane; rice; bananas; vegetables; coffee; livestock; fish

Industry: petroleum; mining; construction materials; food processing; textiles; steel; aluminum; motor-vehicle assembly

Exports: $89.38 billion (primary partners United States, China, India, Cuba)

Imports: $50.04 billion (primary partners United States, Colombia Brazil, China)

Suggested Website

www.cia.org/cia/publications/factbook/index.html

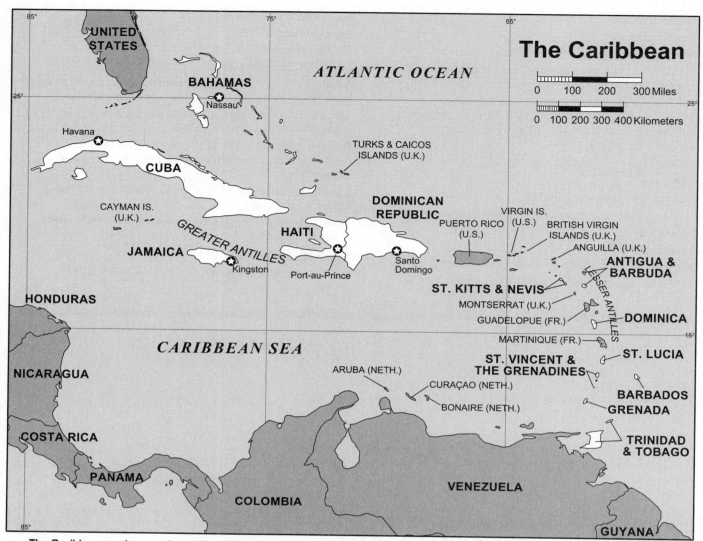

The Caribbean

ATLANTIC OCEAN

UNITED STATES

BAHAMAS
Nassau

TURKS & CAICOS ISLANDS (U.K.)

Havana
CUBA

CAYMAN IS. (U.K.)

GREATER ANTILLES

DOMINICAN REPUBLIC

HAITI

PUERTO RICO (U.S.)

VIRGIN IS. (U.S.)

BRITISH VIRGIN ISLANDS (U.K.)

ANGUILLA (U.K.)

JAMAICA
Kingston

Port-au-Prince

Santo Domingo

ANTIGUA & BARBUDA

ST. KITTS & NEVIS

MONTSERRAT (U.K.)

GUADELOPUE (FR.)

MARTINIQUE (FR.)

LESSER ANTILLES

DOMINICA

ST. LUCIA

HONDURAS

CARIBBEAN SEA

NICARAGUA

ARUBA (NETH.)

CURAÇAO (NETH.)

BONAIRE (NETH.)

ST. VINCENT & THE GRENADINES

BARBADOS

GRENADA

COSTA RICA

PANAMA

COLOMBIA

VENEZUELA

TRINIDAD & TOBAGO

GUYANA

0   100   200   300 Miles

0   100 200 300 400 Kilometers

The Caribbean region consists of hundreds of islands stretching from northern South America to the southern part of Florida. Many of the islands cover just a few square miles and are dominated by a central range of mountains; only Cuba has any extensive lowlands. Almost every island has a ring of coral, making approaches very dangerous for ships. The land that can be used for agriculture is extremely fertile; but many islands grow only a single crop, making them vulnerable to fluctuations in the world market in that particular commodity.

156

The Caribbean

Sea of Diversity

To construct a coherent overview of the Caribbean is an extremely difficult task because of the region's profound geographical and cultural diversity. "The history of the Caribbean is the examination of fragments, which, like looking at a broken vase, still provides clues to the form, beauty, and value of the past." So writes historian Franklin W. Knight in his study of the Caribbean. Other authors have drawn different analogies: Geographer David Lowenthal and anthropologist Lambros Comitas note that the West Indies "is a set of mirrors in which the lives of black, brown, and white, of American Indian and East Indian, and a score of other minorities continually interact."

For the geographer, the pieces fall into a different pattern, consisting of four distinct geographical regions. The first contains the Bahamas as well as the Turks and Caicos Islands. The Greater Antilles—consisting of Cuba, Hispaniola (Haiti and the Dominican Republic), Jamaica, the Cayman Islands, Puerto Rico, and the Virgin Islands—make up the second region. Comprising the third region are the Lesser Antilles—Antigua and Barbuda, Dominica, St. Lucia, St. Vincent and the Grenadines, Grenada, and St. Kitts and Nevis as well as various French departments and British and Dutch territories. The fourth group consists of islands that are part of the South American continental shelf: Trinidad and Tobago, Barbados, and the Dutch islands of Aruba, Curaçao, and Bonaire. Within these broad geographical regions, each nation is different. Yet on each island there often is a firmly rooted parochialism—a devotion to a parish or a village, a mountain valley or a coastal lowland.

CULTURAL DIVERSITY

To break down the Caribbean region into culture groups presents its own set of problems. The term "West Indian" inadequately describes the culturally Hispanic nations of Cuba and the Dominican Republic. On the other hand, "West Indian" does capture the essence of the cultures of Belize, the Caribbean coast of Central America, and Guyana, Suriname, and Cayenne (French Guiana). In Lowenthal's view: "Alike in not being Iberian [Hispanic], the West Indies are not North American either, nor indeed do they fit any ordinary regional pattern. Not so much undeveloped as overdeveloped, exotic without being traditional, they are part of the Third World yet ardent emulators of the West."

EFFORTS AT INTEGRATION

To complicate matters further, few West Indians would identify themselves as such. They are Jamaicans, or Bajans (people from Barbados), or Grenadans. Their economic, political, and social worlds are usually confined to the islands on which they live and work. In the eyes of its inhabitants, each island, no matter how small, is—or should be—sovereign. Communications by air, sea, and telephone with the rest of the world are ordinarily better than communications within the Caribbean region itself. Trade, even between neighboring islands, has always been minimal. Economic ties with the United States or Europe, and in some cases with Venezuela, are more important.

A British attempt to create a "West Indies Federation" in 1958 was reduced to a shambles by 1962. Member states had the same historical background; spoke the same languages; had similar economies; and were interested in the same kinds of food, music, and sports. But their spirit of independence triumphed over any kind of regional federation that "threatened" their individuality. In the words of a former Bajan prime minister, "We live together very well, but we don't like to live together." A Trinidadian explanation for the failure of the federation is found in a popular calypso verse from the early 1960s:

> Plans was moving fine
> When Jamaica stab we from behind
> Federation bust wide open
> But they want Trinidad to bear the burden.

Recently, however, the Windward Islands (Dominica, Grenada, St. Lucia, and St. Vincent and the Grenadines) have discussed political union. While each jealously guards its sovereignty, leaders are nevertheless aware that some integration is necessary if they are to survive in a changing world. The division of the world into giant economic blocs points to political union and the creation of a Caribbean state with a combined population of nearly half a million. Antigua and Barbuda resist because they believe that, in the words of former prime minister Vere Bird, "political union would be a new form of colonialism and undermine sovereignty."

While political union remains problematic, the 15 members of the Caribbean Community and Common Market (CARICOM, a regional body created in 1973) began long-term negotiations with Cuba in 1995 with regard to a free-trade agreement. CARICOM leaders informed Cuba that "it needs to open up its economy

View of the fishing nets and rope on a beach at Mire Cove with small fishing boats anchored nearby.

more." The free-market economies of CARICOM are profoundly different from Cuba's rigid state controls. "We need to assure that trade and investment will be mutually beneficial." Caribbean leaders have pursued trade with Cuba in the face of strong opposition from the United States. In general, CARICOM countries are convinced that "constructive engagement" rather than a policy of isolation is the best way to transform Cuba.

Political problems also plague the Dutch Caribbean. Caribbean specialist Aaron Segal notes that the six-island Netherlands Antilles Federation has encountered severe internal difficulties. Aruba never had a good relationship with the larger island of Curaçao and, in 1986, became a self-governing entity, with its own flag, Parliament, and currency, but still within the Netherlands. In 2010 Curaçao was granted full control over its internal affairs. "The other Netherlands Antillean states have few complaints about their largely autonomous relations with the Netherlands but find it hard to get along with one another."

Interestingly, islands that are still colonial possessions generally have a better relationship with their "mother" countries than with one another. Over the past few decades, smaller islands—populations of about 50,000 or less—have learned that there are advantages to a continued colonial connection. The extensive subsidies paid by Great Britain, France, or the Netherlands have turned dependency into an asset. Serving as tax-free offshore sites for banks and companies as well as encouraging tourism and hotel investments have led to modest economic growth.

CULTURAL IDENTIFICATION

Despite the local focus of the islanders, there do exist some broad cultural similarities. To the horror of nationalists, who are in search of a Caribbean identity that is distinct from Western civilization, most West Indians identify themselves as English or French in terms of culture. Bajans, for example, take a special pride in identifying their country as the "Little England of the Caribbean." English or French dialects are the languages spoken in common.

Nationalists argue that the islands will not be wholly free until they shatter the European connection. In the nationalists' eyes, that connection is a bitter reminder of slavery. After World War II, several Caribbean intellectuals attacked the strong European orientation of the islands and urged the islanders to be proud of their black African heritage. The shift in focus was most noticeable in the French Caribbean, although this new ethnic consciousness was echoed in the English-speaking islands as well in the form of a black-power movement during the 1960s and 1970s. It was during those years, when the islands were in transition from colonies to associated states to independent nations, that the Caribbean's black majorities seized political power by utilizing the power of their votes.

It is interesting to note that at the height of the black-power and black-awareness movements, sugar production was actually halted on the islands of St. Vincent, Antigua, and Barbuda—not because world-market prices were low, but because sugar cultivation was associated with the slavery of the past.

African Influences

The peoples of the West Indies are predominantly black, with lesser numbers of people of "mixed blood" and small numbers of whites. Culturally, the blacks fall into a number of groups. Throughout the nineteenth century, in Haiti, blacks strove to realize an African-Caribbean identity. African influences have remained strong on the island, although they have been blended with European Christianity and French civilization. Mulattos, traditionally the elite in Haiti, have strongly identified with French culture in an obvious attempt to distance themselves from the black majority, who comprise about 95 percent of the population. African-Creoles, as blacks of the English-speaking islands prefer to be called, are manifestly less "African" than the mass of Haitians. An exception to this generalization is the Rastafarians, common in Jamaica and found in lesser numbers on some of the other islands. Convinced that they are Ethiopians, the Rastafarians hope to return to Africa.

Racial Tension

The Caribbean has for years presented an image of racial harmony to the outside world. Yet, in actuality, racial tensions are not only present but also have become sharper in the last half of the twentieth century. Racial unrest broke to the surface in Jamaica in 1960 with riots in the capital city of Kingston. Tensions heightened again in 1980–1981 and in 1984, to the point that the nation's tourist industry drastically declined. A slogan of the Jamaican tourist industry, "Make It Jamaica Again," was a conscious attempt to downplay racial antagonism. The black-power movement in the 1960s on most of the islands also put to the test notions of racial harmony.

Most people of the Caribbean, however, believe in the myth of racial harmony. It is essential to the development of nationalism, which must embrace all citizens. Much racial tension is officially explained as class difference rather than racial prejudice. There is some merit to the class argument. A black politician on Barbuda, for example, enjoys much more status and prestige than a poor white "Redleg" from the island's interior. Yet if a black and a Redleg competed for the job of plantation manager, the white would likely win out over the black. In sum, race does make a difference, but so too does one's economic or political status.

East Indians

The race issue is more complex in Trinidad and Tobago, where there is a large East Indian (i.e., originally from India) minority. The East Indians, for the most part, are agricultural workers. They were originally introduced by the British between 1845 and 1916 to replace slave labor on the plantations. While numbers of East Indians have moved to the cities, they still feel that they have little in common with urban blacks. Because of their large numbers, East Indians are able to preserve a distinctive, healthy culture and community and to compete with other groups for political office and status.

East Indian culture has also adapted, but not yielded, to the West Indian world. In the words of Trinidadian-East Indian author V. S. Naipaul: "We were steadily adopting the food styles of others: The Portuguese stew of tomato and onions . . . the Negro way with yams, plantains, breadfruit, and bananas," but "everything we adopted became our own; the outside was still to be dreaded. . . ." The East Indians in Jamaica, who make up about 3 percent of the population, have made even more accommodations to the cultures around them. Most Jamaican-East Indians have become Protestant (the East Indians of Trinidad have maintained their Hindu or Islamic faith).

East Indian conformity and internalization, and their strong cultural identification, have often made them the targets of the black majority. Black stereotypes of the East Indians describe them in the following terms: "secretive," "greedy," and "stingy." And East Indian stereotypes describing blacks as "childish," "vain," "pompous," and "promiscuous" certainly do not help to ease ethnic tensions.

◼ REVOLUTIONARY CUBA

In terms of culture, the Commonwealth Caribbean (former British possessions) has little in common with Cuba or the Dominican Republic. But Cuba has made its presence felt in other ways. The Cuban Revolution, with the social progress that it entailed for many of its people and the strong sense of nationalism that it stimulated, impressed many West Indians. For new nation-states still in search of an identity, Cuba offered some clues as to how to proceed. For a time, Jamaica experimented with Cuban models of mass mobilization and programs designed to bring social services to the majority of the population. Between 1979 and 1983, Grenada saw merit in the Cuban approach to social and economic problems. The message that Cuba seemed to represent was that a small Caribbean state could shape its own destiny and make life better for its people.

The Cuba of Fidel Castro, while revolutionary, was also traditional. Hispanic culture is largely intact. The politics are authoritarian and personality-driven, and Castro himself easily fit into the mold of the Latin American leader, or caudillo, whose charisma and benevolent paternalism won him the widespread support of his

159

(Courtesy of Robert Buss)

These workers in Port-de-Paix, Haiti, are hand-carrying building materials up a ladder to add a second story to an existing home. Most people build with the intent of someday putting on a second story. When they get a little money they buy a few cinder/cement blocks until they have enough to build. Here they are hauling gravel to make concrete bucket by bucket. The roof is supported by many sticks that will remain there until the work is completed.

people. Castro's relationship with the Roman Catholic Church was also traditional and corresponds to notions of a dualistic culture that has its roots in the Middle Ages. In Castro's words: "The same respect that the Revolution ought to have for religious beliefs, ought also to be had by those who talk in the name of religion for the political beliefs of others. And, above all, to have present that which Christ said: 'My kingdom is not of this world.' What are those who are said to be the interpreters of Christian thought doing meddling in the problems of this world?" Castro's comments should not be interpreted as a Communist assault on religion. Rather, they express a time-honored Hispanic belief that religious life and everyday life exist in two separate spheres.

The social reforms that have been implemented in Cuba are well within the powers of all Latin American governments to enact. Those governments, in theory, are duty-bound to provide for the welfare of their peoples. Constitutionally, the state is infallible and all-powerful. Castro chose to identify with the needs of the majority of Cubans, to be a "father" to his people. Again, his actions are not so much Communistic as Hispanic.

Where Castro ran against the grain was in his assault on Cuba's middle class. In a sense, he reversed a trend that is evident in much of the rest of Latin America—the slow, steady progress of a middle class that is intent on acquiring a share of the power and prestige traditionally accorded to elites. Cuba's middle class was effectively shattered—people were deprived of much of their property; their livelihood; and, for those who fled into exile, their citizenship. Many expatriate Cubans remain bitter toward what they perceive as Castro's betrayal of the Revolution and the middle class. Fidel Castro's health problems and the subsequent designation of his brother Raúl Castro as Cuba's leader marks the passing of an era.

◼ EMIGRATION AND MIGRATION

Throughout the Caribbean, emigration and migration are a fact of life for hundreds of thousands of people. These are not new phenomena; their roots extend to the earliest days of European settlement. The flow of people looking for work is deeply rooted in history, in contemporary political economy, and even in Caribbean island culture. The Garifuna (black-Indian mixture) who settled in Belize and coastal parts of Mexico, Guatemala, Honduras, and Nicaragua originally came from St. Vincent. There, as escaped slaves, they intermixed with remnants of Indian tribes who had once peopled the islands, and they adopted many of their cultural traits. Most of the Garifuna (or Black Caribs, as they are also known) were deported from St. Vincent to the Caribbean coast of Central America at the end of the eighteenth century.

From the 1880s onward, patois-speaking (French dialect) Dominicans and St. Lucians migrated to Cayenne (French Guiana) to work in the gold fields. The strong identification with Europe has drawn thousands more to what many consider their cultural homes.

High birth rates and lack of economic opportunity have forced others to seek their fortunes elsewhere. Many citizens of the Dominican Republic have moved to New York, and Haitian refugees have thrown themselves on the coast of Florida by the thousands. Other Haitians seek seasonal employment in the Dominican Republic or the Bahamas. There are sizable Jamaican communities in the Dominican Republic, Haiti, the Bahamas, and Belize.

On the smaller islands, stable populations are the exception rather than the rule. The people are constantly migrating to larger places in search of higher pay and a better life. Such emigrants moved to Panama when the canal was being cut in the early 1900s or sought work on the Dutch islands of Curaçao and Aruba when oil refineries were built there in the 1920s. They provided much of the labor for the banana plantations in Central America. Further contributing to out-migration is the changing character of some island economies. Many islands can no longer compete in world markets for sugar or bananas and have been forced to diversify. In 2005 St. Kitts closed its last sugar mills, ending a 350-year relationship with what had been the island's main industry. Now hope has been placed in tourism. For agricultural workers the alternatives are retraining or emigration.

The greatest number of people by far have left the Caribbean region altogether and emigrated to the United States, Canada, and Europe. Added to those who have left because of economic or population pressures are political refugees. The majority of these are Cubans, most of whom have resettled in Florida.

Some have argued that the prime mover of migration from the Caribbean lies in the *ideology* of migration—that is, the expectation that all nonelite males will migrate abroad. Sugarcane slave plantations left a legacy that included little possibility of island subsistence; and so there grew the need to migrate to survive, a reality that was absorbed into the culture of lower-class blacks. But for these blacks, there has also existed the expectation to return. (In contrast, middle- and upper-class migrants have historically departed permanently.) Historian Bonham Richardson writes: "By traveling away and returning the people have been able to cope more successfully with the vagaries of man and nature than they would have by staying at home. The small islands of the region are the most vulnerable to environmental and economic uncertainty. Time and again in the Lesser Antilles, droughts, hurricanes, and economic depressions have diminished wages, desiccated provision grounds, and destroyed livestock, and there has been no local recourse to disease or starvation." Hence, men and women of the small West Indian islands have been obliged to migrate. "And like migrants everywhere, they have usually considered their travels temporary, partly because they have never been greeted cordially in host communities."

On the smaller islands, such as St. Kitts and Nevis, family and community ceremonies traditionally reinforce and sustain the importance of emigration and return. Funerals reunite families separated by vast distances; Christmas parties and carnival celebrations are also occasions to welcome returning family and friends.

Monetary remittances from relatives in the United States, England, Canada, or the larger islands are a constant reminder of the importance of migration. According to Richardson: "Old men who have earned local prestige by migrating and returning exhort younger men to follow in their footsteps. . . . Learned cultural responses thereby maintain a migration ethos . . . that is not only valuable in coping with contemporary problems, but also provides continuity with the past."

The Haitian diaspora (dispersion) offers some significant differences. While Haitian migration is also a part of the nation's history, a return flow is noticeably absent. One of every six Haitians now lives abroad—primarily in Cuba, the Dominican Republic, Venezuela, Colombia, Mexico, and the Bahamas. In French Guiana, Haitians comprise more than 25 percent of the population. They are also found in large numbers in urban areas of the United States, Canada, and France. The typical Haitian emigrant is poor, has little education, and has few skills or job qualifications.

Scholar Christian A. Girault remarks that although "ordinary Haitian migrants are clearly less educated than the Cubans, Dominicans, Puerto Ricans and even Jamaicans, they are not Haiti's most miserable; the latter could never hope to buy an air ticket or boat passage, or to pay an agent." Those who establish new roots in host countries tend to remain, even though they experience severe discrimination and are stereotyped as "undesirable" because they are perceived as bringing with them "misery, magic and disease," particularly AIDS.

There is also some seasonal movement of the population on the island itself. Agricultural workers by the tens of thousands are found in neighboring Dominican Republic. *Madames sara,* or peddlers, buy and sell consumer goods abroad and provide "an essential provisioning function for the national market."

■ AN ENVIRONMENT IN DANGER

When one speaks of soil erosion and deforestation in a Caribbean context, Haiti is the example that usually springs to mind. While that image is accurate, it is also too limiting, for much of the Caribbean is threatened with ecological disaster. Part of the problem is historical,

These lush mountain peaks in St. Lucia are volcanic in origin.

(© Glowimages/PunchStock)

for deforestation began with the development of sugarcane cultivation in the seventeenth century. But now, soil erosion and depletion as well as the exploitation of marginal lands by growing populations perpetuate a vicious cycle between inhabitants and the land on which they live. Cultivation of sloping hillsides, or denuding the slopes in the search of wood to make charcoal, creates a situation in which erosion is constant and an ecological and human disaster likely. In 2004 days of heavy rain on the island of Hispaniola generated thousands of mudslides and killed an estimated 2,000 people in Haiti and the Dominican Republic.

A 1959 report on soil conditions in Jamaica noted that, in one district of the Blue Mountains, on the eastern end of that island, the topsoil had vanished, a victim of rapid erosion. The problem is not unique to the large islands, however. Bonham Richardson observes that ecological degradation on the smallest islands is acute. Thorn scrub and grasses have replaced native forest. "A regional drought in 1977, leading to starvation in Haiti and producing crop and livestock loss south to Trinidad, was severe only partly because of the lack of rain. Grasses and shrubs afford little protection against the sun and thus cannot help the soil to retain moisture in the face of periodic drought. Neither do they inhibit soil loss."

Migration of the islands' inhabitants has at times exacerbated the situation. In times of peak migration, a depleted labor force on some of the islands has resulted in landowners resorting to the raising of livestock, which is not labor-intensive. But livestock contribute to further ecological destruction. "Emigration itself has thus indirectly fed the ongoing devastation of island environments, and some of the changes seem irreversible. Parts of the smaller islands already resemble moonscapes. They seem simply unable to sustain their local resident populations, not to mention future generations or those working abroad who may someday be forced to return for good."

■ MUSIC, DANCE, FOLKLORE, AND FOOD

Travel accounts of the Caribbean tend to focus on local music, dances, and foods. Calypso, the limbo, steel bands, reggae, and African–Cuban rhythms are well known. Much of the music derives from Amerindian and African roots.

Calypso music apparently originated in Trinidad and spread to the other islands. Calypso singers improvise on any theme; they are particularly adept at poking fun at politicians and their shortcomings. Indeed, governments are as attentive to the lyrics of a politically inspired calypso tune as they are to the opposition press. On a broader scale, calypso is a mirror of Caribbean society.

Some traditional folkways, such as storytelling and other forms of oral history, are in danger of being replaced by electronic media, particularly radio, tape recorders, and jukeboxes. The new entertainment is both popular and readily available.

Scholar Laura Tanna has gathered much of Kingston, Jamaica's, oral history. Her quest for storyteller Adina Henry took her to one of the city's worst slums, the Dungle, and was reprinted in *Caribbean Review:* "We walked down the tracks to a Jewish cemetery, with gravestones dating back to the 1600s. It, too, was covered in litter, decaying amid the rubble of broken stones. Four of the tombs bear the emblem of the skull and crossbones. Popular belief has it that Spanish gold is buried in the tombs, and several of them have been desecrated by treasure seekers. We passed the East Indian shacks, and completed our tour of Majesty Pen amidst greetings of 'Love' and 'Peace' and with the fragrance of ganja [marijuana] wafting across the way. Everywhere, people were warm and friendly, shaking hands, chatting, drinking beer, or playing dominos. One of the shacks had a small bar and jukebox inside. There, in the midst of pigs grunting at one's feet in the mud and slime, in the dirt and dust, people had their own jukeboxes, tape recorders, and radios, all blaring out reggae, the voice of the ghetto." Tanna found Miss Adina, whose stories revealed the significant African contribution to West Indian folk culture.

In recent years, Caribbean foods have become more accepted, and even celebrated, within the region as well as internationally. Part of the search for an identity involves a new attention to traditional recipes. French, Spanish, and English recipes have been adapted to local foods—iguana, frogs, seafood, fruits, and vegetables. Cassava, guava, and mangos figure prominently in the islanders' diets.

The diversity of the Caribbean is awesome, with its potpourri of peoples and cultures. Its roots lie in Spain, Portugal, England, France, the Netherlands, Africa, India, China, and Japan. There has emerged no distinct West Indian culture, and the Caribbean peoples' identities are determined by the island—no matter how small—on which they live. For the Commonwealth Caribbean, nationalist stirrings are still weak and lacking in focus; while people in Cuba and the Dominican Republic have a much surer grasp on who they are. Nationalism is a strong integrating force in both of these nations. The Caribbean is a fascinating and diverse corner of the world that is far more complex than the travel posters imply.

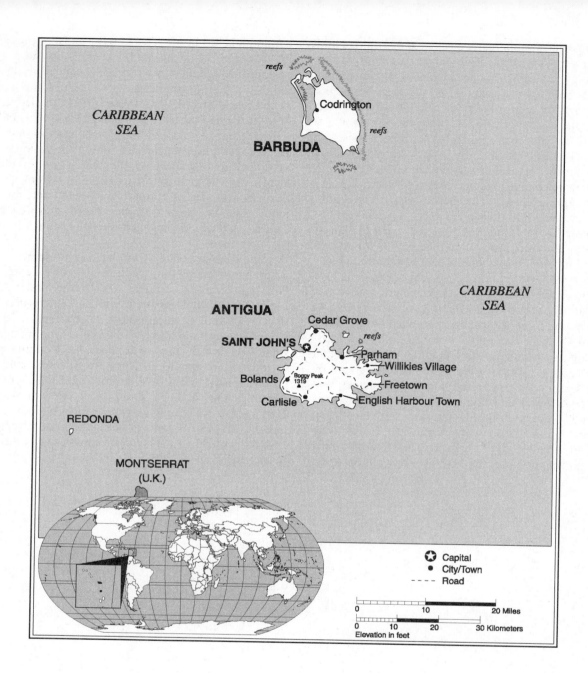

CARIBBEAN SEA

BARBUDA

reefs

• Codrington

reefs

CARIBBEAN SEA

ANTIGUA

Cedar Grove

SAINT JOHN'S

reefs

Parham

Willikies Village

Bolands

Boggy Peak
1319

Freetown

Carlisle

English Harbour Town

REDONDA

MONTSERRAT
(U.K.)

⊕ Capital
• City/Town
--- Road

0   10   20 Miles

0   10   20   30 Kilometers
Elevation in feet

Antigua and Barbuda

ANTIGUA AND BARBUDA: A STRAINED RELATIONSHIP

The nation of Antigua and Barbuda gained its independence from Great Britain on November 1, 1981. Both islands, tenuously linked since 1967, illustrate perfectly the degree of localism characteristic of the West Indies. Barbudans—who number approximately 1,200—culturally and politically believe that they are not Antiguans; indeed, since independence of Britain, they have been intent on secession. Barbudans view Antiguans as little more than colonial masters.

MEMORIES OF SLAVERY

Antigua was a sugar island for most of its history. This image changed radically in the 1960s, when the black-power movement then sweeping the Caribbean convinced Antiguans that work on the sugar plantations was "submissive" and carried the psychological and social stigma of historic slave labor. In response to the clamor, the government gradually phased out sugar production, which ended entirely in 1972. The decline of agriculture resulted in a strong rural-to-urban flow of people. To replace lost revenue from the earnings of sugar, the government promoted tourism.

Tourism produced the unexpected result of greater freedom for women, in that they gained access to previously unavailable employment opportunities. Anthropologist W. Penn Handwerker has shown that a combination of jobs and education for women has resulted in a marked decline in fertility. Between 1965 and the 1980s, real wages doubled, infant mortality fell dramatically, and the proportion of women ages 20 to 24 who completed secondary school rose from 3 percent to about 50 percent. "Women were freed from dependency on their children" as well as their men and created "conditions for a revolution in gender relations." Men outmigrated as the economy shifted, and women took the new jobs in tourism. Many of the jobs demanded higher skills, which in turn resulted in more education for women, followed by even better jobs. And notes Handwerker: "Women empowered by education and good jobs are less likely to suffer abuse from partners."

CULTURAL PATTERNS

Antiguans and Barbudans are culturally similar. Many islanders still have a strong affinity for England and English culture, while others identify more with what they hold to be their African–Creole roots. On Antigua, for example, Creole, which is spoken by virtually the entire population, is believed to reflect what is genuine and "natural" about the island and its culture. Standard English, even though it is the official language, carries in the popular mind an aura of falseness.

FOREIGN RELATIONS

Despite the small size of the country, Antigua and Barbuda are actively courted by regional powers. The United States maintains a satellite-tracking station on Antigua, and Brazil has provided loans and other assistance.

TIMELINE

1632
The English settle Antigua

1834
Antigua abolishes slavery

1958–1962
Antigua becomes part of the West Indies Federation

1981
Independence from Great Britain

1990s
Barbuda talks of secession; Hurricane Luis devastates the islands

2000s
The Bird government announces a "zero tolerance" drug policy
Bird political dynasty comes to an end in 2004

2010
World recession hits hard; tourism reduced significantly

2012
Dispute continues with United States over internet gambling

Snapshot: ANTIGUA AND BARBUDA

Summarized below is a quick look at the country with regard to its development, freedom, health/welfare, and achievements.

Development

Land-use patterns in the islands show that 37 percent of the land is devoted to grazing, 34 percent to woodlands, 11 percent to settlements, 3 percent to tourist areas, and 3 percent to airports. Agricultural use accounts for only 8 percent of the land. Tourism, the leading source of employment, has replaced agriculture as the prime generator of revenue. Perhaps 50 percent of foreign exchange derives from tourism.

Freedom

According to Refworld, Antigua and Barbuda "generally respects freedom of the press, but in practice media outlets are concentrated among a small number of firms affiliated with either the current government or its predecessor. The Bird family continues to control television, cable, and radio outlets. The government owns one of three radio stations and the public television station."

Health/Welfare

The government has initiated programs to enhance educational opportunities for men and women and to assist in family planning. The new Directorate of Women's Affairs helps women to advance in government and in the professions. It has also sponsored educational programs for women in health, crafts, and business skills.

Achievements

Antigua has preserved its rich historical heritage, from the dockyard named for Admiral Lord Nelson to the Ebenezer Methodist Church. Built in 1839, the latter was the "mother church" for Methodism in the Caribbean.

A small oil refinery, jointly supported by Venezuela and Mexico, began operations in 1982.

■ FAMILY POLITICS

From 1951 to 2004, with one interruption, Antiguan politics has been dominated by the family of Vere Bird and his Antigua Labour Party (ALP). Charges of nepotism, corruption, drug smuggling, and money laundering dogged the Vere Bird administration for years. Still, in 1994, Lester Bird managed to succeed his 84-year-old father as prime minister, and the ALP won 11 of 17 seats in elections. Lester admitted that his father had been guilty of some "misjudgments" and quickly pledged that the ALP would improve education, better the status of women, and increase the presence of young people in government.

The younger Bird, in his State of the Nation address early in 1995, challenged Antiguans to transform their country on their own terms, rather than those dictated by the International Monetary Fund. His government would take "tough and unpopular" measures to avoid the humiliation of going "cap in hand" to foreign financial institutions. Those tough measures included increases in contributions for medical benefits, property and personal taxes, and business and motor-vehicle licenses.

In 2003, however, the government angered public employees, who constitute one-third of the labor force, when it failed to pay salaries on time. Tourism was stagnant and the public debt was a very high 140 percent of GDP. Economic difficulties when coupled with persistent scandal and corruption brought 90 percent of the electorate to the polls in 2004 and Bird's ALP was soundly defeated. Prime Minister Baldwin Spencer's government must now live up to the expectations of the electorate. Tourism, the earnings from which slipped from 80 percent of GDP in 1994 to only 50 percent in 2004, has still not recovered, and continues to be a major area of concern. Internet gambling sites have emerged as a revenue supplement to tourism, but this has embroiled Antigua in a trade dispute with the United States, which places restrictions on the business. Even though the World Trade Federation ruled in favor of Antigua and Barbuda, as of early 2012 the United States still refuses to ease restrictions. Agricultural production, consisting primarily of fruits and vegetables, concentrates on the domestic market and does not generate significant foreign exchange earnings. Of great concern was the collapse in 2009 of the country's largest financial institution, Stanford Financial. Its United States CEO was charged by U.S. authorities with massive fraud. Added to these woes is a large budget deficit. Spencer's administration must make some difficult choices in the near future.

? DID YOU KNOW?

English Harbour with its Nelson's Dockyard was vital to British naval power in the Caribbean in the 18th and early 19th centuries. With its garrison of 1,000 soldiers, the crowded harbor serviced the needs of British warships. Nelson's Dockyard remains a popular tourist destination.

FURTHER INVESTIGATION

For more information on Nelson's Dockyard National Park go to http://www.antigua-barbuda.org/agharb01.htm

Statistics

Geography

Area in Square Miles (Kilometers): 171 (442) (about 2½ times the size of Washington, D.C.)

Capital (Population): Saint John's (27,000)

Environmental Concerns: water management; clearing of trees

Geographical Features: mostly low-lying limestone and coral islands, with some higher volcanic areas

Climate: tropical marine

People

Population

Total: 87,884 (2011 est.)

Annual Growth Rate: 1.23%

Rural/Urban Population Ratio: 70/30

Major Languages: English; Creole

Ethnic Makeup: almost entirely black African origin; some of British, Portuguese, Lebanese, or Syrian origin

Religions: 25.7% Anglican; 12.3% Seventh Day Adventist; 10.6% Pentecostal; 10.5% Moravian; 10.4% Catholic

Health

Life Expectancy at Birth: 73 years (male); 77 years (female)

Infant Mortality Rate (Ratio): 14.63/1,000

Physicians Available (Ratio): .17/1,000

Education

Adult Literacy Rate: 85.8%

Compulsory (Ages): 5–16

Communication

Telephones: 41,700 main lines

Cell Phones: 163,900

Internet Users: 65,000

Transportation

Roadways in Kilometers (Miles): 1,165 (724)

Railroads in Kilometers (Miles): 48 (77)

Usable Airfields: 3

Government

Type: parliamentary democracy

Independence Date: November 1, 1981 (from the United Kingdom)

Head of State/Government: Queen Elizabeth II; Prime Minister Baldwin Spencer

Political Parties: Antigua Labour Party; United Progressive Party; a coalition of opposing parties

Suffrage: universal at 18

Military

Current Disputes: tensions between Antiguans and Barbudans

Economy

Currency ($U.S. Equivalent): 2.75 East Caribbean dollars = $1

Per Capita Income/GDP: $22,100/$1.734 billion

GDP Growth Rate: 2%

Inflation Rate: 2.5%

Unemployment Rate: 11%

Labor Force: 30,000

Natural Resources: negligible; the pleasant climate fosters tourism

Agriculture: cotton; fruits; vegetables; sugarcane; livestock

Industry: tourism; construction; light manufacturing

Exports: $68 million (primary partners Caribbean, Guyana, United States)

Imports: $657 million (primary partners United States, United Kingdom, Canada)

Suggested Website

www.cia.gov/cia/publications/factbook/geos/ac.html

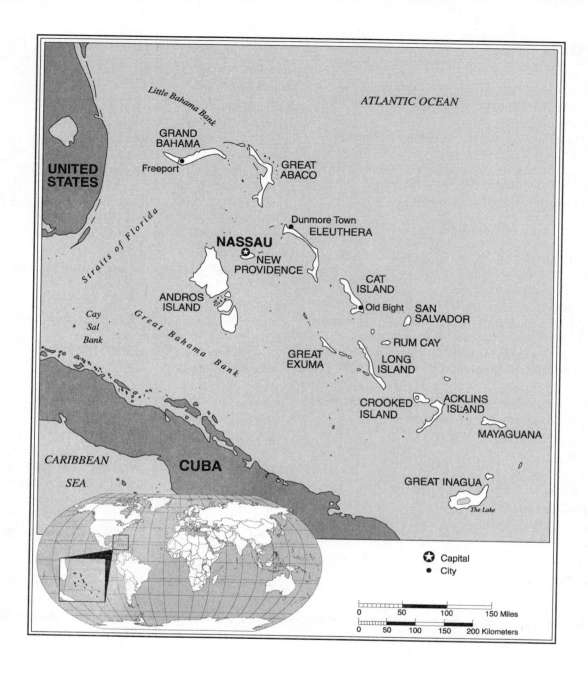

ATLANTIC OCEAN

Little Bahama Bank

GRAND
BAHAMA

Freeport

GREAT
ABACO

UNITED
STATES

Dunmore Town
ELEUTHERA

NASSAU

NEW
PROVIDENCE

CAT
ISLAND

Straits of Florida

ANDROS
ISLAND

Old Bight

SAN
SALVADOR

Cay
Sal
Bank

Great Bahama Bank

RUM CAY

GREAT
EXUMA

LONG
ISLAND

CROOKED
ISLAND

ACKLINS
ISLAND

MAYAGUANA

CARIBBEAN

SEA

CUBA

GREAT INAGUA

The Lake

⊛ Capital

● City

0   50   100   150 Miles
0   50   100   150   200 Kilometers

The Bahamas

(Commonwealth of the Bahamas)

BAHAMAS: A NATION OF ISLANDS

Christopher Columbus made his first landfall in the Bahamas in 1492, when he touched ashore on the island of San Salvador. Permanent settlements on the islands were not established by the British until 1647, when the Eleutheran Adventurers, a group of English and Bermudan religious dissidents, landed. The island was privately governed until 1717, when it became a British Crown colony. During the U.S. Civil War, Confederate blockade runners used the Bahamas as a base. The tradition continued in the years after World War I, when Prohibition rumrunners used the islands as a base. Today, drug traffickers utilize the isolation of the out-islands for their illicit operations.

Although the Bahamas are made up of almost 700 islands, only 10 have populations of any significant size. Of these, New Providence and Grand Bahama contain more than 75 percent of the Bahamian population. Because most economic and cultural activities take place on the larger islands, other islands—particularly those in the southern region—have suffered depopulation over the years as young men and women have moved to the two major centers of activity.

Migrants from Haiti and Jamaica have also caused problems for the Bahamian government. There are an estimated 60,000 illegal Haitians now resident in the Bahamas—equivalent to nearly one-fifth of the total Bahamian population of 313,000. The Bahamian response was tolerance until late 1994, when the government established tough new policies that reflected a fear that the country would be "overwhelmed" by Haitian immigrants. In the words of one official, the large numbers of Haitians would "result in a very fundamental economic and social transformation that even the very naïve would understand to be undesirable." Imprisonment, marginalization, no legal right to work, and even the denial of access to schools and hospitals are now endured by the immigrants.

Bahamian problems with Jamaicans are rooted differently. The jealous isolation of each of the island nations is reflected in the peoples' fears and suspicions of the activities of their neighbors. As a result, interisland freedom of movement is subject to strict scrutiny.

The Bahamas were granted their independence from Great Britain in 1973 and established a constitutional parliamentary democracy governed by a freely elected prime minister and Parliament. Upon independence, there was a transfer of political power from a small white elite to the black majority, who comprise 85 percent of the population. Whites continue to play a role in the political process, however, and several hold high-level civil-service and political posts.

The country has enjoyed a marked improvement in health conditions over the past few decades. Life expectancy has risen, and infant mortality has declined. Virtually all people living in urban areas have access to good drinking water, although the age and dilapidated condition of the capital's (Nassau) water system could present problems in the near future.

The government has begun a program to restructure education on the islands. The authorities have placed a new emphasis on technical and vocational training so that skilled jobs in the economy now held by foreigners

TIMELINE

1492
Christopher Columbus first sights the New World at San Salvador Island

1647
The first English settlement in the Bahamas

1967
Black-power controversy

1973
Independence from Great Britain

1980s
Violent crime, drug trafficking, and narcotics addiction become serious social problems

1990s
New investments create jobs and cut the unemployment rate

2000s
Employment is up, and so is many Bahamians' sense of optimism

2007
Hubert Ingraham elected prime minister

2012
Elections scheduled

Snapshot: THE BAHAMAS

Summarized below is a quick look at the country with regard to its development, freedom, health/welfare, and achievements.

Development

Together manufacturing and agriculture account for only 10 percent of GDP. There has been little growth in either sector. Offshore banking and tourism contribute the most toward economic growth and together account for about half of the jobs on the islands.

Freedom

The Bahamas is a destination, source, and transit country for men, women, and children subjected to forced labor and sex trafficking: Women from South American countries may be subjected to forced prostitution; some workers from Haiti, Jamaica, China, Peru, and the Philippines could be vulnerable to involuntary servitude.

Health/Welfare

Cases of child abuse and neglect in the Bahamas rose in the 1990s. The Government and Women's Crisis Centre focused on the need to fight child abuse through a public-awareness program that had as its theme: "It shouldn't hurt to be a child."

Achievements

The natural beauty of the islands has had a lasting effect on those who have visited them. As a result of his experiences in the waters off Bimini, Ernest Hemingway wrote his classic *The Old Man and the Sea*.

---

will be performed by Bahamians. But while the literacy rate has remained high, there is a shortage of teachers, equipment, and supplies.

The government of Prime Minister Hubert A. Ingraham and his Free National Movement won a clear mandate in 1997 over the opposition Progressive Liberal Party to continue the policies and programs it initiated in 1992. *The Miami Herald* reported that the election "marked a watershed in Bahamian politics, with many new faces on the ballot and both parties facing leadership succession struggles before the next vote is due in 2002." Ideologically, the two contending political parties were similar; thus, voters made their decisions on the basis of who they felt would provide jobs and bring crime under control. In 2002 voters decided that the Progressive Liberal Party would do a better job and elected Perry Christie as prime minister. That apparently did not happen and Hubert Ingraham was again elected prime minister in 2007.

Honest government and a history of working effectively with the private sector to improve the national economy have dramatically increased foreign investment in the Bahamas. Rapid growth in the service sector of the economy has stimulated the migration of people from fishing and farming villages to the commercial tourist centers in New Providence Island, Grand Bahama, and Great Abaco. It is estimated that tourism now accounts for 60 percent of GDP and absorbs half of the labor

? DID YOU KNOW?

The strategic geographical position of The Bahamas just off the coast of Florida has transformed it into a major transshipment point for illicit narcotics destined for the United States and Europe. Human trafficking is also a significant problem for the government.

force. Importantly, today there are more companies owned by Bahamians than ever before.

Despite new investments, many young Bahamians out-migrate. The thousands of illegal Haitian immigrants have added pressure to the job market and still worry some Bahamians that their own sense of identity may be threatened. Another concern is the unrest created in part by global recession. Crime rose by 17 percent in the first quarter of 2010 over the same period in 2009.

FURTHER INVESTIGATION

For more information on drug trafficking and illegal immigration in The Bahamas and other Caribbean countries go to http://www.bbc.co.uk/2/hi/americas/country_profiles/1154642.stm

Statistics

Geography

Area in Square Miles (Kilometers): 5,380 (13,934) (about the size of Connecticut)

Capital (Population): Nassau (248,000)

Environmental Concerns: coral-reef decay; waste disposal

Geographical Features: long, flat coral formations with some low, rounded hills

Climate: tropical marine

People

Population

Total: 313,312 (2011 est.)

Annual Growth Rate: 0.93%

Rural/Urban Population Ratio: 16/84

Ethnic Makeup: 85% black; 15% white

Major Language: English

Religions: 32% Baptist; 15% Anglican; 13.5% Catholic; 8.1% Pentecostal; 22% others or not specified

Health

Life Expectancy at Birth: 69 years (male); 73 years (female)

Infant Mortality Rate (Ratio): 13.49/1,000

Physicians Available (Ratio): 1.05/1,000

Education

Adult Literacy Rate: 95.6%

Compulsory (Ages): 5–14; free

Communication

Telephones: 129,300 main lines

Daily Newspaper Circulation: 126 per 1,000 people

Cell Phones: 428,400

Internet Users: 115,800

Transportation

Highways in Kilometers (Miles): 1,672 (2,693)

Usable Airfields: 62

Government

Type: constitutional parliamentary democracy

Independence Date: July 10, 1973 (from the United Kingdom)

Head of State/Government: Queen Elizabeth II; Prime Minister Hubert A. Ingraham

Political Parties: Free National Movement; Progressive Liberal Party

Suffrage: universal at 18

Military

Military Expenditures (% of GDP): 0.7%

Economy

Currency ($U.S. Equivalent): 1.00 Bahamian dollar = $1

Per Capita Income/GDP: $30,900/$10.81 billion

GDP Growth Rate: 2%

Inflation Rate: 3.4%

Unemployment Rate: 7.6%

Labor Force: 184,000

Natural Resources: salt; aragonite; timber

Agriculture: citrus fruits; vegetables; poultry

Industry: tourism; banking; cement; oil refining and transshipment; salt production; rum; aragonite; pharmaceuticals; steel pipe

Exports: $710 million (primary partners United States, Singapore, Germany, Dominican Republic)

Imports: $2.854 billion (primary partners United States, Venezuela, South Korea, France, India, Japan, Singapore, China)

Suggested Website

www.cia.gov/cia/publications/factbook/index.html

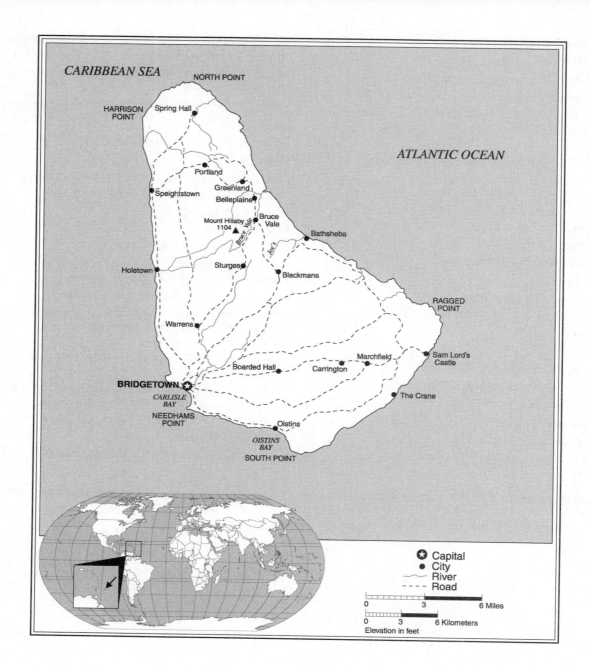

CARIBBEAN SEA

NORTH POINT

HARRISON
POINT

Spring Hall

ATLANTIC OCEAN

Portland

Greenland

Speightstown

Belleplaine

Mount Hillaby
1104

Bruce
Vale

Bathsheba

Holetown

Sturges

Blackmans

RAGGED
POINT

Warrens

Marchfield

Sam Lord's
Castle

Boarded Hall

Carrington

BRIDGETOWN

CARLISLE
BAY

The Crane

NEEDHAMS
POINT

Oistins

OISTINS
BAY

SOUTH POINT

⭐ Capital
● City
River
Road

0   3   6 Miles

0   3   6 Kilometers

Elevation in feet

Barbados

THE LITTLE ENGLAND OF THE CARIBBEAN

A parliamentary democracy that won its independence from Britain in 1966, Barbados boasts a House of Assembly that is the third oldest in the Western Hemisphere, after Bermuda's and Virginia's. A statement of the rights and privileges of Bajans (as Barbadians are called), known as the Charter of Barbados, was proclaimed in 1652 and has been upheld by those governing the island. The press is free, labor is strong and well organized, and human rights are respected.

While the majority of the populations of the English-speaking West Indies still admire the British, this admiration is carried to extremes in Barbados. In 1969, for example, Bajan soccer teams chose English names and colors—Arsenal, Tottenham Hotspurs, Liverpool, and Coventry City. Among the primary religions are Anglican and Methodist Protestantism.

Unlike most of the other islands of the Caribbean, European sailors initially found Barbados uninhabited. It has since been determined that the island's original inhabitants, the Arawak Indians, were destroyed by Carib Indians who overran the region and then abandoned the islands. Settled by the English, Barbados was always under British control until its independence.

A DIVERSIFYING ECONOMY

In terms of wealth, as compared to other West Indian nations, Barbados is well off. One important factor is that Barbados has been able to diversify its economy; thus, the country is no longer dependent solely on sugar and its by-products rum and molasses. Manufacturing and high-technology industries now contribute to economic growth, and tourism has overtaken agriculture as a generator of foreign exhange. Off-shore finance and information services have also become important.

The Constitution of 1966 authorized the government to promote the general welfare of the citizens of the island through equitable distribution of wealth. While governments have made a sincere effort to wipe out pockets of poverty, a great disparity in wealth still exists.

RACE AND CLASS

Barbados is a class- and race-conscious society. One authority noted that there are three classes (elite, middle class, and masses) and two colors (white/light and black). Land is highly concentrated in the hands of a few; 10 percent of the population own 95 percent of the land. Most of the nation's landed estates and businesses are owned by whites, even though they comprise a very small percentage of the population (4 percent).

While discrimination based on color is legally prohibited, color distinctions continue to correlate with class differences and dominate most personal associations. Although whites have been displaced politically, they still comprise more than half of the group considered "influential" in the country.

Even though Barbados's class structure is more rigid than that of other West Indian states, there is upward social mobility for all people, and the middle class has been growing steadily in size. Poor whites, known

TIMELINE

1625
Barbados is occupied by the English
1647
The first sugar from Barbados is sent to England
1832
Full citizenship is granted to nonwhites
1951
Universal suffrage
1966
Independence from Great Britain
1990s
Barbados develops an offshore banking industry
2000s
The Arthur government continues its policy of economic diversification
2010
Fruendel Stuart elected prime minister
2012
House of Assembly elections scheduled

Snapshot: BARBADOS

Summarized below is a quick look at the country with regard to its development, freedom, health/welfare, and achievements.

Development

Between 1971 and 1999, there was an approximate 30 percent decrease in the amount of land used for agriculture. Formerly agricultural land has been transformed into golf courses, residential areas, commercial developments, tourist facilities, or abandoned. This trend continued until 2007 when it began to slow with the first signs of global recession. As of 2012 both the tourist and financial services industries had not recovered.

Freedom

Barbados has maintained an excellent human-rights record. The government officially advocates strengthening the human-rights machinery of the United Nations and the Organization of American States. Women are active participants in the country's economic, political, and social life.

Health/Welfare

By 2007, unemployment had dropped to 10.7 percent, from the 1993 high of 26 percent. Although prices have risen, a sound economy has given people more money to spend on consumer goods, durables, and housing.

Achievements

Bajan George Lamming has won attention from the world's literary community for his novels, each of which explores a stage in or an aspect of the colonial experience. Through his works, he explains what it is to be simultaneously a citizen of one's island and a West Indian.

---

as "Redlegs," have frequently moved into managerial positions on the estates. The middle class also includes a fairly large percentage of blacks and mulattos. Bajans have long enjoyed access to public and private educational systems, which have been the object of a good deal of national pride. Adequate medical care is available to all residents through local clinics and hospitals under a government health program. All Bajans are covered under government health insurance programs.

■ SEEKING A LEADERSHIP ROLE

Given the nation's relative wealth and its dynamism, Bajans have been inclined to seek a strong role in the region. In terms of Caribbean politics, economic development, and defense, Bajans feel that they have a right and a duty to lead.

The Labour Party has continued to push privatization policies. In 1993, an important step was taken toward the greater diversification of the nation's economic base with the creation of offshore financial services. By 1995, the new industry had created many new jobs for Bajans and had significantly reduced the high unemployment rate. Recent discussions on the Free Trade Area of the Americas (FTAA) has stimulated much debate among the smaller Caribbean states. While the Barbados government sees the possibilities of tying into a market of 800 million consumers, it also feels that the larger states must afford smaller nations special and differential treatment. Others are concerned about maintaining the "Bajan way

? DID YOU KNOW?

Barbados has one of the oldest democracies in the Western Hemisphere. In fact, the framers of the United States Constitution borrowed wording from the 1635 Charter of Barbados.

of life" and worry that "the world is falling in on us." Critics charge that any new wealth would be skewed saying, it has the attributes of "fancy molasses." "Very little trickles down, the rich get richer while the poor become marginalized." Other concerns have been expressed about pollution, the possible loss, because of FTAA, of offshore financial privileges, and growing out-migration of young Bajans because of job shortages in 2009 and 2010. Particularly troubling is the continuing malaise in the tourism and financial services industries. In 2011 the nation's public debt rose to 104% of GDP—a dangerous benchmark. A significant budget deficit presents the Stuart government with a difficult scenario.

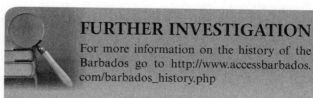

FURTHER INVESTIGATION

For more information on the history of the Barbados go to http://www.accessbarbados.com/barbados_history.php

Statistics

Geography

Area in Square Miles (Kilometers): 166 (431) (about 2½ times the size of Washington, D.C.)

Capital (Population): Bridgetown (112,000)

Environmental Concerns: pollution of coastal waters from waste disposal by ships; soil erosion; illegal solid-waste disposal

Geographical Features: relatively flat; rises gently to central highland region

Climate: tropical marine

People

Population

Total: 286,705 (2011 est.)

Annual Growth Rate: 0.36%

Rural/Urban Population Ratio: 56/44

Major Language: English

Ethnic Makeup: 93% black; 3.2% white; 3.6% Asian and mixed

Religions: 63.4% Protestant (Anglican, Pentecostal, Methodist, others); 4% Roman Catholic; 20.6% unspecified or none

Health

Life Expectancy at Birth: 72 years (male); 76 years (female)

Infant Mortality Rate (Ratio): 11.86/1,000

Physicians Available (Ratio): 1.8/1,000

Education

Adult Literacy Rate: 99.7%

Compulsory (Ages): 5–16

Communication

Telephones: 137,500 main lines

Daily Newspaper Circulation: 157 per 1,000 people

Cell Phones: 350,000

Internet Users: 188,000

Transportation

Highways in Kilometers (Miles): 1,650 (1,025)

Usable Airfields: 1

Government

Type: parliamentary democracy; independent sovereign state within Commonwealth

Independence Date: November 30, 1966 (from the United Kingdom)

Head of State/Government: Queen Elizabeth II; Prime Minister Fruendel Stuart

Political Parties: Democratic Labour Party; Barbados Labour Party; People's Empowerment Party

Suffrage: universal at 18

Military

Military Expenditures (% of GDP): 0.8%

Current Disputes: none

Economy

Currency ($U.S. Equivalent): 2.02 Barbados dollars = $1

Per Capita Income/GDP: $23,600/$6.528 billion

GDP Growth Rate: 1.8%

Inflation Rate: 7.4%

Unemployment Rate: 10.7%

Labor Force: 175,000

Natural Resources: petroleum; fish; natural gas

Agriculture: sugarcane; vegetables; cotton

Industry: tourism; light manufacturing; sugar; component assembly

Exports: $467.4 million (primary partners Brazil, Trinidad and Tobago, United States, St. Lucia, Venezuela, St. Vincent and the Grenadines)

Imports: $1.601 billion (primary partners Trinidad and Tobago, United States, Colombia, China)

Suggested Website

www.cia.gov/cia/publications/factbook/index.html

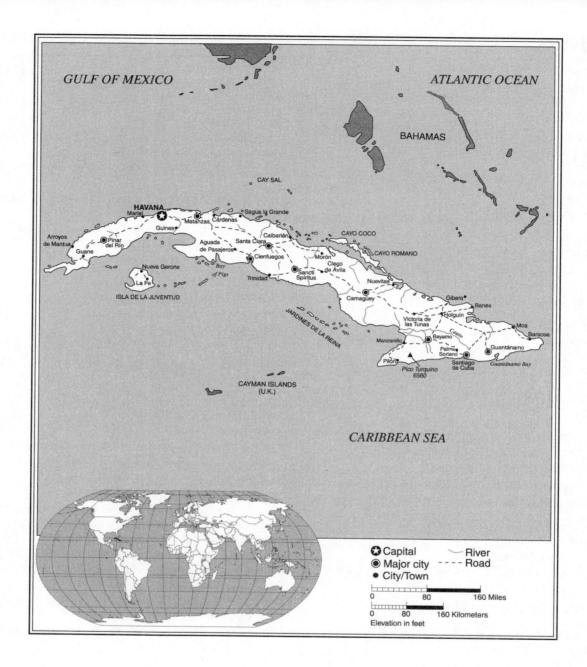

Cuba
(Republic of Cuba)

REFLECTIONS ON A REVOLUTION

Cuba, which contains about half the land area of the West Indies, has held the attention of the world since 1959. In that year, Fidel Castro led his victorious rebels into the capital city of Havana and began a revolution that has profoundly affected Cuban society. The Cuban Revolution had its roots in the struggle for independence from Spain in the late nineteenth century, in the aborted Nationalist Revolution of 1933, and in the Constitution of 1940. It grew from Cuba's history and must be understood as a Cuban phenomenon.

The Revolution in some respects represents the fulfillment of the goals of the Cuban Constitution of 1940, a radically nationalist document that was never fully implemented. It banned *latifundia* (the ownership of vast landed estates) and discouraged foreign ownership of the land. It permitted the confiscation of property in the public or social interest. The state was authorized to provide full employment for its people and to direct the course of the national economy. Finally, the Constitution of 1940 gave the Cuban state control of the sugar industry, which at the time was controlled by U.S. companies.

The current Constitution, written in 1976 and amended in 1992 and 2002, incorporates 36 percent of the articles of the 1940 Constitution. In other words, many of Castro's policies and programs are founded in Cuban history and the aspirations of the Cuban people. Revolutionary Cuba—at least in its earlier years—was very successful in solving the nation's most pressing problems of poverty. But those successes must be balanced against the loss of basic freedoms imposed by a strong authoritarian state.

ACHIEVEMENTS OF THE REVOLUTION

Education

One of the Revolution's most impressive successes has been in the area of education. In 1960, the Castro regime decided to place emphasis on raising the minimum level of education for the whole population. To accomplish this, some 200,000 Cubans were mobilized in 1961 under the slogan "Let those who know more teach those who know less." In a single year, the literacy rate rose from 76 to 96 percent. Free education was made available to all Cubans. The literacy campaign involved many Cubans in an attempt to recognize and attack the problems of rural impoverishment. It was the first taste of active public life for many women who were students or teachers and because of their involvement, they began to redefine sex roles and attitudes.

While the literacy campaign was a resounding triumph, long-term educational policy was less satisfactory. Officials blamed the high dropout rate in elementary and junior high schools on poor school facilities and inadequate teacher training. Students also apparently lacked enthusiasm, and Castro himself acknowledged that students needed systematic, constant, daily work and discipline.

"Scholarship students and students in general," in Castro's words, "are willing to do anything, except to study hard."

TIMELINE

1492
The island is discovered by Christopher Columbus
1511
The founding of Havana
1868–1878
The Ten Years'War in Cuba
1895–1898
The Cuban War of Independence
1902
The Republic of Cuba is established
1940
Cuba writes a new, progressive Constitution
1959
Fidel Castro seizes power
1961
An abortive U.S.-sponsored invasion at the Bay of Pigs
1980s
Mass exodus from Cuba; trial and execution of top military officials for alleged dealing in drugs
1990s
The economy rapidly deteriorates; Castro pursues Economic Liberalization Tensions flare between Cuba and the United Sates over the disposition of a young Cuban refugee, Elian González
2000s
The U.S. trade embargo, supported only by Israel, continues to make life difficult for the Cuban people
2008
Raœl Castro replaces his brother as Cuba's leader
2011
Raûl Castro introduces significant economic reforms

Health Care

The Revolution took great strides forward in improving the health of the Cuban population, especially in rural regions. Success in this area is all the more impressive when one considers that between one-third and one-half of all doctors left the country between 1959 and 1962. Health care initially declined sharply, and the infant mortality rate rose rapidly. But with the training of new health-care professionals, the gaps were filled. The infant mortality rate in Cuba is now at a level comparable to that of developed countries.

From the outset, the government decided to concentrate on rural areas, where the need was the greatest. Medical treatment was free, and newly graduated doctors had to serve in the countryside for at least two years. The Cuban health service was founded on the principle that good health for all, without discrimination, is a birthright of Cubans. All Cubans were included under a national health plan.

The first national health standards were developed between 1961 and 1965, and eight priority areas were identified: infant and maternal care, adult health care, care for the elderly, environmental health, nutrition, dentistry, school health programs, and occupational health. A program of insect spraying and immunization eradicated malaria and poliomyelitis. Cuban life expectancy became one of the highest in the world, and Cuba's leading causes of death became the same as in the United States—heart disease, cancer, and stroke.

Before the Revolution of 1959, there was very little health and safety regulation for workers. Afterward, however, important advances were made in the training of specialized inspectors and occupational physicians. In 1978, a Work Safety and Health Law was enacted, which defined the rights and responsibilities of government agencies, workplace administrators, unions, and workers.

Cuba also exported its health-care expertise. It has had medical teams in countries from Nicaragua to Yemen and more doctors overseas than the World Health Organization. From 2003 to the present Cuban medical personnel have provided health care to Venezuela, which in turn provides Cuba with cheap petroleum.

Redistribution of Wealth

The third great area of change presided over by the Revolution was income redistribution. The Revolution changed the lives of rural poor and agricultural workers. They gained the most in comparison to other groups in Cuban society—especially urban groups. From 1962 to 1973, for example, agricultural workers saw their wages rise from less than 60 percent to 93 percent of the national average.

Still, Cuba's minimum wage was inadequate for most families. Many families needed two wage earners to make ends meet. All wages were enhanced by the so-called social wage, which consisted of free medical care and education, subsidized housing, and low food prices. Yet persistent shortages and tight rationing of food undermined a good portion of the social wage. Newly married couples found it necessary to live with relatives, sometimes for years, before they could obtain their own housing, which was in short supply. Food supplies, especially those provided by the informal sector, were adversely affected by a 1986 decision to eliminate independent producers because an informal private sector was deemed antithetical to "socialist morality" and promoted materialism.

President Raúl Castro promised economic liberalization and from 2010 to 2012 new property laws, legislation has been enacted allowing the creation of private businesses, ownership of cell phones and fewer restrictions on internal movement. Even so, economic growth, at 1.5% in 2011, lagged behind the rest of the region.

Women in Cuba

From the outset of the Revolution, Fidel Castro appealed to women as active participants in the movement and redefined their political roles. Women's interests were protected by the Federation of Cuban Women, an integral part of the ruling party. The Family Code of 1975 equalized pay scales, reversed sexual discrimination against promotions, provided generous maternity leave, and gave employed women preferential access to goods and services. Although women comprised approximately 30 percent of the Cuban workforce, most were still employed in traditionally female occupations; the Third Congress of the Cuban Communist Party admitted in 1988 that both racial minorities and women were underrepresented in responsible government and party positions at all levels. Significant improvement occurred and by the end of 2007 women held about one-third of the seats in the National Assembly.

■ SHORTCOMINGS

Even at its best, the new Cuba had significant shortcomings. Wayne Smith, a former chief of the U.S. Interest Section in Havana who was sympathetic to the Revolution, wrote: "There is little freedom of expression and no freedom of the press at all. It is a command society, which still holds political prisoners, some of them under deplorable conditions. Further, while the Revolution has provided the basic needs of all, it has not fulfilled its promise of a higher standard of living for the society as a whole. Cuba was, after all, an urban middle-class society with a relatively high standard of living even before the Revolution. . . . The majority of Cubans are less well off materially."

Castro, to win support for his programs, did not hesitate to take his revolutionary message to the people. Indeed, the key reason why Castro enjoyed such widespread support in Cuba was because the people had the sense of being involved in a great historical process.

Alienation

Not all Cubans identified with the Revolution, and many felt a deep sense of betrayal and alienation. The elite and most of the middle class strongly resisted the changes that robbed them of influence, prestige, and property. Some were particularly bitter, for at its outset, the Revolution had been largely a middle-class movement. For them, Castro was a traitor to his class. Thousands fled Cuba, and some formed the core of an anti-Castro guerrilla movement based in South Florida.

(AP photo/Jorge Ray/AP050417014789)

Fidel Castro served as prime minister of Cuba from 1959 to 2008.

In recent years there were many signs that the government, while still popular among many people, began to lose the widespread acceptance it enjoyed in the 1960s and 1970s. While it still has the support of the older generation and those in rural areas who benefited from the social transformation of the island, limited economic growth increasingly led to dissatisfaction among urban workers and youth, who were less interested in revolutionary heroes and more interested in economic gains.

More serious disaffection existed in the army. Journalist Georgie Anne Geyer, writing in *World Monitor,* suggests that the 1989 execution of General Arnaldo Ochoa, ostensibly for drug trafficking, was actually motivated by Castro's fears of an emerging competitor for power. "The 1930s-style show trial effectively revealed the presence of an 'Angola generation' in the Cuban military. . . .That generation, which fought in Angola between 1974 and 1989, is the competitor generation to Castro's own Sierra Maestra generation." The condemned officers argued that their dealings with drug traffickers were not for personal enrichment but were designed to earn desperately needed hard currency for the state. Some analysts are convinced that Castro knew about drug trafficking and condoned it; others claim that it took place without his knowledge. But the bottom line is that the regime had been shaken at the highest levels, and the purge was the most far-reaching since the 1959 Revolution.

The Economy

The state of the Cuban economy and the future of the Cuban Revolution are inextricably linked. Writing in *World Today,* James J. Guy predicted that, given the economic collapse of the former Soviet Union and its satellites, "Cuba is destined to face serious structural unemployment: its agrarian economy cannot generate the white-collar, technical jobs demanded by a swelling army of graduates . . . The entire system is deteriorating—the simplest services take months to deliver, water and electricity are constantly interrupted . . . ," and there is widespread corruption and black-marketeering.

Oil is particularly nettlesome. For years after the collapse of the Soviet Union, Cuba had no access to affordable petroleum, at great cost to the economy. That changed in 2003 when Venezuela provided Cuba with discounted oil in exchange for Cuban expertise in the areas of health and sports.

Although Castro prided Cuba on being one of the last bulwarks of untainted Marxism-Leninism, in April 1991 he said: "We are not dogmatic . . . we are realistic. . . . Under the special conditions of this extraordinary period we are also aware that different forms of international cooperation may be useful." He noted that Cuba had contacted foreign capitalists about the possibility of establishing joint enterprises and remarked that more than 49 percent foreign participation in state businesses was a possibility.

In 1993, Castro called for economic realism. Using the rhetoric of the Revolution, he urged the Legislative Assembly to think seriously about the poor condition of the Cuban economy: "It is painful, but we must be sensible. . . . It is not only with decisiveness, courage and heroism that one saves the Revolution, but also with intelligence. And we have the right to invent ways to survive in these conditions without ever ceasing to be revolutionaries."

Slowly the governments of Fidel and especially Raúl Castro began to redefine the revolution along less ideological lines. The government now allows Cubans to establish private businesses; today, Cubans in some 140 professions can work on their own for a profit. At about the same time, the use of dollars was decriminalized, the Cuban currency became convertible, and, in the agricultural sector, the government began to transform state farms into cooperatives. Farmers are now allowed to sell some of their produce in private markets and, increasingly, market forces set the prices of many consumer goods. Managers in state-owned enterprises have been given unprecedented autonomy; and foreign investment, in contrast with past practice, is now encouraged.

Still, the Cuban economy languishes. Mirta Ojito, writing in *The New York Times,* sees older revolutionaries "coming to terms with the failure of their dreams." Cuba, she noted, resembled most other underdeveloped countries, with "many needy, unhappy, sad people." The Revolution was supposed to make Cuba prosperous, "not merely survive," and end the country's dependence on the U.S. dollar. By 1999, dollars in circulation in Cuba had created a parallel speculative economy.

So pervasive had the parallel dollar economy become that in October 2004 Castro decreed that dollars would no longer be accepted for commercial transactions anywhere on the island, although dollar bank accounts would still be legal. Expatriate Cubans, who remit perhaps $1 billion annually to relatives on the island, were told to send euros, British pounds, or Canadian dollars. There was certainly a pragmatic side to Castro's decision. By encouraging people to convert their dollars to what was called the "convertible peso" (after a period of grace the government would charge 10 percent to exchange dollars for pesos; there would be no exchange charge for other currencies), Castro was able to provide his government with the dollars needed to purchase critical inputs for Cuba's economy. In the words of Mexico's former ambassador to Cuba, as reported in *The New York Times*, "I don't think this is a political decision at all. It's a pragmatic move." Cuba had to buy more oil than it had planned, and so it urgently needed dollars. Castro was also responding to U.S. efforts to strengthen economic sanctions against Cuba by setting limits on the amount of money that people could send to relatives on the island.

With the new millennium, Cuba's infrastructure continued to crumble. In 2001, salaries averaged just $15 per month, and the weekly ration card given to each family provided one chicken, just over three pounds of rice and beans, sugar, and two pints of cooking oil. With rising prices, it was not surprising that prostitution, moonlighting, black-marketeering, and begging have rapidly increased. Castro talked with CARICOM states about the possibilities of free trade, but the stifling bureaucracy makes it much easier to export *from* rather than export *to* Cuba.

Freedom Issues

Soon after the Revolution, the government assumed total control of the media. No independent news organization is allowed, and all printed publications are censored by the government or the Communist Party. The arts are subject to strict censorship, and even sports must serve the purposes of the Revolution. As Castro noted: "Within the Revolution everything is possible. Outside it, nothing."

In many respects, until recently, there is less freedom now in Cuba than there was before the Revolution. Cuba's human-rights record is not good. There are thousands of political prisoners, and rough treatment and torture—physical and psychological—occur. The Constitution of 1976 allows the repression of all freedoms for all those who oppose the Revolution. U.S. political scientist William LeGrande, who was sympathetic to the Revolution, nevertheless noted that "Cuba is a closed society. The Cuban Communist Party does not allow dissenting views on fundamental policy. It does not allow people to challenge the basic leadership of the regime." But here, too, there are signs of change. In 1995, municipal elections were held under a new system that provides for run-offs if none of the candidates gains a clear majority. In an indication of a new competitiveness in Cuban politics, 326 out of 14,229 positions were subject to the run-off rule.

■ THE FUTURE

It will be difficult for the government to maintain the unquestioned support of the Cuban population. There must be continued positive accomplishments in the economy. Health and education programs are successful and will continue to be so. "Cubans get free health care, free education and free admission to sports and cultural events [and] 80 percent of all Cubans live in rent-free apartments, and those who do pay rent pay only between 6 and 10 percent of their salaries," according to James J. Guy.

But there must be a recovery of basic political and human freedoms. Criticism of the government must not be the occasion for jail terms or exile. The Revolution must be more inclusive and less exclusive.

Although Castro was never effectively challenged, there are signs of unrest on the island. The military, as noted, is a case in point. Ironically, although Castro lost a good deal of luster internationally as a result of statist economic policies, recent trends in the region away from free trade and toward more authoritarian forms of government have given Cuba strong allies in South America.

Still, many Cubans are frustrated with their lives and continue to take to the sea in an attempt to reach the United States. Thousands have been intercepted by the United States Coast Guard and have been interned.

Fidel Castro embodied the Cuban Revolution and enjoyed staying power. When presented with a gift of a Galapagos tortoise, Castro asked how long they lived. The reply, "More than a hundred years," prompted Castro to say, "How sad it is to outlive one's pets." That longevity for Castro is now at an end. Health problems forced him to hand over the reins of power to his brother, Raúl.

The smooth transition disappointed critics of the regime who hoped that Fidel Castro's passing from the political stage would produce upheaval. In January 1999 *The Economist* asked: "What will follow Fidel?" The magazine suggested that Cubans could be faced with violence and political turmoil, for there were "no plausible political heirs in sight, no credible opposition, and an exiled community eager not only for return but also for revenge." Raúl Castro is less ideologically driven than his brother and is certainly more pragmatic. He realizes that Cuba faces profound economic problems and has taken steps to increase food production. Local farm leaders will be relied on to make more decisions in an effort to stimulate agricultural production, increase the sale and distribution of food, and substitute imports. Private farmers and cooperatives have also been encouraged to bring unused government land into production. It was estimated that more than half of the arable land in Cuba was underused or fallow because of official mismanagement. The government has also decided to remove the prohibition on citizens from owning cell phones, even though their cost is prohibitive for most Cubans. Nevertheless, it signals an opening for Cubans to access information previously unavailable. Impressively, cell phone ownership tripled from 300,000 to over 1,000,000 in just two years. Additionally, it has been made easier for state

Snapshot: CUBA

Summarized below is a quick look at the country with regard to its development, freedom, health/welfare, and achievements.

Development

The government of Raúl Castro has steadily "modernized socialism" in an effort to stimulate the Cuban economy. New laws allowing people to open businesses and sell real estate, measures to reduce state subsidies, and cuts to a bloated bureaucracy illustrate the new direction taken by the government.

Freedom

In a 2011 survey, Freedom House found that 41% of Cubans embrace new economic freedoms introduced by the government. Liberalization of the economy is "the most significant positive change to have taken place in Cuba since communism was introduced a half century ago. . . ."

Health/Welfare

In August 1997, the Cuban government reported 1,649 HIV cases, 595 cases of full-blown AIDS, and 429 deaths, but in 2010 the reported number of deaths had dropped to below 100. Slightly over 6,000 people are living with AIDS. Cuban medical personnel are working on an AIDS vaccine. AIDS has been spread in part because of an economic climate that has driven more women to prostitution.

Achievements

A unique cultural contribution of Cuba to the world was the Afro-Cuban movement, with its celebration of black song and dance rhythms. The work of contemporary prize-winning Cuban authors such as Alejo Carpentier and Edmundo Desnoes has been translated into many languages.

workers to gain title to homes they once rented, real estate can now be bought and sold, and some restrictions on internal movement have been removed.

Raúl Castro appreciates the need for change. But change can also produce a "revolution of rising expectations" which could be difficult to manage. Indeed, a Freedom House survey taken in 2011 indicated that 28% of Cubans surveyed now want increased freedom of expression and the freedom to travel. Over 60% of Cubans approve of Raúl Castro's reforms, but further change must occur if approval is not to be replaced with frustration.

DID YOU KNOW?

Cuba has more health professionals than the World Health Organization working around the world? In Venezuela, in exchange for discounted petroleum, Cuba has sent 30,000 healthcare workers.

FURTHER INVESTIGATION

For more information on the history of Cuba's record in sending medical assistance to other countries go to http://blogs.plos.org/speakingofmedicine/2011/01/24/cuban-doctors-overlooked-champions-of-the-health-and-human-resources-crisis/

Statistics

Geography

Area in Square Miles (Kilometers): 44,200 (114,471) (about the size of Pennsylvania)

Capital (Population): Havana (2,140,000)

Environmental Concerns: pollution of Havana Bay; threatened wildlife populations; deforestation

Geographical Features: mostly flat to rolling plains; rugged hills and mountains in the southeast

Climate: tropical

People

Population

Total: 11,087,330 (2011 est.)

Annual Growth Rate: −0.1%

Rural/Urban Population Ratio: 25/75

Ethnic Makeup: 65.1% white; 24.8% mulatto or mestizo; 10% black

Major Language: Spanish

Religion: 85% nominally Roman Catholic

Health

Life Expectancy at Birth: 75 years (male); 80 years (female)

Infant Mortality Rate (Ratio): 4.9/1,000

Physicians Available (Ratio): 6.4/1,000

Education

Adult Literacy Rate: 99.8%

Compulsory (Ages): 6–11; free

Communication

Telephones: 1,164,000 main lines

Daily Newspaper Circulation: 122 per 1,000 people

Cell Phones: 1,003,000

Internet Users: 1,606,000

Transportation

Roadways in Kilometers (Miles): 60,858 (37,815)

Railroads in Kilometers (Miles): 2,985 (4,807)

Usable Airfields: 136

Government

Type: Communist state

Independence Date: May 20, 1902 (from Spain)

Head of State/Government: President Raúl Castro is both head of state and head of government

Political Parties: Cuban Communist Party

Suffrage: universal at 16

Military

Military Expenditures (% of GDP): 3.8% (est.)

Current Disputes: U.S. Naval Base at Guantanamo Bay is leased to the United States

Economy

Currency ($U.S. Equivalent): 0.98 Cuban pesos = $1 (official rate)

Per Capita Income/GDP: 9,900/$114.1 billion

GDP Growth Rate: 1.5%

Inflation Rate: 4.7%

Unemployment Rate: 3.8

Labor Force: 5,153,000

Natural Resources: cobalt; nickel; iron ore; copper; manganese; salt; timber; silica; petroleum; arable land

Agriculture: sugarcane; tobacco; citrus fruits; coffee; rice; potatoes; beans; livestock

Industry: sugar; petroleum; food; textiles; tobacco; chemicals; paper and wood products; metals; cement; fertilizers; consumer goods; agricultural machinery

Exports: $4.679 billion (primary partners, China, Canada, Venezuela, Spain)

Imports: $12.97 billion (primary partners, Venezuela, China, Spain, Brazil, Canada, United States)

Suggested Website

www.cia.gov/cia/publications/factbook/index.html

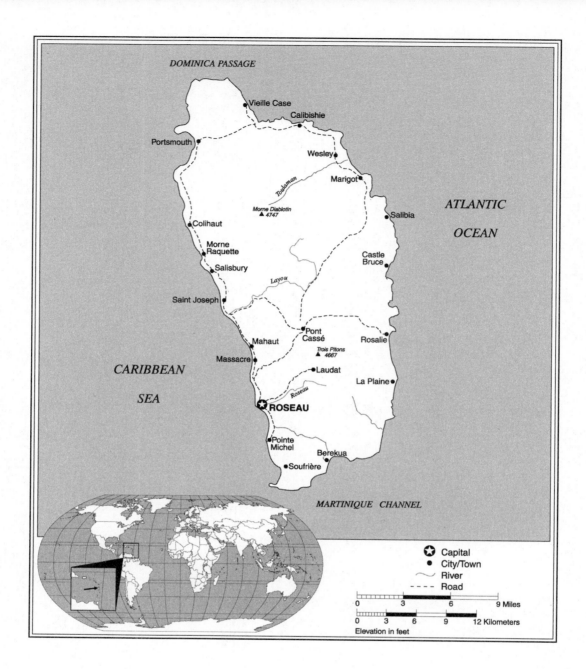

DOMINICA PASSAGE

Vieille Case

Calibishie

Portsmouth

Wesley

Marigot

Toulaman

Morne Diablotin
▲ 4747

Salibia

Colihaut

Morne
Raquette

Castle
Bruce

Salisbury

Layou

Saint Joseph

Pont
Cassé

Mahaut

Rosalie

Trois Pitons
▲ 4667

Massacre

CARIBBEAN

Laudat

La Plaine

Roseau

SEA

★ ROSEAU

Pointe
Michel

Berekua

Soufrière

ATLANTIC

OCEAN

MARTINIQUE CHANNEL

★ Capital
● City/Town
～ River
- - - Road

| 0 | 3 | 6 | 9 Miles |

| 0 | 3 | 6 | 9 | 12 Kilometers |

Elevation in feet

Dominica
(Commonwealth of Dominica)

A FRAGMENTED NATION

Christopher Columbus discovered the island of Dominica on his second voyage to the New World in 1493. Because of the presence of Carib Indians, who were known for their ferocity, Spanish efforts to settle the island were rebuffed. It was not until 1635 that France took advantage of Spanish weakness and claimed Dominica as its own. French missionaries became the island's first European settlers. Because of continued Carib resistance, the French and English agreed in 1660 that both Dominica and St. Vincent should be declared neutral and left to the Indians. Definitive English settlement did not occur until the eighteenth century, and the island again became a bone of contention between the French and English. It became Britain's by treaty in 1783.

Dominica is a small and poor country that gained its independence from Great Britain in 1978. Culturally, the island reflects a number of patterns. Ninety percent of the population speak French patois (dialect), and most are Roman Catholic, while only a small minority speak English and are Protestant. Yet English is the official language. Descendants of the original Carib inhabitants still live in a reserve in the northern part of the island. For years many in the nonindigenous population saw them as drunken, lazy, and dishonest. But others see them as symbolically important because they represent an ancient culture and fit into the larger Caribbean search for cultural and national identity. In 2004 the newly elected chief of the Caribs told the *Chronicle,* a Dominican weekly newspaper, that ". . . we are the rightful owners of this country and we deserve much more than we get. . . . '[We] . . . need a bigger share of development.'" A significant step was taken in this direction in 2005 when the Carib Indians were given a cabinet position in the government of the ruling Dominica Labour Party. There is also a small number of Rastafarians who identify with their black African roots.

Today, Dominica's population is broken up into sharply differentiated regions. The early collapse of the plantation economy left pockets of settlements, which are still isolated from one another. A difficult topography and poor communications exaggerate the differences between these small communities. This contrasts with nations such as Jamaica and Trinidad and Tobago, which have a greater sense of national awareness because there are good communications and mass media that reach most citizens and foster the development of a national perception.

EMIGRATION

Although its people's life expectancy has measurably increased over the past few years, Dominica's annual growth rate has dropped to under 1 percent due to significant out-migration. Out-migration is not a new phenomenon. From the 1880s until well into the 1900s, many Dominicans sought economic opportunity in the gold fields of French Guiana. Today, most move to the neighboring French departments of Guadeloupe and Martinique.

TIMELINE

1493
Dominica is sighted on Christopher Columbus's second voyage

1783
Dominica is deeded to the British by France

1978
Independence from Great Britain

1979–1980
Hurricanes devastate Dominica's economy

1989
Hurricane Hugo devastates the island

1990s
Dominica seeks stronger tourism revenues, especially in ecotourism
The banana industry is in crisis

2000s
The banana industry looks for solutions to its problems
Roosevelt Skerrit elected prime minister in 2004
World recession cuts growth rate to 1 percent

2013
Elections scheduled

Snapshot: DOMINICA

Summarized below is a quick look at the country with regard to its development, freedom, health/welfare, and achievements.

Development

More Americans visit Dominica than any other national group. In 2008, tourist visitors totaled around 460,000, mainly from the United States, the French West Indies, the United Kingdom, and CARICOM. The two largest private employers in Dominica are U.S. companies, and a number of Americans attend Ross University, a U.S. medical school with a campus in Portsmouth.

Freedom

Freedom House, an international human-rights organization, listed Dominica as "free." It also noted that "the rights of the native Caribs may not be fully respected." The example set by former prime minister Mary Eugenia Charles led to greater participation by women in the island's political life.

Health/Welfare

With the assistance of external donors, Dominica has rebuilt many primary schools destroyed in Hurricane Hugo in 1989. A major restructuring of the public health administration has improved the quality of health care, even in the previously neglected rural areas.

Achievements

Traditional handicrafts—especially intricately woven baskets, mats, and hats—have been preserved in Dominica. Schoolchildren are taught the techniques to pass on this dimension of Dominican culture.

■ THE ECONOMY

Dominica's chief export, bananas, has suffered for some years from natural disasters and falling prices. Hurricanes blew down the banana trees in 1979, 1980, 1989, and 1995, and banana exports fell dramatically. A drop in banana prices in 1997 prompted the opposition Dominica Freedom Party to demand that Dominica become part of a single market in order to take advantage of set prices enjoyed by the producers of Martinique and Guadeloupe. Recent talks among producers, Windward Island governments, and the European Union focused on the need for radical changes in the banana industry. The head of the Windward Islands Banana Development and Exporting Company said that the industry should be "market-led rather than production-led." He also noted that the industry was too fragmented, with 10,000 growers all over the islands. This was one reason why costs were high and yields low. With new technology, an acre should produce 20 tons of fruit instead of the four tons now harvested. Together with other banana-producing small states in the Caribbean, Dominica has increasingly turned to nontraditional crops, including root crops, cucumbers, flowers, hot peppers, tomatoes, and nonbanana tropical fruits.

Hard-pressed for revenue, *the Economist* reports that Dominica has traded on its sovereignty for cash. It has sold passports to foreigners, hosted off-shore banks, and voted with Japan in favor of commercial whaling. The "favorite local game" involves playing off China and Taiwan for economic gain.

■ POLITICAL FREEDOM

Despite economic difficulties and several attempted coups, Dominica still enjoys a parliamentary democracy patterned along British lines. The press is free and has not been subject to control—save for a brief state of emergency in 1981, which corresponded to a coup attempt by former prime minister Patrick John and unemployed members of the disbanded Defense Force. Political parties and trade unions are free to organize. Labor unions are small but enjoy the right to strike. Women have full rights under the law and are active in the political system; former prime minister Mary Eugenia Charles was the Caribbean's first woman to become a head of government.

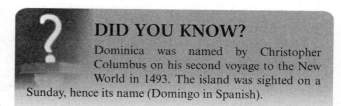

DID YOU KNOW?

Dominica was named by Christopher Columbus on his second voyage to the New World in 1493. The island was sighted on a Sunday, hence its name (Domingo in Spanish).

FURTHER INVESTIGATION

For more information on the history and culture of Dominica go to http://www.dominica.dm/index.php/history-a-culture

Statistics

Geography

Area in Square Miles (Kilometers): 289 (752) (about 4 times the size of Washington, D.C.)

Capital (Population): Roseau (14,000)

Geographical Features: rugged mountains of volcanic origin

Climate: tropical

People

Population

Total: 72,969 (2011 est.)

Annual Growth Rate: 0.213%

Rural/Urban Population Ratio: 33/67

Major Languages: English; French Creole

Ethnic Makeup: 87% black; 8.6% mixed, 2.9% Carib

Religions: 61.4% Roman Catholic; 28% Protestant

Health

Life Expectancy at Birth: 73 years (male); 79 years (female)

Infant Mortality Rate (Ratio): 12.78/1,000

Physicians Available (Ratio): .5/1,000

Education

Adult Literacy Rate: 94%

Compulsory (Ages): 5–15; free

Communication

Telephones: 15,500 main lines

Cell Phones: 98,100

Internet Users: 28,000

Transportation

Highways in Kilometers (Miles): 780 (484)

Usable Airfields: 2

Government

Type: parliamentary democracy

Independence Date: November 3, 1978 (from the United Kingdom)

Head of State/Government: President Nicholas J. O. Liverpool; Prime Minister Roosevelt Skerrit

Political Parties: United Workers Party; Dominica Freedom Party; Dominica Labour Party

Suffrage: universal at 18

Military

Current Disputes: none

Economy

Currency ($U.S. Equivalent): 2.68 East Caribbean dollars = $1

Per Capita Income/GDP: $13,600/1.02 billion

GDP Real Growth Rate: 0.9%

Inflation Rate: 3.5%

Unemployment Rate: 23%

Labor Force: 25,000

Natural Resources: timber

Agriculture: fruits; cocoa; root crops; forestry and fishing potential

Industry: soap; coconut oil; tourism; copra; furniture; cement blocks; shoes

Exports: $47.8 million (primary partners Japan, Egypt, Antigua and Barbuda, Jamaica, Guyana, Trinidad and Tobago)

Imports: $207.1 million (primary partners Japan, United States, Trinidad and Tobago, China)

Suggested Website

www.cia.gov/cia/publications/factbook/index.html

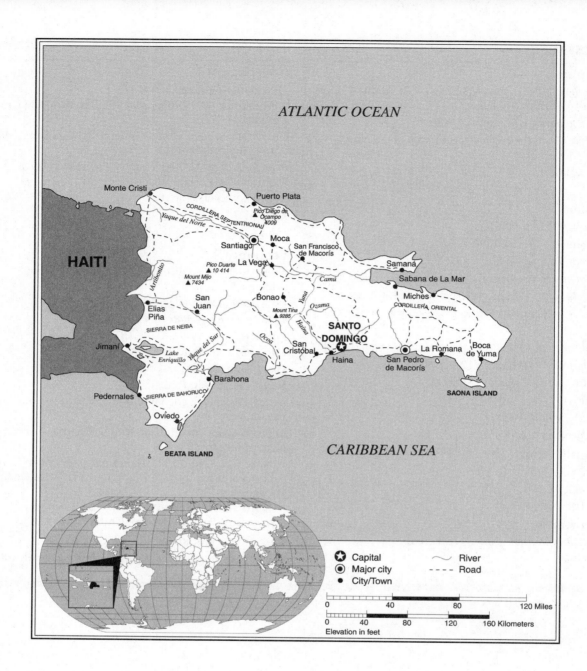

ATLANTIC OCEAN

Monte Cristi

Puerto Plata

CORDILLERA SEPTENTRIONAL

Pico Diego de
Ocampo
▲4009

Yaque del Norte

HAITI

Santiago

Moca

San Francisco
de Macorís

Samaná

Pico Duarte
▲10 414

La Vega

Camú

Sabana de La Mar

Mount Mijo
▲7434

Artibonito

San
Juan

Bonao

Yuna

Miches

CORDILLERA ORIENTAL

Elias
Piña

Ozama

SIERRA DE NEIBA

Mount Tina
▲9285

Haina

SANTO
DOMINGO

Jimaní

Lake
Enriquillo

Ocoá

Yaque del Sur

San
Cristóbal

La Romana

Boca
de Yuma

Haina

San Pedro
de Macorís

Barahona

Pedernales

SIERRA DE BAHORUCO

SAONA ISLAND

Oviedo

BEATA ISLAND

CARIBBEAN SEA

★ Capital   ～ River
◉ Major city   - - - Road
● City/Town

| 0 | | 40 | | 80 | | 120 Miles |
| 0 | 40 | | 80 | 120 | | 160 Kilometers |

Elevation in feet

Dominican Republic

DOMINICAN REPUBLIC: RACIAL STRIFE

Occupying the eastern two-thirds of the island of Hispaniola (Haiti comprises the western third), the Dominican Republic historically has feared its neighbor to the west. Much of the fear has its origins in race. From 1822 until 1844, the Dominican Republic—currently 73 percent mixed, or mulatto—was ruled by a brutal black Haitian regime. One authority noted that the Dominican Republic's freedom from Haiti has always been precarious: "Fear of reconquest by the smaller but more heavily populated (and, one might add, black) neighbor has affected Dominican psychology more than any other factor."

In the 1930s, for example, President Rafael Trujillo posed as the defender of Catholic values and European culture against the "barbarous" hordes of Haiti. Trujillo ordered the massacre of from 12,000 to 20,000 Haitians who had settled in the Dominican Republic in search of work. For years, the Dominican government had encouraged Haitian sugarcane cutters to cross the border to work on the U.S.–owned sugar plantations. But with the world economic depression in the 1930s and a fall in sugar prices and production, many Haitians did not return to their part of the island; in fact, additional thousands continued to stream across the border. The response of the Dominican government was wholesale slaughter.

Since 1952, a series of five-year agreements have been reached between the two governments to regularize the supply of Haitian cane cutters. An estimated 20,000 cross each year into the Dominican Republic legally, and an additional 60,000 enter illegally. Living and working conditions are very poor for these Haitians, and the migrants have no legal status and no rights. Planters prefer the Haitian workers because they are "cheaper and more docile" than Dominican laborers, who expect reasonable food, adequate housing, electric lights, and transportation to the fields. Today, as in the 1930s, economic troubles have gripped the Dominican Republic; the government has promised across-the-board sacrifices.

There is a subtle social discrimination against darker-skinned Dominicans, although this has not proved to be an insurmountable obstacle, as many hold elected political office. Discrimination is in part historical, in part cultural, and must be set against a backdrop of the sharp prejudice against Haitians. This prejudice is also directed against the minority in the Dominican population who are of Haitian descent. For example, during the contested presidential election of 1994, President Joaquín Balaguer Ricardo introduced the issue of race when questions were raised about his opponent's rumored Haitian origins. President Leonel Fernández has worked hard for better relations with Haitians, but the bitter memories and policies of the past undercut his efforts.

Ironically, the tragic Haitian earthquake in 2010 did much to ease tensions between the two nations. The Dominican Republic provided significant human and material support to its beleaguered neighbor. Not all the aid, as reported by *The New York Times,* is altruistic. Dominican companies "may have the most to gain in the immediate future from reconstruction efforts." Then, too, a stable Haiti is in the best interests of the Dominican Republic which is always concerned about an "exodus of Haitians across the border."

TIMELINE

1496
The founding of Santo Domingo, the oldest European city in the Americas

1821
Independence from Spain is declared

1822–1844
Haitian control

1844
Independence as a separate state

1930–1961
The era of General Rafael Trujillo

1965
Civil war and U.S. intervention

1990s
Diplomatic relations are restored with Cuba Hurricane Georges slams into the nation, killing many and causing $1.3 billion in damage

2000s
Leonel Fernández elected president in May 2008

Snapshot: DOMINICAN REPUBLIC

Summarized below is a quick look at the country with regard to its development, freedom, health/welfare, and achievements.

Development

A free trade agreement signed with Central American nations (CAFTA-DR) provided an impetus to investment in the Dominican Republic and reduced losses to the Asian garment industry. Following a sharp economic downturn in the economy due to global recession, in 2010–2011 the Dominican Republic currently enjoys one of the fastest growth rates in the region.

Freedom

Freedom House reported that "violence and discrimination against women remain serious problems, especially for women under the age of 18." Trafficking in women and girls, child prostitution, and child abuse are also major issues. A new (2010) constitution "includes one of the most restrictive abortion laws in the world, making the practice illegal even in cases of rape, incest, or to protect the life of the mother."

Health/Welfare

Sociologist Laura Raynolds notes that a restructuring of labor that moved thousands of women into nontraditional agriculture and manufacturing for export has reduced them to a "cheap and disciplined" workforce. Their work is undervalued to enhance profits. In that the majority of these workers are mothers, there has been a redefinition of family identity and work.

Achievements

Some of the best baseball in the hemisphere is played in the Dominican Republic. Four of its citizens, pitcher Pedro Martinez, and sluggers Sammy Sosa, David Ortiz, Vladimir Guerrero and Albert Pujols have become stars in major-league baseball in the United States. They have raised awareness of their country and have contributed to the welfare of Dominicans.

■ WOMEN'S RIGHTS

Women in the Dominican Republic have enjoyed political rights since 1941. While in office, President Balaguer, in an unprecedented move, named women governors for eight of the country's 29 provinces. Sexual discrimination is prohibited by law, but women have not shared equal social or economic status or opportunity with men. Divorce, however, is easily obtainable, and women can hold property in their own names. A 1996 profile of the nation's population and health noted that 27 percent of Dominican households were headed by women. In urban areas, the percentage rose to 31 percent.

■ AN AIR OF CHANGE

Progress toward a political scene free of corruption and racism has been fitful. The 1994 presidential election was marred by what multinational observers called massive fraud. The opposition claimed that Balaguer not only "stole the election" but also employed racist, anti-Haitian rhetoric that "inflamed stereotypes of Haitians in the Dominican Republic." Widespread unrest in the wake of the election, together with pressure from the Roman Catholic Church, the Organization of American States, and the United States, resulted in the "Pact for Democracy," which forced Balaguer to serve a shortened two-year term as president. New elections in 1996 returned Leonel Fernández to the presidency.

A brief economic recovery was followed by sharp recession. Inflation soared to 10 percent a month in 2003, the slowdown in the global economy cut into the tourist industry, and assembly plants in the free trade zone were forced to cut back. Many of the problems were blamed on President Hipólito Mejía's economic policies, which included a $2.4 billion bailout of the nation's third largest commercial bank—bankrupted by massive fraud. In elections in 2004 Mejía resorted to demagoguery, distributed motorcycles at cut rates, and promised a 30 percent raise to public employees. He lost the election to former president Leonel Fernández, who pledged to cut inflation, stabilize the exchange rate, and restore investor confidence. Fernández largely succeeded and the Dominican Republic enjoyed steady economic growth from 2005 until the onset of global recession in 2008. Robust growth returned in 2010 and 2011. Inflation is under control. The nation still suffers from high unemployment and underemployment; there is also a skewed distribution of wealth. Ten percent of the population control 40 percent of the national income. Fernández was returned to power in 2008 and promised to continue his economic policies.

? DID YOU KNOW?

The Dominican Republic has more baseball players in minor and major league teams in the United States than any other Caribbean region nation. Almost all major league teams own baseball academies on the island where they recruit and train talent.

FURTHER INVESTIGATION

For more information on baseball in the Dominican Republic go to http://mlb.mlb.com/mlb/features/dr/index.jsp

Statistics

Geography

Area in Square Miles (Kilometers): 18,712 (48,464) (about twice the size of New Hampshire)

Capital (Population): Santo Domingo (2,138,000)

Environmental Concerns: water shortages; soil erosion; damage to coral reefs; deforestation; damage from Hurricane Georges

Geographical Features: rugged highlands and mountains with fertile valleys interspersed

Climate: tropical maritime

People

Population

Total: 9,956,648 (2011 est.)

Annual Growth Rate: 1.3%

Rural/Urban Population Ratio: 31/69

Major Language: Spanish

Ethnic Makeup: 73% mixed; 16% white; 11% black

Religions: 95% Roman Catholic; 5% others

Health

Life Expectancy at Birth: 75 years (male); 79 years (female)

Infant Mortality Rate (Ratio): 22.22/1,000

Physicians Available (Ratio): 1.88/1,000

Education

Adult Literacy Rate: 87%

Compulsory (Ages): 6–14

Communication

Telephones: 1,010,000 main lines

Daily Newspaper Circulation: 35 per 1,000 people

Cell Phones: 8,893,000

Internet Users: 2,701,000

Transportation

Highways in Kilometers (Miles): 12,600 (7,825)

Railroads in Kilometers (Miles): 757 (470)

Usable Airfields: 35

Government

Type: republic

Independence Date: February 27, 1844 (from Haiti)

Head of State/Government: President Leonel Fernández is both head of state and head of government

Political Parties: Dominican Revolutionary Party; Social Christian Reformist Party; Dominican Liberation Party; others

Suffrage: universal and compulsory at 18, or at any age if married; members of the armed forces or the police cannot vote

Military

Military Expenditures (% of GDP): 0.7%

Current Disputes: none

Economy

Currency ($U.S. Equivalent): 38.19 Dominican pesos =$1

Per Capita Income/GDP: $9,300/$93.23 billion

GDP Growth Rate: 4.5%

Inflation Rate: 8.6%

Unemployment Rate: 13.3%

Labor Force: 4,732,000

Natural Resources: nickel; bauxite; gold; silver; arable land

Agriculture: sugarcane; coffee; cotton; cocoa; tobacco; rice; beans; potatoes; corn; bananas; livestock

Industry: tourism; sugar processing; ferronickel and gold mining; textiles; cement; tobacco

Exports: $7.792 billion (primary partners United States, Haiti)

Imports: $18.38 billion (primary partners United States, Venezuela, China, Mexico, Colombia)

Suggested Website

www.cia.org/cia/publications/factbook/index.html

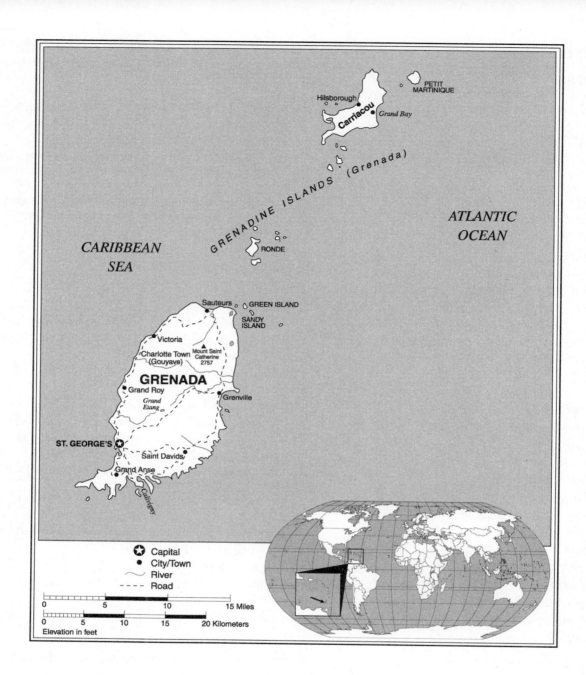

CARIBBEAN
SEA

ATLANTIC
OCEAN

PETIT
MARTINIQUE

Hilsborough

Carriacou

Grand Bay

GRENADINE ISLANDS (Grenada)

RONDE

Sauteurs

GREEN ISLAND

SANDY
ISLAND

Victoria

Charlotte Town
(Gouyave)

Mount Saint
Catherine
2757

GRENADA

Grand Roy

Grand
Etang

Grenville

ST. GEORGE'S

Saint Davids

Grand Anse

Calivigny

⭐ Capital
● City/Town
〰 River
- - - Road

0   5   10   15 Miles

0   5   10   15   20 Kilometers

Elevation in feet

Grenada

GRENADA: A FRESH BEGINNING

On his third voyage to the New World in 1498, Christopher Columbus sighted Grenada, which he named Concepción. The origin of the name Grenada cannot be clearly established, although it is believed that the Spanish renamed the island for the Spanish city of Granada. Because of a fierce aboriginal population of Carib Indians, the island remained uncolonized for 100 years.

Grenada, like most of the Caribbean, is ethnically mixed. Its culture draws on several traditions. The island's French past is preserved among some people who still speak patois (a French dialect). There are few whites on the island, save for a small group of Portuguese who immigrated earlier in the century. The primary cultural identification is with Great Britain, from which Grenada won its independence in 1974.

Grenada's political history has been tumultuous. The corruption and violent tactics of Grenada's first prime minister, Eric Gairy, resulted in his removal in a bloodless coup in 1979. Even though this action marked the first extra-constitutional change of government in the Commonwealth Caribbean (former British colonies), most Grenadians supported the coup, led by Maurice Bishop and his New Joint Endeavor for Welfare, Education, and Liberation (JEWEL) movement. Prime Minister Bishop, like Jamaica's Michael Manley before him, attempted to break out of European cultural and institutional molds and mobilize Grenadians behind him.

Bishop's social policies laid the foundation for basic health care for all Grenadians. With the departure of Cuban medical doctors in 1983, however, the lack of trained personnel created a significant health-care problem. Moreover, although medical-care facilities exist, these are not always in good repair, and equipment is aging and not reliable. Methods of recording births, deaths, and diseases lack systemization in Grenada, so it is risky to rely on local statistics to estimate the health needs of the population. There has also been some erosion from Bishop's campaign to accord women equal pay, status, and treatment. Two women were elected to Parliament, but skilled employment for women tends to be concentrated in the lowest-paid sector.

On October 19, 1983, Bishop and several of his senior ministers were killed during the course of a military coup. Six days later, the United States, with the token assistance of soldiers and police from states of the Eastern Caribbean, invaded Grenada, restored the 1974 Constitution, and prepared the way for new elections (in 1984).

According to one scholar, the invasion was a "lesson in a peacemaker's role in rebuilding a nation. Although Grenada has a history of parliamentary democracy, an atmosphere of civility, fertile soil, clean drinking water, and no slums, continued aid has not appreciably raised the standard of living and the young are resentful and restless."

Grenada's international airport, the focus of much controversy, has pumped new blood into the tourist industry. Moves have also been made by the Grenadian government to promote private-sector business and to

TIMELINE

1498
Grenada is discovered by Christopher Columbus
1763
England acquires the island from France by treaty
1834
Slavery is abolished
1958–1962
Member of the West Indies Federation
1974
Independence from Great Britain
1979
A coup brings Maurice Bishop to power
1983
Prime Minister Bishop is assassinated; U.S. troops land
1995
Former mathematics professor Keith Mitchell is elected prime minister
2000s
Venezuela experiments with new shipping routes to Grenada to expand markets in both nations
2008
Tillman Thomas elected prime minister
2013
Elections scheduled

Snapshot: GRENADA

Summarized below is a quick look at the country with regard to its development, freedom, health/welfare, and achievements.

Development

Hurricanes Ivan and Emily devastated Grenada in 2004 and 2005. The costs of rebuilding have created a significant debt that acts as a drag on the economy. In 2011 the public debt was 110% of GDP, which left little money for public investment or social programs. Nutmeg and cocoa cultivation has largely recovered from the damage.

Freedom

Grenadians are guaranteed full freedom of the press and speech. Newspapers, most of which are published by political parties, freely criticize the government without penalty. The OAS reported ballot fraud in the elections of November 2003, thus giving Prime Minister Keith Mitchell yet another term. He was defeated in 2008, however.

Health/Welfare

Grenada still lacks effective legislation for regulation of working conditions, wages, and occupational safety and health standards. Discrimination is prohibited by law, but women are often paid less than men for the same work.

Achievements

A series of public consultations have been held with respect to the reestablishment of local government in the villages. Some 52 village councils work with the government in an effort to set policies that are both responsive and equitable.

---

diminish the role of the government in the economy. Large amounts of foreign aid, especially from the United States, have helped to repair the infrastructure.

In recent years, foreign governments such as Kuwait, attracted by the power of Grenada's vote in the United Nations, have committed millions of dollars to Grenada's infrastructure. Some of these partnerships, particularly that involving Japan's access to Caribbean fish stocks, may have severe consequences for Grenadians in the future.

Significant problems remain. Unemployment has not significantly decreased; it remains at 12.5 percent (2007) of the workforce. Not surprisingly, the island has experienced a rising crime rate.

Prime Minister Keith Mitchell of the New National Party promised to create more jobs in the private sector and to cut taxes to stimulate investment in small, high-technology businesses. He also stated that government would become smaller and leaner.

Just as the economy had begun to experience its first significant growth in decades, Hurricane Ivan struck the island with a direct hit in 2004. It killed many people, destroyed or damaged 90 percent of the island's structures, and devastated the nutmeg crop, dealing the economy a serious blow. Privatization has continued, attracting foreign capital. As is the case in much of the Caribbean, tourism has become an important source of revenue and employment in Grenada, with a rapid expansion of the service sector. Despite the decline of agricultural exports, Grenada has maintained its position as the world's second-largest exporter of nutmeg. To protect forested areas and what remains of its agricultural base, in 2001 the government developed a "Land Bank" policy. Designed to promote the efficient use and management of all agricultural lands, the government helps those who want to engage in agricultural pursuits but lack access to land, and pressures landowners who have not maintained prime agricultural land in a productive state.

The government of Prime Minister Tillman Thomas, elected in 2008, has limited financial resources to fund either social programs or public projects. This is because of the costs of hurricane reconstruction and the subsequent debt burden as well as the global recession of 2008 that has greatly impacted the island nation.

DID YOU KNOW?

Grenada is known as the "island of spices," especially nutmeg, which grows virtually everywhere. Nutmeg bushes can grow to 70 feet. There is some dispute as to who first introduced nutmeg to Grenada. Some say it was the French in the late 1700s; others claim it was the British in 1843.

FURTHER INVESTIGATION

For more information on Grenada's long association with nutmeg to go http://www.indianchieftravel.com/en/grenada/spotlights/nutmeg-grenada

Statistics

Geography

Area in Square Miles (Kilometers): 133 (340) (about twice the size of Washington, D.C.)

Capital (Population): St. George's (40,000)

Geographical Features: volcanic in origin, with central mountains

Climate: tropical

People

Population

Total: 109,011 (2011 est.)

Annual Growth Rate: 0.538%

Rural/Urban Population Ratio: 61/39

Major Languages: English; French patois

Ethnic Makeup: 82% black; 13% mixed; 5% East Indian

Religions: 53% Roman Catholic; 13% Anglican; 33% other Protestant

Health

Life Expectancy at Birth: 70 years (male); 76 years (female)

Infant Mortality Rate (Ratio): 11.12/1,000

Physicians Available (Ratio): 1/1,000

Education

Adult Literacy Rate: 96%

Compulsory (Ages): 5–6; free

Communication

Telephones: 28,400 main lines

Cell Phones: 121,900

Internet Users: 25,000

Transportation

Highways in Kilometers (Miles): 1,040 (646)

Usable Airfields: 3

Government

Type: parliamentary democracy

Independence Date: February 7, 1974 (from the United Kingdom)

Head of State/Government: Queen Elizabeth II; Prime Minister Tillman Thomas

Political Parties: New National Party; National Democratic Congress

Suffrage: universal at 18

Military

Current Disputes: none

Economy

Currency ($U.S. Equivalent): 2.68 East Caribbean dollars = $1

Per Capita Income/GDP: $13,300/$1.428 billion

GDP Growth Rate: −1.4% (2010)

Inflation Rate: 4%

Unemployment Rate: 12.5%

Labor Force: 42,300

Natural Resources: timber; tropical fruit; deepwater harbors

Agriculture: bananas; cocoa; nutmeg; mace; citrus fruits; avocados; root crops; sugarcane; corn; vegetables

Industry: food and beverages; spice processing; textiles; light assembly operations; tourism; construction

Exports: $38 million (primary partners St. Lucia, Egypt, Antigua and Barbuda, United States)

Imports: $252.8 million (primary partners Trinidad and Tobago, United States)

Suggested Website

www.cia.gov/cia/publications/factbook/index.html

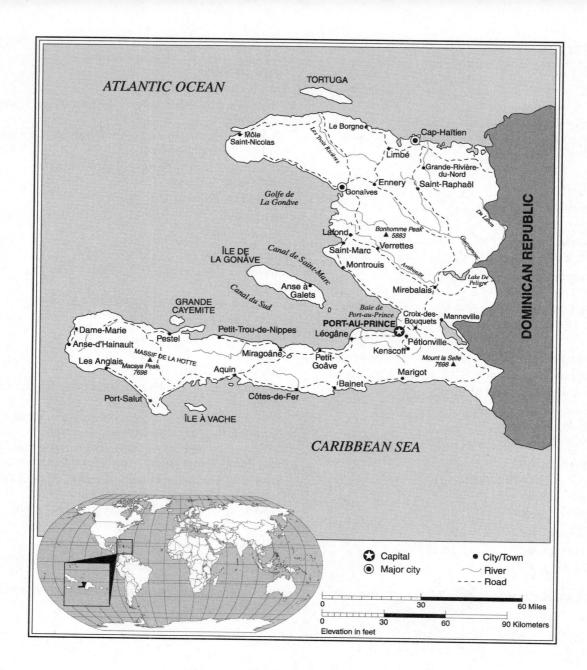

ATLANTIC OCEAN

TORTUGA

Le Borgne

Môle
Saint-Nicolas

Cap-Haïtien

Limbé

Grande-Rivière-
du-Nord

Ennery

Saint-Raphaël

Golfe de
La Gonâve

Gonaïves

Les Trois Rivières

Du Libon

Guayamouc

Bonhomme Peak
▲ 5883

Lafond

Verrettes

ÎLE DE
LA GONÂVE

Canal de Saint-Marc

Saint-Marc

Montrouis

Aribonite

Lake De
Peligre

Anse à
Galets

Mirebalais

GRANDE
CAYEMITE

Canal du Sud

Baie de
Port-au-Prince

Croix-des-
Bouquets

Manneville

Dame-Marie

Petit-Trou-de-Nippes

PORT-AU-PRINCE

Léogâne

Pétionville

Pestel

Anse-d'Hainault

MASSIF DE LA HOTTE

Miragoâne

Petit-
Goâve

Kenscoff

DOMINICAN REPUBLIC

Les Anglais

Macaya Peak
7698

Aquin

Mount la Selle
7698 ▲

Port-Salut

Côtes-de-Fer

Bainet

Marigot

ÎLE À VACHE

CARIBBEAN SEA

★ Capital

● City/Town

◉ Major city

⁀ River

- - - Road

0   30   60 Miles

0   30   60   90 Kilometers

Elevation in feet

Haiti
(Republic of Haiti)

HAITI: A FAILED STATE?

Haiti, which occupies the western third of the island of Hispaniola (the Dominican Republic comprises the other two-thirds), was the first nation in Latin America to win independence from its mother country—in this instance, France. It is the poorest country in the Western Hemisphere and one of the least developed in the world. Agriculture, the main employer of the population, is pressed beyond the limits of the available land; the result has been catastrophic deforestation and erosion. While only roughly 30 percent of the land is suitable for planting, 50 percent is actually under cultivation. Haitians are woefully poor, suffer from poor health and lack of education, and seldom find work. Even when employment is found, wages are miserable, and there is no significant labor movement to intercede on behalf of the workers.

A persistent theme in Haiti's history has been a bitter rivalry between a small mulatto elite, consisting of 3 to 4 percent of the population, and the black majority. When François Duvalier, a black country doctor, was president (1957–1971), his avowed aim was to create a "new equilibrium" in the country—by which he meant a major shift in power from the established, predominantly mulatto, elite to a new, black middle class. Much of Haitian culture explicitly rejects Western civilization, which is identified with the mulattos. The Creole language of the masses and their practice of Vodun (voodoo), a combination of African spiritualism and Christianity, has not only insulated the population from the "culturally alien" regimes in power but has also given Haitians a common point of identity.

Haitian intellectuals have raised sharp questions about the nation's culture. Modernizers would like to see the triumph of the French language over Creole and Roman Catholicism over Vodun. Others argue that significant change in Haiti can come only from within, from what is authentically Haitian. The refusal of Haitian governments to recognize Creole as the official language has only added to the determination of the mulatto elite and the black middle class to exclude the rest of the population from effective participation in political life.

For most of its history, Haiti has been run by a series of harsh authoritarian regimes. The ouster in 1986 of President-for-Life Jean-Claude Duvalier promised a more democratic opening as the new ruling National Governing Council announced as its primary goal the transition to a freely elected government. Political prisoners were freed; the dreaded secret police, the Tontons Macoute, were disbanded; and the press was unmuzzled.

The vacuum left by Duvalier's departure was filled by a succession of governments that were either controlled or heavily influenced by the military. Significant change was heralded in 1990 with the election to power of an outspoken Roman Catholic priest, Jean-Bertrand Aristide. By the end of 1991, he had moved against the military and had formulated a foreign policy that sought to move Haiti closer to the nations

TIMELINE

1492
The island is discovered by Christopher Columbus; named Hispaniola

1697
The western portion of Hispaniola is ceded to France

1804
Independence from France

1957-1971
The era of President François Duvalier

1971
Jean-Claude Duvalier is named president-for-life

1986
Jean-Claude Duvalier flees into exile

1991
A military coup ousts President Jean-Bertrand Aristide

2000s
The suffering of millions continues
Aristide ousted in February 2004

2006
René Préval elected president

2008
Food riots break out as prices rise
Three hurricanes and one tropical storm kill 800

2010
Magnitude 7.0 earthquake destroys Port-au-Prince and kills over 230,000

2011
Popular musician Michel Martelly elected president

(USAID/Prentice Colter, U.S. Air Force)

January 21, 2010. Port-au-Prince, Haiti. Here displaced Haitians receive emergency food aid in an operation led by USAID.

of Latin America and the Caribbean. Aristide's promotion of the "church of the poor," which combined local beliefs with standard Catholic instruction, earned him the enmity of both conservative Church leaders and Vodun priests. The radical language of his Lavalas (Floodtide) movement, which promised sweeping economic and social changes, made business leaders and rural landowners uneasy.

Perhaps not surprisingly in this coup-ridden nation, the army ousted President Aristide in 1991. It took tough economic sanctions and the threat of an imminent U.S. invasion to force the junta to relinquish power. Aristide, with the support of U.S. troops, was returned to power in 1994. Once an uneasy stability was restored to the country, U.S. troops left the peacekeeping to UN soldiers.

Although there was a period of public euphoria over Aristide's return, the assessment of *The Guardian,* a British newspaper, was somber: Crime rates rose precipitously, political violence continued, and Aristide's enemies were still in Haiti—and armed. Haitians, "sensing a vacuum," took the law "into their own hands."

René Préval, who had served briefly as Aristide's prime minister, was himself elected to the presidency in 1996. According to *Caribbean Week,* Préval was caught between "a fiercely independent Parliament [and] an externally-imposed structural adjustment programme. . . ." Préval, presiding over a divided party, was unable to have his choices for cabinet posts approved

by the Legislature, which left Haiti without an effective government from 1997 to 1999.

Aristide was reelected in 2000 in a vote characterized by irregularities and fraud. The result was parliamentary paralysis, as the opposition effectively boycotted Aristide's few initiatives, and a country where virtually every institution failed to function. Violent protests and equally violent government repression finally forced Aristide from power at the end of February, 2004. Meanwhile, the suffering of Haiti's people continued unabated, compounded by heavy spring rains and mudslides that killed perhaps 2,000 people.

For the next year and a half a bitterly divided nation attempted to lay the groundwork for new elections in the midst of rampant crime, gang violence, politically motivated attacks and murders, and widespread police corruption. Some 7,000 United Nations peacekeepers themselves came under assault. Political scientists began to use Haiti as an example of a "failed state." Elections were finally held in February 2006 and René Préval won with 51 percent of a contested vote. He promised to come to the aid of Haiti's poor—but many have made that promise before. Particularly worrisome were been statements by exiled president Jean-Bertrand Aristide that he intended to return to Haiti.

There are few signs of improvement in Haiti. More than 80 percent of the population lives in poverty and 54 percent live in extreme poverty. The economy grew by a modest 3.5 percent in 2007, in large part because of

Snapshot: HAITI

Summarized below is a quick look at the country with regard to its development, freedom, health/welfare, and achievements.

Development

Haiti's agricultural sector, where the vast majority of people earn a living, continues to suffer from massive soil erosion caused by deforestation, poor farming techniques, overpopulation, and low investment. The 2010 earthquake further exacerbated Haiti's economic woes with heavy loss of life and massive property and infrastructure damage.

Freedom

Demobilized soldiers and armed political factions are responsible for much of the violence in Haiti and have come to dominate drug trafficking. The rule of law cannot be maintained in the face of judicial corruption and a dysfunctional legal system. On the positive side, parliamentary democracy was restored in form in 2006.

Health/Welfare

Until 30 years ago, Haiti was self-sufficient in food production. It must now import about a third of its food needs. Two years after the horrific earthquake that claimed over 200,000 lives, hundreds of thousands of people still live in temporary shelters.

Achievements

In the late 1940s, Haitian "primitive" art created a sensation in Paris and other art centers. Although the force of the movement has now been spent, it still represents a unique, colorful, and imaginative art form.

---

help from the International Monetary Fund. Exports of garments and automobile parts to the United States, which assessed no tariffs on these goods, have helped the economy. It is sobering that Haiti's primary source of foreign exchange is in the form of remittances sent from abroad. These moneys are twice the amount earned from exports. Furthermore, 50% of the government's budget depends on foreign aid. Haiti is one of the first countries to feel the impact of rapidly rising food prices worldwide. People are desperate, many eat "cookies" composed largely of earth, and food riots have become increasingly violent. Hurricanes, tropical storms in 2008, and a devastating earthquake in 2010 have only added to the nation's misery.

There are also troubling signs that President Martelly intends to re-create a Haitian military, which had been disbanded. The military has a long history in Haiti of corruption and abuse. Many feel that an updated and well-trained police force would be adequate to meet security needs.

? DID YOU KNOW?

From the air you can plainly see the border between Haiti and the Dominican Republic. Haiti has lost 98% of its forests and the land, from the sky, appears brown. On the other hand, the Dominican side of the border is a lush green. Desperately poor people in Haiti cut the trees to sell as charcoal and the land, stripped of vegetation, washes away in the rain, further exacerbating what is already an environmental disaster.

FURTHER INVESTIGATION

For more information on environmental destruction in Haiti go to http://www.globalpost.com/dispatch/worldview/100127/haiti-earthquake-environment

Statistics

Geography

Area in Square Miles (Kilometers): 10,714 (27,750) (about the size of Maryland)

Capital (Population): Port-au-Prince 2,143,000 (2011 est.)

Environmental Concerns: extensive deforestation; soil erosion; inadequate potable water

Geographical Features: mostly rough and mountainous

Climate: tropical to semiarid

People*

Population

Total: 9,801,664 (2011 est.)

Annual Growth Rate: .888%

Rural/Urban Population Ratio: 48/52

Major Languages: French; Creole

Ethnic Makeup: 95% black; 5% mulatto and white

Religions: 80% Roman Catholic (of which about half also practice Vodun); 16% Protestant; 4% others

Health

Life Expectancy at Birth: 61 years (male); 64 years (female)

Infant Mortality Rate (Ratio): 52.44/1,000

Physicians Available (Ratio): 0.25/1,000

Education

Adult Literacy Rate: 52.9%

Communication

Telephones: 50,000 main lines

Daily Newspaper Circulation: 7 per 1,000 people

Cell Phones: 4,000,000

Internet Users: 1,000,000

Transportation

Highways in Kilometers (Miles): 4,160 (2,588)

Usable Airfields: 14

Government

Type: republic

Independence Date: January 1, 1804 (from France)

Head of State/Government: President Michel Martelly

Political Parties: Front for Hope (coalition); Fusion (coalition Socialist party); National Front for the Reconstruction of Haiti; Struggling People's Organization; Democratic Alliance (coalition); many others

Suffrage: universal at 18

Military

Military Expenditures (% of GDP): 0.4%

Current Disputes: claims U.S.–administered Navassa Island

Economy

Currency ($U.S. Equivalent): 39.8 gourdes = $1

Per Capita Income/GDP: $1,200/$12.44 billion

GDP Growth Rate: 6.1%

Inflation Rate: 9.3%

Unemployment Rate: 40.6%; 66% have no formal jobs

Labor Force: 4,810,000

Natural Resources: bauxite; copper; calcium carbonate; gold; marble; hydropower

Agriculture: coffee; mangoes; sugarcane; rice; corn; sorghum; wood

Industry: sugar refining; flour milling; textiles; cement; tourism; light assembly based on imported parts

Exports: $690.3 million (primary partners United States, Canada, France)

Imports: $3.275 billion (primary partners United States, Dominican Republic, China)

Suggested Website

www.cia.gov/cia/publications/factbook/geos/ha.html

*Note: Estimates explicitly take into account the effects of excess mortality due to AIDS.

Virtually all of these statistics must be weighed against the devasting earthquake of 2010 that killed over 200,000 and destroyed much of the nation's infrastructure.

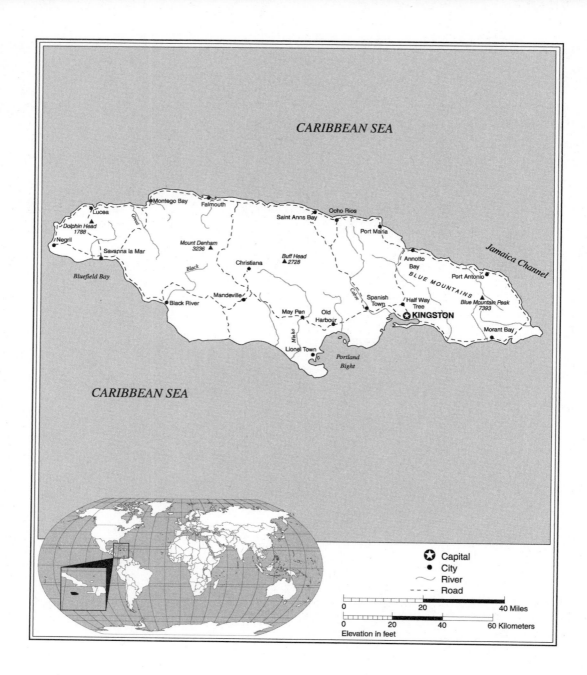

CARIBBEAN SEA

CARIBBEAN SEA

Jamaica Channel

Lucea

Dolphin Head
1788

Negril

Montego Bay   Falmouth

Saint Anns Bay   Ocho Rios

Port Maria

Savanna la Mar

Mount Denham
3236

Buff Head
2728

Annotto
Bay

Port Antonio

Christiana

BLUE MOUNTAINS

Bluefield Bay

Black

Mandeville

Spanish
Town

Half Way
Tree

Blue Mountain Peak
7393

Black River

May Pen   Old
Harbour

★ KINGSTON

Milk

Lionel Town

Morant Bay

Portland
Bight

Cobre

Capital
City
River
Road

0   20   40 Miles

0   20   40   60 Kilometers

Elevation in feet

Jamaica

JAMAICA: "OUT OF MANY, ONE PEOPLE"

In 1962, Jamaica and Trinidad and Tobago were the first of the English-speaking Caribbean islands to gain their independence. A central problem since that time has been the limited ability of Jamaicans to forge a sense of nation. "Out of many, one people" is a popular slogan in Jamaica, but it belies an essential division of the population along lines of both race and class. The elite, consisting of a small white population and Creoles (Afro-Europeans), still think of themselves as "English." Local loyalties notwithstanding, Englishness permeates much of Jamaican life, from language to sports. According to former prime minister Michael Manley: "The problem in Jamaica is how do you get the Jamaican to divorce his mind from the paralysis of his history, which was all bitter colonial frustration, so that he sees his society in terms of this is what crippled me?"

Manley's first government (1975–1980) was one of the few in the Caribbean to incorporate the masses of the people into a political process. He was aware that in a country such as Jamaica—where the majority of the population were poor, ill educated, and lacked essential services—the promise to provide basic needs would win him widespread support. Programs to provide Jamaicans with basic health care and education were expanded, as were services. Many products were subjected to price controls or were subsidized to make them available to the majority of the people. Cuban medical teams and teachers were brought to Jamaica to fill the manpower gaps until local people could be trained.

However, Jamaica's fragile economy could not support Manley's policies, and he was eventually opposed by the entrenched elite and voted out of office. But Manley was returned to office in 1989, with a new image as a moderate, willing to compromise and aware of the need for foreign-capital investment. Manley retired in 1992 and was replaced as prime minister by Percival J. Patterson, who promised to accelerate Jamaica's transition to a free-market economy. The government instituted a policy of divestment of state-owned enterprises.

The challenges remain. Crime and violence continue to be major social problems in Jamaica. The high crime rate threatens not only the lucrative tourist industry but the very foundations of Jamaican society. Prime Minister Patterson called for a moral reawakening: "All our programs and strategies for economic progress are doomed to failure unless there is a drastic change in social attitudes. . . ." A stagnant economy, persistent inflation, and unemployment and underemployment combine to lessen respect for authority and contribute to the crime problem. In 2001, Amnesty International noted that in proportion to population, more people are killed by police in Jamaica than anywhere else in the world. Many of the deaths are the result of clashes with gangs of drug dealers, who usually outgun the police. Jamaica counted 1,000 murders in 2002, more, proportionately, than in South Africa, and less than Colombia or El Salvador. The power of one druglord, Christopher "Dudus" Coke, resulted in the declaration of a state of emergency in Kingston in 2010, as forces loyal to the cocaine and arms dealer fought police and troops to prevent his extradition to the United States. Self-described as a "community leader,"

TIMELINE

1509
The first Spanish settlement

1655
Jamaica is seized by the English

1692
An earthquake destroys Port Royal

1944
Universal suffrage is proclaimed

1962
Independence from Great Britain

1990s
Violent crime and strong-armed police responses plague the island
Percival J. Patterson is elected prime minister

2000s
Gun battles break out in Kingston
Patterson reelected to a fourth term in 2002

2006
Portia Simpson Miller elected Jamaica's first woman prime minister

2007
Bruce Golding elected prime minister

2010
Violent unrest in Kingston fueled by drug gangs and supporters

2011
Three prime ministers hold power. Portia Simpson-Miller elected prime minister in December

Snapshot: JAMAICA

Summarized below is a quick look at the country with regard to its development, freedom, health/welfare, and achievements.

Development

The Jamaican economy, already fragile, suffered a further setback in 2007 with widespread devastation caused by Hurricane Dean. High unemployment and underemployment is a perennial problem. Persistent violent crime and drug activity also have a negative impact on potential investment in the island.

Freedom

Despite the repeal of the controversial Suppression of Crime Act of 1974, the Parliament, in the face of persistent high levels of crime, provided for emergency police powers. Some critics charge that the Parliament in essence recreated the repealed legislation in a different guise. With regard to

freedom of the press, Jamaica improved its standing in 2011 to 16 out of 179 surveyed by the World Press Freedom Index.

Health/Welfare

According to the Encyclopedia of the Nations, in 2011 housing remained one of the government's "most pressing problems. While middle-and upper-income housing is comparable to that in neighboring areas of North America, facilities for low-income groups are poor by any standard. The problem has been aggravated by constant migration from the rural areas to the cities, causing the growth of urban slums."

Achievements

Marcus Garvey was posthumously declared Jamaica's first National Hero in 1964 because of his leading role in the international movement against racism. He called passionately for the recognition of the equal dignity of human beings regardless of race, religion, or national origin. Garvey died in London in 1940. Track star Uslain Bolt claims the title of the "world's fastest human."

Coke won the support of many poor when he provided benefits and services that the government could or would not. Prime Minister Golding denounced the unrest as an "assault on the authority of the state." It remains a violent society, and the nation continues to walk the narrow line between liberty and license.

As is the case in many developing-world countries where unemployment and disaffection are common, drug use is high in Jamaica. The government is reluctant to enforce drug control, however, for approximately 8,000 rural families depend on the cultivation of ganja (marijuana) to supplement their already marginal incomes.

Some of Jamaica's violence is politically motivated and tends to be associated with election campaigns. Both major parties have supporters who employ violence for political purposes. The legal system has been unable to contain the violence or bring the guilty to justice because of a pervasive code of silence enforced at the local level.

The Patterson government moved deliberately in the direction of electoral reform in an attempt to reduce both violence and fraud. Reelected to a fourth term in 2002, Prime Minister Patterson hoped to match Jamaica's political stability with improvements in the nation's social and economic sectors. He successfully addressed inflation through tight monetary and fiscal policies and redressed Jamaica's debt by privatizing inefficient state enterprises.

On the positive side, human rights are generally respected, and Jamaica's press is basically free. Press freedom is observed in practice within the broad limits of libel laws and the State Secrets Act. Opposition parties publish newspapers and magazines that are highly critical of government policies, and foreign publications are widely available.

Jamaica's labor union movement is strong and well organized, and it has contributed many leaders to the political process. Unions are among the strongest and best organizations in the country and are closely tied to political parties.

Long-term Prime Minister Patterson stepped down from office in 2006 and was replaced by Portia Simpson-Miller, Jamaica's first woman leader. Unfortunately, Simpson-Miller's choices for ministerial positions proved a liability. Several were accused of mismanagement and corruption, accusations that colored a bitter election campaign in 2007. Although she lost the election, she again became prime minister late in 2011, following the resignation of Golding and the very brief 10-week term of his successor, Alexander Holness. Jamaica's serious social and economic problems in the meantime remain daunting.

? DID YOU KNOW?

Music known as reggae appeared in Jamaica around 1960 and derives from the traditional rhythms of the Rastafarians. Originally called "ska," reggae was introduced to the United States at the New York World's Fair in 1964. The lyrics often embody a protest theme and are sharply critical of the injustices of society.

FURTHER INVESTIGATION

For more information on reggae go to http://www.rootsreggaeclub.com/culture_reggae_afro/reggae/reggae.htm

Statistics

Geography

Area in Square Miles (Kilometers): 4,244 (10,991) (slightly smaller than Connecticut)

Capital (Population): Kingston (580,000) (metro)

Environmental Concerns: deforestation; damage to coral reefs; water and air pollution

Geographical Features: Mostly mountains, with a narrow, discontinuous coastal plain

Climate: tropical; temperate interior

People

Population

Total: 2,889,187 (2012 est.)

Annual Growth Rate: 0.714%

Rural/Urban Population Ratio: 48/52

Major Languages: English; Jamaican Creole

Ethnic Makeup: 90% black; 7% mixed; 3% East Indian, white, Chinese and others

Religions: 62.5% Protestant; 2.6% Catholic; 21% none specified

Health

Life Expectancy at Birth: 72 years (male); 75 years (female)

Infant Mortality Rate (Ratio): 14.3/1,000

Physicians Available (Ratio): 0.85/1,000

Education

Adult Literacy Rate: 87.9%

Compulsory (Ages): 6–12; free

Communication

Telephones: 263,100 main lines

Daily Newspaper Circulation: 65 per 1,000 people

Cell Phones: 3,103,000

Internet Users: 1,581,000

Transportation

Roadways in Kilometers (Miles): 20,996 (13,046)

Usable Airfields: 27

Government

Type: constitutional parliamentary democracy

Independence Date: August 6, 1962 (from the United Kingdom)

Head of State/Government: Queen Elizabeth II; Prime Minister Portia Simpson-Miller

Political Parties: People's National Party; Jamaica Labour Party; National Democratic Movement

Suffrage: universal at 18

Military

Military Expenditures (% of GDP): 0.6%

Current Disputes: none

Economy

Currency ($U.S. Equivalent): 86.36 Jamaican dollars = $1

Per Capita Income/GDP: 9,000/$24.58 billion

GDP Growth Rate: 1.5%

Inflation Rate: 7.7%

Unemployment Rate: 12.7%

Labor Force: 1,324,000

Natural Resources: bauxite; gypsum; limestone

Agriculture: sugarcane; bananas; coffee; citrus fruits; potatoes; vegetables; poultry; goats; milk

Industry: tourism; bauxite; textiles; food processing; light manufacturers; rum; cement; metal

Exports: $1.65 billion (primary partners United States, Canada, Norway, United Kingdom, Netherlands)

Imports: $6.356 billion (primary partners United States, Venezuela, Trinidad and Tobago, China)

Suggested Website

www.cia.gov/cia/publications/factbook/index.html

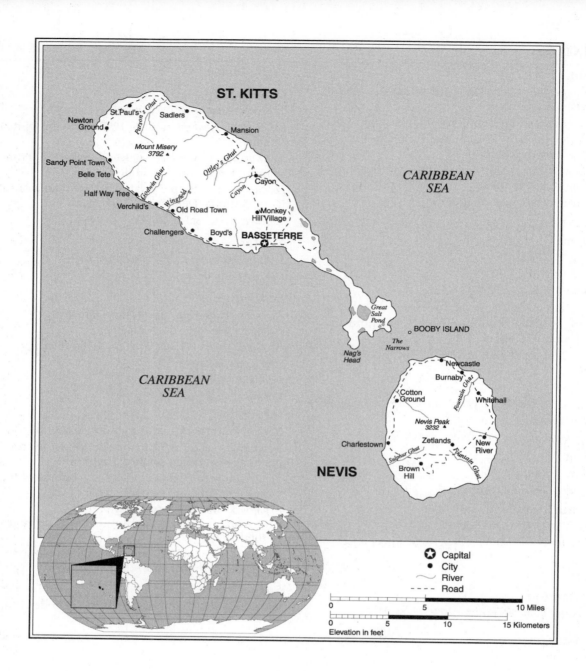

ST. KITTS

Newton
Ground

St.Paul's

Sadlers

Mansion

Parson's Ghut

*CARIBBEAN
SEA*

Mount Misery
3792 ▲

Sandy Point Town

Belle Tete

Godwin Ghut

Ottley's Ghut

Cayon

Cayon

Half Way Tree

Wingfield

Verchild's

Old Road Town

Monkey
Hill Village

Challengers

Boyd's

BASSETERRE ✪

*Great
Salt
Pond*

○ BOOBY ISLAND

*The
Narrows*

*Nag's
Head*

*CARIBBEAN
SEA*

Newcastle

Burnaby

Fountain Ghut

Cotton
Ground

Whitehall

Nevis Peak
3232 ▲

Charlestown

Zetlands

New
River

Sulphur Ghut

Fountain Ghut

Brown
Hill

NEVIS

✪ Capital
● City
〜 River
- - - Road

0				5			10 Miles

0		5		10		15 Kilometers

Elevation in feet

St. Kitts–Nevis

(Federation of St. Kitts and Nevis)

ST. KITTS–NEVIS: ESTRANGED NEIGHBORS

On September 19, 1983, the twin-island state of St. Kitts–Nevis became an independent nation. The country had been a British colony since 1623, when Captain Thomas Warner landed with his wife and eldest son, along with 13 other settlers. The colony fared well, and soon other Caribbean islands were being settled by colonists sent out from St. Kitts (also commonly known as St. Christopher).

The history of this small island nation is the story of the classic duel between the big sea powers of the period—Great Britain, France, and Spain—and the indigenous people—in this case, the Carib Indians. (Although much of the nation's history has centered around St. Kitts, the larger of the two islands, Nevis, only two miles away, has always been considered a part of St. Kitts, and its history is tied into that of the larger island.) The British were the first settlers on the island of St. Kitts but were followed that same year by the French. In a unique compromise, considering the era, the British and French divided the territory in 1627 and lived in peace for a number of decades. A significant reason for this British–French cooperation was the constant pressure from their common enemies: the aggressive Spanish and the fierce Carib Indians. The Caribs, for a while, played a role similar to that of Indians in the French and Indian War in North America a century later. They were adept at forming alliances with either the French or the English to drive one or the other or both from the region.

With the gradual elimination of the mutual threat, Anglo–French tensions again mounted, resulting in a sharp land battle at Frigate Bay on St. Kitts. The new round of hostilities, which reflected events in Europe, would disrupt the Caribbean for much of the next century. Events came to a climactic head in 1782, when the British garrison at Brimstone Hill, commonly known as the "Gibraltar of the West Indies," was overwhelmed by a superior French force. In honor of the bravery of the defenders, the French commander allowed the British to march from the fortress in full formation. (The expression "peace with honor" has its roots in this historic encounter.) Later in the year, however, the British again seized the upper hand. A naval battle at Frigate Bay was won by British Admiral Hood following a series of brilliant maneuvers. The defeated French admiral, the Count de Grasse, was in turn granted "peace with honor." Thereafter, the islands remained under British rule until their independence in 1983.

AGRICULTURE

Before the British colonized the island, St. Kitts was called Liamiuga ("Fertile Isle") by the Carib Indians. The name was apt, because agriculture for most of its history played a big role in the economy of the islands. Tourism and offshore banking and business facilities definitively replaced sugar, which ceased production in 2005, as the largest generator of foreign exchange.

Because the sugar market was so unstable and because world market prices were so low, the decision was made to phase out the sugar industry

TIMELINE

1493
The islands are discovered and named by Christopher Columbus

1623
The British colony is settled by Captain Thomas Warner

1689
A land battle at Frigate Bay disrupts a peaceful accord between France and England

1782
The English are expelled by the French at the siege of Brimstone Hill
The French are beaten at the sea battle of Frigate Bay; the beginning of continuous British rule

1967
Self-government as an Associate State of the United Kingdom

1983
Full independence from Great Britain

1998
A referendum on Nevis secession is narrowly defeated

2010
Denzil Douglas reelected to a fourth consecutive term

Snapshot: ST.KITTS-NEVIS

Summarized below is a quick look at the country with regard to its development, freedom, health/welfare, and achievements.

Development

The country's Development Bank, through its Business Support Unit, has offered workshops to both the tourism and agricultural sectors of the economy. The object is to enhance the bank's technical assistance to its small and medium size business clients.

Freedom

The 2010 United States Department of State human rights report noted that "violence against women was a problem. The law criminalizes domestic violence, including emotional abuse, and provides penalties of up to EC$13,500 ($5,000)

or six months in prison. Although many women were reluctant to file complaints or pursue them in the courts, the Ministry of Gender Affairs handled an annual average of 25 to 30 reports of domestic violence."

Health/Welfare

The demise of the sugar industry in 2005 resulted in the loss of employment for about 4 percent of the population. Affected workers sought employment in other kinds of agriculture, the tourism industry, or out-migrated. Although a minimum wage exists by law, the amount is less than what a person can reasonably be expected to live on.

Achievements

St. Kitts–Nevis was the first successful British settlement in the Caribbean. St. Kitts–Nevis was the birthplace of Alexander Hamilton, the first U.S. secretary of the Treasury Department and an American statesman.

---

altogether. The last mill closed its doors in 2005. Agricultural production will now likely be geared toward local or regional markets.

ECONOMIC CHANGE

Unlike such islands as Barbados and Antigua, St. Kitts–Nevis for years chose not to use tourism as a buffer to offset any disastrous fluctuations in sugar prices. On St. Kitts, there was an antitourism attitude that can be traced back to the repressive administration of Prime Minister Robert Bradshaw, a black nationalist who worked to discourage tourism and threatened to nationalize all land holdings.

That changed under the moderate leadership of Kennedy Simmonds and his People's Action Movement, who remained in power from 1980 until ousted in elections in July 1995. The new administration of Denzil Douglas promised to address serious problems that had developed, including drug trafficking, money laundering, and a lack of respect for law and order. In 1997, a 50-man "army" was created to wage war against heavily armed drug traffickers operating in the region. Agriculture Minister Timothy Harris noted that the permanent defense force "was critical to the survival of the sovereignty of the nation." Simmond's promotion of tourism took root. By 2001, tourism had become a major growth industry in the islands. Major airlines refused to schedule landings in St. Kitts until there were an adequate number of hotel rooms. Accordingly, the government promoted the construction of 1,500 rooms. A positive side-effect are the jobs produced in the construction trades and service industry.

The future of St. Kitts–Nevis will depend on its ability to broaden its economic base. Prime Minister Douglas's economic policies include the promotion of export-oriented manufactures and off-shore banking.

A potential problem of some magnitude looms, however: The island of Nevis, long in the shadow of the more populous and prosperous St. Kitts, nearly voted to secede in a referendum held in August 1998. The Constitution requires a two-thirds majority for secession; 61.7 percent of the population of Nevis voted yes. Not surprisingly, the government is working to fashion a new federalism with "appropriate power sharing" between the islands. That has not diminished the move toward independence for Nevis's 10,000 people. Currently, Nevis enjoys a large measure of autonomy and has its own premier and legislature. Prime Minister Douglas has also said that difference between the two islands should be the subject of constitutional reform, not repeated referenda on secession.

? DID YOU KNOW?

When St. Kitts-Nevis won its independence from Great Britain in 1983, it became the third two-island country in the Caribbean (the others are Antigua and Barbuda, and Trinidad and Tobago). The demand on the part of the citizens of the smaller island of Nevis, with 20% of the population, for an equal say in the government has been a considerable source of friction and is bitterly opposed by the residents of St. Kitts.

FURTHER INVESTIGATION

For more information on the history of the Nevis secession movement go to http://www.nevisindependence.com/history.html

Statistics

Geography

Area in Square Miles (Kilometers): 101 (261) (about 1½ times the size of Washington, D.C.)

Capital (Population): Basseterre (13,000)

Geographical Features: volcanic, with mountainous interiors

Climate: subtropical

People

Population

Total: 50,726 (2012 est.)

Annual Growth Rate: 0.806%

Rural/Urban Population Ratio: 68/32

Major Language: English

Ethnic Makeup: mainly of black African descent

Religions: Anglican; other Protestant sects; Roman Catholic

Health

Life Expectancy at Birth: 72 years (male); 77 years (female)

Infant Mortality Rate (Ratio): 9.43/1,000

Physicians Available (Ratio): 1.09/1,000

Education

Adult Literacy Rate: 97.8%

Compulsory (Ages): for 12 years between ages 5 and 18

Communication

Telephones: 20,600 main lines

Cell Phones: 84,600

Internet Users: 17,000

Transportation

Highways in Kilometers (Miles): 320 (199)

Railroads in Kilometers (Miles): 58 (36)

Usable Airfields: 2

Government

Type: constitutional monarchy within Commonwealth

Independence Date: September 19, 1983 (from the United Kingdom)

Head of State/Government: Queen Elizabeth II; Prime Minister Denzil Douglas

Political Parties: St. Kitts and Nevis Labour Party; People's Action Movement; Nevis Reformation Party; Concerned Citizens Movement

Suffrage: universal at 18

Military

Current Disputes: Nevis has threatened to secede

Economy

Currency ($U.S. Equivalent): 2.68 East Caribbean dollars = $1

Per Capita Income/GDP: $16,400/$918 million

GDP Growth Rate: 1.5%

Inflation Rate: 4.6%

Unemployment Rate: 4.5%

Labor Force: 18,170

Natural Resources: negligible

Agriculture: rice; yams; vegetables; bananas; fish

Industry: tourism; cotton; salt; copra; clothing; footwear; beverages

Exports: $63.1 million (primary partners United States, Canada, Azerbaijan)

Imports: $315.7 million (primary partners United States, Trinidad and Tobago, Bolivia, Barbados)

Suggested Website

www.cia.gov/cia/publications/factbook/index.html

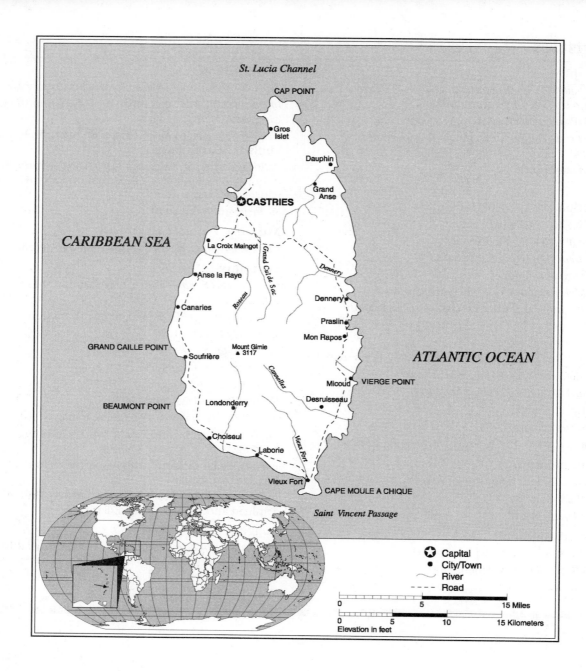

St. Lucia Channel

CAP POINT

• Gros
  Islet

Dauphin •

Grand
Anse

★ CASTRIES

CARIBBEAN SEA

La Croix Maingot •

Grand Cul de Sac

Dennery

• Anse la Raye

Dennery •

Roseau

Praslin •

Mon Rapos •

• Canaries

Mount Gimie
▲ 3117

GRAND CAILLE POINT

• Soufrière

Cannelles

Micoud •   VIERGE POINT

ATLANTIC OCEAN

Desruisseau •

BEAUMONT POINT

Londonderry •

• Choiseul

Vieux Fort

Laborie •

Vieux Fort •

CAPE MOULE A CHIQUE

Saint Vincent Passage

★ Capital
• City/Town
〰 River
--- Road

0		5		15 Miles

0	5	10	15 Kilometers
Elevation in feet

St. Lucia

ST. LUCIA: ENGLISH POLITICS, FRENCH CULTURE

The history of St. Lucia gives striking testimony to the fact that the sugar economy, together with the contrasting cultures of various colonial masters, was crucial in shaping the land, social structures, and lifestyles of its people. The island changed hands between the French and the English at least seven times, and the influences of both cultures are still evident today. Ninety percent of the population speaks patois (a French dialect), while the educated and the elite prefer English. Indeed, the educated perceive patois as suitable only for proverbs and curses. On St. Lucia and the other patois-speaking islands (Dominica, Grenada), some view the common language as the true reflection of their uniqueness. English, however, is the language of status and opportunity. In terms of religion, most St. Lucians are Roman Catholic.

The original inhabitants of St. Lucia were Arawak Indians who had been forced off the South American mainland by the Carib Indians. Gradually, the Carib also moved onto the Caribbean islands and destroyed most of the Arawak culture. Evidence of that early civilization has been found in rich archaeological sites on St. Lucia.

The date of the European "discovery" of the island is uncertain; it may have occurred in 1499 or 1504 by the navigator and mapmaker Juan de la Cosa, who explored the Windward Islands during the early years of the sixteenth century. The Dutch, French, and English all established small settlements or trading posts on the island in the seventeenth century but were resisted by the Caribs. The first successful settlement dates from 1651, when the French were able to maintain a foothold.

The island's political culture is English. Upon independence from Great Britain in 1979, St. Lucians adopted the British parliamentary system, which includes specific safeguards for the preservation of human rights. Despite several years of political disruption, caused by the jockeying for power of several political parties and affiliated interests, St. Lucian politics is essentially stable.

THE ECONOMY

St. Lucia has an economy that is as diverse as any in the Caribbean. Essentially agricultural, the country has also developed a tourism industry, manufacturing, and related construction activity. A recent "mineral inventory" has located possible gold deposits, but exploitation must await the creation of appropriate mining legislation.

U.S. promises to the region made in the 1980s failed to live up to expectations. Although textiles, clothing, and nontraditional goods exported to the United States increased as a result of the Caribbean Basin Initiative, St. Lucia remained dependent on its exports of bananas. About a third of the island's workforce were involved in banana production, which accounts for 90 percent of St. Lucia's exports.

St. Lucia's crucial banana industry suffered significant production losses in 1997 and 2001 in large part because of drought. Exports were half of the normal volume, and St. Lucia fell short of filling its quota

TIMELINE

1638
The English take possession of St. Lucia
1794
The English regain possession of St. Lucia from France
1908
Riots
1951
Universal adult suffrage
1979
Independence from Great Britain
1990s
Banana production suffers a serious decline
2000s
Economic diversification becomes a critical need
2012
Kenny Davis Anthony elected prime minister

Snapshot: ST. LUCIA

Summarized below is a quick look at the country with regard to its development, freedom, health/welfare, and achievements.

Development

Although Hurricane Tomás in October 2010 caused significant damage to St. Lucia's infrastructure, the island nation has largely recovered. Tourism increased by 10% and resulted in a 33% growth in tourism-related revenues.

Freedom

The Heritage Foundation/Wall Street Journal reported that The 2012 Index of "Economic Freedom, which looks at a series of factors, including the rule of law, limited government, regulatory efficiency and open markets, found St. Lucia to be number one in the region, followed by Barbados."

Health/Welfare

The minister of agriculture has linked marginal nutrition and malnutrition in St. Lucia with economic adjustment programs in the Caribbean. He noted that the success achieved earlier in raising standards of living was being eroded by "onerous debt burdens."

Achievements

St. Lucians have won an impressive two Nobel prizes. Sir W. Arthur Lewis won the prize in 1979 for economics, and in 1993, poet Derek Walcott won the prize for literature. When asked how the island had produced two Nobel laureates, Wolcott replied: "It's the food."

---

for the European Union. A 1999 European Union decision to drop its import preferences for bananas from former colonial possessions in the Caribbean together with increased competition from Latin American growers created an urgent demand to diversify St. Lucia's economy. Increased emphasis has been placed on exports of mangos and avocados. Tourism, light manufacturing, and offshore banking have also experienced growth. Despite these attempts unemployment, inflation, a high cost of living, and drug trafficking remain serious problems and have led to periodic unrest.

St. Lucia, like several other islands, has also succeeded in trading on its sovereignty—a vote in the United Nations—to raise revenue. St. Lucia has supported China's claims of sovereignty over Taiwan in the expectation of increased Chinese investment in the island. This action was one response to the collapse of the banana industry in 1997. Prime Minister Anthony has indicated that he will re-establish relations with Taiwan, reversing Sir John Compton's pro-Peoples Republic of China policy.

▪ EDUCATION AND EMIGRATION

Education in St. Lucia has traditionally been brief and perfunctory. Few students attend secondary school, and very few (3 percent) ever attend a university. Although the government reports that 95 percent of those eligible attend elementary school, farm and related chores severely reduce attendance figures. In recent years,

St. Lucia has channeled more than 20 percent of its expenditures into education and health care. Patient care in the general hospital was made free of charge in 1980.

Population growth is relatively low, but emigration off the island is a significant factor. For years, St. Lucians, together with Dominicans, traveled to French Guiana to work in the gold fields. More recently, however, they have crossed to neighboring Martinique, a French department (administrative division), in search of work. St. Lucians can also be found working on many other Caribbean islands.

? DID YOU KNOW?

St. Lucia has a "drive-in volcano." It is possible to drive a car to the very crater lip of the volcano Soufrière. The area around the crater has many hot springs, some of which have been used as sulphur baths since 1785, when France's King Louis XVI had the water channeled for the benefit of his troops.

FURTHER INVESTIGATION

For more information on the geology of the Soufrière volcano go to http://soufrierefoundation.org/about-soufriere/geology

Statistics

Geography

Area in Square Miles (Kilometers): 238 (619) (about 3 times the size of Washington, D.C.)

Capital (Population): Castries (15,000)

Environmental Concerns: deforestation; soil erosion

Geographical Features: volcanic and mountainous; some broad, fertile valleys

Climate: tropical maritime

People

Population

Total: 162,178 (2012 est.)

Annual Growth Rate: 0.38%

Rural/Urban Population Ratio: 72/28

Major Languages: English; French patois

Ethnic Makeup: 82.5% black; 11.9% mixed; 2.4% East Indian

Religions: 67.5% Roman Catholic; 25% Protestant

Health

Life Expectancy at Birth: 74 years (male); 80 years (female)

Infant Mortality Rate (Ratio): 12.39/1,000

Physicians Available (Ratio): 0.47/1,000

Education

Adult Literacy Rate: 90.1%

Compulsory (Ages): 5–15

Communication

Telephones: 41,100 main lines

Cell Phones: 179,300

Internet Users: 142,900

Transportation

Highways in Kilometers (Miles): 1,210 (451)

Usable Airfields: 2

Government

Type: constitutional monarchy within Commonwealth

Independence Date: February 22, 1979 (from the United Kingdom)

Head of State/Government: Queen Elizabeth II; Prime Minister Kenny Davis Anthony

Political Parties: United Workers' Party; St. Lucia Labour Party

Suffrage: universal at 18

Military

Current Disputes: none

Economy

Currency ($U.S. Equivalent): 2.68 East Caribbean dollars = $1

Per Capita Income/GDP: 12,900/$2.142 billion

GDP Growth Rate: 2%

Inflation Rate: 1.9%

Unemployment Rate: 20%

Labor Force: 79,700

Natural Resources: forests; sandy beaches; minerals (pumice); mineral springs; geothermal potential

Agriculture: bananas; coconuts; vegetables; citrus fruits; root crops; cocoa

Industry: clothing; assembly of electronic components; beverages; corrugated cardboard boxes; tourism; lime processing; coconut processing

Exports: $162.3 million (primary partners United Kingdom, United States, Peru, Antigua and Barbuda, Dominica, Barbados, Trinidad and Tobago, Grenada

Imports: $535.4 million (primary partners Brazil, United States, Trinidad and Tobago)

Suggested Website

www.cia.gov/cia/publications/factbook/index.html

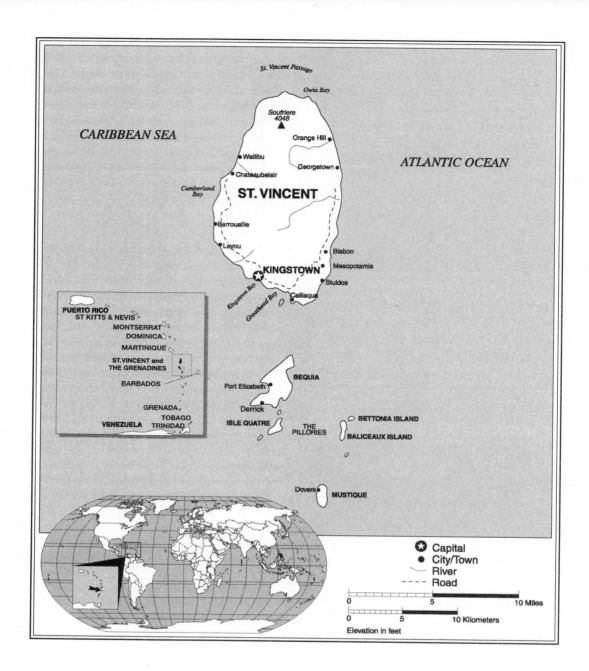

CARIBBEAN SEA

ATLANTIC OCEAN

St. Vincent Passage

Owia Bay

Soufriere
4048

● Orange Hill

● Wallibu

Georgetown

● Chateaubelair

Cumberland
Bay

ST. VINCENT

● Barrouallie

● Layou

● Biabon
● Mesopotamia

✪ **KINGSTOWN**

● Stuldos

Kingstown Bay

Calliaqua ●

Greathead Bay

PUERTO RICO
ST KITTS & NEVIS
MONTSERRAT
DOMINICA
MARTINIQUE
ST. VINCENT and
THE GRENADINES
BARBADOS
GRENADA
TOBAGO
VENEZUELA **TRINIDAD**

BEQUIA

Port Elizabeth ●

Derrick ●

ISLE QUATRE

THE
PILLORIES

● **BETTONIA ISLAND**

BALICEAUX ISLAND

Dovers ●

MUSTIQUE

✪ Capital
● City/Town
〜 River
- - - Road

0			5		10 Miles

0	5		10 Kilometers

Elevation in feet

St. Vincent and the Grenadines

ST. VINCENT AND THE GRENADINES: POOR BUT FREE

Vincentians, like many other West Indians, either identify with or, as viewed from a different perspective, suffer from a deep-seated European orientation. Critics argue that it is an identification that is historical in origin, and that it is negative. For many, the European connection is nothing more than the continuing memory of a master–slave relationship.

St. Vincent is unique in that it was one of the few Caribbean islands where runaway black slaves intermarried with Carib Indians and produced a distinct racial type known as the Garifuna, or black Carib. Toward the end of the eighteenth century, the Garifuna and other native peoples mounted an assault on the island's white British planters. They were assisted by the French from Martinique but were defeated in 1796. As punishment, the Garifuna were deported to what is today Belize, where they formed one of the bases of that nation's population.

In 1834, the black slaves were emancipated, which disrupted the island's economy by decreasing the labor supply. In order to fill this vacuum, Portuguese and East Indian laborers were imported to maintain the agrarian economy. This, however, was not done until later in the nineteenth century—not quickly enough to prevent a lasting blow to the island's economic base.

St. Vincent, along with Dominica, is one of the poorest islands in the West Indies, although there has been some recent improvement. The current unemployment rate (2009) is estimated at 15 percent. With more than half the population under age 15, unemployment will continue to be a major problem in the foreseeable future.

Formerly one of the West Indian sugar islands, St. Vincent's main crops are now bananas and arrowroot. The sugar industry was a casualty of low world-market prices and a black-power movement in the 1960s that associated sugar production with memories of slavery. Limited sugar production has been renewed to meet local needs.

THE POLITICS OF POVERTY

Poverty affects everyone in St. Vincent and the Grenadines, except a very few who live in comfort. In the words of one Vincentian, for most people, "life is a study in poverty." In 1969, a report identified malnutrition and gastroenteritis as being responsible for 57 percent of the deaths of children under age five. Those problems persist.

Deep-seated poverty also has an impact on the island's political life. Living on the verge of starvation, Vincentians cannot appreciate an intellectual approach to politics. They find it difficult to wait for the effects of long-term trends or coordinated development. Bread-and-butter issues are what concern them. Accordingly, parties speak little of basic economic and social change, structural shifts in the economy, or the latest economic theories. Politics is reduced to personality contests and rabble-rousing. Prime Minister Ralph Gonsalves, elected to a second term in 2005, remarked that he was tired of "perpetual warfare of a verbal kind" and has urged national reconciliation.

TIMELINE

1498
Christopher Columbus discovers and names St. Vincent

1763
Ceded to the British by France

1795
The Carib War

1902
St. Vincent's La Soufrière erupts and kills 2,000 people

1979
Independence from Great Britain

1990s
A new minimum-wage law takes effect

2000s
The country's financial problems remain severe

2001
Ralph Gonsalves assumes the post of prime minister

2005
Gonsalves wins second term

2009
Voters reject proposal to end the monarchy and replace it with a republic

2010
Prime Minister Gonsalves wins another term

Snapshot: ST. VINCENT AND THE GRENADINES

Summarized below is a quick look at the country with regard to its development, freedom, health/welfare, and achievements.

Development

Grenada's economy, which grew by a startling 10 percent in 2006, slowed dramatically as a result of global recession. In 2009, the nation experienced a negative growth rate of 6.5 percent and, as of 2011, had not moved into positive territory. Some moneys have been earmarked for infrastructure development and a new international airport is scheduled to open in 2013.

Freedom

The government took a great step forward in terms of wage scales for women by adopting a new minimum-wage law, which provided for equal pay for equal work done by men and women. Violence against women remains a significant problem.

Health/Welfare

Minimum wages established in 1989 range from $3.85 *per day* in agriculture to $7.46 in industry. New minimums were presented to Parliament in 2003. Clearly, the minimum is inadequate, although most workers earn significantly more than the minimum. The government's debt burden makes funding of social programs difficult.

Achievements

A regional cultural organization was launched in 1982 in St. Vincent. Called the East Caribbean Popular Theatre Organisation, its membership extends to Dominica, Grenada, and St. Lucia.

Despite its economic problems, St. Vincent is a free society. Newspapers are uncensored. Some reports, however, have noted that the government has on occasion granted or withheld advertising on the basis of a paper's editorial position.

Unions enjoy the right of collective bargaining. They represent about 11 percent of the labor force. St. Vincent, which won its independence from Great Britain in 1979, is a parliamentary, constitutional democracy. In 2009, voters, in a constitutional referendum, rejected a proposal to end the monarchy and replace it with a republic. Political parties have the right to organize.

■ POLITICS AND ECONOMICS

While the country's political life has been calm, relative to some of the other Caribbean islands, there are signs of voter unrest. Prime Minister James Mitchell was reelected in 1999 for an unprecedented fourth five-year term, but his New Democratic Party lost some ground in the Legislature. In 2001 Ralph Gonsalves and his Unity Labour Party narrowly won election; in 2005 they gained 12 seats in the 15-seat parliament. Gonsalves, as reported by *BBC News,* is known to his followers as "Comrade Ralph" and campaigned on his government's economic record. He could point to meaningful economic growth and the completion of dozens of major projects.

Bananas once accounted for two-thirds of St. Vincent's export earnings. That figure fell to 50 percent in 2004 and to 33 percent in 2005. As is the case with other Windward Islands, St. Vincent's economy has been hurt by the 1999 European Union decision to phase out preferential treatment to banana producers from former colonial possessions. Not surprisingly drug trafficking, marijuana cultivation, and money laundering have increased as a result of the general economic malaise. The government has recently initiated steps to curb marijuana cultivation and to halt money laundering. Drug-related criminal activity continues to grow, however.

In 2001, along with other islands in the Windwards, St. Vincent entered talks with European Union officials with an eye to improving both yields and quality of bananas. There was general agreement that the entire Windward Islands banana industry needed restructuring if the industry is to survive.

? DID YOU KNOW?

St. Vincent was one of the last Caribbean islands to be colonized by Europeans because of the effective resistance of aboriginal Caribs. It was not until the 18th century that the island was colonized. Interestingly, escaped black slaves found a safe haven on St. Vincent where they intermarried with Caribs. The progeny of these unions were known as "Black Caribs," or Garifuna. The British finally crushed the Caribs, and the Garifuna were removed to Central America and existed there in sufficient force to hold off European incursions until the eighteenth century.

FURTHER INVESTIGATION

For more information on the history and culture of St. Vincent and the Grenadines go to http://www.everyculture.com/No-Sa/Saint-Vincent-and-the-Grenadines.html

Statistics

Geography

Area in Square Miles (Kilometers): 131 (340) (about twice the size of Washington, D.C.)

Capital (Population): Kingstown (28,000)

Environmental Concerns: pollution of coastal waters and shorelines by discharges from pleasure boats

Geographical Features: volcanic; mountainous

Climate: tropical

People

Population

Total: 103,537 (2012 est.)

Annual Growth Rate: −0.313%

Rural/Urban Population Ratio: 51/49

Major Languages: English; French patois

Ethnic Makeup: 66% black; 19% mixed; 6% East Indian

Religions: 47% Anglican; 28% Methodist; 13% Roman Catholic, 12% other

Health

Life Expectancy at Birth: 72 years (male); 76 years (female)

Infant Mortality Rate (Ratio): 13.86/1,000

Physicians Available (Ratio): 0.75/1,000

Education

Adult Literacy Rate: 96%

Communication

Telephones: 21,700 main lines

Cell Phones: 131,800

Internet Users: 76,600

Transportation

Highways in Kilometers (Miles): 1,040 (646)

Usable Airfields: 6

Government

Type: Parliamentary democracy, independent sovereign state within the British Commonwealth

Independence Date: October 27, 1979 (from the United Kingdom)

Head of State/Government: Queen Elizabeth II; Prime Minister Ralph Gonsalves

Political Parties: Unity Labour Party; New Democratic Party;

Suffrage: universal at 18

Military

Current Disputes: none

Economy

Currency ($U.S. Equivalent): 2.68 East Caribbean dollars = $1

Per Capita Income/GDP: $11,700/$1.224 billion

GDP Growth Rate: −.04%

Inflation Rate: 3.7%

Unemployment Rate: 15%

Labor Force: 57,520

Natural Resources: negligible

Agriculture: bananas; arrowroot; coconuts; sweet potatoes; spices; small amount of livestock; fish

Industry: food processing; cement; furniture; clothing; starch; tourism

Exports: $64.4 million (primary partners France, Greece, Trinidad and Tobago, St. Lucia, Barbados)

Imports: $348 million (primary partners Singapore, Trinidad and Tobago, United States, China, France)

Suggested Website

www.cia.gov/cia/publications/factbook/index.html

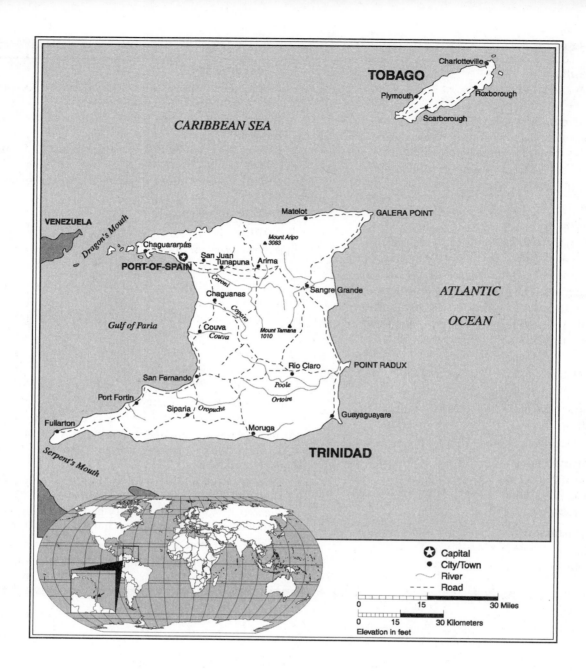

TOBAGO

Charlotteville

Plymouth   Roxborough

Scarborough

CARIBBEAN SEA

VENEZUELA

Dragon's Mouth

Matelot   GALERA POINT

Chaguaramas

Mount Aripo
▲ 3063

San Juan
Tunapuna   Arima

PORT-OF-SPAIN

Coroni

Chaguanas   Sangre Grande

Caroni

ATLANTIC

OCEAN

Gulf of Paria

Couva   Mount Tamana
1010

Couva

Rio Claro   POINT RADUX

San Fernando

Poole

Port Fortin   Ortoire

Siparia   Oropuche

Guayaguayare

Fullarton

Moruga

Serpent's Mouth   TRINIDAD

★ Capital
● City/Town
〜 River
- - - Road

| 0 | 15 | 30 Miles |

| 0 | 15 | 30 Kilometers |

Elevation in feet

Trinidad and Tobago

(Republic of Trinidad and Tobago)

TRINIDAD AND TOBAGO: A MIDDLE-CLASS SOCIETY

The nation of Trinidad and Tobago, which became independent of Great Britain in 1962, differs sharply from other Caribbean countries in terms of both its wealth and its societal structure. A sizable portion of its revenue derives from exports of petroleum and liquified natural gas. A portion of this revenue has been redistributed and has helped to create a society that is essentially middle class. Health conditions are generally good, education is widely available, and the literacy rate is a very high 98 percent.

The country also enjoys an excellent human-rights record, although there is a good deal of tension between the ruling urban black majority and East Indians, who are rural. The divisions run deep and parallel the situation in Guyana. East Indians feel that they are forced to submerge their culture and conform to the majority. In the words of one East Indian, "Where do Indians fit in when the culture of 40 percent of our people is denied its rightful place and recognition; when most of our people exist on the fringes of society and are considered as possessing nothing more than nuisance value?"

The lyrics of a black calypso artist that state the following are resented by East Indians:

> If you are an East Indian
> And you want to be an African
> Just shave your head just like me
> And nobody would guess your nationality.

The prosperity of the nation, however, tends to mute these tensions.

Freedom of expression and freedom of the press are constitutionally guaranteed as well as respected in practice. Opposition viewpoints are freely expressed in the nation's Parliament, which is modeled along British lines. There is no political censorship. Opposition parties are usually supported by rural Hindu East Indians; while they have freely participated in elections, some East Indians feel that the government has gerrymandered electoral districts to favor the ruling party.

Violent crime and political unrest, including an attempted coup by black fundamentalist Muslim army officers in 1990, have become a way of life in the nation in recent years. Prime Minister Basdeo Panday, elected in 1996, noted that there were still agendas, "political and otherwise," that divided Trinidadian society. "How much better it will be," he stated, "if all in our society, and particularly those in a position to shape mass consciousness, will seize every opportunity to promote and mobilise the greater strength that comes out of our diversity. . . ."

Trade-union organization is the most extensive among Caribbean nations with ties to Britain and includes about 30 percent of the workforce. In contrast to other West Indian states, unions in Trinidad and Tobago are not government-controlled, nor are they generally affiliated with a political party.

Women are well represented in Parliament, serve as ministers, and hold other high-level civil-service positions. In 2011 a woman, Kamla

TIMELINE

1498
The island now called Trinidad is discovered by Columbus and later colonized by Spain

1797
Trinidad is captured by the British

1889
Tobago is added to Trinidad as a colonial unit

1962
Independence from Great Britain

1980s
Oil-export earnings slump

1996
Basdeo Panday is elected prime minister

2000s
Further development of the natural-gas industry

2005–2007
Tension between Venezuela and Trinidad over competition for petroleum markets in the Caribbean region

2011
A woman, Kamla Persad-Bissessar, elected prime minister

Snapshot: TRINIDAD AND TOBAGO

Summarized below is a quick look at the country with regard to its development, freedom, health/welfare, and achievements.

Development

The economy has experienced rapid growth thanks to vast reserves of natural gas, which has attracted investors from developed countries. The government has also promoted the use of natural gas, instituting a program to encourage consumers to switch from gasoline.

Freedom

In 2011 the government instituted an emergency curfew in an attempt to address the nation's high homicide and crime rate. While moderately successful, the measure alienated many citizens. An alleged plot by criminal elements to assassinate the prime minister was uncovered in November 2011, but nothing was proven.

Health/Welfare

Legislation passed in 1991 greatly expanded the categories of workers covered by the minimum wage. The same legislation provided for 3 months' maternity leave for household and shop assistants as well as other benefits. An Occupational Safety and Health Act enacted in 2004 provides additional safeguards for workers. Citizens enjoy the highest per capita incomes in Latin America.

Achievements

Eric Williams, historian, pamphleteer, and politician, left his mark on Caribbean culture with his scholarly books and his bitterly satirical *Massa Day Done*. V. S. Naipaul is an influential author born in Trinidad. Earl Lovelace is another well-known Trinidadian author. He won the 1997 Commonwealth Writers' Prize for his novel *Salt*.

Persad-Bissessar, was elected prime minister. Several groups are vocal advocates for women's rights.

In an attempt to redress imbalances in the nation's agricultural structure, which is characterized by small landholdings—half of which are less than five acres each—the government has initiated a land-redistribution program using state-owned properties and estates sold to the government. The program is designed to establish more efficient medium-sized family farms, of five to 20 acres, devoted to cash crops. For years, the economy has moved away from export-oriented agriculture. The last sugar crop for export was produced in 2005.

The islands' economic fortunes have tended to reflect the prices it can command from its exports of oil and liquefied natural gas. Petrochemicals, steel, aluminum, and plastics have contributed significantly to the nation's high growth rate. In 2001, British Petroleum began development of the Kapok gas field. The project gives the nation one of the largest offshore gas-handling facilities in the world. Importantly, the company has indicated that the facility will conform to the most stringent environmental safeguards.

Of some concern to the government are the inroads made by Venezuela into its Caribbean market for refined petroleum. Venezuelan foreign policy has used oil to buy influence in the region and its low prices undercut Trinidad. A possible solution was discussed in 2006 whereby Venezuelan crude would be refined in Trinidad.

■ TOBAGO

Residents of Tobago have come to believe that their small island is perceived as nothing more than a dependency of Trinidad. It has been variously described as a "weekend resort," a "desert island," and a "tree house"—in contrast to "thriving," "vibrant" Trinidad. Tobagans

feel that they receive less than their share of the benefits generated by economic prosperity.

In 1989, the Constitution was reviewed with an eye to introducing language that would grant Tobago the right to secede. The chair of the Tobago House of Assembly argued that, "in any union, both partners should have the right to opt out if they so desire." Others warn that such a provision would ultimately snap the ties that bind two peoples into one. Trinidadian opposition leaders have observed that the areas that have historically supported the ruling party have more and better roads, telephones, and schools than those backing opposition parties. Partly to mollify Tobagans, the government has invested in tourism-related projects on the island.

? DID YOU KNOW?

Trinidadians, with an inventive skill that astounded musicologists, created a whole range of instruments from oil drums, gas tanks, pots and pans to empty metal containers of all descriptions. Collectively, these are known as a steel band. The unique and compelling music from these homemade instruments became popular after World War II and quickly spread to other islands.

FURTHER INVESTIGATION

For more information on the origins of the steel band go to http://www2.nalis.gov.tt/LinkClick.aspx?link=239&tabid=61

Statistics

Geography

Area in Square Miles (Kilometers): 1,980 (5,128) (about the size of Delaware)

Capital (Population): Port-of-Spain (57,000)

Environmental Concerns: water pollution; oil pollution of beaches; deforestation; soil erosion

Geographical Features: mostly plains, with some hills and low mountains

Climate: tropical

People

Population

Total: 1,226,383 (2012 est.)

Annual Growth Rate: −0.86

Rural/Urban Population Ratio: 14/86

Major Language: English

Ethnic Makeup: 40% East Indian; 37,5% black; 20.5% mixed

Religions: 26% Roman Catholic; 22.5% Hindi; 7.8% Anglican; 22% other Protestant; 5.8% Muslim

Health

Life Expectancy at Birth: 69 years (male); 74 years (female)

Infant Mortality Rate (Ratio): 26.73/1,000

Physicians Available (Ratio): 1.2/1,000

Education

Adult Literacy Rate: 98.6%

Compulsory (Ages): 5–12; free

Communication

Telephones: 293,300 main lines

Daily Newspaper Circulation: 139 per 1,000 people

Cell Phones: 1,894,000

Internet Users: 593,000

Transportation

Highways in Kilometers (Miles): 8,320 (5,167)

Usable Airfields: 6

Government

Type: parliamentary democracy

Independence Date: August 31, 1962 (from United Kingdom)

Head of State/Government: President George Maxwell Richards; Prime Minister Kamla Persad-Bissessar

Political Parties: People's National Movement; United National Congress; Congress of the People others

Suffrage: universal at 18

Military

Current Disputes: none

Economy

Currency ($U.S. Equivalent): 6.40 Trinidad/Tobago dollars = $1

Per Capita Income/GDP: $20,300/26.83 billion

GDP Real Growth Rate: 1.1%

Inflation Rate: 10.5%

Unemployment Rate: 6.2%

Labor Force: 636,800

Natural Resources: petroleum; natural gas; asphalt

Agriculture: cocoa; sugarcane; rice; citrus fruits; coffee; vegetables; poultry

Industry: petroleum; chemicals; tourism; food processing; cement; beverages; textiles

Exports: $16.92 billion (primary partners United States, Spain, Jamaica)

Imports: $10.47 billion (primary partners Russia, Brazil, Colombia, Gabon, China, Canada)

Suggested Website

www.cia.gov/cia/publications/factbook/index.html

Articles From the World Press

Topic Guide

All the articles that relate to each topic are listed below the bold-faced term.

1 The Paradoxes of Latin America

Mario Vargas Llosa

Learning Objectives

After reading this article, you will more clearly understand the following:

- Latin American identities
- Cultural diversity
- Myths and stereotypes
- *Mestizaje* (racial mixing)

What does it mean to feel you are Latin American? It means being aware that the territorial boundaries dividing our nations are artificial, imposed arbitrarily during the colonial years. And neither our leaders during the emancipation period nor the republican governments that followed bothered to correct that situation. In fact, they often worsened things by further separating and isolating societies whose commonalities were deeper than their petty differences. This balkanization of Latin America, unlike what took place in North America, where the Thirteen Colonies became the United States, has been one of the conspicuous factors in our underdevelopment. It has engendered nationalism, war and conflict, bleeding our nations and wasting natural resources that could have been used for modernization and progress.

Only in the cultural arena was Latin American integration a reality, the result of experience and necessity—everyone who writes, composes, paints or practices any creative endeavor discovers that what unites us is more important than what separates us. In other areas—politics and economics, especially—attempts to unify governmental actions and markets have always been thwarted by the nationalist reflexes ingrained in the continent. That is why all of the plans conceived to unite the region have failed.

National boundaries, however, do not mark the true differences that exist in Latin America. These differences thrive in the bosom of each country and, in a transverse way, encompass regions and groups of countries. There is a Westernized Latin America that speaks Spanish, Portuguese and English (in the Caribbean and in Central America) and is Catholic, Protestant, atheist or agnostic; and there is an indigenous Latin America, which in countries like Mexico, Guatemala, Ecuador, Peru and Bolivia comprises millions of people. *That* Latin America retains pre-Hispanic institutions, practices and beliefs. But even indigenous culture is not homogeneous, and it constitutes yet another archipelago that experiences different levels of modernization. While some languages and traditions—Quechua and Aymara—are the patrimony of vast social conglomerations, others, like the Amazonian cultures, survive in small communities, sometimes just a handful of families.

Fortunately, *mestizaje*—racial mixing—extends in all directions, bringing these two worlds together. In some countries, Mexico for example, *mestizaje* has integrated the bulk of society both culturally and racially. It represents the greatest achievement of the Mexican Revolution—transforming the two ethnic extremes, Native Americans and Europeans, into minorities. This integration is less dynamic in the other countries, but it is still going on and it will ultimately give Latin America the distinctive identity of a *mestizo* continent. But let's hope it does so without making it totally uniform and erasing its subtle differences, though that is certainly possible in this century of globalization and interdependence among nations.

What is imperative is that, sooner rather than later, liberty and legality will be conjoined, thanks to democracy. Then all Latin Americans, regardless of race, language, religion and culture, will be equal before the law, will enjoy the same rights and opportunities, and will coexist in diversity without being discriminated against or excluded. Latin America cannot renounce its cultural diversity, which is what makes it a model for the rest of the world.

Mestizaje must not be understood exclusively as the fusion of Indians and Spaniards or Portuguese, though, naturally, those are the most important ethnic and cultural components in Latin American reality. The African contribution—and in the countries of the Caribbean basin and in certain regions of Brazil, it is an essential one—is of the highest importance. Africans reached the New World at the same time as did the conquistadors, and we see their influence in all artistic and cultural manifestations, especially in music. Asia, too, has been a presence in the life of the continent since the colonial era, and there are magnificent examples of how the techniques and achievements of Far Eastern plastic and decorative arts came to our lands and were assimilated by native artists and artisans. When you dig into the Latin American past without prejudice, without assuming a *party pris,* you soon discover that our cultural roots are spread all over the world.

Despite Latin America's universality, one of its recurring obsessions has been defining its identity. In my opinion, this is a useless enterprise, dangerous and impossible, because identity is something possessed by individuals and not collectivities, at least once they've transcended tribal conditions. Only in the most primitive communities, where the individual exists only as part of the tribe, does the idea of a collective identity have any *raison d'être*. But, as in other parts of the world, this mania for determining historico-social or metaphysical specificity for an agglomeration has caused oceans of Latin American ink to flow, generating ferocious diatribes as well as interminable polemics.

The most celebrated and prolonged of all is the confrontation between Hispanists, for whom Latin American history begins with the arrival of Spaniards and Portuguese and the resultant linking of the continent with the Western world, and Indigenists, for whom the genuine reality of the New World resides in the pre-Hispanic civilizations and their descendants, and not in the contemporary heirs of the conquistadors, who still today marginalize and exploit Native Americans. Though eclipsed for long periods, this schizophrenic and racist vision of Latin America will never disappear. From time to time, it resurfaces in politics because, like all Manichean simplifications, it allows demagogues to stir up collective passions and provide superficial, schematic answers to complex problems. Every attempt to fix a unique identity for Latin America requires discriminatory surgery that excludes and abolishes millions of Latin Americans, along with many forms and manifestations of its rich cultural variety.

Latin America's wealth lies in its being many things simultaneously—so many, in fact, that it is a microcosm in which all the races and cultures of the world coexist. Five centuries after the arrival of Europeans to its shores, mountain ranges and forests, Latin Americans of Spanish, Portuguese, Italian, German, African, Chinese or Japanese descent are as much "natives" of the continent as are those whose ancestors were the ancient Aztecs, Toltecs, Mayas, Quechuas, Aymaras or Caribes. And the mark that Africans have left on the continent, where they, too, have been living for five centuries, is ubiquitous: in people, speech, music, food, and even in certain ways of practicing religion. It would not be an exaggeration to say that there is no tradition, culture, language or race that hasn't contributed something to the phosphorescent vortex of mixtures and alliances swirling about in all orders of Latin American life. This amalgam is our greatest patrimony: to be a continent that lacks an identity because it contains all identities. And, thanks to its creators, it goes on transforming itself every day.

There could be no more persuasive demonstration of this unique condition than the extraordinary exhibition, "Tesoros/Treasures/Tesouros: the Arts in Latin America, 1492–1820", mounted last year in Philadelphia, Los Angeles and Mexico City. The show presented a vast, absorbingly beautiful and diverse collection of art and artisanal work produced in Latin America over the course of the three centuries between the arrival of Spaniards and Portuguese and the period when the Hispanic and Luso-American colonies became independent republics.

One of the most suggestive conclusions the visitor to the show could reach after spending two or three hours reviewing this careful selection of the best that our ancestors created in architecture, painting, sculpture, gold carving, textile weaving, decoration and all the applied arts in the 328 years when Latin America formed part of the Portuguese and Spanish empires, was that the term "colonial art" is accurate only in an historical and political sense. To define its achievements, forms and contents, it is completely inadequate.

From the first moments of the incorporation of the new continent into Western culture, this art possessed singularities, because it set itself at a distance from the European models and motifs that, on the surface at least, inspired it. It couldn't have happened any other way. The explorers and conquistadors did not reach a virgin land, but a continent of cultures and civilizations that over many centuries had reached a high level of refinement in customs and beliefs, and in systems of social organization.

Those who painted, sculpted, carved, did feather or metal work, or wove fabric and erected temples, altars and pulpits were, in their majority, descendants of those civilizations and cultures that were destroyed and subjugated, but not eradicated with the arrival of Europeans. They survived in the shadows and went on working in the spirit of creators and artisans. The colonial system imposed new beliefs and behavior patterns that changed appearances, but could not change souls. Ancient gods, habits, devotion and mythology disappeared from view but remained in hearts and minds, despite the efforts of the artists themselves. Then, surreptitiously, those phantoms impregnated all manifestations of "colonial" Latin American art, imparting to it shades all its own which, without breaking with the prototypes brought by the colonizers, renewed them with additions or alterations linked to native idiosyncrasies. The facades of churches, their altars, pulpits, retables, frescos and sculptures, would become subtly Americanized, with an irrepressible explosion of local flowers and fruits, with virgins and angels who became Creole or Indian in their skin, their facial or body features, their clothing, colors and landscapes, the distortion of perspective and the syncretism of Christianity and the abolished religions.

It would be an error to attribute this miscegenation exclusively to indigenous artists and image-makers. Europeans transplanted to the American colonies very quickly became *criollos*—Europeans born or raised in the New World—as many pieces in "Tesoros" made manifest. One of its most eloquent revelations was how rapidly, though most certainly involuntarily, European art "Americanized" in Spanish and Portuguese America beginning in the 17th century and then overtly in the 18th. Though the citizens of the New World took another century or century-and-a-half to extrapolate that transformation into the political realm in order to dream of emancipation, when they painted, composed, sculpted or wrote, they stopped being European; they were already, in more than one sense, *criollos,* Spanish or Portuguese Americans, in their works. However, the notion of being something other than European either hadn't occurred to them or remained nebulous. From the cultural and artistic point of view, the process of Latin American emancipation begins during the colonial era, discreetly at first but becoming more manifest with the passage of time.

One subject, only rarely acknowledged explicitly, runs through all the circuits of Latin American culture: the abysmal contradiction between its social and political reality and its literary and artistic production. On one side, income differences between poor and rich, high indices of marginalization, unemployment and poverty, corruption that undermines its institutions, dictatorial and populist governments, illiteracy, criminality and drug-trafficking, the exodus of its people—all this make Latin America the very incarnation of underdevelopment. But the same continent also boasts, and has since the colonial era, a high coefficient of literary and artistic originality.

In the field of culture, it is only possible to talk about underdevelopment in Latin America in sociological terms: the smallness of its cultural market; the fact that so little is read, and the limited sphere of artistic activity. But as soon as we talk about the production of its writers, cineasts, painters and musicians (who make the whole world dance), we realize Latin America cannot be called underdeveloped. Nor, in their time, could the artists in the "Tesoros" show. Some can be favorably compared with the most original creators in the Western world. At its highest level, the art and literature of Latin America left the picturesque and folkloric behind centuries ago and reached levels of sophistication and originality that guaranteed them a universal audience.

How can we explain this paradox? We might consider the great contrasts in Latin American reality, where all geographies, ethnicities, religions and customs coexist with all historical eras. This is the phenomenon Alejo Carpentier imaginatively re-creates in *The Lost Steps* (1953), a novelistic voyage in space from the most modern urban-industrial center to the most primitive rural life, a species of literary time travel from present to past and back again. While the cultural elites modernized, opened themselves to the world, and renewed themselves thanks to a constant comparison with the great centers of thought and contemporary cultural creation, political life remained anchored in a past of *caudillos* and cliques that exercised despotism, looted public resources and kept economic life frozen in feudalism and mercantilism. There was a divorce: The citadels of cultural life—spaces of freedom abandoned to their fate by a political power generally disdainful of culture—found themselves in contact with modernity and evolved. And out of those bastions emerged high-level writers and artists, while the rest of society, for all intents and purposes, remained immobilized in a self-destructive anachronism.

It is impossible to understand Latin America without leaving it and observing it from afar with your own eyes, noting at the same time the myths and stereotypes that have been constructed about it abroad. That mythical dimension is inseparable from the historical reality of the community: Latin America has itself assimilated and metabolized many of those myths and stereotypes, often laboring to be what for ideological and folkloric reasons many Europeans and North Americans have said it was and wanted it to be. We could begin with the colonial chronicle writer Antonio León Pinelo, who "proved" that the Earthly Paradise was in the Amazon region. Our America was never a paradise, but by the same token it was never a hell, though something of both may be found scattered throughout its contradictory reality.

Another question has also been (and continues to be) the object of impassioned polemics: Is Latin America part of the West, culturally speaking, or is it something essentially different, like China, India or Japan? Latin America is an overseas projection of the West that, from colonial times, has acquired its own distinctive features. Those traits, without severing it from the tree from which it sprouts, give it a specific personality. Mind you, that opinion is not held by all Latin Americans. Far from it. It is often refuted with the argument that if it were really the case that Latin America derives from the West, then in its culture and art it would be nothing more than an epigone, an ancillary derivation of Europe.

Those who think that way, at times without noticing it themselves, are nationalists convinced that each people or nation has a unique mental and metaphysical configuration of which its culture is an expression. This is just not so. Culturally speaking, Latin America is so many dissimilar things that only by fragmenting it and excluding a good number of those fragments that make up its reality could it be possible to determine a specific trait valid for the entire continent which, since the arrival at its shores of Columbus' three ships, articulated its history with that of the rest of the world. Its diversity, compatible in its case with a subterranean unity that is its characteristic condition, is in good measure a consequence of the Western sources that nurture it.

It is for that reason Latin Americans express themselves in the main in Spanish, English, Portuguese and French. It is for that reason Latin Americans are Catholics, Protestants, atheists or agnostics. And those who are atheists or agnostics are the way they are based on what they learned from the West, as is the case for Latin America's reactionaries and revolutionaries, its democrats and liberals, its traditionalist or avant-garde artists, its romantics, classicists or postmodernists.

But in their most creative moments, Latin Americans never produced mere "imitations and copies" of what they took from Western culture. The expression *calco y copia* ("imitations and copies") was coined by José Carlos Mariátegui, one of the very rare Latin American Marxists who did not merely repeat like some ventriloquist's dummy the ideas of the European Marxists in whose pages he was educated. He used those lessons to make an original, if not always accurate, analysis of America's social and economic problematic.

Another interesting example of what I'm trying to illustrate is the Brazilian writer Euclides da Cunha, who in *Os Sertões* ("Revolt in the Backlands") (1902) carefully scrutinized what took place in the war at Canudos, in the Brazilian northeast, at the end of the 19th century, making use of all the sociological and philosophical theories current in the Europe of his time. The result of his investigation was exactly the opposite of what he himself had foreseen: Instead of enabling him to disinter the profound meaning of that war unleashed by a messianic movement, he learned that those European conceptual constructs were inadequate for explaining the conflict, which was born from a deep distortion of certain religious values and doctrines that, in the primitive world of Bahía, were transformed into their opposites.

Mariátegui and da Cunha are two examples among many of the way in which Latin America departed from European sources to find its own music, music that sets it apart without placing it at odds with the voices of the Old World. The artistic accomplishments realized by its creators would have been impossible without the skill and the mastery of techniques that American artists learned how to acclimate to their world. Is that not the most valuable trait of what we call Western culture? The perpetual renovation of forms and ideas reacting to criticism and self-criticism. The constant assimilation of imported values and principles that enrich those we already possess. All of it within a coexistence of the differences that only liberty, critical spirit and a vocation for universality make possible.

Those who have tried their utmost to distance Latin America from the West have been those Western writers, thinkers or artists who, disillusioned with their own culture, venture forth in search of others to satisfy their appetite for exoticism, primitivism, magic, irrationality and the innocence of Rousseau's noble savage—and have made Latin America the goal of their utopias. This has produced excellent literary fruit, though, in general, catastrophic political confusion. Like that of those cataclysm

lovers for whom Latin America would appear to have no other reason for being than as a scenario for romantic fantasies that European space, with its boring democracies, no longer tolerates at home. The gravest aspect of this is that Latin America has often striven to represent those fictions Europeans invented for it. That utopian vocation has also impregnated American art, the best testimony to the elusive personality, made of unity and dispersion, of Latin America.

Mario Vargas Llosa is a member of the editorial board of *The American Interest*. The original Spanish version of this essay is available at www.the-american-interest.com.

Challenge Questions

After reading this article, you will be able to answer the following questions:

1. Is Latin America a "western" culture or something else?
2. Is there a Latin American identity?
3. How can we explain the paradox between Latin American political and social "underdevelopment" and the region's extraordinary literary and artistic originality?
4. How can we understand the tension between nationalism and cultural integration?

2 Violence against Women

Dr. César Chelala

Learning Objectives

After reading this article, you will more clearly understand the following:

- Reasons behind domestic violence
- Prevention strategies
- Cultural dimension
- Anti-violence legislation and resolutions

It is under-recognized and underreported, but it is one of the most significant epidemics in the world today: gender violence, manifested primarily as violence against women. Women of an social classes and religions are subject to gender violence; it is a cause of significant harm to their health and quality of life. This age-old epidemic has intensified in some present day settings and demands new, more effective policies to mitigate its destructive impact.

Domestic violence is perhaps the most common kind of gender violence around the world. And while women are not the only targets of domestic violence, they are the most frequent. Few precise figures exist, but the numbers can be shocking. According to some studies, approximately four million women are attacked by their husbands or partners each year in the United States. In Latin America and the Caribbean, numbers vary widely, but it is estimated that approximately 40 percent of women in the region have experienced domestic violence. The World Health Organization has published a report addressing the devastating effects of gender violence around the globe. According to this report, gender violence claims almost 1.6 million lives each year, about three percent of all deaths.

In the United States, violence against women is responsible for a large percentage of medical visits and for approximately one-third of all hospital emergency room visits. Domestic violence is the most frequent cause of injury among women treated in US emergency rooms, more common than motor vehicle accidents and robberies combined.

The Economic Commission for Latin America and the Caribbean (ECLAC) has developed a series of indicators to measure the incidence and trends of domestic violence. Women's groups and journalists in Latin America have gathered information that suggests that up to 80 percent of female murder victims are killed by their husbands or intimate partners. Domestic violence has ah impact not only on the women themselves but also on their families, particularly their children. More than 50 percent of children in foster care are there largely as a result of domestic violence in their homes. In some cases, they are also the direct targets of violence in the home.

Clearly, governments need to do much more to stop gender-based violence against women. In 1994, the Organization of American States (OAS) adopted the only international treaty addressing the prevention and punishment of violence against women: the Inter-American Convention on the Prevention, Punishment and Eradication of Violence against Women, also known as the Belém do Pará Convention. Of the 34 member countries of the OAS, only the United States and Canada have not ratified the Convention.

All countries in the Americas—with the exception of the United States—have ratified the Convention on the Elimination of all Forms of Discrimination against Women (CEDAW), one of the most important instruments on women's rights. Several countries have also ratified the Optional Protocol to CEDAW, which enables women to file complaints individually with the United Nations when violations of their rights are not properly addressed in the court system of their home country. Today, almost 30 countries in the Americas have enacted laws against domestic violence or characterized this form of violence as a crime. Yet as UNIFEM has recognized, "while these countries have signed and ratified these instruments, the challenge is to get their precepts actually implemented."

In 1993, the Pan American Health Organization (PAHO) declared domestic violence a public health issue and recommended that governments implement policies for its prevention and control. Since then PAHO has been working actively to publicize and combat this problem. The basic health interventions related to domestic violence include prevention strategies, care for victims, medical-legal certification of cases, treatment of the aggressors (with psychotherapy, for example), and notifying the authorities.

Various cultural, economic, and social factors—including shame and fear of retaliation—contribute to women's reluctance to report acts of violence against them. Legal and criminal systems in many countries make the process difficult, and frequently, fear keeps women trapped in abusive relationships.

Almost 80 percent of all serious gender-violence injuries and deaths occur when female victims of violence try to leave a relationship or after they have left it.

The stubborn fact, even today, is that in many countries, violence against women is seen as normal behavior, especially in the domestic setting. The belief that men have a right to abuse women perpetuates the violence. In that sense, domestic violence is a manifestation of perverse power relationships.

Although physical violence and sexual violence are easier to see, other forms of violence include emotional abuse, such as verbal humiliation, threats of physical aggression or abandonment, economic blackmail, and forced confinement to the home. Many women consider psychological abuse and humiliation even more devastating than physical violence. The experience of violence makes female victims more susceptible to a variety of problems such as depression, suicide, and alcohol and drug abuse.

Studies in Bolivia and Puerto Rico found that 58 percent of battered women had been sexually assaulted by their partners; in Colombia that figure was 46 percent. Sexual violence also increases women's risk of contracting sexually transmitted diseases, including AIDS (because of forced sexual relations and/or inability to persuade men to use condoms). It also increases the number of unplanned pregnancies and may lead to various gynecological problems such as chronic pelvic pain and painful intercourse.

Few governments in the region offer women real alternatives to staying in abusive relationships. Shelters are scarce and some shelters do not allow children. Demand exceeds space in every country of the region. According to one study, there were 3,800 animal shelters in the United States in 1990, but only 1,500 shelters for battered women. Making matters more difficult, judges, police officers, and other government officials often consider domestic violence a "private matter," beyond the scope of the law.

A comprehensive approach to domestic violence includes action at three levels: the national level, the community level, and in the health sector. National measures should include the development of alliances aimed at creating and implementing policies and laws to prevent domestic violence, respond to violent situations, and prosecute offenders. When adequate resources are available, the broad approaches of national or regional campaigns can be reinforced at the local community level. Health care workers are often the best positioned to identify, counsel, and refer victims of physical abuse, and health centers can act as points of coordination. This is the kind of issue that requires all hands on deck. The public sector, private sector, and non-governmental organizations must an play a part. As OAS Secretary General José Miguel Insulza observed, "The human prosperity we long for, energy security, and environmental sustainability cannot surely be attained without true democracy permanently rooted in the principles of equality, equity, social justice, and full respect for women's rights."

Violence against women is a very complex problem with multiple causes, facets, and intersections. Centuries-old cultural beliefs and social norms have created unequal relationships of power between men and women that can be self-reinforcing. As the UN Declaration on the Elimination of Violence against Women has stated, violence against women is a manifestation of power relationships and "is one of the crucial mechanisms by which women are forced into a subordinate position compared with men."

> **Because violence against women is the result of learned ideas and behavior, education is an essential part of the solution.**

Though some progress has been made and many governments in the Americas have made commitments to work towards a solution, results to date have been modest. Because violence against women is the result of learned ideas and behavior, education is an essential part of the solution. The behavior of today's children and youth will grow out of the kind of education they are receiving in school and at home.

One important fact is that any action to control violence against women will be more effective if men are also participating in these efforts. When men work with other men on this issue, recidivism rates decrease and first-time violence is prevented as well.

Because violence against women is caused by many factors, it demands a multifaceted response and the involvement of various sectors (legal, educational, labor, justice, criminal, and public health). The epidemic has been ignored for too long. The time to give it priority is now.

From *Americas,* bimonthly magazine, May/June 2009, pp. 53–55, published by the General Secretariat of the Organization of American States. Copyright © 2009 by the Organization of American States. Reprinted by permission.

Challenge Questions

After reading this article, you will be able to answer the following questions:

1. Is violence against women more prevalent in Latin America?
2. Are cultural beliefs and social norms factors in violence against women?
3. How can education reduce the incidence of violence against women?
4. How is domestic violence linked to power relationships?

3 The Return of *Continuismo*?

Shelley A. McConnell

Learning Objectives

After reading this article, you will more clearly understand the following:

- The nature of *continuismo*
- Possible emergence of dictatorships
- Challenges to democracy
- Possible role for the OAS

Political struggles concerning presidential term limits have reemerged over the past year in Latin America. These struggles show that the region's institutional rules of democracy are still in flux. They also are raising fears that Latin America may witness a return to "*continuismo*"—a past tendency of some presidents to extend their stay in office through constitutional change, electoral fraud, or force.

In the 1980s and 1990s, Latin American countries undergoing transitions to democracy after two decades of authoritarian rule designed their constitutions to prevent a return to dictatorship. The central aim was to assure military subordination to elected civilian leaders and prevent armed overthrow of still-fragile democratic governments. However, Latin Americans were also conscious of the region's history of continuismo.

Countries returning to democracy therefore revived constitutional constraints on presidential reelection that had been developed under prior periods of democratic governance. These provisions either limited presidents to a single term in office or prohibited consecutive election, obliging presidents to step down for one or two terms before seeking office again. Countries without past democratic experience adopted similar precautions, and long-standing democracies already had them.

In subsequent years, such limits were in some cases loosened and immediate reelection to a second presidential term became common. This seemed like good news. Publics rewarded presidents who governed well by allowing them to continue serving. Argentina, Brazil, Colombia, the Dominican Republic, Peru, and Venezuela—and more recently Bolivia and Ecuador—all amended their constitutions to allow presidents to seek immediate reelection to one additional term. Chile, Costa Rica, El Salvador, Nicaragua, Panama, and Uruguay required an interval of at least one presidential term before a leader could seek reelection, and in some cases also imposed a two-term limit. Guatemala, Honduras, Mexico, and Paraguay retained prohibitions on reelection.

Some presidents tried to evade the limits, but these efforts generally failed. In 2000, the Peruvian legislature interpreted President Alberto Fujimori's bid for a third term as legal because it was to be only his second term under the 1993 constitution, but soon afterwards his government's bribery of legislators was exposed and he was forced to resign anyway. In Argentina, two-term president Carlos Menem wanted to run for an immediate third term, but the courts ruled his proposed candidacy unconstitutional.

In 2009, however, wrangling over presidential term limits resumed. In Venezuela, President Hugo Chávez championed a referendum that erased the term limits his own government had enacted. In Nicaragua, the Constitutional Chamber of the Supreme Court of Justice struck down limits on presidential reelection, allowing Daniel Ortega to seek an additional term in 2011 immediately following his current term; it would be his third term overall.

The trend is not confined to leftist leaders. The Colombian legislature last year authorized a referendum to decide whether to amend the constitution to permit immediate reelection of a president serving his second term. If the judiciary allows the referendum to be held, its passage would permit President Álvaro Uribe to run for a third term in 2010. In addition, Dominican Republic President Leonel Fernández, already in his third term overall, negotiated a constitutional amendment allowing him to run again, albeit only after he spends a term out of office.

It is not immediately obvious whether the relaxation of presidential term limits will spread, but Latin American countries historically have looked to one another for political precedents. The Organization of American States (OAS), which since 1990 has taken a leading role in protecting democratic governance in the Western Hemisphere, has raised no objection to the constitutional changes. In any case, to understand the possible consequences for democracy, one needs to distinguish among the ways that these constitutional amendments have proceeded in different countries.

■ VENEZUELANS VOTE—AGAIN

After Chávez's initial victory at the polls in 1998, Venezuela held an almost continuous series of referendums and elections, centering politics around the president's relationship with the electorate. His government moved quickly to bring promised change, enacting a new constitution through an elected constituent assembly dominated by Chávez's supporters. In a break with Venezuela's past practice of allowing presidents reelection only after a 10-year period out of office, the 1999 constitution permitted immediate reelection to a second term and simultaneously lengthened the presidential term to six years.

New elections were held in 2000 and Chávez won his first six-year term. After surviving a coup attempt and a recall referendum, the president rode high oil prices to a 63 percent reelection victory in 2006.

The following year, Venezuela held a referendum on a broad set of constitutional changes proposed by the president and authorized by the legislature. These included lifting all limits on presidential reelection. In what seemed like a public rebuke of Chávez's charismatic authority and transformational agenda, some 3 million of his past supporters stayed away from the polls and the referendum lost by a margin of 1.4 percent.

Yet just 14 months later, in February 2009, Chávez put forward another proposal for indefinite reelection, and this time it passed. Analysis of this referendum suggests that it succeeded in part because of lavish public spending in advance of the vote and government dominance of the media, and also because the referendum question had been restructured so that governors and mayors as well as the president would win expanded reelection rights. This change garnered support for the measure from politicians across the country. They in turn helped mobilize the "yes" vote.

The legality of the referendum's timing was contested. Opponents argued that the proposition was not substantively different from the one rejected in 2007, and so could not legally have been brought before the public again within the same presidential term. However, because opposition parties had boycotted the 2005 legislative elections, claiming the campaign conditions were not fair, they held no seats in the National Assembly and could not block the proposed change. Legislators from Chávez's party predictably authorized the referendum. Voters approved it by a comfortable margin, with 6.3 million in favor and 5.2 million against.

This public process imbued the outcome with substantial legitimacy, but deep political polarization has meant that critics of Chávez's "twenty-first-century socialism" equate indefinite reelection with the end of democracy. Proponents respond that the public retains the right to vote Chávez out; indefinite reelection is not dictatorship as long as Venezuela's elections are free and fair, with a secret ballot and an honest count. This binds the question of democracy's future firmly to the quality of elections, which already have been a matter of concern because of Chávez's dominance of the electoral branch of the government.

■ NICARAGUA'S "JUDICIAL COUP"

Ortega governed Nicaragua from 1979 to 1990, first as the leader of a revolutionary junta, and after 1984 as the elected president. He was defeated at the polls in 1990, and again in 1996 and 2001, but his party consistently won about 40 percent of the vote. In 2000, Ortega was able to negotiate an interparty agreement to reform the constitution so that presidents could be elected with just 35 percent of the vote if the candidate had a 5 percent lead over all others. Using this rule, he regained the presidency with a 38 percent plurality in 2006.

Two years into his second term, Ortega's Sandinista National Liberation Front (FSLN) party began sounding out the legislature about removing limits on presidential reelection. A 1995 constitutional amendment had set a two-term limit for the presidency and prohibited immediate reelection. Lawmakers could undertake constitutional changes only with a 60 percent vote, which meant the FSLN would need 56 of the 92 votes in the legislature to alter the reelection rules. However, the party had only 38 seats, and it was unable to muster support from opposition parties.

In the fall of 2009, Ortega and a group of 109 mayors challenged the legality of the two-term limit and the prohibition on immediate reelection of the president, together with electoral limits on the vice president and mayors. They first took their complaint to Nicaragua's Supreme Electoral Council, a fourth branch of government coequal to the Supreme Court, with the authority to decide electoral matters. That body promptly demurred, ruling that it was not empowered to decide the issue. The president and mayors then sought an injunction in the courts, claiming that the limits on reelection violated the constitutional principle of nondiscrimination before the law.

Justice proved unusually speedy in this affair. Within three days, the injunction passed through the Managua Court of Appeals, was accepted for consideration by the Supreme Court's Constitutional Chamber, and was ruled upon. The Constitutional Chamber ruling found in favor of the complaint, arguing that constitutional Article 147, limiting reelection based on one's job, was void because it contradicted the principle of nondiscrimination in the constitution's preamble and the guarantee of equality before the law in Article 27.

The ruling prepared an anticipatory defense against foreign criticism by citing international human rights covenants that uphold the right to seek office. However, that right has never been absolute, and the Chamber left intact language within Nicaragua's constitution that limits presidential candidacy on the basis of age, familial relationship to the president, and criminal record.

The problems with this process were legion. Since 2000, the Supreme Court had been composed of 16 members, half appointed from the FSLN and the other half from the Liberal party. Its Constitutional Chamber is composed of six Supreme Court justices, including both Sandinistas and Liberals. Oddly, the Liberal members did not attend the off-hours session to decide this case, and later claimed they were not notified of it. To fill the empty seats, the FSLN appointees called up substitute justices from their own party. As a result, the ruling was issued entirely by Sandinista supporters.

The Liberal justices then filed a communiqué rejecting the ruling. They claimed that the session of the Constitutional Chamber had been improperly formed, and that the Sandinista justices had usurped the role of the National Assembly and legislated from the bench. They denounced the ruling as the product of a conspiracy, calling it a "judicial coup" against the constitution.

But they were powerless to overturn it. By contrast, the Supreme Electoral Council quickly accepted the ruling and announced it was "etched in stone."

The constitutional change was firmly rejected in the court of public opinion. Nicaragua had had a revolution in 1979 to overthrow a president who practiced continuismo, and there was bitter irony in seeing the revolutionary party head down that path. The Constitutional Chamber's ruling was particularly disturbing in light of allegations of widespread fraud in the 2008 municipal elections, which generated public uncertainty concerning the governing party's willingness to hold a fraud-free presidential election in 2011. In a rare display of unity, all four opposition parties, the two most influential business associations, the Catholic Church, and a score of civil society organizations denounced the constitutional change.

■ COLOMBIA'S TAILORED TINKERING

Colombia represents a case of constitutional amendment by legislative acquiescence. As Uribe in 2009 began the final year of his second term as Colombia's president, he enjoyed stunning approval ratings from a public grateful for the tangible improvements his policies had made in personal security. A Gallup poll conducted in July 2009 showed 68 percent of respondents approving of Uribe's performance, and 58 percent said they thought Uribe should be allowed to run for a third term in 2010.

A drive by Uribe's supporters to collect signatures initiated legislative consideration of a referendum on whether to permit second-term presidents to seek consecutive reelection. This would not be the first constitutional change tailor-made to facilitate Uribe's career; in 2005, the Colombian legislature amended the constitution to allow him to seek reelection to a consecutive term.

In May 2009, the Colombian Senate approved the proposal. The lower house followed suit, but with a different version, creating a delay while a special committee reconciled the two texts. In August, the Senate approved the amendment with 56 votes in favor, and in early November the House passed it with 85 votes in favor to just 5 against. However, an opposition boycott of the vote in the Senate and 76 abstentions in the House showed that the issue was politically divisive. Given Uribe's popularity, congressmen who voted against the third term risked offending their constituents and losing their seats in legislative elections scheduled for March 2010. As a result, many absented themselves or abstained rather than directly opposing the amendment.

The proposal was then sent to the Constitutional Court, which was not expected to complete its review until February 2010. There would then be only a narrow window in which to hold the referendum before the May presidential election. As 2009 came to an end, time was against Uribe; a worsening economy and a corruption scandal were slowly sapping his support. Meanwhile, election authorities found that donors to the signature drive had exceeded allowed financial limits, putting the legality of the entire amendment process in doubt. The

election authorities' judgment was not binding, but the Constitutional Court, known for its independence, was expected to take it into account. Speculation rose that the amendment might not survive judicial scrutiny.

If the referendum is held, one-quarter of registered voters will have to cast ballots for it to be considered valid. If turnout is low, Uribe might obtain a majority but still be unable to run for reelection. Colombia prides itself on being South America's oldest continually operating democracy, and even citizens who have supported Uribe might consider the amendment unwise. Should he win a third term, he would be positioned to make new high court appointments and dominate the judiciary. That would further erode checks and balances in a country where presidential powers are already considerable, and where the state has come under criticism for human rights violations.

Sizeable segments of the press and the intelligentsia in Colombia oppose the proposed change. For his part, Uribe has been cagey, refusing to be pinned down on whether he would run if doing so were legal. Certainly his government's staunch support for the referendum implies that he hopes to. Meanwhile, his refusal categorically to rule out another run has made it difficult for his supporters to rally around an alternative candidate.

■ THE DOMINICAN PARTY PACT

In October 2009, the Dominican Republic amended more than 40 articles of its constitution. Two issues—a prohibition on abortion and alteration of citizenship rights—dominated the media spotlight. The amendment of provisions for presidential reelection was less controversial because, while it removed term limits, it also prohibited consecutive election.

For much of the twentieth century, the Dominican Republic was governed by strongmen who held the presidency for extended periods. A crisis due to alleged electoral fraud in 1994 was resolved via an interparty agreement to amend the constitution. Under the new legal framework, presidents could be reelected to any number of four-year terms as long as they stepped aside for at least one term between their periods in office.

In 2002, the constitution was amended to allow a sitting president to seek immediate reelection one time. Whereas other Latin American presidents who changed constitutional rules to stand for reelection met with success at the polls, President Hipólito Mejía lost his 2004 reelection bid to Leonel Fernández, who had first served as president from 1996 to 2000. In 2008, Fernández was able to take advantage of Mejía's constitutional change to seek immediate reelection, and won a third term as president. He was then ineligible to run again.

The 2009 amendments drafted by President Fernández returned the Dominican Republic to the provisions of the 1994 constitution, which allowed an unlimited number of presidential terms as long as there was a pause between each one. This meant that, although Fernández would be obliged to step down as scheduled in 2012, he would be eligible to run for a fourth presidential term in 2016 or thereafter. The 2009 amendments underwent substantial legislative scrutiny before being passed in September.

Public concern was allayed because Fernández did not concoct an amendment that would permit him to seek immediate reelection to a fourth term, but instead returned the Dominican Republic to a prior presidential reelection rule that had enjoyed widespread legitimacy. Moreover, Fernández forged consensus on the 2009 draft with the main opposition leader, Miguel Vargas Maldonado, and consulted the island's third party as well. Legislative support was consequently strong, with 122 voting in favor to just 14 against.

The absence of a requirement for public ratification of constitutional amendments, while not unusual in Latin America, meant that the process was top-down, controlled from start to finish by those in power. Ordinary citizens had no opportunity to vote to retain term limits.

The interparty consensus-building behind the Dominican Republic's amendments should not be assumed to stem solely from a commitment to democratic principles and respect for the opposition. A less generous interpretation might construe the constitutional change as a pact meant to perpetuate the two leaders' dominance of their respective parties and give Fernández another shot at the presidency. Absent a cap on the total number of terms any one person may serve, former presidents have an incentive to block would-be successors and entrench themselves as their party's perennial candidate. Doing this impedes the entry of fresh faces and ideas into the political system, and reduces democracy within parties.

■ THE CHALLENGE TO DEMOCRACY

The Venezuelan and Nicaraguan decisions to permit indefinite reelection of presidents, the Colombian legislature's approval of a referendum permitting a second-term president to seek immediate reelection, and the Dominican Republic's enabling of its president to seek a fourth term marked 2009 as the year in which prospects for continuismo reappeared on the region's horizon. Latin America is witnessing an all-too-familiar pattern of presidents' manipulating the constitutional framework to seek additional terms in office. Although the cases we have seen are not yet sufficient to establish a trend, precedents have been set that might serve as a rationale for other Latin American countries to soften reelection constraints.

Such changes could easily exacerbate Latin America's hyper-presidentialism, in which the presidency tends to dominate other branches of government. Where institutional checks and balances are weak, elections could become the only means to hold presidents accountable, exposing election authorities to enormous political pressure. Indeed, the danger of such a slippery slope heightened concerns in Honduras about President Manuel Zelaya's alleged interest in relaxing constitutional limits on reelection, and these concerns helped trigger a military coup that suspended democracy there in June 2009. The Venezuelan referendum approving indefinite presidential reelection, held just four months earlier, loomed large as a precedent. It shaded interpretations of Zelaya's warm relations with Chávez and raised the perceived stakes of preserving Honduras's prohibition on reelection.

The recent constitutional changes to presidential reelection rules have occurred in a context of regional support for democracy, at a time when new instruments for the collective protection of democracy have been developed. The most comprehensive of these is the Inter-American Democratic Charter, which was signed in 2001 by all 34 countries in the OAS. This accord, which defines democracy and empowers the OAS to assist members whose democracy is eroding, was developed to prevent a repetition of Peruvian President Fujimori's "slow motion coup" in 2000, in which he dismantled the checks and balances in government to seek a third term as president. Nonetheless, the Democratic Charter has not deterred experimentation with third and fourth terms or even indefinite reelection, because these do not violate the definition of democracy articulated in the Democratic Charter's Articles 3 and 4.

Part of the dilemma may be that the OAS membership roster includes Canada and the English-speaking Caribbean states, which have parliamentary systems. In a parliamentary system there is no cap on the number of terms a prime minister can serve. If a political party holds the majority in the legislature, its leader becomes prime minister, so turnover in the executive branch depends more on internal party politics and voter support for political parties than on any constitutional limits. Thus, for example, Jamaican Prime Minister P.J. Patterson served from 1992 to 2006, inheriting the post that his party had won under Michael Manley and then winning three elections.

Such systems give the parliament the ability to hold a vote of no confidence that can force a prime minister to call new elections. But they draw on a democratic political culture, as much as checks and balances, to prevent abuse of power, since British colonialism inculcated different values and customs from those bequeathed by the Iberian colonial experience. Absent term limits of their own, Caribbean members of the OAS may be reluctant to criticize their Latin American counterparts whose presidents seek extended reelection; the inevitable comparisons might leave them vulnerable to accusations of hypocrisy.

While it might seem reasonable to consider Colombia's proposed three terms and the alternation model in the Dominican Republic as less troubling for democracy than the unlimited reelection now permitted in Venezuela and Nicaragua, any OAS evaluation of these amendments based on their content is a political non-starter. Member states rarely criticize one another on matters of internal politics. The principle of sovereignty grounds the organization's every move, a reaction to a long and difficult history of US intervention in the region.

Moreover, Washington's ongoing ideological confrontation with some leftist presidents in Latin America makes voicing bilateral objections to the recent constitutional changes in Venezuela and Nicaragua a prickly business. No Latin American leader wants to appear to back US meddling in a sister republic. For its part, the United States has criticized Chávez and Ortega for removing limits on reelection, and has discouraged Uribe from seeking a third term—but if Colombia passes the proposed referendum and Uribe wins reelection again, the United States will not likely cool relations with a right-wing president who is an ally in the fight against drugs and terrorism.

■ APPLYING THE DEMOCRATIC CHARTER

Meanwhile, the primary instrument for preventing democratic erosion in the hemisphere—the Inter-American Democratic Charter—is ill-suited to framing or even informing political struggles over institutional rules for presidential reelection. The specifications for democracy in the Charter call for periodic, free, and fair elections held with universal suffrage and a secret ballot. However, the document does not draw lessons from past experience with continuismo, nor is it intended to endorse any specific constitutional design or best practices. The Democratic Charter is therefore silent on whether lengthy presidencies would be likely to compromise elements of democracy it deems "essential," such as "the separation of powers and independence of the branches of government."

Even if it were advisable for the Democratic Charter to offer guidelines or to identify a range of appropriate democratic practices, amendment of the Charter to address this matter is unlikely. Indeed, opening the text for discussion would probably weaken rather than strengthen it—the regional consensus on liberal representative democracy is more fragile now than it was when the document was signed in 2001.

The Democratic Charter may nonetheless prove useful. No president's popularity lasts forever. Sooner or later, a president seeking to stay in office will face the choice of rigging the vote or stepping down. And the Charter allows for suspending the OAS membership of any state whose leaders do not come to power democratically. The organization's willingness to use this sanction was illustrated by its suspension of Honduras's membership in the wake of the June 2009 coup d'état.

The Democratic Charter also endorses the rule of law; therefore, distinguishing among countries in terms of the legality of their constitutional amendment processes is essential. The party collusion in the Dominican Republic may be viewed as thoughtful consensus-building or as an elite pact to provide President Fernández with a route to a fourth term in office. Either way, the constitutional change was made legally.

In Colombia, the path to constitutional change has followed pre-established procedures and allowed scrutiny from both the legislature and the Constitutional Court. The boycott of the vote in the Senate and mass abstentions in the lower house may have detracted from the amendment's perceived legitimacy, but they did not affect its legality. The signature collection process violated political finance regulations, but in Latin America such transgressions are rarely considered serious enough to void electoral outcomes or jeopardize a popular president.

With respect to the cases of indefinite reelection—cases that pose a more imminent prospect of empowering a president to govern for life—the constitutional changes in Venezuela and Nicaragua are markedly different. The Venezuelan process arguably violated restrictions on introducing a referendum proposal twice in the same presidential term, and it did so in a context where the president's willingness to be constrained by law was already questionable. However, the referendum was properly authorized by the legislature, and the public approved it in a clean vote with a decisive margin.

By contrast, Nicaragua's partisan manipulation of the Supreme Court was not accepted as legal by opposition justices. Indeed, they provided the OAS with possible grounds for launching an inquiry by proclaiming that the Constitutional Chamber's revocation of term limits represented a rupture of Nicaragua's democratic and institutional order. That language echoed Article 20 of the Inter-American Democratic Charter, which states that an unconstitutional rupture of the constitutional order in a member state is cause for OAS diplomatic action with or without an invitation from the government in question.

Despite Ortega's good record of accepting defeat in past presidential races, the partisan nature of the Constitutional Chamber's decision has given rise to concerns that the governing party may not be averse to distorting electoral rules to favor his reelection in 2011.

■ WILL HISTORY REPEAT?

Whether or not the erosion of presidential term limits will spread to additional countries is uncertain. The legislative vote in Colombia, the judicial process in Nicaragua, and the referendum in Venezuela have all revealed deep political divisions regarding the relaxation of term limits, and voters elsewhere may reject such changes if given the chance to do so through a ratification procedure. Leaders, too, may choose to retain electoral limits even when the leaders enjoy continuing public support—as in Brazil, where President Luiz Inácio Lula da Silva will leave office on January 1, 2011, when his second term expires. Judging by the current cases, reelection limits are more likely to be eased where presidents are relatively powerful and the institutions that constrain them are concomitantly weak.

If similar initiatives arise elsewhere to extend the number of presidential terms allowed, whether they are consecutive or not, constitutional amendment processes will bear watching. Where sitting presidents are willing to bend the law to secure expanded reelection rights, they may not flinch at tampering with elections. There is a role for the OAS in reporting on deterioration of the rule of law and monitoring elections to prevent fraud. Ideally, such measures will not be needed; in and of itself, repeated reelection is not undemocratic. Nonetheless, for those conscious of Latin America's political history, there is understandable concern that the seeds of continuismo may have been replanted.

___

Shelley A. McConnell, an assistant professor at St. Lawrence University, served for nine years as senior associate director of the Carter Center's Americas Program.

From *Current History,* February 2010, pp. 74–80. Copyright © 2010 by Current History, Inc. Reprinted by permission.

Challenge Questions

After reading this article, you will be able to answer the following questions:

1. Why do many Latin American constitutions have term limits for presidents?
2. What mechanisms are used to alter constitutions to allow re-election?
3. Is democracy in danger in Latin America?
4. What dangers does *continuismo* present to the region?

4 Hemispheric Echoes

Larry Birns and Nicholas Birns, PhD

The Reverberations of Latin American Populism.

After reading this article, you will more clearly understand the following:

- Nature of Latin American populism
- Mass-based politics
- Multipolarity
- Challenge to United States policy

■ A RESURGENT POPULISM

In the immediate post-Cold War world, Latin America did not ignite much diplomatic interest. Though the growth of democratic processes in formerly authoritarian countries was brusquely hailed, the region was seen as a grateful laboratory for the Washington Consensus, and not as a sphere of potential controversy. The revival of populism in Latin America has changed this framework. The region is now genuinely out of the doldrums and is the source of genuine headlines in the world press.

Most of the changes are due to the stirrings promoted by well-intentioned populist figures hoping to promulgate major organic reforms. Outside observers once saw Latin American populism as hyperbolic rhetoric that might win elections and ignite occasional political ruckuses, but not as a particularly serious governing creed. Recently, however, populism has come to the fore in a new way, fueled by a desire to bring the organs of government into a genuinely closer dialogue with a disempowered and alienated citizenry. The neoliberal prescriptions handed down from Washington in the past two decades—insisting on balanced budgets and fiscal austerity in carrying out public works or income-redistribution programs—have stoked some resentment. Latin Americans are now more vociferously seeking redress for the economic distortions and the resulting inequalities long present in their societies.

The recent upsurge of populism in the region comes as a direct riposte to Washington Consensus dogma. The populist regimes now in power in Latin America—Nicaragua, Argentina, Bolivia, Ecuador, Venezuela, Chile, and Brazil—are diverse and have varying bases of support. The rural *campesinos* and urban laborers who account for the core of Evo Morales's support in Bolivia differ demographically from the base behind the successful campaign of Rafael Correa in Ecuador. But all of these leaders are motivated by a desire for government to be results-oriented and as close as possible in policy and spirit to the aspirations of the governed.

Though the fabled Hugo Chávez of Venezuela may sometimes comport himself in an overly emotive style reminiscent of the brimstone balcony declarations of old-style *caudillos,* today's Latin American populist standard-bearers are democratically elected. They have managed to keep their eyes peeled on the social imperatives which carried them to power because they know that if they fail at improving their citizens' living standards, they must be prepared to figuratively—sometimes even literally—end up biting the dust. In Bolivia and Ecuador, so-called populists ran on platforms dedicated to serving the goals of the poor and indigenous populations. Once in office, these leaders revoked their commitments by pleading that the requirements of the marketplace had forced them to invalidate their earlier pledges to adhere to their platforms. The electorates proceeded to unceremoniously dispose of them by means of economic blockades and work stoppages. This was true for Lucio Gutierrez in Ecuador who paid with his presidency when he broke his word with the nation's native people.

■ POPULISM—YESTERDAY AND TODAY

Hugo Chávez is a former military officer. Yet most of the current populist presidents come from civilian backgrounds. The dogmas of these leaders are very diverse, but today's populists are consistent in their opposition to untrammeled free markets and are skeptical of any manifestation of US hegemony in the region. They tend to reject wholesale modernization, favor a mixed over a heavily planned economy, and are predisposed to identify with the outlook of the global South rather than the technologically-propelled major northern powers. Despite Chávez's braggadocio and hip outbursts, populist leaders have been far from the caricature (created by populism's detractors) of the unrestrained, wild-eyed demagogue. These detractors include the conservative-dominated media in many Latin American countries and some of the more tendentious US policy analysts and press. Close scrutiny of the various populist-style governments reveals that these leaders are far more than ranting ideologues. More often than not, they are thoughtful dreamers who want to use the state to achieve their population's aspirations.

Populists such as Evo Morales and Rafael Correa are not one-shot phenomena who quickly fade once in power; rather, they are the political heralds of a tendency popularly termed the "pink tide," meant to signify the process by which populism has surged from one country to another. Populist movements have nurtured each other as a result of unabashed generosity, particularly that exhibited by Venezuela.

Populism has started to reengineer the economic equation in those countries in which it has gained power. In recent years, neo-liberal-flavored institutions and policies—such as relentless privatization and deflationary policies—have tended to slash public sector employment as a percentage of the economy. However, the new populist governments have invariably increased public-sector spending and have not hesitated to increase the number of government jobs and expand the state's areas of responsibility through bureaucracy as well as via a rich variety of community-based organizations. This process, rather than radical redistribution of wealth, has been the principal domestic macroeconomic multiplier used by this genre of policy makers to regularize the economy while sustaining social norms. As for economic norms, these have undeniably shifted in the past thirty years. During this period, Latin American populism has provided a significant, if ultimately limited rejoinder to the generally unhindered sweep of free-market initiatives, especially in the wake of the collapse of Soviet Communism. Populism may be considered best as a partial societal response to a world economic habitat where the free-market remains paramount but finds itself under growing challenge.

Populist democracies have also innovated in international economic terms. Here, the most visible initiative has come in the area of debt reduction. Argentina's President Kirchner's determination not to bend to IMF-imposed conditionality was hardly welcomed by advocates of fiscal restraint. The IMF mandated the imposition of a harsh regime affecting debt servicing that would have most likely hamstrung the resilience of the country's economy for as much as a decade. Argentina's resistance has inspired other leaders to ask that their country's immediate future not be sacrificed to the single-factor monetarist prescriptions of Washington and other global finance centers.

One can ask, is there a new vision for restoring economic productivity at play in the region? Populism's resilience could herald a new and different kind of era, one in which the concept is not *per force* a dirty word. Latin American left-leaning governments could demand a new respect from the international arena for the impressive achievements they are already recording.

But how did these slow but noticeable changes come to pass? In the late 1990s, amid the confidence brought on by the worldwide preeminence of Washington's unipolar model of globalization, Latin America duly marched in stride. At the time, the region was still taken seriously as a premium location for orthodox financial transactions. But a sensational shift would begin to take place that would affect US trade policy. This change was brought about by a *de facto* grassroots implementation of something akin to a Lockean Social Contract. It was increasingly obvious that IMF-mandated neo-liberal economics and the fiscal stringencies inspired by the Washington Consensus were neither eternal nor universal. However, it was also argued by many conventional global fiscal managers that at the time Latin America had no viable alternative. Bolivian activists such as Felipe Quispe and Evo Morales were seen as vendors of snake oil: even if a populist regime gained power, it eventually would go down in flames as a result of political and economic realities. These orthodox tribunes prophesied that without any viable alternative, the populist leaders would have to eventually lash themselves to a neo-liberal formula in order to survive.

The White House's pressure on the world community to endorse its effort to dislodge Saddam Hussein may have helped to compromise its gravitational pull over the region. An unexpected example in this respect is Chile, the only South American country at the time to have initialed a free-trade pact with the United States. Washington surely counted on Santiago's congruency with its main foreign policy guideline: its unpopular sortie in Iraq. But during the UN March 2003 deliberations, Soledad Alvear, Chile's foreign minister at the time, presented one of the strongest cases heard before the UN Security Council against the US thesis that it had the unilateral right to invade a member state for good cause. Seen for decades as well disposed to the United States, Chile's unwillingness to back the Iraq invasion registered a pivotal shift in its behavior. Overweening US diplomacy may well have accelerated the electoral success of parties whose leaders are no longer automatically prepared to capitulate to US policy mandates. After 2003, the "pink tide" leadership came into its own.

■ THE MAJOR ACTORS–CHÁVEZ, LULA, KIRCHNER, AND MORALES

While Washington's eyes were riveted on Iraq, a foiled coup in Venezuela and the election of new Argentine and Brazilian presidents were changing the ideological equation in Latin America. In the April 2002 coup attempt against Cháfez, it seemed at first that his administration had been overthrown and that the White House could now prepare to add another "democratizing" feather to its cap. But Chávez held on and managed to survive the attempted coup, which had been bitterly nursed by a disaffected middle-class and business-led opposition. The coup itself had been kindled by an inflammatory rightist media, 85 percent of which was controlled by owners who loathed Chavez.

The failed coup all but destroyed an extensive mythology that democratization was at the forefront of US policy goals for the hemisphere, since Chávez had ruled Venezuela in an entirely constitutional manner for his entire tenure in office. Thereafter, Chávez was not just a big-mouthed radical and controversial president, but quickly became the best-known exemplar of the "pink tide"—a wave of left-leaning social reformers who were being elected to office by strong majorities throughout a turbulent South America. Soon after Chávez came to power, his policies served as the inspiration for the separate agendas set up in each "pink tide" country. What united these agendas was the populist impulse—the belief that the presidency could be used to provide leadership and social justice for every corner of the nation.

Luis Ignacio Lula da Silva almost won the Brazilian presidency in 1989; his initial series of defeats could be partially credited to fears that his policies, as well as his personality, would come to antagonize Washington. Lula's election in 2002 marked a tipping point in the spread of electorally-viable populist candidates in South America. Although Lula's populist tendencies noticeably diminished into his presidency by his surprising emphasis on monetarist economic policies and an institutional continuity in foreign policy-making, Lula still used the presidential voice to rally the citizens with calls for social justice.

Argentina had traditionally been less inhibited about quarreling with a Washington-centered vision of world affairs than Brazil. When Nestor Kirchner was elected president of Argentina in April 2003, ending a kaleidoscopic series of temporary tenants of the Casa Rosada, he sent a signal to Washington that strengthening the country's internal stability would take precedence over repaying its debt, as mandated by the IMF. Kirchner has since strengthened relations with a host of countries in Europe, Asia, and Africa and has become an important force on the side of the world stage that does not swiftly move to accommodate itself to Washington's desiderata.

A great success of the "pink tide" was the 2006 election of coca farmer, indigenous activist, and professed socialist, Evo Morales, as president of Bolivia. Morales, who came to power in an unimpeachably democratic process, has managed so far to only barely placate his largely indigenous supporters while unsuccessfully making conciliatory gestures to the rest of the Bolivian polity. Even a clearly hostile US State Department has nominally accommodated itself to his presidency as demonstrated by the relatively lukewarm treatment he has received from the State Department through much of his tenure. But this acquiescence was coupled with a rather dire warning to the victor by Secretary of State Condoleezza Rice, who insists that she has her own definition of democracy. Even Paul Wolfowitz, attempting to rebrand himself from Iraq hawk to World Bank highflying dove, reached out to Morales in hopes of finding common ground.

WHERE THE TIDE IS RISING: CHILE, MEXICO, AND PERU

Even countries that are not overtly populist are still subject to contending forces that cause them to be far from quiescent regarding US policy. The election of the Socialist Michelle Bachelet to the Chilean presidency in 2006 was an important event, although Chile is not yet considered part of the "pink tide." But this fact cannot give comfort to those in Washington who counted on Santiago's automatic backing. As the daughter of military officers tortured by the Pinochet dictatorship, Bachelet is not likely to be a major sword carrier for the White House.

Andres Manuel Lopez Obrador's headstrong decision to squander his moral capital in what became an increasingly ineffective populist-sponsored protest against Mexico's last presidential election undermined his reputation. In spite of the enormous support he had mustered when he contested last year's close election *mano a mano*, his support had since dwindled, while Felipe Calderon buttressed his conservative rule. Though no occupant of *Los Pinos* is likely to take on the United States in a directly confrontational way, Mexico has become used to regular post-September 11 brush offs by the Bush administration and can expect more of the same under President Calderón. It is unlikely that the Bush administration's guest workers program—affecting as many as eleven million undocumented workers in the United States—will solve the problem of illegal immigration. Therefore, the troubled border is likely to persist as a prime irritant between the United States and Mexico and can be expected to periodically invoke ringing populist outbursts from Mexico.

In Peru, former President Alan Garcia, much reviled when he left office in 1990, made an unexpected return to power last year. Though, as with the returned Sandinistas in Nicaragua, his once-venerable Aprista party has shed any genuinely populist associations, even a defanged APRA cannot fully sympathize with the road to prosperity pioneered by the Washington Consensus. However, Washington has tried to woo Lima, while Ollanta Humala's populist movement—which espoused indigenous rights—has yet to achieve the successes of some of its more articulate counterparts elsewhere on the continent. Yet the movement has been further refining its socioeconomic credo and proposed administrative system, making it into a formidable rival of Garcia, particularly if the Garcia presidency stumbles.

MULTIPOLARITY: THE "PINK TIDE" AND THE MONROE DOCTRINE

Populism often causes Washington to distrust indigenous ideals and can turn race and culture into something of a shibboleth used to fan paranoia and a fear of change. Populism, in the eyes of the State Department and conservative Washington think tanks, has become a convenient, encapsulating slogan to depict Chávez and Morales and their school as irresponsible radicals who would not make seemly diplomatic partners.

One of the key differences between the current face-off between the United States and a left-leaning segment of Latin American nations and how that relationship has been previously carried out is the absence of a Monroe Doctrine to invoke with respect to interventions by foreign powers in the hemisphere. Most recently, Soviet interest in the region, especially after the Cuban

Revolution, gave US policy makers sufficient reason for Washington to play a hegemonic card. The force of this move was heightened by the irony that the Monroe Doctrine was first invoked against the Czarist Russia-led Holy Alliance, which had made rhetorical threats about re-conquering Spain's former Latin American colonies after the colonial era had ended. The post-Cold War era experienced echoes of the Monroe Doctrine but not any systematic use of it as a guiding principle for foreign policy.

With Venezuela seeking a multipolar alliance relationship with such declared or tacit opponents of the United States as Iran, China, North Korea, and Russia, the current situation is very much set for the invocation of a new and somewhat transformed round of populist-driven indictments of current US policy worldwide. Unlike Castro's Cuba, which needed Soviet logistical and financial support to guarantee its survival, Venezuela is not a beachhead requiring constant monitoring, but a large, wealthy country situated on the South American mainland and sitting astride immense reserves of oil and natural gas—the largest in the hemisphere. What is even more difficult for Washington is that the case against Chávez cannot be made credibly, while that against the United States can. There is no dynamic of Chávez being a puppet under the control of some extra-continental power. When he deals with China, Russia, or Iran, it is entirely on equal terms.

US policy initiatives directed against Chávez cannot hide behind the purported altruism of the Monroe Doctrine to disguise what some observers see as Washington hankering after continued regional hegemony. The emergence of autochthonous leaders such as Kirchner,

Morales, and Ecuador's Correa, inspired to different degrees by Chávez's example and with unimpeachably legitimate democratic credentials of their own, renders somewhat implausible any attempt at a binary division of the hemisphere into black hats and white hats. We now see democratically elected regimes that have adopted traditional populism for the twenty-first century in a way that attracts the votes of the discontented but is also able to enact its ideological convictions in practical terms once in office. Populism has put the region back into global diplomatic play. Washington may now have to deal with more unrest than was ever expected in its own so-called backyard.

Challenge Questions

After reading this article, you will be able to answer the following questions:

1. What accounts for the rise of populism in Latin America?
2. What do populist leaders hope to achieve?
3. Why is populism described as "leftist" ("pink tide")?
4. What is the effect of populism on United States foreign policy?

5 Dollarization Declines in Latin America

José M. Cartas

Latin Americans are placing more value in their own currencies.

Latin American countries are among the most dollarized in the world. While the extent of dollarization—when foreign currency is used in place of the local currency—varies widely among countries in the region, in most cases the ratio of foreign currency deposits to total bank deposits (one very common measure of dollarization) exceeded 30 percent at the end of 2009, and was sometimes much higher. Latin America is not alone in this respect: other emerging economies, such as the former Soviet Union countries and southeastern european countries also show a high degree of dollarization, ranging from 30 percent to 70 percent.

But some Latin American countries have managed to achieve a significant reduction in dollarization over the past 10 years, particularly countries with very high

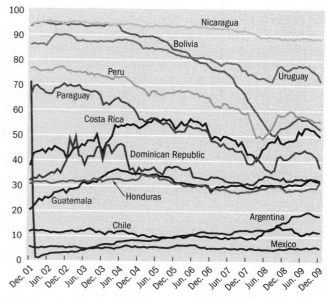

The degree of dollarization has declined in Latin America over the past decade (percent of foreign currency deposits to total bank deposits)

dollarization in 2001. The most prominent examples are Bolivia, Paraguay, and Peru, where the share of foreign currency deposits fell from 93 to 53 percent, 66 to 38 percent, and 76 to 56 percent, respectively. While this

What Is Dollarization?

Cocirculation–also commonly known as dollarization–results when a foreign currency, often the U.S. dollar, is used as a means of payment and store of value in parallel with the national currency. Several factors may affect the degree of dollarization of an economy. One factor is a country's legal framework. Some countries, for example, do not allow banks to take deposits in foreign currency. Conversely, others have adopted, de jure or de facto, a foreign currency as legal tender. Another factor is inflation. Residents of countries with high and variable inflation may prefer doing business in a foreign currency whose value is more stable. The interest rate differential between instruments denominated in national and foreign currency also influences the preferences of the public, together with expectation of future exchange rate movements.

About the Database

The data are derived from the standardized report forms (SRFs) currently used by 114 countries to report monetary data to the IMF's Statistics Department. The SRF's uniform presentation across countries according to instrument, currency, and sector, allows for high-quality cross-country analysis. They can be accessed via International Financial Statistics Online at www.imfstatistics.org/imf. Excluded from this analysis are Brazil, Colombia, and Venezuela, which do not allow accounts in foreign currency, and Ecuador, El Salvador, and Panama, which are fully dollarized economies. Foreign currency deposits refer to deposits in the domestic banking system and include deposits indexed to a foreign currency.

downward trend has slowed recently, with the interruption associated with the global financial crisis, dollarization levels in these countries remain well below those prevailing as of 2001. This tendency to dedollarize represents an increasing preference for holding the national currency, which may be linked to the improved confidence that comes with the elimination of high inflation and the implementation of sounder economic and financial policies.

Dollarization has not been declining steadily in all Latin American countries. In Chile and Mexico, dollarization was already relatively low at the beginning of the decade and has remained fairly stable. In Argentina, dollarization fell to near zero with the policy of deposit "pesofication" at the beginning of the decade, but subsequently has increased. In some countries of Central America, dollarization showed more fluctuation over the decade, without a clear trend.

Challenge Questions

After reading this article, you will be able to answer the following questions:

1. What accounts for the rise of populism in Latin America?
2. What do populist leaders hope to achieve?
3. Why is populism described as "leftist" ("pink tide")?
4. What is the effect of populism on United States foreign policy?

6 The New Mercantilism: China's Emerging Role in the Americas

Eric Farnsworth

Learning Objectives

After reading this article, you will more clearly understand the following:

- China's search for raw materials and export markets
- Latin American development
- Differences in Chinese and United States economic approaches toward Latin America
- Labor, human rights and environmental protection

My first visit to China was in 1986; my second was in 2010. The difference between the two visits was profound. Within one generation, it seemed as if everything except the Forbidden City and the Great Wall had changed. Cars had replaced bicycles, shining office towers had replaced ramshackle tenements, and consumerism had replaced the dreary economic hopelessness that many Chinese previously endured.

Which is not to say all is well there. Newly acquired wealth exists side by side with abject poverty. Stunning natural beauty contrasts with choking pollution. And overseeing the country's dramatic change is the Communist Party leadership, which remains jealous of its 60-year monopoly on political power and is unwilling to tolerate any challenge to its rule.

To maintain legitimacy and power, the government has made a strategic bet—that it can keep political control by allowing and even encouraging economic liberalization. Growth and job creation are the keys to making this strategy work, and have become a virtual obsession of Chinese leaders. According to the International Monetary Fund, China accounted for almost a fifth of world growth in 2010. Exports have been and continue to be critical to this success; China uses an undervalued currency as a tool to keep global demand for its exports high.

Production, however, requires inputs, and exports require raw materials. Thus, over the past 10 years, China has been on a global hunt for the raw materials that it needs to keep its production lines humming and its people employed, including the additional millions who join the work force every year. Coal, oil and gas, ores and minerals, soy and other agricultural goods: Chinese demand for these has caused a secular shift in global commodities markets.

China's leaders, moreover, are not content to leave their procurement efforts to the vagaries of global markets. Rather, they seek long-term, guaranteed access to raw materials, in some cases even looking to control the means of production and in-country infrastructure such as ports and rail. Raw materials are then turned into value-added products and re-exported from China around the world.

This is a transparently mercantilist strategy, with domestic political requirements at its core. It is a strategy designed, fundamentally, to keep the ruling party in power. It is not a strategy to project power or to contribute to the development of the impoverished abroad. Nor is it a strategy primarily to build political alliances, though political influence will naturally increase with enhanced trade linkages. (China has asked trading partners, for instance, to support the diplomatic isolation of Taiwan.)

It is a strategy, however, that is changing the world. In Latin America, in particular, the impact has been significant, with game-changing implications for economic growth, long-term development, governance, and US policy.

■ THE DRAGON ENTERS

Traditionally, China had virtually no footprint in Latin America or the Caribbean. It was a region that Chinese leaders considered the "backyard" of the United States and were reluctant to enter. Similarly, Latin American and Caribbean leaders gave almost no thought to China, the exceptions being smaller nations that recognized Taiwan as a result of Taiwanese financial incentives, and extralegal groups like Peru's Shining Path that purposefully fashioned themselves after Maoist revolutionaries.

Latin American and Caribbean trade and investment generally flowed on a north-south axis, with European connections also playing an important role, particularly in economic relations with Brazil and South America's Southern Cone. Japan, too, played an important, though tertiary, trade role.

In recent years, however, China has entered the region forcefully. Between 2000 and 2009, China's imports from Latin America and the Caribbean ballooned from approximately $5 billion to $44 billion. Exports to the region have followed a similar trajectory, rising from $4.5 billion to $42 billion over the same time period. China is now Brazil and Chile's largest trade partner, and may soon be Peru's as well. The United Nations Economic Commission for Latin America and the Caribbean estimates that China will displace the European Union as the second-largest regional trading partner by 2015, and will trail only the United States.

The US share of regional trade, meanwhile, is declining. From 2002 to 2008, the US share of exports to the region fell from 48 to 37 percent, while China's grew from 4 to 10 percent. This trend is likely to continue, especially as China locks in trade arrangements for the long term.

Bilateral free trade agreements are now in force between China and Chile, Costa Rica, and Peru. Additional agreements are just a matter of time. China buys primarily raw materials from Latin America. In fact, commodities make up fully 80 percent of Chinese purchases—driven, again, by China's domestic development needs. As a result of China's dash for growth, cyclical commodities markets have stabilized and prices have remained at historic highs. Conversely, most of what China sends back to Latin America and the Caribbean is in the form of competitively priced manufactured goods, actually threatening the manufacturing base of countries like Mexico, the Central American states, and even Brazil.

This is the very definition of mercantilism. China buys raw materials from the region, engages in value-added production at home, and then re-exports the finished products to Latin America and the Caribbean, thereby undercutting the region's own efforts at value-added production.

At the same time, Latin America and the Caribbean have clearly benefited from selling to China over the past decade. Weak economic growth, averaging little more than 1 percent per year in the 1980s and 1990s, has given way to regional growth rates in the range of 4 to 6 percent. Brazil's growth alone has risen from an average of 1.7 percent annually in the 1998–2003 period to 4.2 percent since 2004. In 2010, Brazil's economy grew an estimated 7.5 percent; projections suggest a sustainable rate of 5.5 percent through 2014. Much of this is a result of trade with China. And the rest of the commodities-exporting nations in the region have experienced similar growth.

■ TAKING ADVANTAGE

Those countries without much in the way of commodities sales to China, including Mexico and nations in Central America and the Caribbean Basin, have not done as well. In addition to having only limited commodities to sell in the first place, these countries are truly dependent on the US economy as their primary export market for both goods and services, and also the primary economy from which remittances are sent.

Sluggish recovery in the United States will continue to limit Mexican, Central American, and Caribbean Basin growth rates for the foreseeable future, especially as manufactures from the region come under continuing pressure from Chinese imports.

On the other hand, for those nations, primarily in South America, that have been in a position to take advantage, exports of primary goods to China have been one of the key factors keeping their economies out of the depths of the recent recession and leading them to rapid recovery.

It has also had the effect, however, of shielding such countries from the need to reform their economies to promote broad-based development and to position themselves more competitively for the long run. When nations are able to sell as much as they can produce of any particular product, the thinking is generally to continue doing so and reap the rewards. When economies are growing, there is little political imperative or incentive for reform.

China promises only a commercial relationship without political or policy interference.

Yet Latin America continues to lack knowledge-based, value-added innovation and production. Education rates remain comparatively low. Workforce development and the liberalization of labor codes have lagged. Investment in research and development barely registers in most countries. And national development strategies are virtually nonexistent.

Of course, China has aggressively and successfully promoted its own value-added production, in part by insisting on technology transfer and other capacity-building measures whenever Western companies look to gain access to the Chinese marketplace. It is a strategy that has paid off handsomely for the Chinese, who are starting to compete head to head with others on highly sophisticated products.

There is no reason at all why Latin America should not replicate this model (abstaining, of course, from obviously negative aspects of Chinese practices, such as theft of intellectual property). Brazil is beginning to take this approach, insisting on in-country investments, technology transfer, and joint research and development platforms that help to develop local valued-added capabilities and expertise. Others should, too. For example, Bolivia, South America's poorest nation, should refuse to give Beijing access to its massive deposits of lithium unless the Chinese first agree to joint research and development of the technology needed to build the car batteries for which the lithium is intended. Rather than merely mining lithium, Bolivia might then aspire to become a developer of battery technology, reaping rewards from a potentially huge demand for clean energy transportation alternatives.

The ability to promote labor and environmental protections, human rights, and the rule of law is being commensurately reduced.

■ LET'S MAKE A DEAL

Expanding trade always attracts attention, but headlines are drawn by investment deals—including blockbuster announcements by Chinese officials detailing massive regional investments that they intend to make. The reality of China's investments in the region is, however, somewhat more complex than the headlines would indicate. The actual flow of money has been limited despite announced figures, as China takes steps to learn about and understand markets before actually committing funds. Even so, investments and acquisitions have begun to surge.

Oil and gas deals have been leading the charge, hitting over $13 billion in 2010, up from zero in 2009. China's oil giant Sinopec has been particularly active, announcing in December 2010 that it would acquire Occidental Petroleum Corporation's assets in Argentina for $2.45 billion. This followed hard on Sinopec's October announcement that it would buy 40 percent of the Spanish company Repose's Brazilian assets for $7.1 billion, the biggest acquisition by a Chinese firm in Latin America to date. Additional significant announcements are on the horizon, as Sinopec, China National Offshore Oil Company, and others vie for assets.

Oil and gas are not the only sectors involved, of course. Mining, power generation, fishing, and agriculture deals have also recently occurred and will continue to occur given China's strategic play to lock in access to raw materials. Because they are commodities producers, Argentina, Brazil, Chile, and Peru have benefited handsomely, while Colombia is also on track to benefit and is currently negotiating a free trade agreement with China.

Infrastructure projects are next in line, given Latin America's significant underinvestment in the infrastructure required to take advantage of its emerging role in the global economy. Roads, bridges, railways, ports, and information technology and telecommunications, for example, will all require huge investments in the near term to help make the region more competitive. As well, signature projects in Brazil, as that nation gets ready to host the World Cup in 2014 and the Olympic Summer Games in 2016, will soon come on line.

The Chinese government is supportive of overseas projects generally, and the Bank of China offers attractive finance. With such backing, Chinese companies have been known to make above-market offers on infrastructure projects and for assets such as oil and gas and mineral deposits that otherwise have attracted little attention, guaranteeing that China will be in position to bid successfully.

China has also done investment deals with Venezuela, Ecuador, Cuba, and Bolivia—leftist-run countries that one would predict, if ideology were an overriding factor in Chinese decisions, might attract the lion's share of investment. To date, however, China's commercial relations with Ecuador have been rocky. An April 2010 promise by Beijing to loan $20 billion to Venezuela in order to lock in access to that country's heavy oil remains pending. And Bolivia's takeover of its gas fields did not impress the Chinese, who are looking for long-term certainty in their investments.

In fact, Chinese companies have no problem dealing with populist or authoritarian leaders, but neither are they unduly attracted to doing business in countries ruled by them. With them, it is strictly business. If a decent, risk-adjusted return can be made, and access to a necessary resource guaranteed, the investment will likely be made. Otherwise, it will not. This is a matter not of charity or ideology, but of China's need to meet its domestic demands in the most efficient and effective manner possible.

It must be said that total Chinese foreign direct investment (FDI) in Latin America and the Caribbean is dwarfed by the stock of US investment in the region, and will be for some time. But Chinese investment is increasing rapidly. In 2009, for example, some 17 percent of total Chinese FDI went to Latin America. And Chinese investment is just at the beginning of the curve as the nation pursues its strategy of locking in access to raw materials.

China appears to be less interested in majority control of enterprises than in taking significant minority stakes, which allow Chinese investors to learn the ins and outs of a heretofore unknown marketplace while guaranteeing long-term access to raw materials. Chinese portfolio investment, on the other hand, has only just begun, but it will play an increasingly important role in the region as Chinese investors, like their Western counterparts, seek higher returns in emerging markets in an era of slow growth elsewhere.

■ RETURNS ON INVESTMENT

As investment increases, the quality of FDI is important to consider. Not all investment is the same. For example, US investors and corporations operating abroad generally follow anticorruption provisions codified in the Foreign Corrupt Practices Act. They abide by corporate governance and reporting requirements. They comply with US and local labor laws and human resources requirements. They transfer technology and management expertise to local markets. They provide access to the global marketplace for local production. They source locally. They pay taxes, even when tax laws, as in Brazil, are complex and impenetrable.

US businesses often pursue corporate social responsibility activities, including humanitarian relief, thereby contributing to local economies and social development. They hire from the local economy, using a limited number of expatriates to manage operations while building businesses from local hires. And they abide by US government foreign policies—for example, when countries like Myanmar (formerly Burma), Cuba, or Iran are sanctioned.

Of course, not every company is perfect, and nongovernmental organizations have aggressively highlighted instances in which they believe corporate malfeasance has occurred. To the extent it has, wrongdoers should be held accountable. But in the main, US investors are required by their boards to follow these general guidelines as a matter of course.

Chinese companies, on the other hand, are less likely to abide by these guidelines, though their record is not as lengthy or detailed as that for US investors. One issue that almost universally galls observers of Beijing's investment in the region is China's lack of interest in hiring local workers. Labor forces for construction and operations are routinely brought from China to Latin America and the Caribbean. Many if not most of the jobs that could go to locals are reserved for Chinese nationals.

It is a difficult case to make, as a result, that one of Chinese investment's primary benefits to the region has been job creation. Disgruntlement over this trend can be expected to rise as investment increases, unless active steps are taken to reverse course.

More broadly, the political implications of different investment models are important. The United States and other like-minded nations have traditionally used economic and financial incentives to encourage reforms in Latin America and the Caribbean. Tools have included bilateral and regional trade agreements, market access agreements, defense and security relations, equipment sales and transfer, training and capacity building, and foreign assistance. Areas of interest to US policy makers run the gamut from democracy to human rights, from labor rights to the environment, from investor protections to intellectual property provisions.

The US trade agreement with Colombia, for example, was signed in 2006 but remains pending, given Washington's expressed concerns over labor rights and protections in Colombia. A trade agreement with Peru was held up pending the resolution of environmental concerns. The North American Free Trade Agreement required side agreements on both labor and environmental issues before Congress approved it. A unilateral Andean trade preferences program requires that recipient nations cooperate fully on counternarcotics and also maintain appropriate investment climates. And so on.

China, on the other hand, promises a commercial relationship without political or policy interference in the nations in question. Chinese investors are not hung up on whether a host nation's government is capitalist or populist, authoritarian or democratic, corrupt or not. They certainly do not care if the government is pro-United States or anti-United States.

The Chinese do not care if their investments prop up local bad guys or undercut collective international efforts to enforce norms of behavior. Their emphasis is on doing business effectively and undisturbed. For domestic purposes, they have pursued a strategy of business for business's sake in Latin America and the Caribbean, as they have around the world; they are not attempting to change the world.

◼ CONQUISTADORS

And yet, the world is changing, because by acting in this manner, Beijing offers to the countries of Latin America and the Caribbean the opportunity to forge a path independent of the United States and liberal economic orthodoxy. This is attractive to them, particularly when the US economy is struggling, and to the extent that US leaders at times have been overbearing and self-interested in their actions toward the region. Regional elites have often chafed at what they consider to be the United States'

patronizing tendency to use trade and investment to leverage sensitive domestic political changes.

At the same time, the ability of the United States and other Western nations to promote labor and environmental protections, human rights, and the rule of law in Latin America and the Caribbean is being commensurately reduced by the increase in Chinese economic activity. The region is beginning to have other options, a trend cheered by those who most disdain the perceived historic role that the United States has played in the region, and by those who mistakenly view trade itself as an exploitative mechanism that primarily benefits the United States. (This view is particularly pronounced within the human rights and development communities, without the recognition that trade and investment are among the most potent tools that the United States has for promoting the agendas that they themselves hold dear.)

This is ironic. For years, Latin American and Caribbean elites and observers have railed against the United States for its alleged exploitation of Latin America's natural resources, claiming that the North Americans came to conquer, despoil the landscape, impoverish the region, and make off with the riches of the continent.

An entire literature has arisen around these themes, the most famous example of which, perhaps, is Uruguayan journalist Eduardo Galeano's *Open Veins of Latin America: Five Centuries of the Pillage of a Continent*. Though it was written in 1971, the book remains popular with a new generation of leaders, including Venezuelan President Hugo Chávez, who mischievously presented a copy to President Barack Obama at the Summit of the Americas in Trinidad and Tobago in April 2009.

Even Hollywood has gotten into the act. Filmmaker Oliver Stone's 2010 documentary "South of the Border" purports to show that the United States, global capitalism, and the corporate media have caused the ills of the Western Hemisphere. The primary explanation for a lack of development and opportunity in Latin America is the predatory and exploitative behavior of the developed world, with the private sector at the vanguard, supported by the raw military, financial, and political muscle of a hegemonic United States.

This line of thinking is a tired and tiresome approach to analyzing the Americas, and has been widely and repeatedly debunked. At the same time, one often hears across Latin America—including from populist, anti-US leaders—that building relations with China and welcoming Chinese trade and investment are national priorities.

China is now Brazil and Chile's largest trade partner, and may soon be Peru's as well.

For countries such as Brazil, Chile, and Peru, links with China are intended to help build economies. For the new administration of President Juan Manuel Santos in Colombia, China links provide a means to develop a healthier, less dependent relationship with the United States. For others, they are seen as a means of diversifying relations away from traditional trade and investment patterns and the political connections that develop alongside them, while providing new economic options that will allow greater flexibility in governing.

Venezuela's Chávez is the best example of this latter category, particularly regarding the president's desire to diversify the markets for his country's heavy crude away from the United States. Accomplishing this will require massive investments in infrastructure, including specially built refineries, along the Venezuela-to-China supply chain. Economically, this makes zero sense. Politically, it makes a great deal of sense to Chávez. And if it guarantees the Chinese access to Venezuelan crude over the long term, it is win-win, even though the arrangement may take years to materialize fully.

■ HARD THINKING

At a time when Latin American economies are growing, and when many countries are gaining a new sense of confidence and of a direction apart from the United States, the region is running headlong into an economic embrace of China. This is not to suggest that China will supplant the United States in investment any time soon, or that Chinese economic linkages will lead to political meddling or adventurism from Beijing.

In fact, neither the pronouncements nor the behavior of the Chinese to this point support the contentions of conservative US commentators that Beijing entertains strategic political or military designs on the Western Hemisphere. There is no evidence that China aspires to take over the Panama Canal or otherwise project power into the region. The United States will remain the strongest nation in the Western Hemisphere, albeit less able over time to determine the outcome of regional events.

Still, as economic links with China proliferate, it must be asked whether China is good for the Americas beyond the short-term economic gain it provides, no matter how beneficial this has been and will continue to be for the foreseeable future. One wonders why regional leaders and observers, so quick to condemn the United States for its alleged pillaging of the continent, have not seen fit to raise their voices to question the Chinese approach—an approach that is straightforwardly mercantilist and is lacking in any of the benevolent or pro-development

impulses that can be found in US engagement with the region, including the promotion of international norms and Western values.

China's involvement in the region is not illegitimate, illegal, or even necessarily threatening, despite being economically unbalanced. But people in the region do need to think hard about the best means to ensure that Chinese engagement benefits the region over the long term, and not just in the short run.

Correspondingly, the United States needs to meet its own obligations in the hemisphere—from passing pending trade agreements to engaging with the people of the region in a manner that is conducive to cooperation and mutual respect. Perhaps then the silly idea so frequently heard in policy circles and around the region—that Chinese economic engagement is unquestionably positive for the Americas, while US economic engagement is exploitative and should be resisted—can be put to rest. The outcome of this debate will, in any event, help determine Latin America and the Caribbean's political direction, as well as its development prospects, for many years to come.

Challenge Questions

After reading this article, you will be able to answer the following questions:

1. What might be the consequences of the Chinese economic penetration of Latin America and the position of the United States in the region?
2. What dangers does Chinese economic policy pose for Latin American development?
3. What is the connection between Chinese domestic politics and its foreign trade and investment policies?
4. What is meant by the term "mercantilism"?

7 The Real War in Mexico

Shannon O'Neil

How Democracy Can Defeat the Drug Cartels.

Learning Objectives

After reading this article, you will more clearly understand the following:

- Drug-related violence
- Threats to Mexico's democratic institutions
- Historical link between drug-trafficking organizations and political parties
- United States role in combating drug-trafficking

Brazen assassinations, kidnappings, and intimidation by drug lords conjure up images of Colombia in the early 1990s. Yet today it is Mexico that is engulfed by escalating violence. Over 10,000 drug-related killings have occurred since President Felipe Calderón took office in December 2006; in 2008 alone, there were over 6,000. Drug cartels have begun using guerrilla-style tactics: sending heavily armed battalions to attack police stations and assassinating police officers, government officials, and journalists. And they have also adopted innovative public relations strategies to recruit supporters and intimidate their enemies: displaying *narcomantas*—banners hung by drug traffickers—in public places and uploading videos of gruesome beheadings to You Tube.

Washington is just waking up to the violence next door. Last December, the U.S. Joint Forces Command's *Joint Operating Environment, 2008* paired Mexico with Pakistan in its discussion of "worst-case scenarios"—states susceptible to "a rapid and sudden collapse." In January, Michael Hayden, the departing CIA chief, claimed that Mexico could become "more problematic than Iraq," and Michael Chertoff, the departing secretary of homeland security, announced that the Department of Homeland Security has a "contingency plan for border violence, so if we did get a significant spillover, we have a surge—if I may use that word—capability." The U.S. media breathlessly proclaims that Mexico is "on the brink."

This rising hysteria clouds the real issues for Mexico and for the United States. The question is not whether the Mexican state will fail. It will not. The Mexican state does, and will continue to, collect taxes, run schools, repair roads, pay salaries, and manage large social programs throughout the country. The civilian-controlled military has already extinguished any real guerrilla threats. The government regularly holds free and fair elections, and its legitimacy, in the eyes of its citizens and of the world, is not questioned.

The actual risk of the violence today is that it will undermine democracy tomorrow. What has changed in Mexico in recent years is not the drug trade but that a fledgling market-based democracy has arisen. Although an authoritarian legacy persists, power now comes from the ballot box. This transformation has coincided with the rise of Mexico's middle class, which, now nearly 30 million strong, has supported more open politics and markets.

But Mexico's democratic system is still fragile. And by disrupting established payoff systems between drug traffickers and government officials, democratization unwittingly exacerbated drug-related violence. The first two freely elected governments have struggled to respond, hampered by electoral competition and the decentralization of political power. Yet in the long run, only through true democratic governance will Mexico successfully conquer, rather than just paper over, its security challenges. For the safety and prosperity of Mexico and the United States, Washington must go beyond its current focus on border control to a more ambitious goal: supporting Mexico's democracy.

■ DRUG PARTIES

Mexico's escalating violence is in part an unintended side effect of democratization and economic globalization. The chaos, anarchy, and violence of the Mexican Revolution—which began nearly a hundred years ago—scarred the country and enabled the rise of a strong state dominated by a single political party. Created in 1929, the National Revolutionary Party, later renamed the Institutional Revolutionary Party (PRI), systematically extended its control over Mexico's territory and people. It quelled political opposition by incorporating important social groups—including workers, peasants, businesspeople, intellectuals, and the military—into its party structure.

The PRI's reach went beyond politics; it created Mexico's ruling economic and social classes. Through an inwardly focused development model (and later by giving away oil money), the government granted monopolies to private-sector supporters, paid off labor leaders, and doled out thousands of public-sector jobs. It provided plum positions and national recognition for loyal intellectuals, artists, and journalists. Famously called "the perfect dictatorship," the PRI used its great patronage machine (backed, of course, by a strong repressive capacity) to subdue dissident voices—and control Mexico for decades.

Ties between the PRI and illegal traders began in the first half of the twentieth century, during Prohibition. By the end of World War II, the relationship between drug traffickers and the ruling party had solidified. Through the Mexican Ministry of the Interior and the federal police, as well as governorships and other political offices, the government established patron-client relationships with drug traffickers (just as it did with other sectors of the economy and society). This arrangement limited violence against public officials, top traffickers, and civilians; made sure that court investigations never reached the upper ranks of cartels; and defined the rules of the game for traffickers. This compact held even as drug production and transit accelerated in the 1970s and 1980s.

Mexico's political opening in the late 1980s and 1990s disrupted these long-standing dynamics. As the PRI's political monopoly ended, so, too, did its control over the drug trade. Electoral competition nullified the unwritten understandings, requiring drug lords to negotiate with the new political establishment and encouraging rival traffickers to bid for new market opportunities. Accordingly, Mexico's drug-related violence rose first in opposition-led states. After the PRI lost its first governorship, in Baja California in 1989, for example, drug-related violence there surged. In Chihuahua, violence followed an opposition takeover in 1992. When the PRI won back the Chihuahua governorship in 1998, the violence moved to Ciudad Juárez—a city governed by the National Action Party (PAN).

With the election of Vicente Fox, the PAN candidate, as president in 2000, the old model—dependent on PRI dominance—was truly broken. Drug-trafficking organizations took advantage of the political opening to gain autonomy, ending their subordination to the government. They focused instead on buying off or intimidating local authorities in order to ensure the safe transit of their goods.

Democratic competition also hampered the state's capacity to react forcefully. Mexico's powerful presidency—the result of party cohesion rather than institutional design—ended. As Congress' influence grew, legislative gridlock weakened President Fox's hand, delaying judicial and police reforms. Conflicts also emerged between the different levels of government. Federal, state, and local officials—who frequently belonged to different parties—often refused to coordinate policies or even share information. At the extreme, this led to armed standoffs—not with drug dealers but between federal, state, and local police forces, such as the one that occurred in Tijuana in 2005.

THE HIGH TIDE

As democratization tilted the balance of power from politicians to criminals, the economics of Mexico's drug business also changed. Mexico has a long history of supplying coveted but illegal substances to U.S. consumers, beginning at the turn of the twentieth century with heroin and marijuana. It continued through Prohibition, as drinkers moved south and Mexican rumrunners sent alcohol north. The marijuana trade picked up in the 1960s and 1970s with rising demand from the U.S. counterculture.

In the late 1970s and 1980s, U.S. cocaine consumption boomed, and Mexican traffickers teamed up with Colombian drug lords to meet the growing U.S. demand.

In the 1980s and 1990s, the United States cracked down on drug transit through the Caribbean and Miami. As a result, more products started going through Mexico and over the U.S.-Mexican border. In 1991, 50 percent of U.S.-bound cocaine came through Mexico; by 2004, 90 percent of U.S.-bound cocaine (and large percentages of other drugs) did. Like other Mexican industries, the drug cartels learned to maximize the comparative advantage of sharing a border with the world's largest consumer. As the transit of drugs to the United States grew, Mexican traffickers gained more power vis-à-vis the Colombian cartels.

These changes in business and enforcement accelerated the consolidation and professionalization of Mexico's drug-trafficking organizations. Rising profitability meant larger operations and more money, and as political and market uncertainty grew, the cartels developed increasingly militarized enforcement arms. The most famous of these branches is the Zetas, who were recruited from an elite Mexican army unit in the 1990s by the Gulf cartel. This group now acts independently, supplying hired guns and functioning as a trafficking organization itself. For many Mexicans, its name has come to signify terror and bloodshed.

From this increasingly sophisticated operational structure, Mexico's drug-trafficking organizations aggressively moved into the markets for heroin and methamphetamine in the United States, as well as the expanding European cocaine market. They extended their influence down the production chain into source countries such as Bolivia, Colombia, and Peru. They established beachheads in Central American and Caribbean nations—which in many cases have much weaker institutions and democracies than Mexico—where they worked their way into the countries' economic, social, and political fabric, to devastating effect. They widened and deepened their U.S. distribution route. In the words of a recent Justice Department report, Mexican drug cartels now represent the "biggest organized crime threat to the United States," with operations in some 230 U.S. cities. They also diversified their domestic operations, with participants expanding into kidnapping, extortion, contraband, and human smuggling.

A HISTORY OF VIOLENCE

The current surge in violence is largely a result of these long-term political and economic processes, but President Calderón self-proclaimed war on drug trafficking has also contributed. Soon after coming into office in December 2006, Calderón sent the army to Nuevo León, Guerrero, Michoacán, and Tijuana, beginning a new phase of government action that now involves some 45,000 troops. Record numbers of interdictions, arrests, and extraditions to the United States have interrupted business as usual. With the older kingpins gone, the second and often third generations of criminal leaders are now vying for territory, control, and power. Many of these aspiring leaders come from the enforcement arms of the cartels—and are accordingly inclined to use even more violence as they try to gain control of fragmented markets. Both the rewriting and the enforcement of illicit contracts mean blood in the streets.

The number of drug-related deaths in 2008 far surpassed those for any other year in Mexican history. Disputes between rival criminal organizations have led to open gun battles on major city streets, often in broad daylight. Death threats have forced dozens of law enforcement and government officials to resign. Extortion rings in many cities prey on businesses, forcing owners to pay to protect their operations and employees. The fear of kidnapping plagues the upper, middle, and working classes alike.

But as concern mounts on both sides of the border, the current situation should be put into perspective. Although unparalleled in scale, today's bloodshed is not unprecedented in type. In the early 1990s, conflict between the Tijuana and Sinaloa cartels engulfed not only the city of Tijuana but also the entire country in violence—including the assassinations of Cardinal Juan Jesus Posadas Ocampo, a Catholic archbishop, and Luis Donaldo Colosio, the pri's presidential candidate These events stirred up fear in both Washington and Mexico City, spurring the United States to strengthen border controls and revive security collaboration with Mexican counterparts (which had all but disappeared in the wake of the murder of the U.S. Drug Enforcement Administration agent Enrique "Kiki" Camarena in 1985). The violence did not decline until 1997, when the Tijuana cartel successfully solidified its hold over the border crossing to San Diego.

As the carnage subsided in Tijuana, it skyrocketed in Ciudad Juárez, which borders El Paso, Texas. There, the violence initially reflected intracartel fighting following the demise of the Juárez cartel leader Amado Carrillo Fuentes, who died while undergoing plastic surgery to change his appearance. It escalated as both the Tijuana and the Sinaloa organizations attempted to take over the territory of the shaken cartel. This wave of bloodshed did not end until 1999, when Vicente Carrillo Fuentes, Amado's brother, gained clear control of the Juárez cartel.

Simmering narco-conflicts again exploded in 2005, this time in the border town of Nuevo Laredo, when the Sinaloa cartel tried to take over the U.S.-Mexican crossing there (the busiest land border between the two countries), which the Gulf cartel had controlled for years. Shootouts in broad daylight with automatic rifles and rocket-propelled grenades prompted the temporary closing of the U.S. consulate in Nuevo Laredo, and the body count quickly rose to over 180. Among the dead were the editor of the largest daily newspaper in the city and the new police chief—who was killed just six hours after his swearing in. President Fox sent in the army, and Secretary Chertoff revived Operation Stonegarden, an initiative to provide up to $400 million in funding to local law enforcement agencies on the U.S. side of the border. Stability returned when the cartels reached a truce in 2007, with the Sinaloa cartel paying the Gulf cartel for access to the Laredo border crossing.

■ THE LAST WAR

This history does not diminish the current danger. It does, however, highlight the inefficacy of rehashing past policy approaches. This is not the first time Mexico has brought out the military to quell drug related violence. President Miguel de la Madrid mobilized troops in the mid-1980s to fight drug gangs, and every subsequent Mexican president has followed suit (although Calderón current effort far surpasses former shows of force). The United States, too, provided equipment, training, and capacity building at various points throughout the 1980s and 1990s. If history is any lesson, these approaches will neither stem the violence nor provide real border security.

Instead, the United States needs to develop a comprehensive policy to bolster North American security—one that treats Mexico as an equal and permanent partner. Mexico must continue to challenge the drug cartels, and the United States, in turn, must address its own role in perpetuating the drug trade and drug-related violence. But more important, Mexico and the United States need to work together to broaden their focus beyond immediate security measures—fostering Mexico's democracy and growing middle class. Only then can they overcome the security challenges facing both nations.

> **The United States needs to take a hard look at its own role in the rising violence in Mexico.**

To start, the United States needs to take a hard look at its own role in the escalating violence and instability in Mexico. This means enforcing its own laws—and rethinking its own priorities. When it comes to the gun trade, U.S. law prohibits the sale of weapons to foreign nationals or "straw buyers," who use their clean criminal records to buys arms for others. It also forbids the unlicensed export of guns to Mexico. Nevertheless, over 90 percent of the guns seized in Mexico and traced are found to have come from the United States. These include not just pistols but also cartel favorites such as AR-15s and AK-47-style semiautomatic rifles. To stop this "iron river" of guns, Washington must inspect traffic on the border going south—not just north—and increase the resources for the Bureau of Alcohol, Tobacco, Firearms and Explosives. (Even with recent additional deployments, a mere 250 ATF officers and inspectors cover the 2,000-mile border.) This effort should also include a broader program of outreach and education, encouraging responsible sales at gun shops and shows and deterring potential straw buyers with more explicit warnings of the punishment they would face if caught. Reducing the tools of violence in Mexico is a first step in addressing U.S. responsibility.

Even more important than guns, although less discussed, is money. Estimates of illicit profits range widely, but most believe some $15 billion to $25 billion heads across the U.S. border into the hands of Mexico's drug cartels each year. This money buys guns, people, and power. Compiled from thousands of retail drug sales in hundreds of U.S. cities, much of this money is wired, carried, or transported to the U.S.-Mexican border and then simply driven south in bulk. Mexican criminal organizations then launder the funds by using seemingly legal business fronts, such as used-car lots, import-export businesses, or foreign exchange houses. Laundered money not used to fund criminal operations or pay off officials in Mexico is often sent back to the United States and saved in U.S. bank accounts.

Targeting illicit funds is one of the most effective ways of dealing with drug trafficking. (Incarcerating individuals only briefly disrupts criminal operations, since people are swiftly replaced.) Washington has begun working with Mexican authorities to stop the flow of illicit funds. There have been some successes, such as the passage of an asset forfeiture law in Mexico, the addition of Mexican cartels to the U.S. drug kingpin list, and the strengthening of Mexico's financial intelligence unit. The United States should continue and deepen this bilateral cooperation, further developing financial tools and infrastructure to increase the information and intelligence sharing needed to dismantle money-laundering schemes. At home, the United States should work to replicate the successes of the interagency Foreign Terrorist Asset Tracking Center, which was ramped up after 9/11 to thwart terrorist financing, by creating a similar structure to go after drug-related money.

Law enforcement, however, is not enough. The supply of drugs follows demand. The United States needs to shift the emphasis of its drug policy toward demand reduction. Studies show that a dollar spent on reducing demand in the United States is vastly more effective than a dollar spent on eradication and interdiction abroad and that money designated for the treatment of addicts is five times as effective as that spent on conventional law enforcement. The United States needs to expand its drug-treatment and drug-education programs and other measures to rehabilitate addicts and lessen drugs' allure for those not yet hooked. Reduced demand would lower the drug profits that corrupt officials, buy guns, and threaten Mexico's democracy.

■ THE OTHER SIDE

As the United States deals with the problems in its own backyard, it should also be helping Mexico address its challenges. Until just last year, the United States provided less than $40 million a year in security funding to its southern neighbour—in stark contrast to the $600 million designated for Colombia. This changed last June with Congress' passage of the Merida Initiative, which called for supplying $1.4 billion worth of equipment, software, and technical assistance to Mexico's military, police, and judicial forces over three years.

Despite its many laudable elements, the Merida Initiative does not go far enough fast enough. For one thing, it is just too small. The current budget for Plan Colombia is twice as large as Mexico's 2009 allotment—and that

is for a country that does not share a border with the United States. And even the support for Plan Colombia pales next to the billions of dollars U.S. drug consumers supply to Mexico's enemies in this confrontation. Compared to other U.S. national security threats, Mexico remains an afterthought.

The spending has also been far too slow. Although $700 million had been released by Congress as of April 2009, only $7 million had been spent. Despite the touted urgency, a cumbersome consultation process between the two countries, combined with a complicated dispersement process (since all of the assistance is in kind, not cash), has meant little headway even as the deaths mount. Most important, the focus of this aid is too narrow, reflecting a misunderstanding of Mexico's fundamental challenge. Unlike Colombia, which had to retake vast swaths of territory from guerrilla groups, paramilitary organizations, and drug cartels, the Mexican state has been able to quell the rising violence when it has deployed large and well-armed military units. So far, the cartels have put up limited resistance in the face of true shows of force by the state—for instance, when the government sent in 7,000 troops to Ciudad Juárez in March 2009. Firepower is not the main issue; sustainability is.

Mexico's Achilles' heel is corruption—which in an electoral democracy cannot be stabilizing the way it was in the days of Mexico's autocracy. Under the PRI, the purpose of government policy was to assert power rather than govern by law. The opacity of court proceedings, the notorious graft of the police forces, and the menacing presence of special law enforcement agencies were essential elements of an overall system of political, economic, and social control. Rather than acting as a check or balance on executive power, the judiciary was often just another arm of the party, used to reward supporters and intimidate opponents. Law enforcement, too, was used to control, rather than protect, the population.

The decline of the PRI and the onset of electoral competition transformed the workings of the executive and legislative branches quite quickly, but the changes have had much less influence over the judicial branch or over law enforcement more generally. Instead, even after the transition to democracy, accountability mechanisms remain either nonexistent or defunct. Most of Mexico's various police forces continue to be largely incapable of objective and thorough investigations, having never received adequate resources or training. Impunity reigns: the chance of being prosecuted, much less convicted, of a crime is extremely low. As a result, Mexicans place little faith in their law enforcement and judicial systems. And as today's democratic government struggles to overcome this history through legislative reform, funding new programs for vetting and training and creating more avenues for citizen involvement, it faces a new threat: increasingly sophisticated, well-funded, and autonomous criminal organizations intent on manipulating the rule of law for their own benefit.

The Merida Initiative provides some funding for institution building, but that is dwarfed by the amount spent on hardware. Furthermore, although Mexico's lawlessness is most intractable at the state and local levels, the Merida funding focuses almost solely on the federal level. This neglects some 325,000 officers—90 percent of the nation's police. It leaves out those on the frontlines who are most likely to face the ultimate Faustian bargain—money or death—from organized crime. The United States should expand Merida's focus to incorporate local and state-level initiatives and training, including vetting mechanisms similar to those envisioned for federal agents, training for local crime labs, training for judges and lawyers, and support for community policing programs. In the end, all lasting security is local.

■ DISORDER ON THE BORDER

Improving security will depend above all, however, on other dimensions of the complex U.S.-Mexican relationship—including trade, economic development, and immigration. To really overcome Mexico's security challenges, the United States must move beyond a short-term threat-based mentality to one that considers all these elements in the strategic relationship with its southern neighbor.

The foremost challenge in Mexico today, at least according to most Mexicans, is in fact the growing economic crisis. Even during Mexico's protectionist days, its fortunes rose and fell along with those of its northern neighbor. Today, the economies and general well-being of Mexico and the United States are even more linked. Some 80 percent of Mexico's exports—well over $200 billion worth—go to the United States. Mexico's tourism industry—which brings in $11 billion annually—depends on 15 million American vacationers each year. The large Mexican and Mexican American populations living in the United States—estimated at 12 million and 28 million, respectively—transfer nearly $25 billion a year to family and friends in Mexico.

This relationship runs the other way as well. After Canada, Mexico is the second most important destination for U.S. exports, receiving one-ninth of U.S. goods sent abroad. It is either the primary or the secondary destination for exports from 22 of the 50 U.S. states. Hundreds of thousands—if not millions—of American jobs depend on consumers and industries in Mexico. And increasingly, U.S. citizens depend on Mexico for even more, as over one million individual Americans—from young professionals to adventurous snowbirds—now live there.

The U.S. recession is hitting Mexico's economy exceptionally hard. In January, Mexico's GDP shrank by nearly ten percent year on year as manufacturing tumbled. In March, the Peso sodded to a 16-year low against the dollar. The government now predicts a three-and-a-half percent decline in GDP for 2009, and many private economists are bracing for an even greater fall. Policymakers are beginning to worry about rising unemployment, poverty, and even social unrest. Some ten million Mexicans still live on just $2 a day, and economists predict that the downturn will push more Mexicans into poverty.

Nowhere else are the asymmetries between two such interlinked neighbors so severe. In its own self-interest, the United States should work with Mexico on a new economic development strategy. The United States can start by lessening the barriers to trade with Mexico. This will require resolving the current trucking dispute (fulfilling U.S. obligations under the North American Free Trade Agreement [NAFTA] by allowing Mexican trucks to operate on both sides of the border) and avoiding protectionist measures, such as the recent "Buy American" provision in the stimulus package. It will also require investing in the border itself. Nearly one million people and $1 billion in trade cross the border every day, overwhelming the existing infrastructure and border personnel and leading to long and unpredictable border delays, which limit Mexico's competitiveness. The U.S. Department of Transportation currently estimates that $11 billion more will need to be spent on the U.S. side of the border to catch up with the growing traffic.

The United States should also help create opportunities within Mexico. This means expanding development assistance, rather than just security assistance. At less than $5 million for 2009, current U.S. development aid to Mexico is paltry. Increased assistance should focus on supporting Mexico's efforts to expand its education and infrastructure programs and encourage local entrepreneurship and job creation.

Intertwined with both the economy and security is immigration. Economic opportunities in the United States, and their absence at home, draw millions of Mexicans north. Subsequent remittances provide a lifeline for millions of Mexican households and have brought many families out of poverty and into the bottom rungs of Mexico's middle class. At the same time, immigration to the United States pulls away many of Mexico's best and brightest, limiting the spillover benefits of their work on the larger economy and society.

Most studies show that immigration provides net benefits to the United States, including providing flexible workers to labor-scarce economic sectors, lowering the prices of domestically produced labor-intensive goods and services, and contributing to entitlement programs such as Social Security. The illegality of these human flows, however, has its costs. It depresses local wages and puts pressure on local health and education services, and it can undermine labor rights. In terms of security, the presence of millions of unauthorized workers in the United States gives unsavory elements a place to hide among a larger population forced to live underground. Illicit profits can be hidden in the flow of honestly earned money going back to Mexico, complicating efforts against money laundering.

The United States views immigration as a domestic concern, but when it comes to Mexico, this perspective is both inaccurate and counterproductive. During her April 2009 visit to Mexico, Janet Napolitano, the U.S. secretary of homeland security, announced, with Patricia Espinosa, the Mexican foreign secretary, a new high-level joint working group to make immigration safer and more orderly. This is a step toward greater consultation and cooperation. Still, fundamental and comprehensive immigration reform in the United States is necessary to address the economic and security concerns on both sides of the border. New policies should be designed not only to improve border security and management. They should also regularize the status of the unauthorized work force already in the United States, ensure employer verification and responsibility, and create an expanded flexible worker program to meet changing U.S. economic demands.

Finally, U.S. policy toward Mexico must become more coherent. The U.S. diplomatic presence in Mexico—which includes an embassy, nine consulates, and 14 consular agencies—is one of the largest diplomatic missions in the world. It houses representatives from not only enforcement and investigative agencies, such as the ATF, the Drug Enforcement Administration, and the Department of Homeland Security, but also 37 additional agencies and departments, ranging from the Department of Agriculture to the U.S. Agency for International Development. Disorganization has led to a lack of policy coherence, as no organization is able or willing to take the lead in guiding the overall bilateral relationship. Washington needs to strengthen coordination among the agencies, bringing together the multiple interests and agendas they represent into a more coherent strategy.

■ MENDING FENCES

U.S. leaders and the press commonly tout President Calderón's commitment to fighting the Mexican cartels as something exceptional. Congressman Connie Mack (R-Fla.) has said, for example, "This is a president who has taken the drug cartels head-on, and has not flinched in the fight to rid Mexico of these cowards." Although true, this image misses the real political dynamic behind Calderón fight. Rather than a quixotic lone crusader, he is a shrewd politician responding to voter demands.

> **Rather than a lone crusader, Calderón is a politician responding to voters' demands.**

Like his predecessor, Calderón was elected by Mexico's burgeoning middle class—now nearly one-third of the population. Long noted for the disparities between the extremely wealthy and the desperately poor, Mexico now has an economic center that is rapidly expanding. The middle class has grown thanks to NAFTA and Mexico's broader economic opening, a boom in immigration to the United States that has sent billions of dollars back to families at home, and a decade of economic stability and growth that has enabled average citizens to work, save, and plan for the future. Mexico's middle-class families work in small businesses, own their cars and homes, and strive to send their children to college. And as voters, they threw out the PRI in 2000, bringing an end to its 70-year rule. Since then, they have been behind halting steps to create new civil-society organizations and to

demand public transparency, judicial reform, and safety. It is these voters who tilted the election in Calderón's favor in 2006—and it is to them he is responding.

Security ranks second only to the economy in terms of voter priorities. Polls show that the middle class (as well as other segments of society) wants the government to take on the narcotraffickers, even if it creates more violence in the short run—and even though many think the government cannot win. Calderón's ratings have risen as he has confronted organized crime, with fully two-thirds of the public supporting his actions.

Mexican middle-class preferences for law and order, fairness, transparency, and democracy benefit Mexico, but they also benefit the United States. Although hardly an antidote for all challenges, a secure and growing middle class would help move Mexico further down the road toward achieving democratic prosperity and toward an increasingly able partnership with the United States. But if this center is diminished or decimated by economic crisis, insecurity, or closing opportunities, Mexico could truly descend into crime-ridden political and economic turmoil.

The best the United States and Mexico can hope for in terms of security is for organized crime in Mexico to become a persistent but manageable law enforcement problem, similar to illegal businesses in the United States. But both the United States and Mexico should hope for more in terms of Mexico's future, and for the future of U.S.-Mexican relations. U.S. policies that help increase accountability, expand economic and social opportunity, and strengthen the rule of law in Mexico will all encouragea more inclusive and more stable democracy there. This will require a difficult conceptual shift in Washington—recognizing Mexico as a permanent strategic partner rather than an often-forgotten neighbor.

Shannon O'Neil is Douglas Dillon Fellow for Latin America Studies at the Council on Foreign Relations and Director of the CFR task force on U.S.–Latin American relations.

From *Foreign Affairs*, July/August 2009, pp. 63–77. Copyright © 2009 by Council on Foreign Relations. Reprinted by permission. www.ForeignAffairs.com

Challenge Questions

After reading this article, you will be able to answer the following questions:

1. Why must trade, economic development, and immigration be considered in any discussion of the drug-trafficking problem?
2. What steps can the United States take to aid Mexico?
3. How significant is corruption in the fight against the drug cartels?
4. Is a secure and growing middle class part of any solution?

8 Central America's Security Predicament

Michael Shifter

Learning Objectives

After reading this article, you will more clearly understand the following:

- The sources of instability in Central America
- The problems caused by drug-trafficking
- The impact of increased criminal activity and violence

In retrospect, it was probably naïve to expect that, with the signing of the last of the Central American peace accords (Guatemala, 1996), the heightened civil strife that beset the region for decades would give way to a greater measure of social peace. Although Central America can celebrate the virtual end of political violence over the past 15 years, the five countries of the isthmus that in the 1980s were in the international spotlight on account of instability—Guatemala, El Salvador, Honduras, Nicaragua, and Costa Rica— are, to varying degrees, still notably troubled.

That this is true even of Costa Rica—the Central American nation most known for (relative) tranquility, social progress, and democratic performance—speaks to the depth of the problems in the region. Indeed, at the end of 2010 Costa Rica found itself increasingly contending with drug-fueled violence and also experiencing a tense standoff with neighboring Nicaragua over a disputed border area. Yet, despite Costa Rica's difficulties, the country's position remains comparatively advantageous. It is better equipped institutionally than its more vulnerable neighbors to withstand the global pressures and strains that contribute to societal disintegration.

The region has registered, to be sure, some impressive economic, political, and social gains in recent years, including higher levels of political competition within countries. These achievements have mostly been eclipsed, however, by an overall deterioration in security conditions and by continuing economic stagnation. Unfavorable external conditions and internal decay and fragmentation have produced societies with increasingly urgent problems.

Central America has been squeezed by rising energy costs—the region has little choice but to import its oil and gas—and has suffered disproportionately from the financial and economic crisis that originated in the United States in 2008 and continues to be acutely felt. Remittance flows from the United States, which are critical to sustaining the region's economies, have sharply dropped as a result of the economic downturn.

Meanwhile, precarious political institutions and endemic poverty and inequality have rendered governance challenges daunting. The results of the 2010 Latinobarómetro report, a region-wide public opinion survey, reveal that Central Americans are particularly tepid in their support of democracy.

Such ambivalence is understandable in light of the ominous tendencies of both organized and common crime in the subregion. Pervasive fear often corresponds to objective data on violence. According to a study carried out in 2008 by the Latin American Public Opinion Project, high crime levels significantly erode interpersonal trust and tend to fray the social fabric on which democracies are constructed. The study found that, in the five Central American countries, roughly 14 percent to 19 percent of citizens said they had been victims of crime during the preceding 12 months.

Other research has highlighted the explosive growth of private security companies that often outstrip official police forces and typically function without controls or regulation. A 2009 United Nations Development Program report showed that in Guatemala and Honduras private security personnel outnumber police forces by five to ten times. No Central American country has more police than private security officers. Economic costs associated with anti-crime measures absorb an increasing share of national budgets throughout the subregion.

Regrettably, Central America is often overlooked compared with other regions within Latin America. While South America, led by Brazil, has drawn praise for its remarkable ascent, and Mexico has dominated headlines because of its unrelenting and particularly brutal criminality, Central American nations have been off the international radar and are at best treated as an afterthought.

Yet what is taking place both north and south of Central America is contributing to the deepening predicament of the region, which has become a hub for drug trafficking routes. Only recently has concern substantially increased in Washington and elsewhere regarding a set of countries that occupied center stage—and generated moderately high hopes and expectations—just two decades ago.

■ GUATEMALAN GANGLAND?

Recent developments in Guatemala have especially alarmed observers and policy officials. Guatemala is Central America's largest country and also the one where a decades-long civil war took the greatest toll, with 200,000 dead. Longstanding inequities highlighted by sharp ethnic divisions— Guatemala's population is majority indigenous—have posed formidable challenges for governing the country.

Guatemala has among the region's lowest tax rates, with notoriously fierce resistance from wealthy sectors to contributing their fair share, and this has made it even more difficult to redress the glaring disparities.

However, while political violence and old-fashioned militarism have subsided, there has been a striking surge in the penetration of organized crime in all spheres of the nation. Analysts often refer to dark forces and parallel structures that engage in illicit activities and operate with nearly assured impunity. Judicial and police institutions are riddled with corruption. The country's governance structures are too weak and ineffective to cope with such powerful pressures. In this context, the International Commission Against Impunity in Guatemala (CICIG) performs a fundamental role. A special judicial body assembled in cooperation with the United Nations, the CICIG began its work in 2007 with the aim of supporting efforts by the country's flawed criminal justice system to root out criminal networks operating inside government bodies.

A succession of murky and complicated incidents in recent years has highlighted disturbing trends in the country. In May 2009, the killing of a Guatemalan lawyer, Rodrigo Rosenberg, became a major political controversy after a video was made public in which Rosenberg, before he died, blamed President Alvaro Colom for his assassination. The CICIG investigated the Rosenberg case and in January 2010 announced detailed findings concluding that Rosenberg staged his own murder in an attempt to call attention to the killing of his son, in which Rosenberg believed Colom had had a hand.

The CICIG investigations also led to the arrest of a former president, Alfonso Portillo, on corruption charges and in response to an extradition request from the United States on money laundering charges. And the commission contributed to the arrest in March 2010 of a former national police chief, Baltazar Gómez, for involvement with drug trafficking and blocking an investigation of corrupt police officers.

In June 2010, however, the head of CICIG, a Spanish lawyer named Carlos Castresana, resigned out of frustration, complaining that the Guatemalan government had not been following the commission's recommendations and that there was an active campaign to discredit the CICIG among groups with an entrenched interest in continued impunity.

The resignation was provoked by the Colom government's appointment of Conrado Reyes as attorney general—after the CICIG had identified Reyes as having ties to drug trafficking and illegal adoption rings. Castresana's decision created a political firestorm, and the country's Constitutional Court ultimately rejected Reyes's appointment on grounds that the selection process may have been influenced by organized crime. The UN then appointed Costa Rican Attorney General Francisco Dall'Anese, a renowned advocate against organized crime, to succeed Castresana as the CICIG's head.

Another illustration of the sort of convoluted intrigue that increasingly characterizes Guatemala occurred in early December 2010, when a Guatemalan court sentenced eight people to prison for lengthy terms for involvement in the February 2007 murders of three Salvadoran members of the Central American Parliament and their driver. The CICIG had worked closely with Guatemalan prosecutors on the case, and among those sentenced was a former Guatemalan congressman charged with masterminding the killing. The court ruled that the four men had been murdered at the behest of a Salvadoran legislator who had been expelled from his party over allegations of criminal activity. The murders were actually carried out by four Guatemalan police officers, who were slain in a high-security prison just days after being arrested.

And in January 2011, a bomb attack on a bus in Guatemala City claimed seven lives. In recent years, the country's public transport has been increasingly subjected to extortion by organized crime groups (a member of the Mara 18 gang was charged in the January attack). In 2010, according to Guatemalan police, bus drivers paid out over $1.5 million in extortion money. Local rights groups report that 119 of the country's bus drivers and 51 other transport workers were murdered last year.

As if the security situation and the fragility of political institutions were not serious enough, Guatemala has been profoundly affected by the brutal and bloody cartel battles being waged in Mexico. Fighting among Mexican drug cartels and the aggressive response by the government of Felipe Calderón not only have resulted in more than 30,000 deaths since the start of the Calderón administration. They also have pushed the cartels further south, into northern Guatemala, where they increasingly wreak havoc in an already battered nation that has few defenses.

Members of Los Zetas, a Mexican drug trafficking group, and the Sinaloa drug cartel now routinely attack local law enforcement officials and control substantial swaths of territory, according to a US State Department report. As the journalist Steven Dudley has written in *Foreign Policy,* "as Mexico and Colombia cracked down on their own drug trafficking problems, the criminals sought new refuge, and Guatemala fit the bill: a weak government, a strategic location, and a bureaucracy whose allegiance came cheap." At present the homicide rate in Guatemala is four times that in Mexico.

On December 19, 2010, the Guatemalan government, worried that the situation was spiraling out of control, declared a state of siege in the northern province of Alta Verapaz, large areas of which had reportedly been taken over by Mexican drug traffickers. As an *Associated Press* dispatch observed two days later, "Gangs roamed the streets with assault rifles and armored vehicles, attacking whomever they pleased and abducting women who caught their eye. Shootouts became so common residents couldn't tell gunfire from holiday fireworks." Local leaders from the province, which had become a prime corridor for drug trafficking from Honduras to Mexico, said they had been requesting the intervention of federal authorities for two years.

Undisciplined and fractured political parties aggravate the dire situation in a country that the International Crisis Group has called a "paradise for criminals." Colom's party, for example, holds barely a fifth of the seats in the legislature. This has made promises of greater social inclusion nearly impossible to achieve. According to the World Bank, more than half the population lives in poverty.

While it still may not be accurate (or constructive) to depict Guatemala as a "failed state" or "narco-state," mounting evidence points to conditions of rampant lawlessness that warrant considerable alarm. The real risk is that, with a presidential election scheduled for the fall of 2011, unchecked criminality could trigger reflexes for more authoritarian approaches that evoke what was widely thought to be a bygone era.

■ HONDURAS IS MURDER

Together with Guatemala and El Salvador, Honduras forms part of the so-called "Northern Triangle," a doorway for cocaine traffic into Mexico. The World Drug Report of 2010, published by the UN Office on Drugs and Crime, documents that this territory has the highest murder rates of any region in the world, with more than 50 homicides each year per 100,000 people. *The Economist* notes that Honduras currently has the highest murder rate in the world, at 67 per 100,000; the murder rate in the United States, by contrast, is 5.4 per 100,000.

According to the UN report, Honduras is the Central American country that is most affected by the drug trade. With dense jungle territories and the longest Caribbean coastline, Honduras is positioned as the first corner of the triangle, leading into trade routes that eventually reach Mexico and the United States. The Mexican cartels have penetrated Honduras, as have expanding criminal gangs with readily accessible firearms. The Sinaloa cartel is reported to have assassinated Honduras's top counter-drug official in December 2009 over the seizure of a pseudoephedrine shipment. A plot by the Zetas to kill the minister of security was thwarted in early 2010.

Honduras's highly unsettling security situation has been exacerbated by a still-unresolved political crisis that has undermined governance and, in turn, has tended to benefit drug trafficking organizations and criminal gangs. More than a year and a half after Honduras suffered a military coup that dislodged the constitutionally elected government of Manuel Zelaya (who is in exile in the Dominican Republic), the country remains profoundly polarized between Zelaya's supporters and those associated with the de facto government that took control in June 2009, led by Roberto Micheletti.

In accordance with previously scheduled elections, a new government headed by Porfirio Lobo of the National Party took office in January 2010 and has struggled to navigate and overcome the country's sharp divisions. Conciliatory measures to defuse tensions have borne scant fruit. Distrust and bitterness on both sides compound the difficulties of addressing the country's daunting policy agenda, which includes not just expanding criminality but also high levels of unemployment and deepening social and economic distress.

A truth commission directed by Guatemala's former foreign minister and vice president Eduardo Stein has sought to pursue a balanced approach and heal the wounds, but the undertaking has not garnered broad support and has been criticized from both sides. A clear measure of the country's polarization can be seen in the reaction to a July 2009 diplomatic cable by US ambassador Hugo Llorens, which was leaked by Wikileaks, in which Llorens clearly called the ouster of Zelaya unconstitutional. Whereas coup supporters were upset that the United States adopted a critical stance toward a move they regarded as justified, coup opponents were puzzled that Washington failed to respond to such a depiction with more forceful action against the de facto government.

Honduras continues to be a significant source of discord and strain in inter-American relations. The coup caused member states of the Organization of American States (OAS), the hemisphere's chief political body, to expel Honduras—only the second country, after Cuba (1962), to have met such a fate. Despite substantial pressure to recognize the Lobo government that has been exerted by the United States and all but one of Honduras's Central American neighbors (Nicaragua), key players in regional political affairs still deem the government illegitimate—including Venezuela (Zelaya was an ally of Venezuela's president, Hugo Chávez) and, most crucially, Brazil (Zelaya took refuge in Brazil's embassy in Tegucigalpa, the capital of Honduras, before going into exile). The continued ostracism of the country from regional forums has complicated Honduras's ability to secure needed funds from multilateral financial institutions and has slowed down the government's attempts to ameliorate the nation's acute socioeconomic ills.

Indeed, the economic impact of the political crisis since June 2009 has been quite significant. It is estimated that 200,000 jobs were lost as a direct result of it. Some 36 percent of the workforce was unemployed or underemployed in 2009. Not surprisingly, foreign investment also suffered, with the Honduran central bank reporting a drop of almost 50 percent from 2008 levels, though the global economic downturn surely played a part in that as well. More recently, access to international capital has eased.

One particularly troubling phenomenon in Honduras, which reflects the confluence of security and political crises, has been the killing of journalists (which is also a serious problem in Mexico, though less so in other Central American nations). In 2010, eight journalists in Honduras were murdered. Several of them reported on organized crime, whereas others, according to rights groups, may have been targets of political crimes. In any case, all of the murders have gone unpunished.

In a July 2010 report, the Committee to Protect Journalists accused the Honduran government of "fostering a climate of lawlessness that is allowing criminals to kill with impunity." Buttressing that assessment was a December 2010 report issued by Human Rights Watch, entitled "After the Coup: Ongoing Violence, Intimidation, and Impunity in Honduras." The report documented some 47 attacks or threats against journalists, human rights defenders, and political activists during Lobo's first year in office.

EL SALVADOR TESTED

El Salvador, since the two sides to the country's bitter and bloody civil war signed a peace agreement in 1992, has seen a huge upsurge in gang violence. There are an estimated 30,000 gang members in a country of just over 6 million. This phenomenon, which has become more associated with El Salvador than with other countries in Central America, has to some degree offset the welcome peace dividends that accompanied the end of political violence. The legacies of the armed conflict—along with a proliferation of firearms, enduring socioeconomic woes, and transnational contacts with US-based gangs (an element of which is increased deportations from the United States back to El Salvador)—have resulted in a toxic mix.

Many observers were hopeful that, with the election of President Mauricio Funes in 2009, El Salvador would be better able to develop the institutional capacity to cope with its monumental security and social problems. After nearly two decades of rule by the rightist Arena party, Funes is El Salvador's first elected president from the FMLN (Farabundo Martí National Liberation Front), the party of the demobilized guerrilla movement that fought in the civil conflict (1979–92). Funes's election carried enormous symbolic significance and heightened expectations for a region seeking to bridge longstanding ideological chasms.

Funes, governing largely as a moderate pragmatist, has tried to model his government after that of Luiz Inácio Lula da Silva, Brazil's hugely successful former president. Operating within significant constraints, Funes has accorded more emphasis to poverty-alleviation strategies than his predecessors, presiding over important advances in education and health care. His administration's foreign policies have been notably centrist. El Salvador's posture toward the United States has been accommodating, and regarding the Honduras controversy the Funes administration has been supportive of President Lobo, strongly urging other Latin American governments to recognize his elected government.

According to public opinion surveys, Funes's political approach has wide appeal in a country weary of partisan rancor. Yet the president faces fierce resistance from his FMLN party, which is pressing for a more radical agenda, as well as from factions of the opposition Arena, and he has yet to build a solid governing structure. To do so will require considerable political skill and a measure of luck, but most importantly concrete results in improving El Salvador's security and economic conditions. This will not be easy, especially in light of declining remittances coming from the United States to a country that relies heavily on such flows.

In confronting the security challenge, Funes has moved to criminalize gang membership and has also tried to appeal to Central American neighbors to pursue more coordinated efforts to reduce the spread of criminality, which poses the greatest threat to rule of law in the region. It is far from clear, however, that such measures, however well intentioned, will succeed in arresting the overall deterioration. The growing presence of Mexican drug trafficking organizations in El Salvador could well overwhelm efforts to deal with the gang phenomenon, which has been around since the 1990s.

NICARAGUA'S STRONG MAN

Beyond and beneath the Northern Triangle, one finds a greater measure of tranquility. With 14 murders per 100,000 citizens, Nicaragua is almost a model of social peace compared to Guatemala, Honduras, and El Salvador. Part of the explanation for this is the country's more consistently professional police force, which has been maintained since the transition from Sandinista revolutionary rule to democratic, elected government in 1990.

While crime is less rampant, however, the perpetuation in power of Daniel Ortega remains a concern. Ortega, who has led the Sandinista National Liberation Front since 1979 and was president of Nicaragua from 1985 until his defeat at the polls in 1990, was elected president in 2006 after a number of failed runs for the office. Now he is scarcely disguising his intention to stay on as president: He plans to run again in 2011 despite the fact that doing so is unconstitutional. Through shrewd manipulation of institutions (for example, illegally extending the terms of two Sandinista judges); frequent use of decree authority; cynical and convenient political pacts with prominent opposition figures (especially the former president Arnoldo Alemán); and some moderately successful social programs, Ortega appears to be in a strong position to pull it off.

This is particularly so because there is no guarantee the voting process will be free and fair. Local elections in 2008, in which no outside observers were permitted, were widely deemed to be fraudulent. Ortega's brand of strongman rule, marked by the steady erosion of checks and constraints on executive authority, recalls certain features of the dictatorship of Anastasio Somoza (1967–1979), against which Ortega and his fellow Sandinistas fought in the 1970s. To date, Ortega has been able to proceed with his blatant power grab with little response from the rest of the hemisphere, which is politically fragmented and is not focused on the Nicaraguan situation.

Despite Ortega's alliance with President Chávez, and despite Nicaragua's participation in the Chávez-led regional group ALBA (Bolivarian Alliance for the Americas), ideology has for Ortega clearly taken a back seat to sheer power politics. He appears ready to do whatever is necessary to remain in power. Ortega has, for example, been quite accommodating with international financial institutions and even parts of Nicaragua's private sector. And, occasionally harsh rhetoric notwithstanding, he has been open to dealing with the United States, even fully honoring the 2005 Central American Free Trade Agreement.

In October 2010—in a move few regard as unrelated to Ortega's quest to remain in power—some 50 Nicaraguan troops were sent to a disputed zone on the country's border with Costa Rica, presumably to help dredge the San Juan River. That led Costa Rica to mobilize some of its police force (Costa Rica abolished its military in 1948), resulting in a tense standoff. The OAS has intervened but, despite the adoption of several resolutions, has so far been unable to get Ortega to withdraw the soldiers. The Costa Rican government has also appealed to the International Court of Justice in The Hague for a resolution of the conflict.

Not surprisingly, the dispute has aroused nationalist sentiment in both countries, and has thus boosted Ortega's political standing as he prepares for the 2011 race amid intense controversy over a 2009 Supreme Court ruling that exempted him from the constitutional ban on consecutive reelection. In alliance with Alemán, Ortega also has successfully turned to the national assembly to support legislation that would provide a new framework for the country's defense and security policies, including the formation of an intelligence-gathering network.

Critics warn of further erosion of the rule of law and the prospect of growing militarization of Nicaraguan society. Some observers are also worried about the politicization of the country's police forces, which so far have been an important factor in guarding against the rise and penetration of organized crime that have afflicted Guatemala, Honduras, and El Salvador.

■ VULNERABLE COSTA RICA

Although Costa Rica on nearly all institutional and social measures is more advanced than its Central American neighbors, it is far from immune to some of the wider phenomena creating security problems in the region. At the end of 2010 the government of President Laura Chinchilla of the center-left National Liberation Party was clearly preoccupied with the tense impasse with Nicaragua.

By resorting to the OAS and the International Court of Justice, Chinchilla, Costa Rica's first woman president and a noted expert on public security matters, was pursuing diplomatic and legal options to keep the situation from getting out of control. Further, as the only Central American country with relations with China (established under the previous administration of Oscar Arias), Costa Rica is focused on attracting investment and boosting trade.

Chinchilla's professional background and expertise may turn out to be useful in addressing the problem of drug-related violence, which is putting a strain on Costa Rican institutions. Unlike its neighbors, Costa Rica does not have armed forces, so it cannot deploy military units as other countries have done to bolster police presence and combat spreading criminality. Thus, while Costa Rica does not face the risk of "militarizing" what is fundamentally a law enforcement issue, it is vulnerable to a problem that its police forces may not be fully equipped to handle.

As a result, in accordance with a Joint Maritime Agreement, the United States military, with some 46 warships and 7,000 troops off the coast, has been granted permission to enter the country should the need arise. Although the decision has generated some minor controversy in the country, for the most part the bilateral deal has not so far posed a serious political problem. For Costa Ricans, along with other Central Americans, security has become an increasingly salient concern.

■ CENTRAL AMERICA'S TRAVAILS

Survey after survey point to the same finding: Security is the overriding issue for most Central Americans. Available data tend to bear out the widespread perception: The end of political, armed conflict 15 years ago has not been accompanied by higher levels of social peace. On the contrary, fear and lawlessness today are rampant in the region. This situation is the product of precarious governance structures, including ineffective judicial institutions and incoherent political parties, along with a far from propitious external environment. High energy costs and the consequences of the severe economic downturn in the United States—particularly in sectors of the economy in which Hispanics are disproportionately active—have hit Central America with unusual force.

Mechanisms of integration, both within the Central American subregion and across the hemisphere, have to date not responded adequately to the worsening problems—particularly the organized crime in Guatemala, Honduras, and El Salvador, and the authoritarianism in Nicaragua. The US-backed Mérida Initiative, started under the George W. Bush administration and extended under President Barack Obama, has essentially sought to assist Mexico, through the provision of various kinds of equipment and training, in its enormously difficult fight against drug-fueled violence and organized crime. Within that package of some $1.6 billion over three years, however, relatively few resources have been directed further south, to Central America, despite the problems aggravated by drug trafficking and the war on drugs.

To its credit, the Obama administration has become increasingly concerned with the deteriorating security situation in Central America. In August 2010, the State Department launched the Central American Regional Security Initiative, which lists a set of laudable aims and proposes to devote $165 million to supporting law enforcement and judicial institutions in the region as well as an array of social and economic programs. In September the administration added Honduras, Nicaragua, and Costa Rica to the United States' list of countries with major drug trafficking or producing problems.

257

Given the magnitude of the challenge and the high stakes involved, however, it is not clear whether such efforts, however worthwhile, will be sufficient to deal effectively with problems that require sustained, high-level political attention and a more robust and energized multilateral system. For Washington, a broader strategy would, for example, focus seriously on stemming continuing flows of arms and money from the United States to the region; fostering more genuine cooperation among Central American governments and other Latin American countries, particularly Mexico; and rethinking an anti-drug policy that has yielded such disappointing results.

Although Central America's crime problem cannot be reduced to drugs—illicit activities flourish in a number of different areas—it is a key factor in the overall situation and, if properly addressed, would help mitigate the worst consequences of criminality.

■ SHARED RESPONSIBILITY

The urgent need for a comprehensive approach was highlighted in August 2010, when 72 migrants—most of them from Central America—were executed by the Zetas, the Mexican drug trafficking group. In pursuit of profit, the Zetas help migrants from Guatemala, Honduras, and El Salvador cross the border into Mexico on the way to the United States, then hold some of them hostage and force their families to pay ransom or insist that they help with drug smuggling. If they refuse, they are often executed, as happened in this case.

Such extortion practices and human trafficking, in addition to other tragic stories associated with the narcotics trade and gang violence, are all too common among the United States' closest neighbors, whose citizens make up an increasing share of the US population. For reasons of national interest—not to mention out of a sense of shared responsibility—Washington should seek to catalyze a broader hemispheric effort, marshalling both economic and political resources to address a colossal problem, one that shows no signs of abating and indeed threatens to metastasize.

Challenge Questions

After reading this article, you will be able to answer the following questions:

1. Why is security of paramount importance for Central Americans?
2. Why are the levels of violence and criminal activity lower in Nicaragua and Costa Rica than in the other three Central American states?
3. How are the global economic crisis and high energy costs related to national security concerns in Central America?
4. What might be some possible solutions to the region's instability?

9 In Honduras, Land Struggles Highlight Post-Coup Polarization

Elisabeth Malkin

A settlement of farmworkers on the Marañones plantation. The workers are laying claim to the land, which is owned by one of the richest men in Honduras.

Learning Objectives

After reading this article, you will more clearly understand the following:

- Why farmers demand redistribution of land
- The sources of rural violence
- The role of politics in land struggles

The settlement on the giant Marañones plantation looks like a refugee camp, where children play between rows of huts and chickens peck at garbage heaps. But the farmworkers living here plan to stay, laying claim to land owned by one of the country's richest men.

At the gate, a handful of men sit guard with shotguns and machetes under a red flag painted with defiant words: "Justice, Liberty, Land."

"If they give land to the people, the problem can be resolved," said Marcos Tulio Paredes, one of the community's leaders.

In the past few weeks, a long-running battle over land in Bajo Aguán, this fertile valley near Honduras's northern coast, has flared. At least 15 people have been killed in recent weeks alone, including two of the workers' leaders, and the people here are on edge, fearful that the unrest could spread.

The conflict in Bajo Aguán is the most volatile example of the social divide that burst into view in this tiny impoverished country two years ago, when the country's power brokers orchestrated a military coup to expel the president at the time.

A veneer of normality has returned. A new president was elected on schedule, and the ousted former president finally returned from exile in May. But the political polarization that the coup revealed and the violence it stoked—including the murders of journalists and government opponents—have persisted, and no place more so than in Bajo Aguán.

"The opportunity was lost to introduce some very significant reforms that were sorely needed in Honduras," said Kevin Casas-Zamora, an expert on Central America at the Brookings Institution in Washington. "Honduras is a country with obscene social imbalances, and very little is being done to address that."

In Bajo Aguán, where oil palm tree plantations occupy most of the farmland, President Porfirio Lobo has alternated between sending troops and brokering agreements between farmworker groups and the businessmen who own vast sections of the valley. But events rapidly slip beyond the government's control.

"This is a country where there are no institutions," said Elvin Hernández, a researcher at the Jesuit-supported Reflection, Research and Communication Team in the city of El Progreso. "It is the law of the strongest and Aguán is the place where you see that most clearly."

The government appeared to move forward on negotiating a solution last week, when Congress approved a mechanism to guarantee bank loans that would allow the farmworkers to buy land. An estimated 4,000 families will be eligible for 15-year loans to buy more than 11,000 acres.

But the 1,400 families camped on the Marañones plantation since last year have been frozen out of the latest pact. Without a title, they fear they could be evicted at any time.

"It is better to die here," said one leader, who asked that her name not be used because she had received threats. "We don't have anywhere else to go. We can't give up on the struggle. Where would that leave the deaths of our comrades? In vain?"

The presence of hundreds of troops sent here after the latest round of violence could also set off more conflict. "It's a very critical situation," said Sandra Ponce, the Honduran attorney general for human rights. "What is latent elsewhere has already developed in Bajo Aguán."

The conflict here goes back to the early 1990s, when wealthy landowners bought up plantations from farmer cooperatives. Farmworker groups argue that these purchases were illegal because members of the cooperatives were tricked by their leaders or signed deals they did not understand.

The largest single landowner in the region is Corporation Dinant, owned by Miguel Facussé, the octogenarian patriarch of one of the handful of families controlling much of Honduras's economy. The company owns about one-fifth of all the agricultural land in Bajo Aguán, more than 22,000 acres of well-groomed plantations that supply oil for export and for its snack foods, margarine and cooking oil business. It acquired that land legally, said Roger Pineda, the company's treasurer.

259

"The country needs agrarian reform," Mr. Pineda said. "Too many people don't have land. But not on the lands that are already under production. It can't be, 'I like your car, and then I take it.' "

Just days before he was ousted in June 2009, former President Manuel Zelaya intervened in the disputes, signing an agreement to start talks on redistributing land. In December that year, farmworkers staged coordinated land invasions to put pressure on Mr. Lobo.

The occupations cost Dinant $20 million in lost revenue last year, Mr. Pineda said. In addition, pressure by rights groups this year prompted a German investment bank to withdraw a loan, he said.

The choreography of evictions in Bajo Aguán unfolds violently but fails to sap the workers' resolve.

In June, 300 families who had been living for 11 years on a farm of orange groves outside the hamlet of Rigores were expelled by soldiers and police officers who gave them two hours to gather their possessions. Then the men torched and bulldozed their houses, their two churches and their school. Three days later, the farmworkers came back to the farm and began to rebuild.

Against the backdrop of negotiations, murders have continued. More than 40 people, most of them workers, have been killed in the region since the beginning of last year, said Ms. Ponce, the government's human rights prosecutor. "Not a single investigation has been concluded," she said. When impunity is the rule, she added, "it does not contribute to discouraging the violence."

The workers have accused the landowners' security guards of carrying out the killings. Mr. Pineda denied that, except in the case of five workers killed by Dinant guards during a land invasion last year.

Adding to the combustible mix is the rise of drug trafficking in the region, which has become an important transshipment point, like much of Central America. Drug traffickers may be encouraging some groups to take over land that could be used for landing strips, Ms. Ponce said.

The latest violence flared up last month when four Dinant security guards, a company employee and a teenager were found dead after an unknown group invaded the Paso de Aguán plantation. Five more people were killed the next day.

In late August, two farmworker leaders, both of them involved in negotiations with the government, were also killed. One of them, Secundino Ruíz Vallecillo, was shot by a motorcyclist as he was driving home after making a withdrawal from the bank. Eliseo Pavón, his close friend and the group's treasurer, was slightly wounded in the attack.

Mr. Pavón waved off the government's theory that the motive was robbery and accused the landowners of ordering his friend's slaying.

"They think that with this they can weaken the group, stop the fight," he said. "But it won't happen."

From *New York Times.com*, September 15, 2011. Copyright © 2011 by New York Times. Reprinted by permission.

Challenge Questions

After reading this article, you will be able to answer the following questions:

1. How were large landowners able to take land away from farmers?
2. Why does the government seem ineffective in addressing the issue of land reform?
3. What might be the position of large landowners?
4. Does drug-trafficking play a role in struggles over land?

10 Argentina's Troubled Transition

Hector E. Schamis

The country has a democratic system whose health and stability depend largely on the economic cycle.

Learning Objectives

After reading this article, you will more clearly understand the following:

- "Superpresidentialism"
- Argentina's "boom-bust" economic cycles
- Dangers to Argentina's democratic institutions
- Ideology and foreign policy

A transfer of power from one elected president to another is at the core of a constitutional system, marking the renewal of democratic commitment. In the case of Argentina in December 2007, the commitment vows were not just political but matrimonial as well: The outgoing president, Néstor Kirchner, transferred power to his wife, Cristina Kirchner. Nepotism, of course, is a rather common fact of political life, and not only in Latin America. Democratic renewal, however, is always good news—especially in a country like Argentina. The political transition of 2007 serves as an indicator that Argentina has, to a large extent, recovered from its twin crises of 2001 and 2002: the worst economic collapse in the nation's history, and a political crisis that left democracy on the verge of a breakdown.

Yet many of the tensions of democratic governance that contributed to that crisis persist in Argentina today, and the country continues to face multiple difficulties in trying to build durable and robust democratic institutions. In particular, Argentina suffers from a deeply rooted tendency to concentrate inordinate power in the executive branch, a phenomenon some observers have called "superpresidentialism." This tendency, and the perverse political incentives it generates, predated the great crisis of 2001; actually, they help to explain it. Thus, it is important to consider how this form of politics became the norm in Argentina.

While superpresidentialism in Argentina may partly be a legacy of old-fashioned personality-oriented populism, it is mainly a product of the "Menem decade"—the period in the 1990s that saw a deterioration in the procedural aspects of democracy. During this era, it became prevalent to view the institutions of democracy as mere tools to gain power, and to exercise that power in zero-sum fashion. Today, as the "Kirchner decade" unfolds, examining the earlier period can offer important insights into the nature of democracy under Presidents Néstor and Cristina Kirchner.

Indeed, despite observable economic growth and the popularity of the first couple, Argentina continues to face a number of significant challenges that were evident a decade ago. It has an ill-defined foreign policy. It continues to postpone much-needed correctives to the management of macroeconomic policy. And the country has a democratic system whose health and stability depend largely on the economic cycle. As recent history has shown, rapid economic growth, fueled by high prices for Argentine exports, can hide such political woes for a while. But once international commodity prices change—and prices always change, sooner or later—familiar problems may haunt the country again.

■ THE SHADOW OF THE 1990S

As Argentina entered the twenty-first century, the Menem decade cast a long shadow. Peronist Carlos Menem had been elected in 1989 amid hyperinflation, which had forced the early departure of President Raúl Alfonsín. Menem's greatest success was to defeat the economic instability that had afflicted the country for decades. This success resulted largely from the "convertibility law," a program that Menem's economy minister, Domingo Cavallo, submitted to the Congress in early 1991, whereby the Argentine peso was pegged to the US dollar and a currency board set monetary and exchange rate policy. As a result, the government could increase the money supply only by expanding foreign exchange reserves. The strategy quickly paid off: Inflation dropped to single digits after just three months.

Stability in prices and exchange rates in turn made possible a comprehensive program of economic transformation, which included trade liberalization, deregulation, and privatization. A commitment to monetary policy based on rules, rather than discretion, was deemed necessary to boost credibility. This would allow the private sector to borrow in both domestic and international capital markets and would expedite economic reforms. After the debt crisis of the 1980s, which had virtually eliminated most sources of credit, foreign investment in Argentina began to rise again. In 1992, the country obtained debt relief under a plan sponsored by US Treasury Secretary Nicholas Brady, and the terms of trade (the relative prices of exports and imports), which had collapsed in the late 1980s, became favorable again.

By 1992, the government had managed to achieve growth and stability—on which Menem capitalized to accumulate unprecedented levels of discretionary power in the executive branch. First the president obtained a broad delegation of authority from the Congress. Then he packed the nation's supreme court. Soon Menem was exercising what has been termed "rule by decree." He also advanced a constitutional reform project that would allow him to run for reelection in 1995.

But just as his reelection drive was reaching full speed, a number of economic problems with potentially serious repercussions became apparent. One was the central government's weak fiscal position. Although one-time receipts from the sale of nationalized assets had helped the government nearly erase its deficit by 1993, no lasting means of controlling deficits were put in place. This omission was at least partly deliberate, in keeping with Menem's strategy for achieving constitutional reform and winning reelection. While exchange rate stability was meant to appeal to the urban middle classes, federal spending was kept high in order to win votes from the provinces for the president's constitutional reform process. Sooner or later Menem's maneuvering was bound to run up against macroeconomic fundamentals—as indeed it did when world economic conditions became less supportive in the second half of the 1990s.

The first signs of trouble appeared in the banking sector. The convertibility law had mandated that Argentina's monetary base be backed with international reserves, but it provided only a narrow definition of the money supply. This loophole allowed authorities to expand "bank money" by cutting reserve requirements—the equivalent of a monetary stimulus. This stimulus, in combination with continued strong capital inflows, produced a credit boom that increased the exposure of the banking system. When Mexico devalued its peso in December 1994, Argentina experienced its first major episode of financial turbulence since the inception of the currency board.

Menem, however, was unwilling to implement much-needed financial restructuring during the run-up to the May 1995 presidential election. This compounded the fragility of the banking sector later on. Matters were not helped by additional financial volatility in emerging markets toward the end of the 1990s, the appreciation of the us dollar, the continuous devaluation of Brazil's currency, and drops in commodity prices. As a result, Argentina approached the end of the 1990s in recession, with a weak fiscal base and serious debt exposure.

■ CRISIS AND COLLAPSE

In 1999, after Menem's second term in office ended, Fernando De la Rúa of the Radical Civic Union party became president. De la Rúa had campaigned in favor of extending the life of the currency board, despite clear signs of its exhaustion as a viable economic strategy. De la Rúa's ideas about economic policy may have been wrong, but they were not wrong in the political sense, at least at the time. Argentine voters, after decades of enduring high inflation that at times went out of control, were demanding stability and rewarding at the ballot box politicians perceived as capable of delivering it.

Moreover, the electorate had begun to value low inflation over full employment, and thus displayed a higher tolerance for recession.

By 2000, as a result, the currency board appeared to be in place to stay—just as there began to emerge the kinds of problems that generally accompany stabilization policy based on a nominal exchange rate as an anchor. Typically, such programs lead to a falling real interest rate and to appreciation of the real exchange rate in favor of the local currency. Initially, this sparks a burst in investment, a boom in imports—and a gradual deterioration of the current account. With an open capital account, inflows of capital can finance the trade deficit in the short term. Still, an excessive current account deficit often induces inconsistent fiscal policies that affect the credibility of the currency peg. At this point, the sustainability of the monetary regime itself comes into question. Runs on the currency become widespread, and significant losses in foreign exchange reserves usually result as the government tries to defend the parity. Inevitably, the fixed exchange rate arrangement collapses, and devaluation follows.

In Argentina the boom phase of the economic cycle had begun to end by the turn of the decade, and the bust was already taking shape. Because of currency board restrictions, the government could not intervene with stimulative policies as a recession gathered momentum. This weakened the government's fiscal position even further as revenues shrank. Throughout 2001, this dynamic steadily increased Argentina's country risk index, which translated into exorbitant interest rate increases and worsening debt repayment problems.

By December of that year the government, determined to continue making debt payments, did so by using central bank reserves, an action that undercut the very foundation of the currency board. It also rolled over obligations with private pension funds, which constituted a de facto expropriation. The rules that had governed the economy since 1991 were thereby broken. Making matters worse still, the government froze bank deposits to prevent a massive run to the dollar—imposing yet another loss of wealth on millions of citizens.

At that point the Argentine economy became ungovernable—but it was a long-simmering political crisis that served as the death knell for both the currency board and the De la Rúa administration. The first symptom of that crisis had come earlier, in October 2000, when the vice president resigned. At that point the coalition in power broke down and the president turned his back on his own party and surrounded himself with a clique of unelected, nonpartisan advisers. Among them was Cavallo, once Menem's economic czar and the architect of the currency board. On his return to government, he demanded broad autonomy over the conduct of economic policy, just as he had done in the 1990s.

Cavallo's autocratic style reinforced a policy making approach that was already based on executive decrees. It further marginalized the Congress. And it harmed the overall process of democratic representation. By the time unrest broke out in the streets toward the end of 2001, the government had alienated itself from political society and the party system, and the ensuing power vacuum forced the president's resignation. Menem-style politics based on unilateral decision making and discretionary rule had backfired.

After the collapse of the De la Rúa government, Argentina devalued its currency and defaulted on its foreign debt. The country plunged into the worst recession in its history. After a series of interim presidents served, a joint session of Congress appointed Peronist Senator Eduardo Duhalde as president in hopes that he could stabilize the country during the crisis. Accordingly, he defined his priorities in terms of trying to regain stability and address widespread poverty through across-the-aisle collaboration. He pictured himself as a transitional leader whose goal was to complete De la Rúa's term in office and transfer power to a popularly elected president.

In a country that had been governed by presidential decrees for over a decade, Duhalde's aims—to overhaul the institutional procedures of democracy—were valuable. Yet he faced too many obstacles to fully accomplish his goals. The most notable of the obstacles was the erosion of the party system. The De la Rúa debacle widely discredited the Radical party. Yet Duhalde's own Peronist party, now suddenly in power, was deeply fragmented along territorial lines, thanks to incentives that gave the upper hand to regional bosses in control of subnational political systems. As a result, three Peronist candidates competed for the presidency in the April 2003 election. Duhalde's preferred candidate, the left-of-center governor of Santa Cruz province, Néstor Kirchner, emerged victorious. Democracy, though bruised, had survived.

■ THE POWER GRAB

A considerable degree of continuity marked the transition from the Duhalde to the Kirchner administrations. Duhalde stepped down as he had promised, giving himself credibility. But several of his people stayed in key parliamentary seats and in the cabinet, most notably Roberto Lavagna, the economy minister. The transition as a result was characterized by significant coherence in programs—in policies to reinvigorate the economy on the basis of a competitive exchange rate, to negotiate with the privatized public utility sector on rates and fresh investment, and to restructure the defaulted national debt under conditions that did not affect long-term growth and poverty alleviation. This was an unusual political scenario. There was not only continuity of names and ideas—there was a tacit political pact between a sitting president and a former president who retained significant influence. To an extent, it seemed more like French cohabitation than anything Argentina had seen before.

The new arrangement reinforced stability, and Kirchner found more auspicious domestic and international economic conditions than his predecessors had. Argentina restructured its foreign debt, obtaining an unprecedented reduction of 70 percent, and improved its fiscal condition. At the same time, prices for its major exports began to rise again. With a competitive exchange rate, the country developed a large trade surplus that, beginning in 2003, fostered rapid growth and mounting foreign exchange reserves.

Yet, at exactly this moment, the political situation began to change, and not necessarily for the better. Riding the economic boom, Kirchner sought to cut ties with Duhalde. An opportunity to do so arrived with the October 2005 midterm election. As his "Front for Victory" emerged triumphant from this contest, Kirchner sacked all independent-minded members of his cabinet—including Lavagna, the person most responsible for the economic recovery. Kirchner exploited a weakened opposition by co-opting leaders from other parties and playing on regional and factional divisions. He blatantly employed the government's fiscal resources to grease the wheels of Peronist party politics. Moreover, he began to flirt with unconstitutionality by continuously extracting from the Congress extraordinary powers to make unilateral decisions regarding critical matters such as foreign debt negotiations and the budgetary process.

After the 2005 election, it was clear that a Kirchner would run for the presidency in 2007—it just remained to be seen whether it would be Néstor or his wife, Senator Cristina Kirchner. To that end the Kirchners sought, first, to take over the Peronist party in Buenos Aires province, so as to disassemble the once-powerful Duhalde machine. Second, they sought to further divide the Peronist party so that weaker, smaller factions would be subordinated to the presidency. Third, they worked to co-opt the opposition parties so they could gain support in districts where they had little or no organization of their own. With this strategy fully deployed, the nomination of the candidate would take place in due time, once the public opinion polls revealed which of the two Kirchners was more likable. This was not the first case of nepotistic advancement in Argentina's political history, but never before had it been so easy to carry it out at such a high level.

■ KIRCHNER TO KIRCHNER

As it turned out, Cristina Kirchner got the nomination and won the election in October 2007 with 45 percent of the vote. Meanwhile, Argentina has regained stability and its economy has recovered from the deep crisis of 2001. Yet the issues that were at stake in 2002 have not been fully and satisfactorily addressed.

The first of these outstanding issues is Argentina's continued lack of a foreign policy in the strict sense of the term—that is, a purpose-driven strategy and a set of permanent goals that outlive an incumbent government. Because of this failing, Argentina's place in the international arena has been poorly defined, leading to erratic positions that have undermined the country's credibility.

In the 1990s, for example, the Menem government adopted what amounted to automatic alignment with the United States, a policy that pursued little else than to replay the old illusion of being a first world country.

263

Since 2002, however, Argentina's approach to foreign affairs has been rather the opposite, characterized by a "Latinamericanism" that has rhetorical but no substantive value. This has been expressed in a foreign policy style similar to that of Venezuela's Hugo Chávez: always loud and provocative, with occasional public displays of disrespect for the administration of George W. Bush.

Thus, Argentina continues to formulate foreign policy on the basis of sheer ideology rather than a system of values grounded in an international normative order. This approach ignores numerous historical lessons that ideology alone is not a good compass for orienting a coherent foreign policy. In fact, a government can be quite right-wing and still confront the United States, as the Argentine dictator Leopoldo Galtieri did when he embarked on a war against the United Kingdom over the Falklands in 1982; and a government can be quite left-wing and still cooperate with the United States, as the Chilean and Peruvian socialist governments have done by signing trade agreements.

To be credible in the world, Argentina needs to add a normative dimension to its foreign policy, so that permanent values—such as democracy, international law, human rights, and the rejection of protectionism in the industrialized world, to name a few—can be prioritized. With this sort of normative blueprint, the country's identity could be defined and projected regardless of who occupies the Casa Rosada (the seat of the executive in Argentina) or, for that matter, who lives in the White House.

Seasoned observers hoped that a Cristina Kirchner presidency would make a difference in this arena. At least during the campaign, she expressed empathy with other women in positions of leadership (Angela Merkel, Michelle Bachelet, and even Hillary Clinton) who eschewed bellicosity and appeared to incline toward moderation. Cristina Kirchner seemed more likely to cultivate Brasilia than Caracas as an alliance partner. Unfortunately, such early readings of her intentions proved too optimistic, if not downright naïve. With the discovery only three days after the inauguration of the new president that Venezuelan soft money had interfered with the Argentine political process, any hopes for improvement in Argentina-U.S. relations vanished.

According to a U.S. prosecutor in Florida, the Venezuelan government sent an envoy to Buenos Aires last August with $800,000 for Mrs. Kirchner's election campaign. Arrested in Florida, the alleged envoy testified that the Venezuelan and Argentine governments had also offered him $2 million for his silence. At this moment, revealing their ignorance about the American legal system, both the new president and the ex-president of Argentina leveled a barrage of wild accusations at the us government, saying the arrest had been staged as part of a conspiracy to dominate Argentina. As a result, the country's capacity to project credibility and predictability in the international scene is back to square one.

■ LIMITED RECOVERY

A second outstanding issue, along with foreign policy, is the economy. Without a doubt Argentina has recovered from the crisis of 2001, but the recovery is not based on an investment-attracting program. Thus, it is not an upturn that can sustain growth over time. On the contrary, Argentina's strong economic performance since 2002 has been driven by a deliberately high exchange rate and favorable international commodity prices. With both of these variables beginning to show signs of exhaustion, the recovery's longevity is clearly in question. Indeed, the ongoing appreciation of the currency is evident in a real estate bubble that continues to swell and a trade surplus that is gradually shrinking. And global commodity prices will be hitting their ceiling soon, as can be seen in China's declining demand for Argentine commodities and the first signs of a recession in the United States.

The future, consequently, may not be as spectacular as the Kirchners would hope. Less favorable international conditions will slow growth, probably putting pressure on the government's fiscal position and complicating overall macroeconomic policy. In the meantime, the new government faces pressing decisions. Argentina's debt to the Paris Club (the forum of mostly European creditors), technically in default since 2001, has to be renegotiated and restructured. Only after this is done will Argentina be able to attract fresh investment, especially in the privatized energy sector (mostly owned by European consortia), which is poorly maintained and generally unable to satisfy demand.

In addition, the overheated economy has to be cooled off, something Néstor Kirchner refused to do. And macroeconomic information has to be made reliable. In international financial circles, it is by now a truism that Argentina's official economic information is fictitious. It is not only that the government misreports the inflation rate—a scandal that repeats itself over and over—but doubts also exist about the government's actual fiscal position, the country's money supply, the unemployment rate, and the rate of growth itself. Every 30 days the government issues dubious economic data with grand pomp; the effect is a credibility deficit among foreign investors.

■ IN MENEM'S MIRROR

With coming changes in exogenous economic conditions, including a weakening of international prices for the nation's exports, there will be changes not just in Argentina's economic performance but also, in all likelihood, in the country's political stability. This points to the third and most serious of the outstanding issues in the current transition: the fact that the political system has virtually no autonomy vis-à-vis the economy. In Argentina there is only one type of cycle, the economic one, which the political process follows and reinforces. When the economy grows, whoever is in power stays on—first Menem and now the Kirchners. When the economy slows down and becomes unmanageable, whoever is in power has to leave early—Alfonsín, De la Rúa, and to some extent Duhalde.

This is Argentina's Achilles heel. Democracy is supposed to be an autonomous sphere that functions on the basis of institutional arrangements that allow the government to, among other things, moderate the effects of economic cycles. In other words, democracy is suitable for the design and implementation of countercyclical economic policy, but to accomplish this requires a dense institutional fabric—including organized political parties that are embedded in civil society, an independent legislature that is committed to performing its oversight role, and an executive branch that is willing to live up not only to the text of the constitution but also its spirit.

The problem is that Néstor Kirchner as president eroded these necessary functions of a democratic state. Political parties, including the party in government, are weaker today than in 2003. The opposition has been further co-opted and fragmented on the basis of electoral deals among individuals, not on the basis of ideas or programs. The Congress, as a result, has become a mere appendage of the executive. Even approval of the budget—the most important type of bill for every legislature—has been reduced to a simple administrative procedure that can be resolved in a few hours. That all this has happened over five years during which the economy was growing rapidly and the government was running surpluses—propitious conditions for institution building—makes the lack of institutional progress all the more troubling.

With Cristina Kirchner now in power, there is not much hope for change. The Kirchners have been partners in a manner of governing that has contributed to an institutional decay that served their goal of staying in power. In a clear display of continuity, Cristina Kirchner has already asked the Congress to renew emergency presidential powers to legislate. Thus, Argentina's democracy is alive, and perhaps even well, but it is a democracy that has no true political parties, that exhibits a sparse institutional configuration, and that is based on the discretion of the superpresident. In fat years and with public opinion favoring the president, this system can be sustainable. But, if history since the return of democracy in 1983 is

any guide, in lean years and with societal dissatisfaction, this system only contributes to instability. The main challenge for Argentine democracy is to change this form of politics, so the political cycle is not always reduced to mimicry of the economic cycle.

To a great extent, the Kirchners' political approach is a reflection of what may be called Menem's mirror. What was once right is now left, and vice versa, but otherwise the picture has not changed. Whether democratic procedures are circumvented, twisted, and violated to quickly achieve market efficiency and enter the first world, as in Menem's narrative, or in pursuit of social justice and independence from the United States and the IMF, as the Kirchners put it, makes little difference. In terms of the quality of the democratic process, and prospects for democratic stability, Argentina remains in the long shadow of the 1990s.

Hector E. Schamis is a professor at American University's School of International Service. He is the author of *Re-Forming the State: The Politics of Privatization in Latin America and Europe* (University of Michigan Press, 2002).

Challenge Questions

After reading this article, you will be able to answer the following questions:

1. What is the connection between Argentina's democratic system and economic cycles?

2. What are the dangers to democracy of extraordinary executive power?

3. What might be some of the consequences of a foreign policy based on ideology rather than more traditional norms?

4. How does the global economy influence Argentina's economic cycles?

11 *Machisma*

Cynthia Gorney

How a mix of female empowerment and steamy soap operas helped bring down Brazil's fertility rate and stoke its vibrant economy.

Learning Objectives

After reading this article, you will more clearly understand the following:

- The relationship between women's empowerment and Brazil's declining birth rate
- The roles played by factors such as rapid industrialization, easy access to birth control measures, and the media in reproductive decisions
- Reprioritization of the place of family life in Brazil

José Alberto, Murilo, Geraldo, Angela, Paulo, Edwiges, Vicente, Rita, Lucia, Marcelino, Teresinha. That makes 11, right? Not including the stillbirth, the three miscarriages, and the baby who lived not quite one full day. Dona Maria Ribeiro de Carvalho, a gravelly-voiced Brazilian lady in her 88th year, completed the accounting of her 16 pregnancies and regarded José Alberto, her oldest son, who had come for a Sunday visit and was smoking a cigarette on her couch. "With the number of children I had," Dona Maria said mildly, her voice conveying only the faintest reproach, "I should have more than a hundred grandchildren right now."

José Alberto, who had been fishing all morning at the pond on his ranch, was still in his sweatpants. His mother's front room in the mid-Brazil town of São Vicente de Minas was just big enough to contain three crowded-in armchairs, a television, numerous family photos, framed drawings of Jesus and the Blessed Virgin, and the black vinyl couch upon which he, Professor Carvalho, retiring head of his university's School of Economics and one of the most eminent Brazilian demographers of the past half century, now reclined. He put his feet up and smiled. He knew the total number of grandchildren, of course: 26. For much of his working life, he had been charting and probing and writing about the remarkable Brazilian demographic phenomenon that was replicated in miniature amid his own family, who within two generations had crashed their fertility rate to 2.36 children per family, heading right down toward the national average of 1.9.

That new Brazilian fertility rate is below the level at which a population replaces itself. It is lower than the two-children-per-woman fertility rate in the United States. In the largest nation in Latin America—a 191-million-person country where the Roman Catholic Church dominates, abortion is illegal (except in rare cases), and no official government policy has ever promoted birth control—family size has dropped so sharply and so insistently over the past five decades that the fertility rate graph looks like a playground slide.

And it's not simply wealthy and professional women who have stopped bearing multiple children in Brazil. There's a common perception that the countryside and favelas, as Brazilians call urban slums, are still crowded with women having one baby after another—but it isn't true. At the demographic center Carvalho helped found, located four hours away in the city of Belo Horizonte, researchers have tracked the decline across every class and region of Brazil. Over some weeks of talking to Brazilian women recently, I met schoolteachers, trash sorters, architects, newspaper reporters, shop clerks, cleaning ladies, professional athletes, high school girls, and women who had spent their adolescence homeless; almost every one of them said a modern Brazilian family should include two children, ideally a *casal,* or couple, one boy and one girl. Three was barely plausible. One might well be enough. In a working-class neighborhood on the outskirts of Belo Horizonte, an unmarried 18-year-old affectionately watched her toddler son one evening as he roared his toy truck toward us; she loved him very much, the young woman said, but she was finished with childbearing. The expression she used was one I'd heard from Brazilian women before: *"A fábrica está fechada."* The factory is closed.

The emphatic fertility drop is not just a Brazilian phenomenon. Notwithstanding concerns over the planet's growing population, close to half the world's population lives in countries where the fertility rates have actually fallen to below replacement rate, the level at which a couple have only enough children to replace themselves—just over two children per family. They've dropped rapidly in most of the rest of the world as well, with the notable exception of sub-Saharan Africa.

For demographers working to understand the causes and implications of this startling trend, what's happened in Brazil since the 1960s provides one of the most compelling case studies on the planet. Brazil spans a vast landmass, with enormous regional differences in geography, race, and culture, yet its population data are by tradition particularly thorough and reliable. Pieces of the Brazilian experience have been mirrored in scores of other countries, including those in which most of the population is Roman Catholic—but no other nation in the world seems to have managed it quite like this.

"What took 120 years in England took 40 years here," Carvalho told me one day. "Something *happened*." At that moment he was talking about what happened in São Vicente de Minas, the town of his childhood, where nobody under 45 has a soccer-team-size roster of siblings anymore. But he might as well have been describing the entire female population of Brazil. For although there are many reasons Brazil's fertility rate has dropped so far and so fast, central to them all are tough, resilient women who set out a few decades back, without encouragement from the government and over the pronouncements of their bishops, to start shutting down the factories any way they could.

Encountering women under 35 who've already had sterilization surgery is an everyday occurrence in Brazil, and they seem to have no compunctions about discussing it. "I was 18 when the first baby was born—wanted to stop there, but the second came by accident, and I am *done*," a 28-year-old crafts shop worker told me in the northeastern city of Recife, as she was showing me how to dance the regional two-step called the *forró*. She was 26 when she had her tubal ligation, and when I asked why she'd chosen irreversible contraception at such a young age—she's married, what if she and her husband change their minds?—she reminded me of son number two, the accident. Birth control pills made her fat and sick, she said. And in case I'd missed this part: She was done.

So why two? Why not four? Why not the eight your grandmother had? Always the same answer—"Impossible! Too expensive! Too much work!" With the facial expression, the widened eyes and the startled grin that I came to know well: It's the 21st century, *senhora*, are you nuts?

Population scholars like José Alberto Carvalho maintain a lively argument about the multiple components of Brazil's fertility plunge. ("Don't let anybody tell you they know for sure what caused the decline," a demographer advised me at Cedeplar, the university-based study center in Belo Horizonte. "We'll never have a winner as the best explanation.") But if one were to try composing a formula for crashing a developing nation's fertility rate without official intervention from the government— no China-style one-child policy, no India-style effort to force sterilization upon the populace—here's a six-point plan, tweaked for the peculiarities of modern Brazil:

1. Industrialize dramatically, urgently, and late, causing your nation to hurtle through in 25 years what economists used to think of as a century's worth of internal rural-to-urban relocation of its citizens. Brazil's military rulers, who seized power in a 1964 military coup and held on through two decades of sometimes brutal authoritarian rule, forced the country into a new kind of economy, one that has concentrated work in the cities, where the housing is cramped, the favela streets are dangerous,

babies look more like new expense burdens than like future useful farmhands, and the jobs women must take for their families' survival require leaving home for ten hours at a stretch.

2. Keep your medications mostly unregulated and your pharmacy system over-the-counter, so that when birth control pills hit the world in the early 1960s, women of all classes can get their hands on them, even without a doctor's prescription, if they can just come up with the money. Nurture in these women a particularly dismissive attitude toward the Catholic Church's position on artificial contraception. (See number 4.)

3. Improve your infant and child mortality statistics until families no longer feel compelled to have extra, just-in-case babies on the supposition that a few will die young. Compound that reassurance with a national pension program, relieving working-class parents of the conviction that a big family will be their only support when they grow old.

4. Distort your public health system's financial incentives for a generation or two, so that doctors learn they can count on higher pay and more predictable work schedules when they perform cesareans rather than waiting for natural deliveries. Then spread the word, woman to woman, that a public health doctor who has already begun the surgery for a cesarean can probably be persuaded to throw in a discreet tubal ligation, thus ensuring a thriving, decades-long publicly supported gray market for this permanent method of contraception. Brazil's health system didn't formally recognize voluntary female sterilization until 1997. But the first time I ever heard the phrase "a fábrica está fechada," it was from a 69-year-old retired schoolteacher who had her tubes tied in 1972, after her third child was born. This woman had three sisters. Every one of them underwent a ligation. Yes, they were all Catholic. Yes, the church hierarchy disapproved. No, none of them much cared; they were women of faith, but in some matters the male clergy is perhaps not wholly equipped to discern the true will of God. The lady was pouring tea into china cups at her dining table as we talked, and her voice was matter-of-fact. "Everyone was doing it," she said.

5. Introduce electricity and television at the same time in much of the nation's interior, a double disruption of traditional family living patterns, and then flood the airwaves with a singular, vivid, aspirational image of the modern Brazilian family: affluent, light skinned, and small. Scholars have tracked the apparent family-size-shrinking influence of *novelas*, Brazil's Portuguese-language iterations of the beloved evening soap operas, or *telenovelas*, that broadcast all over Latin America, each playing for months, like an endless series of bodice-ripper paperbacks. One study observes that

the spread of televisions outpaced access to education, which has greatly improved in Brazil, but at a slower pace. By the 1980s and '90s all of Brazil was dominated by the Globo network, whose prime-time novelas were often a central topic of conversation; even now, in the era of multichannel satellite broadcasting, you can see café TVs turned to the biggest Globo novela of the season.

While I was there it was *Passione,* featuring the racked-by-secrets industrialist Gouveia family, who were all very good-looking and loaded up with desirable possessions: motorcycles, chandeliers, racing bicycles, airplane tickets, French high-heeled shoes. The widow Gouveia, resolute and admirable, had three kids. Well, four, but one was a secret because he was born out of wedlock and had been shipped off to Italy in infancy because. . .uh, never mind. The point is that there were not many Gouveias, nor were there big families anywhere else in the unfathomably complicated plotline.

"We asked them once: 'Is the Globo network trying to introduce family planning on purpose?'" says Elza Berquó, a veteran Brazilian demographer who helped study the novelas' effects. "You know what they answered? 'No. It's because it's much easier to write the novelas about small families.'"

And, finally, number 6: Make all your women Brazilians.

This is volatile territory, Brazil and women. Machismo means the same thing in the Portuguese of Brazil as it does in the rest of the continent's Spanish, and it has been linked to the country's high levels of domestic violence and other physical assaults on women. But the nation was profoundly altered by the *movimento das mulheres,* the women's movement of the 1970s and '80s, and no American today is in a position to call Brazil retrograde on matters of gender equity. When President Dilma Rousseff was running for office last year, the fiercest national debates were about her political ideas and affiliations, not whether the nation was ready for its first female president. One of Rousseff's strongest competitors, in fact—a likely contender in future elections—was a female senator.

Brazil has high-ranking female military officers, special police stations run by and for women, and the world's most famous female soccer player (the one-name-only dazzling ball handler Marta). When I spent an evening in the city of Campinas with Aníbal Faúndes, a Chilean obstetrics professor who immigrated decades ago to Brazil and has helped lead national studies of reproductive health, Faúndes returned again and again to what he regards as the primary force pushing fertility change in his adopted country. "The fertility rate dropped because women decided they didn't want more children," he said. "Brazilian women are tremendously strong. It was just a matter of them deciding, and then having the means to achieve it."

The Cytotec episode offers sober but illuminating evidence. Cytotec is the brand name for a medication called misoprostol, which was developed as an ulcer treatment but in the late 1980s became internationally known as an early-abortion pill—part of the two-drug combination that included the medication known as RU-486. Even before the rest of the world received the news about pill-induced abortion, though—it entered the French and Chinese marketplaces in 1988, amid great controversy, and was subsequently approved in the U.S. for pregnancy termination—Brazilian women had figured it out on their own. No publicity campaign explained misoprostol; this was pre-Internet, remember, and Brazilian law prohibits abortion except in cases of rape or risk to the woman's life.

But that law is ignored at every level of society. "Women were telling each other what the dose was," says Brazilian demographer Sarah Costa, director of the New York City-based Women's Refugee Commission, who has written about Brazil's Cytotec phenomenon for the medical journal the *Lancet.* "There were street vendors selling it in train stations. Most public health posts at that time were not providing family planning services, and if you are motivated to regulate your fertility, even if you have poor services and poor information, you'll ask somebody, What can I do? And the information *will* flow."

The open availability of Cytotec didn't last long. By 1991 the Brazilian government had put restrictions on it; today it is available only in hospitals, although women assured me that packs of Cytotec could still be obtained over the Internet or in certain flea markets. But the public health service now pays for sterilizations and other methods of birth control. Illegal abortion flourishes, in circumstances ranging from medically reliable to scary. It may not be entirely easy or safe for a Brazilian woman to keep her family small, but there's no shortage of available ways to do so. And in every respect, women of all ages told me, this is what they now expect of themselves—and what contemporary Brazil, in turn, appears to expect from them.

"Look at the apartments," said a 31-year-old Rio de Janeiro marketing executive named Andiara Petterle. "They're designed for a maximum of four people. Two bedrooms. In the supermarkets, even the labels on frozen foods—always for four people."

The company Petterle founded specializes in sales research on Brazilian women, whose buying habits and life priorities seem to have been upended just in the years since Petterle was born. It wasn't until 1977, she reminded me, that the nation legalized divorce. "We've changed so fast," she said. "We've found that for many young women, their first priority now is their education. The second is their profession. And the third is children and a stable relationship."

So raising children hasn't vanished from these modern priorities, Petterle said—it's just lower on the list, and a tougher thing to juggle now. She has no children herself, although she hopes to someday. As Petterle talked, I heard what was becoming a familiar refrain: Contemporary Brazilian life is too expensive to accommodate more than two kids. Much of the public school system is *ruim*—useless, a disaster—people will tell you, and families scrape for any private education they can afford. The nationwide health system is ruim too, many insist, and families scrape for any private medical care they can afford. Clothing, books, backpacks, cell phones—all these things are costly, and all must somehow be obtained. And everything a young family might need is now available, as the mall windows relentlessly remind passing customers, with *financiamento,* short- or long-term.

Want your child to have that huge stuffed beagle, that dolly set in the fancy gift box, that four-foot-long, battery-powered, ride-on SUV? Buy it on the installment plan—with interest, of course. Consumer credit has exploded throughout Brazil, reaching middle- and working-class families that two decades ago had no access to these kinds of discretionary purchases paid off over time. While I was in Brazil, the business magazine *Exame* ran a cover story on the nation's new multi-class consumerism. The São Paulo journalist who wrote the story, Fabiane Stefano, described the bustle she witnessed inside a travel agency that had recently opened in a downscale city neighborhood. "Every five minutes a new person came in," she said. "Eighty percent of these people were going to the Northeast to see family. It takes three days to get there by bus, only three hours by plane." This was each customer's first time flying. "The guy had to explain to them that in an airplane they wouldn't see their luggage for a while."

It would be a gross oversimplification to suggest that Brazilians are having fewer children just because they want to spend more money on each one. But these questions about material acquisition—how much everything now costs, and how much everyone now desires—both interested and troubled nearly every Brazilian woman I met. Smaller family size has been credited with helping boost the economies of rapidly developing countries, especially the mammoth five now referred to as BRICS: Brazil, Russia, India, China, South Africa. National economic growth brings no assurances of family well-being, though, unless that prosperity is managed thoughtfully and invested in coming generations. "This is something I've been thinking about, the way we're dropping the fertility rate in Brazil and the other BRICS countries, but I don't see any real work on getting more ethical," says the marketer Andiara Petterle. "We could be just *one* billion people in the world, and with the mentality we have now, we could be consuming just as many resources."

The morning I had coffee with a group of young São Paulo professional women, we sat at a sidewalk table across from a shop that carried eight different glossy parenting magazines. Each was thick with ads: the Bébé Confort Modulo Clip convertible stroller; the electronic "cry analyzer" to identify the reason your baby is crying; the wall-mounted DVD player that projects moving images over the crib ("Distracts better than a mobile!"). We studied the fashion photographs of beautiful toddlers in knits and aviator sunglasses and fake furs. "Look at these kids," said Milene Chaves, a 33-year-old journalist, her voice hovering between admiration and despair. She turned the page. "And it seems you have to have a decorated room too. I don't need a decorated room like this."

Chaves had a long-term boyfriend but has no children, not yet. "And when I do, I want to simplify things," she said. The half dozen friends around her agreed, the magazines still open on the table before us: attractive objects, they said, but so excessive, so disturbingly too much. These São Paulo women were in their 20s and 30s, with two children or one or none. They followed precisely the patterns described to me by national demographers. When I asked them whether they ever felt nostalgia for the less materialistic life of their elders, two generations back—eight children here, ten there, with nobody expecting decorators to gussy up the sleeping quarters—I was able to make out, among the hooting, the word *presa.* Imprisoned.

But their answers were nearly drowned out by their laughter.

Challenge Questions

After reading this article, you will be able to answer the following questions:

1. What is *machisma?*
2. How might the Roman Catholic Church in Brazil view birth control?
3. What impact has materialism had on family size?
4. Is there a relationship between national prosperity and declining birth rates?

12 Go Before You Die

Patrick Graham

A Road Trip through the "New" Colombia.

On a February night not long ago, I had dinner in Bogotá with Marea, a childhood friend. She had married a Colombian and moved there twelve years ago, when many Colombians of her class were desperate to get out. "One day, I'd like to drive to the coast," she said as we sat by the fire and her live-in maid prepared dinner. The way she said it made the trip sound vaguely romantic, a bit dangerous or at least unusual, more exploration than mere tourism; and indeed, until only quite recently, traveling Colombia by car was just not done, at least not by those in her social stratum. On the highways, left-wing guerrillas have held up traffic and gone "fishing," taking potentially lucrative hostages like Marea from their cars and into the mountains, where they have been held for ransom, sometimes for years. Those who can afford it have simply flown from town to town or, better, straight out of the country to Miami or Europe. A few years ago the government began encouraging citizens to use the country's highways during vacations in well-protected "caravans." The campaign was called *Vive Colombia, Viaja par Ella* ("Live Colombia, Travel Through It") and consisted of heavily armed convoys of holiday makers many miles long—the only way to travel through Colombia and survive.

But since 2002, when President Alvaro Uribe took office, Colombians' mental maps have been radically redrawn. In five years, Uribe has carved out a country within a country, increasing security on highways and in towns while leaving vast areas of lowland jungle and mountains to the guerrilla armies. As a result, the number of kidnappings has dropped from nearly 3,000 in 2002 to fewer than 700 in 2006, and the murder rate is the lowest in two decades, having receded from 29,000 to 17,000 in the same period. Over dinner, Marea described what she called the "Uribe revolution," which she said had boosted the nation's pride as well as its economy. In contrast to the dithering and corruption of earlier presidents, she said, "Uribe is intense and honest. People trust him and he seems strong." Uribe, who studied at Harvard and Oxford, has survived fifteen assassination attempts and is reputed to do several hours of yoga every day. He won reelection in May 2006 with 62 percent of the vote.

The key to Uribe's "revolution" has been an attempt at willful forgetting: his decision, soon after his inauguration, to negotiate peace deals with the nation's right-wing paramilitaries, which agreed to demobilize 30,000 militiamen in exchange for little or no prosecution—this after decades of butchering Colombians, dealing drugs, and murdering union activists and leftwing politicians. Today, paramilitary-backed candidates often run virtually unopposed in elections, and one paramilitary leader claimed during the previous congressional session that they controlled 35 percent of the legislature. The right-wing drug armies, which maintain control over large parts of the country, have essentially been allowed to launder themselves, with some of their ruthless former leaders now holding office or walking about as legitimate businessmen. This dissonance was well illustrated in January of last year when Salvatore Mancuso, one of the most brutal paramilitary bosses, appeared before a court in a properly sober suit to make a voluntary confession—without risk of prosecution, of course—and surprised everyone by displaying a pleasantly professional, eighty-seven-page PowerPoint presentation that detailed, with diagrams and maps, the various civilians he'd kidnapped or killed.

The sunny unreality of Uribe's new Colombia, a Colombia fit for free exploration—*Viaja par Ella*—has seeped into the consciousness of a nation desperate for normalcy after years of strife. On the day I arrived, the *New York Times* happened to publish a travel piece on Bogotá (BOGOTA IS NOT JUST FOR THE BRAVE ANYMORE), and this made the front pages in Colombia's own newspapers. On the radio in my cab, while I was traveling to Marea's house for dinner, talk was of nothing else. One of the country's private television stations, Caracol, had recently produced a booklet called "Nomad's Guide: A guide describing the marvelous aspects of Colombia," which outlined various possible routes around the country that Colombians were encouraged to discover. It opens with a letter from Paulo Laserna Phillips, the president of Caracol, who led a group of journalists and celebrities on a series of trips covering 10,000 kilometers to prove that Colombia is, at least in parts, safe.

One of the main routes the tourist caravans have taken is from Bogotá to the Caribbean coast through the Middle Magdalena Valley, the Magdalena being the cappuccino-colored river that, because it runs through the center of the country, is invariably compared to the Mississippi. Despite the fact that this valley was until recently the epicenter of the war between right- and left-wing militias, Colombians told me the road had recently become safe for cars traveling alone without police or army protection.

No one I knew had tested this theory in the off-season, and this was what I decided to do. I told one Colombian I met, a businessman working in the hotel industry, that I was planning to make the trip. He insisted there would be no problem—but, he added, we should be off the road by dark.

Did he mean that it was unsafe? I asked him.

"No," he said, smiling. "But you'll be tired. It's better to rest at night."

Bogotá is built on a plateau below a ridge of the Andes, and the farther south one travels the poorer and more dangerous the neighborhoods become. Motorcycle riders in orange vests marked with their license-plate numbers—a law designed to deter bikeborne assassins—weaved in and out of the traffic along with groups of brightly colored cyclists heading to the countryside. (Colombia produces fanatical cyclists, several of whom rode with Lance Armstrong's team.) I was traveling with Scott Dalton, a Texan photographer who has lived in Colombia since the late 1990s. Scott, whose long hair had earned him the nickname Mono Gringo—the blond gringo—had recently finished a controversial documentary on a gang of young urban *paracas,* as the paramilitaries are called, and has a knack for getting along with people at the extreme ends of the country's political spectrum. It seemed like a good idea to bring him along. Originally, we had planned to rent a car, but the concept of a drop-off on the coast was unknown to the Colombian rental companies. Instead we hired Nestor, a Bogotá taxi driver whom Scott had worked with before.

Colombia is often described as "twice the size of France," as if France were somehow a unit of measurement. The topography is impossible; it looks as if the country was once farbigger but has been compacted violently, causing large plains to collapse into deep folds. In the south, the Andes split into three separate ranges; much of the rest of the country is tropical forest and savannah. The geography alone makes Colombia difficult to govern, and the population of 44 million, the second-largest in South America, has fractured into wildly different regional cultures. There is, for instance, an important distinction between the Cachacos, as the people from Bogotá are called, with their reputation for formality and restraint, and the fast-talking, slow-moving Costeños of the Caribbean coast.

As we descended the Andes on steep, choppy hills, we passed men harvesting sugarcane and loading the long stalks onto donkeys. After several hours of carsickness-inducing curves and changing pressure in our ears, the Magdalena River appeared, flowing between low dry hills. Now the air was hot and humid—it felt like stepping out of an airplane after landing in the tropics. In the small towns, loud music blasted from bars and restaurants. The women wore noticeably less clothing, and the men sported variations on Panama hats. Among the campaign posters, of which a surprisingly large number featured female candidates, were billboards of three female torsos in yellow bikinis. These were Aguila (Eagle) beer girls, who appear so often in Colombia that they are a sort of national flag.

Soon we were in Honda (CITY OF PEACE, TOURISM AND COLONIAL HISTORY, said a sign), a weekend destination for Cachacos seeking to escape Bogotá's cool, wet weather for the warmth of the *tierra caliente.* A large steel bridge ran high above the muddy river. The water below foamed into irregular waves between boulder-covered shores from which hundreds of fishermen were tossing nets into the rapids with long wooden prongs. Honda was once very wealthy, the main port of the upper reaches of the Magdalena; narrow cobbled streets of the old city still run past seventeenth century houses that are gradually being renovated for weekenders from the capital. But much of the town is ramshackle and run-down. Honda has an odd feel to it, both stately and unfinished, as if it had been abandoned by its original inhabitants and taken over by people who didn't expect to stay long. The layout is confusing, with dozens of bridges traversing narrow gorges. One of them, an old iron span, had collapsed and still lay at the bottom of one of the ravines. We ended up on the far side of the river at a restaurant called The Breezes of the Magdalena. Here a wind flowed down the canyon; and from a shaded cement platform, we watched fishermen in dugout canoes perform complicated maneuvers with nets while kids in inner tubes rushed by them through the standing waves of the rapids. Lunch came, a fish consommé with lime and cilantro, steaming despite the heat. Many tourists come here, a boy told us, "even some Japanese once."

After Honda, the river slows as it widens on the plain. The landscape had the appearance of several continents at once: the houses were European, with Mediterranean-style terra-cotta shingles, but across the valley rose sandstone buttes and small mountain-shaped hills like in Southeast Asia. The precise, wire-fenced fields looked North American, but the forests and palm trees lining the pastures seemed as tropical as the reddish monkeys that occasionally could be seen atop them. On the drive I had started Gardćia Márquez's *The General in His Labyrinth,* a fictionalized retelling of Simón Bolívar's final few months as he traveled down the Magdalena River to the coast and to his death. By coincidence, Scott and I ended up following almost the same route, although Bolívar took the river, much of which left-wing guerrillas have made too dangerous to travel today.

García Márquez writes about the dying Bolívar stopping in these towns on his way along the Magdalena River, barely able to sleep as fever and disappointment eat away at him. In flashbacks, Bolívar recalls the victories that liberated much of South America from Spain and his ultimate failure to unite South America in an "invincible league of nations." García Márquez portrays Bolívar with fraternal warmth, a younger brother's hero worship. The portrait is like a written version of a nineteenth-century folk painting, self-consciously naive and idiosyncratic. Bolívar is not so much a person as an innocent and cunning man-child striding across the continent, loving women and withering away with fever. The novel is an elegy to Bolívar's refined, almost delicate machismo. At one point on this road, El Libertador fondly reminisces about what was essentially the rape of a slave, "a beautiful mulatta in the flower of her youth" whom he has liberated:

> The General carried her to the hammock, giving her no respite from his soothing kisses, and she gave herself to him not out of desire or love but out of fear. She was a virgin. Only after she regained her courage did she say:
> "I'm a slave, sir."
> "Not anymore," he said. "Love has set you free."

The Middle Magdalena Valley is where the *autodefensas,* as the paramilitary groups have often called themselves, got their start in the early 1980s, as vigilante groups, set up by ranchers and businessmen with the help of the army, to combat kidnappings and extortion by the leftwing militias who then controlled much of the countryside. These vigilante groups, often working with the security services, went on a socialcleansing spree, massacring everyone from suspected guerrilla collaborators to journalists, human-rights workers, indigenous people, prostitutes, presidential candidates, and as many as 3,000 members of one political party. Killers were given nicknames like Black Vladimir and "Two Thousand," the latter moniker indicating the number of people murdered.

It was also in the Middle Magdalena Valley that the *autodefensas* first began working with another group of upwardly mobile landowners: the narco-traffickers. The two groups essentially merged, forming powerful mafias with standing armies that were based on the giant tracts of land controlled by such drug bosses as Pablo Escobar, whose Hacienda Nápoles once covered 5,500 acres in the Middle Magdalena outside Medellín. We decided to make the Hacienda Nápoles our next destination. When we arrived, we found Escobar's swimming pool half-empty and covered in algae, with trees growing through the cement tiles of the deck. A large bullfrog kicked across one comer as calmly as a retiree. It was his pool now.

"That's Pablo's punishment—swimming around in his own muck," Scott said, and walked into the house to photograph its collapsing walls. Shortly after Escobar's death in 1993, treasure hunters had taken apart the two-story house to look for hidden stacks of dollars, knocking down walls and much of the roof. Even part of the pool deck had been tom up.

To get to the hacienda we had driven off the road through an arch with fading blue letters. A newer sign beside it announced that the property had been taken over by the Colombian government. A few hundred yards down the driveway, past some ponds, a group of large, painted plaster dinosaurs, all of them collapsing like a Disney version of Ozymandias, were surrounded by grazing donkeys. Nearby, another sign read: PARQUE ZOOLOGICO NATURAL NAPOLES. This was Escobar's Neverland Ranch. He, too, was fond of adolescents, in his case pubescent girls. He kept an assortment of wild animals here, including rhinos and gazelles, and locals were invited to parties at which Don Pablo handed out presents. The house, built around two sides of the pool, was smaller and less flamboyant than I expected, at least for someone who had once offered to payoff Colombia's national debt. The rounded corners of the windows, removed long ago, suggested a distinct architectural style. (Call it "narcotecture.")

The pioneer of violent drug kingpins and something of a populist folk hero, Escobar won a seat in congress, owned a newspaper, blew up a national jetliner, and was eventually hunted down by U.S. and Colombian law enforcement on a Medellin rooftop in 1993. On our drive through the Middle Magdalena Valley, we met former employees of Escobar's who reminisced about his generosity, talking about him the way some Iraqis talk nostalgically about Saddam Hussein. The cocaine trade, like the oil industry, seems impervious to regime change: Escobar was quickly replaced by the associates who had betrayed him, including "Don Berna," who now controls Medellin from a nearby correctional facility and is in the process of being officially demobilized as a paramilitary leader. Despite the more than 1 million hectares of coca destroyed in the past ten years and the almost 600 traffickers extradited to the United States since 2002, prices have remained essentially level—a 25 percent spike this year has been due only to Mexico's crackdown on its own cartels. The most noticeable effect of the billions spent by the United States on Plan Colombia, 70 to 80 percent of which goes to the armed forces, has been a substantial increase in the government's ability to wage its counterinsurgency war.

We had reached Escobar's ranch shortly before sundown, and it was getting dark. A bat began its erratic, low-flying patrol over the putrid green water of the pool, darting at bugs. The sound of the cicadas swelled to a grating pitch. A twelve-year-old boy named Julián had ridden up on his mountain bike to watch the gringos poke around. He wore red shorts, and a shirt was thrown over his shoulder. Like the other families we met who were living in the outbuildings of Hacienda Napoles, Julián and his family were among the 1.8 million refugees displaced by what he called "the violence," the fighting among right-wing paramilitaries, the Colombian army, and leftwing guerrillas. Decades of war have left Colombia with the largest population of internally displaced people in the world outside of Sudan and Iraq. *"Chicharras,"* he said when we asked him about the sawing sound of the bugs. "They make their noise only from six to six-thirty."

"If it was more than half an hour, Pablo would have had them all killed," Nestor said as he got back into the taxi.

"Are you going to Mompox, Land of God?" asked a man selling soft drinks beside where we waited for the ferry. Whenever people mentioned Santa Cruz de Mompox (pronounced Mornposs), they almost invariably added *Tierra de Dios,* "Land of God." Scott and Nestor chuckled at his Costeño accent, his coastal way of swallowing words. Above us, the foundation of a huge new bridge that would connect Mompox to the highway had only a dirt track leading up to it, stranded like a hippopotamus in a puddle.

Mompox, which in 1810 became the first city in the New World to declare independence from Spain, is central to the Bolívar myth. I had wanted to arrive in Mompox by river like Bolívar had, but the water was now too low. It was here that Bolívar collected four hundred troops who would help liberate much of the rest of the continent. "To Caracas I owe my birth, but to Mompox I owe my glory," he is supposed to have said (though Cartagena claims the quote as well). On the waterfront in Mompox, the town has erected a stone pillar with the dates and directions of Bolívar's visits. Built on an island that separates two branches of the Magdalena, the city was once a crucial port to the interior, providing refuge for the wealthy from massive raids by British buccaneers on Cartagena during the sixteenth and seventeenth centuries. By the late nineteenth century Mompox was dying. The branch of the Magdalena that provided river traffic was silting up, suffocating trade and leaving Mompox preserved in its isolation. Guerrilla activity and bad roads later cut it'off from Cartagena's substantial tourist trade.

It seemed strange that a city built in 1537 in the New World as a major trading center should have accumulated, after almost five hundred years, so little modern suburban rind. A few miles outside of town, the dirt road abruptly turns to asphalt, and soon one arrives at a whitewashed colonial town of narrow streets and squat but elegant buildings. In any other country, Santa Cruz de Mompox would be a marquee tourist attraction, a place where wealthy expatriates would renovate atmospheric, cheap villas and learn Spanish. But Mompox just felt lost. Our hotel was a classic single-story mansion with rooms off a main courtyard behind thick walls. The Spanish-speaking couple in the front hall were the first tourists we'd seen since leaving Bogotà three days earlier.

We wandered out of the hotel into the soupy air and through the town, where the afternoon light slanted across the streets and forced us to hug the shaded wall. Much of the town's life seemed to be hidden in the courtyards. Every now and then we caught glimpses of thick foliage in these courtyards—waxy, dark leaves and rich, energetic flowers framed by iron-grilled windows; otherworldly tableaus in which one might expect to find crouching a wide-eyed lion from a Rousseau painting. In front of one set of huge, green wooden doors that seemed to have been built for giant ancestors, an elderly bald man sat in a rocking chair. He led us inside, around the house he had been fixing up over the past half century. In an open dining room at the back of the courtyard, he picked up a photo of himself dressed as a bishop, from when he played a small role in the film version of García Márquez's *Chronicle of a Death Foretold* starring Rupert Everett. The film had been shot in Mompox. He called himself a "superstar" and laughed. At ninety-one, he looked a bit like the turtles that were creeping around his courtyard garden among the fan palms and potted bougainvillea.

"Things have changed for the worse," he said without malice. "Thank God we've had peace—with the paramilitaries and the guerrillas. This is one of the few places where you can say that in Colombia."

At dusk, we passed a group of quiet but not solemn people attending a funeral mass in the street because it was too hot inside the baroque church of San Agustín. Floating plants swirled in the eddies of the glassy river, and across it the far bank was just a green savannah, empty of development. Mompox reminded me of French villages in the 1970s that were chipped and flaking and moving according to their own social rhythms, despite tourists, before being scrubbed and manicured in the Eighties and turned into boutique malls. Built to exploit the New World, Mompox in old age has proved surprisingly unable to exploit itself.

We reached the coast at Cartagena and then traveled on to Santa Marta—the town where SimÓn Bolívar finally escaped his labyrinth, dying in a colonial hacienda at the edge of the city. Having shrunk by an inch, according to García Márquez, and strangled by coughing, Bolívar was hallucinating, then "driven to despair by the recurrent attacks of hiccupping."

"Damn it," he sighed. "How will I ever get out of this labyrinth!"

Santa Marta, and the coastal state of Magdalena in which it resides, is arguably the capital of what Colombians call *parapolítica,* or "parapolitics": the merging of the paramilitary groups with the political process. Magdalena's governor, Trino Luna, is widely suspected of having used the paramilitary groups to intimidate rivals during his successful 2003 election bid. (He wound up running unopposed.) Last March, when Colombian prosecutors indicted him on these charges, they indicated that the mayor of Santa Marta, José Francisco Zuñiga, was under suspicion as well. Santa Marta today is cheap, full of drugs and caterers to sex tourists—we bumped into a platoon of creepy German men at dinner one night. The hacienda is now a museum, with a parade ground and a monument that looks like it was designed by Albert Speer.

Early the following morning, along with two local guides—Omar and Javier—and an athletic Englishman named Paul who insisted on being called a "backpacker," we headed out of town toward the Sierra Nevada de Santa Marta national park. In 1939, after leading an American expedition to the area, Thomas D. Cabot published a report in the Journal of the American Geographical Society that began, "It is difficult to write of the Sierra Nevada de Santa Marta of Colombia without using superlatives: so far as I know, it is the highest coastal mountain mass in the world, one of the highest from its immediate base, and the nearest to New York offering extensive scope to the alpinist." Cabot was right: it is the tallest coastal mountain range in the world, with a pyramid-shaped formation of snow-covered central mountains that climbs out of the Caribbean and reaches an astonishing 5,800 meters. This massif rising out of the sea like a "biogeographic island" (as one Colombian environmentalist puts it) contains every climatic zone in tropical America. Because this is Colombia, only perhaps a few thousand people go there every year. This might be because much of the 3,800-square-kilometer park is unsafe to visit: left-wing guerrillas control the higher altitudes, right-wing paramilitaries grow coca and opium lower down, and the Kogi—thought to be one of the most genuinely preserved pre-Colombian cultures—and Arhuaca Indians who live there are ambivalent about tourists. After years of fighting and kidnapping, the park has seen more visitors this year than in the past decade. According to park guides, a disproportionate number of the visitors are young Israelis who don't seem to be put off by Colombia's reputation.

As we left the dry, cactus-covered hills on the coast and drove into the rainforest, we passed roadside stands displaying rows of fruit I had never seen before, including *caimito,* which oozed white milk from a gorgeous deep-purple but bland-tasting pulp. It was burning season in the park, the time when *campesinos* cleared extra land and clouds of smoke hung over the steep green valleys. Despite this being a national park, most of the hills here had until recently been planted with coca, but an eradication program had recently fumigated the crops. Many of the *campesinos* had just moved to more remote fields across the valley, and now the old terrain was used for grazing cattle.

On one section where the path switchbacked steeply, Omar pointed to a pair of disintegrating pants, the kind tourists wear that can be unzipped into shorts, hanging off a small shrub like a discarded scarecrow. Omar tapped the side of his nose with his finger. A few months earlier, he said, a coked-up forty-four-year-old Brit had collapsed in the humidity and died, shitting his pants in the process. Omar swore there was still money in the pocket that nobody wanted to touch. Nearby, small bright green coca leaves growing on slender bushes staggered down a hill above a small tin-roofed house. They had fumigated here last year; across the valley cows grazed and the hillside smoked where the *campesinos* were clearing more land.

"They will harvest soon," said Omar. "Now the *campesinos* plant the coca among the yucca so that it doesn't get fumigated."

A few hours later, it started to rain as we descended a steep, rust-colored hill. Rubbery red flowers grew up tall out of broad-leafed plants, and beautiful white flowers, reminiscent of lilies, hung from tree branches upside down like ghostly bats. The Colombians call the tree *borrachero,* which translates roughly as "get-you-drunk," or "go-on-a-bender," or "get-really-tucked-up." The flowers produce a drug called scopolamine, a sedative that causes amnesia and hallucinations. Indian tribes in Colombia are said to have used it to drug the wives of dead chieftains so they could be buried alive. Its properties are especially useful if you want to empty people's bank accounts or sexually abuse them. Colorless and odorless, *borrachero* is easily slipped into someone's drink or inside an offered cigarette. Circe-like women put it on their breasts, ask unsuspecting men to lick them, and soon the entranced men are offering up their PIN numbers. Doormen later tell the owners of robbed apartments that the owners themselves were cooperating with the thieves. According to Omar, the Israeli tourists were really fond of *borrachero* and would make tea with it. A few months earlier, though, one of them had lost her mind, and now Omar wouldn't let them make it any more.

"The tea will make you crazy—it's much stronger than marijuana," said Adan Bedoya, a small-time drug producer who also owned the bed-and-breakfast—actually a series of tin-roofed houses and open-sided buildings alongside the trail—where we stayed that night.

In his early sixties, Adan was doing pretty well, but he wasn't profiting from cocaine. For producers at Adan's level, drugs are actually a poor business. It's not until the paste is refined and then distributed that the margins increase exponentially. Adan figured that each of his four hectares (ten acres) of coca plants yields about one kilogram of paste, which he then sells for 2.5 million pesos a kilo. After paying his workers and buying the chemicals, he makes about $1,000 every four months—not even enough to bribe the police if he is caught with the chemicals.

The next morning, Adan took us to his coca lab. It wasn't much—just a large, wide container like a sandbox with a cement floor, covered with a black tarp and surrounded by a canopy of trees that hid it from the air. The place stank of gasoline, and it grew hot under the tarp while we watched. As part of the demo, Adan threw some coca leaves down and cut them up with a weed whacker. He added sea salt and lime and walked over the pile like a winemaker. The next step was to soak it in gasoline, and, like a television show cook turning to his prepared ingredients, he went over to a barrel that was already full of soaking coca leaves and drained off the gasoline. The cocaine, he said, was now suspended in the gas, and the leaves were just mulch. The following step required mixing the gasoline with sulphuric acid. Adan demonstrated each step as he gradually refined the mass from flammable liquid to gunk and finally ro a paste. The last step involved what looked like an abrasive bathroom cleaner. The final result was a spoonful of greenish goo. A dog with a hole in the side of his face watched us for a while; he tried to take a drink from a black hose, but water poured down his cheek.

"This is educational," Paul the "backpacker" said. "They should bring coke addicts here."

"The tourists always want to put it in their mouths—if it puts your mouth to sleep, it's cocaine," said Adan.

"Some tourists come here and say, I'm glad 'I saw this because I'll never do it again.' It begins with gasoline and acid. The whole process is bad for you."

Hernán Giraldo, the right-wing paramilitary leader whom the newspapers call "Lord of the Sierra," lives inside the national park in the town of Mamai, where we met him almost by accident when we walked past his bungalow. Soon we were sitting in the shade on his veranda, drinking cold soda that had been brought to us by a young man with a flat, broad face and a pistol bulge under his shirt at the waistband. Across the dirt road, men with DAS, the Colombian FBI, stood wearing flak jackets, and near them was a knot of army soldiers. All of them were watching us. Some young women had gathered in a hallway, and men who could only have been Giraldo's bodyguards pulled up more chairs, though their guns were more discreet than their walkie-talkies.

"The ones with legal problems are still waiting to find out what will happen to them. I am also charged," Giraldo said, casually listing the charges against him: "homicide, belonging to a private militia, conspiracy to commit a crime. I haven't been in Santa Marta for sixteen years because of legal problems."

The previous night Adan had told us the story, a legend really, of how Giraldo had escaped four assassination attempts, one of which left 446 bullet holes in his car. And how he had taken on Colombia's most powerful paramilitary leader, Carlos Castaño, and survived—something that could not be said for thousands of others, including several Colombian presidential candidates.

"We have been looking at tourism possibilities," Giraldo said. On our way into the small mountain town, Scott and I had passed some men in a forest clearing who were planting flowers and putting a palm-frond roof on a long, new building. This, as it turns out, was to be Giraldo's hotel. "The Sierra Nevada is very beautiful—there is a hot spring not far away. The hotel you saw will have a natural swimming pool, room for sixty people, and a restaurant. It will be in a very natural style and finished quickly—we are in a hurry. Now we are working with the army because we want the tourists to be safe."

Giraldo had the look of someone who had once been poor but had known just what to do to afford the jewel-encrusted gold rooster that now hung on a large chain and poked out of his open shirt. His thick gold rings covered in precious stones looked like gifts a Renaissance pope might have given an NFL team. His mustache was trimmed, his face clean-shaven, but there was nothing pampered about the way he looked at us. His Panama hat elegantly framed a face that demanded to be called Don Hemán.

"I came here in 1969 as a colonizer. It was all mountains with few people—not even any guerrillas. We grew coffee, chocolate, and sugarcane and raised cattle, a bit of everything. In 1979, the guerrillas arrived and started charging taxes. But we didn't think that the campesinos should have to collaborate if they didn't want to. The guerrillas called me personally because I was a community leader. They wanted 10 percent of everything I produced and wanted to control the schools and teach guerrilla politics. They demanded to know how much everybody made, who lived where, and they wanted our children to join the FARC. They wanted us to pay a war tax, but we had no money. When they first tried to kill me, I was wounded by five grenades and bullets. They tried four times. We turned to the army and the police, and they accompanied us for a small amount of time. And then they abandoned us. FARC then came to kill some campesinos, and we felt obliged to arm ourselves. This was in 1980. At first we had hunting rifles. Over time we bought weapons and some were given to us. We formed an autodefensa in 1983 and defended the region. And so more people came because it was safe and more business grew up between here and the ocean. We lived well until we had to demobilize. We had an agreement with the government to provide security alongside the army and security services. We don't know if the FARC and the ELN will begin to probe the area now, but we will stay here and try to live."

The "legal problems" Giraldo referred to are something of a euphemism, and his history was somewhat incomplete. During the late 1970s and 1980s, he traded in marijuana, mostly the celebrated Santa Marta Gold. Giraldo is said to have switched to cocaine in the early 1990s, building his private army and buying hotels, fish farms, and ranches along the way. Now he was switching to tourism. Or at least he was now providing services for the money tourists were paying him already. Like every other visitor, we involuntarily had given a twenty-five dollar tax to Giraldo's paramilitaries for protection inside the national park when we paid for our tour at the Turcol agency offices in Santa Marta.

Giraldo is arguably one of the most powerful drug dealers in the world. In a 2001 article, *Newsweek* said that he "may one day rival the late Medellin-cartel kingpin Pablo Escobar in both wealth and power." The legend includes—apart from the usual kidnapping and murder—his cutting up four construction workers with chainsaws after they finished a secret cocaine storage facility; killing the head of the park we were sitting in; massacring twenty unionized banana workers (for which he was sentenced to a twenty year prison term he hasn't served); and ordering the successful murders of three Colombian drug agents, as well as the attempted murders of two DEA officers working in Colombia. At one point, Giraldo was said to be sending $1.2 billion worth of cocaine each year to the United States from his stronghold in the Sierra Nevada mountains using dozens of "go-fast" speedboats, a figure that put him among Colombia's top five drug traffickers.

While developing their new ecotourism business, Giraldo and about a hundred of his men were under house arrest in MamaÏ, waiting for the final stages of his negotiations with the government. In the past few weeks, 1,166 members of his private army had demobilized, and the rest were waiting to hear about charges that had been brought against them. Confessions and a return of some property would later result in a very short prison sentence. Giraldo is perhaps the most egregious example of President Uribe's "revolution"—the demobilization of *autodefensas* that has in fact legitimized a drug mafia. Today, along with other paramilitary leaders, he is under arrest in a former recreational facility outside Medellin, secure in the knowledge that if he confesses to his crimes he will not be extradited to the United States. Not surprisingly, Giraldo described himself to us as a "defender of the people against the guerrillas," speaking those words with the confidence of someone who knows that the government has to believe his version of the truth.

As Scott and I drove into Barranquilla from Santa Marta, we followed an old red Renault 4 with a pair of dummy legs and a large penis hanging off the back bumper. People dressed as apes and assorted trans-gendered beings assaulted our car with shaving cream-like foam as we entered the suburbs. It was the first morning of the city's Carnaval, and the husband of my childhood friend Marea had arranged for us to join one of the companies taking part in the Battle of the Flowers parade. Shabby in areas, full of apartment buildings, and very hot, Barranquilla isn't that impressive; but Colombians love it, and the city has a reputation for being a lot of fun. After lunch, our host came downstairs in a blue costume that made him appear to be a cross between an Italian clown and a Saudi woman. He handed us some shirts that had once belonged to his mother. I chose one that was such a strange collection of patterns it was difficult to know what fashion moment produced it, but I thought it might be mistaken for part of a costume. It was heavy for the heat and smelled musty.

For several hours, we stood around baking in an industrial area of the city, drinking rum and ice from plastic cups and waiting for the parade to start. A woman in blackface had white lines where sweat streaked down her neck. A satyr plastered with silvery pancake makeup was being attached to a pair of hind legs on rollers. A few dozen bands with drums and various brass instruments lined up with their groups along the avenue, playing a few bars and then stopping. Dancers in elaborate African-inspired bathing suits or traditional Spanish formal-wear practiced for a few minutes, entertaining small crowds from other companies. The only shade came from the high concrete wall of a factory, where men went to piss and people sat out of the sun, some of them smoking pot.

The parade started to move. On one side of the road, the wealthier Colombians sat in shaded stands. On the other side, the poorer classes stood or sat on plastic chairs and occasionally came out and danced with us as we went by. Thankfully, people on both sides of the road seemed less interested in watching us than in spraying one another with foam. The last time I had been in a large, crowded parade was during Ashura, the Shia festival of mourning in the southern Iraqi city of Karbala, where chanting men beat themselves with chains and sliced open their heads with swords. That display was about death and mourning whereas this one was Dionysian,

but in each of them I could feel the way the spirit of the crowd pulled me in, held me.

The next day, when Scott and I flew back to Bogotá, the plane took us across much of the ground we had covered, over the cordilleras and the river valleys that had been off-limits to visitors for so many years. No longer—1.5 million tourists came to Colombia last year, and one cannot help but be glad that they (and Colombians, too) can now more safely enjoy the country's extraordinary places, like Mompox, Hacienda Nápoles, the Sierra Nevada de Santa Marta. Foreign investment has increased more than four times in as many years; last March, Cartagena was visited by none other than Bill Gates, who announced that Microsoft would fund nine educational centers in Colombia to teach demobilized paramilitary troops how to use computers.

But many Colombians wonder what good can come of a peace deal with the paramilitaries that whitewashes three decades of massacres, drug dealing, and corruption—much of which continues, albeit with a lower body count. One notorious paramilitary leader, Rodrigo Tovar, negotiated his demobilization even as he was ordering the deaths of hundreds more people. A list of more than 550 names was later found on his laptop; the files also included instructions for teaching unemployed peasants to act like soldiers on demobilization day, so that real units could remain armed and in control of "vulnerable zones." Men like Tovar and Hernán Giraldo cannot be extradited, and they are unlikely to serve significant prison terms in their own country. For the victims, there has been no justice at all. Alvaro Uribe has made the country safe for travel again, but Colombians have paid an intolerable toll.

Patrick Graham's last article for Harper's Magazine, *"Beyond Fallujah"* (June 2004), was the winner of an Overseas Press Club award.

Challenge Questions

After reading this article, you will be able to answer the following questions:

1. What can explain the persistence of violence in Colombia?
2. What steps has the government taken to reduce coca cultivation and narco-trafficking?
3. What impact has the drug culture had on Colombian society?

13 Wolf Sheds Fleece: Venezuela's Drift to Authoritarianism

Learning Objectives

After reading this article, you will more clearly understand the following:

- Authoritarianism
- Media freedom
- Rule of law

Hugo Chavez worries ever less about maintaining a semblance of democracy.

Opponents of Hugo Chavez have often bewailed his knack of cloaking authoritarianism in outwardly democratic forms. So perhaps they should be grateful that the Venezuelan president is increasingly abandoning the pretence. On January 23rd—a date on which the country commemorates the 1958 uprising that ousted its last military dictator—cable-television operators were told to stop carrying RCTV, a pro-opposition channel. It was the latest in a series of recent moves that have placed Mr Chavez's elected regime within a hair's breadth of dictatorship.

Three years ago RCTV's broadcasting licence was not renewed, confining it to cable. Now the government has ruled that, despite being a cable channel, it (and many other channels) must obey a broadcasting law that requires it, among other things, to transmit the president's lengthy speeches live, whenever he feels like it. The urge came over him almost immediately, at a political rally. When RCTV declined to oblige him, its fate was sealed.

The Inter-American Commission on Human Rights (part of the Organisation of American States) complained that RCTV and the other channels had been punished without due process, and called for their rights to be restored. The response of the regime, which has repeatedly snubbed the regional body, was to blow a raspberry.

Venezuelans are due to vote for a new parliament in September. Last year, Mr Chavez won a referendum he had called to abolish term limits for presidents and other senior elected officials. Now, opinion polls are showing unprecedented levels of discontent over crime, inflation, and power and water shortages. There were big anti-government protests in Caracas, the capital, after RCTV was shut off, which were countered by the government's more modest rally.

These problems, and the resulting discontent, may well intensify in coming months. Even the president's undoubted charisma has not rendered him immune. In one recent poll, 66% said they did not want him to continue in office when his present term ends in three years.

If the September elections were run according to the constitution, which mandates proportional representation, Mr Chavez would surely lose his strong parliamentary majority. But a new electoral law allows the largest single group to sweep the board. The government-dominated electoral authority redrew constituency boundaries this month, with the effect of minimising potential opposition gains. The closure of RCTV, one of the main outlets for anti-Chavez voices, seems to follow the same logic.

In his annual address to Parliament, earlier this month, the president announced (to no one's surprise) that he was now a Marxist. He no longer pays lip-service to the separation of powers, which in practice disappeared some time ago. The head of the Supreme Court, Luisa Estella Morales, said last month that such niceties merely "weaken the state". A leading member of the ruling United Socialist Party, Aristobulo Isturiz, called for the dismantling of local government, which Mr Chavez wants to replace with communes.

The 1999 constitution guarantees property rights and the existence of private enterprise. But the president now says that private profit is the root of all evil. Callers to the government's consumer-protection body, Indepabis, find its hold-music is a jingle about evil capitalists. Insisting that his recent currency devaluation was no excuse for price rises, Mr Chavez had Indepabis close down hundreds of stores for "speculation". He told Parliament to change the law on expropriations and seized a French-controlled supermarket chain to add to the government's new retail conglomerate, Comerso.

The opposition parties, wrangling over "unity" candidates for parliament, are ill equipped to deal with this onslaught. But there are signs of tension within the regime itself. On January 25th, the vice-president, Ramon Carrizalez, resigned, along with his wife, the environment minister. He cited personal reasons, but that a close ally, the minister of public banking, also quit (over unexplained "health problems") set tongues wagging.

Rumours from within the recesses of the regime attribute Mr Carrizalez's departure to manoeuvring by the public-works minister, Diosdado Cabello, who is widely regarded as the second-most-powerful figure in the government. Mr Carrizalez was also defence minister and was replaced in that job by a general close to Mr Cabello. Thereby Mr Cabello, who is reputed to have designs on the presidency, has further consolidated his grip on the army.

The president's determination to cling to power and intolerance of dissent have sapped his popularity and may, if the elections go badly for him, sap his ability to govern. He is—as Vladimir Villegas, a journalist and former ally, wrote this week—now trapped in the autocratic scheme he has chosen to follow. That scheme bears scant resemblance to the liberal democracy under which he was elected.

Challenge Questions

After reading this article, you will be able to answer the following questions:

1. How can a country move from democracy to dictatorship?
2. How does a government control an opposition media?
3. What can account for the popularity of President Chavez?
4. How can the ineffectiveness of opposition political parties be explained?

14 Chavez Struggles to Fix Venezuela's Housing Crisis

Christopher Toothaker

Learning Objectives

After reading this article, you will more clearly understand the following:

- Why Venezuela has a serious shortage of housing
- One consequence of rural to urban migration
- Government rhetoric and Venezuelan reality

For more than a year, thousands of Venezuelans have been living in disaster shelters, sleeping in bunks and sharing bathrooms.

Their long wait for government homes shows how far President Hugo Chavez still has to go to fulfill his promises of aid for the poor after nearly 13 years in office.

Opposition politicians estimate that more than 30,000 people remain in the shelters waiting for Chavez to deliver. And yet, his inability to keep such grand promises doesn't seem to be a serious handicap as he seeks re-election next year.

"I trust Chavez will get us into an apartment. I just don't know when that could occur, and waiting so long is becoming more and more difficult," said Christian Ortiz, who spent a second Christmas in the crowded shelter with his wife and two children.

For months, Ortiz and his family have been watching construction workers shoulder steel rods and pour cement as they build a government apartment building two blocks away from the community center where they are living. They expect to eventually be assigned one of the 400 apartments in the half-finished building, and are hoping that 2012 will be their year.

Caracas has long had large hillside slums of "ranchos" slapped together with bricks and concrete, many built on unstable ground that regularly collapses in rainstorms. Torrential rains and landslides in late 2010 destroyed homes in parts of Caracas and forced tens of thousands of evacuees to move into disaster shelters nationwide.

A year later, Chavez's government is struggling to cope with a shortage of affordable housing so severe that it could easily take a decade or more to remedy.

Those living in disaster shelters are only part of the problem. A recent government survey found that more than 3.1 million of the nation's roughly 29 million people have inadequate housing.

Chavez set a goal of building about 150,000 homes this year, and he said on Saturday that more than 125,000 housing units have been completed. His opponents question the official figures, and the government hasn't provided a detailed breakdown of homes built by the government and private construction companies, nor has it specified whether the figures include refurbished housing.

"It's December and we have the same homeless people waiting for houses for a year due to lack of commitment and inefficiency," opposition lawmaker Julio Borges said at a recent news conference. He accused the government of inflating its figures and providing far fewer homes than it claims.

"If 100,000 houses were built as they say, to whom did they give them?" Borges asked.

Housing Ministry officials did not respond to requests for an interview.

Chavez's construction effort has leaned not on local builders but instead has enlisted construction companies from allied countries such as Iran, China, Russia, Brazil and Cuba.

The leftist leader has also expropriated buildings and vacant lots where construction crews have been cleaning debris and laying foundations. The government has seized 1,045 parcels of land and buildings this year, including 461 properties and assets from construction companies, according to a report by Conindustria, the country's largest industrial chamber.

Chavez recently said his government has poured 52 billion bolivars, or about $12 billion, into housing projects this year, according to the state news agency. That helped the construction sector grow 10 percent in the third quarter of the year and contributed to overall quarterly growth of 4.2 percent, according to the Central Bank.

The lofty goal of constructing more than 150,000 homes in a year hasn't been reached, critics say, in part due to excessive bureaucracy and lack of communication among dozens of companies and institutions that Chavez has tapped. The country's construction chamber has also complained about shortages of supplies, including cement.

In addition to construction firms, the government has enlisted the Housing Ministry, state-run oil and petrochemical companies and a host of pro-Chavez state governors and other officials to oversee the projects.

The government also has used an unorthodox variety of buildings to temporarily house displaced families: an unfinished shopping mall, a horse-racing track and even tent-like shelters in a courtyard behind Chavez's presidential palace.

Some of the homeless have moved into privately owned hotels that opened their doors to evacuees at the government's request.

When Chavez was sworn in as president in 1999, the country already suffered a major shortage of housing, a problem that grew from heavy migration to urban slums and a construction industry that had focused on building homes largely for the middle class and the affluent.

The country's housing deficit has long been more severe than those of many other Latin American nations, said Paulina Villanueva, who heads the Villanueva Foundation, a Caracas-based think tank that analyzes urban planning.

The problem goes back to the 1940s and '50s, when the growth of Venezuela's oil industry and the decline of its farming economy prompted many to migrate to the cities in search of jobs, Villanueva said. She said that for much of Chavez's presidency, the government seems to have had priorities other than the housing crisis.

Many poor Venezuelans live crammed in slum housing with zinc roofs, sometimes lacking running water. Others have seized abandoned buildings where they live as squatters.

Hundreds of such squatters fill an unfinished 45-story skyscraper in Caracas that has been abandoned since the mid-1990s. Often known as the Tower of David after the late entrepreneur David Brillembourg, who invested in the building, the high-rise's helicopter pad marks a strong contrast to the smashed windows that leave many occupants exposed to the wind and rain.

Chavez has fed the hopes of many Venezuelans by vowing to provide a roof for every family in need, and the government is heavily promoting its efforts. Banners flying beside newly built red brick buildings tout the "Great Housing Mission," while during the televised inauguration of one apartment complex in western Lara state, a giant inflatable likeness of Chavez wobbled in front of the building.

Opposition politicians have tried to use the government's performance against Chavez in the run-up to the October presidential vote, when he will seek another six-year term. But thus far, the potential for political fallout seems limited.

Ortiz and many others living in the shelters still hold out hope that Chavez will eventually come through, and the president's approval rating has been hovering around 50 percent in recent polls.

"We trust Chavez. He promised us a house, and we're sure we'll have one sooner or later," said Katiuska Hernandez, 32, who gathered her belongings in boxes as she and her family left a shelter temporarily to spend the holidays with relatives. "The problem is the delay. This process has taken too much time."

Some have grown so impatient living in the shelters that they have begun venting frustration in small protests where they hold hands to block streets and demand results.

Chavez has urged patience. When heavy rains earlier this month forced more Venezuelans into disaster shelters, he offered about $350 in cash assistance to each displaced family.

"We are resolving numerous problems such as housing all at once," Chavez said last month.

On a breezy hilltop overlooking the Caribbean Sea near Caracas, a flagship housing project is being built by a joint company formed by the Venezuelan and Cuban governments.

Chavez calls it Caribia Socialist City, and the government says it will become a model self-sufficient community with a state-run supermarket, small farms and schools.

The Socialist City may be a metaphor for how far Chavez still has to go in addressing the housing shortage. Plans call for about 80,000 homes to be built. So far, after more than three years of construction, the Housing Ministry has said that about 600 families have been able to move into the first apartments.

Challenge Questions

After reading this article, you will be able to answer the following questions:

1. What are the forces that drive rural to urban migration?
2. Why has the government failed to meet its own housing goals?
3. What part have natural disasters played in the crisis?
4. Why has Chavez been described as "leftist" and how does that relate to the housing crisis?

15 In Cuba Property Thaw, New Hope for a Decayed Icon

Peter Orsi and Andrea Rodriguez

Learning Objectives

After reading this article, you will more clearly understand the following:

- Cuba's new economic model
- Societal changes during the Cuban Revolution
- Redevelopment of Havana

Along Havana's northern coastline, storms that roll down from the north send waves crashing against the concrete seawall, drenching vintage cars and kids playing games of chicken with the salty spray.

Fisherman toss their lines into the warm waters, shirtless men play dominoes on card tables, and throngs of young people gather on weekend nights to laugh, flirt and sip cheap rum.

This is the achingly beautiful and most instantly recognizable part of Havana's cityscape: the Malecon seafront boulevard, with its curlicue lampposts and pastel buildings rising into an azure sky.

Just about anywhere else in the world, it would be a playground for the wealthy, diners in four-star restaurants and tourists willing to spend hundreds of dollars a night for a million-dollar view.

But along the Malecon, many buildings are dank, labyrinthine tenements bursting beyond capacity, plagued by mold and reeking of backed-up sewer drains. Paint peels away from plaster, and the saline air rusts iron bars to dust. Some buildings have collapsed entirely, their propped-up facades testimony to a more dignified architectural era.

Now, for the first time since the 1959 revolution, a new law that permits the sale of real estate has transformed these buildings into extremely valuable properties. Another new law that allows more people to go into business for themselves has entrepreneurs setting up shop and talking up the future. And a multimillion-dollar revitalization project is marching down the street improving lighting, sidewalks and drainage.

The year has seen some remarkable first steps toward a new Cuban economic model, including the sacrificing of a number of Marxism's sacred cows. The state is still firmly in control of all key sectors, from energy and manufacturing to health care and education, but increasingly people are allowed to engage in a small measure of private enterprise. Officials say the changes are irreversible, and this is the last chance to save the economy.

Yet Cubans will tell you that change comes slowly on the island. Strict controls on foreign investment and property ownership mean there's precious little money to bankroll a capitalist revival. Even some Malecon denizens who embrace the reforms see a long haul ahead.

"It's not that I see the future as black, more like I'm seeing a little spark from someone 3 kilometers away who lit a match," said Jose Luis Leal Ordonez, the proprietor of a modest snack shop. "But it's a match, not a lantern."

Leal's block, the first one along the promenade, has offered a front row seat to five decades of Cuba under Fidel Castro. The residents of Malecon 1 to 33 have watched the powerful forces of revolution play out beneath their balconies, and today they're bracing for yet another act as Castro's younger brother Raul turns a half-century of Communist dogma on its ear.

Given that Cuba's national identity has been inextricably bound up with its powerful neighbor 150 kilometers (90 miles) to the north, it is perhaps fitting that the Malecon is the legacy of a "Yanqui."

The year was 1900 and the country was under U.S. control following the Spanish-American War. Governor General Leonard Wood, who commanded the Rough Riders during the war with friend Teddy Roosevelt as his No. 2, launched a public works program to clean up unsanitary conditions and stimulate the economy. A key element was the Malecon.

At that time Havana ended about a block from the sea, separated from the waves by craggy rock. Raw sewage seeped into the bay nearby, so fishermen and bathers avoided this part of the waterfront. Only later would high-rise hotels and casinos spring up to make the Malecon a world-famous tourism draw.

For those early American occupiers, "The idea was to create a maritime drive so the city, which until now had its back to the sea, would begin to face the ocean," said architect Abel Esquivel. Since 1994, he has been working with the City Historian's office to restore the crumbling Malecon.

As the boulevard and promenade took shape, buildings sprang up on this block. One of the first was a three-story boarding house for singles and childless couples who occupied 12 apartments.

Today those have been subdivided horizontally and vertically, again and again, to take advantage of every last inch of space, and some 70 families live crammed into every nook and cranny.

Leal runs his cafeteria in the home where he was born 46 years ago, at the dark crux of an interior passageway.

It caters mostly to neighbors and goes unnoticed by tourists on the sun-drenched walk outside.

A lifelong supporter of the revolution, Leal is grateful for the opportunity to live rent-free and earn two master's degrees on the state's dime. Still, after years of frustration working for dysfunctional government bureaucracies, he quit his state job. He opened his snack shop May 1, and already it brings more income than before, enough even for his daughter's upcoming "quinceanera," her coming-of-age 15th birthday party.

He is one of the people on this block who is buying into Castro's entrepreneurial challenge.

Another is Omar Torres, who operates a private restaurant known as a "paladar" on a second-story terrace with sea and skyline views. He praised the government for lifting a ban on the serving of lobster and steak and allowing him to more than quadruple the number of diners he can seat.

Downstairs, an artist runs an independent gallery selling paintings of "Che" Guevara and cityscapes to tourists. Although he doesn't own the house, he's so confident in the future that he's using the income to remodel his rental.

Elsewhere folks are letting out rooms to travelers, and newly licensed street vendors are now legally peddling peanuts in tightly wrapped paper cones.

"Cubans dream of truly feeling like masters of their own destiny, for the state not to interfere in personal matters," Leal said. "Until now the state told you that you couldn't even sell your home."

From its early days, the Malecon was a place to see and be seen, to celebrate a success, drown a sorrow or woo a sweetheart. By the 1920s it was a favorite strip for middle-class Cubans who motored up and down to show off their vehicles.

Havana developed without a strong central plan or dominant core, and the Malecon became one of its most important communal spaces, said historian Daniel Rodriguez, a Cuban-American researcher at New York University.

"I think the closest thing Havana has to an urban center is this long seawall," Rodriguez said. "It's a long, ribbony main square."

Today the concrete promenade stretches 6 kilometers (4 miles) from the harbor to the Almendares River, the last section completed in 1958 under strongman Fulgencio Batista.

Those were heady times, when the city's nightclubs pulsed with a mambo beat and mafia casinos on the Malecon drew planeloads of American tourists. But their days were numbered.

The following January, the young rebel Fidel Castro marched triumphantly into Havana and in short order began seizing mansions and apartment buildings and redistributing them to the poor, triggering a tectonic shift in housing as well as the rest of the economy and society.

Castro declared private real estate incompatible with the revolution's ideals. "For the bourgeoisie," he said,

things like "country, society, liberty, family and humanity have always been tied to a single concept: private property."

In a country where everyone is guaranteed a place to live, millions are jammed into dilapidated, multigenerational homes. The government is landlord to vast ranks of tenants who pay nothing or a nominal rent of around $2 a month. Sapped of any sense of ownership, some cannibalized the old buildings, ripping out wood, cinderblocks and decorative tiles to use or sell. That, combined with the punishing climate, has stifled upkeep and hastened decay in the buildings on the Malecon.

One of them, the Hotel Surf, was a beauty when Griselia Valdes arrived here as an 18-year-old newlywed in 1963. The entryway was tiled in pink and black with white benches and a restaurant on the ground floor. The rooms even had air-conditioning.

The glass bricks that lined the front wall are long gone, demolished by big storms. A drainpipe dumps over a spider web of electrical wires hanging at eye level in a passageway, while rainwater filters through the walls and spills into the lobby. The elevator was taken out years ago, but with the motor left rusting at the top of the shaft, people fear it could come crashing down any day.

"Mostly it is us who have abused the building with the subdivisions, with the banging and the crashing," Valdes said. "From neglecting it, from indolence."

Jan Ochoa Barzaga, who lives in the hotel's basement, is pessimistic about how much Raul Castro's reforms can change things. The factory worker finds it very frustrating that his girlfriend, like many others in Cuba, received a free university education from a generous government, but is languishing in a low-paid job.

Ochoa Barzaga tried to make the sea passage off the island in 2009, but was caught and returned home. If he had another opportunity to leave, he wouldn't think long.

"If they opened it up again," said the 32-year-old. "I'd be out of here."

The Malecon continued to serve as center-stage throughout Fidel Castro's rule, with the military conducting war games along the seawall during the 1960s after the failed Bay of Pigs invasion. In 2000 a flag-waving Castro personally led marches along the seawall to demand Cuban raft-boy Elian Gonzalez's return from the United States.

Four years earlier, with Cuba buckling under a severe economic crisis following the collapse of the Soviet Union, thousands marched through the streets with makeshift plywood and inner-tube rafts and set off from the Malecon in a desperate gamble to reach Florida. Many failed.

On Aug. 5 of that year, riotous protests erupted on the boulevard and surrounding streets that were likely the biggest challenge to Castro since he took power. Amid looting and dozens of arrests, Castro addressed the crowd from atop a military vehicle.

"We were witnesses to all that," said Torres, the private restaurant owner, who saw the multitudes from his balcony. "You began to reconsider the meaning that Fidel has for Cubans, because in a moment of chaos and uncertainty, his presence was something else. Even the rioters began shouting, 'Fidel! Fidel!'"

That image of a robust, charismatic father figure faded when illness forced him from power five years ago.

The future is left to Raul, who at 80, is five years younger than his brother. He has dropped one bombshell after another with his economic reforms. None caused more of a stir than the measure legalizing the real estate market.

There's no sign of an imminent gold rush along this block of the Malecon, or anywhere else. Few individuals hold title to these homes; most rent from the government. Meanwhile the new law contains protections against individual accumulation of property or wealth, and officials insist this is no wholesale embrace of capitalism.

"All these changes, necessary to update the economic model, aim to preserve socialism, strengthen it and make it truly irrevocable," Raul Castro said in December 2010.

There's also the question of money: Cuba has only a tiny middle class with the kind of coin to not only buy a seafront home but afford the maintenance needed to keep the corrosive air at bay. The new law bars anyone not a permanent resident from buying property, including exiles who still imagine a day when they might return.

For Jorge Sanguinetty, who grew up a few blocks from the Malecon and was an economist for central planning under Fidel Castro before fleeing in 1967, the history of the seawalk is personal.

"I was like Tom Sawyer or Huck Finn. I used to go fishing there, walking through the rocks. We could see the salt from the waves on our windows during the storms," Sanguinetty recalled, saying he still dreams about it more than 40 years later. "You have to see a sunset (on the) Malecon. They are absolutely sensational."

Sanguinetty, founder of the international development group DevTech Systems, is writing a book about potential redevelopment in Cuba and has followed the issue closely over the years. He said the same forces that caused the Malecon's decay also added to its charm.

"The stagnation of Havana had this unintended consequence: Even though many things have fallen apart and are no longer salvageable, Havana will remain very desirable because uncontrolled development didn't take place," he said by phone from his office in Miami. "So there are many jewels there architecturally, and the Malecon is one of the most beautiful jewels in the crown."

When it comes to the Malecon, the City Historian's Office wields near-total control. A largely autonomous institution, it collects undisclosed millions of dollars each year from the hotels and tourist restaurants it runs in restored buildings, and plows a big chunk of that back into rehabilitating more. The office recently said it has more than 180 projects, on top of the hundreds already completed.

The result has been an architectural rebirth that's on display in the gleaming Spanish-American cultural center, a rescued former tenement next door to Leal's building. A few doors away is a near-total rehab with brand-new apartments upstairs from a state-run restaurant, a mixed-use model that could be repeated.

There are also reminders that money is tight. Residents here remember how in the early 2000s, at the site of the collapsed Hotel Miramar, a fancy hotel from 1902 where tuxedoed waiters once attended to a fashionable clientele, Fidel Castro and Chinese President Jiang Zemin laid the cornerstone for a $24 million hotel to be built with help from Beijing.

Construction mysteriously froze after just a few weeks. Today, bricks form a single uncompleted first story and a faded artistic rendering tacked to a fence depicts the glassy, hyper-modern structure that never got built.

Despite the decay and unfulfilled hopes, the residents say they live in a magical place that creates a sense of community that doesn't exist even one block inland.

"I'm right on what we call the balcony of the city," said Leal, the cafeteria owner. "For me there's no place more sacred than where I live."

Challenge Questions

After reading this article, you will be able to answer the following questions:

1. How is Havana's Malecon symbolic of the Cuban Revolution?
2. What are the benefits or costs of an authoritarian government?
3. Why does Cuba have a small middle class?
4. Why has Raul Castro changed the government's economic policies?

16 The Stomachs of Strongmen

Ann Louise Bardach

Learning Objectives

After reading this article, you will more clearly understand the following:

- Connection between major health issues and authoritarian rulers
- Symbiotic relationship between Venezuela and Cuba
- Fidel Castro as a revolutionary symbol

The tribute concert Aug. 12 for Fidel Castro's 85th birthday, at the Karl Marx Theater in Havana, was billed as the Serenata de la Fidelidad (the Serenade to Fidelity). In terms of flat-footed plays on the name of Cuba's maximum leader, I prefer "The Fideliad"—which speaks to his epic, exhausting and endless run, which began in 1959.

Some 5,000 concertgoers turned out for the homage by 22 singers, including Omara Portuondo of the Buena Vista Social Club, but the guest of honor was not present. Instead, he settled for a quiet celebration with family, his 80-year-old brother and presidential successor, Raúl, and his devoted disciple, President Hugo Chávez of Venezuela. The irrepressible Mr. Chávez broke the news on Twitter late Saturday: "Here with Fidel, celebrating his 85th birthday! Viva Fidel!"

Over the last decade, the two leaders have celebrated quite a few birthdays together. For his 75th in 2001, Mr. Castro trooped to Caracas for a bash with Mr.Chávez, who hosted a Champagne gala, followed by a nautical tour of Venezuela's rainforests. The visit, Mr. Chávez said, "gives us an opportunity to let him know how much we love him."

It's unclear how many birthdays are left for either leader. Both are now facing their greatest challenges yet, not from opposition movements or dissidents, but from their own failing bodies. Mr. Castro nearly died in 2006 during a botched colon surgery to treat a pernicious case of chronic diverticulitis. He passed his 80th birthday lying in a hospital bed, connected to an antibiotic and nutrient drip. Sitting beside him was Hugo Chávez, who has been there at every stage of Mr. Castro's five-year convalescence, casually jetting into Havana as if it were a stroll around the block.

Now the 57-year-old Venezuelan is fighting for his own life, after a baseball-size tumor was removed from his abdomen in Havana's top hospital in June. It was Fidel Castro, not an oncologist, surgeon or family member, who delivered the bad news to Mr. Chávez post-surgery, and who outlined his prognosis and treatment—along with his usual tips on public relations and political strategies. It is likely, based on his surgeries, symptoms and treatment, that Mr. Chávez has metastasized colorectal cancer. After surgery and radiation, he is probably undergoing at least six months of chemotherapy, again in Havana, where he just finished his second round.

As it turned out, Mr. Castro spent much of his birthday giving his friend a pep talk. "We spoke about everything," Mr. Chávez related upon his return to Caracas. "He said to me: Chávez, 'You yourself can begin to convince yourself that everything's over. . . . No, no, it's not over.'"

Ironically, the hemisphere's most indomitable strongmen and determined foes of the United States and free market economics have both been felled, at least for now, by abdominal woes—their guts, as it were. It's just one more anomaly shared by the leader of the country with the world's largest reserve of oil and that of a debt-saddled island in the Caribbean.

The symbiosis between Cuba's emeritus or former (and in most ways, still de facto) commander in chief and the Venezuelan colonel-turned-oil-sultan is the most powerful and fascinating political alliance in the Americas. Five years before becoming president in 1999 and two years after a failed coup attempt, Mr. Chávez was released from prison and flew to Havana in hopes of meeting his revolutionary hero. Waiting to welcome him at the airport was the man himself. It's been a lovefest ever since, with Mr. Chávez declaring that Venezuela is sailing in Cuba's "sea of happiness."

More crucially, after Cuba lost its Russian patron and plummeted into economic free fall, Mr. Chávez gave his friend one of the most magnanimous gifts in history—around 100,000 barrels of oil every day, gratis, with no strings attached—for as long as Cuba wanted it. In exchange, Mr. Castro sent thousands of doctors to Caracas—a deal derided by some critics as "oil for ointment." No one doubts who got the better deal.

Unlike the quid-pro-quo-demanding Soviets, who picked up most of Cuba's tab for three decades, Mr. Castro now receives adoration from a leader who happily calls him "mi padre."

Not without reason. In 2002, when a coup appeared to have dislodged Mr. Chávez from power, it was Mr. Castro who spent night after night on the phone, tutoring his charge in a strategy to regain power and dispatch his enemies. "Don't resign! Don't resign! I kept telling him," Mr. Castro recounted in his autobiography.

Since then, Ramiro Valdés, Cuba's pre-eminent policeman and spymaster, has made Caracas a second home, reorganizing Venezuela's military, police force and Internet services (a fiber-optic cable connects the two countries like an umbilical cord). Cuban advisers are dotted throughout Venezuela's ministries, offering counsel on everything from literacy to opposition movements and elections. There will not be another coup, or many more elections.

"Deep down," says the Venezuelan convalescent in chief, "we are one government." They don't call it "Venecuba" for nothing.

Hence, if the health of either man further fails—and both are walking the razor's edge—all bets are off. One cannot overstate the symbolism that surrounds Fidel Castro in Latin America; Mr. Chávez's legitimacy as a Bolivarian revolutionary depends, in large part, on his being mentored by Mr. Castro. And if Mr. Chávez succumbs to illness or is (somehow) voted out, Cuba's oil spigot could well be turned off by a less generous successor. Raúl Castro, who is trying to salvage Cuba's bankrupt economy with all manner of fixes and reforms, is especially dependent on Venezuelan munificence.

Despite the ailing titans, change is happening in Cuba—in ways big and small and previously unthinkable. Take for instance the marriage of a transsexual woman and an H.I.V.-positive gay man on Mr. Castro's birthday. Hailing it as their "gift" to him, the happy couple cruised in a convertible through Havana, where gay men could once be hauled into work camps for being "anti-revolutionary." The bride had her sex change surgery at the National Center for Sexual Education, run by Mariela Castro Espín, Raúl Castro's free-spirited daughter, who has turned Havana into the San Francisco of the Caribbean.

Tolerance for entrepreneurship is also increasing. Cubans will soon be able to sell their homes, for the first time since the Castros took power. And the Obama administration has lifted many of the pointless and onerous restrictions on travel to Cuba.

Of course, if Marco Rubio, the hard-line Cuban-American senator from Florida, snares the vice-presidential slot for the Republicans, Democrats will feel pressure to tighten the screws of the embargo once again. And should the Republicans prevail in 2012, relations will almost certainly return to the Stone Age of nonengagement—hinged on the mantra that "Fidel will go any day now."

While he appeared frail and off balance during his one brief "live" appearance at the Communist Party powwow in April, I would argue against any bet on Mr. Castro's date with his maker. A worthy rival of Lazarus, he has survived three major surgeries and the loss of a good deal of abdominal viscera, not to mention the administrations of 10 United States presidents.

Certainly, there are enough family members in key government ministries—most notably Raúl Castro's powerful son and sons-in-law—to ensure a degree of dynastic rule into the future. But the lavish concern and solicitation of the elder Mr. Castro toward his Venezuelan charge suggests a deeply felt fear should his island lose Mr. Chávez's patronage.

That said, in case Mr. Chávez slips his mortal coil before his Cuban ally does, the über-strategist Fidel Castro has no doubt cobbled together some sort of contingency plan—as he was forced to do after the Soviets pulled out. Trust and sentimentality are not part of his political credo. Discussing an early betrayal by a compañero turned informer, Mr. Castro said he learned a crucial lesson: "You shouldn't trust someone just because he's a friend." Or depend on him.

"Fidel is a force of nature," observed his friend the writer Gabriel García Márquez. "With him, you never know." Or as they lament in Miami, "Immortal until proved otherwise."

Challenge Questions

After reading this article, you will be able to answer the following questions:

1. What might happen if an authoritarian leader falls victim to incapacitating illness?
2. What is meant by the term "Venecuba"?
3. How dependent is Cuba's economy on Venezuelan aid?
4. What is the relationship between Venezuelan oil and its foreign policy?

17 Planting Hope on Hispaniola

Tommy Ventre

Learning Objectives

After reading this article, you will more clearly understand the following:

- Environment
- Peasant attitudes
- Habitat loss
- Reforestation

In a country whose national symbol could be a motorcycle with a blown-out muffler, the Dominican Republic's Armando Bermúdez National Park is an oasis of tranquility.

Not much has changed in the park since its founding over half a century ago by Rafael Trujillo, a dictator whose cold-blooded rule lasted for more than 30 years. Punctuated by three 3,000-meter peaks (the Caribbean's highest), draped in stands of Hispaniolan pine, and crisscrossed by streams and waterfalls, the park covers more than 1,000 square kilometers in the Cordillera Central, the central mountain range of the Dominican Republic. By one count, the uninhabited park receives only a few hundred paying visitors a year.

But although much has remained the same inside Armando Bermúdez, changes are taking place in the way people living outside the park—indeed, across the entire island—think about the environmental treasures it represents. It's been a slow shift, arguably tracing its roots back to the 1970s when Joaquin Balaguer (Trujillo's one-time protégé) set aside 10 percent of the country's land area as parks or scientific reserves. Awareness is rising about crucial environmental themes like the roles healthy forests play in everything from agriculture to water purification. Dovetailing with this increasing awareness is the government's growing desire to address some of the same issues. For evidence of this shift, look no further than the country's new environment and natural resources secretariat, a far cry from Balaguer's draconian anti-logging laws that were enforced by soldiers with machine guns. The spirit of the law is largely the same today (no cutting is allowed without a permit), but the agents charged with enforcing it now answer to the civilian bureaucracy.

These changes are taking place in a critical location. The island of Hispaniola, which the Dominican Republic (the DR) shares with Haiti, extends over 78,000 square kilometers—large enough to be home to a dazzling array of endemic bio-diversity, but small enough for that same biodiversity to be wiped out in the evolutionary blink of an eye.

But do changes in attitude—both of the government and the governed—ensure that changes are taking place on the ground? The answer, like the problems facing the island's ecosystems, is complex.

GOOD INTENTIONS, SOME PROGRESS

Directly to the south of Armando Bermúdez is another protected area of about the same size called José del Carmen Ramírez National Park, whose extensive cloud forests host wild orchids and bromeliads and the source of the Río Yaque del Sur. Taken together, the Yaque del Sur's watershed and that of the longer Río Yaque del Norte, rising in the same mountain range, cover more than 25 percent of the country's land area. Much of it is prime agricultural land.

The two parks are the cornerstone of the Dominican national park system, a vast network of more than 60 parks, reserves, refuges, and sanctuaries overseen by the seven-year-old Secretariat of the Environment and Natural Resources. The endemism of the mountain range in which they lie is astonishing: the Nature Conservancy reports that more than 90 percent of the amphibians and reptiles there exist nowhere else in the world. The same goes for half the area's butterflies, more than 40 percent of its plant species, and 35 percent of its birds.

Armando Bermúdez and José del Carmen Ramírez are symbols of what can happen when things are done correctly. The government's commitment to the area is evident in the signage, easily accessed entrances, and well-staffed park ranger stations. This official air, in turn, means laws are followed and boundaries respected. It's amid this environment that the Cordillera Central has become a center for ecotourism in the Caribbean, with several outfits in Jarabacoa, Constanza, and other towns offering whitewater rafting, horseback riding, mountain biking, and guided hikes up 3,087-meter Pico Duarte.

Off to the west, in the mountains just southeast of the Dominican city of Dajabón, lies Nalga de Maco National Park. Like Armando Bermúdez and José del Carmen Ramírez, it has towering peaks, thundering waterfalls, and stunning biodiversity.

But there are some key differences. For one, the river it helps to feed doesn't exist solely in the DR; the Río Artibonito flows westward into Haiti (where it is called the Rivière Artibonite) after forming at the confluence of the Río Libón and Río Joca. No river on Hispaniola is longer than the Artibonito, and none more important to Haiti's farmers. The valley through which it runs is that nation's principal rice-growing region; thanks to the Peligre Dam constructed in 1950, the river irrigates more than 35,000 hectares of land.

Nalga de Maco also differs from those other parks in that it only loosely resembles a protected area. There are no grand entrance gates, no signs, nothing to suggest that it's a federally administered national park except a one-room office in Rio Limpio, a tiny mountain town at the park's northwestern edge. More often than not, a visitor to that office will find it empty, as I did on weekly visits to Rio Limpio toward the end of my Peace Corps service in early 2007. The environment secretariat's website lists the park staff as an administrator, three rangers, and three forest extensionists. In a 280-square-kilometer park, that's one staff person for every 40 square kilometers. (Armando Bermúdez and José del Carmen Ramírez, in contrast, feature 26 ranger stations and 6 observation towers and combine to average one staffer per 24 square kilometers.)

No formal guiding groups exist for visitors who want to enter the park, as I found out in March 2006. A friend and I spent four hours finding someone who knew the path to the summit of Nalga de Maco, the 1,991-meter peak from which the park gets its name. That someone was Jairo, a 22-year-old Rio Limpio resident who told us he learned the trails as a boy while walking them with his father. In the early part of our trek, in the foothills at the mountain's base, we passed more than a few farmers and laborers with hoes and axes slung over their shoulders. On our way down a day later, we saw the same men standing in clearings where just a day before had been lush growth. Embers could still be seen smoldering in parts of the new clearings. Jairo told me it was illegal to clear land there because it was within park boundaries. "But who's going to enforce it? The law does not reach [the residents] here," he said.

This episode illustrates a stark truth of developing-world environmental policy, according to Bill Kaschak, who spent eight years working for the International Resources Group directing a USAID-funded project that advised the Dominican government as it developed new environmental policies. Decisions may be made at high levels of government, but those decisions don't always affect what happens on the ground. In 2000, when the Dominican government resolved to protect its environment and use its natural resources in sustainable ways, the result was the creation of the environment secretariat. Seven years later, the framework remains incomplete.

In some cases, Kaschak says, the money just isn't available for implementation, a fact reflected in the lax enforcement in Nalga de Maco. But a more pressing concern is the culture question. "It's about attitude, knowledge, behavior—what people perceive and how they interpret that," he says. The creation of the policy framework was helpful in that it established, in Kaschak's terms, a "body of technicians" to enforce the legal dimensions of the policies. The difficulty now is not in establishing whether the will to erect the framework exists—it does, at least in the DR—but in the time it may take the culture to become comfortable acting within that framework.

■ GREEN AND PEASANT LAND?

In the Dominican Republic the fact that the environment is facing any number of threats has been recognized, and a partial framework has been created for doing something about it. Laws are on the books now to regulate

everything from carbon emissions to whalewatching, a big-time tourism draw on the Saman Peninsula in the country's northeast. But what about places where such a framework doesn't exist? What about Haiti?

Since 1988, four coups and/or U.S. military interventions have wracked the nation, robbing it of the stability needed to set up strategies to address pressing issues like the state of the environment. Development agencies that might fill the void find tough sledding too. The Peace Corps, for instance, long a driver of environmental awareness during 46 consecutive years on the Dominican side of the island, has suspended its Haiti program four times since 1987, including twice since 2004.

So if government doesn't exist, and if workers from other countries are ordered to leave (as nonessential employees of the U.S. State Department were in May 2005), who remains to safeguard the Haitian environment?

Haitian peasants, decided Chavannes Jean-Baptiste.

In 1972, the young Catholic-layman-turned-agronomist began work on what would become the Peasant Movement of Papaye (MPP), with the goal of teaching sustainable agriculture to impoverished farmers in the Haitian countryside. In the 35 years since, Haiti's population has grown from 5.5 million to more than 8.7 million, half of whom earn less than $60 per year, according to globalsecurity.org. As the population has grown, trees have disappeared. Forests cover less than 2 percent of Haiti's land mass, and Jean-Baptiste says conservative estimates suggest 20 million trees are felled for charcoal production each year.

That's led to the erosion problems Jean-Baptiste has placed at the center of his efforts. In a healthy system, according to Jean-Baptiste, erosion can be expected to result in 1 metric ton of soil loss per hectare per year. Current estimates put soil loss in Haiti at 1,600 metric tons per hectare per year. In a situation that extreme, erosion ceases to be merely an agricultural or environmental issue and becomes an acute humanitarian problem as well: since 2004, flooding caused in part by erosion and deforestation has killed or displaced several thousand Haitians. "I can say that the country will go from catastrophe to catastrophe if nothing is done to change the situation," Jean-Baptiste says.

For almost four decades, Jean-Baptiste has been working to do just that. In 2005, he received a Goldman Environmental Prize for his work with MPP, whose members have planted more than 20 million trees. Perhaps more important to Jean-Baptiste, the number of rural Haitians taking part in MPP projects has topped 60,000 to date.

"You cannot save the environment without the formal engagement of peasant organizations," Jean-Baptiste argues. "They must be the principal actors." If anything positive came out of the floods of the past decade, he believes, it's that they have increased public awareness among Haitians of the degradation of the country's environment: "The problems one encounters working on environmental protection in Haiti are diverse, but in my opinion the biggest problem is one of education and information."

The new awareness is a first step toward a resolution of the problems, but ultimately what's needed is a national strategy, though it may be slow in coming. Jean-Baptiste serves as the chair of the federal government's new council on peasant issues, and he's frank about how close such a strategy currently is to reality: "It demands a degree of political will that doesn't exist in Haiti at the moment."

■ NURSING THE FORESTS

Almost a year after my first visit, I returned to Nalga de Maco with Chris Bright, a former senior researcher at Worldwatch, and Gaspar Pérez, the manager of a nearby agroforestry nursery started by Bright's nonprofit group, Earth Sangha. Bright was in the country to see the latest progress at the nursery, but he also wanted to see some virgin tropical moist forest.

We approached the mountain on a different trail than the one I had used with Jairo a year earlier, but the lack of regulation was just as evident. To our left, as we climbed was a plantation of Honduran pine, the exotic softwood of choice for entrepreneurs trying to make some money in the timber trade. To our right was a slope overtaken by thickets of an invasive shrub the Dominicans call calliandra. Banana plantations and bean fields were also visible.

When we finally found the stand Pérez had in mind, we saw the type of ecosystem that once dominated the island: ferns, mosses, palms, and trickling streams that ran through an eternally damp forest floor. Just beyond the parcel's vine-entangled border, however, lay a huge hillside expanse of felled trees, charred brush, and smoldering ash. Interplanted among the piles of debris: more banana trees.

Pérez would later say he felt embarrassed that Bright and I had seen it. "It isn't supposed to be like that. It wasn't like that when I was younger."

Unfortunately, the same can be said for much of the mountainous region in the country's northwest. Logging has become big business in places like the Dajabón province. Flatbed trucks descend from the hills daily, loaded with huge trunks of mature native Hispaniolan pine and younger logs of Honduran pine. There are more of the former these days, but that might not be true in a few years: Hispaniolan pine is on the World Conservation Union's (IUCN) "red list" of threatened species, while the most popular selection for replanting programs sponsored by the Dominican forestry department is the faster-growing Honduran species, introduced solely for low-grade timber production.

The forestry department, an arm of the environment secretariat, has small regional nurseries throughout the country, including two in Restauracin, a section of Dajabón province labeled the nation's "leading forestry municipality" by environment secretary Max Puig. The secretariat's commitment to reforestation is such that planting trees is touted as though it were a civic duty. Posters in many of the agency's field offices depict Dominican President Leonel Fernández with his sleeves rolled up planting a sapling, and public-service announcements on the afternoon radio urge families to plant trees near their houses. In many instances, though, those posters and radio spots are the closest any Dominican can get to entering the process. A gap exists between rhetoric and action.

Closing this gap became the focus of my Peace Corps service. Despite living in the DR's "leading forestry municipality," families in Los Cerezos, the community in which I served as a volunteer, simply couldn't get their hands on any trees to plant. The government nurseries, while a boon for the absentee owners of the area's vast timber plantations, offered little to the small family farms that in many respects are on the leading edge of deforestation.

When I arrived in May 2005, two farmers, in a community of roughly 500 people, had contracted with the forestry office to introduce managed plantings on their land. A handful of others had received trees from the forestry nurseries through a now-defunct local NGO. Those who hadn't been included in any sort of planting program or tree giveaway asked for a Peace Corps volunteer to help get them involved. They had seen the posters and heard the ads. Many had even attended day-long, government-administered workshops on concepts like agroforestry, soil structure, and the dangers of deforestation. They knew the virtues of forest renewal and wanted desperately to help promote it.

But over time it became apparent that the government, whatever its intentions, couldn't possibly accommodate every Dominican farmer who wanted to reforest his land. Moreover, there were no other options. In response, a small association of farmers in Los Cerezos formed a Peace Corps-facilitated partnership with Bright's nonprofit and built their own nursery. It's located right inside their community and is producing around 6,000 trees per year.

"The project is designed to create opportunities for local people while also strengthening farm culture and preserving the landscape," Bright says. "The farmers there know very well that they shouldn't clear forest, but they've never had any other options that they can afford. With their nursery and our program, now they do."

Bright hopes to expand his group's program into Haiti once the Los Cerezos project begins to produce lasting results. Chavannes Jean-Baptiste, for his part, doesn't place much faith in projects that attempt such expansions. Arrangements like that are too simple, he says, especially for a place where the problems are so complex. "Today, there's a lot of talk about binational projects," says Jean-Baptiste. "The European Union, for example, encourages them. But I think they're poorly conceived because they don't take into account the characteristics of each area. I get a lot of people who come in with great intentions during planning stages, but when the time comes to start doing some work, they're nowhere to be seen."

The majority of these projects fail, he says, because they violate basic principles of development work, including longterm planning and integrated approaches to problems.

But if Bright and Jean-Baptiste differ on the value of cross-border projects on Hispaniola, they share the conviction that more options must be created for the island's residents. Jean-Baptiste sees job creation through public-works projects in the Haitian countryside as a way to relieve pressure to cut trees, but he also wants to introduce environmental education to the peasant class. For him, the makings of a solution lie in awareness.

Gaspar Pérez and his counterparts in the DR already have varying degrees of that awareness; what they need are avenues through which to act on it. Whether those avenues are created by a slowly evolving policy framework or by something else doesn't matter. What matters is that people have a chance to act.

And that's the common thread that runs through Hispaniola. There, as anywhere, real change will only begin at the grassroots, where attitudes meet action. Attitudes have begun to change, perhaps spurred by the creation of a national park more than five decades ago. With luck, it won't take another five decades for action to have caught up.

Tommy Ventre works for the Fairfax, Virginia-based environmental nonprofit Earth Sangha. He was a Peace Corps volunteer in the Dominican Republic from 2005 to 2007.

From *World Watch*, January/February 2008, pp. 8–13. Copyright © 2008 by Worldwatch Institute. Reprinted by permission. www.worldwatch.org

Challenge Questions

After reading this article, you will be able to answer the following questions:

1. Why is environmental degradation more serious in Haiti than in the Dominican Republic?
2. What is the role of the peasantry in protecting the environment?
3. How are governments acting to preserve the ecosystem?
4. How important is eco-tourism as a means to protect the environment?

18 Aftershocks

David Heymann

Hundreds of thousands are likely to have died, millions are in need, their homes having been lost. Many wait for medical care. Safe water is in short supply and the rainy season starts in May. Could it have been different in Haiti? Would good planning have eased the pain of the shocks?

Learning Objectives

After reading this article, you will more clearly understand the following:

- Natural disaster
- International aid
- Government paralysis in the face of disaster
- Human and economic costs of the earthquake

In northern Haiti, high above the city of Cap Haitien, stand the ruins of Sans Souci—a magnificent palace built just after the proclamation of independence from France in the early 1800s by King Henri I of northern Haiti. According to historical accounts, Sans Souci was often referred to as the Versailles of the new world, but in 1842 an earthquake destroyed the city and its palace, leaving behind a spectacular ruin now classified as a World Heritage Site by UNESCO.

Fast forward to this January, to the images from Port au Prince of the ruined presidential palace, with towers imploded on crumbled walls, and to the human suffering caused when tragedy struck again. Two palaces in ruin, two cities devastated, countless lives lost and tragic human suffering.

There is little written about the 1842 earthquake in Cap Hatien, but the records that exist suggest that up to two-thirds of the inhabitants were killed. This year's earthquake also took a large toll, but it will be weeks until the full extent of the tragedy is known.

■ WARNINGS

Haiti has had numerous smaller earthquakes since Sans Souci became a ruin—each a warning that the security of its population was and is at risk, as in other countries situated at or near the junction of tectonic plates. And these warnings have largely gone unheeded by Haiti's succession of failed governments.

■ BE PREPARED

Within hours of the earthquake, Dr Jean Pape, a Haitian medical doctor who has dedicated his career to working with people with AIDS, sent an e-mail from Port au Prince to his colleagues around the world listing priorities during the immediate aftermath: clearing obstructed roads; burying the dead; providing water, food, shelter and medical care; and rebuilding lost infrastructure.

The government could not provide these necessities. It had not prepared for such an event. Like the presidential palace, what infrastructure existed had not survived the shock. These immediate needs are now being addressed by the international community: governments, international and non-governmental organisations(NGOs), supported by donations from people around the world.

But often additional resources required by governments for disaster preparation in vulnerable countries cannot be made available. Development agencies of other governments are not always able to help plan for emergencies and develop the necessary resilience.

Once a disaster has occurred, however, and an emergency has been declared, funding becomes available to NGOs, aid agencies and the United Nations through special mechanisms and funds to respond to humanitarian crises, and public appeals provide the rest.

Some governments in areas of earthquake risk are prepared. Iran's response to the shock in Bam at the end of 2004 is a good example. Several strategic decisions taken by the Iranian health authorities as they developed their emergency plan in the years before the Bam quake made a rapid and effective response easier.

In the first 48 hours, twelve thousand injured people needing treatment were airlifted to hospitals in neighbouring provinces by a team from the army, ministry of interior, ministry of health and the Red Crescent Society.

Humanitarian assistance from more than forty different countries and organisations was supported by government logistics and communications described in the preparedness plan. They first worked to rescue those beneath the rubble and assumed immediate primary healthcare responsibilities in ten field hospitals.

Before humanitarian agencies arrived, the city of Bam was divided into twelve medical zones. Each of these linked up according to plan, with a provincial hospital and medical school that sent medical teams to work side-by-side with the international humanitarian agencies providing routine medical care and psychological support.

Care was provided in hospital tents and to families in their temporary tent shelters provided, as planned, by the army. They replaced medication lost during the earthquake for those suffering from conditions such as hypertension and diabetes.

Organisations that could help countries prepare and develop similar plans, such as Merlin in Britain, the International Federation of Red Cross and Red Crescent Societies in Switzerland and the United Nations system, struggle to raise funds for governments to prepare for emergencies. Other development priorities often take precedence, and money to plan and create emergency and resilience capacity is limited or not available.

While those who are responding now have the opportunity to strengthen Haiti's capacity to cope better with the next disaster by building more resilient infrastructure while in emergency mode, the devastation provides us with yet another reminder of the need to devote resources outside crisis situations to help countries prepare better.

That includes strengthening health systems so they can more easily rebound, as well as drafting contingency plans that set aside resources for government sectors to respond. Of course, investments in capacity building must be carefully targeted to ensure wise use.

■ SUSTAINABLE SUPPORT

Without such investment in resilience capacity, development agencies and NGOs must instead stand ready to mobilise the resources to respond to the needs of those, such as Dr Pape, once an emergency develops. They need to be prepared to continue to provide resources and support as services and healthcare are re-established, often in the face of diminishing funds as new emergencies develop. In Haiti, as in many cases, it is uncertain whether these organisations will be able to sustain the support necessary in the long term.

The tragedy in Haiti is a tale of two ruined palaces and 175 years of warnings that were not heeded. Its government has not been able to respond and the international community has found the resources and taken charge.

It has established logistics and communications, and provided support for the humanitarian response, often with unnecessary competition and duplication because of lack of government coordination. It is hoped there will be sufficient money for infrastructure reconstruction and re-establishing services such as healthcare, possibly even improving on those existing before the earthquake, for people fortunate enough to survive.

As it struggles to deal with the present, the government of Haiti has had another warning that preparedness and resilience must be developed for the next event, no matter how distant it may seem. Donor agencies have had the same warning and must re-examine their preparedness and response to emergencies so that more emphasis is placed on building capacity in vulnerable nations to equip them to withstand and respond better to the next disaster.

Challenge Questions

After reading this article, you will be able to answer the following questions:

1. Why were Haitian authorities so unprepared for a natural disaster?
2. How effective was the response of the international community?
3. Why are 500,000 (as of January 2012) people still housed in makeshift shelters?

Internet References

(Some websites continually change their structure and content, so the information listed here may not always be available.)

GENERAL SITES

CNN Online Page
www.cnn.com
U.S. 24-hour video news channel. News is updated every few hours.

C-SPAN Online
www.c-span.org
See especially C-SPAN International on the Web for International Programming Highlights and archived C-SPAN programs.

GlobalEdge
http://globaledge.msu.edu/ibrd/ibrd.asp
Connect to several international business links from this site. Included are links to a glossary of international trade terms, exporting data, international trade, current laws, and data on GATT, NAFTA, and MERCOSUR.

International Information Systems (University of Texas)
http://inic.utexas.edu
Gateway has pointers to international sites, including all Latin American countries.

Library of Congress Country Studies
http://lcweb2.loc.gov/frd/cs/cshome.html#toc
An invaluable resource for facts and analysis of 100 countries' political, economic, social, and national-security systems and installations.

Political Science Resources
www.psr.keele.ac.uk
Dynamic gateway to sources available via European addresses. Listed by country name, this site includes official government pages, official documents, speeches, election information, and political events.

Relief Web
www.reliefweb.int
UN's Department of Humanitarian Affairs clearinghouse for international humanitarian emergencies. It has daily updates, including Reuters and VOA, and PANA.

Social Science Information Gateway (SOSIG)
http://soig.esrc.bris.ac.uk/
Project of the Economic and Social Research Council (ESRC). It catalogs 22 subjects and lists developing countries' URL addresses.

United Nations System
www.sosig.ac.ulc/
The official website for the United Nations system of organizations. Everything is listed alphabetically, and data on UNICC and Food and Agriculture Organization are available.

UN Development Programme (UNDP)
www.undp.org
Publications and current information on world poverty, Mission Statement, UN Development Fund for Women, and much more. Be sure to see the Poverty Clock.

UN Environmental Programme (UNEP)
www.unep.org
Official site of UNEP with information on UN environmental programs, products, services, events, and a search engine.

U.S. Agency for International Development (USAID)
www.usaid.gov
Graphically presented U.S. trade statistics with Latin America and the Caribbean.

U.S. Central Intelligence Agency Home Page
www.cia.gov/library/publications/the-world-factbook/
This site includes publications of the CIA, such as the World Factbook, Factbook on Intelligence, Handbook of International Economic Statistics, CIA Maps and Publications, and much more.

U.S. Department of State Home Page
www.state.gov/www/ind.html
Organized alphabetically (i.e., Country Reports, Human Rights, International Organizations, and more).

World Bank Group
www.worldbank.org
News (press releases, summary of new projects, speeches), publications, topics in development, and countries and regions. Links to other financial organizations are available.

World Health Organization (WHO)
www.who.ch
Maintained by WHO's headquarters in Geneva, Switzerland, the site uses Excite search engine to conduct keyword searches.

World Trade Organization
www.wto.org
Topics include foundation of world trade systems, data on textiles, intellectual property rights, legal frameworks, trade and environmental policies, and recent agreements.

MEXICO

The Mexican Government
www.gob.mx/wb/egobierno/egob_General_Information
This site offers a brief overview of the organization of the Mexican Republic, including the Executive, Legislative, and Judicial Branches of the federal government.

CENTRAL AMERICA

Central America News/Planeta
www.planeta.com/ecotravel/period/pubcent.html
Access to data that includes individual country reports, politics, economic news, travel, media coverage, and links to other sites are available here.

Latin World
www.latinworld.com
Connecting links to data on the economy and finance, businesses, culture, government, and other areas of interest are available on this site.

SOUTH AMERICA

South America Daily

www.southamericadaily.com
Everything you want to know about South America is available from this site—from arts and culture, to government data, to environment issues, to individual countries.

CARIBBEAN

Caribbean Studies

www.hist.unt.edu/web_resources/caribbean.htm
A complete site for information about the Caribbean. Topics include general information, Caribbean religions, English Caribbean Islands, Dutch Caribbean Islands, French Caribbean Islands, Hispanic Caribbean Islands, and the U.S. Virgin Islands.

Library of Congress Report on the Islands of the Commonwealth Caribbean

http://memory.loc.gov/frd/cs/cxtoc.html
An extended study of the Caribbean is possible from this site. **We highly recommend that you review our website for expanded information and our other product lines. We are continually updating and adding links to our website in order to offer you the most usable and useful information that will support and expand the value of your book. You can reach us at: *www.mhhe.com/cls*.**

The United States
(United States of America)

GEOGRAPHY
Area in Square Miles (Kilometers): 3,794,100 (9,826,675) (about half the size of Russia)
Capital (Population): Greater Washington, DC (4.4 million)
Environmental Concerns: air and water pollution; limited freshwater resources, desertification; loss of habitat; waste disposal; acid rain
Geographical Features: vast central plain, mountains in the west, hills and low mountains in the east; rugged mountains and broad river valleys in Alaska; volcanic topography in Hawaii
Climate: mostly temperate, but ranging from tropical to arctic

PEOPLE
Population
Total: 313,232,044
Annual Growth Rate: 0.963%
Rural/Urban Population Ratio: 18/82
Major Languages: English; Pacific Islander; many others
Ethnic Makeup: 80% white; 13% black; 4% Asian; 3% Amerindian and others
Religions: 51% Protestant; 24% Roman Catholic; 2% Mormon; 2% Jewish; 4% others; 17% none or unaffiliated

Health
Life Expectancy at Birth: 76 years (male); 81 years (female)
Infant Mortality: 6/1,000 live births
Physicians Available: 1/417 people
HIV/AIDS Rate in Adults: 0.6%

Education
Adult Literacy Rate: 99% (official)
Compulsory (Ages): 7–16; free

COMMUNICATION
Telephones: 141 million main lines (2009)
Telephones: 255 million cellular
Mobile Phones: 286 million (2009)
Internet Users: 245 million (2010)
Internet Penetration (% of pop): 77%

TRANSPORTATION
Roadways in Miles (Kilometers): 4,042,768 (6,506,204)
Railroads in Miles (Kilometers): 139,679 (224,792)
Usable Airfields: 15,079

GOVERNMENT
Type: federal republic
Independence Date: July 4, 1776
Head of State/Government: President Barack H. Obama is both head of state and head of government
Political Parties: Democratic Party; Republican Party; Green Party; Libertarian Party
Suffrage: universal at 18

MILITARY
Military Expenditures (% of GDP): 4.06%
Current Disputes: boundary and territorial disputes with Canada, the Bahamas, Haiti and other countries; water-sharing disputes with Mexico; "war on terrorism"

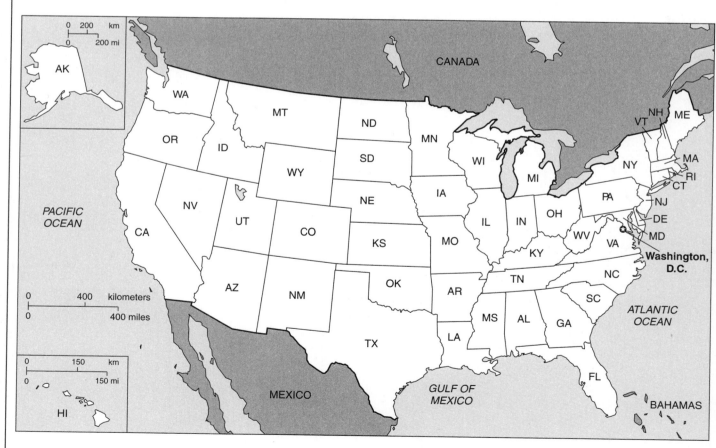

ECONOMY

Per Capita Income/GDP: $47,200/$14.66 trillion
GDP Growth Rate: 2.8%
Inflation Rate: 1.4%
Unemployment Rate: 9.6% (2010)
Labor Force by Occupation: 79% services; 20% industry; 1% agriculture
Population Below Poverty Line: 15%

Natural Resources: many minerals and metals; petroleum; natural gas; timber; arable land
Agriculture: food grains; feed crops; fruits and vegetables; oil-bearing crops; livestock; dairy products
Industry: diversified in both capital and consumer-goods industries
Exports: $1.27 trillion (primary partners Canada, Mexico, China)
Imports: $1.903 trillion (primary partners, China, Canada, Mexico)

Canada

GEOGRAPHY

Area in Square Miles (Kilometers): 3,854,083 (9,984,670) (slightly larger than the United States)

Capital (Population): Ottawa (1.2 million)

Environmental Concerns: air and water pollution; acid rain; industrial damage to agriculture and forest productivity

Geographical Features: permafrost in the north; mountains in the west; central plains; lowlands in the southeast

Climate: varies from temperate to arctic

PEOPLE

Population

Total: 34,030,589

Annual Growth Rate: 0.79%

Rural/Urban Population Ratio: 19/81

Major Languages: English and French

Ethnic Makeup: 28% British Isles origin; 23% French origin; 15% other European; 6% others; 2% indigenous; 26% mixed

Religions: 43% Roman Catholic; 23% Protestant; 18% others; unaffiliated 16%

Health

Life Expectancy at Birth: 79 years (male); 84 years (female)

Infant Mortality: 5/1,000 live births

Physicians Available: 1/498 people *HIV/AIDS Rate in Adults:* 0.3%

Education

Adult Literacy Rate: 99%

Compulsory (Ages): primary school

COMMUNICATION

Telephones: 18.3 million main lines (2009)

Telephones: 23.1 million cellular (2009)

Internet Users: 27 million (2011)

Internet Penetration (% of pop): 79%

TRANSPORTATION

Roadways in Miles (Kilometers): 647,655 (1,042,300)

Railroads in Miles (Kilometers): 29,926 (46,552)

Usable Airfields: 1,404

GOVERNMENT

Type: confederation with parliamentary democracy

Independence Date: July 1, 1867

Head of State/Government: Queen Elizabeth II; Prime Minister Stephen Harper

Political Parties: Bloc Québécois; Liberal Party; New Democratic Party; Green Party; Conservative Party of Canada

Suffrage: universal at 18

MILITARY

Military Expenditures (% of GDP): 1.1%

Current Disputes: maritime boundary disputes with the United States, and sovereignty dispute with Denmark

ECONOMY

Per Capita Income/GDP: $39,400/$1.33 trillion

GDP Growth Rate: 3.1%

Inflation Rate: 1.6%

Unemployment Rate: 8%

Labor Force by Occupation: 76% services; 13% manufacturing; 6% construction; 2% agriculture and 3% others

Natural Resources: petroleum; natural gas; fish; minerals; timber; wildlife; coal; hydropower

Agriculture: grains; dairy products; tobacco; fruits and vegetables; forest products; fish

Industry: oil production and refining; natural-gas development; fish products; wood and paper products; chemicals; transportation equipment

Exports: $461.8 billion (primary partners United States, United Kingdom, China)

Imports: $436.7 billion (primary partners United States, European Union, Japan)

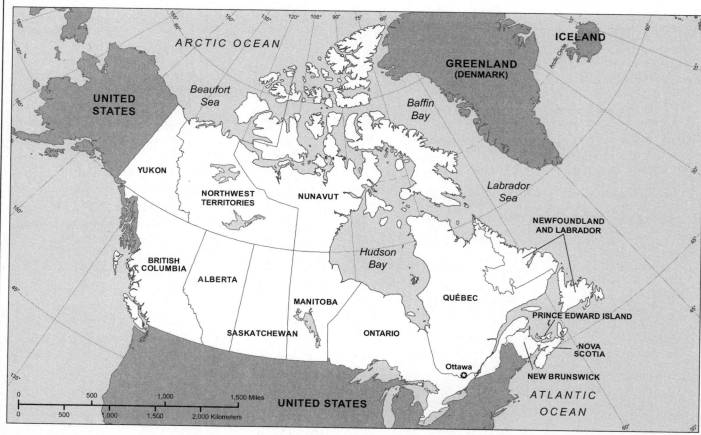

Glossary
of Terms and Abbreviations

Agrarian Relating to the land; the cultivation and ownership of land.

Amerindian A general term for any Indian from America.

Andean Pact (Cartagena Agreement) Established on October 16, 1969, to end trade barriers among member nations and to create a common market. Members: Bolivia, Colombia, Ecuador, Peru, and Venezuela.

Antilles A geographical region in the Caribbean made up of the Greater Antilles: Cuba, Hispaniola (Haiti and the Dominican Republic), Jamaica, the Cayman Islands, Puerto Rico, and the Virgin Islands; and the Lesser Antilles: Antigua and Barbuda, Dominica, St. Lucia, St. Vincent and the Grenadines, St. Kitts–Nevis, as well as various French departments and Dutch territories.

Araucanians An Indian people of south-central Chile and adjacent areas of Argentina.

Arawak An Indian people originally found on certain Caribbean islands, who now live chiefly along the coast of Guyana. Also, their language.

Aymara An Indian people and language of Bolivia and Peru.

CACM (Central American Common Market) Established on June 3, 1961, to form a common market in Central America. Members: Costa Rica, El Salvador, Guatemala, and Nicaragua.

Campesino A Spanish word meaning "peasant."

Caudillo Literally, "man on horseback." A term that has come to mean "leader."

Carib An Indian people and their language native to several islands in the Caribbean and some countries in Central America and South America.

CARICOM (Caribbean Community and Common Market) Established on August 1, 1973, to coordinate economic and foreign policies.

CDB (Caribbean Development Bank) Established on October 18, 1969, to promote economic growth and development of member countries in the Caribbean.

The Commonwealth (Originally the British Commonwealth of Nations) An association of nations and dependencies loosely joined by the common tie of having been part of the British Empire.

Compadrazgo The Mexican word meaning "cogodparenthood" or "sponsorship."

Compadres Literally, "friends"; but in Mexico, the term includes neighbors, relatives, fellow migrants, coworkers, and employers.

Contadora Process A Latin American intiative developed by Venezuela, Colombia, Panama, and Mexico to search for a negotiated solution that would secure borders and reduce the foreign military presence in Central America.

Contras A guerrilla army opposed to the Sandinista government of Nicaragua. They were armed and supplied by the United States.

Costeños Coastal dwellers in Central America.

Creole The term has several meanings: a native-born person of European descent or a person of mixed French and black or Spanish and black descent speaking a dialect of French or Spanish.

ECCA (Eastern Caribbean Currency Authority) A regional organization that monitors the integrity of the monetary unit for the area and sets policies for revaluation and devaluation.

ECLA (Economic Commission for Latin America) Established on February 28, 1948, to develop and strengthen economic relations among Latin American countries.

FAO (Food and Agricultural Organization of the United Nations) Established on October 16, 1945, to oversee good nutrition and agricultural development.

FSLN (Frente Sandinista de Liberación Nacionál) Organized in the early 1960s with the object of ousting the Somoza family from its control of Nicaragua. After 1979 it assumed control of the government. Voted out of power in 1990, the FSLN again won the presidential election in 2009.

FTAA (Free Trade Area of the Americas) An effort to integrate the economies of the Western Hemisphere into a single free trade arrangement.

GATT (General Agreement on Tariffs and Trade) Established on January 1, 1948, to provide international trade and tariff standards.

GDP (Gross Domestic Product) The value of production attributable to the factors of production in a given country, regardless of their ownership. GDP equals GNP minus the product of a country's residents originating in the rest of the world.

GNP (Gross National Product) The sum of the values of all goods and services produced by a country's residents in any given year.

Gran Colombia Territory comprised of Venezuela, Colombia, and Ecuador in the early national period (1820s).

Group of 77 Established in 1964 by 77 developing countries. It functions as a caucus on economic matters for the developing countries.

Guerrilla Any member of a small force of "irregular" soldiers. Generally, guerrilla forces are made up of volunteers who make surprise raids against the incumbent military or political force.

IADB (Inter-American Defense Board) Established in 1942 at Rio de Janeiro to coordinate the efforts of all American countries in World War II. It is now an advisory defense committee on problems of military cooperation for the OAS.

297

IADB (Inter-American Development Bank) Established in 1959 to help accelerate economic and social development in Latin America.

IBA (International Bauxite Association) Established in 1974 to promote orderly and rational development of the bauxite industry. Membership is worldwide, with a number of Latin American members.

IBRD (International Bank for Reconstruction and Development) Established on December 27, 1945, to make loans to governments at conventional rates of interest for high-priority productive projects. There are many Latin American members.

ICAO (International Civil Aviation Organization) Established on December 7, 1944, to develop techniques of international air navigation and to ensure safe and orderly growth of international civil aviation. Membership is worldwide, with many Latin American members.

ICO (International Coffee Organization) Established in August 1963 to maintain cooperation between coffee producers and to control the world market prices. Membership is worldwide, with a number of Latin American members.

IDA (International Development Association) Established on September 24, 1960, to promote better and more flexible financing arrangements; it supplements the World Bank's activities.

ILO (International Labour Organization) Established on April 11, 1919, to improve labor conditions and living standards through international action.

IMCO (Inter-Governmental Maritime Consultative Organization) Established in 1948 to provide cooperation among governments on technical matters of international merchant shipping as well as to set safety standards. Membership is worldwide, with more than a dozen Latin American members.

IMF (International Monetary Fund) Established on December 27, 1945, to promote international monetary cooperation.

IPU (Inter-Parliamentary Union) Established on June 30, 1889, as a forum for personal contacts between members of the world parliamentary governments. Membership is worldwide, with the following Latin American members: Argentina, Brazil, Colombia, Costa Rica, Haiti, Mexico, Nicaragua, Paraguay, and Venezuela.

ISO (International Sugar Organization) Established on January 1, 1969, to administer the international sugar agreement and to compile data on the industry. Membership is worldwide, with the following Latin American members: Argentina, Brazil, Colombia, Cuba, Ecuador, Mexico, Uruguay, and Venezuela.

ITU (International Telecommunication Union) Established on May 17, 1865, to develop international regulations for telegraph, telephone, and radio services.

Junta A Spanish word meaning "assembly" or "council"; the legislative body of a country.

Ladino A Westernized Spanish-speaking Latin American, often of mixed Spanish and Indian blood.

LAFTA (Latin American Free Trade Association) Established on June 2, 1961, with headquarters in Montevideo, Uruguay.

Machismo Manliness. The male sense of honor; connotes the showy power of a "knight in shining armor."

Marianismo The feminine counterpart of machismo; the sense of strength that comes from controlling the family and the male.

Mennonite A strict Protestant denomination that derived from a sixteenth-century religious movement.

MERCOSUR Comprised of Argentina, Brazil, Paraguay, and Uruguay, this southern common market is the world's fourth largest integrated market. It was established in 1991.

Mestizo The offspring of a Spaniard or Portuguese and an American Indian.

Mulatto A person of mixed Caucasian and black ancestry.

Nahuatl The language of an Amerindian people of southern Mexico and Central America who are descended from the Aztec.

NAFTA (North American Free Trade Agreement) Established in 1993 between Mexico, Canada, and the United States, NAFTA went into effect January 1, 1994.

NAM (Non-Aligned Movement) A group of nations that chose not to be politically or militarily associated with either the West or the former Communist bloc.

Nueva Palmira (Duty) Free Zone. Located at the mouth of the Uruguay River and administered by the Uruguayan government.

OAS (Organization of American States) (formerly the Pan American Union) Established on December 31, 1951, with headquarters in Washington, DC.

ODECA (Central American Defense Organization) Established on October 14, 1951, to strengthen bonds among the Central American countries and to promote their economic, social, and cultural development through cooperation. Members: Costa Rica, El Salvador, Guatemala, Honduras, and Nicaragua.

OECS (Organization of Eastern Caribbean States) A Caribbean organization established on June 18, 1981, and headquartered in Castries, St. Lucia.

PAHO (Pan American Health Organization) Established in 1902 to promote and coordinate Western Hemisphere efforts to combat disease. All Latin American countries are members.

Patois A dialect other than the standard or literary dialect, such as some of the languages used in the Caribbean that are offshoots of French.

Peon Historically, a person forced to work off a debt or to perform penal servitude. It has come to mean a member of the working class.

PRI (Institutional Revolutionary Party) At one time the dominant political party in Mexico.

Quechua The language of the Inca. It is still widely spoken in Peru.

Rastafarian A religious sect in the West Indies whose members believe in the deity of Haile Selassie, the deposed emperor of Ethiopia who died in 1975.

Rio Pact (Inter-American Treaty of Reciprocal Assistance) Established in 1947 at the Rio Conference to set up a policy of joint defense of Western Hemisphere countries. In case of aggression against any American state, all member countries will come to its aid.

Sandinistas The popular name for the government of Nicaragua from 1979 to 1990, following the ouster of President Anastasio Somoza. The name derives from César Augusto Sandino, a Nicaraguan guerrilla fighter of the 1920s.

SELA (Latin American Economic System) Established on October 18, 1975, as an economic forum for all Latin American countries.

Suffrage The right to vote in political matters.

UN (United Nations) Established on June 26, 1945, through official approval of the charter by delegates of 50 nations at an international conference in San Francisco. The charter went into effect on October 24, 1945.

UNESCO (United Nations Educational, Scientific, and Cultural Organization) Established on November 4, 1946, to promote inter-national collaboration in education, science, and culture.

UPU (Universal Postal Union) Established on July 1, 1875, to promote cooperation in international postal services.

Windward Islands String of islands extending from the Leeward islands south to Trinidad, but not including Barbados.

World Bank A closely integrated group of international institutions providing financial and technical assistance to developing countries.

Bibliography

SOURCES FOR STATISTICAL REPORTS

U.S. State Department, *Background Notes* (2010).
The World Factbook (2011).
The Statesman's Yearbook (2010).
Demographic Yearbook (2010).
Statistical Yearbook (2010).
World Bank, World Development Report (2010).

GENERAL WORKS

Mark Brill, Music of Latin America (New York: Prentice-Hall, 2010)

Mark A. Burkholder and Lyman L. Johnson, *Colonial Latin America,* 8th ed. (New York: Oxford University Press, 2012).

David Bushnell and Neill Macaulay, *The Emergence of Latin America in the Nineteenth Century,* 2nd ed. (New York: Oxford University Press, 1994).

Shawn William Miller, *An Environmental History of Latin America* (New York: Cambridge University Press, 2007)

Thomas E. Skidmore and Peter Smith, *Modern Latin America,* 7th ed. (New York: Oxford University Press, 2009).

Barbara A. Tenenbaum, ed., *Encyclopedia of Latin American History,* 5 vols. (New York: Charles Scribner's Sons, 1996).

NATIONAL HISTORIES

The following studies provide keen insights into the particular characteristics of individual Latin American nations.

Argentina

Jonathan C. Brown, A Brief History of Argentina (New York: Facts on File, 2011)

Bolivia

Herbert S. Klein, *A Concise History of Bolivia,* 2nd ed. (New York: Cambridge University Press, 2011).

Brazil

Robert M. Levine, *The History of Brazil* (Greenwood, 2003).

Thomas Skidmore, *Brazil: Five Centuries of Change,* 2nd ed. (New York: Oxford University Press, 2009).

Caribbean Nations

Franklin W. Knight, *The Caribbean: The Genesis of a Fragmented Nationalism* (New York: Oxford, 2011).

Louis A. Perez Jr., *On Becoming Cuban: Identity, Nationality and Culture* (Chapel Hill: University of North Carolina Press, 2008 paperback ed.).

Central America

John A. Booth, Christine J. Wade, Thomas W. Walker, *Understanding Central America: Global Forces, Rebellion, and Change,* 5th ed. (Boulder: Westview Press, 2009).

Chile

Simon Collier and William F. Sater, *A History of Chile, 1808–2002,* 2nd ed. (New York: Cambridge University Press, 2004).

Colombia

Frank Safford and Macro Palacios, *Colombia: Fragmented Land, Divided Society* (New York: Oxford University Press, 2001).

Mexico

Michael C. Meyer and William L. Sherman, *The Course of Mexican History,* 9th ed. (New York: Oxford University Press, 2010).

Jorge G. Castaneda, *Mañana Forever? Mexico and the Mexicans* (New York: Knopf, 2011).

Ricardo Pozas Arciniega, *Juan Chamula: An Ethnolographical Recreation of the Life of a Mexican Indian* (Berkeley, CA: University of California Press, 1962).

Peru

Peter Klaren, *Peru: Society and Nationhood in the Andes* (New York: Oxford, 1999).

Daniel Masterson, *The History of Peru* (Westport, CT: Greenwood Publishing, 2009).

Venezuela

H. Michael Tarver and Julia C. Frederick, *The History of Venezuela* (Palgrave, 2006).

NOVELS IN TRANSLATION

The Latin American novel is perhaps one of the best windows on the cultures of the region. The following are just a few of many highly recommended novels.

Jorge Amado, *Clove and Cinnamon* (New York: Vintage, 2006).

Manlio Argueta, *One Day of Life* (New York: Vintage, 1991).

Miguel Ángel Asturias, *The President* (Prospect Heights, IL: Waveland Press, 1997).

Mariano Azuela, *The Underdogs* (New York: Penguin, 2008).

Alejo Carpentier, *The Kingdom of This World* (New York: Farrar, Straus, Geroux, 2006).

Carlos Fuentes, *The Death of Artemio Cruz* (New York: FS&G, 1991).

Jorge Icaza, *Huasipungo: The Villagers* (London: Arcturus Books, 1973).

Gabriel García Márquez, *One Hundred Years of Solitude* (New York: Harper, 2006).

Mario Vargas Llosa, *Death in the Andes* (New York: Picador, 2007).

Victor Montejo, *Testimony: Death of a Guatemalan Village* (Willimantic, CT: Curbstone Press, 1987).

Rachel de Queiroz, *The Three Marias* (Austin: University of Texas Press, 1991).

Graham Greene's novels about Latin America, such as *The Comedians* (New York: Penguin, 1966), and *The Power and the Glory* (New York: Penguin, 2003), and V. S. Naipaul's study of Trinidad, *The Loss of El Dorado: A History* (New York: Vintage, 2003), offer profound insights into the region.

Index